Lifespan Human Development

Second Edition

Sueann Robinson Ambron
Stanford University

David Brodzinsky
Douglass College, Rutgers University

Holt, Rinehart and Winston
New York   Chicago   San Francisco   Philadelphia
Montreal   Toronto   London   Sydney   Tokyo
Mexico City   Rio de Janeiro   Madrid

Library of Congress Cataloging in Publication Data

Ambron, Sueann Robinson.
    Lifespan human development.

    Bibliography: p. 631
    Includes index.
    1. Developmental psychology.   I. Brodzinsky, David.
II. Title.
BF713.A46   1982   155   81-13506
ISBN 0-03-059812-5   AACR2

CBS COLLEGE PUBLISHING
Holt, Rinehart and Winston
The Dryden Press
Saunders College Publishing

CREDITS (continued on p. 630)
We wish to thank the following photographers, authors, and publishers for
permission to reproduce their work.

Cover: Odyssey Productions, Robert A. Frerck

Prologue: p. 1 Gloria Karlson; p. 3 Beryl Goldberg; p. 4 Beryl Goldberg; p. 6 (upper
left) Mimi Cotter; p. 6 (upper right) Beryl Goldberg; p. 6 (lower left) Gloria Karlson; p.
6 (lower right) Beryl Goldberg; p. 8 Holt, Rinehart and Winston Photo Library; p. 9
Holt, Rinehart and Winston Photo Library; p. 11 Mimi Cotter; p. 12 Holt, Rinehart
and Winston Photo Library; p. 15 Beryl Goldberg; p. 23 Gloria Karlson

Preface

The second edition of *Lifespan Human Development*, designed for first courses at the college level, seeks to integrate the basic concepts and principles of physical, cognitive, and psychosocial development at each major stage of life—prenatal, infancy, toddlerhood, preschool period, middle childhood, adolescence, young adulthood, middle adulthood, and old age. All the major topics of human development are fully presented, yet *Lifespan Human Development* can be covered in one semester.

This book may be used for courses without prerequisites, and in which many students are encountering the basic concepts of psychology for the first time. Each technical term is introduced with a clear, concise definition followed by concrete applications and illustrations. While the book provides a solid foundation in modern psychological and developmental theory and research, it concentrates less on the pure research literature and more on the practical implications of this research—on what it tells the reader about the children and adults they meet in everyday life. Presented in this way, the study of human development provides an essential background for students in psychology, nursing, education, social welfare, and home economics; for workers in community service; and for parents and prospective parents.

CHANGES IN THIS EDITION

One major change in this edition is the substantial expansion of the Prologue, "Lifespan Development: Issues, Theories, and Research." This chapter-length introduction to the text provides an overview of developmental psychology, including the nature and function of theories in science, and an outline of the major contemporary developmental theories. Research methods and ethical considerations in studying human beings are also discussed.

The *adulthood section* of the book also has been increased, from three to six chapters (now accounting for nearly one third of the book). This change represents an attempt to provide a more balanced coverage of the major periods of life—to make the second edition a truly lifespan text. The chapters on adulthood provide a comprehensive and up-to-date picture of the developmental tasks confronting most adults in the areas of physical and mental functioning, personality development, family life, social relations, career development, and death and dying.

Over half of the *boxed features* that highlight current issues and apply recent findings are new to this edition, and all are up to date. Among the new topics are prenatal testing, father-infant interactions, child-rearing in American subcultures, the National Day-Care Study, what adopted children need to know, teenage pregnancy, psychological factors in premenstrual tension, women in male-dominated occupations, midlife pregnancy, wife-beating, and exercise and the elderly.

Substantial sections of new material have been added throughout the book. The many more referenced sources in this edition strengthen the research base without sacrificing the text's easily comprehensible presentation.

The *Observational Activities* are new to the second edition. These activities will help students relate the chapter content to actual encounters with children and adults and will give them an opportunity to explore a particular aspect of or issue relating to development that they have read about. They may also stimulate good class discussion. There are two activities at the end of each major life period, plus one following the Prologue, which provides a general set of guidelines for the observational activities. Some topics explored in the observational activities include adult-infant interaction, preparing for fatherhood, children's numerical knowledge, friendships in middle childhood, teenage values, the value of children to young adults, perceptions of career development, and media stereotyping of the elderly.

OUTSTANDING FEATURES OF THE BOOK

Readability   The readability of the book is promoted, first, by careful organization: topics follow logically, and each is given an accurately descriptive heading. Second, the text is written to present even the most abstract concepts in lively prose that is easy to retain. Numerous colorful examples emphasize and clarify ideas. Finally, important technical terms are introduced in bold type, defined immediately in the text and again in the Glossary.

Stage Charts   Because the developmental theories of Erikson, Piaget, Kohlberg, and Duvall flow from one period of development into the next, the student needs to be oriented to these theories as a whole at each stage. To find the place in the theory, special charts are inserted at the appropriate points in the text. These charts present the entire theory in outline form.

Highlight Features   Distributed throughout the text are distinctive features highlighting relevant topics of particular interest. Where work and generativity are being discussed, for example, a feature portrays the challenge of being a female in male-dominated occupations.

Summaries and Further Readings   Every chapter concludes with a summary, organized into short, coherent paragraphs, that provides a handy review for the student. Also following each chapter is a list of annotated readings which will lead interested students to more information about matters that have aroused their curiosity.

Glossary   The end-of-text Glossary is a lifespan dictionary in miniature, defining all the important terms used in the text.

Supplements   Instructors will find the accompanying *Instructor's Manual* helpful in arranging their curricula. The Manual contains chapter outlines, research projects, and, short-answer and essay questions for tests which are correlated to each chapter of the book. The accompanying *Self-scoring Workbook* contains review questions and independent projects involving student observation and experimentation.

The *Slide Program for Developmental Psychology*, free upon bookstore purchase of 100 or more copies of the text, consists of 100 color slides and will allow instructors to visually reinforce facts and concepts.

ORGANIZATION OF THE BOOK

The second edition has a chapter length prologue in addition to its eight major parts. Each part covers the physical, cognitive, personality, and social development of the individual in one of the broad stages of growth.

The Prologue, "Lifespan Development: Issues, Theories, and Research," sketches the concerns of developmental psychology, summarizes the major theories of development, and provides an overview of how research on human development is done.

Part One, "Birth and Infancy," follows the development of the individual from conception through the first year of life. Chapter 1 describes the mechanisms of genetics and the many dimensions of prenatal development. Chapter 2 examines the birth process and describes the characteristics of the newborn. The infant's rapid physical growth and cognitive and social development are traced in Chapter 3.

Part Two, "Toddlerhood," contains two chapters on the period from one to about two years of age. Chapter 4 deals with the toddler's physical growth and cognitive and language development, while the social influences that mold the toddler's personality are discussed in Chapter 5.

Part Three, "Preschool Years," takes the child to age five or six. Physical and perceptual development are described in Chapter 6, growth in cognition and language in Chapter 7, and emotional development and social relations in Chapter 8.

Part Four, "Middle Childhood," follows the developing person through the grade school years to pubescence. Chapter 9 describes physical growth and considers various aspects of personality that arise in this period. Chapter 10 examines cognitive and moral development and discusses problems in the diagnosis and treatment of reading and learning disabilities. Chapter 11 focuses on the child's social relations at home, with peers, and at school.

Part Five, "Adolescence," treats the physical changes that occur at puberty and their effects on the individual's personality and social life. Chapter 12 tells how adolescents reach a mature level of sexual and cognitive development, and in Chapter 13 the issue of identity is explored.

Part Six, "Young Adulthood," presents the major developmental tasks confronting people as they make the transition to adulthood. Chapter 14 focuses on physical, cognitive, and personality changes experienced by young adults, and Chapter 15 examines parenting and family relations and occupational development.

Part Seven, "Middle Adulthood," takes the individual through the middle years of adult life, from approximately 40 to 60 years of age. Physical, cognitive, and personality development are described in Chapter 16. Chapter 17 examines midlife marital and family relations, as well as experiences and adjustments at work.

Part Eight, "Late Adulthood," completes the lifespan with chapters on aging and death and dying. Chapter 18 explores various factors that influence physical and cognitive adaptation in the later years as well as issues of identity and personality adjustment among the elderly. Chapter 19, which focuses on family life and adjustment to retirement, brings to a close issues of development with a look at the final changes that accompany death and dying.

ACKNOWLEDGMENTS

Many instructors of developmental psychology contributed in-depth evaluations of the manuscript. For their thoughtful reviews and many suggestions, we thank Joan McNeil, Kansas State University; Barbara V. Meyers, Avila College; April O'Connell, Santa Fe Community College; Phil Osborne, Hesston College; Bruce Roscoe, Central Michigan University; Donald G. Sprague, North Idaho College; Rena Toliver, Hartnell College; Susan K. Whitbourne, University of Rochester; and John Wilson, Golden West College.

This revision would not have been possible without the writing skills of Rodie Siegler. Also, our thanks to Cherlyn Granrose, Temple University, for her work on several adulthood sections.

The editorial staff of Holt, Rinehart and Winston also deserves mention. For their dedication and support, our thanks to Dan Loch, Lauren Procton Meyer, Fran Bartlett, Jeanette Johnson, Joe Samodulski, Annette Mayeski, and Christine Smith.

Contents

Chapter 5   Social Relationships   181

Part Three   Preschool Years   219

Chapter 6   Physical and Perceptual Development   221

Chapter 7   Cognition and Language   240

Chapter 8   Personality and Society

Part Four   Middle Childhood   301

Chapter 9   Growth and Personality   303

Chapter 10 Learning and Cognition 328

Chapter 11 Home, Peers, and School 356

Chapter 15   Family and Occupational Development 475

Part Seven   Middle Adulthood   507

Chapter 16   Physical, Cognitive, and Personality Development   509

Chapter 17   Family and Occupational Development   535

Part Eight   Late Adulthood   561

Chapter 18   Physical, Cognitive, and Personality Development   563

Chapter 19 Family Life, Retirement, and the Final Years 590

Prologue

❖❖❖❖❖❖

Lifespan Development: Issues, Theories, and Research

At times all of us, in the midst of living our lives, may pause to reflect on the meaning of life's course and our own passage through it. Before long, however, we are likely to discover that there is no single definition. No sooner have we achieved a perspective from which to examine ourselves, than that perspective changes. We become student, worker, spouse, parent, home-owner, supervisor, grandparent, and retiree. Early childhood seems far away, and we have trouble imagining our own death. How are we to make sense of it?

Development psychology is one of many disciplines which help people understand the nature of life. It is a relatively new field, which focuses on the changes that normally occur—in body, thought, and behavior—over the course of a life span. Some of these changes are obvious—the three inches marked up by the toddler in the second year. Others are uncovered only by study and research within a given culture; for example, the assumption of sex-role behavior in middle childhood, or the changes in self-image in middle age.

It has long been recognized that the most dramatic developments occur in childhood. This is so even if we exclude the merely physical: the acquisition of language, for example, rivals nearly any other life accomplishment we can think of. By contrast, it was assumed that relatively few developments occurred in adult life. These assumptions were reflected in the uneven growth of research. While child psychology became a full-fledged scientific discipline in the 1930s, the study of normal adults (as opposed to clinical samples) has grown slowly. Even today there are relatively few psychologists who have addressed themselves to the entire life span—or to that part of it we call adulthood. Middle age is much less understood than middle childhood. Of the adult portion of the life span, only *gerontology*, the study of the aged, has attracted a major research constituency.

This is, however, changing. Not the least reason for the change is the considerable interest of adults in themselves. We have come to be interested not only in the development of our children, or the psychological legacy of childhood, but in the very real growth we all experience from day to day.

THE STUDY OF HUMAN DEVELOPMENT

Bernice Neugarten, a prominent psychologist who specializes in middle and later adulthood, describes **development** as those processes which are biologically programmed or inherent in the person, and those ways in which the person is irreversibly transformed by interaction with the environment. "As a result of one's life history with its accumulating record of adaptations to both biological and social events, there is a continually changing basis within the individual for perceiving and responding to new events" (Neugarten, 1973). Developmental psychologists are interested in behavioral changes over the life span, and they identify the basis for these changes in the *interaction* of biological and environmental factors.

Specialists in human development study virtually everything about people: the way they grow and develop, the way their personalities are formed, the way they think and learn, and the way they respond to the special demands of their culture. And yet these individuals do more than just study development. They ask (and sometimes answer) questions that are important to all members of society.

For example, among the questions asked by developmental specialists are: Does contact between mother and child within the first few hours of life lead to improved communication in the two-year-old? To reduction of child abuse? Or to no significant differences in behavior? . . . Can elementary school teachers foster artistic creativity in the young schoolchild, and if so, how? . . . Can we as a society identify parents or children at risk from child abuse? And can we intervene? . . . Do we know if there are significant differences in the development of children raised in single-parent as opposed to two-parent homes? Or differences between children raised primarily by fathers as opposed to mothers? . . . Does the development of identity in adolescence affect intimacy relationships in young adulthood? . . . Is there such a thing as "mid-life crisis," and if so, in what areas of life does it have an impact? . . . How does aging influence the older person's adaptation to a changing world? And can we intervene to make the process of adaptation easier?

Most of us recognize the importance of such questions to parents, and to ourselves as developing adults. In addition, these questions have a practical application for those who formulate social policy. The research of specialists in human development has had an influence on such diverse social issues as child custody law, day care, education, media programming, occupational planning and development, retirement policy, and the care and welfare of the dying person.

As we shall see, however, not all developmental research addresses social problems. Much of it is basic research, which attempts to understand the processes governing development without regard for the practical implications of the findings. Yet both types of research—basic and applied—contribute to our understanding of the way in which people behave, think, and feel. And in so doing, they enable us to make decisions that will improve the quality of all our lives.

The Subject Matter of Human Development

For the sake of convenience, and in order to highlight specific growth processes, developmental psychologists divide their study of the person into several areas. These include physical development, cognitive development, and psychosocial development.

Physical development is the growth and biological aging of the individual—changes in size and shape as well as in physical and sensory capacities. Puberty is a development on the physical calendar; so is the slight decline in hearing that often occurs during the fifth decade of life.

Random selection of sample subjects allows human development researchers to study an unbiased representation of the population.

Cognitive development refers to the psychology of thinking and processes involved in thought, including problem solving, memory development, creativity, and the capacity for abstract thought. In this content area is intelligence as measured by the standardized test. Material tested varies with age of subjects, but generally intelligence tests measure acquired knowledge, such as basic arithmetic, verbal skills, social knowledge, and some forms of planning ability.

Psychosocial development describes the personality and emotional structures of individuals, as well as their usual ways of interacting. We shall talk about the kinds of development that are normal in a given social environment: that is, our focus will be on the ways people come to relate in orderly sequence to parents, friends, mate, job, children, and society itself. We shall also be interested in the *social roles* which people adopt and in the ways they come to differentiate themselves from others. For example, when and with what understanding do individuals assume the role of "working woman" or "retired person"? To what extent do people derive identity from parenting?

Most investigators tend to concentrate their research on only one or two areas of human development. Human beings, however, are not so simple. There is a constant interfacing of the different areas of functioning within the developing person. For example, mature sexual intimacy (a psychosocial

Are fathers and mothers equally competent to raise young children? Research in child development contributes knowledge and opinions on such questions which influence court decisions in the realm of child care.

achievement) depends, in part, on genital maturity (a physical development). Similarly, people cannot reach the highest levels of moral development until they are capable of abstract and hypothetical thought.

The Role of Theory

During the first half of this century much of the research in developmental psychology sought to discover and chart the course of development. Investigators often followed a specific line of inquiry, for example: When does X develop? How is X influenced by Y? The aim of this research was a *description* of development, not an *explanation* of it. As developmental psychology matured as a discipline researchers were no longer satisfied with simply describing the emergence and development of behaviors and skills. They wanted to understand the basis of development—to be able to explain why specific behaviors emerged at particular times. This shift in focus from questions of "what" and "when" to "why" and "how" heralded the emergence of formal theory in the study of human development.

According to Salkind (1981) a theory is a "group of logically related statements . . . that explain events that have happened in the past as well as predict events that will occur in the future." Thus, theories have both an *explanatory* and a *predictive* role. A theory serves as a basis from which to test hypotheses, and provides a framework for understanding the data that derive from our experiments.

In the study of human development we encounter a variety of theories. Some seek to identify universal principles governing *all* of development. Others focus on one aspect—for example, personality or intellectual development—and seek to explain that. Finally, some theories that contribute to our understanding of development are applicable to much larger areas of human concern (and in this sense are not theories of development at all). For example, behavioral theories, as the name suggests, offer explanations of the behavior of the rat, the chimpanzee, the human being of all ages, and even in a single muscle cell of the human arm.

There is no single theory of development. Rather, there are several different theories, each with a different focal point. Our willingness to accept one or more of these theories, even provisionally, influences the way we view people and the data we are likely to collect about them (Overton & Reese, 1973; Reese & Overton, 1970). For example, Arnold Gesell, one of the early pioneers of developmental psychology, believed that eye-hand coordination and other early demonstrations of intelligence were determined by the inner logic of neurological maturation—and by that alone (Gesell & Amatruda, 1941). If we accept Gesell's assumption of a maturational basis of early intelligence, however, we will not allocate our funds or energies to programs that attempt to speed up development by providing "enriched" nursery environments. Theories of development, therefore, influence not only the way we study people but the way we raise and educate them.

Development is perhaps most dramatically seen in the physical development and increasing motor abilities of the growing child. This was the first aspect of development to be studied.

MAJOR CONTEMPORARY THEORIES: AN INTRODUCTION

Psychosexual/Psychosocial Development: Freud and Erikson

Psychosocial development describes the personality and emotional structures of individuals. It shows how the emotional and biological needs of individuals become reconciled with the requirements of the society in which they live. We are describing psychosocial development, for example, when we say that an individual is "immature" or "unable to form relationships" or when we say that another person, conversely, is mature, dependable, and productive. Much of what we know about psychosocial development is based on the work of Sigmund Freud and his followers.

Freud (1856–1939) was a Viennese physician who specialized in what were called "nervous" or "mental" diseases. (Today Freud would probably be called a psychiatrist.) What is important to us is that Freud was a true developmentalist when it came to the study of personality. He believed that personality grew and developed, was formed and elaborated, much as a physical structure is. In emotional growth as well as physical growth people pass through stages. From his adult patients Freud learned that a failure to develop in one stage inhibited later development, often causing maladjustment. He concluded that adult personality was profoundly affected by early experience.

Stages in Psychosexual/Psychosocial Development

In no area was Freud's developmental thinking more startling, or more significant, than in the area of sexuality. Freud did not believe that sexuality arrived full blown in adolescence. Central to his theory was the assumption that different bodily modes of sexual expression become available to children as they develop. Freud defined sex as any type of bodily stimulation that is pleasurable, and he proceeded to show that the sexuality of adolescence and adulthood is the end stage of a long and orderly sequence.

At birth, according to Freud, the *oral* region is very sensitive to any kind of stimulation. Newborn infants will instinctively suck on any object brought to the mouth, even when they are not hungry. The lips and mouth are a source of sexual pleasure. Sometime in the second year the *anal* area replaces the oral area as a primary source of gratification. The shift from oral to anal stimulation concurs with the neurological development of the anal sphincter muscles, a development that enables children to gain control over their bowel movements. The next stage of development occurs between the ages of three to five or six and is designated as the *phallic* stage. Sexual gratification is achieved during this stage through genital stimulation (or masturbation). In other words, gratification is achieved without regard to the feelings of others—it is a self-centered approach to sexuality. During the elementary school years, the child enters the next period of development, the *latency* stage. This is the time when much of the psychic energy formerly invested in sexual desires is displaced or channeled to other behaviors—for example, mastering culturally

Sigmund Freud (1856–1939) believed that personality grows and develops in a series of ordered stages of psychosexual nature, and that failure to develop in one stage inhibits later development.

relevant skills. From a psychosexual perspective, then, this period is a lull. With the advent of adolescence, however, sexual desires burst forth once again, and the person enters into the final or *genital* stage. In contrast to the phallic period, sexual gratification is now based on mutuality of feelings, an adult intimacy between the self and another. Every stage of sexual development is associated with what we would ordinarily call psychological or social strivings. For example, in the phallic stage children must come to terms with their sexuality within the family: they must master their attraction to the parent of the opposite sex. With the emergence of genital sexuality, the adolescent must cope with the emotional turmoil that results from the need to attract and be intimate with others.

Freud's findings have been reinterpreted by Erik Erikson (b. 1902) a Danish psychotherapist who studied with the Freudian group in Germany before coming to the United States in the 1930s. Erikson's first interest was children. His first scientific observations were drawn from children at play. In his own Freudian-based theory Erikson showed that the sequence of bodily sensations Freud had identified were also a sequence of social experiences that had meaning for children within a given culture (Erikson, 1963). The stage of oral gratification is also the stage at which the infant establishes (or fails to estab-

Erik Erikson (b. 1902) developed the theory that social forces influence the person's development. He maintained that a series of crises occurs in response to demands society places on the developing individual.

lish) a sense of trust in the nurturing figure. The stage of anal control is also the time when the child gains control of other naughty impulses that become the object of parental discipline. For Erikson, to move from the oral stage to the anal stage is also to move from a relationship with a nurturing parent, whom one learns to trust or mistrust, to a relationship with a disciplining (toilet-training) parent, from whom one derives feelings of autonomy or shame. Unlike Freud, Erikson is primarily concerned with the ways in which *social* forces influence the person's development. His theory delineates a series of crises that occur in response to demands that society places on the developing individual—demands to conform to adult expectations about self-expression and self-reliance.

Erikson agrees with Freud's finding that early experience exerts a continuing influence on development. We do not simply graduate from the oral stage, with its crisis of trust. The crisis becomes less critical, but is nevertheless reexperienced in all later stages of development. (It is part of what we endure in developing adult intimacy, for example.) For Erikson as for Freud, each

stage of psychosocial development builds upon, and incorporates, the outcome of earlier stages.

Whereas Freud believed that the final psychosexual crisis occurred in
adolescence, Erikson saw additional psychosocial crises developing in adulthood. Indeed, Erikson's theory is one of the few theories of development that
extends through the full life span. He has written extensively, not only on
personality development in childhood and adolescence, but, as we shall see
later in the book, on the *normal* changes that occur in the developing adult.

Cognitive Development: Piaget

Cognitive development refers to the psychology of thinking, or what we usually
call intelligence. Included in this area of study are the processes involved in
problem-solving, memory development, creativity, and the capacity for both
logical and abstract thought. When we speak of cognitive development we
mean the orderly changes that occur in the way people intellectually understand and cope with their world.

Until about the 1930s children were considered to be miniature adults,
at least so far as intelligence was concerned. That is, children were thought
to differ from adults in the *quantity* of knowledge they had managed to acquire.
With the growth of cognitive research, and the revolutionary thinking of scientists such as Heinz Werner and Jean Piaget, it became clear that children
think and learn in ways that are quite different from adults. The mental activities of the young child differ *qualitatively*, and in a predictable way, from
the mental activities of older children and adults.

We can understand why this is so if we accept the argument of the
philosophical school called *constructivism*. According to this school of
thought all that we know of reality is based on our mental constructions. We
do not passively discover knowledge ready-made: we actively *construct* knowledge. Whatever the reality is, our knowledge of it is always a function of the
particular system by which we organize information.

Jean Piaget (1896–1980), a Swiss psychologist, biologist, and philosopher,
developed a remarkable theory about how children think, based on the philosophical assumptions of constructivism. Piaget showed that children construct knowledge in a way that differs from that of adults. Therefore, what
children know makes a different kind of sense from what adults know.

Piaget's own account of his discoveries demonstrates how great minds
see problems where others see solutions—and vice versa. In the 1920s Piaget
was working with Theophile Simon, the co-developer of the famous Simon-
Binet IQ tests. Piaget's job was to administer hundreds of IQ tests to children
at different ages, in order to establish the age norms when children would be
expected to pass each of the test items. According to the test instructions
children were to receive credit only if their answers were correct in the adult
sense. However, Piaget became fascinated with the children's *incorrect* answers. He noticed that the same incorrect answers were given by children in
the same age groups (Piaget, 1952). He began questioning children about how
they happened to arrive at their incorrect answers and concluded that at

Children's ideas about the world are often based upon assumptions that adults would find absurd.

different ages children used different methods to solve problems. Young children were not simply less intelligent than older children and adults. According to Piaget their thinking was *qualitatively different*. The essential problem in studying cognitive development was to uncover the different methods of thinking used by children at different ages.

Piaget subsequently rejected the practice of giving children questions that had correct and incorrect answers. Instead he asked open-ended questions and presented social dilemmas to them. He was then able systematically to study the reasoning behind children's answers. For example, he asked children what makes something "alive." He found that at a particular age children believe that anything that moves is alive. Therefore, they assign the attributes of life to a seemingly bizarre array of objects. It is quite common for five-year-olds to talk about the sun and moon following them when they are riding in the car or to describe the clouds as raining because they are "sad." The ideas are not absurd from the child's perspective because they are consistent with basic assumptions about the nature of reality.

As children develop, they replace one set of assumptions with another set of assumptions, thereby reorganizing the methods by which they construct knowledge. Children undergo many developmental changes before they finally adopt adult assumptions about the world (Piaget, 1950).

Stages of Cognitive Development

Like Freud, Piaget formulated a sequence of *stages* of development. These stages refer to levels of mental reasoning, showing how the child constructs knowledge anew at every stage of development.

Jean Piaget (1896–1980) formulated the theory that children's thinking is qualitatively different from that of adults and goes through a series of cognitive stages.

In the first stage of cognitive development, from birth to approximately two years of age, thinking is limited to immediate sensory experience and motor behaviors (and so this is called the *sensory-motor stage*). It is a hands-on, trial-and-error type of thinking. Infants "know" objects only in terms of their direct actions upon the objects. Thus, a nipple is known only as something to be sucked, looked at, touched, etc., and the only qualities of the nipple that can be known are those that are revealed by sucking on it, looking at it, etc. The infant cannot understand that nipples and other objects and events can exist somewhere in space-time when he or she is not directly acting on them. That is, the infant functions according to the principle of "out of sight, out of mind" (Piaget, 1952). Thus, if an infant under the age of nine months is playing with a rattle and, in full view of the infant, we take the rattle away and place it under a nearby blanket, the infant will make no attempt to retrieve it. The rattle simply does not have an independent existence for the infant. It exists only as long as he or she is able to perceive it directly. This is so because infants are incapable of mentally constructing a symbol to represent the object that is no longer visible. (A *symbol* is something such as a word, image, or activity that represents something else. Without a system of symbols to represent things, infants are prisoners of their immediate experience.)

The second stage of development, which lasts approximately from two to seven years of age, is known as the stage of *preoperational thought*. During this stage children become increasingly capable of symbol formation. They master the ability to use many different kinds of symbol systems to represent the objects and events they experience. One of these symbol systems is language.

Although the ability mentally to represent experiences emerges in the second stage of development, children's representations remain limited, by adult standards. Children can only represent states of being; they cannot conceive of the transformation from one state to another. It is during the third major period of cognitive development, the state of *concrete operations*, that children become capable of thinking about how things change—and not just how they appear at different times. This stage of development begins at about seven years of age and is not superseded until early adolescence. The difference between concrete operational thinking and earlier stages is apparent in what is perhaps Piaget's most famous experiment. He presented children with two identical glasses of water and asked them if there was the same amount of water to drink in one glass as there was in the other. The two glasses of water looked the same, so all the children agreed that there was the same amount to drink in both glasses. Then Piaget took one glass of water and poured it into a glass of a different shape—one that was taller and thinner. Again he asked the children if there was the same amount of water to drink in the original glass as there now was in the taller and thinner glass. Children at the preoperational stage denied that the two amounts of water were the same. Most thought that there was more water to drink in the tall, thin glass. Children at the concrete-operational stage, however, recognized that although the appearance of the quantities of water was different, the amount of water in the glasses remained equivalent. Preoperational children had no way of relating the state of the quantity of water in the first glass to its transformed state in the second glass; concrete-operational children had developed the ability to do so.

Piaget found that the first three stages of mental reasoning are acquired by children all over the world at about the same ages and in the same sequence. Regardless of whether or not someone has attempted to teach them the solutions, children will shift their reasoning from one form to the next within a particular age range. Once the new form of reasoning is acquired, they will think in qualitatively different ways about the things that they experience. The moon no longer follows them; it is simply there.

The final stage of cognitive development is the stage of *formal operations,* or what we usually call abstract thought. This stage may be attained as early as eleven or twelve, although apparently some people attain it much later in adolescence, and some people not at all (Piaget, 1972). The stage of formal operation differs from earlier stages in an interesting way. In the concrete-operational stage children acquire the capacity mentally to represent transformations, but only transformations of concrete objects and events—that is, things that they actually experience. In other words, children master the ability to think about things. In the formal-operational stage children master the ability to think about thoughts. By this we mean that children are able to reason not only about things that they actually experience, but about things that have no concrete existence. They can reason about abstract ideas.

Adolescents, unlike younger children, can reason about ideals and philosophy. Adolescents are, in fact, known to be idealistic and fond of talking about the meaning of justice, or love, or other abstract concepts. They are able to enter into such discussions because in the formal operational stage they acquire the capacity for *propositional reasoning* (Inhelder & Piaget, 1958). They can begin with assumptions that need not have any basis in reality and lead to conclusions that logically follow from the assumptions.

As with Freudian stages of psychosocial development, we will find that in order to understand any cognitive stage we must keep in mind the child's progress through all earlier stages. Children do not simply graduate from one stage to another: the form of reasoning most recently mastered never entirely replaces earlier forms of reasoning. Piaget has stated that people typically function at the formal-operational stage for only a few hours a day, and that most of the time they resort to trial and error forms of reasoning (Piaget, 1960). And most of us have the experience of approaching some new piece of machinery with the sensorimotor skills of infancy. In cognition, as in other areas, we are the living sum of our earlier development.

The Learning of Behavior: B. F. Skinner and Other Behaviorists

The theories we have reviewed so far consider biology and maturation to be crucial factors shaping the course of development. In Erikson's theory, for example, sexual maturity is partly responsible for the adolescent's need to attract and become intimate with others. In Piaget's theory, too, neurological maturation is, in part, what makes possible the acquisition of cognitive operations. These theories recognize, to varying degrees, the role of the physical and social environments in development—but only insofar as these environmental factors interact with biological factors.

By contrast, one major theoretical approach to psychology attributes primary importance to environmental factors and relatively little importance to biological and maturational factors. This theoretical approach, called *behaviorism*, explains human development as the accumulated effects of learned responses. Children's behavior changes as they learn new responses, as a result of experiences in new environments—the high chair, the kindergarten, the third grade, the baseball diamond, and so forth. The difference between children and adults is a *quantitative* one: adults have many more responses in their behavioral repertoires, and they have been exposed to many more different environments.

According to behaviorists there are no developmental "stages": people at different ages do not have access to different kinds of learning mechanisms. The mechanisms of learning hold for people of all ages, and even for animals. Just as behaviorists posit continuity instead of a series of qualitative shifts

Behaviorists argue that children's behavior changes in response to elements in their environment rather than as the result of biological or maturational factors.

across development from infancy to adulthood, they posit continuity across species. In fact, the first laws of learning were established by a physiologist who worked with dogs, Ivan Pavlov (1849–1936). He demonstrated that hungry dogs automatically learned to salivate at the sound of a bell when the sound was paired with an offering of food. As a specialist in the physiology of digestion Pavlov knew that salivation at the sound of a bell was a response not naturally in the animal's behavioral repertoire. It was a *learned* response. Moreover, it was learned because the environmental situation made it seem appropriate—or *reinforced* it (with the offering of food).

B. F. Skinner (b. 1904), an American psychologist, has extended Pavlov's work by showing that even complicated responses that originate with the organism are shaped by the environment. Working primarily with rats, Skinner has shown that responses that are followed by rewards are likely to be repeated in similar situations in the future. In one experiment hungry rats were placed in cages that contained a horizontal metal bar which, when pressed, emitted a pellet of food. The rats, when first placed in the cages, made a random series of exploratory responses. A probable response that occurred during their exploration was the pressing of the bar. As soon as a rat accomplished this, it received a food pellet. The pairing of a seemingly random response with a reward increased the likelihood that the rats would repeat the bar-pressing behavior under similar environmental conditions. Thus, the initial exploration was "shaped" by the experimenter through the use of reinforcement. A new learned response had been established (Skinner, 1938).

Skinner went on to discover a series of principles regarding reinforcement and learning. For example, he found that rats retained a learned response longer if reinforcement (pellets of food) did not follow every single bar press during the learning process, but occurred on an intermittent schedule, so that some responses are reinforced but others are not.

The principles of Pavlov and Skinner were believed to hold equally for humans as well as for animals. For example, we shall see that infants learn to engage in extensive vocalization because their first random sounds are rewarded by parents in various ways. Similarly, children learn to respond with fearful behaviors to dogs, or doctors, or whatever when their first encounters with these stimuli are paired with pain or some other unpleasantness. Behavioral scientists believe that what we call development is simply what we learn. Since we never stop learning, behavioral psychologists contribute to our understanding of development across the whole human life span.

As with other theories, behaviorism disregards some aspects of the human experience and emphasizes others. What behaviorism emphasizes is, of course, behavior—what the person (or organism) actually *does*. What the organism may think or feel is not a matter for direct study. According to the behaviorists the mental processes that cannot be observed must be considered irrelevant to psychology. Thus, behavioral scientists limit study to objective, observable behavior, and they describe behavioral changes in terms of stimulus and response. In most cases they conduct their research in controlled laboratory environments, with animals. The findings are then generalized to explain human behavior. In the strict sense behaviorists do not offer a theory of human development; their laws of learning apply equally well to other organisms.

Social Learning Theory

An increasingly significant variation of behaviorism is a school of psychology known as *social learning theory*. The foremost figures in this school are Clark Hull, John Dollard, Neil Miller, Albert Bandura, and Robert Sears. These theorists differ from the more traditional behaviorists in that they give greater recognition to the nature of the organism in explaining how behaviors are learned. To understand human beings, therefore, they work predominantly with humans. They also accept the study of some processes that are not observable; these underlying processes (called "intervening variables") are recognized as helping to determine overt behavior. Despite these differences social learning theory incorporates most of the basic principles and mechanisms of learning. The social learning theorists, like the behaviorists, view development as the gradual accumulation of responses rather than as a series of qualitative changes in underlying patterns of emotional or cognitive organization.

Perhaps the greatest contribution of social learning theory is its recognition that responses can be acquired without exposure to direct reinforcement (Bandura and Walters, 1963). Much of what children learn occurs through their natural tendency to imitate or model the behavior of others. If they witness a model (such as a parent) being reinforced, their imitation of the model's behavior will result in "vicarious reinforcement." Social learning theorists feel that vicarious reinforcement is as strong a conditioner of behavior as direct reinforcement. Parents are children's most effective models during the early periods of development. Later, as the person's world broadens, peers and other significant people outside the family become models.

Much of the research in social learning theory has sought to specify the conditions that enhance learning through imitation and modeling. For example, researchers have shown that people are more likely to imitate a model whom they personally hold in high regard and whom they experience as being similar to themselves than a model who is not highly regarded and experienced as different. We will encounter social learning explanations of many behavioral patterns that are important in our culture—among them aggression and sex-role behavior (such as "boyishness" or "femininity").

How Theories Differ

A common notion holds that there are different theories in science competing for the ultimate solution to a set of common problems. This notion probably stems from the media's tendency to dramatize science and scientists. In actuality it is usually impossible to test one theory against another to determine which is the "right" one, for each theory defines its own areas of investigation and its methods (Reese & Overton, 1970). Thus, theories of development differ from one another according to what are the most important aspects of behavior to be studied. For example, Piaget would not deny the validity of the principles of behavioral conditioning and modeling, but he would argue that they provide a trivial and simplistic picture of what human development is all about (Piaget, 1971). He might even argue that behaviorists studying the development of intelligence in children look at children's correct answers while he looks at their incorrect answers. It would be difficult for researchers working within these different theories to agree on a common set of problems to be studied since they are looking at different things. We might say that each theory is true to its own topics of investigation, but to the extent that different theories define different topics of investigation, they do not compete with one another. While there have been some attempts to extend theories formulated in regard to one area of investigation to another area, they have not been generally successful. For example, Miller and Dollard (1941) have attempted to apply laws of learning and conditioning to account for areas of personality development first proposed by Freud.

Ultimately, it appears that scientific theories in human development, as well as in psychology and other sciences in general, stand or fall not on the weight of scientific evidence (for all theories seem to be able to establish their own foundations of evidence) but on how *useful* they are. If a theory can make sense out of behavioral phenomena that appear otherwise quite puzzling, and if there is enough consensus that the phenomena in question are important to understand, then the theory will flourish. As attempts are made to extend the theory, to capture increasingly wider areas of relevance, the theory will grow and change.

RESEARCH

Formulating theory is only one part of scientific investigation. Conducting research is equally important. Most of what you will read about in developmental psychology is based on findings from research studies. Much of this research, of course, is designed with a specific framework in mind, a framework that defines terms and suggests questions to be investigated. Whether researchers collect specimens, take measurements, or devise elaborately controlled laboratory experiments, they proceed with some attention to theory. Results may or may not support the theory. In some instances, a set of findings may suggest an entirely new theory by bringing together a new constellation of evidence.

In gathering the data they need to test their ideas, scientific researchers seek the most accurate information available. They know, however, that their preconceptions about the phenomena they wish to study will affect their selection and organization of facts and the connections they perceive among them. They use empirical methods of investigation—methods based on observations or experience of the real world—which enable them to approach the phenomena under study as objectively as possible.

EXPERIMENTAL DESIGN

There are two basic experimental designs available to the psychologist who studies development over the life span—the cross-sectional design, and the longitudinal design.

In a **cross-sectional study**, different age groups are tested or observed at one point in time. For example, if a psychologist wants to compare the level of moral reasoning of thirty- and sixty-year-olds, he might administer a questionnaire to subjects in those age categories, within the relatively short period of a week or two. If the thirty-year-olds demonstrated higher levels of moral reasoning than the sixty-year-olds, the researcher might conclude that young adults are morally more sensitive than older adults. He might go further and hypothesize that adults lose their ability to draw moral conclusions as they age. A cross-sectional study has the advantage of being quick and relatively inexpensive. Moreover, it gives the psychologist a good overview of the process under investigation.

A second way of studying the problem would be to follow a group of individuals over a given time period. In a **longitudinal design**, the researcher would not compare the sixty- and thirty-year-olds; instead he would compare a group of sixty-year-olds to themselves as tested thirty years earlier. From a large sample, he would determine whether people became more or less morally sophisticated as they grew older. The study would proceed over thirty years and, in order to make best use of time and funds, would probably study more than one trait.

If the phenomena being measured could be expected to show changes in a shorter period, subjects might be studied in a *short-term longitudinal design*. For example, to observe the variables that influence the child's transition from preoperational to operational thought, the psychologist might study subjects over the period of six months. The short-term longitudinal study is sensitive to small changes in the individual, and allows the researcher to observe transitional periods.

The choice between a cross-sectional or longitudinal design, when it arises, is an important one. In studying any aspect of human development—be it moral reasoning, IQ, self-esteem, sexuality—the design of the experiment may influence results. This is so because each design has certain built-in biases. The cross-sectional design brings to light not only the effects of age and aging, but what psychologists call *generation* or *cohort effects*. A sixty-year-old is different from a thirty-year-old not only because he is thirty years older, but because he has lived through different historical events and trends. Suppose that a moral reasoning questionnaire attempted to find out the subjects' attitudes toward war or conscientious objectors. The sixty-year-old may relate those questions to his World War II service; the thirty-year-old will remember Vietnam. It might be inappropriate to conclude from the results that people become more warlike or less tolerant of conscientious objectors as they grow older. It might be more appropriate to attribute the difference to a generation effect—to the difference between having fought "the good war" and having been asked to fight a questionable one.

Because we live in a fast-paced technological age, generation effects (if unrecognized by the researchers or their reader) can be especially troublesome. For example, researchers in intelligence and creativity have found it difficult to determine the effects of aging by means of a simple cross-sectional study. For succeeding generations, the difference in education, nutrition, media exposure, and so on, are simply too great.

In the longitudinal study, data are restricted to a single cohort. However, the longitudinal study presents its own difficulties. For one thing, a longitudinal study represents a tremendous research commitment. There are no quick results. In some cases the original researchers are unable to direct the study to its conclusion. More troublesome is the fact that the subjects who tend to drop out of the study do not constitute a random sample. They are generally the least motivated, least healthy, and least competent subjects. Consequently, the results at the end of the longitudinal study may reflect the characteristics of the better-endowed subjects, rather than the average subject the researcher set out to study. For example, a longitudinal study on a given sample may show greater sexual activity in eighty-year-old men than in seventy-year-old men. This interesting finding might mean that sexual activity increases with age; or it might mean that those who survived into their eightieth year, being a vigorous and elite group, were also more sexually active than average men in the elderly population.

A final, more subtle, problem with the longitudinal study is that some changes in individuals are reflections of *time of measurement* rather than aging. If we return to the sexuality example, we can see that changes in cultural attitudes and expectations could affect a person's behavior as well as her response to testing. A young woman interviewed in the 1950s might say that she has sexual intercourse with her husband an average of once a week, and never in any but the standard position. Interviewed twenty-five years later, in the mid-70s, she says that she has intercourse three to four times a week and has tried a variety of sexual positions. This may mean that the middle-aged woman has greater sexual desires and is more open to variety than she was as a young woman. However, times have changed since the 1950s. The subject may simply be less embarrassed to answer questions than she was twenty-five years ago. Or she may have been influenced by an historical event, such as the publication of *The Joy of Sex* (Comfort, 1972). The point is that the longitudinal design in itself does not enable us to make sound generalizations about the effects of aging. As with the cross-sectional design, careful interpretation is needed.

Conceptualizing a Study

The first thing that a researcher must do in an investigation is to state the problem precisely—that is, to specify what phenomena and what relationships will be studied. The researcher usually phrases the problem as a question, using words that are as unambiguous as possible. Suppose, for example, that a researcher who has been working with delinquent children discovers from talking with them that many of them seem to be quite ingenious in their misbehavior. The researcher wonders if there is some connection between creativity and delinquency. Thus, the question: *What is the relation between creativity (as measured by a test of creativity) and delinquent behavior (as indicated by arrest records) for youths between the ages of ten and fourteen?* After the researcher has stated the problem, he or she can then review the studies that already have been done in the area to be investigated. This survey of the existing literature will usually help the researcher to sharpen his or her conception of the problem.

Variables

The phenomena under study in scientific investigations are called *variables.* In the area of human development variables may be age, sex, socioeconomic class, aggressive behavior, anxiety, cognitive level, self-concept—or virtually any factor associated with human beings.

There are two kinds of variables: independent and dependent. The *independent variable* is the hypothesized *cause* in the relationship being studied; it is the variable that is manipulated or varied by the researcher. The *dependent variable* is the hypothesized *effect* of the relation; it should vary with changes in the independent variable.

Research Methods

Once the researcher has posed the question to be studied, and has defined the way in which the variables will be measured, a research method must be chosen. The specific method decided upon depends on the problem under investigation, and the way in which the variables have been defined. Some research questions lend themselves to experimental methods; others can best be tested by correlational procedures.

In *experimental methods*, researchers have direct control over at least one of the independent variables. They manipulate that variable and observe the dependent variable to see if it changes as the independent variable is changed. Suppose, for example, that a researcher asks this question: Will increasing the frustration experienced by three-year-olds increase their aggressive behavior? The researcher defines frustration as the condition of three-year-olds when they are offered an attractive toy which is then suddenly withdrawn; aggression is defined as hitting or pushing other children, and it is measured by the number of times the subjects perform such acts in a given period of time. The researcher can design an experiment in which a group of three-year-olds are observed in a playroom, exposed to the frustrating experience, and then observed again. The observers record the incidence of aggressive behavior is the dependent variable; it is assumed to be caused by the experimentally induced frustration, the independent variable. The experimenter can change the degree of frustration to see if this affects the amount of aggression that ensues.

In many developmental studies there is no independent variable because none of the variables in the study can be controlled by the researcher. In a study of the relationship between IQ and aggressive behavior, for example, the following question might be asked: Do ten-year-olds who score high on the Stanford-Binet IQ test exhibit less aggressive behavior than ten-year-olds who score lower? In this case the variable, IQ, cannot be manipulated by the researchers. All they can do is measure and correlate it to behavior. The method used in such studies is thus called *correlational.* Because researchers cannot control the independent variable in such a study, *they* cannot be sure that one variable actually caused the effects on another variable. (Perhaps bright ten-year-olds have some other characteristic in common that directly affects their aggressive behavior.) Correlational research provides indirect causes by demonstrating how the changes in one variable are *associated with* changes in other variables.

Correlational methods are especially useful when people are studied in *naturalistic* settings, such as the playground, home, or classroom. In such studies the researchers choose not to manipulate any variables, not to administer any tests. Instead they base data on careful and systematic observations of people's behavior.

Research Data

The information generated in psychological research is based on knowledge about some sample of the population from which conclusions are drawn about an entire population. In sampling, the researchers take a portion of the population to represent the entire population. They study ten or fifty or three hundred infants and say that the conclusions apply to all infants like those in the study.

Sampling

In selecting sample subjects researchers may use the principles of random selection to ensure that every member of the population being studied has the same chance of being chosen for the study. Random sampling produces an unbiased sample of the population that may be taken to represent the entire group.

Suppose a study is planned to determine the effect of a reading-readiness program on kindergarten children. If the subjects are selected through random-sampling techniques, they are likely to have the same range of reading readiness skills at the beginning of the study as the entire group of all kindergarteners. Some of the children will be very ready to read, some will lack the ability to make certain visual discriminations necessary for reading, and so on. The randomly selected sample group will have these characteristics in proportions that are related to the proportions in the population as a whole. This means that if the researchers manipulate one variable of the reading readiness of the sample group, they can measure the degree to which the same manipulation will affect the population as a whole. Using the principles of random selection to choose subject samples allows researchers to know how confidently they can generalize the results of their research.

Reliability and Validity

Measures must be *reliable* if the data produced in a study are to be accurate. Reliability means that if researchers measure the same phenomenon today, tomorrow, or next week, they will get approximately the same results. *It* also means that if someone else uses the same measuring procedures in a duplicate study ten years from now, the results should be the same.

Measures must also be *valid* if they are to produce useful data. A measure has validity if it really measures what it says it does. When a variable must be inferred from behavior, such as aggression, the researchers need to ask whether the behavior they are measuring actually demonstrates that variable.

Random selection of sample subjects allows child development researchers to study an unbiased representation of the population. Do the children in the photograph represent a random sample?

For example, suppose a four-year-old builds a tower with blocks and then knocks the tower over. Is this an expression of aggression, hostility, frustration, or the happy exuberance that comes from a feeling of control over the environment? How can the researcher determine what the behavior means? This question must be answered before research results can be validly applied to behavior outside the research situation.

It is possible for a measure to be reliable and yet be invalid. If a test for creativity is reliable, it will produce the same scores if administered under the same conditions. If the test is valid, it actually measures the creative quality. Good research rests on measures that are both reliable and valid.

Data Collection

Researchers gather data in a variety of ways. Workers in the field of human development often rely on observation for data collection, but they also use interviews, objective tests, and other methods and combinations of methods.

Observation of behavior involves, very simply, watching and recording what subjects do and say. It may take place in a laboratory, in which the environment is highly controlled by the researcher, or in a natural environment. Researchers strive to attain reliability by having all the observers record what they see on standard forms and by comparing the reports of two observers making the same observation. The chief problem with the observation method is that the observers may introduce biases into the recording of the behavior. This problem can be alleviated by careful construction of instruments that clearly define the behavior to be recorded. Rather than asking observers to record incidences of dependency on the teacher in a classroom, for example, a researcher may ask observers to note every time a child asks permission from the teacher before doing something. The second record would be much more objective than the first.

Another problem inherent in observation is that the presence of observers may change the behavior of the subjects. Observers should be as unobtrusive and nonjudgmental as possible, especially in studies involving a natural environment.

Interviews and **questionnaires** are another means of data collection. Oral interviews can be used effectively in collecting data from children because the interviewer can adapt the questions to the child, rephrasing or explaining when the child does not understand. Interviews can be highly structured situations in which the wording, order, and time given to answer each question is fixed—or they may be more flexible and open-ended.

Numerous objective *tests* have been devised to measure intelligence, aptitudes for a wide variety of skills, achievement in general and specific areas of knowledge, personality, and attitudes. Paper and pencil tests answered by multiple choice are most common.

Results and Discussion

The unprocessed information that an investigator gathers in research is called the raw data of the study. At the end of an observational study of behavior, for example, the researcher would have a stack of recording forms filled out by observers—or a computer run of results. If the study is purely descriptive, the raw data comprise the information sought by the study and need only to be codified as the end product of the research.

In most psychological research the raw data do not constitute the end product of the study. If the research begins with a hypothesis, the investigators collect data and then return to their hypothesis to see whether the data refute it. Often this means that they will try to determine whether the results are *significant*—that is, could not have occurred by chance. If a statistical test shows that the probability of obtaining the specific results by chance was five times out of a hundred or less, the results will be usually accepted as being statistically significant.

Once the raw data have been analyzed statistically, the researchers may then go on to discuss or explain their results. They will also relate the results of their research to other studies and to broader theoretical constructs in developmental psychology.

Ethical Considerations

Any research involving human subjects raises ethical questions. Child development research requires special attention to ethical considerations because children are generally considered to be more vulnerable than adults and because it is often difficult to communicate with children so that they can understand all of the implications of a particular research procedure. The specification of what types of experimental procedures violate ethical standards has recently become a topic of intense debate among psychologists and politicians. Some of the standards that have emerged from this debate include the need for investigators to obtain the prior consent of all participants in a psychological study. As much as possible, "the investigator [must] inform participants of all features to the research that reasonably might be expected to influence willingness to participate . . ." (American Psychological Association, 1973). The participants must understand that even if they initially give their consent to participate in a study, they are free to change their minds and withdraw their consent at any time. If the research involves any physical risk or mental discomfort, harm, or danger, the investigator must justify such effects in terms of the potential benefits of the research findings and inform the participants of any and all potential risks. In research involving human subjects investigators typically must have their procedures reviewed by an independent review board consisting of their peers and, often, members of the lay community. The approval of such committees for the protection of human subjects must be obtained prior to soliciting participants in a study (U.S. Department of Health, Education, and Welfare, 1971).

The difficulties in applying these standards to children who participate in research are obvious. Children are not capable of giving their consent for their own participation. Permission must be obtained from the child's parents or guardians, and the researcher must explain to them the nature of the study and describe any risk of stress or harm to the child. Where the research design permits full disclosure of these matters to the subject, the ethical researcher will explain them to the child as well, using language that the child can understand. With preschool children the explanation of the research procedure can often be expressed in terms of a game that the investigator wants the child to play.

In designing a study researchers should be aware of the need to minimize both short-term and long-term adverse effects on the subject. In explaining the experiment to the child's parents, researchers must be frank about the level of anxiety, frustration, or stress that will be involved and must be in a position to predict the effects of this discomfort on the child. After the experiment has been performed, it may also be necessary to explain to the child (in the child's terms) the reasons for any discomfort in the experiment. For example, the researcher might encourage the child to express feelings about the experience, so that all concerned will be aware of the child's perception and better able to relieve any difficulties that have arisen.

Children are not the only group of subjects which present the researcher with ethical questions. Other groups, particularly those who are institutionalized or are relatively powerless, have generated concern. For example, it is acknowledged that special care must be exercised in designing studies involving elderly patients in nursing homes, prisoners, or inmates of mental institutions. One issue is the potential subject's right to decline to participate. If a prisoner's privileges (or, for that matter, a college student's grade) depend on participation, some would argue that the individual does not really have "freedom to decline." When nursing home patients are involved in developmental studies, the powerlessness of the subjects (and the disregard which society in general shows this group) give cause for concern. Is the research likely to invade the older patient's privacy, or compromise his adjustment to what is, after all, his only home? Sometimes the issues involved are complex. For example, if the researcher has a scientific basis for believing that a certain manipulation will so improve adjustment as to reduce mortality rates of patients in the first year, is he ethically justified in setting up a control group which does not benefit from the manipulation? To what extent is he justified in manipulating the environment at all?

With human beings, in general, an important issue is the use of concealment or deception by the researcher. Sometimes, as the APA guidelines recognize, deception appears to be a "methodological requirement" of the study. For example, a group of subjects may be told that a study involves perception of shapes; what is actually observed is the way in which subjects can be persuaded to change their responses (distort their perceptions) as a result of peer pressure brought to bear by "subjects" (actually confederates placed by the researcher). Only after the study is completed is the subject informed of its nature. Although many studies of this sort appear quite harmless, others (for example, those in which the subject is made to believe that he is administering painful shocks to another) have drawn criticism. Many psychologists condemn the practice of deceiving research participants. They feel that experiments in which the researcher must lie to the subject are not worth doing (Mussen, 1960).

SUMMARY

▶ The scientific study of human development is a relatively new and growing field. It is concerned with the physical, cognitive, and psychosocial changes that occur in individuals across the whole life span.

▶ Many theories of human development have been proposed during the twentieth century, and each has supporters. Scientific theories have a predictive and an explanatory role. They serve as a basis from which to test hypotheses, and provide a framework for understanding the data that derive from experiments.

▶ Sigmund Freud (1856–1939) and Erik Erikson (b. 1902) based their theories of development on psychosexual/psychosocial factors. Freud found that there were five stages in sexual development—oral, anal, phallic, latency, and genital—and that failure to develop in one stage inhibited later development. Erikson believed that social forces exert a strong influence on an individual's movement from one stage to the next. Building on Freud's stages, Erikson went on to specify psychosocial stages throughout the life span.

▶ Jean Piaget (1896–1980) developed a theory of cognitive or intellectual development that specified how an individual's thought processes are different at various ages. Piaget discovered four stages from birth through adolescence—sensorimotor, preoperational thought, concrete operations, and formal operations.

▶ Behaviorism, another major theory of development, attributes primary importance to environmental factors. According to behaviorists, an organism learns behaviors which are rewarded or reinforced by the environment. B. F. Skinner (b. 1904) and other behaviorists believe that development is comprised of what an individual learns throughout life. An increasingly significant variation of behaviorism is social learning theory, which gives greater recognition to the nature of the organism in explaining how it learns behavior.

▶ The basic experimental designs available to the developmental psychologist are the cross-sectional and longitudinal designs. The cross-sectional design involves testing different age groups at a single point in time. Longitudinal designs, in contrast, test the same sample of people more than once over a given period of time. Each method has its strengths and weaknesses, and data derived from each must be carefully interpreted.

▶ In conducting scientific research the first step is conceptualizing the study—i.e., stating the problem precisely. Then the variables are determined. The independent variable is the hypothesized cause, which can generally be controlled by the researcher; the dependent variable is the hypothesized effect. In many studies the variables cannot be controlled by the researcher, who must then use correlational methods to determine how the changes in one variable are associated with changes in other variables.

▶ The information, or data, generated in research may be based on a random sample of the population under study. Two important factors in any research project are reliability—producing the same results at different times under the same conditions—and validity—ensuring that the study measures what it says it measures.

▶ Researchers collect data through observation, interviews, tests, and other methods. The researchers then analyze the data statistically and explain the results in terms of other studies and the broader theoretical constructs in the field being studied.

▶ Researchers in human development must be especially aware of ethical considerations. In any studies involving children, or, indeed, any living subjects, adverse short- or long-term, effects must be minimized and appropriate consent obtained. This problem is of great concern to researchers today.

FURTHER READINGS

Ariès, Philippe. *Centuries of childhood: A social history of family life,* **Robert Baldick (trans.). New York: Vintage, 1962.**
This fascinating history of childhood from early medieval to modern times includes discussions of children's games, dress, social behavior, and education. It also traces the development of the family from the fourteenth century to the present. Ariès makes extensive use of primary sources such as paintings and diaries, and his history is full of rich detail and the lives of children in early times.

Asimov, Isaac. *The intelligent man's guide to science.* **New York: Basic Books, 1963.**
These two volumes, the first of which deals with the physical sciences and the second with the biological sciences, cover both the content and the methodology of the various sciences. Especially useful as a popular introduction for readers who feel that science is too abstract, difficult, and mysterious for them to understand.

Bronfenbrenner, Urie (Ed.). *Influences on human development.* **Hinsdale, Ill.: Dryden, 1972.**
A collection of readings in child development that covers a broad range of topics and includes many examples of the use of statistics in research. Among the many topics covered are early deprivation, the effects of television violence on children, group upbringing experiments, birth order in relation to achievement, and the socialization of student activists.

Ginsburg, Herbert, and Opper, Silvia. *Piaget's theory of intellectual development.* **Englewood Cliffs, N.J.: Prentice-Hall, 1969.**
Beginning with a short biography of Piaget, this book outlines his research and theoretical work from infancy through adolescence. The authors also discuss the implications of Piaget's work in the area of education.

Irwin, D. Michelle, and Bushnell, M. Margaret. *Observational strategies of child study.* **New York: Holt, Rinehart and Winston, 1980.**
This practical book surveys a variety of observational techniques for studying children, with relevant applications and lab assignments.

Salkind, Neil J. *Theories of human development.* **New York: Van Nostrand, 1981.**
This book presents a clearly written critical analysis of the major theories and issues in human development.

Skinner, B. F. *About behaviorism.* **New York: Knopf, 1974.**
The famous American behaviorist discusses the basic principles of human conditioning and reinforcement.

Observational Activities

Prologue

Instructions for Observational Activities

Each part of this new edition ends with exercises in observation designed to help you experience some of the situations you have read about in the pertaining chapters. In most cases the children you will observe will be easy to find: friends' children, children on public playgrounds, in parks, in supermarkets, campus child-care centers, shopping malls, and restaurants. You will not generally need to interact with your subjects, but you should—out of courtesy—inform the child's caretaker that you are observing the child as part of a college course whenever you feel that you might be noticed.

Your procedure for the exercises will consist of the following steps, which you might want to write down on your record sheet:

1. Purpose of your observation.
2. Place or location of your observation.
3. Date of your observation.
4. Subject(s)' age, sex, and any special characteristics you need to note.
5. Length of your observation in minutes.
6. If permission was granted for the observation, and if so by whom.
7. Careful record of your observation with notes describing the incident and setting in enough detail that it can be analyzed later. Be careful to stick to the facts—what actually was done and said by the subject. Try not to interpret actions or give them emotional labels (i.e., angry, sad, confused).
8. Brief paragraph of conclusions or findings developed from your observation. Most colleges and universities have a Human Subjects Committee to evaluate and approve of research that involves people. Your instructor will be able to give you guidance on structuring your observations so that you meet requirements.

Adult-Infant Interaction

When a caretaking adult responds to a baby's needs or wants, the baby learns to behave in a way that will get what is wanted or needed from that adult. Observe an adult with an infant of no more than three months of age (home, infant-care center, or public area). Watch the adult-infant interaction when the baby clearly wants the adult's attention. Write a description of the interaction, paying special attention to the following:

1. How does the baby go about getting the adult's attention?
2. What does the baby seem to want from the adult?
3. How does the adult respond?
4. What is the baby's response after the adult's attention?

In analyzing your notes, include a final paragraph that deals with these questions:

1. Would you do anything different in the same situation?
2. If so, what and why?

PART ONE

Birth and Infancy

Chapter 1

❖❖❖❖❖❖❖

Prenatal Development

or the third time in one day Aunt Catherine has had to break up a fight. Erik and Elva, supposedly on their best behavior while staying at her house, have been bickering almost constantly. "They get it from their father," Grandma says. Their mother, Grandma's child, was always sweet and compliant.

"No, it's the way they're being brought up," Aunt Catherine says. "There's no discipline in that house."

What is it that makes Erik and Elva the way they are? What makes them tall for their age, addicted to strawberry ice cream, good in spelling, impossible to put to bed, clumsy with dishes, and rough with the cat? Did they inherit these characteristics in their genes, as Grandma thinks (the bad ones of course coming from their father), or is Aunt Catherine right, and everything the result of what they have been fed, permitted, and taught?

Grandma and Aunt Catherine can argue the matter all afternoon, as philosophers and scientists have argued it since the beginning of history. The debate, usually titled "Nature versus Nurture," continues today, and not just in living rooms but in academic journals as well.

Scientists have been able to clarify some of the terms of the debate. They have discovered that a person's inheritance is not "in the blood," as people used to say, but in every cell of her body. Each cell contains a nucleus, and each nucleus has a set of chromosomes bearing thousands of genes that make up the person's genetic potential. No two people ever born have quite the same combination of genes, except identical twins.

People get their unique combination of genes at the moment they are conceived, and nothing will ever change it. If they live to be a hundred years old, they will die with exactly the same combination. But environment starts to influence their development the very moment *after* conception and will continue to do so all the rest of their lives.

When a baby is born, it already has been subject to environmental influences for nine months. Science has reliably identified some of the characteristics that are primarily the result of genetic makeup and some that have been decisively influenced by the environment; and there are many more characteristics that cannot be solely attributed to either influence. In any case, whenever it is known that the baby was born with a particular characteristic, even if it will not become apparent until later, it is called a **congenital** characteristic. If the baby is born blind, for example, its blindness is called a congenital defect, but it may be due to syphilis in the mother, which affects the developing baby in her womb, or it may be due to a genetic factor.

A **gene** is the hereditary material that governs one trait. Some traits, such as blood type, seem to be determined almost entirely by one gene. Environment has little effect on these traits. Many other traits, however, are affected not only by the environment of the organism but by the combined influence of several genes. Taking this genetic pattern as an immensely complex whole, it can be said that heredity endows the person at conception with the potentiality to develop in a certain direction. Without this potentiality no development can take place, not even in the most favorable environment.

The genetic pattern is no more than a potentiality, however. In a completely adverse environment it will disintegrate because the cells containing it will die; in an environment that is unfavorable in certain ways it will fall short of its full development in corresponding ways. Thus, both a sound genetic pattern and a favorable environment are necessary for healthy development. Both affect the individual in so many ways that it is impossible except in a few cases to estimate which factor has had the greater influence.

GENETIC INFLUENCES

Half of a person's genetic material comes from the father and half from the mother. These two halves come together to form a unique combination of genetic potentialities when the sperm cell fertilizes the egg cell.

The fertilized egg—the first cell in which the father's genes are joined with the mother's—is called the **zygote**. Less than two days after the sperm unites with the egg, the zygote divides into two cells. Then these two cells each divide again, and the process of division goes on, forming a new human being.

In a few rare cases the cells dividing from the zygote become separated into two masses and develop into two individuals. These two individuals are called identical twins, or *monozygotic twins.* They usually develop together in one amnion, the sac that surrounds the embryo, both bathed by the same amniotic fluid. Fraternal twins, on the other hand, develop from two different zygotes—*two eggs* each fertilized by a different sperm. Fraternal twins usually have separate amniotic sacs. Except for monozygotic twins, it is impossible for any two people to have exactly the same heredity (Figure 1.1).

Mechanisms of Heredity

A baby is conceived when a sperm (the male cell) fuses with an egg (the female cell) in the fallopian tube of the mother. There fertilization takes place; the head of the sperm, which contains its nucleus, is engulfed by the egg, and the nuclei of the two germ cells, or *gametes,* are combined to become the nucleus of the zygote, the first cell of the new organism.

The most important material in that nucleus is a substance called deoxyribonucleic acid, or DNA (Figure 1.2). The DNA in the nucleus of a fertilized egg constitutes the genetic "blueprint" for a new, unique individual. How is this possible? The DNA is a relatively simple molecule. It is made up of a sugar, phosphates, and only four other components. But the arrangement of

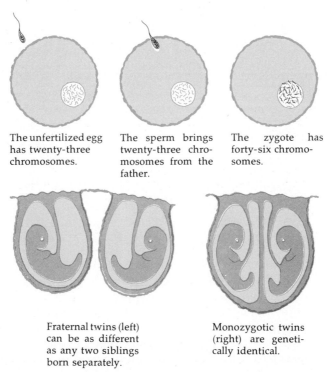

The unfertilized egg has twenty-three chromosomes.

The sperm brings twenty-three chromosomes from the father.

The zygote has forty-six chromosomes.

Fraternal twins (left) can be as different as any two siblings born separately.

Monozygotic twins (right) are genetically identical.

Figure 1.1 Except for monozygotic twins, it is impossible for any two people to have exactly the same heredity.

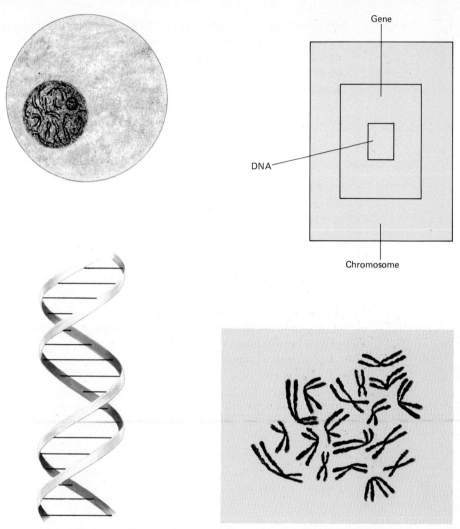

Figure 1.2 A human cell, top left. The dark mass within the cell is the nucleus containing the chromosomes. An enlargement of some chromosomes is shown bottom right. They contain the basic chemical of heredity, deoxyribonucleic acid, or DNA. A portion of a DNA molecule is shown at lower left. At each level of the spiral, shown by horizontal bars, are particular chemical pairs. The arrangement of these pairs along the molecule determines which kinds of proteins will be formed in the cell. The relationship of DNA, gene, and chromosome are shown top right.

these four components forms a kind of code that provides the pattern for the development of the fertilized egg by determining the placement of amino acids in a protein. The precise placement and combination of amino acids in a protein determine its structure and function in the body. All life, and life processes, are based on proteins and the interactions among different proteins.

Technically, therefore, it is not quite correct to speak of inheriting blue eyes or sound teeth. What we inherit is a set of biochemical instructions. If all goes well and those instructions are carried out through the amino acids in body-building proteins, we may indeed have blue eyes or sound teeth. If something goes wrong, we might end up with no eyes or poor teeth. But if our genetic instructions are for blue eyes, one thing we certainly will not end up with is brown eyes.

For all their simplicity the DNA molecules are numerous and can act as a pattern for the formation of many proteins. The part of the molecule that results in the formation of a single protein in the developing person is the *gene.* Most of a person's traits are influenced by several genes. Thus, our knowledge of inherited characteristics, except in a few clear-cut cases, is extremely limited and tentative. This is especially true of the inheritance of such characteristics as intelligence and personality.

Nevertheless, for our purposes here we are justified in thinking of a gene as a segment of a DNA molecule that directs the development of a single trait. It can be thought of as a location on the DNA molecule, like a dot on a map. When we speak of the gene for eye color, we are referring to the part of a DNA molecule that directs the formation of proteins affecting eye color.

The DNA molecules in our bodies are on rodlike structures called *chromosomes* in the nucleus of each cell. Although we have thousands of traits, our cells normally contain only twenty-three pairs of chromosomes, with one chromosome in each pair coming from the mother and one from the father. We can trace this combination of the mother's and father's genetic material back to the zygote: the unfertilized egg has only twenty-three chromosomes, as does the sperm cell; when the egg is fertilized, the resulting zygote has forty-six chromosomes linked up in twenty-three pairs.

Both chromosomes in a pair contain gene factors for the same traits, so there are two factors for each trait. But the two factors may have different effects: one blood-type factor, for example, might be for type A blood and the other for type O. These differing forms of any given gene, which give different instructions for the form a characteristic should take, are known as the **alleles** of that gene. The tremendous number of possible combinations of alleles means that every human being is conceived with a unique genetic endowment.

Cell Division

Our body cells constantly divide and produce new cells in order to maintain growth and good health. This process of cell division is known as **mitosis.** It continues throughout our lives as new cells emerge to replace old ones that wear out and are absorbed into the surrounding tissues and fluids. Cell division occurs most rapidly when a child grows and, later in life, when the body is recovering from an injury, as when new skin is formed to heal a cut.

Cell division begins when the chromosomes replicate to form a second set of chromosomes exactly like the original. Then this set separates from the original, is surrounded by a membrane, and becomes the nucleus of a new cell. The new cell produced through mitosis has the same number of chromosome pairs as the parent cell.

Human sperm and egg cells are produced by a slightly different process of cell division known as **meiosis**, or reduction division. Meiosis, like mitosis, begins with the replication of the original chromosomes. But the ensuing cell divisions result in four cells instead of two. Each new cell has only half the number of chromosomes found in the parent cell. In this way the sperm cell and the egg cell end up with twenty-three single chromosomes instead of twenty-three *pairs* of chromosomes. This is important because, if the sperm cell and the egg cell each carried twenty-three chromosome pairs, the zygote resulting from their union would have forty-six chromosome pairs instead of the normal twenty-three, and would die.

Gene Dominance

What happens when the two alleles an individual receives from its mother and father contain differing instructions for the development of the characteristic they govern? In many cases the answer to this question lies in the principle of **gene dominance** and **gene recessiveness**.

One example of this principle is found in eye color (see Figure 1.3). The allele that instructs the body to produce pigment for the iris (the only pigment possible being brown) is sometimes paired in the zygote with an allele for unpigmented irises (which look blue). Like all babies, a baby with differing genes for eye color will be born with blue eyes, but in time its eyes will turn brown because the effect of its allele for unpigmented eyes will be suppressed by the presence of the allele for pigmentation. Thus, the brown allele is called

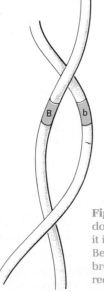

Figure 1.3 Alleles for eye color on a pair of chromosomes. The dominant allele (capital B) calls for brown eyes. In this individual it is paired with a recessive allele (lowercase b) calling for blue eyes. Because the dominant allele prevails, this individual will have brown eyes. To have blue eyes a person must have both alleles recessive (bb).

dominant and the blue recessive. Later, as such individuals grow up and form their own germ cells, the chromosome pairs will separate in meiosis, and 50 percent of the germ cells will carry the recessive gene. Figure 1.4 illustrates this case and every other possible combination for blue eyes and brown eyes. The figure shows, for example, how it happens that some mixed couples (one parent with brown eyes and one with blue) have no children with blue eyes while other mixed couples have as many blue-eyed children as brown-eyed ones.

When both alleles give the same direction for the determination of a trait, the individual is said to be *homozygous* for that trait. If both of an individual's eye-color alleles call for blue eyes, for example, the individual is homozygous for eye color. However, when one allele calls for brown eyes and the other for blue eyes, the individual is said to be *heterozygous* for eye color. Such an individual will have brown eyes because the allele for brown eyes is dominant over the allele for blue eyes.

Complete dominance is rare among inherited traits. More often the effects of both alleles appear in the individual. This condition is referred to as a *codominance* or *incomplete dominance*. Sometimes an individual will show the effect of one allele more than the other, but neither will be completely dominant. Incomplete dominance is characteristic of many hereditary diseases in man, including sickle-cell anemia, Parkinson's disease, gout, and a predisposition to diabetes.

Some inherited traits are **polygenic;** many genes are involved in the for-

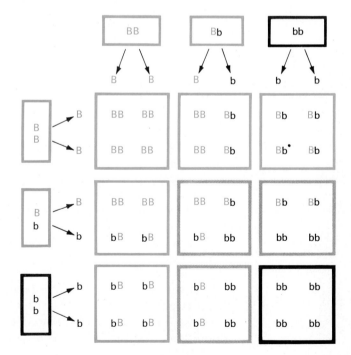

Figure 1.4 Inheritance of eye color. B is the allele for brown eyes; b is the allele for blue. The small boxes left and above represent the genotypes of parents. The alleles separate in meiosis to form the germ cells (sperm or eggs). Then these alleles recombine in the offspring. As the illustration shows, only two blue-eyed parents will have all blue-eyed children. However, when a brown-eyed parent of mixed genotype (Bb) mates with a blue-eyed parent or with another Bb, the probability is that some of the offspring will have blue eyes.

mation of the trait, rather than only one pair. Our chins and teeth are examples of features whose development is affected by several genes; so too is our intelligence (Scarr-Salapatek, 1975).

Sex Determination

We have seen how such physical traits as eye coloring are passed on through genes from parents to children. But what determines whether a child is female of male? The answer again, depends on the laws of inheritance, but in this case the mechanism involved is relatively simple: for human beings, sex is determined by a single pair of sex chromosomes. One of these is called the X chromosome, and the other, which is usually found only in males, is a smaller one called the Y chromosome.

At conception an egg cell from the mother is fertilized by a sperm cell from the father. All egg cells and some sperm cells—about half of them—carry the X chromosome. The other sperm cells carry the Y chromosome. When a sperm cell carrying an X chromosome unites with an egg cell, the zygote has the combination XX because all eggs carry the X chromosome. An XX zygote will normally develop into a female baby. When a sperm cell carrying the Y chromosome unites with an egg, the resulting zygote has the combination XY and will normally develop into a male.

The general rule, then, is for all zygotes to be either XX females or XY males. But there are exceptions to this rule, usually originating in some accident during meiosis which causes the egg or sperm to carry an abnormal number of X or Y chromosomes. The abnormality will then be transmitted to the fertilized egg. Thus, it has been found that females can, in rare instances, have an XXX, XXXX, or some other combination; males can have an XXY, XYY, or other combination. All of these are abnormalities, and fortunately they are extremely rare. Persons having them are likely to suffer from confusion of biological sex characteristics, mental retardation, physiological defects, or sterility. It has been suggested that one of these combinations, the XYY (a double dose of the male sex chromosome), is associated with a predisposition to criminal behavior. In reality the connection seems to be a bit less direct. XYY people are likely to be of low intelligence and therefore may commit crimes out of sheer impulsiveness or stupidity (Witkin et al., 1976). They are also likely to be taller than average and to suffer from severe, disfiguring acne. But they do not seem to have any specific predisposition to crime. Again, the XYY combination is extremely rare.

The X chromosome sometimes carries what are called *sex-linked recessive traits.* Some well-known examples are red-green color blindness, night blindness, muscular dystrophy, and hemophilia. Experiments have shown that the genes for these conditions appear only on the X chromosome. Since the female (XX) has two X chromosomes, she will express these recessive traits only if she carries the genes on *both* of her X chromosomes. This does not happen except in vary rare instances; thus, women usually do not suffer from sex-linked diseases such as hemophilia. But they may serve as carriers of such conditions. The male (XY) has only one X chromosome, which he receives from his mother. If that X chromosome carries a recessive gene, the male will develop that trait because there are no corresponding genes on his Y chromosome that could mask the effect of the recessive gene on the X chromosome.

Inherited Characteristics

We have already spoken of characteristics such as color blindness and blood type as inherited traits. But it is not really traits that a person inherits, only genes; these genes provide the potential to develop particular traits under certain environmental conditions. Remembering that heredity never acts alone but is always interacting with the environment, we can examine some of the cases in which heredity is known to have a decisive effect on the individual's development. Comparing fraternal and identical twins can be an especially useful method of exploring the comparative effects of heredity and the environment. Both types of twins share the same environment, but only the identical twins share the exact same heredity.

Physical Features

The genes that people inherit from their parents have a great influence on their physical appearance. The color of their eyes, hair, and skin, their height, and their bone structure all are results of the hereditary process. In some cases the instructions contained in the genes may be counteracted by the effects of disease, nutrition, or other environmental factors. But normally the genetic influence predominates.

A classic study (Kallman & Sander, 1949) of monozygotic (identical) twins, who are identical in their genetic makeup, provided some striking examples of the inheritance of physical features. Although all the persons included in the study were over sixty years of age, each one was remarkably similar to his or her twin. The twins tended to show the same degree of graying of hair and the same kinds of eye and tooth changes. They became about equally feeble at about the same rate, and in some cases they died within weeks of each other.

Of course, some traits seem more affected by hereditary factors and others more by environmental conditions. Another study (Newmann, Freeman, & Holzinger, 1937) found that the height of monozygotic twins remained very close whether they were brought up together or separately. On the other hand the weight of monozygotic twins brought up separately differed more than the weight of those who grew up in the same environment. Evidently weight is more easily affected by environmental factors than height.

Personality

It is difficult to measure precisely the effects of heredity on an individual's personality. Certain environmental factors—including nutrition and the dynamics of family life—obviously have an effect on personality, but the influence of heredity can also be demonstrated.

Sometimes a child looks so much like his parent that the hereditary relationship is immediately obvious.

Again, the study of twins is an important aid in determining the effects of genetic inheritance on personality. In some cases monozygotic twins brought up separately show remarkable similarities in personality and behavior. In one study (Lindeman, 1969) the researcher found striking similarities between twins separated shortly after birth and brought up in different circumstances. While Tony had the security of a large family, Roger was moved from one foster home to another and finally ended up living with relatives of his father. Also, Tony was raised in an Italian Catholic household, whereas Roger was raised in a Jewish household. Yet at age twenty-four, when the brothers discovered each other by chance, they showed amazing similarities, from their attitudes toward religion and work to such minor details as the way they held a cigarette or coffee cup. One had volunteered for military service just eight days before the other.

Various behavioral characteristics and personality disorders may also be transmitted through genetic inheritance. Thomas and Chess (1977), for example, have argued that temperament differences among young infants in such areas as activity level, irritability, mood, regularity in biological functioning (eating, sleeping, and bowel movements), and sociability, are influenced strongly by genetic factors. This speculation has received support in recent twin studies by Torgersen and Kringlen (1978) and Matheny (1980). In another twin study, Eysenck (1964) has shown that monozygotic twins are twice as likely to follow similar patterns in adult criminality and alcoholism, as are fraternal twins. Other research has indicated that monozygotic twins brought up separately will often have similar tendencies toward crime and schizophrenia.

These studies of twins suggest that the effects of heredity on personality must be significant. Yet, as we shall see in later chapters, the impact of socialization practices, and more general environmental conditions, on personality development, is at least equal to, if not greater than, heredity.

Intelligence

The study of the influence of heredity on intelligence is both complex and controversial. In part this is because there is no commonly accepted definition of intelligence. Does intelligence mean the ability to acquire knowledge, the capacity to think creatively, an aptitude for abstract and intellectual reasoning, or the ability to adjust to changing conditions? Are gifted poets intelligent even if they cannot solve simple mathematical problems? Are people with a great deal of "common sense" more intelligent than, say, a highly educated but somewhat naive research chemist?

Resemblances between monozygotic twins in physical development, character, intelligence, and life history have been the subject of many studies.

There are no simple answers to such questions, but intelligence tests have nonetheless been devised and administered to millions of people. The results show a correspondence between heredity and the ability to perform in IQ tests. For example, the correlation between IQ scores for identical twins is .87, whereas for fraternal twins, the correlation ranges between .55 and .62 (Plomin & DeFries, 1979). Perhaps most striking is the finding (Newmann, Freeman, & Holzinger, 1937) that monozygotic twins reared in different homes scored more similarly on intelligence tests than did dizygotic twins who grew up together.

Another approach to studying the influence of heredity on intelligence is to compare adopted children with their biological and adoptive parents. Overall, research has found a much closer relationship in intellectual functioning between adoptees and their biological parents than between these children and their adoptive parents. Furthermore, adoptive parents are more similar in intelligence to their biological children than their adoptive children (DeFries & Plomin, 1978; Munsinger, 1975).

In the light of such evidence it cannot be denied that heredity has a strong influence on performance on IQ tests. Some investigators have proceeded to estimate, primarily on the grounds of twin studies, just how much heredity contributes to a person's intelligence and how much is contributed by the environment. The educator Arthur Jensen put the figures at 80 percent for heredity and 20 percent for environment. This estimate led him to argue that if the aim of compensatory educational programs is to boost children's IQ scores, they are futile (Jensen, 1969).

Because compensatory education is more often offered to minority group children who may score low on IQ tests, Jensen's arguments have invited racial interpretation—and angry debate. One of the most telling replies came from the psychologist Urie Bronfenbrenner (1972), who attacked Jensen's estimate that the influences on a person's intelligence are 80 percent genetic. Bronfenbrenner found that the twin studies used by Jensen did not justify any estimate at all because they involved too many uncontrolled factors. He pointed out, for example, that when monozygotic twins are separated and brought up in different homes, the homes are often quite similar in cultural environment. Other investigators (Newmann, Freeman, & Holzinger, 1937) had previously speculated that intelligence was, at most, 50 percent determined by heredity, and a later analysis (Fehr, 1969) arrived at about the same figure.

Jensen's position conforms to what Scarr-Salapatek (1975) calls the "myth of heritability"—namely, that if intelligence *is* largely determined by genetic factors, it must not be very malleable or changeable. Scarr-Salapatek soundly rejects this assumption, noting that what we inherit is not a fixed ability or level of competence, but a "range of reaction"—a genetic potential for development—that is expressed in complex ways as a result of continual transaction between one's genetic code and the environment. To the extent that the person is raised in a more favorable or stimulating environment, there is a greater chance that the person's full potential will be reached. As an example, Scarr and Weinberg (1976) report that lower-class black children adopted by middle-class white families scored significantly higher on IQ tests than one would expect—based on IQ data for black children raised in their own homes. These results suggest that environmental enrichment, which presumably was experienced by the black children in the Scarr and Weinberg study following adoption, is sufficient to facilitate intellectual functioning. Scarr and Weinberg are careful not to endorse the adoption of black children by white families as a social policy. What they do endorse, however, is that "*if* higher IQ scores are considered important for educational and occupational success, then there is a need for social action that will provide black children with home environments that facilitate the acquisition of intellectual skills tapped by IQ measures" (p. 738).

Birth Defects

Most babies are born whole, healthy, and relatively normal. They have all the proper parts, and their systems and organs work more or less as they should. But many babies are not so fortunate. In the United States 100,000 to 150,000

Is intelligence inherited? When children are bright and eager to learn, how much is due to the genes received from their parents, and how much to the environment in which they grow up?

infants are born each year with congenital malformation (of the brain, for example), abnormal chromosomes (e.g., Down's syndrome), or a genetic disorder, such as muscular dystrophy or cystic fibrosis (National Institutes of Health, 1979). These problems may be severe enough to result in infant mortality or mild enough to be corrected or controlled by surgery, diet, or therapy.

As noted, some defects are genetic. The harmful genes that cause them may have been in the family for generations, passed down from parent to child. Hemophilia is a case in point. Others result from damage to a parent's ovum or sperm before pregnancy begins, through disease, radiation, or other environmental causes.

Still other birth defects are developmental; they occur while the fetus is developing in the womb. Sometimes they are simply accidents, but certain infections, drugs, and radiation can all cause such damage. How much harm these agents do depends a good deal on the stage of pregnancy at which the fetus is exposed to them. We shall discuss such environmentally caused defects later in this chapter.

Finally, a few defects result from injury during the birth process. The most important cause of such injury is **anoxia,** or deprivation of oxygen. We shall look at some of its effects when we discuss labor and birth in Chapter 2.

Genetic Defects

Sometimes the hereditary process passes along the potential for serious diseases or metabolic defects. Glaucoma, certain forms of muscular dystrophy, and a predisposition to diabetes can all be inherited. Some types of mental retardation also result from inherited metabolic deficiencies. In these cases the body usually has a genetic inability to manufacture some important enzyme. Without this enzyme it cannot properly utilize some element in the diet. As a result poisonous by-products build up in the bloodstream and injure the brain and central nervous system. Phenylketonuria (PKU), an inability to metabolize a common amino acid, is one such disorder. Another is galactosemia, the inability to handle one of the carbohydrates in milk. Fortunately, such defects are relatively rare. PKU, for example, probably occurs in fewer than one in ten thousand newborn infants. If diagnosed early enough, such diseases can often be controlled by careful diet, so that retardation is limited or avoided.

One well-known genetic disorder is Down's syndrome (mongolism). This defect can be found in about one of every five hundred babies born in the United States; it occurs most frequently in the children of very young mothers or mothers over forty years of age. It is not caused by a mutant gene, but by the presence of an extra chromosome, or part of one. This may result from the failure of the paired chromosomes to separate properly when an egg or sperm is formed. The condition is thus similar in origin to the sex-linked abnormalities discussed earlier. Victims of Down's syndrome can be recognized by an unusual skin fold in the corner of the eyes, a broad nose, and a protruding tongue. They suffer from mental retardation, and may have heart

Parents can be relieved of fears that their unborn child may carry a hereditary defect. A study of their genealogy or an amniocentesis test may assure them that the baby will in all probability be normal.

malformations, respiratory disorders, and be at heightened risk for leukemia. Before modern surgery and antibiotics they probably would not have lived beyond the age of ten or twelve years.

Genetic factors may also contribute to diseases that we classify as mental illnesses. Often the causes of such mental disorders are unclear, and scientific authorities differ as to whether they result from hereditary or environmental factors. This is especially true in the case of schizophrenia, perhaps the most commonly diagnosed mental disorder in the United States. Some early studies of monozygotic twins (Kallman, 1938) point to a strong hereditary factor associated with certain types of schizophrenia. More recent research also seems to support the idea of a genetic component in schizophrenia and other such disorders (e.g., Mednick, Schulsinger, & Schulsinger, 1975). Yet other research suggests that stresses in family life and environmental experiences can affect when and how hereditary predispositions to certain disorders are displayed.

It should be noted that although birth defects have been attributed almost exclusively in the past to the genetic makeup of women, recent research has implicated paternal inheritance in certain abnormalities. For example, recent studies of children with Down's syndrome having increasingly identified the father as the carrier of the chromosome abnormality (Holmes, 1978; Magenis, et al., 1977).

Genetic Counseling

One of the newer methods of coping with genetic disorders is genetic counseling. Before a couple decide to have children, they have their genealogy studied to learn whether they are likely to be carrying genes that could transmit defects to their offspring. For example, a woman who knows that congenital blindness has occurred in her family could find out how likely it is that she carries the defective gene. She can also find out whether she alone could transmit the blindness to her children, or whether it could only happen if her husband also carries the gene. In some cases biochemical tests can be performed to show for certain whether the harmful gene is present. With such knowledge the couple can decide whether they should avoid having children at all, or whether the chances of a healthy baby are good enough for them to risk going ahead.

STAGES OF GESTATION

The prenatal phase of human life lasts an average of 266 days. During these nine months, the zygote divides into as many as 200 billion cells. The fetus grows within the mother's uterus until it is strong enough to sustain life outside her womb.

There are three principal stages of gestation. The first, the **ovum stage**, lasts from ten to fourteen days. During this period all cells are exact replicas of the zygote. When the tiny cell mass, or blastocyst, has implanted itself in the wall of the uterus, the **embryo stage** begins. Differentiated tissues and important body systems—such as the circulatory and digestive systems—begin to develop. The embryo stage lasts about six weeks, usually until the end of the eighth week of pregnancy. Then the **fetal stage** begins. During the thirty weeks of the fetal stage all the individual body systems develop toward readiness for birth, and the fetus as a whole grows dramatically in size.

Ovum Stage

Cell division begins on the first day after conception. While the zygote is splitting into new cells, it moves through the mother's fallopian tubes toward the uterus (Figure 1.5). The cluster of cells is nourished at this time by the yolk of the ovum.

By the time the cell cluster arrives at the uterus, it may contain as many as thirty-two cells. The process known as differentiation is about to begin, when the cells will separate into groups according to their future roles. At this point the cluster is a blastocyst, a hollow ball of cells. One half of the ball consists of two distinct layers of cells, and this half will eventually become the baby. The other half contains only a single layer of cells. This will form

❖❖❖

Prenatal Testing

There are several technologies available that allow doctors to evaluate the condition of the fetus during pregnancy. In the past decade this prenatal diagnosis of disease and defects has become "a vital new option in the reproductive (genetic) counseling of many families at increased risk for such conditions in their offspring (National Institutes of Health, 1979, pp. 1–2). For example, prenatal testing has been helpful to "at-risk" couples who, until now, may have been afraid to chance a pregnancy because they would not know the condition of the offspring until birth.

One prenatal diagnostic technique is known as *amniocentesis*. This test is usually performed after the fourteenth week of pregnancy, when the baby's basic systems are all in place and functioning. A hollow needle is inserted into the uterus through the mother's abdomen, and a small amount of the amniotic fluid surrounding the fetus is removed. This fluid contains, among other things, loose cells discarded by the developing fetus. The cells are separated from the fluid, grown in a culture, and examined for evidence of defects. If there are no defects—as is true in some 95 percent of the cases—the mother is spared several months of needless anxiety. If there are abnormalities, she may decide to have an abortion or go ahead with the pregnancy, in the latter case having time to prepare for the needs—special nursing care, for example—of an abnormal child.

Amniocentesis is nearly 100-percent accurate in detecting Down's syndrome, sex-chromosome abnormalities, and over 70 serious metabolic disorders. It has also been very useful in prenatal testing for Tay-Sachs disease, a degenerative disease of the brain that is 100 times more frequent among Jewish infants than infants from any other segments of the population.

Amniocentesis, however, is not advisable as a routine procedure except for those mothers who are at risk. Included in this category would be women thirty-five and older, women with a family history of Down's syndrome or the other abnormalities described, and cases in which the mother has experienced three or more spontaneous abortions. There are several reasons for limiting use of the procedure. Amniocentesis involves a slight risk of miscarriage or infection. There is also the risk, as in any test, of positive results that are false or misleading. Most malformations and many genetically implicated problems cannot be determined by amniocentesis. Also, as noted, the procedure is usually done at thirteen to fourteen weeks. It then requires two to three weeks of lab work. By this time, the mother is in a rather advanced stage of pregnancy, both in terms of the risks associated with abortion and the mother's probable emotional attachment to the fetus.

Another technique useful for detecting certain types of gross defect is *ultrasound*, which is sometimes used in conjunction with amniocentesis. By scanning the uterus with sound waves of extremely high frequency, doctors can get a picture of the outline of the fetus. (The procedure does not cause discomfort and also lessens the need for X rays.) Anencephaly, a rare and fatal defect in which parts of the skull or brain are missing or malformed, has been detected in this way. Serial ultrasound has also been used to detect the rate of fetal growth, a vital measurement in those cases in which retarded intrauterine growth is suspected.

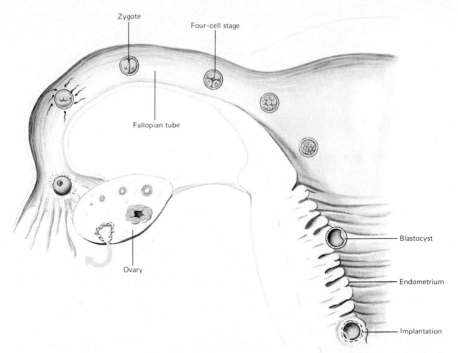

Figure 1.5 Ovulation, fertilization, and implantation. The ovary discharges an egg into the fallopian tube, where it is penetrated by a sperm. The zygote begins cell division as it moves down the fallopian tube toward the uterus. When the cluster of cells has formed a hollow ball, it is called a blastocyst. About six days after conception the blastocyst begins to implant itself in the wall of the uterus.

the housing and life-support system for the fetus, including the placenta, the umbilical cord, and the amniotic sac.

The blastocyst floats for some time in the uterus. By about the sixth day after conception it begins to implant itself in the uterine wall. This is a critical point in gestation, for if the blastocyst does not implant itself properly, at the right time and in the right place, the cell mass will die before it can reach the embryo stage. But if all goes well, the blastocyst will be firmly embedded about two weeks after conception.

Embryo Stage

During the forty-six-day embryo stage the embryo grows to a length of over one inch (2.5 cm). By the end of the embryo stage many body systems will be in operation, and the embryo will show the beginnings of human appearance.

The embryo takes nourishment and oxygen and releases waste products, such as carbon dioxide, through the **umbilical cord**, which links it with the placenta. The umbilical cord contains three blood vessels through which the embryo's blood circulates to and from the placenta (Figure 1.6).

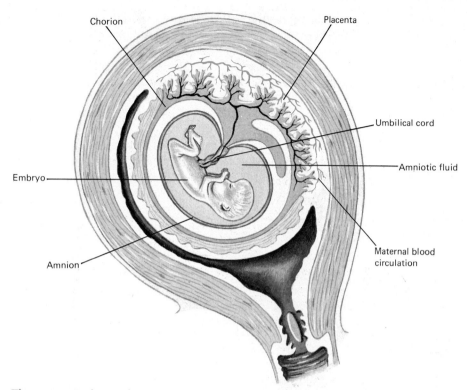

Figure 1.6 Embryo. The embryo's blood, conducted by the umbilical cord, circulates through the placenta. It picks up oxygen and nutrients and discharges wastes into the mother's blood without actually mixing with it. The amniotic fluid protects the embryo from shock and helps to regulate its temperature.

The **placenta** is a disk-shaped mass of tissue six to eight inches (15–20 cm) long and one inch (2.5 cm) thick. Implanted in the inner wall of the uterus, it serves as a two-way filter between the bloodstreams of the mother and the embryo. It makes it possible for the mother to carry on life functions—digestion, excretion, circulation, respiration—for the embryo. Into the placenta, by way of two arteries in the umbilical cord, the embryo deposits waste material, such as carbon dioxide. The mass of blood vessels on the mother's side of the placenta then absorbs the waste into her bloodstream. The embryo also receives, through the vein in the umbilical cord, fresh nutrients—oxygen, amino acids, sugar, fats, minerals—from the mother's bloodstream. It also receives hormones, antibodies, and other necessary substances by the same route.

The bloodstreams of the mother and the embryo do not mix; the placenta cell walls act as a screen. Thus, the unborn child receives only materials whose molecules are small enough to pass through the screen.

At the same time as the embryo is taking shape, the **amniotic sac** is developing into a protective chamber. By the end of the eighth week this sac completely surrounds the embryo. The watery fluid inside keeps the embryo from being jostled by any sudden movements of the mother or by accidents that may happen to her, such as a fall or a blow. The amniotic sac also keeps the embryo at a constant temperature.

During the embryonic period three layers of cells are differentiated. The outer layer, or **ectoderm,** develops into sensory cells, skin, and the nervous system. The middle layer, or **mesoderm,** becomes the excretory system, muscles, and blood. The inner layer, the **endoderm,** forms the digestive system, lungs, and thyroid gland.

By the end of the third week of development the embryo's heart is beating and its nervous system is forming rapidly. After the fourth week the legs are curled, and the eyes have appeared as dark circles. During the fifth and sixth weeks arms and legs can be seen. After eight weeks all of the major body organs are present. The liver is making blood cells, and the kidneys are removing waste products. The mouth, nose, eyes, and head are clear and distinct. The head is roughly half of the total body size at this time. Fingers and toes are blunt, and ribs show under the skin.

The eight-week time span of embryonic development is a particularly vulnerable period in human growth. The embryo can very easily be affected by chemicals, drugs, hormones, or viruses in the mother's system. Rubella (German measles) is a common danger during this stage of pregnancy.

Fetal Stage

The fetal stage begins in the ninth week of pregnancy and continues until the birth of the baby, usually about thirty weeks later (Figure 1.7).

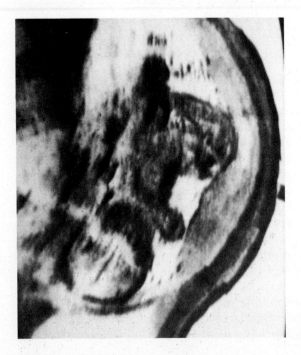

Ultrasound photograph of fetus in utero. The baby's head is down, in birth position. Its toes can be seen above. Amniotic fluid, of which the amniotic sac holds about four quarts, appears as the lighter area.

Figure 1.7 Fetus. When all the major physical structures are recognizable and the circulatory and nervous systems are operating, the embryo has entered the fetal stage. The spongy material shown at left of the fetus and the amniotic sac is the placenta, with its rich network of blood vessels.

The mother first feels the fetus move in the fourth to fifth month of pregnancy. It can open and close its mouth, swallow, and make certain head movements. It may even suck its thumb. The fastest growth period for the fetus is the fourth month, when it almost doubles in length, reaching six inches (15 cm) from crown to rump. Limbs become sensitive to touch, and a heartbeat can be heard with a stethoscope.

After five months the skin of the fetus is fully developed. Hair, nails, and sweat glands are apparent. The fetus sleeps and wakes. In the sixth month the eyelids are open, and the fetus can open and close its eyes. It may now weigh as much as twenty-four ounces (672 g). During the seventh month the eyes can distinguish light from dark. The brain has more control over body systems than before, and an infant born prematurely at the end of this time has a fair chance of survival. In the last two months the fetus gains about eight ounces (224 g) per week.

PRENATAL ENVIRONMENTAL INFLUENCES

Securely implanted in the wall of the uterus, the embryo is bathed in amniotic fluid, kept at a constant temperature, and protected from physical shock. The uterine environment is remarkably effective in protecting and nourishing the growing child. The great majority of women have uncomplicated pregnancies and give birth to healthy babies.

For many years, in fact, it was believed that the baby in the uterus was completely insulated from all outside influences, but now we know that this is not entirely true. Environmental influences ranging from radioactivity and stress in the outside world due to drugs, chemicals, hormones, and viruses in the mother's bloodstream can affect prenatal development. Even though the placenta acts as a filter, keeping the blood of the mother and the fetus from mixing, a number of potentially dangerous substances can pass through it. And, of course, if the mother's blood lacks the nutrients required by the growing fetus, it may not develop fully.

Lack of proper nourishment or the introduction of harmful substances will affect the fetus in different ways at different stages of prenatal development. This is because the body organs and parts develop at different speeds but through definite phases. First they go through a phase of rapid multiplication in the number of cells. Then there is an increase in both the number of cells and in cell size. In the third and final phase of development, cell size continues to increase rapidly, but cell division slows down.

The second phase, when a body part or organ system is growing most rapidly both in cell number and size, is known as the **critical period** of development for that part or system. If an environmental factor, such as a chemical or virus, interferes with growth during the critical period, development of that organ system will be permanently affected. The organ does not have another chance to develop, because the third phase begins at a preset time, even if the developmental potential has not all been achieved.

The effect of environmental influences will vary, therefore, in accordance with the stage of prenatal development in which the environmental factor is encountered. During the first three months of pregnancy tissues and important body systems begin to develop in the embryo. Adverse influences during this period will affect the basic structure and form of the body and may have particularly serious effects on the nervous system. Physical development can be arrested and irreparable malformation may occur. For example, women who took the drug Thalidomide during the first three months of pregnancy gave birth to many children with serious defects, but it did not appear to have adverse effects when taken toward the end of pregnancy.

Teratogens

When it was discovered that the development of the unborn can be affected by many outside influences, scientists went to work to find out exactly how. The scientific study of congenital abnormalities caused by prenatal environmental influences is known as **teratology** (from the Greek *teras,* meaning "marvel" or "monster"), and the environmental agents that produce abnormalities in the developing fetus are called **teratogens.** A teratogenic agent may be a chemical such as a drug or hormone, a virus or other organism, or radiation. The effects of some teratogens, particularly newly developed drugs, are just becoming known. As medical researchers discover new teratogens and their effects, it may become possible to eliminate many congenital defects.

Diseases

In rare cases infants have been born with cases of smallpox, malaria, measles, chicken pox, mumps, or syphilis that have been transmitted from the mother. The placenta cannot filter out extremely small disease carriers such as viruses; they are able to migrate through the placenta and infect the fetus.

German measles, or rubella, is the most widespread of the viruses that have a teratogenic effect. If a pregnant woman contracts rubella in the first three months of pregnancy, she is likely to give birth to a child with a congenital abnormality. Heart disease, cataracts, deafness, and mental retardation are among the abnormalities caused by rubella.

Other viruses—mumps, polio, influenza—also have teratogenic effects, but the probability that these viruses will harm the fetus is not as great as with rubella, and the defects they cause are not serious.

Certain microorganisms can also cross the placenta and infect the fetus. One is the protozoan *Toxoplasma gondii,* commonly carried by cats. Adults are often infected, apparently without showing any particular ill effects. Fetuses, though, are very sensitive to this organism. An infected infant may die before birth or may be born with toxoplasmosis, a serious disease that affects the brain, eyes, and other organs.

Disorders not caused by any virus or organism can also have teratogenic effects. Women suffering from diabetes are six to ten times as likely to give birth to infants with congenital malformations as nondiabetic mothers, and their infants often have respiratory difficulties soon after birth. Diabetic mothers are also very prone to stillbirths and have a tendency to deliver unusually large infants. Toxemia is a rather frightening condition that endangers both mother and fetus. Its cause is unknown, but it is characterized by high blood pressure, swelling and weight gain due to a buildup of fluid in the body tissues, and the presence of protein in the mother's urine. In severe cases the woman may go into convulsions or coma. The strain this places on the mother's system is, of course, carried over to the fetus, and women with toxemia frequently give birth to premature babies or to babies smaller than average for their gestational age—that is, their age since conception. If untreated, toxemia can be fatal to both mother and child.

Toxemia is one of several diseases that can cause anoxia in the baby. **Anoxia** is a condition in which the brain of the baby does not receive enough oxygen to allow it to develop properly. Anoxia can cause the child to be born with certain forms of epilepsy, mental deficiency, cerebral palsy, and behavior disorders. Learning disorders, which affect some 10 percent of normally intelligent school-age children in the United States, have also been linked to anoxia. These problems, when they are caused by brain damage during the prenatal period, are difficult to treat. If the amount of brain damage is not too severe, however, it may be possible to compensate for the disorder to some extent. Epilepsy can often be controlled with drugs, for instance, and many victims of cerebral palsy can learn some control of their affected muscles.

Drugs, Alcohol, and Nicotine

Chemicals can cause a wide range of congenital abnormalities. The severity of the abnormality depends on the amount of chemical the mother is exposed to, the developmental stage of the fetus, and the period of time over which the mother's exposure to the chemical takes place. Exposure to chemicals during pregnancy thus should be avoided whenever possible, and care should be taken in the use of drugs.

Most of the drugs that can interfere with prenatal development have been identified only within the last ten or twenty years. Certain drugs used in the treatment of cancer are known to cause malformation in babies; others used for the treatment of thyroid malfunction in pregnant mothers have caused goiter and other symptoms in the newborn child. Even such a seemingly harmless drug as tetracycline, an antibiotic that is commonly prescribed for colds and flu, is now known to cause minor congenital abnormalities of the baby's skeleton and teeth. There is also a chance that some common tranquilizers, such as Valium, Librium, and Miltown, may cause harelip and other defects, though this is far from being certain.

Pharmaceuticals are not the only drugs that can affect the baby prenatally. Women who are addicted to heroin, morphine, or methadone give birth to addicted babies. Soon after birth, the babies show symptoms of withdrawal—fever, tremors, convulsions, difficulty in breathing, and intestinal disturbances. The severity of infant withdrawal depends on the period of the mother's addiction, the size of her doses, and how soon before delivery she

Research indicates that the expectant mother who smokes cigarettes runs the risk of harming her unborn child.

last took the drug. Some infants die during withdrawal. For those infants who do survive, a number of behavioral disturbances have been noted. Kolata (1978) found that such babies are more often characterized by unusually strong reflex reactions, excessive crying, irritability, disturbed sleep, and later by poor attention and hyperactivity.

Cigarette smoking, already shown to have dire consequences for the smoker, now also has been found to be hazardous for the unborn and the newborn child. According to a recent Surgeon General's Report (U.S. Public Health Service, 1980) studies of hundreds of thousands of pregnancies both here and abroad and encompassing various ethnic, racial, and cultural groupings indicate that the unborn fetus and neonate are significantly affected by cigarette smoking during pregnancy. Furthermore, the report claims that, in some cases, "these damaging effects have been repeatedly shown to operate independently of all other factors which influence the outcome of pregnancy." Maternal smoking increases the risk of spontaneous abortions, bleeding during pregnancy, premature rupture of the amniotic sac and fetal deaths and deaths of newborns. Smokers during pregnancy give birth to babies that are 200 grams lighter (on the average) and smaller in all dimensions (e.g., length and head circumference) than babies of comparable nonsmokers.

These various deficiencies and damaging effects are increased or reduced according to the number of cigarettes smoked. For example, the greater the amount of smoking during pregnancy, the greater the reduction in birth weight. One study (Davies et al., 1979) indicates that when pregnant women in their last trimester stopped smoking for just forty-eight hours there was a significant increase of 8 percent in the oxygen available to the fetus from the mother's blood.

The effects of alcohol in pregnancy are less clearly known than those of smoking, as there have been few good studies of pregnant women for whom drinking was the only problem. Fetal Alcohol Syndrome (FAS)—a pattern of severe physical and mental deficiencies, including retardation and limb abnormalities—has been associated with chronic alcoholic mothers. But even this relationship requires further study that would take into account environmental variables (Thompson, 1979). For example, poor prenatal care has been associated with alcohol abuse (and with drug abuse), and both factors are implicated in premature labor and smaller-than-normal babies (Eriksson et al., 1979). Alcohol does cross the placenta into the fetal bloodstream, and changes in fetal activity can be detected after the mother has had one or two drinks. However, the changes are not consistent. Sometimes the heartbeat speeds up, sometimes it slows down; one fetus becomes more active, another less active. More research will be needed before we can say for certain whether a mother who drinks is endangering her unborn child.

Hormones

Even some substances that are natural and normal in the body can cause trouble if they occur at the wrong time or in the wrong amount. The sex

❖❖

Advice on Alcohol in Pregnancy

WASHINGTON, April 23 (UPI)—The director of the National Institute on Alcohol Abuse and Alcoholism wants the Government to warn pregnant women that more than two drinks a day, or a total of about three ounces of whiskey, may harm their unborn children.

Dr. Ernest P. Noble said he reached that decision on the basis of a finding by a panel of 40 experts that human and animal evidence shows excessive alcohol consumption can lead to physical and behavioral abnormalities in offspring.

"These animal studies have become so convincing that I feel it's important we should caution people about it," he said in an interview.

Among the human birth defects believed caused by heavy alcohol drinking are facial abnormalities, heart defects, abnormal limb development and lower than average intelligence.

Dr. Noble said that he had forwarded the recommendation to the Department of Health, Education and Welfare.

"As far as I'm concerned, being the director of this institute, a physician, and a scientist, I'm convinced there is enough concern here that people should be aware of it," he said.

"What we are saying essentially is that if you have six drinks or more a day, and that's taken throughout pregnancy, or maybe during a certain phase of pregnancy, there's a significant risk for abnormalities in the young.

"Below six drinks, the risk is questionable," he added. "In order to be on the safe side, we are saying that two drinks a day or less is what people ought to be taking."

Dr. Noble said he was talking about a limit of about three ounces of an alcoholic beverage such as whiskey or gin daily which he said was equal to two mixed drinks, or two glasses of beer or two glasses of wine.

He said there also was evidence suggesting that "binge drinking" could be a problem, too.

"In other words, a person taking a big, big slug of alcohol and maybe not drinking at all for the rest of the pregnancy could also have that kind of a damaging effect," he said. (*The New York Times*, April 24, 1977, p. 26.)

---

hormones are a case in point. One of their normal functions is to ensure that the fetus develops the proper physical characteristics for its genetic sex—that an XX fetus acquires female sex organs and an XY fetus male organs. Occasionally, though, a fetus somehow gets an overdose of hormones for the wrong sex. This may result in a pseudohermaphrodite—a child whose sexual characteristics are somewhere in between those of both sexes. Tests on saliva and blood (chromosome analysis) can be used to determine the true sex. The condition then can often be helped by hormone therapy or surgery after birth, depending on how severe it is.

Ironically, a woman may receive damaging overdoses of hormones (usually female) in perfectly well-meaning medical ways. Oral contraceptives are preparations of female hormones, and sometimes a woman keeps on taking them for a short time before she realizes she is pregnant. Also, women who have a history of miscarriages are often given hormones as a means of sustaining the pregnancy. Recently, considerable attention has been centered on women who were given diethylstilbestrol (DES) during the first trimester of their pregnancy. It has been found that female offspring of these women are at greater risk for vaginal tract and cervical abnormalities (O'Brien et al., 1979), which may lead to problems when they become pregnant themselves (Barnes et al., 1980). Other hormones used to sustain pregnancies have been linked to specific behavioral outcomes. Reinisch (1981), for example, found that women who received synthetic progestins (a masculinizing hormone) during the first three months of pregnancy produced children who showed increased levels of aggression as compared to children whose mothers did not receive the hormone.

Chemicals

Chemicals in the environment are being increasingly linked with teratogenic effects on the fetus. Some of these chemicals may damage the genetic material itself; others probably interfere with development after conception.

In some cases we know that the chemical can damage the genes, but we do not know whether it normally reaches the sperm and egg cells. If it does not, it would harm only the person exposed to it, not a future fetus. Among these chemicals are some common sulfur compounds—sulfur dioxide, which is a major component of air pollution, and bisulphite, a food preservative—and a number of substances used in many hair dyes.

In other cases the evidence for damage to the fetus is clearer. Mercury, for example, is often used to coat seeds as a protection against fungus growth when they are planted. If a woman gets mercury into her system during pregnancy, her child may be mentally retarded. Then there is a whole group of compounds, known as organic hydrocarbons, that are used in fungicides, insecticides, and herbicides. Various of these compounds have been linked with abortions, stillbirths, and birth defects in domestic animals and perhaps in humans.

Absorption of lead into the body is also associated with physical and mental damage, including mental retardation in cases of acute lead poisoning and learning problems and hyperactivity in less severe cases. The most significant data on lead poisoning deals with postnatal exposure to lead in the environment. Eating chipped-off pieces of lead-based paint, for example, is an important source of lead poisoning among children between the ages of one and five. However, there is also some evidence that certain cases of lead poisoning may have their origin in prenatal contact with lead, though the exact nature of this exposure is uncertain. One study (Wibberly et al., 1977) found that the placentas of stillborn infants and infants who died shortly after being born contained much higher levels of lead than were found in the placentas of infants who survived. In another study (Routh, Mushak, & Boone, 1979) children with higher than normal levels of lead in their blood suffered from reduced head size (microcephaly) and more general growth retardation. If there is an association between the blood lead and microcephaly, the fact that most of these children had histories of low weight at birth suggests that they may have been exposed to lead when they were still fetuses.

Radiation

The effects of prenatal exposure to radiation were tragically demonstrated by the babies born after the atomic explosions in Japan during World War II. If a woman in her first twenty weeks of pregnancy was within a half-mile of the center of the explosion, her chances of delivering a normal baby were very small. Expectant mothers farther from the center of the explosion gave birth to babies with congenitally dislocated hips, malformed eyes, heart disease, leukemia, and mental retardation.

Exposure to X rays and other small, controlled amounts of radiation is now known to damage the fetus. Larger doses of therapeutic radiation, such as those required for the treatment of cancer, may be injurious to the fetus and can sometimes cause spontaneous abortion. There really seems to be no completely safe level of radiation; even the various levels of natural radiation found in different parts of the world can be correlated with the higher or lower chances that babies born in those parts of the world will have congenital abnormalities.

The Mother

Since the mother's body is the chief element in the unborn baby's environment, her physical condition can significantly affect its development. Among the maternal factors known to influence the fetus are diet, prolonged stress, reactions associated with a certain blood component, and the mother's age.

Age

Teen-age mothers and those over thirty-five have a higher risk of miscarriage, premature birth, and some birth defects than mothers in the prime child-bearing years. Some of the reasons are fairly obvious. Very young mothers have not yet completed their own development, and their reproductive system may not be quite ready to function. In older women the reproductive system may be past its most efficient functioning. In both cases pregnancy puts an extra strain on a body that is not fully able to bear it. Furthermore, there is some reason to think that a woman's ova may deteriorate with age, leading to a greater risk of birth defects. Women have all their ova in partly developed form when they are born. So a woman who becomes pregnant at age thirty-seven is "using" an ovum that has been more or less exposed to thirty-seven years' worth of harmful chemicals, radiation, virus infections, and whatever else has happened to her body. This may explain why, for instance, Down's syndrome is most common in children born to mothers over forty.

It is quite possible, however, that men's sperm may also be susceptible to chemicals and radiation effects over time. Furthermore, there may be genetic disorders that cause changes in sperm structure. Kolata (1978) notes that there is growing evidence linking a number of birth defects to preconception exposure of certain substances in males. Furthermore, as we noted earlier, recent studies have suggested that fathers may be the carrier of the chromosome abnormality in Down's syndrome.

Diet and Physical Condition

Only in recent years has the mother's nutrition been considered important to the development of the fetus. Doctors and researchers realized that pregnancy puts additional demands on the mother's body, but they used to assume that the fetus's nutritional needs would be met first, even at the mother's expense.

The current opinion, however, is that the prenatal development of the fetus and its growth and development after birth are directly related to maternal diet. Women who follow nutritionally sound diets during pregnancy give birth to babies of normal or above-normal size. Their babies are less likely to contract bronchitis, pneumonia, or colds during early infancy. Their teeth and bones are better developed, and their mothers have fewer complications during pregnancy and on the average spend less time in labor.

But if the mother's diet is low in certain vitamins and minerals when she is pregnant, the child may suffer from specific weaknesses. Insufficient iron may lead to anemia in the infant, and a low intake of calcium may cause poor bone formation. If there is not enough protein in the mother's diet, the baby may be smaller than average and may suffer from mental retardation.

One study (Vore, 1973) links malnutrition in the prenatal period and infancy to deficits in the development of the central nervous system and the brain. These deficits reduce the child's ability to learn, and the damage cannot be repaired.

Babies born of women who follow nutritionally sound diets during pregnancy are of normal or above normal size and are less likely to contract diseases during early infancy.

The Rh Factor

The Rh-positive factor is a common inherited, genetically dominant trait in the blood that can result in a situation dangerous to the child. When blood containing the Rh factor (that is, Rh-positive blood) is introduced into blood without the Rh factor (Rh-negative), antibodies to combat the Rh factor are produced. If any Rh-negative woman mates with an Rh-positive man, the resulting child may have Rh-positive blood. Any small rupture in the capillaries of the placenta will release the Rh factor into the mother's bloodstream, causing her body to produce the antibodies needed to fight it. The antibodies in the mother's blood will then cross the placenta into the fetal bloodstream and attack its Rh-positive red blood cells, depriving it of oxygen. The result may be a miscarriage, possible brain defects, or even death to the fetus or newborn child. Only in circumstances involving an Rh-negative mother and an Rh-positive child does this danger exist.

This condition in the child is called *fetal erythroblastosis.* Firstborn children are not threatened, as the mother's blood has not had time to produce a large amount of antibodies, but the risk increases with each pregnancy. In the past erythroblastosis was always fatal, but now medical techniques can minimize the harmful results of Rh incompatibility. After the birth of an Rh-positive child the Rh-negative mother can be given an injection of the drug Rhogan to reduce the buildup of antibodies in her blood. If this is not done, future Rh-positive children will be endangered by the high antibody level.

Stress

If a mother is extremely anxious—about her pregnancy, her abilities as a mother, or any other problem in her life—the unborn child may be affected. Mothers who are relatively free of emotional stress, on the other hand, tend to give birth more easily, and their babies usually develop normally. Although the baby's nervous system is separate from the mother's, strong emotions in the mother such as rage, fear, and anxiety cause a great increase of hormones and other chemicals in her bloodstream. These substances pass through the placenta wall, and it is believed that they can reproduce the mother's physiological state in the fetus.

One researcher (Sontag, 1944) found that the bodily movements of the fetus increased considerably when the mother was undergoing stress. He suggested that if this stress is prolonged or often repeated, it could have enduring consequences for the child—particularly if it occurs during the first trimester of pregnancy. Other researchers (Copans, 1974), however, point out that the effect of maternal stress is as yet unknown.

TO HAVE OR NOT HAVE CHILDREN

The concept of family planning has gained impetus and real meaning from the fact that we now have reliable means and methods of contraception. There are nonprescription products, such as condoms and vaginal foams, which

A joyful attitude helps to minimize stress and creates an atmosphere beneficial to the unborn child. A mother's emotions may affect the development of her unborn child through hormones that pass from her bloodstream to that of the fetus.

can be purchased at drugstores. Using these materials, however, is not nearly as reliable as using the Pill, the intrauterine device (I.U.D.), and the diaphragm, all of which require a visit to a clinic or a private physician. Birth control through voluntary surgical sterilization is becoming more common, though most people dislike the fact that fertility can rarely be restored. Some people, including those whose religion forbids other methods of contraception, use the "rhythm method" (periodic abstinence), though it is the least reliable technique of family planning.

Despite the use of contraceptives, pregnancies may occur. If the child is unwanted or the risk of fetal abnormalities is high, abortion may be chosen as a secondary method of birth control. About 10–15 percent of pregnancies end in spontaneous abortion or miscarriage during the first three months. Most abortions, however, are induced.

The method used for inducing abortion, at least in the United States, depends on the stage of pregnancy. In the earliest stage a flexible tube is inserted through the cervical canal into the uterus and a vacuum is created that gently empties the uterus of its contents. Before six weeks "menstrual

Raising children can be a profoundly rewarding experience. However, it requires time, energy, and patience.

extraction" is the suction technique used; during the first trimester "suction curettage" (also known as "vacuum aspiration") is performed. A local or general anesthetic may be used, and the entire procedure—which can be done in a hospital, clinic, or physician's office—may take three to ten minutes. An abortion at this stage is considered to be nine times safer than childbirth.

Between twelve and fifteen weeks (or even during the first trimester) a more delicate abortion procedure may be performed. Known as dilation and curettage (D & C), it usually requires hospitalization and general anesthesia. The cervix is opened wide enough to allow a blunt instrument, known as a curette, to be inserted into the uterus, where it is used to remove fetal tissue. This procedure involves a risk of cervical infection and of perforation of the uterus.

After sixteen weeks abortion techniques may be used that induce labor, thus resulting in miscarriage. A strong salt solution is injected through the abdomen into the amniotic sac. This usually causes contractions twelve to twenty-four hours later and expulsion of the fetus and placenta within forty-eight hours. Hemorrhaging, intrauterine infection, and "salt poisoning" are some of the risks of this method, and hospitalization is often advised. An alternate method of inducing labor with a somewhat lesser risk of hemorrhaging is done by injecting prostaglandin, a hormone found in human semen. Common side effects include nausea, diarrhea, and vomiting, and the success of the procedure varies with the stage of pregnancy. Local anesthetic is the usual practice when performing either of the labor-inducing procedures.

Abortions before the third trimester (in other words, within the first twenty-four weeks of pregnancy) were legalized in the United States in 1973. Yet abortion remains a controversial procedure, at least in those cases in which pregnancy poses no danger to the mother and in which there is no risk of fetal abnormalities. Many people fervently oppose abortion on religious and moral grounds. Some have also claimed that it may have damaging psychological effects on women. Postabortion guilt and depression have been attributed to both emotional and physiological factors. On the other side of the issue, some have claimed that bringing an unwanted child into the world can be damaging to both mother and infant. They believe that emotional and financial unpreparedness on the part of single mothers or married couples can make the child a source of stress and conflict and the target of abuse and neglect.

SUMMARY

▶ Every individual is influenced by genetic factors and by the prenatal environment. The individual's genetic potentialities are inherited from both parents, but the combination of genes that the individual receives is unique. A gene is the part of a chromosome that directs the formation of a single trait. Chromosomes are found in the nucleus of every living cell.

▶ Some physical features, such as eye and skin color, as well as certain rare diseases are inherited. Mental illness, intelligence, and personality may be affected by inheritance, but it is hard to say exactly how much.

▶ In gestation the zygote develops into a fully formed baby through three stages. During the short ovum stage the zygote enters the uterus while undergoing cell division. When this tiny cell mass embeds itself in the uterine wall, the embryo stage begins. When tissue differentiation and system development are essentially complete, the fetal stage begins and the baby grows rapidly until it is ready for birth.

▶ Environmental agents that adversely affect an individual's development before birth are called teratogens. Some teratogens are diseases that infect the mother and injure the child. Others are drugs or chemicals that cross from the mother's bloodstream into the child's. A third type of teratogen is radiation such as X rays and nuclear particles.

▶ New and improved contraceptive techniques offer the option of family planning. Abortion, though a highly controversial issue, is now a legal procedure for terminating unwanted pregnancy. Abortion techniques vary according to the stage of pregnancy.

❖❖

FURTHER READINGS

Apgar, Virginia, and Beck, Joan. *Is my baby all right? A guide to birth defects.* New York: Trident, 1972.
In one out of every sixteen births, a baby is born with a defect that will significantly affect later life. Apgar and Beck explain the causes of both genetic and environmental birth defects. The intricate steps of development that take place in the human fetus, and how the pattern can go wrong, are carefully described by the authors.

Dilfer, Carol Stahmann. *Your baby, your body fitness during pregnancy.* New York: Crown, 1977.
This book focuses on achieving total body fitness during and after pregnancy. In addition it discusses the benefits of calisthenics and acrobatic exercises.

Galinsky, Ellen. *Beginnings: A young mother's account of two premature births.* Boston: Houghton Mifflin, 1976.
Galinsky writes revealingly about her two difficult pregnancies and tells what it is like to leave a "preemie" in incubation. Her second baby did not survive.

Montagu, Ashley. *Human heredity.* Cleveland: World, 1963.
The author not only explains what is scientifically known about the science of heredity but clarifies the nature or nurture issue. The second half of the book is a discussion of common physical and functional traits that are inherited genetically.

Nyhan, W. *The heredity factor.* New York: Grosset & Dunlap, 1976.
This well-written, comprehensive book provides an explanation of genetics, genetic counseling, and genetic defects for the general reader.

Salk, Lee. *Preparing for parenthood.* New York: McKay, 1975.
Written for parents-to-be, this book is concerned with helping them understand and deal with their own feelings about birth and assuming a new role.

Whelan, Elizabeth. *A baby . . . maybe.* New York: Bobbs-Merrill, 1975.
This engaging book discusses the decision of whether or not to have children, presenting the arguments on both sides.

Chapter 2

❖❖❖❖❖❖

Birth and the Neonate

*A*lthough we are all aware that birth may involve a number of complications—the mother's pelvis may be too narrow to allow the passage of the baby's head, for example, or the baby may emerge bottom first instead of head first—these problems, and others, fortunately are the exceptions. The large majority of mothers and babies come through childbirth in good health. Though this reassuring information is always at hand, first-time parents tend to worry.

Many parents combat anxiety and fear by participating in one of the programs known as prepared childbirth. They read factual material on childbirth, attend lectures, and discuss what they learn with other prospective parents. They also practice breathing routines and exercises that prepare both parents for the birth experience. Home study and self-directed exercises can often accomplish the same aim.

Popular report sometimes pictures advocates of prepared childbirth as opposing the use of anesthesia or other drugs in labor, but this is not quite accurate. The purpose of prepared childbirth is to reduce maternal anxiety and to teach the mother to facilitate rather than resist labor and delivery. Whether to use drugs—and how much—is a decision that must be left to the mother and her physician. However, many women remain conscious and require minimal or no analgesic medication. They can then bring voluntary

effort to bear in the delivery, which has provided many mothers and participating fathers with a great sense of accomplishment.

LABOR

Is this labor? Has the time come at last? Many mothers ask themselves these
questions more than once in the late weeks of pregnancy. When labor finally
does arrive, it progresses through three stages: dilation, expulsion, and placental. The first stage, **dilation,** may only be two hours long, or it may last
sixteen hours or more. Each contraction, at first, is thirty to forty-five seconds
in duration and comes about fifteen to twenty minutes after the last one. The
contractions are involuntary; the mother cannot start them or stop them at
will or make them come faster or slower. Their function is to dilate the cervix
until it is wide enough to let the baby through—usually about four inches (10
cm).

In the course of the first stage the contractions come more and more
frequently, until finally they are only a minute or two apart. Each contraction
also becomes longer; toward the end of the first stage they may last ninety
seconds. The mother's mood also changes as the first stage progresses. At first
she feels the contractions with a sense of jubilation or relief, for she has been
waiting nine months for this moment. When she has spent some hours in
labor, however, and the contractions are both longer in duration and quicker
in succession, she may become serious and determined.

At the end of the first stage there may be a series of contractions that
are very intense. The cervix has been stretched around the baby's head. The
mother may feel ready to give up, but this phase, known as **transition,** is soon
over. It rarely lasts more than half an hour, and is often much shorter (see
Figure 2.1).

In the second stage, **expulsion,** the involuntary contractions continue to
be long in duration and closely spaced, but now the mother has a strong urge
to bear down voluntarily with her abdominal muscles. In between contractions she may drift off into a state of forgetfulness, but she rouses with each
new contraction and pushes down with all her strength. She sweats, flushes,
and grunts, and the baby's scalp comes into view, only to disappear again
when the contraction ends. This is known as **crowning.** With each contraction
more and more of the baby's head can be seen. Many obstetricians routinely
perform an *episiotomy*—making a small slit in the skin outside the vagina
toward the anus—to prevent this tissue from tearing, for the slit heals much
more readily than a jagged tear. When the baby's head comes out as far as its
widest diameter, it stays out, and in a short time it is free. The head may be
molded—elongated in shape due to passage through the cervix—but the soft
skull bones that have been squeezed together soon recover their normal
shape.

Some babies will give their first cry at this point. With the next contractions the shoulders emerge, and the rest of the body slips out easily. The
mother experiences a great feeling of release and elation.

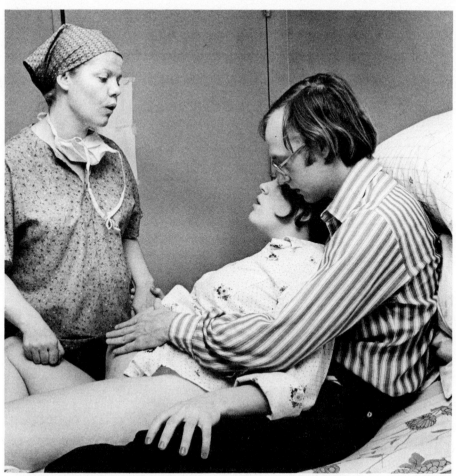

The Lamaze childbirth class prepares the mother for dealing with the pain of giving birth and allows the father to share in the delivery-room duties.

As soon as delivery is complete, the umbilical cord is clamped and cut. Then a nurse takes the baby, wrapped in a receiving blanket, to perform a series of procedures that vary from hospital to hospital. Typically, the baby is given drops in its eyes to prevent infection, both mother and baby are given plastic identification bracelets, and fingerprints of the mother and sometimes footprints of the baby are taken. Also, a series of tests known as the Apgar Scoring System are made at one and five minutes after birth to evaluate the baby's muscle tone, heart rate, breathing effort, color, and reflex response. These tests either provide assurance that the baby's life-sustaining functions are operating normally, or else they alert the hospital staff promptly to the presence of a potentially dangerous problem. During the third, or **placental,** stage the placenta and the attached membranes and cord, commonly called the **afterbirth,** are expelled from the uterus. Labor is now completed.

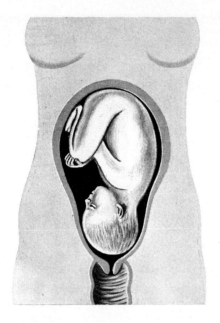 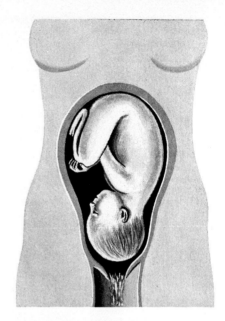

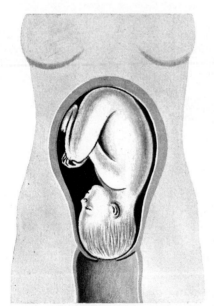 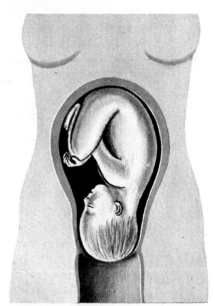

Figure 2.1 Dilation of the cervix. Upper left: In pregnancy the cervix is closed and sealed with a mucous plug. Upper right, breaking water: The amniotic sac ruptures, and the amniotic fluid runs out through the cervix. Lower left: Labor contractions force the baby's head down, dilating the cervix. Lower right: the cervix stretches to permit the baby's head to pass through.

Alternate Birth Centers

Hospitals operate at a bustling, crisis-oriented pace. Such institutions are for sick people, and pregnancy is not considered an illness by supporters of a new kind of environment for giving birth—the Alternate Birth Center (ABC). Alternate Birth Centers were developed—because many parents objected to what they felt to be the impersonal, needlessly technological, and increasingly expensive childbirth procedures in the conventional hospital setting. As a growing number of mothers chose to give birth at home, the risks involved became a serious public health hazard in parts of the United States (Arms, 1975). The ABC, then, is a response to both the dissatisfaction with hospitals and the hazards of home births.

They were all but unheard of in 1969. Within a decade at least a thousand were established and the trend is expected to continue. In 1978 the medical establishment officially endorsed many elements of this alternate care; recommending that it be included in conventional maternity services (Interprofessional Task Force on Health Children, 1978). Out-of-hospital facilities for the management of low-risk deliveries were also established.

Alternate Birth Centers provide a relaxed, homey atmosphere for the pregnant woman, her family, and the newborn. The most dramatic aspect of an ABC compared with the conventional hospital is the room where the deliveries take place. Unlike the sterile chamber resembling an operating room to which laboring mothers are generally sped at the most uncomfortable, critical moment, the birthing room, a cheerfully decorated suite resembling a bedroom, is also the location of the mother's predelivery hours. Women in labor move about freely (Caldeyro-Barcia, 1979). They eat, drink, or rest as they choose, accompanied by their husbands, families, and friends. An attending nurse, midwife, or doctor, who is present throughout, delivers the baby into this low key, family-oriented environment. It is dimly lit, quiet, and peaceful. The new mothers, and those with them, report a sense of control and contentment in contrast to the anxiety and isolation commonly experienced in the traditional delivery room (Montrose, 1978).

Following birth, the new family remains in the birthing room, in close physical contact. The newborn is placed on the mother's bare skin and has the first opportunity to suckle and enjoy eye contact. A soothing warm bath may be administered. In these first hours bonding of parent and child has a unique chance to commence. In many birth rooms siblings may share these special experiences. Although this option is controversial, some proponents believe that future rivalry between siblings is reduced (Leonard et al., 1978). The entire family leaves the ABC together, usually earlier than from the traditional setting.

For safety birthing-room facilities keep a significant amount of emergency equipment hidden within the suite itself and deliver only low-risk mothers. Nonetheless, of these approximately 10 percent develop problems best handled in a more conventional setting. When located in a hospital, birthing rooms are usually adjacent to traditional delivery and operating rooms. Out-of-hospital ABCs transfer laboring mothers by ambulance, if necessary, to a cooperating nearby hospital.

Supporters of birthing rooms claim that there are physical, physiological, psychological, and medical benefits. But it is still too early for conclusive research findings. It will be interesting to find out whether for children who begin life in a birthing room there are significant differences in maternal and paternal behavior and incidence of child abuse. Meanwhile more and more people are enjoying the opportunity to share the experience of childbirth.

The length of the entire process varies greatly, as does the actual experience of labor. Fifteen hours is an average figure for the duration of birth from the first contraction to the expulsion of the afterbirth. But this average covers a spectrum of labor as long as twenty-four hours and as short as three hours or less. Labor is usually longer for first babies than for later ones.

Mother and baby may or may not stay together after delivery, depending on the policy of the hospital and the doctor. Many believe it wise to isolate the baby for several hours at first in order to reduce exposure to germs, while others believe it is more important to give the parents and the baby the psychological satisfaction of resting together after their great experience. When this is done, the baby has a crib beside the mother's bed and is said to be "rooming in."

Complications

Variations from the norm that occur during the delivery of a baby can usually be dealt with successfully by the obstetrician and the hospital staff. The baby may, for example, come out bottom first in what is called a **breech presentation.** Sometimes one foot is the first thing to appear, and sometimes the umbilical cord comes out alongside the head. The doctor must manage these variations with great skill if the baby is to be delivered unharmed. If contractions slow down or stop, hormones may be used to make them resume. The use of forceps may also be required if the mother's contractions become irregular or decrease in strength. At one time it was reasonably common to use forceps during the first stage of delivery or in the early part of the second stage. This procedure, known as high-forceps delivery, can cause brain damage to the child because of the considerable force needed to pull the baby's head out. For this reason, high forceps are rarely used today. Low-forceps delivery—that is, the use of forceps in the actual delivery stage—is seldom damaging to the infant. Consequently, it is still commonly used in many hospitals.

Throughout the labor process both mother and fetus are constantly observed for signs of birth complications. In particular, the fetal heartbeat is monitored during labor and when there is cause for concern, a surgical operation known as a cesarean section is performed. In *cesarean birth* the baby is delivered through a surgical incision made in the mother's abdomen and uterus.

Drugs During Labor

What is good for the mother is not always good for the fetus. For decades the pains of labor have been eased with many types of drugs, from mild painkillers such as analgesics to general anesthetics that obliterate all sensation. Recently researchers have begun to take a careful look at the possible effects of these drugs on the fetus, especially in light of the extreme danger of some drugs taken earlier in pregnancy. A review of the various studies (Bowes et al., 1970)

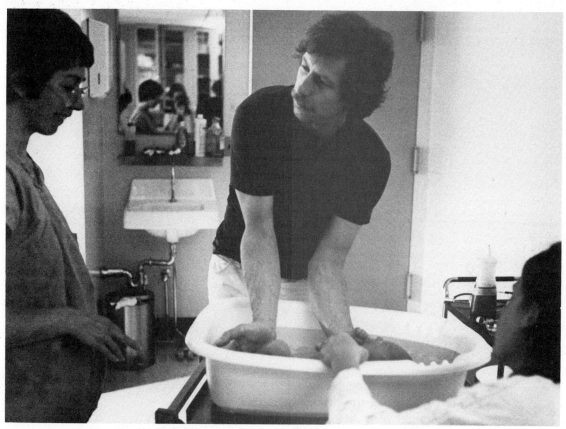

The gentle birth method of delivery is believed to ease the newborn's transition from the mother's womb to the outside world.

explains that most of the medication administered during labor crosses the placenta by diffusion. No study found that the drugs caused long-term harm to the fetus, but they did find more sluggish behavior in babies whose mothers took labor medication.

A more recent study (Scanlon et al., 1974) which compared infants whose mothers were given a routine regional anesthetic known as epidural anesthesia (which is administered in the lower spine) with those whose mothers did not receive the drug during labor, adds to the evidence of short-term effects. The former sample of newborns showed significant decreases in muscle tone and strength in the first eight hours of life compared with the latter group, and they were described as "floppy but alert." However, neurobehavioral testing of "higher" central nervous system function showed little difference between the two groups.

Differences in visual attentiveness, weight gain, general brain activity, and sucking behavior observed in various studies generally fade away within a few weeks. However, the possibility of more subtle long-term effects of labor drugs on behavior and development is still the subject of controversy.

❖❖

Gentle Birth

How does it feel to a baby to be forced out of the uterus, through the vagina, and into the world? What are the baby's first impressions of the world it is being thrust into? At least one expert, French obstetrician Frederick Leboyer, believes that being born is a terrifying experience. And the terror is intensified, in Leboyer's view, by the violence of modern delivery techniques.

Most babies are born into an operating room full of blinding light and noisy bustle. Hardly do they emerge before they are handled, washed, tagged, weighed, and footprinted. Some obstetricians even follow the time-honored ritual of holding the baby by the ankles and giving it a slap to start it breathing.

Leboyer feels that all this is a brutal introduction to life outside the womb. He has developed an alternative method of delivery called nonviolent or gentle birth, a method that is designed to make the transition from the womb to the outside world as comforting as possible. Gentle birth is a logical extension of prepared childbirth techniques, with the difference that prepared childbirth focuses on the experience of the mother and father, whereas Leboyer's method focuses on the experience of the baby.

The Leboyer technique involves a number of radical changes in the delivery procedure. As soon as the infant begins to emerge, the physicians and nurses attending the birth lower their voices and the lights in the operating theater are turned down. Everyone handles the baby with the greatest possible tenderness. Immediately after delivery it is placed on its mother's belly, where it can start breathing before the umbilical cord is cut. After a few minutes the obstetrician places the baby in a lukewarm bath, an environment very like the amniotic fluid. In this way the difference between the fetal environment and the world is minimized.

Leboyer has written a book that describes his delivery technique and has prepared a film showing an actual birth by his method.

Although we don't remember our own birth, impressions of it may remain in the unconscious memory. Sigmund Freud conjectured that the experience of birth and the shock of being separated from one's mother could set the pattern for later feelings of anxiety (Freud, 1924). One of Freud's students, Otto Rank, further developed this notion of the "birth trauma." Rank felt that birth is such a terrifying experience that it leaves a lasting mark on every individual. Others have questioned this theory, noting, for example, that the newborn child's nervous system may be so undeveloped that it cannot yet register any experience as strongly and sharply as Rank suggests (Allport, 1961).

One recent study (Nelson et al., 1980) found no differences between the Leboyer and conventional methods of delivery on infant and maternal behavior; nor were differences noted for the incidence of birth complications for the infant or mother. Whether the Leboyer method of delivery offers a safer entrance into the world, therefore, remains a controversial issue.

Anoxia

Anoxia, or the deprivation of oxygen, can cause severe brain damage. Mild incidents of anoxia have been blamed for minor cases of brain damage, learning disabilities, and behavior difficulties. The fetus can be subjected to anoxia before birth, as mentioned in Chapter 1. If the mother is anemic, for example, her blood is deficient in iron, and its oxygen-carrying capacity may be so low that oxygen in the blood of the fetus falls to dangerous levels. Anoxia can also strike the baby at birth, either by a rupture of blood vessels in the brain or by a failure of the umbilical circulation to provide oxygen before the baby is ready to take its first breath. There are many things that can happen during birth to interfere with or cut off the umbilical circulation. Occasionally the mother's blood pressure may drop because of bleeding. Sometimes part of the cord emerges before the baby's head is delivered, and the cord is then squeezed against the wall of the birth passage by the emerging head. This often happens in a breech presentation, and is a chief reason why such a presentation is regarded as a problem. Sometimes, too, very strong contractions can momentarily pinch the cord against the baby's head or body within the uterus. Neonates suffering a mild loss of oxygen at birth seem to be more irritable than others for about the first week. Their muscular activity is more tense and rigid, and their response to visual stimulation and pain less sensitive (Graham et al., 1956). Studies that trace the effects of anoxia through childhood years indicate that these children score significantly lower on tests of intellectual capability, particularly when other indications of respiratory distress were evident during delivery (Broman, 1979).

PREMATURITY AND LOW BIRTH WEIGHT

A baby is considered premature if it is born at thirty-seven weeks of gestation or earlier (the normal gestation period is forty weeks). But it is often difficult to tell just when gestation began, and some babies are born small even after forty weeks in the womb. These low-birth-weight babies, weighing under five and a half pounds (2.4 kg), have many of the same disadvantages whether they were born early or simply born small. For this reason they are treated as babies "at risk" for developmental physical problems. They can be measured and tested, especially for reflexes, to determine the exact dimensions of their underdevelopment.

The premature baby is not physically ready to adapt to the world outside the uterus. It has less fat to insulate its body and therefore less ability to keep warm. It may be lacking in immunity to infection and in the muscular strength necessary to expand its lungs for breathing. The capillary network in its lungs may also be inadequate to provide a sufficient exchange of gases. As soon as possible after birth, therefore, the baby is placed in a warmed crib or an incubator. In many cases it is given oxygen at first, though too much of it for too long may result in blindness.

Because its body, being underdeveloped, is delicate, the "preemie" must be handled with care. In fact, until fairly recently it was felt that the less handling the better. The infant was best off left undisturbed in its incubator, as far as possible, until it reached normal birth weight. But recent studies have made increasingly clear that warmth, food, oxygen, and protection from disease are not all that a newborn needs—even a newborn who ought, de-

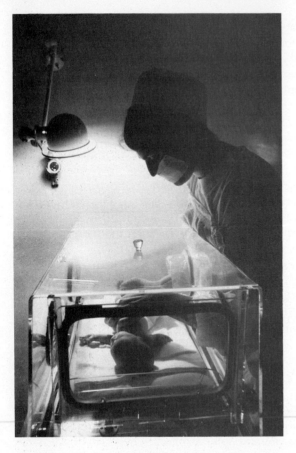

Early human contact is an important factor in the development of the premature baby. Research has revealed that "preemies" need to be cuddled and talked to as much as full-term babies.

velopmentally speaking, to be still in its mother's womb. Sensory stimulation is important, and so is the human contact that other babies have virtually from the moment of birth. The lack of this early stimulation may even be one of the reasons for the difficulties that low-birth-weight children experience in later life. Nowadays, therefore, low-birth-weight babies are deliberately given more stimulation—cuddled, fondled, rocked, talked to, removed from the incubator for feeding, and supplied with eye-catching crib toys.

Studies following the development of premature babies over a period of years have kept track of their motor and perceptual performance, their intelligence, and any behavior disorders they may show. One study (Field, Dempsey, & Shuman, 1979) of premature infants with a respiratory distress syndrome (RDS) at birth, followed them through the first four years of life and compared their mental and motor development with that of healthy full-term babies. The gap between the two groups narrowed significantly during their second year, and by the end of it, the test scores of the RDS group were within the normal range, though at its lower end. In this and other studies (Ambrus et al., 1970; Fitzhardinge et al., 1976; Harrod et al., 1974; Johnson et al., 1974) the gap in test results is much greater in motor development than mental development. According to the authors of the 1979 study, the fact that there is any significant difference in mental scores between the two groups may be due to the testing device. The Bayley Development Assessment, which was used in all these studies, requires some coordination and fine motor skills even in mental tests. At the age of four, both groups scored comparably on IQ and social maturity tests, but there were some differences in hearing and language development as well as minimal brain dysfunction, and these may indicate some risk of future learning disabilities.

Other research (Sigman et al., 1981) indicates that although a child's development undoubtedly is affected by neurological and medical complications associated with early birth, family and sociocultural factors also play a major role in the eventual outcome of the child. Specifically, these investigators found that firstborn children and children from higher socioeconomic levels were less affected by prematurity than were later-born children and children from lower socioeconomic levels. The researchers suggested that the presence of appropriate caretaking resources can offset many of the problems associated with prematurity.

PHYSICAL CHARACTERISTICS OF THE NEWBORN

It takes a while for many babies to become beautiful. At first the skin of the neonate is thin, sensitive, and very ruddy in appearance. Some have little white bumps around the nose and on the cheeks; darker-complexioned babies often have bluish colorations on the back or the buttocks. Some are born with a full head of hair as well as a fine down on the ears, the lower back, and the shoulders. This down, called the *lanugo*, is most common in premature infants.

The eyes of the newborn seem small. The lids are puffy, the eyes have a dull color because pigmentation has not yet developed, and the gaze has an absent, almost unseeing quality. Most babies have blood spots on the eyes for the first few days, due to pressure during delivery. The nose, too, often suffers some temporary distortion from having been pressed down during birth, and the head is molded.

The neonate's body has a frail look; it does not yet have the thick fatty tissue that gives a baby the usual soft roundness. It keeps its legs bent in at the knee with its feet flexed outward, which tends to give the limbs an awkward look. In fact, the newborn looks best when wrapped snugly in a receiving blanket. Many of these characteristics come as a surprise to first-time parents, but their baby's appearance changes rapidly for the better.

Respiration

The fetus receives a steady supply of oxygen through the umbilical cord; the newborn must breathe for itself. Normal breathing is a reflex action triggered by a chemical imbalance; an excess of carbon dioxide in the blood stimulates

Learning to be a parent involves the acquisition of a host of new skills.

the respiratory center of the brain, and without thinking about it, we take a breath. This process, which prompts each successive breath, also prompts our first gasp. The oxygen level in the neonate's blood drops when the umbilical cord is clamped, shutting off the oxygen supply; the breathing reflex follows almost immediately. Squeezing through the birth canal has already prepared the lungs for their first breath.

As the neonate takes its first few breaths, its lungs expand. The smaller bronchi and the tiny lung buds, or *alveoli*, are first collapsed or filled with fluid, so the first few breaths must be vigorous enough to expand them. With the opening of the alveoli the capillaries unfold, and the way is cleared for an increasing volume of blood to the lungs.

This adaptation does not occur all at once. Even during fetal life a certain amount of blood is pumped through the lungs, but changes in the circulatory system are necessary before the lungs receive the entire output of the right ventricle of the heart.

The newborn breaths with the diaphragm in what is called abdominal breathing, rather than with the chest. It favors its nose rather than its mouth. The breathing of a newborn baby is often very uneven. Because control of the soft palate and the larynx is still immature, or because some fluid may remain in the respiratory passages for a while, many babies make wheezing and snorting noises as they breathe.

Circulation

When the umbilical cord is clamped and cut, one major branch of the circulatory system, as it existed in the fetal stage, closes down. The main blood vessels to and from the placenta shut off shortly after birth.

As circulation through the umbilical cord stops, circulation through the lungs increases. In the fetal heart the pulmonary circulation—blood pumped to and from the lungs—is not separate from the general body circulation, as it is in an adult. There is an opening between the right and left auricles known as the *foramen ovale*, and a small shunting vessel known as the *ductus arteriosus* between the aorta and the pulmonary artery. The foramen ovale permits incoming blood to flow into either auricle, and the ductus arteriosus permits blood pumped out by both ventricles to enter the general circulation. After the baby is born, however, the foramen ovale gradually seals up and the ductus arteriosus constricts and shuts off. When these closures are complete, the right ventricle pumps blood only to the lungs, as it does in an adult.

The newborn's heart beats rapidly, from 120 to 140 beats per minute. During the first weeks of life the blood is very rich in hemoglobin, the substance that carries oxygen to the tissues.

Digestion

The neonate is well equipped to make the change from passively receiving nutrition from the mother's blood to actively seeking food with its mouth. It has a strong sucking reflex, and has sucking pads on the inner surface of each cheek. After a day or two of sucking the newborn develops what looks like a blister but is really a callus on the surface of the lip.

Babies are usually fed about twelve hours after birth, depending on the policy of the hospital. If the baby is breast-fed, the mother's milk begins to flow the second or third day after birth. At first the breast produces a substance called *colostrum*, which provides an abundant supply of antibodies to the newborn. Whether the baby is on breast milk or on bottle formula, the diet is sometimes supplemented by a sugar-water mixture for the first few days.

Often, because of the overactivity of the reflex that stimulates the intestinal tract once the stomach is filled, the newborn will have a bowel movement after, or even during, each feeding. Breast-fed babies generally have more frequent and looser bowel movements than bottle-fed babies. Weight loss of about half a pound (.225 kg) in the first few days of life is normal.

Although the baby produces a surprising number of enzymes at birth, one enzyme in the liver known as a transferase is deficient in almost 50 percent of newborns. This temporary deficiency results in mild jaundice—the skin takes on a yellow tint.

Skeleton

The skeleton of the newborn has been enriched by the calcium received from the mother's body, but many bones are still mainly cartilage at birth. Some are only connective tissue, and bone formation takes place after the baby is born.

The main characteristic of the neonate's skeleton is its flexibility. The skull, for example, is made up of several bones that touch each other at certain places called the **sutures,** and other places are actually separated by soft areas of the connective tissue called **fontanelles** (Figure 2.2). The largest of the fontanelles, near the top of the head, is the last to close, around a year after birth.

The skull bones themselves are quite soft and are often molded temporarily to an egg shape during birth, then flattened and somewhat distorted when the baby sleeps on one side. None of these distortions remain after the first year.

Temperature Regulation

The adult body has a number of mechanisms to help it maintain its internal temperature while the air around it changes. The neonate is more vulnerable to its surroundings. Two of the most basic reactions—secretion of sweat to lose heat and shivering of the muscles to raise body temperature—are simply not yet developed in the neonate. The neonate is also at a disadvantage in maintaining body temperature because its layer of fatty tissue is thin and therefore does not provide much insulation.

Although the newborn is largely dependent on others to make sure that it is not subjected to extremes of heat or cold, its body is not totally lacking in defense mechanisms. When it cries, its body temperature is raised because the metabolism rate is increased. It may also warm itself up by becoming more active.

Immunity to Infection

Before birth the baby receives a valuable supply of antibodies directly from its mother especially toward the end of pregnancy. These antibodies protect it at birth when it is suddenly confronted with an environment filled with germs, many of which invade its skin, digestive tract, and respiratory tract almost instantly. The protection given by some of the mother's antibodies lasts for about a month in the baby. Other antibodies from the mother, against diseases such as measles, polio, and hepatitis, lasts from six to twelve months. Immunities are also obtained through the mother's breast milk. The mother's antibodies protect the baby against most of the common infectious diseases,

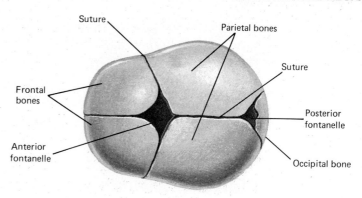

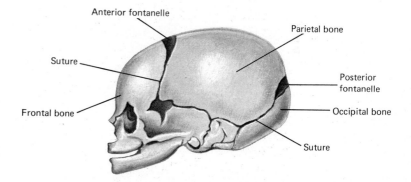

Figure 2.2 The fontanelles. The newborn's skull bones are separated by the fontanelles, areas of cartilage and tough connective tissue that do not entirely ossify (turn to bone) until the child is about one year old.

but the baby's immunity level will be only as high as the mother's. In any event, the neonate immediately begins to produce his own antibodies. And he soon receives immunizing injections from the physician.

POSTPARTUM SEPARATION

Some studies suggest that in the initial period following birth a special bond may form between the mother and child. Researchers (Condon and Sander, 1974a; Perry, 1980) have shown that newborns in the first minutes and hours of life see, hear, and move in rhythm to the mother's voice, creating a beautifully synchronized "dance" with her. Babies also perform several sensory and motor behaviors that help to win the mother's affection. They unmistakably react to the mother's odor, touch, glance, and body warmth, while acting upon her by crying, following her movements with their eyes, and sucking or licking her nipples.

This stimulation of the nipples triggers the secretion of the hormones oxytocin and prolactin in the mother. Oxytocin hastens contraction of the uterus and reduces bleeding after delivery. Prolactin, besides prompting milk

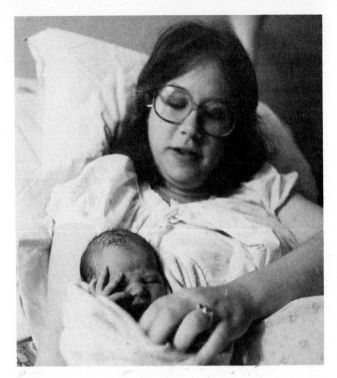

Research has suggested that a special bond may form between mother and child in the initial period following birth. Newborns move in rhythm to the mother's voice and react to the mother's touch, odor, glance, and body warmth.

production, may also be the Cupid's arrow of biology. A "love hormone" in birds, it may work in a similar way in humans, activating the bond between mother and newborn and thus improving the child's chance of survival.

Whatever hormones underlie the mother-child bond, timing also may play an important role. Klaus and Kennell (1976) suggest that a "maternal-sensitive time" exists in the first few hours after birth. It is during this period that the mother is most predisposed to form a bond with the infant. Other researchers, however, have failed to find evidence in support of this position (Svejda, Campos, & Emde, 1980). At the present time, therefore, the importance of early and sustained contact between mother and infant remains controversial.

Although the specific timing of the mother-child bond has been questioned, most researchers are in agreement that prolonged separation of the infant from its parents during the postpartum (afterbirth) period may be detrimental to the infant's development.

Such separations may occur when babies fall sick soon after delivery and are taken from their mothers for intensive care by hospital staff. They most often take place when an infant is born prematurely and placed in an incubator, thus postponing physical contact and the feeding relationship between mother and child for as long as two or three months.

Assuming that parental self-confidence and the baby's responsiveness contribute significantly to happy parent-infant relationships (Goldberg, 1977), both sides start out with some handicaps in such a situation. Many parents have some sense of failure when they cannot bring their newborn home in triumph, but have to leave it at the hospital because of prematurity or illness. Their readiness to take full charge of the child is thereby put into "cold storage," and their previous confidence is affected by the knowledge that their baby has special medical needs that they cannot fulfill themselves.

When the baby is finally released to them, it is still not so ready for interaction as a full-term newborn. More of its energy is required for survival, less is available for eye-contact and social responses like smiling and vocalization, so the parents don't get much reassuring feedback from the child. An emotional factor to compound the child's physical unresponsiveness is that it had relatively little social interaction during its stay in the hospital; indeed, some of its contact with others may have been associated with unpleasant medical procedures. So the child's experiences may not lead it to anticipate social encounters with any eagerness.

All these circumstances may contribute to the widely documented fact that postpartum separation has a negative effect on the relationship between mother and infant. Mothers are less inclined to cuddle such children and hold them close while they feed them (Leifer et al., 1972; Quinn & Goldberg, 1977) and generally show less emotional involvement with their babies than the mothers of full-term infants. Recent studies have found that infants changed much faster than parents who, in the fourth month, may still be geared to the infant's initial rather than current behavior (DiVitto & Goldberg, 1979), and that the less-than-normal maternal response after postpartum separation may last up to nine months (Brown & Bakeman, 1977). Premature and ill newborns have also been found to be at increased risk of later abuse or neglect (Hunter et al., 1978; Klein & Stern, 1971). A combination of factors appears to be involved, one of them being a lack (or limited number) of early mother-infant and family-infant interactions.

One study (Field, 1977) suggests that there may be another factor that is slightly more important than early separation in terms of later mother-infant behavior: the baby's style of interaction at birth. Premature infants, for example, score lower than "normal" infants in terms of their reaction to various sights and sounds. This initial deficit may adversely affect the mother's later responsiveness to her child.

Nevertheless, even this study of prematures did not suggest that early separation had no subsequent effects. There may be important benefits for mother and child in leaving them together for at least thirty minutes after delivery (whenever possible) and then for most of the time during each of the first few days of the postpartum period, as many hospitals are now doing under the rooming-in plan. In the case of premature or ill infants many hospitals are finding it advisable to arrange for periodic visits to the nursery by the mother. Even providing for this limited handling and touching of the infant would seem to contribute to mother-child bonding. It would also allow staff members to observe the mother's behavior and provide support and guidance if she appears to be having problems in coping with a child whom she may perceive as "difficult."

Learning To Be a Parent

"The closest we ever got to preparing for parenthood was playing with dolls," said a thirty-one-year-old mother of an infant daughter quoted in a recent issue of *Parents'*. Her remark reflects the feelings of many new mothers and fathers who, despite extensive reading and excited anticipation, find themselves unprepared for the realities of parenting.

The job of becoming a parent, involves the acquisition of a host of new "how-to" skills. Many parents-to-be take advantage of infant-care classes offered through their hospital or at the homes of obstetric nurses or other certified practitioners. At weekly sessions, open to both the prospective mother and father, a wide range of less-than-esoteric topics are covered, including how to fit a diaper securely to prevent leakage; what end of the baby gets washed first, and at what point the baby can start eating solid foods. Aside from the valuable practical advice, new parents have found that the classes gave them the opportunity to share their concerns and anxieties about the newborn and about becoming parents. Upon leaving the hospital, parents can often avail themselves of excellent follow-up care, which may include counseling with their personal physician or psychiatrist. Even after the diaper stage a variety of facilities are available to assist people in the parenting process. These are provided by governmental social-service agencies, churches, and child-development centers.

In almost every locality mothers' groups and parent workshops have been formed, which meet at a local YMCA, church, or home of the group leader; babysitting is provided. On the agenda may be a discussion of mother-child separation problems, the emotional development of the toddler, or quick-relaxation techniques for recouping energy. Some groups are more structured and are led by a trained psychologist or experienced social worker. All are aimed at fostering mutual support through the discussion of child-rearing issues (Hoffman, 1978).

One innovative program is the Parent-Child Developmental Center in New Orleans, which offers comprehensive guidance to sixty to eighty low-income mothers and their children over a three-year period. Staffed by psychologists, social workers, and health-care professionals and paraprofessionals from the local community, the center's goal is to share the insights of the experts with the mothers. The mother and infant spend one morning discussing with the staff a particular area of development, such as nutrition and how it relates to self-feeding. On the other morning mothers learn about buying food and clothing, cooking, sewing, toy-making, and family health. The premise is that successful parenting will occur when the mothers have the support and skills the center offers. A follow-up study on the children whose mothers had completed the center's program showed that a year later their IQ scores were considerably higher than the control group. This indicates the carry-over effects of continued home stimulation (Gross & Gross, 1978).

Other research (Badger & Burns, 1980) indicates that parent training programs may also benefit the personal development of the parent. Teen-age mothers who frequently attended a twenty-week postnatal parent-education program were found to be better equipped to plan and limit the size of their family than were infrequent attenders. They also were better able to act on plans to complete school and find a job. In addition, they had more positive attitudes about the importance of a stimulating environment for their infants. These findings suggest that the problems usually associated with early parenthood may be reduced through intensive educative programs.

BEHAVIOR OF THE NEONATE

Babies set up communications with their parents right from the start. Parents with a sharp ear can tell their infant's demanding cries from its plaintive wailings, and learn that the demand means "I'm hungry," the plaint, "I'm hurting." Babies, in turn soon know whether their messages are getting across, and sense what their parents intend to do with them when they pick them up.

This communicative behavior has been reported by many parents, but is difficult to study scientifically. Much more open to objective study are the neonate's *reflexes*—its involuntary motor responses to specific stimuli. Normal, mature reflexes are now so readily recognized that testing them usually forms an important part of the physical examination given neonates. These tests aid in neurological evaluation and are valuable as a measure of prematurity.

A rather complex example is the startle reflex, or *Moro* reflex, described by Ernst Moro in 1918. If the baby's position is suddenly changed or support seems to fall away, it will grimace and sometimes cry; it will also extend its legs and arms and then bring its arms up in a motion like an embrace. Most babies seem to lose the Moro reflex in about three months (Kessen, Haith, & Salapatek, 1970). Another reflex, the *grasp* reflex, is elicited by touching the baby's palm; it takes hold of whatever has touched it. In the first weeks of life many babies can hold their own weight by the strength of their grasp.

Stroke the sole of the neonate's foot, and its toes will usually spread outward in what is called the *Babinski* reflex. Later in life normal reaction to this stimulus is just the opposite—the toes will curl downward. A number of reactions, however, appear to be precursors of later capabilities. For example, hold the neonate in an upright position so that the feet touch a solid surface, and it reacts with an automatic walking response, placing the foot down in a heel-toe sequence. This response is another reflex that is useful in determining prematurity; only the full-term neonate walks on the whole foot, whereas prematures walk on tiptoes.

Reflex: BABINSKI	*BABKIN*	*DOLL'S EYE*
Description Tickle the sole of the baby's foot, stroking from the heel toward the toes, and the big toe will lift up while the other toes spread out.	*Description* Press both of the baby's palms and its eyes will close, its mouth will open, and its head will turn to the side.	*Description* Turn the baby's head with your hand and its eyes will stay fixed instead of moving with the head.
Diagnostic use Absence of this reflex may indicate immaturity of the central nervous system, a lesion in the motor area of the brain, or defects of the spinal cord.	*Diagnostic use* If this reflex is absent at birth, or if it reappears after having vanished at the normal age of three to four months, the central nervous system may be malfunctioning.	*Diagnostic use* This reflex usually vanishes at about one month of age, when the baby achieves good visual fixation. If it reappears later, it may indicate damage to the central nervous system.

The *Babkin* reflex is a response that can be demonstrated by pressing the palms of both the baby's hands. The baby reacts by opening its mouth, turning the head from the side to straight forward, and occasionally by raising the head.

The two responses associated with feeding are perhaps the most important reflexes. The first of these is the *rooting* reflex, which is produced by stroking the baby's cheek, its chin, or the corner of its mouth. The baby responds by turning toward the side that was stroked and searching restlessly with its mouth as if it were looking for something to suck.

The *sucking* reflex itself, the newborn's response when its lips are touched, is by far its most interesting and complex activity. When a baby sucks, it is coordinating a number of activities with remarkable efficiency. It is using its cheeks to create suction and its tongue and palate to squeeze the nipple. It is at the same time synchronizing these two activities with swallowing, as well as with breathing through the nose. The extensive research devoted to this response is quite understandable. It has been used as an index of various perceptual reactions and studied for its own complexity in connection with the newborn's learning and adaptive capacity.

Reflex: PEREZ	PLANTAR GRASP	ROOTING
Description Stroke the baby's spine from tail toward head, applying some pressure, and it will cry out and its head will go up.	*Description* Press your thumbs against the balls of the baby's feet and the toes will flex.	*Description* Stroke the baby's cheek at the corner of its mouth and its head will turn toward your finger and its mouth will make sucking movements.
Diagnostic use This reflex should vanish in four to six months. If it does not, the baby's central nervous system may be severely depressed.	*Diagnostic use* Absence of this reflex may indicate damage to the spinal cord.	*Diagnostic use* If this reflex does not vanish in three to four months, the central nervous system may be malfunctioning.

Reflex: GALANT	MORO	PALMAR GRASP
Description Stroke the baby's back to one side of the spine and the trunk will arch toward that side.	*Description* Three kinds of stimulus elicit this reflex. Holding the baby horizontal, drop it a few inches in your hands. Or just let the head drop a few inches. Or make a sudden loud noise, for example by slamming the door. The baby's arms will fling out and then come together as its hands open and then clench.	*Description* Press *one* of the baby's palms (not both, as for the Babkin reflex) and its fingers will grasp the object.

Reflex: GALANT	*MORO*	*PALMAR GRASP*
Diagnostic use Absence of this reflex may indicate a spinal injury or depression of the central nervous system.	*Diagnostic use* If this reflex is weak or absent at birth, the central nervous system is severely disturbed. However, persistence of this reflex beyond the age of four to six months is abnormal.	*Diagnostic use* If this reflex is absent or weak at birth, the baby may have an injured spinal cord or a depressed central nervous system. However, persistence of this reflex beyond the age of four to six months is abnormal.

Sensory Capabilities

Neonates perceive the world through many senses. They react to pain, heat, and cold—and certainly to touch. They respond to change in balance. They seem to distinguish certain kinds of sounds, smells, and even tastes.

Much of what newborns perceive depends on what researchers call their "state": if they are asleep, the type of sleep; or if they are awake, the type of wakefulness and whether they are hungry or have just been fed. They will not perceive visible things if they are asleep, of course, but there are also states of wakefulness that seem to affect what they perceive or how they perceive it.

The reverse is also true: stimulation affects state. A sudden change of position, a startling sight or sound, make neonates more alert and active. Rocking, on the other hand, can stop their crying and lull them to sleep.

Reflex: STEPPING	*SUCKING*	*WITHDRAWAL*
Description "Walk" the baby, moving it forward, and it will make stepping movements.	*Description* Put your finger or nipple in the baby's mouth and it will suck rhythmically.	*Description* Prick the sole of the baby's foot with a pin and its knee and foot will flex.
Diagnostic use If this reflex reappears after having vanished at the normal age of 3–4 months, the baby may have an injury of the upper spinal cord.	*Diagnostic use* Depressed sucking may be due to medication given the mother in childbirth.	*Diagnostic use* Absence of this reflex may indicate a damaged sciatic nerve.

Researchers (Gordon & Foss, 1966) have speculated that rocking may have this effect because newborns require kinesthetic stimulation—the feeling of being in bodily motion—and further that this stimulation may help to regulate their internal temperature.

It has also been found (Pederson & Ter Vrugt, 1973) that the more vigorous rocking is, the more effective it is in controlling the infant's crying. Knowing this can make life easier for the parents; it may have implications for the social development of the infant as well. One psychologist (Ainsworth, 1971) has suggested that the security of the attachment between mother and infant may depend to some extent upon the mother's ability to control the infant's crying.

Experiments for visual reactions have established that babies are born with the pupillary reflex—their pupils widen in darkness and narrow in brightness. They also seem to have visual preferences. They like figures with strong contrasts and a certain degree of complexity. In experiments where newborns have been shown a simple triangle, they seemed to spend most of their time looking at one of the angles (Salapatek & Kessen, 1973). Because of the immaturity of the neuromusculature of the eye, however, newborns cannot accommodate their vision to various distances. Research indicates that in the first month of life, infants see best when objects are at a distance of seven to eight inches (Haynes, White, & Held, 1965).

Experiments on hearing indicate that newborns can discriminate between distinct sounds, and are capable of detecting the location of sound in the environment (Ling, 1972). The coordination of sensory systems during this early period of life, however, remains poorly developed. For example, McGurk, Turnura, & Creighton (1977) found that visual tracking of a moving object by newborns was unaided by the addition of sound to the moving object. The investigators concluded that there appears to be a "relative independence of auditory and visual perception during the neonatal period."

Other research has shown that newborns are capable of perceiving changes in smell and taste. They flinch, for example, from some sharp odors, such as ammonia or vinegar, but have no reaction at all to many odors that adults find repulsive.

Learning

Learning of the sort that we shall describe throughout the life span begins in infancy. For example, in one study the baby's palms were pressed to produce the Babkin response, and at the same time a buzzer was sounded. After this was done many times, the experimenters were able to produce the response with the sound alone (Kaye, 1965). In another experiment a tone was repeatedly followed by a puff of air that made the baby's eyes blink. Later, the tone alone was sufficient to produce the blink (Little, 1971).

More complex experiments have used a combination of stimulus and response accompanied both by a signal, such as a tone, and a reward for good response, such as a squirt of milk in the baby's mouth. The use of a reward has had especially interesting results in experiments devoted to the sucking capabilities of the newborn. In one series of studies, which tested each of the two components of sucking separately—suction and compression of the nipple—the results showed that newborns definitely react to feedback. They will adjust their sucking to obtain the most efficient flow of liquid, in a kind of adaptive learning (Sameroff, 1972).

It is generally felt that one of the best signs of learning in the neonate

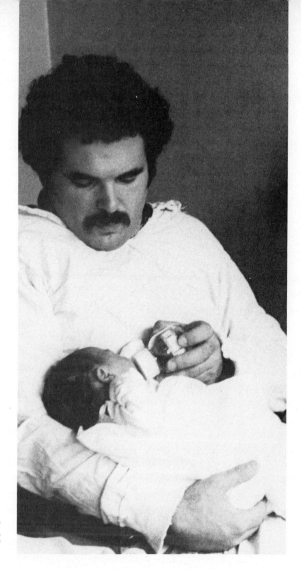

Father and newborn baby in the hospital. The policy of many hospitals is to allow the father to start giving care to his child practically from birth.

is the process called **habituation,** in which the baby seems to become familiar with a stimulus and has a decreasing reaction to it. Habituation can be demonstrated by a two-step testing procedure. In the first step a stimulus such as a checkerboard with four squares is presented several times, and the baby's response time is recorded. The second step consists of presenting a brand-new stimulus, such as a 144-square checkerboard. Infants seem to grow bored with the first stimulus and perk up for the second, suggesting that in the course of the repetitions they had made some record of the first stimulus.

Individual Differences

The experiments cited in this chapter have yielded many important generalizations about neonates. But it must not be forgotten that these generalizations describe only a normal range among the babies studied, not every baby.

Babies develop at their own individual rate. What is more, they are born with their own temperament, and they manifest this individuality almost immediately. Some babies are placid and easily contented; others are active and easily ruffled or distressed. They may, for example, show less tolerance for stomach distress and may cry more as a result. Very soon, however, each baby brings its individual temperament into interaction with the environment. Parents may accept their baby's nature and try to channel its restlessness or its placidity in a desirable direction; or they may show their frustration over such behavior. The quality of their interaction will be just as important as the kind of temperament the child starts out with.

A useful method of evaluating newborn behavior and assessing individual differences in behavior and temperament is known as the Brazelton Neonatal Behavioral Assessment Scale (Brazelton, 1973), which can be administered between the second day through six weeks after birth. As described by Sostek (1978) this scale has been very useful in showing the relationship between the newborn's earliest response patterns and later infant behavior, including interaction with the mother. The scale includes an assessment of the newborn's neuromotor functions and information-processing capacity as well as responses to stimuli, both animate and inanimate.

For many years psychologists interested in discovering how personality is formed concentrated most of their attention on the child's early environment. Then Thomas, Chess, and Birch (1968) identified certain characteristics of temperament that are apparent soon after birth: (1) motor activity, (2) regularity of such functions as eating and sleeping, (3) acceptance of something or someone new, (4) adaptability of behavior, (5) sensitivity to stimuli, (6) intensity of responses, (7) general cheerfulness and friendliness, (8) distractibility, and (9) attention span and persistence. They rated a number of babies as high, medium, or low in those nine characteristics and followed the children's development for more than ten years.

With many children these characteristics appeared in typical clusters. The three types of temperament formed by these clusters were called "easy," "difficult," and "slow to warm up." However, 35 percent of the children studied could not be classified in any of the three types.

In general these investigators concluded that any demand that conflicts strongly with a child's temperamental characteristics may put the child under severe stress. Thus, parents and teachers who understand the child's temperament, and know what it can and cannot do, may be in a position to avoid many problems in development and behavior.

Other long-term studies have found sociability to be a remarkably stable characteristic, especially in boys (Kagan & Moss, 1962; Schaeffer & Bayley, 1963). The infant's degree of activity, too, is a fairly constant characteristic (Halverson & Waldrop, 1976). Those who were the most active a month before their birth became the most active infants and developed certain motor skills relatively early. The individual's level of activity tended to remain relatively constant into adolescence (Kagan & Moss, 1962; Neilon, 1948) and into maturity (Tuddenham, 1959).

SUMMARY

▶ Natural or prepared childbirth is a program enabling prospective parents to prepare themselves for the experience of having a baby. They study and discuss the stages of childbirth with other parents and practice breathing routines and exercises.

▶ Labor progresses through three stages: dilation, expulsion, and placental. Although the length of labor varies considerably from woman to woman, the average labor lasts about fifteen hours from the first contraction to the birth of the baby.

▶ Complications are unusual, and a hospital is equipped to handle them. Though anesthesia administered during labor is known to cross the placenta, it is not known that these drugs cause any permanent damage to the neonate. Anoxia at birth may be caused either by ruptured blood vessels in the brain or delay before the baby begins breathing. When oxygen loss is acute, there is damage to brain cells.

▶ Although premature babies are not fully adapted to the world outside the uterus, early stimulation and special care can help them overcome this initial handicap.

▶ The neonate makes several physiological adjustments to become an independent organism. The respiratory center in the brain reacts to a chemical imbalance in the blood, and this triggers breathing. Circulation through the lungs increases, the umbilical cord is cut, and the heart gradually develops its mature form.

▶ Both the neonate and the mother may benefit from remaining in physical contact with one another following birth. Postpartum separation may affect the child's subsequent behavior and attachments and may impair the mother's ability to relate to her child.

▶ In evaluating the neonate's behavior scientists study the child's neuromotor functions, information-processing capabilities, and responses to various stimuli. The range of normal development is very wide, and individual differences in neonate behavior and temperament are to be expected.

FURTHER READINGS

Dick Read, Grantly. *Childbirth without fear: The original approach to natural childbirth* **(4th ed.). Wessel, H., and Ellis, H. F. (Eds.). New York: Harper & Row, 1972.**

The English obstetrician Dick Read wrote this book in 1944 and changed the course of obstetric history. He has proven from his own experience as a physician that childbirth is a natural physiological process not meant to be painful. The book contains a history and rationale of natural childbirth and an explicit step-by-step guide for expectant mothers that stresses a positive mental attitude toward the birth process.

Elkins, Valmai Howe. *The rights of pregnant parents.* **New York: Two Continents, 1977.**

Up-to-date advice on how couples can choose a supportive obstetrician, find helpful prenatal classes, and avoid difficulties in the hospital.

Guttmacher, Alan F. *Pregnancy, birth and family planning: A guide for expectant parents in the 1970s.* **New York: Viking, 1973.**

In plain, nontechnical language Dr. Guttmacher offers practical advice on every aspect of childbearing, from the emotional and physical changes that occur during pregnancy to such things as diet, rest, exercise, clothing, and sexual relations.

Lamaze, Fernand. *Painless childbirth: The Lamaze method.* **New York: Pocket Books, 1972.**

Unlike the Dick Read method, the Lamaze system of training for childbirth stresses physical as well as mental preparation, including special breathing and relaxation techniques to be used during labor. The Lamaze method is now used in most prepared-childbirth classes.

LeBoyer, Frederic. *Birth without violence.* **New York: Knopf, 1975.**

This book describes the controversial gentle-birth procedure advocated by LeBoyer. It includes interesting pictures of newborns.

Montagu, Ashley. *Life before birth.* **New York: New American Library, 1964.**

A famous anthropologist examines myths and facts about the influences during pregnancy that affect the unborn child. Montagu feels that the interval between conception and birth is far more important to subsequent growth and development than we have realized.

Nilsson, Lennart. *A child is born.* **New York: Delacorte Press, 1976.**

Beautiful photographs detail the developing life within the womb. The text for parents includes information on birth procedures.

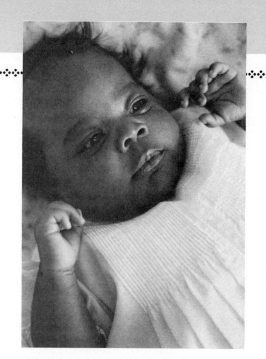

Chapter 3

❖❖❖❖❖❖❖

The Young Infant

At birth we have all our limbs, organs, and senses; we can breathe, cry, suck, and swallow; we even have a temperament. But we still have a long way to go before we will be able to hit a home run, write a term paper, or get a driver's license. No other animals—not even elephants or whales, who have plenty of growing to do—must go through such a long period of development before they are able to survive in the world without assistance from adults.

At times during this period our development seems to proceed at a rather leisurely pace, and at other times we grow astonishingly fast along every dimension. The fastest development takes place during infancy, the first year of life.

PHYSICAL GROWTH

Most people equate growth with an increase in height and weight. These are the most obvious signs, but there are also less apparent kinds of growth in the infant. Muscles increase not only in size but in the precision and control with which they can be used; as bones harden, the skeleton is transformed from a gelatinous mold into a sturdy frame; the brain cells grow and become specialized. These changes are subtle and sometimes related.

Weight and height gain are more obvious indicators of growth. On the average, an infant's birth weight doubles in the first five months and triples by the end of the first year, while his length increases 20 percent in the first three months and 50 percent in one year.

Parents tend to become concerned when their baby, especially if he is their first, appears to be too small, or is late in teething or walking. However, there are no hard and fast measures—only guidelines and overall patterns. Children at the same age develop at noticeably different rates, and even great differences are considered normal. The child's rate of growth is determined not only by his heredity, but also by a number of other factors, including what and how much he eats. As will be shown later in this chapter, poor nutrition in early childhood can have devastating and long-lasting—sometimes permanent—effects on all aspects of a child's development.

Development in Body Structures

As the body grows, new tissues and structures emerge, differentiate, and specialize in function. Of an individual's total weight at birth, roughly 20 percent is muscle, 15 percent internal organs, and 15 percent nervous system. In the adult these proportions are about 45 percent, 10 percent, and 3 percent, respectively. The proportion of water making up the body drops from about 75 percent at birth to about 60 percent at age twelve. The tissues lying under the skin, mostly fat, increase rapidly in thickness during the first nine months of life, then decrease until the child is about two and a half. Boys, as they grow, tend to have more muscle; girls, more fat.

At birth the skeleton is composed largely of cartilage and in an X ray looks somewhat like a puzzle whose pieces are on the verge of being locked into place. Most of the bones are still separated, and the relatively large spaces between them give the infant's joints flexibility. Infants' bones contain more water and proteinlike substances than do mature bones, and they have a lower mineral content. It may appear that the softness of a baby's skeleton is advantageous, allowing the body to bounce. But young bones, though they do not fracture as easily, are more liable to deformity than they are later in life, because they are less resistant to pressure and muscle pull. Because children's bones are so easily bent, it is vital that their diet (and that of the mother during pregnancy) be adequate. A deficiency of vitamin D, for instance, can produce the condition known as rickets, in which the strengthening of the bones is retarded. They bend permanently under the child's weight when it begins to walk, resulting in such deformities as swayback or bowlegs.

As for muscles, infants are probably born with all the muscle fibers they will ever have. Muscle growth results from increases in the length and thickness of these fibers. The structure, attachment, and nervous control of muscles also develop systematically. On the whole children's large muscles function better than their small, fine ones. Throughout the entire growing period children are more skillful in activities involving large movements than in those requiring precision.

Overlaying the muscles are two layers of tissue; the subcutaneous layer, which is chiefly fat, and the cutaneous tissues, which include skin, hair, and nails. A thick layer of fat pads the frames of many infants and small children and gives them their characteristic chubby look. The layer of fatty tissue thickens rapidly during the first nine months and then decreases. By the time the child is five it is normally only about half as thick as it was at nine months.

Teeth begin to form when the fetus reaches its sixth week. By birth all twenty baby teeth and a few permanent teeth are developing, although they will not usually begin to make their appearance until around the middle of the first year. During the prenatal period the crowns of the baby teeth (the parts that will show) form and calcify deep in the jaws. Most of the permanent teeth have begun to grow and calcify by the time an infant is six months old (Figure 3.1). This is still another of the many reasons why good nutrition is so important in the young child; a balanced diet, supplemented with additional vitamins and with fluoride, is essential to the development of sound teeth.

The baby teeth appear in a predictable sequence, but the age at which they erupt varies greatly. So does the amount of discomfort that accompanies teething. The first teeth usually erupt between four and twelve months of age, with the average at seven months. A small number of babies are actually born with one or two teeth, while a few children do not get their first tooth until sixteen months. Neither extreme is cause for concern.

Differential Maturation

Rapidly as the body grows in infancy, it develops according to orderly and predictable patterns (Figure 3.2). One pattern is its tendency to develop first at the head and then in the rest of the body, moving downward in what is called a *cephalocaudal* ("head-to-tail") sequence. Even in the fetus the head forms first. The arm buds form before the leg buds, the nervous system grows from the brain downward, and the facial muscles develop before other muscles. Accordingly, babies have a well-developed sucking reflex before they can do much of anything else. They gradually gain control of head, neck, and trunk muscles, in that order. They learn to use their arms before they can control their legs. The cephalocaudal growth pattern helps explain why children sit before they can stand and crawl before they can walk.

In a second sequential pattern development occurs first at the center of the body and later at the extremities, or in a *proximodistal* ("near-to-far") direction. First the baby can control its trunk and then its arms, hands, and

Figure 3.1 Development of the teeth. Twenty baby teeth appear in five stages, shown here from left to right, usually starting at about six months of age. The infant's jaw contains the buds of some permanent teeth even before the first baby teeth break through the gums.

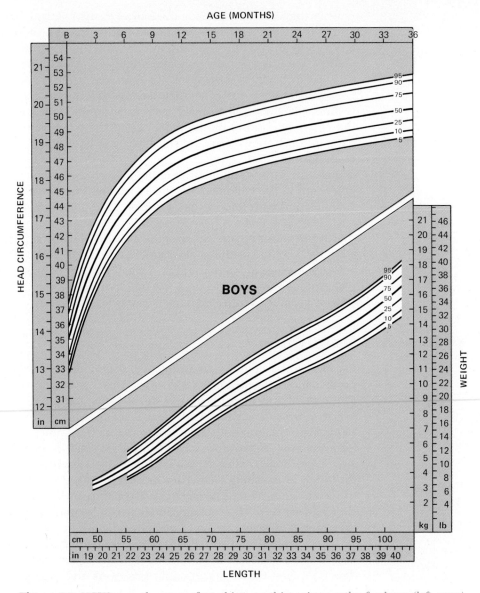

Figure 3.2 NCHS growth curves from birth to thirty-six months for boys (left page) and girls (right page) (in percentages).

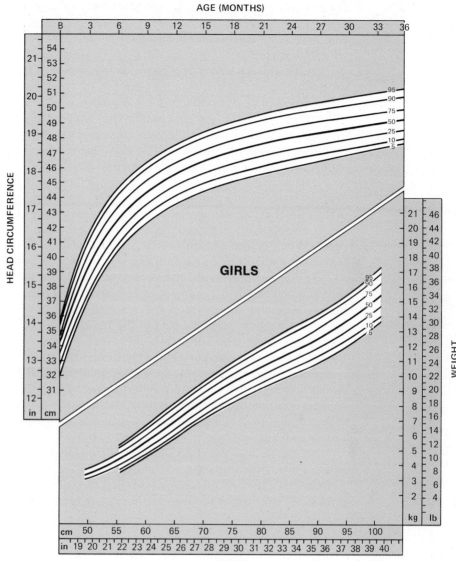

AGE (MONTHS)

HEAD CIRCUMFERENCE

GIRLS

WEIGHT

LENGTH

fingers; first its hips and then its legs, feet, and toes. Proximodistal growth explains, for instance, why babies are able to reach out in a somewhat random way for a large object long before they are able to pick up something small with their fingers.

Still a third pattern of general development is that a baby's physical responses move from a general reaction to a controlled, specific one—a process known as *differentiation.* For example, when young babies see something they want (a toy, say, or a bottle), they express their pleasure and desire by widening their eyes, panting with excitement, wiggling all over, and waving their arms madly at the object. The older baby, who is no less pleased and excited, simply smiles and reaches for the object.

The nervous system illustrates some of these patterns. The brain is the primary organ of the central nervous system. Infants possess most, if not all, of the cells that will ever compose the brain, though the cells will later become larger and more specialized. At the age of one year the brain has already reached 60 percent of adult weight, and the brain of a five-year-old is 90 percent the weight of an adult brain.

In the newborn child the best-developed parts of the brain are those that function chiefly to control such essential reflex behavior as sucking, swallowing, emptying the bladder, and coughing. These reflexes come from the midbrain (a rather primitive part of the brain) and the spinal cord, whereas voluntary control arises in high brain centers. These higher centers are also the seat of sense perceptions and intelligence. Gradually, as these higher centers assume some of the functions formerly controlled by the midbrain and spinal cord, many of the baby's reflexes start to disappear. For example, the walking reflex of the newborn, described in Chapter 2, originates in an entirely different area of the central nervous system from the part that controls voluntary walking.

By six months the child has gained considerable control over voluntary movements. Different parts of the brain develop in accordance with these movements. First are the cells controlling the upper trunk, neck, and upper arm; those controlling the legs and head follow.

DAILY ROUTINES

Before birth a child's needs are taken care of more or less automatically. Nourishment is constantly supplied through the umbilical cord. The fetus rests or is active as its own body requires, without much direct reference to what is going on outside. After birth, though, some thought has to be taken of these matters. Someone has to provide food at suitable times and in suitable forms and quantities. Similarly, someone must make sure that outside conditions do not keep the child from getting a proper balance of rest and activity. From instinct through folk wisdom to scientific studies a good deal of thought has gone into this matter of a baby's daily routines.

Eating

In our culture an infant is either breast- or bottle-fed, depending in most cases on the mother's preference. Either way the mother (or other caregiver) establishes a degree of physical contact with the infant. She also evokes a certain amount of cooperation, which is essential. Stressful or abrupt feeding may disrupt the relationship, leading the infant to associate feelings of discomfort with the mother and with the satisfaction of physical needs.

It has long been recognized that breast- and bottle-feeding do not have exactly the same effects. The baby's sucking technique, the speed of milk intake, and even the composition and taste of the milk differ. Moreover, the mother's physical state is greatly affected by nursing (Newton, 1972).

In women who breast-feed their newborn infants the uterus returns more quickly to normal size after delivery than in mothers who do not breast-feed. It has been found, too, that women who breast-feed generally have an easier time losing the extra weight gained during pregnancy. Nursing also inhibits the menstrual cycle. Thus it serves as a kind of natural birth-control device, allowing the mother to postpone the physical stress of a new pregnancy until her body is more ready for it. (It is *not*, however, an absolutely certain means of birth control. Breast-feeding mothers can become pregnant, and occasionally do.)

For the infant breast-feeding has certain physical advantages. Breast-fed babies seem to develop fewer food allergies than their bottle-fed peers. Also, they benefit from receiving a natural "formula" that is specifically designed for the needs of human infants, not calves or goats. The child derives certain antibodies from the milk. In addition, the milk is more easily absorbed, which is especially beneficial for preterm babies whose intestines are more sensitive and may not be ready for formula.

The psychological results of breast- and bottle-feeding are more difficult to specify, because so many hard-to-control variables enter into the picture. For one thing there are fashions in feeding; approved techniques vary from time to time and from one socioeconomic group to another. Not so many years ago a really modern-minded woman would not have dreamed of breast-feeding her baby; a few years later it had become the popular thing to do. Thus many women may choose a method of feeding not because it is what they really want, but in obedience to social pressure.

Also, breast- and bottle-feeders, as groups, may differ in other ways. One study, for example, found that expectant mothers who planned to breast-feed their children differed significantly on certain psychological tests from those who planned to bottle-feed. The researchers interpreted the test results as suggesting that the would-be breast-feeders placed more importance on the exchange of affection with other people (Brown et al., 1961). Obviously, such an attitude would influence other aspects of a mother's relationship with her baby. And, indeed, other research suggests a greater pleasure among breast-feeding mothers in the "physicalness" of human relationships. More breast-feeding than bottle-feeding mothers, for instance, reported that they occa-

Crib Death

The baby seemed to be perfectly well—except for a little head cold perhaps. He had his bath and his supper, spent a few minutes quietly playing with his parents, and was finally put to bed in his own room with the lights out. At their own bedtime, the parents looked in on him and saw that he was quietly sleeping, very much as usual. So they went to bed themselves. The next morning, wondering why he had not awakened them with his usual cries for attention and breakfast, they found their baby dead in his crib.

Every year 7,000 to 10,000 babies die of Sudden Infant Death Syndrome (SIDS), popularly known as Crib Death. Until very recently the nature of this disease—if one can call it a disease—has been so shrouded in mystery that a good deal of misinformation had accumulated about it. The typical case may have any or all of a wide variety of features. Most of the victims are boys between one and six months old. Many of them had been born prematurely and had experienced respiratory problems. In one study of the offspring of 4,000 pregnancies fifteen infants succumbed to SIDS. The three reliable variables that emerged from comparison of the SIDS cases with two control groups all seemed related to poor oxygenation of the fetus. In addition the SIDS infants had lower Apgar scores than the control groups and, in general, were under hospital care for a longer period of time (Lipsitt, Sturner, & Burke, 1979).

These then are some of the characteristics of babies who die of SIDS. But many SIDS babies have *none* of these characteristics, and many babies with *all* of these characteristics never suffer anything remotely like SIDS. What can be the cause of these mysterious deaths?

At postmortem examination, the bodies of SIDS babies reveal few clues to the cause of their deaths. It is clear that they have not been strangled or smothered by their bedclothes. They have not choked or drowned as a result of mismanaging a propped bottle or vomiting. They have not been poisoned by chemicals in the water supply or medications their mothers took during pregnancy. They have no internal abnormalities such as enlarged thymus glands or bleeding tumors. And still they die, without a struggle, without an outcry, without warning. Why?

One possible cause of crib death is spasm of the vocal cords. If a baby's larynx went into spasm long enough to cut off his oxygen supply for a critical amount of time, the baby would die. But there is little evidence to support this as the major cause of crib death.

Recent studies are beginning to suggest other causes. Many of the babies, for example, had abnormalities of the central nervous system, defects which had caused the infants difficulty even in their first five days of life. In some cases, body temperatures were not properly regulated at first; in others, there were a variety of abnormalities, all transitory and attributable to seemingly minor disorders of the nervous system.

Recent investigations also indicate that some SIDS babies have lesions of the respiratory center in the brain stem. These lesions may cause disorders of breathing, especially during sleep. Although many normal babies have episodes of apnea (cessation of breathing) during normal sleep, the SIDS baby seems to be more likely to have profound and prolonged difficulty (Steinschneider, 1975). In the presence of such a disorder even a mild respiratory illness might trigger an episode of apnea that if sufficiently prolonged, could lead to anoxia, cardiac arrest, and death.

Finally, there appears to be a definite association between smoking during pregnancy and the occurrence of SIDS. In fact, a review of various studies on this subject states: "It is now . . . clear that maternal cigarette smoking contributes to an infant's risk of dying from SIDS (Rhead, 1977). Even "passive smoking" (exposure to cigarette smoke) seems to contribute to the risk of SIDS, though the reasons are not yet clear nor has it been determined whether prenatal exposure is more important than postnatal exposure.

Though the solution to crib death appears to be complicated by multiple (potentially) causative factors, recently a system has been developed that may prevent the deaths of babies considered to be at risk. The system involves the use of a monitor that measures the rate of breathing and heartbeat. Through blinking lights and beeper sounds the monitor "warns" that an episode of apnea is occurring. Parents then have seconds to revive the baby, in some cases by administering cardiopulmonary resuscitation. Monitor systems are now being used in many hospitals in the United States and can be obtained for private use.

---

sionally or frequently rested or slept in bed with their babies (Newton et al., 1968), and Masters and Johnson (1970) found that breast-feeding mothers were generally eager to get back to active sexual life with their husbands as soon as possible after delivery.

Yet whether infants are breast-fed or bottle-fed seems to have little impact on their later emotional development. Research examining the long-term influence of feeding mode has found no differences between these two groups of children (Schmitt, 1970). It is the quality of the mother-infant relationship, and not the mode of feeding, that determines future adjustment.

Experts agree that breast-feeding is not the best choice for all mothers and infants. Some mothers are unable to nurse; others find it physically painful (for instance, it may make their nipples sore), socially embarrassing, or impossible because of a career commitment. While some mothers feel guilty about choosing the bottle, most are quickly reassured when they see that the baby does well on formula. For those infants who would probably do better on breast milk (preterm babies, for example) but whose mothers may be unwilling or unable to breast-feed, some hospitals have established breast milk banks where donor milk is stored.

Weaning

In our culture weaning—the end of breast- or bottle-feeding—is usually begun by the last quarter of the child's first year, though nowadays some parents start cup feeding much earlier.

Children differ in their readiness to be weaned. Children's natural curiosity about new food tastes, textures, and smells prepares them for weaning. When babies show signs of beginning to be bored with the bottle or breast—

Through feeding, the infant establishes a degree of physical contact and cooperation with the mother.

when, for instance, they regularly chew on the nipple, play with their hands, or flirt with the person who is feeding them—it is a pretty good clue that they will find drinking from a cup an exciting new experience. Also, nursing requires that an infant remain still and in a horizontal position. This may no longer be "acceptable" to the infant who is beginning to crawl or walk. In effect, such infants wean themselves.

The sucking instinct of some babies, however, is not quite satisfied in infancy, and they become attached more fervently than ever to the bottle or breast as they get older. Some bottle-fed babies also develop a passionate attachment to the bottle when it has been used as either a pacifier or a parent substitute. When babies are put to bed with a propped bottle instead of being fed in an adult's arms until they become sleepy, the bottle gets all the credit for their feeling of well-being and therefore takes on undue importance. (It should also be noted that a young baby might choke if left alone with a bottle.)

The process of weaning should be gradual. A baby who is weaned too abruptly may balk completely. The usual procedure is to start by feeding a small amount of milk from a cup at each meal. The amount is slowly increased, until the cup can be offered exclusively.

Sometimes it is the mother who postpones weaning. She may be reluctant to end this emotional tie with her child, or may fear that the child will not get enough milk from the cup. Or she may just be afraid that the process will upset the child. These last two fears are almost always unfounded. By the time they are ready to be weaned, most babies can do with considerably less milk than they are used to taking from the bottle or breast, and if children are weaned when they themselves indicate signs of readiness, they seldom become very upset.

Diet

Nutrition may well be the most important factor in an infant's environment, affecting as it does growth, functioning, and resistance to disease. Poor nutrition results in stunted growth. Even when an initially poor diet is improved in later childhood, the losses in growth potential are never fully made up.

Malnutrition occurs in infancy when substances vital to the growth and maintenance of the body are missing from a baby's diet or are present in insufficient quantity. Not only is malnutrition responsible for generally poor health, increased susceptibility to disease, stunted growth, and deformities of the body, but it can also impair mental development. Outright deficiency diseases, such as rickets (caused by an insufficient amount of vitamin D in the diet), scurvy (due to a lack of vitamin C), and beri-beri (from too little vitamin B_1), are less common in Western societies today than formerly. But a more insidious form of malnutrition, protein deficiency, is nearly as common as ever.

Proteins form part of almost all animal cells. They provide building materials for the formation of tissues during growth. They also play an important role in building up immunities to disease. An insufficient amount of protein in a child's diet causes underweight and less-than-normal growth of the skeleton and nervous system. Subnormal growth of the brain interferes with intellectual capacity and ability to adapt to environmental conditions. Once the damage has been done, it can never be completely overcome. Because high-protein foods tend to be among the most expensive, protein deficiency is most common among the children of poor families. It generally develops only after weaning, since an infant who is getting enough milk to satisfy its hunger is automatically getting enough protein.

Because diet is so important, the subject of what and how much to feed a child has been given a great deal of attention. In a classic experiment (Davis, 1935) infants and toddlers were allowed, for a year or more, to select their own diet from a variety of wholesome, natural, and unrefined foods. The children ate eagerly and consumed astonishingly large quantities at meals, then stopped with an air of finality. At the conclusion of the experiment their appetites, digestion, and overall physical condition were well above average. Some of the implications of this study are still quite controversial. Still, it does seem clear that if parents offer a child a diet of overall high nutritional value,

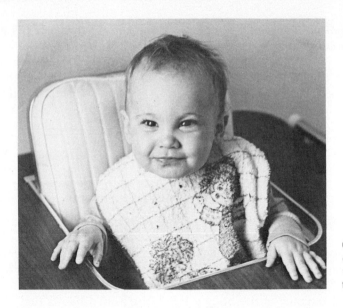

Given a good selection of foods, infants will usually get the nutrients they need.

they need not be worried about getting the child to eat precisely measured, carefully selected portions of food.

The chief element in the diet of the very young child is, of course, milk (or some high-protein substitute, such as soybean emulsion). In feeding a baby both rate of weight gain and signs of hunger should be considered. Overfeeding, which has a harmful effect on health and eating habits, should be discouraged almost as much as underfeeding. Appetite varies with each child and from day to day for any one child. A baby's appetite, weight gain, the interval it is willing to wait before feedings, and its response to new foods are all important in determining when so-called solid foods (that is, food other than milk or formula) should be introduced into the diet, and when portions should be increased.

The infant's diet may also be related to one of the most serious nutritional problems confronting Americans today—obesity. The reasons for becoming overweight are varied. Some people seem to inherit the tendency to be fat. Others suffer from hormonal imbalances that lead to uncontrolled weight gain; still others have developed poor eating habits. One interesting theory suggests that obesity in later life is directly linked to being overfed in infancy. Presumably, overfeeding the infant increases both the number and the size of fat cells in the body, thereby increasing the chances of obesity in later childhood and adulthood. Although this theory has gained considerable attention among researchers and pediatricians, some doubt has been cast upon its validity. Recently, two groups of researchers (Dine et al., 1979; Roche, 1981) failed to find any relationship between infant fatness and later obesity. But even if fat babies do not necessarily grow up to be fat children and/or fat adults, regulating what the infant eats is still a good idea. Medical research suggests that diseases such as diabetes, hypertension, and heart disease may be prevented, or at least minimized, by limiting the amount of sugar and salt taken into the body from the very beginning of life.

Digestive Disorders

Practically all young babies do some "spitting up" during or after feedings. The muscle valve at the upper end of the stomach may not be well enough developed to hold down all the contents when a full baby is picked up or jostled. If the baby has swallowed air while nursing, some milk may lie on top of the air bubble; when the baby is burped, therefore, it will bring up not only the bubble but also a little milk. Infants also have occasional spells of mild indigestion or gas. None of these conditions are anything to worry about.

More alarming are the symptoms of colic. As it is usually used, "colic" is a catchall word that describes the symptoms of infants who have regular or prolonged bouts of crying, with apparent intestinal discomfort, during their first few months of life. More precisely, however, colic is a condition in which the abdomen becomes distended with gas, apparently resulting in severe pain. It tends to begin when the infant is only a few weeks old and is usually over or definitely on the wane by the time the child is three months old. The baby's distress—and the parent's concern—often seem to be relieved by feeding; hence, colicky babies tend to gain weight somewhat more rapidly than others.

No one really knows what causes colic. X rays of colicky babies do not show any structural irregularities of the digestive tract. One investigation (Ferreira, 1960) seemed to show that babies whose mothers were under greater than average emotional stress during pregnancy were more likely to be colicky.

Unfortunately, there are no reliably effective remedies. Pediatricians occasionally prescribe a tranquilizer for a severely colicky baby (and sometimes for the nerve-racked parents as well), but generally babies simply outgrow the problem without medical treatment.

A surprisingly large number of babies are allergic to one or more foodstuffs, some of the most common of which are eggs (especially the whites), citrus fruits, and, not least of all, cow's milk. The allergy usually reveals itself by digestive upsets, such as vomiting or diarrhea, or by a skin rash of some kind, frequently eczema or hives. When the allergic substance has been identified (often through some cooperative detective work by doctor and parents), it is removed from the diet. If it is an essential nutrient, some other foodstuff that the child can tolerate is substituted for it. Even a milk allergy creates no real problem nowadays, since formulas made with soy protein are readily available. Many pediatricians now recommend that eggs and citrus fruits not be introduced into the infant's diet before the end of the first year.

Although some people remain allergic to certain foods all their lives, others outgrow some or all of their infant allergies, often in a remarkably short time.

Sleeping

Just as activity is necessary to the child, so is rest. Rest conserves the energy that is required for the growth and maintenance of the body. It may take the form of quiet play, relaxation, or sleep. A child who gets too little rest may

Very young infants usually sleep most of the time between feedings. Gradually they increase their waking time during the daylight hours.

become overactive and may show signs of emotional instability, such as excessive fussiness, overreaction to stress situations, and loss of acquired skills. Fatigue also increases a child's susceptibility to illness and accidents.

During the first few weeks of life the average number of hours spent sleeping is between sixteen and seventeen, and neither sleeping nor waking periods are long (Parmelee, Schultz, & Disbrow, 1961). Occasionally a newborn baby sleeps as long as eight hours at one time, but the average time, day or night, is four or five hours. The longest wakeful period seldom exceeds two hours. From the end of the first month to about three months the average total sleeping time in a twenty-four-hour period shortens to fifteen hours. Most babies also start to consolidate their sleep periods and to straighten out their daytime and nighttime hours. Before long they begin to sleep through the night, skipping the nighttime feeding. By the time they are one most of the required sleep is obtained at night, but one or more daytime naps of from one to three hours are still necessary.

In the early months of life the child's sleep is relatively shallow and easily broken. The young baby wakes because of internal proddings, especially of hunger; often this awakening is abrupt and accompanied by a sharp cry.

An older baby's sleep is more like an adult's, characterized by heavy and light periods. During the heavy periods the baby is almost motionless, its breathing is quite regular, and it makes very little sound. During the lighter sleeping periods it moves more, its respiration is much less regular, and it

Sleep, Over the Life Span

The amount and quality of sleep vary with age. A young baby needs more rest and shorter intervals between rest than a toddler. As a child's abilities increase and his experience widens, he tends to resist naps and bedtimes; slowing down simply becomes more difficult.

Between the ages of five and ten, total sleep time changes relatively little. At adolescence, it declines steeply. During adulthood, that is, between ages twenty and sixty, the amount of sleep changes little (Timiras, 1972). The average duration of sleep is about seven and a half hours a night (Bromley, 1974).

The quality of sleep, however, does change quite dramatically over the life span. During the early months of life sleep is relatively shallow. The infant awakens because of internal proddings, especially hunger and wetness. Often his wakening is abrupt and accompanied by sharp cries. An older baby sleeps more peacefully, and during childhood and adolescence a person does not awaken spontaneously: his sleep is relatively uninterrupted.

In young adulthood, interruptions become more frequent; moreover, they tend to become both more frequent and longer as the person ages. People in their forties spend considerable time awake in bed. And many of the elderly suffer from insomnia or constant awakenings. They tend to wake earlier than young adults, and to have experienced less satisfying sleep (Bromley, 1974).

The characteristic activity patterns of the brain during sleep patterns (which indicate the stage of depth of sleep achieved) also vary with age. Among the sleep stages identified by the electroencephalograph (EEG) are the lightest stage, Stage 1 sleep, which is characterized by Rapid Eye Movement (REM) and dreaming, and deep Stage 4 sleep, which is characterized by slow wave activity. The proportion of time spent in Stage 4 sleep is greatest at four to five years of age. It declines in later childhood and again at adolescence. And it continues to decline over the life span, until, at age fifty or so, the person spends only half the amount of time in Stage 4 as he did at age twenty (Timiras, 1972). In the middle adult years more time is spent in the intermediate stages, Stages 2 and 3.

In the older person, the deep Stage 4 sleep is virtually absent and the proportion of Stage 1 (REM) sleep has also declined. The latter decline seems to be correlated with decline in intellectual functions. The greater the amount of time the older person spends in REM sleep, the better he tends to perform on tests measuring intellectual and other psychological variables (Timiras, 1972). Some researchers have suggested that total sleep time, too, may offer an indication of the older person's functioning. Whereas "senile" elderly patients slept about 20 percent less than healthy young adults, bright and active older people slept about the same amount as young adults (Luce & Segal, 1966).

Some theorists have suggested that during sleep the brain carries out processes necessary for cognitive advances during the day. If this is so, the high levels of sleep in childhood may occur because this is the time during which the greatest acquisition of concepts and information takes place. The falling off of sleep during adulthood may similarly reflect reduced abilities, or at least reduced growth, in problem-solving and creative abilities.

makes faces and noises. Older babies wake more smoothly and fall asleep more easily than young infants. By about sixteen weeks the wakening mechanism is usually functioning so well that crying upon awakening is uncommon.

PERCEPTION AND LEARNING

How do we know what infants realize and perceive? Science has no window on their mental processes, but ingenious experiments have been devised to find out what they do and do not respond to. The response measured may be a smile or an eye movement, or it may be a change in heartbeat or breathing. In one study of visual perception (Ahrens, 1954), for example, two-month-old infants were presented with different arrangements of dots, angles, and bars drawn on cardboards. The dots evoked the most smiles, which suggests that infants build their perceptions of facial features beginning with the eyes.

In a somewhat more sophisticated experiment (Fantz, 1961) two- to four-month-old infants were shown three black-and-white patterns (a face, a piece of newspaper, and a bullseye) and three colored circles without patterns. The face pattern proved to hold their attention for the longest period.

Sight

Much more is known about the sight of infants than about their other senses. There are several different processes necessary to vision. They do not all work well at birth, but they soon improve. The **pupillary reflex** (Figure 3.3) consists of an automatic narrowing of the pupil of the eye in bright light and a widening in dim light. Babies exhibit the pupillary reflex almost immediately after birth, even if they are premature. Therefore, we know that the newborn baby can distinguish between light and dark. However, during the first two days only gross changes, from very bright light to totally dark and back again, activate the reflex. It takes a few weeks to respond to subtler changes.

Visual coordination (Figure 3.4) is the ability of the eye muscles to turn

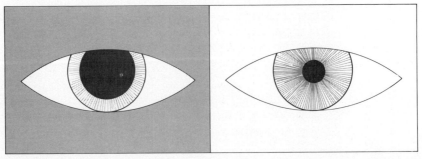

Figure 3.3 Pupillary reflex. The pupils of the newborn automatically contract in bright light and dilate in dim light.

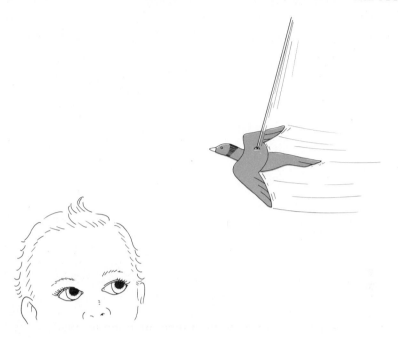

Figure 3.4 Visual coordination. An infant soon learns to follow a moving object with his eyes.

the eyes in the direction of an object. It is achieved when babies can follow a moving object with their eyes, which most of them do a few weeks after birth.

The infant's next step in refining visual perception is **convergence**—focusing both eyes to produce a single image. Babies start making rough attempts at convergence in their first hours of life but do not perfect it until the end of the second month.

During the first three months vision is blurry because the muscles cannot yet adjust the lens curvature to focus the light rays (reflected by objects) sharply on the retinas. This adjustment is called **accommodation of the lens** (Figure 3.5). It begins in the second month and is fully developed by the third or fourth month (Haynes, White, & Held, 1965).

Even then, however, the baby's visual perception can hardly be called equivalent to the adult's. The neural pathways and visual receptor mechanisms are not yet fully developed. Around the age of eight weeks babies may smile in apparent recognition at their mother or father bending over them, but experiments indicate that such recognition is partial at best. Their eyes cannot yet absorb the complete face before them, only the forehead and eyes. The clear recognition of something familiar is still some weeks away.

But long before they can recognize faces, and even before the physical processes of vision are fully developed, babies seem predisposed to look around and examine the world. In a recent study (Mendelson & Haith, 1976) newborn infants were tested for visual scanning activity. Even in darkness,

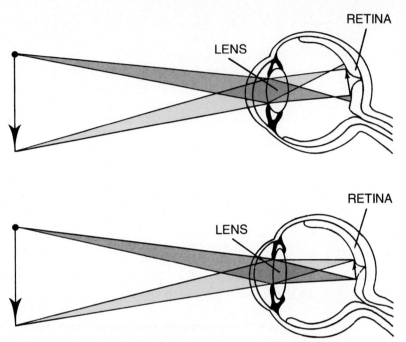

Figure 3.5 Accommodation of the lens. The images of an object will not be focused sharply on the retina unless the lens is flattened or allowed to return to its more globular shape, depending on the distance of the object from the eye. Some cameras can also be adjusted for distance, and for the same purpose: to produce a sharp image on the film. But camera lenses are not flexible, and so the adjustment must be made by moving the lens closer to or farther from the film.

when there was nothing to be seen, they scanned quite actively, which suggests that humans are born with some built-in procedures for learning about their world. In light the infants tended to scan areas that contained many contours—lines, edges of shapes, and so on. These areas would, of course, be more likely to offer useful information than would blank, undifferentiated areas such as a bare wall. Even though newborn infants certainly do not form any clear concept or memory of what they "see" by this early scanning, they are already building up a fund of experience that will help them later.

Objects of Attention

Indications are that while the baby is very young, its perceptions are organized along very different lines from the adult's. An infant's perceptive frame of reference changes, however, almost from month to month. During the first three months an object must have relatively well-defined characteristics to attract the baby's attention—such characteristics as movement, sound, sharp color contrast, or distinctive contours and patterns. The youngest babies seem interested in very simple patterns, older ones in more complex designs. However, there must not be too much novelty. Apparently babies must be able to perceive the new object as in some way "like" things they have seen before. If it is totally new and different, they cannot fit it into any frame of reference and soon seem to lose interest.

One well-known experiment illustrates this dual attractiveness of moderate familiarity and moderate novelty (Haaf & Bell, 1967). Four drawings were shown to a group of four-month-old boys. The first drawing resembled a human face; the second was the outline of a face with an eye missing, an extra mouth in the forehead, and lines and squiggles filling the outline at random. The third drawing was a face outline that was blank except for a nose; and the fourth had no facial features at all, only the outline filled with the same squiggles as the second drawing. The babies paid more attention to the first drawing, the most recognizable face, and almost as much attention to the second drawing. The experimenters concluded that what interested the babies most was neither complexity nor amount of detail, but "faceness."

Novelty is a particularly effective attention-getter for infants when it is combined with movement. This may account in part for the fascination that television has for some babies. They also seem to appreciate the sound that fittingly accompanies the visual images, as we can see from an ingenious experiment with babies of four months (Spelke, 1978). Two films were shown simultaneously to these infants: they could watch either a toy kangaroo or a toy donkey who bounced around at different speeds while a central speaker played one of their sound tracks. There was significantly more watching of whichever film was played with its own sound track.

Depth Perception

The ability of a baby to perceive depth during the first year has been established by a famous experiment using a "visual cliff" (Gibson & Walk, 1960; Walk, 1966). A sheet of heavy plate glass was laid over a surface with a checkerboard pattern. On one side the checkerboard pattern was directly under the glass; on the other side it was several feet below, giving the impression of a cliff. Just along the brink of the "cliff" a wide plank was laid over the glass.

Six-month-old babies were placed on the plank and coaxed by their mothers from the far side of the deep area. They could have crossed it in perfect safety, for the glass was strong and securely anchored. The question was, would they see the depth and be afraid to cross it, or would they be reassured by the feel of the glass under their hands and knees and take no notice of the depth? As it turned out, the visual impression was stronger. Most of the babies could not be tempted into venturing off the plank on the "cliff" side. They had no hesitation about crossing on the other side, where there was no visible drop. And when the checkerboard pattern on the deep side was raised to within a few inches of the glass—making the "cliff" look much less dangerous—some babies were willing to risk the crossing. Evidently, then, infants do have a definite awareness of depth.

How much judgment is acquired is not clear. Some authorities maintain that babies have built-in depth perception at birth; others believe they are taught by the experience of seeing objects at various levels and distances.

The Nonvisual Senses

To some extent the nonvisual senses—hearing, touch, taste, and smell—seem to develop without practice. A crying baby, for example, will probably quiet down the first time it is picked up and rocked. Of course, it was rocked a great deal before it was born, and there is no reason to doubt that it felt that. Its mother's heartbeat was also familiar before birth and apparently continues to soothe the baby during infancy.

Babies can hear the difference between high-pitched and low-pitched sounds; they even seem to sense the direction from which a sound is coming (Leventhal & Lipsitt, 1964). Babies also begin early to listen to people's voices, and they seem "programmed" to respond to human language, but the way babies react to sounds depends on the conditions in which they hear them. They may be startled and frightened by a loud noise when they are alone in the crib but remain quite undisturbed by a similar noise when safe in an adult's arms. This sense of security is transmitted from parent to child long before the child has any notion of the concept "mother" or recognizes mother and father as specific, unique persons.

Taste is relatively undifferentiated at birth but develops rapidly in the first two weeks. The first tastes babies learn to tell apart are sweet and bitter—

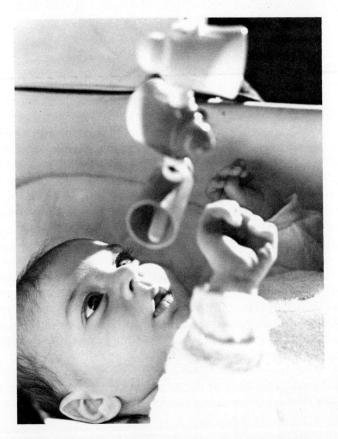

Brightly colored plastic toys over the crib help the baby to distinguish shapes and, eventually, colors.

and they greatly prefer sweet. Salty tastes seem to be halfway along the desirability scale; babies will accept them when they are hungry but reject them in favor of milk or glucose when these are offered. Well-fed babies learn to discriminate more carefully among foods than do babies who are not so well fed, and the substitution of water for milk may elicit a surprised lift of the eyebrows by the ripe age of ten days.

The sense of smell is present in primitive form at birth. Newborn infants seem to be insensitive to faint odors but show a distinct aversion to sharp, unpleasant smells such as ammonia.

Tactile perception (touch) is a delight to the baby from the moment it first stuffs its fist into its mouth or grasps its feet with its hands. A little later the realization that these are its own fingers and toes lends further zest to these explorations. Soon the method of investigation by touch and taste is firmly established. Gripping and handling objects is necessary to the motor development of infants, and handle them they do, especially when they are able to get around on their own.

One aspect of tactile perception, the infant's sensitivity to pain, increases rapidly right after birth. Throughout infancy the head is more sensitive to pain than the arms and legs, and girls are more sensitive than boys. Sensitivity to heat and cold varies greatly among individual babies, but all of them show some response.

Moving and Manipulating

The control a child achieves over its body depends on the structural readiness of that body and the functional readiness of the brain. Even during the prenatal period the muscles involved in grasping, sitting, and walking are exercised, but these motions cannot become voluntary until there is sufficient maturation of the nerves and muscles. Most of the child's basic physical accomplishments are achieved, on the average, during the first year and a half of life. Infants will use their arms and hands to reach for whatever attracts their attention; they will sit up to survey their surroundings; they will creep from one place to another to explore a larger world; they will stand up to survey new vistas; and ultimately they will demonstrate their growing independence by taking a few steps all by themselves.

In this progressive mastery of motor skills two patterns can be seen. The first is the baby's will to gain greater mobility, to get around. The second is the need, which is more inborn than imitative, to stand upright. The famous physician Benjamin Spock (1976) aptly describes this second drive as a celebration of "that period millions of years ago when man's ancestors got up off all fours." At the same time that children learn to balance on their feet they are also learning to manipulate things skillfully with their hands.

Grasping

As we saw in Chapter 2, the grasping reflex is present at birth. About one month after birth the grasping reflex starts to become distinctly weaker, and by four months it is gone. At about the time it disappears, the child begins to reach out for things, and some time after the middle of the first year it can voluntarily grasp, transfer, and manipulate objects. Characteristically, the palm and side of the hand are used more than the fingers to pick up small objects during this period. This method is called the "palmar scoop."

After children learn to grasp, they must learn to let go. Initially they drop an object because their hand relaxes involuntarily when their attention and muscular energy are diverted elsewhere, but by six to eight months they have usually learned to let go on purpose. This new skill often becomes a favorite game, with the child dropping a rattle or other object on the floor, having someone pick it up and hand it back, only to drop it again.

Children gradually gain control over their fingers and thumbs, and by eight or nine months the forefinger and thumb work smoothly in opposition. This enables babies to use their hands to pick up and hold smaller things, and by one year they can execute this manipulation skillfully even on very small objects. Many one-year-olds delight, for instance, as they crawl around, in picking up (and sometimes eating) tiny specks of dust and dirt.

Rolling Over

Rolling over is usually children's first maneuver with their whole body, and it cannot be accomplished until they have gained considerable control over their head, torso, and legs. To roll from front to back, babies raise their head and one shoulder, arch their back, and twist, giving a shove with their legs, and over they go. Many babies start to master this stunt well before the age of five months; a month or so later they usually learn to roll from back to front as well. Rolling may become one of their favorite pastimes, and they will practice it for the sheer pleasure of the movement itself. Later they will roll over with some other purpose in mind, such as reaching for a toy. Rolling over eventually leads to some complex maneuvers as pulling up into a standing position.

Sitting Up

As with rolling over, children must gain strength in their neck and back and control over their head before they can sit up. Newborn babies demonstrate what is known as "head lag." Although they can usually raise their head from the mattress very slightly when prone (lying on their stomach) and may be able to turn it from side to side, when they are held upright their head is floppy and either drops backward or sags forward on their chest. However, as they practice raising their head while they are prone, their neck and shoulder muscles strengthen; eventually they are able to get their head and chest well off the bed and can hold their head erect when they are picked up.

Many babies can sit with the support of pillows by the age of four months. At an average of twenty-eight weeks children can sit up briefly by themselves, leaning forward on their hands. By forty weeks the muscles of the back are usually strong enough for children to sit straight and steadily for a fairly long period of time, and most have strong enough abdominal muscles to get to a sitting position on their own. Neurologic reactions are just as important as strength in the development of sitting. They serve to protect

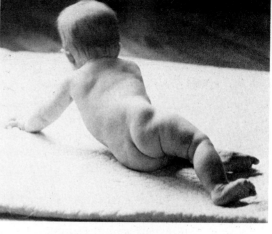

Above, grasping; *top right*, rolling over; *right*, sitting up; *below*, creeping.

children when they lose their balance: hands go out to the back, front, or sides to break the fall.

Creeping and Crawling

Although most babies can use their arms and legs to turn themselves around on their stomachs by the middle of the first year, they do not usually begin to creep—that is, to get around on all fours—until they are over seven months old. A child may become remarkably skillful at getting around this way, and even after it has learned to walk, it may occasionally revert to creeping as a speedier means of locomotion. Although most children creep before they can walk, some do not. Creeping, therefore, may not be a necessary stage of motor development.

When babies start to creep, they may not go forward at first; they may go backward, sideways, or in circles instead. But somehow, they usually end up where they want to go, and once they get there, they may well demonstrate that they know how to pull themselves up to a standing position while holding onto a piece of furniture. This ability to pull up usually occurs about the same time creeping begins.

Sooner or later babies discover that all this activity need not be confined to a single level. They can pull themselves up by the leg of the coffee table, crawl onto the top, and view the living room from this new height; or they can crawl up the stairs and look down through the bannister posts.

COGNITIVE DEVELOPMENT

Cognition is knowing. Sometimes the term is used to mean a kind of knowing that is more definite, more certain, and more lasting than immediate sense perception. Sometimes it is used to mean the parts or dimensions of knowing that can be distinguished from emotion. Sometimes it seems to include all of the mental life. According to one list (Kagan & Kogan, 1970) cognition includes imagery, perception, thought, reasoning, reflection, problem-solving, and all verbal behavior. Its development in infancy is practically inseparable from the development of the senses and motor skills.

The Sensorimotor Period

During the first weeks of life babies have not yet discovered the repetitiveness of events or any cause-and-effect relationships. Thus, for them each impression is an event belonging exclusively to the moment, without past or future. The Swiss psychologist Jean Piaget (1952; 1954) describes the cognitive processes of infants from birth to twenty-four months as **sensorimotor intelligence,** for until individuals are about two years old their mental lives are completely given over to regularizing their sensations and controlling their muscle or motor activity.

In the sensorimotor period children cannot use language or logic to organize their experiences of the world. All their "knowledge" is dependent

Babies will suck their thumbs in reaction to stimulation of their faces or hands.

on sensorimotor skills. With the development of these skills organized patterns of perception and behavior are formed. These patterns are called **schemas** by Piaget and are the way infants deal with information that, in the early months of life, derives from their immediate internal and external environment.

The infant's first schemas are reflexes, of which sucking is one example. Initially, the child will make sucking motions with its mouth whenever its lips or face are stimulated. This is a very simple schema. In time, however, this familiar pattern is modified and expanded by means of two processes—assimilation and accommodation. **Assimilation** is the process whereby increasingly more objects and environmental situations are included in the individual's behavioral repertoire. **Accommodation** is the modification of sensorimotor patterns to deal with these new situations.

The sucking reflex, for example, is specifically adapted to the nipple. Eventually, however, the infants will seek to exercise it on anything they can get into their mouth—a blanket, a thumb, toys, or a pacifier. In other words, infants *assimilate* new objects into the original schema, and new schemas are thus derived. Infants also learn to modify the sucking pattern in a way that results in the most efficient behavior for dealing with a given object. That is, they *accommodate* their behavior or "technique" to suit the different properties of the different objects they have assimilated into the original schema. These same processes are involved in the elaboration of other early schemas, such as kicking, grasping, and looking.

Assimilation and accommodation are the manifestations of the infant's sensorimotor intelligence. The two processes work together and, according to Piaget, gradually promote the infant through the sensorimotor period. By the end of this period the infant's concrete actions have laid the groundwork for intellectual activity.

As Piaget sees it, sensorimotor intelligence consists of six stages, in each of which the child attains certain abilities. No child, however, is a "pure" example of any particular stage, since one aspect of the infant's behavior normally advances faster than another. The child's development proceeds along a gradual path—new abilities are gained and old ones are retained—rather than in abrupt leaps from one stage to another. Furthermore, there are no precise age levels for a given stage: environmental and physiological factors result in individual variations. However, each stage is a necessary preparation for the next, and the sequence of the stages, according to Piaget, does not vary with different children.

Piaget's Six Stages of Sensorimotor Development

Stage 1: *Reflex Activity (1st month of life)* In this early stage the child's behavior is essentially limited to exercising innate skills—that is, reflex actions, like sucking, that are the product of heredity. Initially these actions are automatically triggered by external stimulation. By the end of this stage, through visual and other sensory experiences with the environment, infants are able to use their innate skills in a somewhat discriminating and proficient (though basically primitive) manner. When really hungry, for example, infants now appear able to distinguish the nipple from other objects and surfaces and to maneuver their heads and mouths in order to find it.

Stage 2: *Primary Circular Reactions (1–4 months)* Infants begin to refine some of their reflex actions and to express repetitive behaviors such as opening and closing their fists, hand sucking, foot kicking, etc. The reason Piaget calls such behaviors circular is that the infants are reacting to the pleasure they have derived from chance actions or unplanned behavior by seeking to repeat this behavior in a trial-and-error fashion. Infants also begin to develop primitive anticipations on the basis of past experience. For example, they start to make sucking motions on being put into a posture that signals to them that they are about to be fed.

Stage 3: *Secondary Circular Reactions (4–10 months)* In the previous stage infants were preoccupied with their own bodily activities, such as the movement of their hands. In this stage they begin to turn their attention toward objects and occurrences in the external environment. Infants begin to perceive some connection between a given action and its consequences in the "outer" world. Through accidental body movements, for example, an infant may cause a toy to make a sound. Finding this event interesting or pleasurable, the infant is motivated to try to reproduce the action or series of movements that resulted in the sound. The infant's behavior is now becoming somewhat intentional or purposeful, involving a more refined trial-and-error process than observed previously.

Stage 4: *Coordinating Secondary Schemas (10–12 months)* The infant begins applying patterns of behavior learned in the previous stage to new or prob-

Piaget's Periods of Cognitive Development

SENSORIMOTOR PERIOD (BIRTH TO 24 MONTHS)

Stage 1 (birth to 1 month). Egocentric perceptions; does not differentiate between self and other objects. Reflex activity.

Stage 2 (1–4 months). Shows curiosity and primitive anticipations. Beginning of hand-mouth coordination.

Stage 3 (4–8 months). Increased manipulation and contemplation of objects. Begins to imitate and construct perceptual classes and relations. Repeats rewarding activities. Development of eye-hand coordination.

Stage 4 (8–12 months). Imitates and anticipates more actively. Uses familiar actions or responses to deal with new situations.

Stage 5 (12–18 months)

Stage 6 (18–24 months)

PREOPERATIONAL PERIOD (2–7 YEARS)

PERIOD OF CONCRETE OPERATIONS (7–11 YEARS)

PERIOD OF FORMAL OPERATIONS (11 YEARS ON)

lematic situations. Piaget noted how his infant son Laurent had already developed the habit of hitting hanging objects and then, in the fifth month, of actually striking the objects to make them swing. Previously an end in itself, this "scheme of striking" was used by Laurent in Stage 4 as a *means:* in an effort to grasp a box of matches held by Piaget, the son first struck at a cushion that Piaget held up as an obstacle. According to Piaget the infant's behavior has become much more intentional and thus, for the first time, intelligent.

Stage 5: *Tertiary Reactions (12–18 months)* The child becomes interested in objects in themselves. For example, infants may repeatedly move or drop different items, like a piece of food or a toy, from various positions and heights, and then watch how the object "responds." From these "experiments" children begin to understand more about the nature of the external environment. Children also become more proficient at imitating simple behaviors of adults—such as pointing a finger to the forehead—than they were in previous stages.

Stage 6: *Invention of New Means through Mental Combinations (18–24 months)* This stage heralds the beginning of thought. Children begin to solve practical problems by thinking them out before taking action, rather than simply using hit-or-miss physical means to achieve an end. As Piaget noted in observing his son Laurent, children of this stage who find that a desired object is beyond their reach may use some other object—such as a stick—to bring the desired object closer to them. The mental imagery or internalized symbolism this requires can also be seen in children's imitative behavior. In the past the child

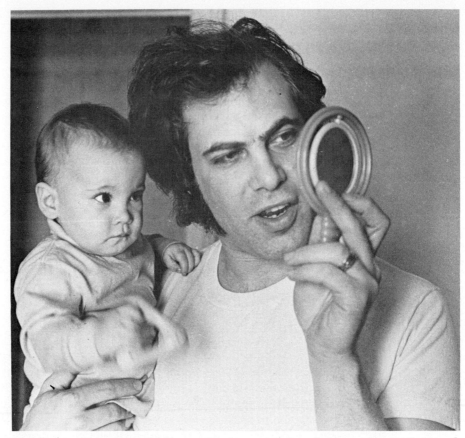

As infants mature, they are able to perceive connections between given actions and their consequences.

could only imitate behavior in the presence of a model. Now the child can observe the behavior, make an internal representation, and reproduce the behavior later on, when the model is absent. For example, Piaget's daughter Jacqueline watched a young boy throw a temper tantrum in his playpen; on the next day she copied that tantrum in her own playpen.

Infants' mental imagery now permits a very different conception of objects. In the earliest stage, when an object or person goes out of sight, the infant acts as though it no longer exists. In the course of the sensorimotor period the infant slowly begins to realize that objects have a reality of their own, separate from his or her body or actions. It is not until Stage 6, however, that the concept of *object permanence* is truly acquired. An object—say, a spoon—can be shown to the child and then concealed in the adult's hand. The spoon can then be moved from one hiding-place to another as the child watches. At Stage 6 infants will search for the spoon in the last place where the adult's hand was seen to enter. They understand that the object exists even when concealed. And they now have the ability to make a mental image of the object, so that they can "follow" it through a series of invisible displacements.

The Preliminaries to Language

Only weeks after birth babies begin to make a few basic gestures and sounds and to gain an approximate notion of certain key expressions, tones of voice, and words. Soon they are spending hours babbling and cooing to themselves though they do not yet speak or understand language systematically. But soon their gestures become more precise and by the end of the first year they have begun to use a few words. Now, instead of simply waving their arms about, they may reach out or point to the bottle or toy they want; instead of simply crying or murmuring, they may say the word—"mama," "up," "bye-bye"—that makes their meaning relatively clear. They start to work at using sounds to make themselves understood.

How does this momentous development come about? We are still a long way from knowing all the answers, but modern technology has made it possible to learn one thing at least: it seems that babies are somehow "programmed" to respond to human speech in a distinctive way as early as the first day or so of life (Condon & Sander, 1974b). Long before they have any notion of meaning in the speech sounds that reach their ears, their movements are synchronized to them, as they are not to other sounds. Clearly, then, the language environment of babies is important from the very beginning of postnatal life, and not merely when they are "ready to talk."

Traditionally, research in language learning has been hampered by two major obstacles: the large number of languages, and the fact that none of us have the faintest recollection of how we learned to speak. We all know how greatly the spoken or written word helps in forming and remembering a mental image or even a feeling. Small wonder, therefore, that our earliest, wordless years are often blanks in our minds.

In recent years the fact that there are many languages, has become an aid rather than an obstacle to progress. Psycholinguists have discovered that a number of factors underlie the ways in which all children acquire speech, no matter what their native tongue. That is, the words differ from language to language, but the ways in which infants use them are astonishingly similar. We know, for instance, that in at least six languages infant speech is characterized by the same type of syllable repetition to describe the same types of objects, and that diminutives are formed in predictable ways. Thus, the English "choo-choo" corresponds to German "Töf-töf" (car), the English "doggy" to the German "Hundi."

The first sounds infants make are crying or screaming, shortly followed by cooing and then babbling. One researcher (Engel, 1973) has suggested another stage—a period of humming. In daily records of her son's vocalizations she noted that his humming sounds, which were quite different from singing, soon assumed sentencelike upward and downward intonations, and acquired meaning. A pointed finger accompanied by a level-pitched "mmmm" indicated that he was pointing the object out to her. When he actually wanted to have it, his pitch rose in a manner similar to the adult query or request intonation: "mmm?"

Engel believes that early screaming and crying, while certainly forms of expressions, cannot be considered real language; neither can gurgling, which is merely the pleasure-denoting equivalent of crying. Babbling—the playful repetition of sounds, usually in the second six months of life—is in her view the first true attempt at linguistic expression. It first appears at a time when the infant already understands the meaning of a few spoken words, and disappears as soon as language has been mastered, having then outlived its usefulness. Significantly, it often reappears in later life when linguistic expression is in some way reduced or damaged, as in stuttering or while learning a foreign language.

Imitation

Speech may be divided into two basic elements: sounds and intonations (changes in pitch). Since intonation can and does take place independently of speech sounds, it is of particular interest in tracing the linguistic development of infants.

The study of intonations suggests that imitation is an important factor in the child's acquisition of language. Analysis of infant vocal sounds revealed a closer and closer similarity of the babies' speech sounds to the intonations they heard from the adults around them.

According to Engel's experience with her own child (1973) language begins with the sounds of "m" and "b," which appear during the humming period. These consonants become associated with a vowel—usually "a," which is the one that results most naturally from simply closing and opening the mouth while voicing these consonants.

The first of these wordlike formations was produced by Engel's son as "am" (meaning "I'm hungry"), although the more usually observed sequence is "ma" (meaning the same thing). These and similar syllables are first emitted in short sequences rather than singly (ma-ma, da-da, bye-bye). Later they proliferate and expand through imitation—first by ear alone, then by ear and eye combined: babies don't only imitate the sound they hear their parents make, but they try to copy it more accurately by imitating the lip movements that produce it. With this development babies, as they approach toddlerhood, are well on the way to "real" speech and communication with adults.

SOCIAL RELATIONSHIPS

Babies derive their sense of self largely from others. As their parents hold them and pat their back, and as they respond by smiling and gurgling, they gain a sense of physical self. As one psychologist (Murphy, 1972) puts it, "All these actions provide sensations which gradually become organized into a cognitive map of himself—perhaps with the feeling 'There is such a lot of me and all so luscious.'"

How does this happen? Infants become aware of themselves because someone touches them and they touch themselves. They become aware of being the same person from day to day because things happen to them regularly. They learn that their arms and legs are part of them—that they do not disappear forever under a peekaboo blanket—because somebody plays with them. In short, what infants feel about themselves and their world cannot be taken for granted; it is entirely dependent on the care and attention they receive in the first year of life.

Attachment

Infants under six months of age do not fully recognize or relate to their caregivers as separate human beings. Though they may cry when their parents turn their attention to something else, nearly anyone who provides the desired stimulation or satisfaction will quickly be accepted as a substitute.

It is usually at about seven months or so that a special attachment develops, usually to the parents (or parenting figure) but sometimes toward others. Nearly 90 percent of all infants form such special attachments by the

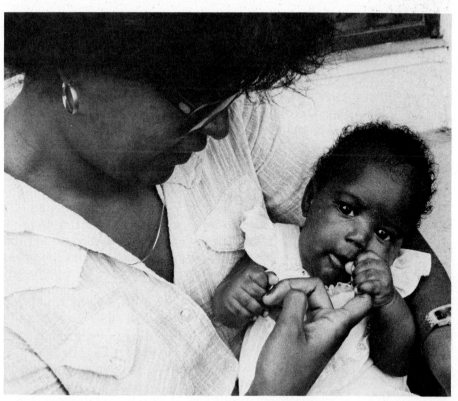

Infants usually form a special attachment to their parents by the end of the tenth month. This attachment is characterized by exchanging glances, seeking of physical contact, and vocalization.

end of the tenth month (Schaffer & Emerson, 1964). Now the infant cries loudly when its parents disappear, even if there are many other people present to provide comfort and stimulation. When its parents are present, the infant tends to engage in attachment behaviors toward them—exchanging glances, seeking physical contact, vocalizing, and so on. When a parent leaves, the infant may follow on all fours.

At this stage the infant is in the process of developing its first meaningful attachment to another person. This is in fact a social relationship, one that involves all the possibilities of warmth and rejection, care and neglect. The quality of the parent-child relationship is the determining factor in development in many species.

It appears that parent-infant attachments occur in other animal species as well as humans. In almost every primate species that has been studied infants seem to be strongly attractive to adult and juvenile animals. The infant is treated with tolerance and solicitude even by individuals who are normally rather belligerent or aggressive. In some species the infant is so attractive that it is common for others besides the mother to take an active interest in caring for it.

A particularly early and striking form of attachment is found in certain flock animals, such as geese, chicken, ducks, and swans. These birds are able to walk very soon after hatching, and they are instinctively programmed to follow the first moving object they perceive, which in most cases is the parent bird. There seems to be a short period, called the sensitive period, during which the following response can be fixed, or **imprinted,** in the young goose. If the mother goose is not present, the infant will follow whatever does appear—even if it happens to be a six-foot honking scientist. Konrad Lorenz, the famous researcher and writer on animal behavior, has succeeded in attaching goslings to himself and to a variety of mechanical decoys. Imprinting does not seem to take place in mammals. Nevertheless, striking attachment behaviors have been observed in many species.

Parent-Infant Attachment

Attachment in the human baby is unquestionably more complex than attachment in other animals, although there are some similarities. First, in all species studied so far attachment takes place at about the time the young become mobile. Human infants become attached to their parents at about four to seven months and learn to creep at about seven to nine months.

Like animals, humans suffer some harm when their attachments are disrupted. Several animal experiments have become important precisely because they suggest the effects of poor mothering and inadequate attachment. The most famous of these is, in a sense, an attempt to discover the very basis for attachment: what accounts for the firm and healthy relationship between the mother and the newborn?

For many years it was assumed that feeding was the answer. The infant clung to its mother and eventually came to prefer her because she was the one who extended the breast or bottle. The striking studies with monkeys conducted by psychologist Harry Harlow and his associates (1962, 1966) were designed to test this assumption. The experimenters constructed two surrogate, or substitute, monkey mothers. One was a body made of bare chicken wire; the other was covered with soft cloth. A feeding bottle could be attached to either one. Each baby monkey had both kinds of surrogate mother, but some were fed only by the wire mother, and others only by the cloth one.

If mother-child attachment were based primarily on feeding, the baby monkeys should have become attached to whichever surrogate mother had the bottle. Instead, the experimenters found that all the monkeys developed the classic clinging attachment to the cloth-covered mother surrogate, preferring "her" presence between feedings and in stressful situations. The wire mother was ignored except at feeding time.

These experiments clearly demonstrated that tactile stimulation, as manifested in the clinging response, was the critical bond between mother and infant. Nevertheless, the comfortable cloth surrogate was not, in the end, an adequate mother, for "her" babies did not develop normally. Most of the female monkeys, at maturity, were unable to nurse their own young, and a few were even vicious toward them. Apparently feeding and tactile contact do not of themselves constitute adequate mothering for monkeys. Anyone who has observed a live monkey mother busily cuddling and grooming her young knows that primate mothering is complex behavior. It is especially so in the human.

It seems, then, that parenting is a matter of social stimulation as well as physical care. If a mother (or other caregiver) props a bottle in an infant's mouth and then leaves, a physical need is being met, but that is all. The infant needs both tactile and social stimulation if it is to develop an attachment to the caregiver. When the parent strokes and smiles at the infant during feeding and at other times, a relationship is formed.

A recent study of individual differences in mother-infant attachment, in which the mother was the primary caregiver, suggests that certain problems in attachment might well have antecedents in the neonatal period. In a sample of 100 neonates the children who showed early interactive deficits (including signs of unresponsiveness to visual, auditory, and tactile stimuli) were found to be "anxious/resistant" by the end of the first year:

> (They) find it difficult to be comforted by contact with the adult after separation. While they actively seek contact, this is mixed with stiffness, struggling to be put down, continued crying, and, often, signs of anger (p. 209).

The study suggests that a child's early interaction problems might contribute to problems in the mother's behavior—difficulty in holding and feeding the child, problems in face-to-face interactions, limited responsiveness and availability—which then exerted its own influence on the quality of the attachment relationship during the first year (Waters, Vaughn, & Egeland, 1980).

Another study suggests that the quality of mother-child attachment in infancy may in turn affect the later quality of play and problem-solving behavior of the child. Of forty-eight infants, those who were securely attached at eighteen months were found to be "more enthusiastic, persistent, cooperative, and in general, more effective" by the age of two than were the infants who were insecurely attached (Matas, Arend, & Sroufe, 1978).

Both of the above studies suggest a certain degree of continuity between early and later behavior and experiences. It should be remembered, however, that there are individual differences in how children respond to and are affected by interactions with others, especially parents. Moreover, according to Kagan (1979), various studies suggest that while early parental behavior does affect the child, experiences in infancy do not necessarily predict how the child will behave in later years:

> . . . there is so much change in environmental demands during the opening years, it should not be surprising that psychologists have been unable to trace the ten-year-old's profile to the experiences of infancy (p. 888).

Fathers and Infants

Until recently studies of attachment focused almost entirely on the relationship between the infant and its mother. The father was thought to be much less important—a notion that fitted in nicely with the usual division of family responsibilities in our society. But now we are finding that infants become attached to their fathers virtually as soon as to their mothers, and just about as strongly. One researcher (Lamb, 1977) found this to be true whether or not the father shared major responsibility for taking care of the child. When both parents were present, the infant was about as likely to turn to the father for attention and affection as to the mother.

A review of a series of studies (Parke & Sawin, 1977) indicates that the social and intellectual growth of the infant are importantly and perhaps uniquely influenced by fathers. It suggests that the father-infant attachment is as strengthened by early and extended contact as is the mother-infant bond. It also suggests that in spite of traditional images there is evidence to support the view that "the father is just as capable of caring for babies as the mother, and ought to at least share the burden" (p. 109). It was found, for example, that fathers participated as actively as mothers in nurturing and stimulating babies when fathers were allowed to visit mother and child in hospital rooms. Differences in the kinds of interactions were also observed. For example:

> When they have the chance, fathers are more usually attentive and playful (talking to the baby, imitating the baby), but they are less active in feeding and caretaking activities such as wiping the child's face or changing diapers (p. 111).

Yet, when they are involved in traditionally female tasks, such as feeding the infant, fathers can be quite successful. They seem as sensitive and responsive to the infant and elicit positive responses from their child.

Physical Contact

Like monkeys, human infants have an inborn need to cling. Newborns will grasp any finger that touches their small palm. Later they will show their attachment by clinging to their parents, burrowing into their laps, or pulling on their hair. The extent to which parents encourage and supply this physical contact is an important factor in the infant's social development.

Particularly crucial is the *quality* of the adult-infant contact. Is the baby picked up only in the course of routine feeding and diaper change? Or is it held for the sheer pleasure of it? There are many differences between parent-infant pairs, and researchers believe that the subsequent social patterns of the infants can be traced to these differences. One researcher, for example (Ainsworth, 1972), found that when parents held their babies relatively long, the babies appeared to be particularly relaxed and "well-rounded." They enjoyed being picked up, but were cheerful when put down. Other infants, who were held more frequently but for shorter periods, did not respond so positively and were likely to fuss when put down.

Some researchers—and many parents—have suggested that physical contact between the adult and baby is at least partly influenced by the baby itself (Bell, 1968; Schaffer & Emerson, 1964). Parents may find that their first baby is a "cuddler" who delights in being held, while a second child is restless in their arms, eager to be put down to explore toys and surroundings. It seems that some infants are biologically predisposed to seek a high degree of physical contact—from mother, father, stuffed dog, or security blanket. Others are naturally more goal- or task-oriented and dislike situations that cuddle them, confine them, or otherwise restrict their energies.

Smiling

Smiling, like physical contact, is an early means of communication between adult and child. In fact, nearly everyone smiles at a baby, hoping the baby will smile in return. Doting grownups gather before the hospital nursery window, imagining smiles on the faces of the newborn infants. A smile is important because, in our culture, it initiates a social relationship.

An infant may smile when it is only a few hours old, but this is not yet a social smile. Like most early attachment behaviors, the smile is at first bestowed indiscriminately. Nevertheless, it is from the start an important influence on the parent-child relationship. A smiling baby is a virtual advertisement for parenthood: it makes any parent feel proud, contented, and singularly blessed. The adult will respond with babbling, frequent cuddling, and so on. A grumpy, serious baby may not inspire the same attention. Some studies have supported the general observation that the parent's and child's actions have mutual effect on one another. In one such investigation (Gewirtz & Boyd, 1977) mothers were conditioned to smile or respond positively to the contingent vocalizations and head turns of their two- to three-month-old babies.

The adult's responsive smile transforms the spontaneous smile of infants into an exchange—the first real social interaction. In effect, the adult's smile shows infants that they can have an impact on a person in their environment. Long before they can talk, they have discovered an important social tool. A smile will get them many things they like—a smile in return, some cuddling, or talk and play.

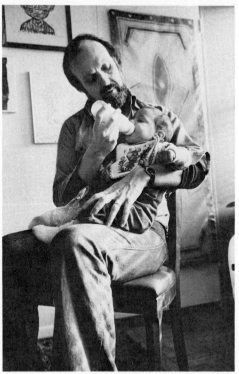

The father/infant relationship is now the subject of much interest and research.

The frequency of the infant's smiling behavior seems to be congenitally influenced. Some infants appear to be smilers almost from birth, while others do not smile even with strong encouragement. Despite these congenital differences an infant's smiles will generally increase if the parents reinforce them with their own smiles or other stimulation.

Basic Trust

The position of the newborn infant may be difficult for us to imagine. From the time of late childhood we have been able to make realistic comparisons of our parents with other parents, of our family life-style with other life-styles. Infants or very young children are absolutely unable to make such comparisons. They must accept as the real and total world the particular family situation in which they find themselves.

Noting this, psychoanalyst Erik Erikson (1963) has characterized infancy

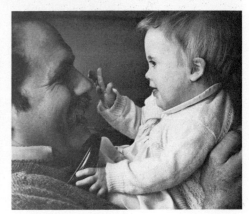

as the period during which the child develops basic and long-standing expectations about the world. During infancy the great issue is trust versus mistrust. Basic trust involves a positive orientation toward oneself, the world, and others. Mistrust is manifested in negative feelings such as fear and insecurity.

According to Erikson, when the infant's needs are met in a consistent and affectionate way, it is satisfied that the world is a safe place. The child trusts its caregivers basically because of their consistent attentiveness, but also because they convey a stable sense of their own worthiness.

When the needs of infants are not recognized, their world is chaotic, unpredictable. Sometimes their cries are met with milk and cuddling; sometimes they are ignored or pushed harshly aside. If they are left to cry for long periods, they cannot conclude, as we might, that their parents are neglectful, for they have no experience to judge people by. It is their *world* that seems neglectful. Perhaps it really is an arbitrary and unfriendly place, or perhaps

❖❖

The Quality of Father-Infant Interaction

Parents who work outside the home like to say that the *quality* of time spent with an infant or young child is fully as important as the *quantity* of time.

This is an argument that might be expected to appeal to fathers, most of whom are absent from the home during the day. Lamb (1979), in a review of research on paternal influence, notes that most fathers studied did not assume major roles in their infants' care. Probably the average father spent less than ten hours a week interacting with his infant.

And yet there was a special *quality* to father-infant interaction. Fathers were more likely than mothers to indulge in joyous and stimulating play (Parke & O'Leary 1976; Yogman et al., 1976). In most households it was fathers who tossed their infants in the air and romped with them on the floor. Fathers were also more likely to poke the infant in the ribs and make a game of mimicking his expressions (Trevarthen, 1974).

In other ways, too, fathers distinguish themselves from mothers, who are usually the primary caregivers. According to one study (Rebelsky & Hanks, 1971) fathers spend less time talking to their infants. Although there is some question as to whether this is so, it does appear that fathers are less likely than mothers to engage in high-pitched vocalizations and other intimate "conversations" with their infants. Fathers are also less likely to constrain their infants—for example, by holding them by the arms to keep them still.

All this suggests that fathers are qualitatively different from mothers—at least in their play styles. But this may not be so. The different play styles may simply reflect differences in the quantity of time that fathers and mothers typically spend with their infants. One study shows that when a father undertakes primary care for his infant, he is more likely to act like the usual mother described in the research (Field, 1978). He engages in high-pitched vocalizations and intimate "conversations" that reflect *not* his fatherhood but rather his day-in-day-out familiarity with his infant's needs. In other words, when exposure to infants and caretaking duties are equal, parent-child interaction patterns may actually be quite similar.

Studies do not tell us if mothers who are secondary caretakers return from the office to throw their briefcases on the chair and their infants in the air.

---

only *they* do not get attention. Under such circumstances infants develop a basic mistrust of the world and a sense of their own unimportance.

Basic mistrust is soon manifested in behavior. When infants are not regularly satisfied in their need for physical contact, nourishment, and so on, they react with prolonged crying. Ainsworth found that the amount and frequency of infant crying reflected the degree of responsiveness the parents had shown in the past. Where adults do not respond or respond too slowly to crying, infants increase both the frequency and duration of their crying episodes (Ainsworth, 1972). It seems as if they no longer trust that someone will come right away.

Erikson's Crises in Psychological Development

BASIC TRUST VERSUS BASIC MISTRUST (FIRST YEAR OF LIFE)

If the infant gains a sense of familiarity with its sensations and experiences, it comes to feel that the world is benevolent or at least reliable. In this way it learns to trust itself and its capacities. If it fails to do this, it may develop basic mistrust instead.

AUTONOMY VERSUS SHAME AND DOUBT (SECOND YEAR OF LIFE)

INITIATIVE VERSUS GUILT (THE PRESCHOOL YEARS)

INDUSTRY VERSUS INFERIORITY (MIDDLE CHILDHOOD)

IDENTITY VERSUS ROLE CONFUSION (ADOLESCENCE)

INTIMACY VERSUS ISOLATION (YOUNG ADULTHOOD)

GENERATIVITY VERSUS STAGNATION (PRIME OF LIFE)

EGO INTEGRITY VERSUS DESPAIR (OLD AGE)

By learning to love and trust his parents, a baby prepares to form other social attachments comfortably and happily.

Once babies adopt an orientation of mistrust, their environment works to reinforce it. Their parents now conclude that they are bad or cranky babies who simply cannot be attended every time they cry. Other members of the family shout at them; the neighbors bang on the walls. And when they are held, it is usually by some desperate person who hopes to shut them up. Later they become the toddlers we see crying in the supermarket: their mothers slap their faces and they wail all the more. Their behavior begins to resemble that of many maladjusted adults, such as neurotics who cannot trust relationships but continue to be demanding or possessive even when it is clear that their behavior drives others away. Basic mistrust leads to self-defeating behavior patterns, a reduced sense of self-esteem, and an inability to deal positively with others.

Fear of Strangers

A direct result of the infant's first attachment is *stranger anxiety*, which appears at approximately eight months in American infants. Once infants become specifically attached to the parent or parenting figure, they can be easily upset by the approach of an unfamiliar adult, especially if the parents are not present. They fix their eyes on the stranger and stare, unmoving, for a short time; then they are likely to cry, scream, and show other signs of distress. If a parent is present, they will cling to the parent in panic.

Stranger anxiety is not a reaction to strangers as such, but rather a reaction to a discrepant schema. By now babies have incorporated the schema of their parents' faces and probably those of some others as well. They will be frightened by faces that fail to conform to their schemas, whether these are strange faces or merely the mother's face with unaccustomed dark glasses or the father in a hat. It is the discrepancy that triggers the infant's reaction. Interestingly enough, strangers are not nearly so frightening when they turn their back (Zegans & Zegans, 1972).

Stranger anxiety is generally greatest when the parent-infant attachment is intense (Schaffer & Emerson, 1964). It is virtually nonexistent in institutionalized children. Fear of strangers also seems to be influenced by the position of the child in the family and, in some cases, by the extent of the child's contact with persons outside the home. In one study (Collard, 1968) firstborn children and widely spaced children showed the most intense fear of strangers. Among the firstborns children from isolated rural areas showed greater fear than children from urban centers.

Interestingly, father-infant contact may affect the child's ability to deal with strangers. A review of father-infant studies (Parke, 1979b) indicates that when the father is actively involved in caring and playing with the infant, the infant is less disturbed by new social situations involving strangers. This finding seems to be supported by cross-cultural studies. It was suggested that one possible reason for this correlation might be that "more egalitarian families not only share caretaking more but expose the infant to a wider range of other individuals, which, in turn, might reduce the impact of a strange adult" (Parke, 1979b, p. 572).

In specific instances the infant's reaction depends on momentary feelings of insecurity. A parent's presence makes the infant more secure in most exploratory behavior, including the exploration of new faces. Thus, a mask constituting a discrepant facial schema will provoke crying and other signs of fright when it is worn by a strange experimenter. The same mask, worn by the parenting figure, is more likely to elicit laughter and smiles (Sroufe & Wunsch, 1972). Indeed, laughter is, like fear, a reaction to a discrepant schema; which reaction occurs depends on children's developmental status as well as their feeling of security at the moment. Only after they have incorporated the schema for crawling will they laugh at the incongruity of their mother crawling along the floor (Sroufe & Wunsch, 1972) or scream at the sight of a drunken man crawling in the street.

This brings up an important point about the concept of the fear of strangers. Rheingold and Eckerman have pointed out that it is by no means the developmental milestone we once thought. Schaffer (1971) made the same qualification when he said:

> The trouble is that fear of strangers is by no means an on-off phenomenon which the infant either has or does not have. On the contrary, it appears to be highly sensitive to all sorts of conditions both within the child and in the situation and particularly so to the appearance and behavior of the stranger (p. 65).

This viewpoint is supported in a review of the literature (Clarke-Stewart, 1978) which indicates that stranger anxiety is not consistently shown across situations, kinds of behavior, age of onset, and/or type of stranger. Investigations (Bretherton & Ainsworth, 1974; Brooks & Lewis, 1976) are tending to view the child's reaction to a stranger as a complex phenomenon composed of fear (emotion) and wariness (cognition), attachment, affiliation, and exploration behaviors; the balance among these determines the child's response. In other words, this behavior is composed of varied, interactive patterns between the child and others.

Institutionalization and Foster Care

Children with unresponsive or inconsistent parents will cry for long periods in an attempt to attract attention. But what of children who have no parents or regular caregivers, children who are fed by a propped-up bottle? At first they too, will indulge in prolonged crying; but after a time they will do the only thing they *can* do. They will gradually reduce their crying and subside to a state of quiet indifference. When their demands are unmet, they become altogether undemanding. That is a tragic adjustment.

Infants who for various reasons could not be kept at home have been cared for in institutions like orphanages, children's homes, or hospitals where they were more or less deprived of ordinary parenting. The quality of institutional care has varied, of course, but in the most depriving institutions many children became as unresponsive to adults as the institutional caretakers were to them (Spitz, 1945).

Several studies found institutionalized children to be retarded in sensorimotor, cognitive, and social development. Differences appeared only after three or four months of life, and the negative effects seemed to increase with the length of stay in the institution. The peak of smiling came later in institutionalized infants, presumably because of lack of stimulation from caregivers (Provense & Lipton, 1962). Visual discrimination, reasoning, and concept formation suffered. Behavior was often disturbed. Most important, language learning was seriously, perhaps irreversibly, retarded. Other studies failed to show such severe effects. As one would expect, a good deal depended on the quality of care in the institution.

It might seem reasonable to conclude that the lack of a permanent attachment is the likely cause of retarded development in institutionalized children. There is evidence, however, that the lack of stimulation may be a more important factor. It is conceivable that an institutionalized infant, given a stimulating developmental program, and opportunities for one-to-one emotional involvements, could be as advanced as an infant raised at home.

Several studies suggest that when the conditions of institutionalization are improved, children experience a remarkable rise in IQ and in social capacities as well. A most interesting study was conducted (Skeels, 1966) over a period of thirty years. The subjects of the study were twenty-five children raised in an orphanage and classified as mentally retarded. At the age of two, thirteen of the children—most of them girls—were transferred to another institution where each was adopted by an older mentally retarded child in a kind of "big sister" arrangement. Though the transferred children continued to live in an institutional setting, each now had a caregiver or mothering figure. The children who remained in the original orphanage did not have this advantage.

Twenty years later the transferred group was significantly higher in IQ than the orphanage group. Whereas only one member of the orphanage group had completed high school, almost half of the transferred group had attended high school, and one had even gone to college. Most of the transferred children had eventually been perceived as normal and adopted into a family setting. All of them had grown up to be normal, self-supporting adults, whereas four members of the orphanage group were still in institutions. Clearly not all the children were simply and irreversibly "mentally retarded."

Often children who lack a permanent home of their own may be placed in foster homes. For some children this is an opportunity to participate in normal family life. But the foster parents are performing a paid service; they do not adopt the child. This can make the arrangement precarious from the child's point of view. In fact, it is common for a foster child to be brought up in a series of different homes.

Despite its imperfections, however, the foster home environment has definite advantages over the institution for the child's development. In general, institutionalized children transferred to a foster home showed fewer personality disturbances and higher intelligence scores than children who remained in institutions. Comparisons of institutionalized and foster children have shown that foster children were emotionally more secure and better adjusted, even when they spent their first three years of life in a particularly depriving institution (Goldfarb, 1945a). Children who were brought into a foster home as infants were decidedly better adjusted than children who spent the first three years in institutions (Goldfarb, 1945b).

SUMMARY

▶ The most obvious indicators of growth are height and weight, and these increase rapidly during the first year of life. Individual children vary in their rates of growth, depending on their heredity patterns and socioeconomic circumstances.

▶ As a child grows, its skeleton hardens, its muscle fibers lengthen and thicken, and its nervous system matures. Growth progresses according to orderly and predictable patterns: cephalocaudally—from head to tail; proximodistally—from trunk to extremities; and from general to specific reactions.

▶ A properly diversified diet, an appropriate emotional climate, a sensible feeding schedule, and gradual weaning contribute to the infant's healthy growth. Breast-feeding has certain advantages, but bottle-feeding is more satisfactory for some infants. Minor digestive disorders such as colic and food allergies are usually outgrown without medical attention. Malnutrition, however, can cause permanent damage.

▶ Sleep is a positive body function that allows for growth and maintenance of the body. Infants gradually increase their total waking time and consolidate their sleeping time. Their sleep also becomes more like an adult's, alternating between heavy and light periods.

▶ Seeing is a complex learning experience which depends on physical maturation as well as skill in using the eyes. Among the first objects infants attend to are faces, particularly the eyes. Young infants are attracted by stimuli that are moderately different from those they already know. By six months of age infants have depth perception.

▶ Development of motor skills likewise depends on both maturation and practice. When infants are ready to perform an action, they are usually eager to work at it. In predictable sequences they learn to grasp and then to let go; to roll over, sit up, creep, stand, and eventually walk.

▶ Cognition is knowing. During the first period of cognitive development the sensorimotor period, children's learning and thinking are entirely bound up with sensation and action. They form organized patterns of perception and behavior, called schemas, by which they interpret and deal with the world. As their experience widens, they assimilate new elements into the schemas and modify or accommodate the schemas to make them more useful in dealing with the environment.

▶ Piaget views babies as very active participants in their sensorimotor development, which he divides into six stages. Innate reflex actions form the basis of deliberate, practiced motor activity. After gaining some control over the limbs, infants start to investigate and manipulate objects and begin to imitate simple actions. Thought as a means of solving problems develops between the ages of eighteen and twenty-four months, as does the concept of object permanence.

▶ Preparation for language begins almost at birth, and includes crying and all the other prelinguistic vocalizations. Hence a linguistically stimulating environment is important from the start.

▶ The attitudes infants have toward themselves and the world around them seem to be derived from the care and attention they receive. Their attachments before the age of six months or so are relatively indiscriminate; then they form a primary attachment to the parent or parenting figure. As in other species, human attachment takes place at about the same time the infant becomes mobile.

▶ The quality of the first attachment is crucial for the child's development. It is not sufficient merely to meet the infant's gross physical needs. Physical contact, smiling, responsiveness, stimulation, and a positive orientation to all these activities are also necessary. Depending on the way their needs are met at this time, children form an attitude of basic trust or mistrust toward the world.

▶ Children raised in institutions are frequently impaired in almost all aspects of their development. However, institutionalization need not be harmful if there is opportunity for attachment and plenty of perceptual and cognitive stimulation, such as would be provided in a good home.

FURTHER READINGS

Brazelton, T. Terry. *Infants and mothers: Differences in development*. New York: Dell, 1969.
   A leading pediatrician describes development on a month-to-month basis during the first year of life for infants of different temperaments.
Chess, Stella, Thomas, A., and Birch, H. G. *Your child is a person: A psychological approach to parenthood without guilt*. New York: Viking, 1972.
   One thing that has become clear in the field of child development in recent years is the importance of the earliest period of life for the shaping of an individual's

personality. The authors trace this process, showing the effects of continuing interaction between the child's own temperament and the environment which in the child's experience constitutes the world.

Dunn, Judy. *Distress and comfort.* **Cambridge, Mass.: Harvard University Press, 1977.**

Dunn examines the problems of the developing child. In this diligently researched, clinical appraisal, the author draws her conclusions from numerous, recent case studies and experiments.

Fraiberg, Selma. *Every child's birthright: In defense of mothering.* **New York: Basic Books, 1977.**

An eloquent account of how a baby's future healthy development is founded on early attachment to a caring person. The book also discusses the need for adequate day-care for the babies of working mothers.

Gunther, M. *Infant feeding.* **Chicago: Regnery, 1971.**

Dr. Gunther is qualified both as a researcher and a practicing physician to write with authority on infant feeding. Viewing breast-feeding as the basis of infant feeding, she offers a full explanation of all the processes involved in lactation.

Kagan, Jerome, et al. *Change and continuity in infancy.* **New York: Wiley, 1971.**

Kagan conducted longitudinal research on a large sample of children, who were studied from the age of four months to four years. The author hypothesized that there are continuities in the behavior of an individual child over time if the observed behavior can be related to an underlying personality trait. Differences of sex and social class in cognitive and behavioral development were also studied.

Klaus, Marshall H., and Kennell, John H. *Maternal-infant bonding.* **St. Louis: Mosby, 1976.**

Written by eminent pediatricians specializing in this field, this book reviews the research on the importance of mother-infant bonding. It includes practical suggestions for how doctors, nurses, and hospitals can contribute to early mother-infant contact.

McCall, R. B. *Infants: The new knowledge about years from birth to three.* **New York: Vintage Books, 1980.**

This unique book does not tell parents what to do but rather explains how the child is growing and developing. In clear and simple terms an expert psychologist has described the radical revision of our understanding of infant capabilities that has occurred in recent years.

McCall, R. B., Eichorn, D. H., and Hogarty, P. S. *Transitions in early mental development.* **Monograph of the Society for Research in Child Development, Serial #171, 1977.**

This study was a reanalysis of data collected on mental development in the Berkeley Growth Study. The authors describe developmental change and transitions during the first five years of life.

Stern, D. *The first relationship: Infant and mother.* **Cambridge, Mass.: Harvard University Press, 1977.**

This book provides a clear description of research on the mother-infant relationship, as well as practical applications.

White, Burton L., and Watts, J. C. *Experience and environment: Major influences on the development of the young child.* **Englewood Cliffs, N.J.: Prentice-Hall, 1973.**

A report on a major research undertaking at Harvard on the development of intellectual and social competence from birth to the age of six. The data are based on observations in the homes of the children being studied. The researchers were interested in the development of language, the senses, abstract thought, and social competence. Interesting case studies are included as well as a full discussion of the methodology and testing used.

Observational Activities

Part One   Birth and Infancy

Environmental Factors and the Health of the Unborn Baby

Evidence continues to build on the effects of environmental factors on the health of an unborn baby. The general rule is that the embryo is most susceptible to damaging factors in the earliest stages of a woman's pregnancy.

For example, one environmental factor that can have a negative effect on the unborn child involves toxoplasmosis, which is carried by cat feces. Pregnant women are advised not to care for a cat's litter box during their pregnancy. Toxoplasmosis can cause blindness, mental retardation, fetal death, and cardiac anomalies. Cigarette smoke can cause prematurity and growth retardation in the unborn child; drugs, alcohol, and medication of various sorts all are linked to some abnormalities in the developing fetus. And yet many women ignore the evidence and continue to smoke, drink alcoholic beverages, or take drugs during pregnancy.

Identify six female friends who smoke. Ask them to tell you if they would continue to smoke if they were pregnant, knowing that smoking might endanger the health of their unborn child. Record their answers and their reasons for those answers. (If you prefer to check on an environmental factor other than smoking, do so.) Briefly summarize your findings and draw some conclusions.

Preparing for Fatherhood

In his book *Preparing for Parenthood* Dr. Lee Salk urged men to participate actively with their pregnant wives in learning about prenatal care and child-rearing. In Salk's experience fathers who do so become far more involved in the care of their children than fathers who do not.

Identify your individuals—two expectant fathers and two men who are fathers of children under age two. You may want to arrange with two pregnant women to interview their husbands, or you may be able to locate expectant fathers through a local class of expectant parents. Interview the four men either in person or by phone, and ask the following questions:

Questions for the two expectant fathers
1.   Will this be your first child?
2.   If not, are you preparing for this child in a way that is different from your past preparation?
3.   Does your wife attend prenatal classes? If so, do you attend with her?
4.   What part do you plan to play in the actual birth of your child?
5.   What are three important aspects of being a "good" father to your child?

   Questions for the two fathers
1.   Did your wife attend prenatal classes? If so, did you attend with her?
2.   What part did you play in the actual birth of your child? Were you present during your wife's labor and delivery?
3.   If you did participate in prenatal classes and the childbirth experience, how do you think this affected your role as a father?
4.   Would you prepare differently for your next child?
5.   What are three important aspects of being a "good" father to your child?

Analyze your findings, and compare them with those of your classmates to determine the differences between expectant fathers and fathers of young children.

PART TWO

Toddlerhood

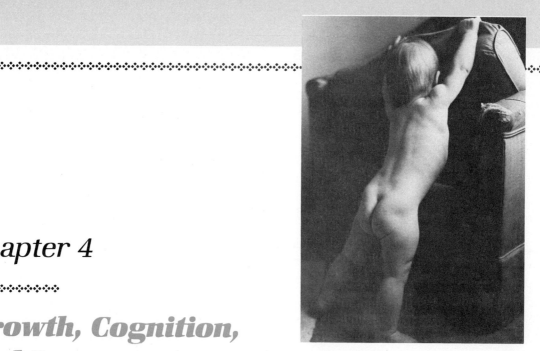

Chapter 4

❖❖❖❖❖❖

Growth, Cognition, and Language

*I*ncessant activity characterizes toddlers. When babies reach this stage they no longer depend on someone to carry them around. They are up off the ground and on their own. No matter how swiftly they got about on all fours, toddling is more satisfactory. They can see better standing on their own two feet, and they can use their hands to carry things.

Toddlerhood lasts from about fifteen months to two or two-and-a-half years of age. Despite an occasional show of obstinacy, toddlers are delightful. They are beginning to show goal-directed behavior, to talk in short sentences with an ever-increasing vocabulary, and to play with other children. By the time they are three, children have a better mastery of their bodies. They walk erect, have no trouble turning sharp corners, and are able to ride a tricycle. And just as important, they will have learned to cope in an amiable and more socially acceptable fashion.

PHYSICAL DEVELOPMENT

As in infancy, so in toddlerhood, physical development follows more or less predictable patterns. The child's growth in the second year or year and a half is largely a continuation of the process we studied in Chapter 3. Although the

143

tremendous rate of growth in the first year of life will never again be equaled, children are still, until the age of about twenty-four months, growing faster than they will again until the onset of puberty.

Body Growth

At age one children are quite different from what they were when they first emerged into the world. Their height, at twenty-eight to thirty-one inches (70 to 77.5 cm), is roughly one-third greater than at birth, and their weight has gone from as little as five pounds (2.25 kg) to somewhere between seventeen and twenty-six pounds (7.65 and 11.7 kg). By age two they may be thirty-two to thirty-seven inches (80 to 92.5 cm) tall, and will have gained another four to seven pounds (1.8 to 3.15 kg) in weight—not so dramatic a gain as before, but still very significant for such small people.

In one way they have completed even more of their growth than these figures suggest. The brain, by the end of the first year of life, has already reached about 65 percent of its final adult weight. This has important consequences for the child's behavior, for it means that in some respects the nervous system can be seen as almost fully developed. For instance, the perceptual abilities we examined in Chapter 3 have reached just about their full functioning capacity.

Body Proportions and Skeletal Growth

The toddler's proportions are already different from those of the newborn. By age one the neck has begun to lengthen slightly; so have the long bones of the arms and legs, in relation to the torso. In accordance with the cephalocaudal principle we described in Chapter 3, the arms take an early lead. By age two they will have lengthened by about 60 to 75 percent, whereas the legs will be only about 40 percent longer than at birth. Thereafter, though, the legs will quickly catch up and soon become longer than the arms.

Rapid skeletal growth occurs during toddlerhood and can easily be detected through X-ray studies. See Figure 4.1. The processes of ossification and calcification are well under way during this period. The spine is slowly beginning to harden and to take on the S shape that is characteristic of adult humans. The toddler's bones are still very soft, however, and accidental deformation can occur—for example, if the child always sleeps in the same position, or if disease or dietary deficiencies interfere with the hardening process.

In addition to the lengthening of the long bones of the limbs, other important skeletal changes are going on in toddlerhood. The number of bones in the body actually changes. A number of smaller bones join together to form larger units, while elsewhere new bones are being formed from what was originally cartilage, as in the wrists and ankles. The fontanelles—those open spaces in the cranium—are closing as bone growth catches up with the rapid enlargement of the brain.

Most children enter toddlerhood armed with at least a few of their

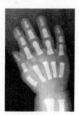

Birth

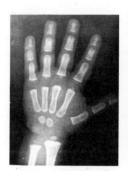

One year

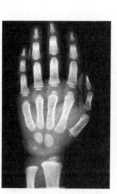

Two years

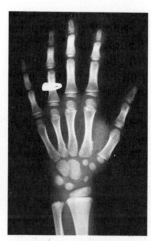

Five years

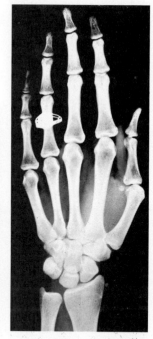

Eighteen years

Figure 4.1 X ray pictures show how the bones of the hand develop from birth to maturity.

twenty baby teeth—also called milk teeth or deciduous ("falling") teeth. The thirty-two permanent teeth are already formed in the gums, though they will not begin to erupt until around age six or seven.

As the teeth grow, so does the face. The pattern of facial growth is established during the first three years and is marked by more or less proportionate increases in facial size. Influencing both the growth of the face and the position of the teeth is the growth of the jaws. The relationship between the upper and the lower jaw determines facial balance and efficiency in chewing.

Motor Skills

The motor areas of the toddler's brain—the centers that control and coordinate movement—continue to develop until about the fifteenth month. As we might guess, the arms and hands are ahead of the legs and feet. The one-year-old child has already learned to grasp objects between the fingers and opposed thumb (pincer grasp), as an adult would do, and has usually achieved independent control of the fingers. Right- or left-handedness is beginning to emerge, and a child is becoming able to grasp an object in one hand and manipulate it with the other. Typical one-year-olds take vast delight in wiggling all these individual little appendages, which seem suddenly to have

Learning to walk involves the coordination of many factors, including learning ability and maturation of the skeletal and muscular systems and of the neuromuscular mechanism.

acquired a life of their own. But they are only beginning to get their legs and feet sufficiently under control to attempt that crowning goal of their young existence, walking upright.

Children's motor control thus depends very much on the maturation of the central nervous system. But when they are ready to perform, whether it be walking or some other skill, they should be encouraged to do so and given plenty of opportunity to practice. If they are not ready, they should be left alone, inasmuch as no amount of pushing can get them to do what they are not yet physically capable of doing. Forcing children to try a skill they are not ready for can result in misery and frustration; sometimes it may even make them reluctant to try it when they are ready. Every child is an individual who has his or her own rate of physical development and his or her own pace of learning.

Walking

Walking is a tremendous milestone in children's lives. It enables them to expand their environment immensely and, by freeing their hands for manipulation, makes the possibilities for exploration almost limitless. Walking requires not only learning but also maturation of the skeletal and muscular systems and the neuromuscular mechanism. Well-developed sight and hearing are needed to help children keep their balance and steer their course. After all, they must be able not merely to place one foot in front of the other, but also to see where they are going.

Most children can stand with support at between eight and ten months, and alone by one year. The average age of unassisted walking is between thirteen and fourteen months, although, of course, some children walk much earlier and others walk much later.

A child's first independent steps are jerky and uneven. Feet are spread out and toes turned outward. The arms are held out for balance. Children weave as they walk, and they fall frequently. As they practice, they move on to "toddling," a kind of flat-footed paddling about. Soon they become bold and strong enough to undertake positively daring feats—climbing stairs, running, balancing on one foot. As the muscles grow stronger and balance improves, walking patterns also become more mature. By the time they are two and a half, most children walk quite well.

Oddly, the proficient and well-coordinated creeper may not be the earliest walker. Babies who are adept creepers may be too busy scooting around on their hands and knees examining their world to take the time to practice standing. Less proficient creepers, on the other hand, may spend a great deal of time pulling themselves to a standing position; because they have greater need to learn to walk than the youngster who gets around well on all fours, they may be earlier walkers.

By fifteen months, when average children are standing and walking alone, they need physical space for their exploration and energetic play. The typical toddler is quite literally "all over the place"—under the sink, out the door, across the yard, or into new mischief behind the couch. Every bookcase and tabletop is a potential playground; every ashtray, vase, clock, or piece of china is fair game. The danger to—and from—the environment increases at about eighteen months, when most children are starting to run as much as they walk. At this age toddlers are beginning to pick up their toys and carry them around. They stack objects on the floor and furniture, then push the pile over to see it fall. They are finding out how to operate on their surroundings. They are constantly learning from the results, but the price of this knowledge is a certain amount of breakage and general messiness.

By about two years children run easily, and they can jump with both feet, negotiate a staircase with relative safety, kick toys and balls (still somewhat clumsily), and turn the pages of a book fairly well. Many of them have started to draw with crayons or pencil, although they are not yet interested in trying to make recognizable faces or figures. At this age a lot of children are distinctly impatient with being held. Although they frequently want and need the reassurance of being in a parent's arms, they want it when *they* want it. The friend or visitor who picks up a two-year-old at the wrong moment is likely to find himself holding a squirming, howling child who, at the moment,

No corner is safe from
a toddler's inquisitive-
ness.

is not the least bit desirous of attention or affection. They have their own life
to live, and they insist on being left alone to get on with it.

PERCEPTION

Perception is the process of taking in information about the world around
us—its color and smell, brightness and noisiness, temperature, texture, and
taste. To do this we need at least two different kinds of ability. First, our senses
must be able to take in the signals that the environment makes available: light
rays, waves of sound, odors, tastes, the pressure of objects against our skin.
But all of this information will be of no use to us unless our minds are able
to organize—unless we are able to make sense of the raw data our senses are
registering.

Maturation of the Physical Senses
By the time a child is one year old, the physical senses are almost fully developed. The eyes can focus accurately and can properly register line and
color; the ears can distinguish variations in the pitch and quality of sound;
the nervous system can carry signals promptly to the correct receiving center

❖❖

Caution: Toddlers Ahead

When two-year-old Susan said she had swallowed all the aspirin, her mother was skeptical. But she decided to humor the child and watched, astonished, as she toddled into the kitchen, climbed onto the countertop, and reached for the top shelf of the cabinet to display an empty bottle of baby aspirin. Susan had to be rushed to a hospital emergency room and have her stomach pumped out.

Incidents such as this are not uncommon. Accidents cause more childhood deaths than the five leading fatal diseases combined. What's more, most of these accidents occur at home and can be prevented. Children under five are at special risk. They are, after all, tempted by their unlimited curiosity about a newly accessible and fascinating world, threatened by their very limited understanding of the dangers of that world, and handicapped by their incomplete physical development and experience, which cannot sufficiently protect them from the hazards around them. Adults can do many things to protect their small children. One of the most important of these is to keep dangerous objects out of the child's reach. These include anything small enough to fit into a child's mouth and be swallowed or aspirated—buttons, parts of toys, pills, jewelry, and even some foods, such as nuts or popcorn.

Sharp instruments like knives and scissors are obviously dangerous, but the sharp edges of cans a child may find in the garbage or the sharp edges of carelessly produced toys are equally hazardous. Few parents would offer matches and lighters and electrical appliances to a toddler, but for a creeping, crawling, or toddling child, even electric wall sockets must be shielded. How inviting they look for sticking fingers, tools, or toys into!

Toxic substances pose yet another problem. According to the United States Public Health Service each year 500,000 children swallow household materials left in easily accessible places—under the kitchen sink or on the floor of a linen closet. Many of these swallowings prove fatal. As the case of Susan demonstrates, children may happily swallow whole bottles of medicine—especially syrupy liquids or tablets with sugar coating. Even bottles with safety caps aren't foolproof against the inquisitive child. Many parents report that kids cope with the so-called childproof containers more easily than grownups do.

The toddler years are filled with homely common dangers. Most parents learn to guard against the things their children are "getting into" at the moment. They keep the cribside up once children begin to roll over and sit up; they use a safety harness when babies begin to stand up in the carriage; they try to keep electric wires from dangling temptingly where a creeping child can pull them and bring a lamp or toaster crashing down.

But the trick is to look ahead to the next stage and realize that children who are creeping today may tomorrow, without warning, suddenly pull themselves up by the leg of the coffee table and climb on top. Or gleefully scale a flight of stairs on hands and knees and suddenly realize they cannot get down. Parents must somehow manage to protect their child from all reasonably anticipated hazards without making a nervous and fearful wreck out of either the baby or themselves.

in the brain. Some maturation, it is true, is still in progress: for instance, vision and hearing are accurate only to a limited distance, beyond which the child may have difficulty recognizing even quite familiar objects. This is why toddlers so easily get lost in stores. Confronted with a multitude of "big people" moving about a dozen yards away, the toddler may not be able to tell which of them is Mommy, or even to recognize her voice when she calls. But the ability to do so is steadily improving, and in another year or so will be complete. From now on perceptual development will depend largely on the second of the two processes cited above—organization.

Organization of Sensory Data

As we have seen, organization and learning are nothing new to toddlers. They have been eagerly working at them since the day they were born. In forming their first schemata—their mother's face, or the bottle whose arrival meant warm milk and comfort—they were already organizing their sensations, filing in their minds the discovery that certain collections of events tended to occur together, and that when this did happen, they could expect certain other occurrences to follow.

Not only was each such discovery an exciting revelation in itself, and a means of increasing control over their world, it also supplied them with material for making still more discoveries. Thus, having arrived at schemata for fingers and toes, they then found that these wiggly things were parts of themselves. A schema for a rubber duck, plus another schema of the bath as always including a rubber duck, helped them toward the realization that all those rubber ducks were in fact the same duck—an object that continued to exist from one bath to another, even though it was out of sight.

Perceptual discoveries go on throughout life. There are always new parts of the physical and social world to be located, identified, and connected with what is already known; and there are always new concepts, new understandings about relationships, to be built up on those physical discoveries. Though toddlers cannot yet essentially distinguish between things and their meaning, they are getting well into this process of discovery and construction. By one year of age they have a fairly clear notion of their own bodies. They can locate their own mouths accurately enough to feed themselves with a spoon—although they may not always hit the target on the first try. They have learned where their eyes, ears, and nose are, and they find these organs quite intriguing. They can scratch precisely at the place where they itch, and if something hurts, they have a pretty good idea of where it hurts. At this age many children have found their own genitals, and they may enjoy playing with them now and then.

Perception and Motor Development

As we noted, toddlers cannot yet really conceptualize a meaning or a relationship apart from the physical object or action that embodies it. Furthermore, their perceptual development is still closely linked to their motor de-

Providing children with a rich environment which they are free to experience is important for their psychological development.

velopment. Increased mobility exposes them to a larger environment, with more objects to perceive, more actions to perform, and hence more opportunity for schemata to be formed. Also, their ability to handle and manipulate objects is improving; this permits them to examine and experiment with objects more elaborately. For example, they become able to stack one block on top of another, and find this quite a delightful game; then, some months later, their control improves to the point where they can manage a six-block tower without toppling it, and this is even more fun.

The link between perception and motor development is so close that most tests of intelligence for infants and toddlers are based on measurements of motor skills. By measuring what children can do, we get an idea of what they are capable of understanding. For example, the Cattell Baby Test for children aged two to thirty-two months includes the following items: at three months, infants can follow an object being swung around their head, and at sixteen months they can put beads in a box. Another test, the Bayley Scale of Infant Development, provides an "age placement" for each of 163 items, referring to the age in months at which 50 percent of children can be expected to be capable of performing that particular task. The age placement for building a tower of two blocks is about fourteen months, that for reaching a toy with a stick is about seventeen months, and that for building a six-cube tower is about twenty-two or twenty-three months.

Perception and the Environment

We saw in our discussion of institutionalized children in Chapter 3 that when the young children's surroundings do not provide sufficient stimulation, their maturation may be retarded, sometimes even impairing their intelligence and mental health. A favorable environment, rich in intellectual as well as emotional stimulation, is therefore an important factor in full development of each child's potential.

The child's surroundings can be divided into a physical and psychological environment; but the two are closely interdependent, and nowhere is their interaction more evident than in matters of perceptual development. Even the adult personality undergoes profound and traumatic changes under conditions of sensory deprivation, as in imprisonment or isolation. This must hold true all the more for a small child, who has not yet built up the inner resources to counteract external deprivation.

From babyhood on, children avidly reach out for sensory experience and ways to integrate the perceptual stimuli they receive. This hunger for discovery grows along with them as they leave the crib and begin to crawl. By the time they reach the toddling stage, they are exploring the world every waking moment, disemboweling toys and furniture, emptying garbage pails and medicine cabinets, and eating thumbtacks, wallpaper, and detergents with equal relish.

Research suggests that the way in which the environment is structured by parents plays a major role in determining the extent of infants' and toddlers' exploratory behavior. One study (Belsky, Goode, & Most, 1980), for example, found that mothers who used more attention-focusing behaviors, such as pointing and highlighting, in interaction with their young children were more likely to enhance the children's exploratory behavior. This result is an example of a more general research finding indicating that children's emerging competence in the second and third years of life is strongly affected by the home environment and parental behaviors (Bradley, Caldwell, & Elardo, 1979; White & Watts, 1973).

Learning Theory

No one had to teach Annie how to blink or sneeze or cry. She was born with the ability to perform these reflex actions and with the tendency to perform them more or less automatically and involuntarily in response to certain stimuli—a flash of light, a tickling sensation, a pricking pin. Learning, however, is another matter. Annie was born with the rooting reflex that set her nuzzling about when her cheek touched her mother's breast, but she had to learn to interpret the cues she received so as to know where to search most efficiently for the nipple. Later she had to learn how to combine her swallowing reflex with the actions of biting and chewing in order to deal appropriately with such new foods as a bit of bread or fruit.

Learning theory describes the process by which a person acquires or modifies a pattern of behavior. It happens in response to specific circumstances (stimuli), which may or may not have been arranged on purpose. That is, it is a *person's reaction to an environment.*

It is important to remember both of the terms in this formula—*person* and *environment.* Much of the early research into human learning seemed to contain the underlying assumption that the environmental stimuli were all-important and the individual character of the learner rather unimportant. Yet when children are presented with a set of stimuli, all their previous experience affects the way they perceive it and the behavior by which they react to it. Think, for instance, of three individuals who suddenly become aware of a live garter snake at their feet. One person screams and flees; one jumps back and looks around for a rock to kill the snake; the third bends down to examine it, then picks it up with an "Isn't it cute?" sort of smile and allows it to coil comfortably around her wrist. The stimulus is the same for all, but evidently what has been learned from previous encounters with such stimuli is very different.

There is, of course, a great deal of interest in the question of how children learn; and despite individual differences certain general principles can be seen. It is apparent even to the casual observer, for example, that children frequently learn by doing what they have observed someone else do. Toddlers are particularly adept imitators. A little girl will cross her arms over her chest in an exact imitation of her mother; a little boy will "shave" with the precise strokes used by his father.

Classical Conditioning

Children learn not only by imitation but by a process known as **conditioning.** Two models of this type of learning—classical conditioning and operant conditioning—have been advanced.

In dogs salivation is a reflex or an unconditioned response to food. All dogs salivate when they start to eat. As discussed in the prologue the Russian physiologist Ivan Pavlov, working at the turn of the century, constructed an experiment in which he rang a bell every time he brought his dogs food. He *conditioned* the dogs to salivate at the sound of a bell—the first demonstration of what has come to be known as **classical conditioning.**

The same process can influence responses in humans. For example, some babies may cry as soon as they see the doctor because several times before the doctor stuck them with a needle. The neutral stimulus (the doctor) is associated with the unconditioned stimulus (the needle) again and again until the doctor alone evokes the same response (crying) as the needle.

But suppose the doctor has a potted plant on the window sill of the examining room. Will the baby become conditioned to fear potted plants as well as doctors? Not necessarily. Researchers have found that conditioning sometimes works differently with different stimuli. For example, in a 1929 experiment by Valentine (described in Scarf, 1974) a little girl just over a year old was shown an ornate pair of opera glasses. Each time she reached for

Toddlers sometimes learn new behaviors by observing and then imitating the actions of others.

them, she heard a harsh, startling blast on a whistle. Her response showed no sign of fear, either of the whistle or of the opera glasses. Later the same day the experiment was repeated with a new stimulus—a live "woolly bear" caterpillar. The results were dramatically different:

> She had seen such insects before, but had never touched one. She shifted away slightly, then turned back to look at it. At this moment her father blew a loud blast on the whistle. She screamed in terror and turned away from the insect.

The sequence was repeated several times, and each time the child showed fear. Something made it easier for her to become afraid of a furry, crawling live thing than of an inanimate tool. Some researchers think this may be a reflection of our evolutionary heritage: that is, during the millions of years our ancestors were evolving from apes to modern humans, it may have been very useful to be able to acquire certain fears quickly.

In summary, then, there are two aspects of classical conditioning that are important: (1) stimulus and response and (2) the subject.

Stimulus and Response

In a classical conditioning situation the subject "learns" to associate the real or *unconditioned* stimulus with the associated or *conditioned* stimulus. Thus, in Pavlov's experiment of food (unconditioned stimulus) becomes associated with the bell (conditioned stimulus), and the dog's response is to salivate at the ringing of the bell when the food is *not* present. We say the dog has become conditioned to the bell.

The Subject

In the classical situation the conditioning or environmental influence is paramount. The subjects learn, not by acting, but by being acted upon. However, there are great differences as to the effectiveness of different conditional stimuli in eliciting a conditioned response among infants and toddlers. They do not necessarily respond as do adults or animals. As we have seen with the opera glasses and furry caterpillars, the young human organism does not respond predictably or automatically. Furthermore, there are wide differences among small children as to with what stimuli their unconditioned responses can be effectively conditioned. Only by actual experiments can the factors affecting classical conditioning be determined (Fitzgerald & Brackbill, 1976).

Operant Conditioning

The discovery that responses could be predictably produced and altered—that behavior could be changed—ushered in a new era in the study of learning processes both in animals and in humans. In the 1930s B. F. Skinner formulated the learning model known as **operant conditioning.** One important difference between classical and operant conditioning is that in classical conditioning the subject's response follows the stimulus—the baby sees the doctor and then cries. In operant conditioning, on the other hand, the response precedes the reward—a rat presses a lever and then gets food. Gradually the sight of the lever becomes the stimulus and the food becomes the reward. Because the individual's behavior is instrumental in affecting the outcome, this kind of conditioning is also called **instrumental conditioning.**

A 1959 experiment (Rheingold, Gewirtz, & Ross) used operant conditioning to teach three-month-old infants to vocalize. The researcher immediately rewarded (reinforced) any random vocalization the infant made by smiles, pats on the tummy, and conversational cooings. In just six days of conditioning there was a measurable increase in vocalization. When the rewards were stopped, vocalization dropped back to its preexperimental level.

Operant conditioning depends more on what follows than what precedes it. As Skinner (1968) has written:

> Operant behavior, as I see it, is simply the study of what used to be dealt with by the concept of purpose. The purpose of an act is the consequences it is going to have. Actually, in the case of operant conditioning, we study the consequences an act has had in the past. Changes in the probability of response are brought about when an act is followed by a particular kind of consequence.

Reinforcement

The concept of **reinforcement** rests on the fundamental tenet of psychology that when behavior is followed by a desirable consequence, that behavior is likely to be repeated. Reinforcement motivates learning, first at home and later in social situations and at school. Lois invites Jimmy to take a turn riding her new tricycle because she has been praised many times for sharing.

Behavioral psychologists commonly use the term "stimulus" to refer to the conditions that are used in reinforcement. If behavior is followed by a pleasant stimulus, as in the Rheingold experiment described above, the reinforcement is *positive*. If the behavior is followed by the removal of an unpleasant stimulus, the reinforcement is *negative*. In general, reinforcement is most effective if it is intermittent—that is, if the behavior is reinforced most of the times, but not every time, that it occurs.

It is important to distinguish between negative reinforcement and punishment, two conditioning tools that are often confused. In **negative reinforcement** an unpleasant stimulus is *removed* in order to *encourage* a particular response. In **punishment** an unpleasant or painful stimulus is *applied* in order to *discourage* a given kind of behavior. In animal studies the difference is easy to see. For example, imagine a rat placed in a box with an electrified floor grid. Current is passed through the grid, shocking the rat. Eventually the rat learns that by doing some specific thing—perhaps tugging a string—it can stop the shock. The relief from shock is a negative reinforcement for the behavior of tugging the string. On the other hand, suppose another rat has to choose between two bars in its box. One bar, when pressed, yields a food pellet, the other a shock. In this case the shock is a punishment—it occurs as a consequence of the rat's behavior and serves to discourage the pressing of the wrong bar.

Punishment

Judging from animal studies, negative reinforcement seems in general to be more effective than positive reinforcement in establishing new behavioral responses. The trouble with trying to use this insight in teaching children is that it is hard to devise an initial unpleasant stimulus that will not be unfair or somehow harmful to the child, especially if the child catches on to the fact that it is deliberately imposed. This raises some questions. What is the aim of punishment? What forms of punishment are most effective? Under what circumstances does punishment bring about desired results? And what characteristics of the punisher are most effective? Punishment is a common but poorly understood means for bringing about desired behavior in children. The forms of punishment can range from a gentle reprimand to physical assault sufficiently severe to warrant the label "child abuse." In addition to verbal and physical punishment are the techniques of withdrawing such positive reinforcers as a favorite toy or a week's allowance. The withdrawal of affection or attention is an effective form of punishment, although such child psychotherapists as Chaim Ginott feel that love and respect toward a child should be unwavering; disapproval should be directed toward the offending behavior, not the child.

Physical Punishment

Experiments involving the use of physical punishment cannot, of course, be performed with children as subjects because of ethical considerations. However enough is known about the efficacy of various other forms of punishment to make the use of physical punishment "neither justified, desirable, nor necessary" (Parke, 1977). Although physical punishment may seem to be effective, there are too many undesirable side effects. Parke also speculates that an important reason for the immediate effectiveness of physical as well as verbal punishment is that punishment symbolizes to the child the withdrawal of love and respect. Bandura (1967) believes that the parent or teacher who uses physical punishment may unwittingly serve as an aggressive model to be imitated by the child. And, indeed, in one experiment (Gelfand et al., 1974) six- to eight-year-old children were exposed to rewarding, punishing, or unresponsive adults in learning a game involving marbles. These children were then given the chance to train other children in the game. As it turned out, most children used a training technique that was strikingly similar to the one they each had experienced. Physical punishment, then, is very likely to teach a child aggressive techniques as an unintended consequence.

In another experiment (Redd, Morris, & Martin, 1975) it was shown that children avoided the adult who employed punishment as a means of control. The punitive adult was better able to keep children working at a task than either a supportive or unresponsive adult. However, the children's avoidance of a person who resorts to punishment, especially physical punishment, as a technique will undermine that person's effectiveness as an influence in the future. When escape from a punishing adult is not possible, further punishment may lead to passivity and withdrawal, or the child may adapt to the punishment, rendering it ineffective.

Factors Affecting Punishment

Recently Ross D. Parke (1977) reviewed field and laboratory experiments with children that tested a variety of factors affecting punishment. The *timing* of punishment—that is, the length of time between the undesired action and the punishment—can make a difference. A number of studies (Parke & Walters, 1967; Cheyne & Walters, 1969) show that punishment is more effective the sooner it follows the undesired action. *Intensity* increases the effectiveness of punishment—in animal studies, when electric shock is used. With children, however, intensity may produce such a high level of anxiety that the child cannot engage in the learning process necessary to inhibit the undesired behaviors.

Another variable is the *nature of the behavior* shown by the socializing agent. Studies (Sears, Maccoby, & Levin, 1957) show that the more affectionate and nurturant the teacher or parent, the more effective he or she will be as a punishment agent.

Reasoning—that is, providing a rationale with the punishment—is another important factor (LaVoie, 1973; Parke & Murray, 1971). Given a reason for the desired behavior, children respond more effectively and continue to exhibit the desired behavior for a longer period than they do in response to any other factor mentioned. The reasons given, however, must match the intellectual level of the child. Young children understand an object-oriented appeal—that is, an admonition that is concrete and related to the physical

Some child development specialists feel that disapproval should be directed toward the offending behavior, not the child.

consequences of an action. ("Don't touch the toy. It is fragile and might break.") Children five years and older respond to rules, such as a property rule. ("Don't touch that toy. It belongs to John.") An empathetic appeal ("I will be very unhappy if you touch that toy") is relatively ineffective with young children. Short explanations are more effective than long ones. And finally, inconsistent punishment is less effective than punishment that is consistent. Inconsistency confuses the learning process. Furthermore, the adult who uses punishment inconsistently builds up a resistance in the child to future attempts to suppress or extinguish undesirable behavior by later, consistently administered punishment (Deur & Parke, 1970).

The Child as Participant

The recipient of these variously administered punishments, the child, does not remain a passive participant. Children modify the behavior of adult socializers in regard to the punishment meted out. In one study (Parke & Sawin, 1975) it was found that children who offered reparations for offending behavior

("I'll clean it up") were likely to receive the least amount of punishment, whereas those who acted in a defiant fashion would receive the most. In a related study (Parke et al., 1974) children were asked to predict the reaction of a teacher to a child's response to a reprimand. Even four-year-olds have well-defined and accurate ideas about the various ways an adult will react to different responses of children to reprimands: children expect defiance to lead to more punitiveness than either pleading for mercy or making reparations. This knowledge on the part of the children no doubt leads to inconsistent behavior on the part of socializing adults. Who can resist the child who smiles and says, "I'm sorry. I'll fix it." In order to maintain consistency teachers and parents may need to improve their understanding of the tactics children use to mitigate expected punishment.

Alternatives to Punishment

What other techniques for controlling undesirable behavior are available as alternatives to any punishment at all? In one study (Perry & Parke, 1975) children who were prohibited from playing with a toy were provided with a less attractive toy. They touched the prohibited toy less when the alternative toy was provided. Thus, a prosocial alternative can be provided to reduce prohibited behavior. Similarly, reinforcing children for behavior such as cooperation and helpfulness which is incompatible with aggression will reduce such undesirable behavior. In one study (Brown & Elliot, 1965) nursery-school teachers were asked to ignore aggressive behavior and to encourage the alternatives. A marked reduction of aggression in the classroom was the result. Even speaking in a soft and quiet manner can reduce aggression without resorting to punishment of any kind. As Parke (1977) points out, although socialization implies control, children must be viewed and treated as self-respecting and self-determining human persons, when evaluating the goals and techniques for influencing their behavior.

COGNITION AND LANGUAGE

When asked to tell a story, a two-year-old replied with the following tale:

> About a girl. I think she was frightened by a rabbit. In the woods. He was eating carrots. The rabbit ate the girl up. Then a fox came out. The fox bited the rabbit. A witch was coming. She stole the bunny ... First they catch the witches and then they put them in jail. That's all. (Ames & Ilg, 1976)

From such a story one may wonder what is going on in the head of the toddler. Just how do toddlers view the world around them? And what are the processes that help to shape their view of the world?

Cognition is learning and knowing. It is the concept that is concerned with what goes on in the human mind. The study of cognition in very young children is still fairly new. Although Jean Piaget published his first studies of children's cognitive development in the period from 1923 to 1932, most of the work on cognition has been done since 1960. Piaget regards cognition as one kind of biological adaptation—the organism's constant effort to bring about a harmonious interaction between its own schemata and the environment. It is a "system of living and acting operations" that strives for equilibrium, or a balancing between what the individual already knows and what the individual perceives in the world (Piaget, 1950).

LATER STAGES OF SENSORIMOTOR INTELLIGENCE

According to Piaget, the toddler is in the last phases of the sensorimotor period. As we saw in Chapter 3, by the end of the first year most children have already passed through four of the six stages Piaget discerns in this earliest period of cognitive development. From a few reflex behavior patterns, an unfocused curiosity, and the vaguest of perceptions of the world, infants have progressed to well-developed schemas of self and other people, and to a growing recognition of relatively permanent objects outside themselves. They have also gained considerable skill in handling objects and responding appropriately to events that happen around them. They have begun to understand spoken language and to experiment with using it themselves.

One-year-old children show deliberate intention in their activity—they do things because they want to produce certain results. They are becoming aware of the world as a place where things happen independently of themselves. At the same time they are finding that many events are predictable, and they are learning to anticipate some of them. Their understanding of objects and their movements is becoming more accurate. Most striking of all, they are developing great skill at imitating the behavior of those around them; their games with adults and others are livelier and more exploratory. These all set the scene for the next two stages of cognitive development.

Tertiary Circular Reactions

The fifth stage—from about the twelfth through the eighteenth month—has been called "the climax of the sensorimotor period" (Ginsburg & Opper, 1979). All the cognitive abilities of earlier stages are now expanded and applied to increasingly complex situations. Children become systematic in their explorations of the environment. They are ready to try novel solutions to problems and to learn by trial and error. For the first time they show curiosity about an object for its own sake and seem intent on learning everything they can about it. In this stage the exploration of novelty is an end in itself.

Piaget observed that his son Laurent, while playing with a soap dish, accidentally dropped it. The novelty of the situation immediately caught the child's interest, and he set about repeating the event, dropping the soap dish several times in succession. Within a few days he began dropping a variety of things—the soap dish, a celluloid swan, a bit of bread—from different heights and onto different surfaces—his pillow, the mattress. He seemed to be studying the effects of the different ways of dropping and the different behavior of each object as it landed. Instead of simply repeating an observed event, he was deliberately seeking new ways to vary and experiment with the phenomenon.

At this stage children have enough understanding of the behavior of objects even to devise completely new means to reach a desired goal. When Lucienne was one year and five days old, Piaget arranged the following problem for her: a pivoting box was placed on a table, and atop the box, just out of her reach, was a toy bottle. In Piaget's own words:

> Lucienne at first tries to grasp the box, but she goes about it as though the handkerchief were still involved [Grasping a handkerchief was a previous problem.] She tries to pinch it between two fingers, in the center, and tries this for a moment without being able to grasp it. Then, with a rapid and unhesitating movement she pushes it at a point on its right edge. . . . She then notes the sliding of the box and makes a pivot without trying to lift it; as the box revolves, she succeeds in grasping the bottle (Piaget, 1952).

At first the child attempted to pinch the box, a maneuver she had used successfully to obtain the handkerchief. Then, by trial and error, she discovered a new method. By pushing the box, Lucienne managed to bring the bottle closer. Her actions were directed both by the goal and by previous schemata that gave her an understanding of what was happening.

Piaget applies the label "tertiary circular reaction" to this behavior. As we saw earlier, much of the behavior of young children is circular: they want to repeat an action that has already given pleasure. Primary circular reactions involve repeating an action—such as opening and closing the fist—solely for its own sake. Secondary circular reactions involve a second dimension—chil-

---

Piaget's Periods of Cognitive Development

SENSORIMOTOR PERIOD (BIRTH TO 24 MONTHS)

Stage 1 (birth to 1 month)
Stage 2 (1 to 4 months)
Stage 3 (4 to 8 months)
Stage 4 (8 to 12 months)
Stage 5 (**12 to 18 months**). Perception and behavior become more exploratory and experimental. Discovers new ways to solve problems and attain goals. Begins to understand that external objects have independent existence.
Stage 6 (**18 to 24 months**). Beginning of imagination and speech.

PREOPERATIONAL PERIOD (2 TO 7 YEARS)

PERIOD OF CONCRETE OPERATIONS (7 TO 11 YEARS)

PERIOD OF FORMAL OPERATIONS (11 YEARS ON)

dren learn that their actions have particular results, and they obtain gratification from repeating the actions and observing those results. Tertiary, or
third-level, circular reactions bring a third factor into play. Children are grat-
ified by the result of their actions, and in addition they intentionally search
for *novel* ways of bringing about the same result. At this stage, and for the first
time in their lives, children deliberately try to do things in new ways. They
appreciate novelty, and they find it in new and creative forms of play.

The Beginning of Symbolic Thought

Now we have reached a great divide—the transition to deliberate symbolic
thought.

Until now the child's mental processes have manifested themselves entirely through actions. So far as we know, children have had no way of mentally
symbolizing an action without actually performing it, or imagining an object
present when it is not. Their world has included no "as if" dimension (at least

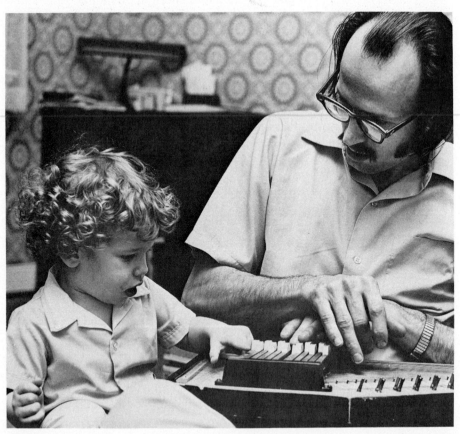

According to Piaget, exploration becomes an end in itself between the twelfth and
eighteenth months as children become more curious about new objects.

not in waking thought; they do dream, and this is an area that calls for further study).

All this changes during the mental revolution that takes place in the sixth stage, which occurs from about eighteen months to two years: children gain the ability to imagine things. This amounts to no less than a change to a higher plane of reality—the one on which they will spend the rest of their lives. Now they are capable of thought that transcends the immediate situation.

This really enormous change often first appears in play. A child may be engaged in the enjoyable game of throwing alphabet blocks out of the playpen, one by one, for Mommy to pick up and bring back. One day, quite suddenly, this familiar pastime may take on a new dimension that will cause Mommy to catch her breath: this time, when the last block is thrown out, the game does not end. Without breaking the rhythm of his movements the toddler once more bends down with an outstretched hand, straightens up, lifts his arm and throws—an *imaginary* block.

Piaget describes his play with Lucienne when she is one year and four months of age. The girl is playing with one of her usual toys, her father's watch chain. Piaget now takes the chain from her, places it in a matchbox, and closes the opening of the box to a narrow slit. Lucienne does not yet know about opening and closing the box, but she has played with the box and chain before. Up to now she could always get the chain out, either by turning the box over or by reaching inside with her fingers.

> It is of course this last procedure that she tries first: she puts her finger inside and gropes to reach the chain, but fails completely. A pause follows during which Lucienne manifests a very curious reaction.... She looks at the slit with great attention; then, several times in succession, she opens and shuts her mouth, at first slightly, then wider and wider! [Then] ... Lucienne unhesitatingly puts her finger in the slit, and instead of trying as before to reach the chain, she pulls so as to enlarge the opening. She succeeds and grasps the chain (Piaget, 1952).

Lucienne has solved the watch-chain problem—not by trial and error, as she has done before, but by *thinking* of a solution. She is only a beginner at this business of symbolic thought, and she is not yet able to carry out the whole process in her head. Thus, she works out the problem partly by physical means—she opens and closes her mouth to help her imagine opening the box. The physical movement is still, for her, part of the intellectual process. But already she has made a tremendous advance over her earlier ways of thinking. From now on the history of Lucienne's intellectual growth will be a chronicle of genuinely symbolic, imaginative mental activity.

This totally new dimension of cognitive functioning—imagination—quickly enters into all the child's activities. From now on when children confront a problem, they are no longer limited to trial and error to find the solution. They need not immediately charge into action. They can, though on a primitive level at first, do what an adult can do when solving a problem. They can envision a solution first and then act to bring about the result anticipated in their imagination.

Children begin to think in symbolic terms when they can envision a solution to a problem before acting upon it.

Imitation, which becomes so important in language acquisition, is an aspect of learning and cognition that interested Piaget. In his book *Play, Dreams and Imitation in Childhood* (1962), he notes that in modes of imitation a revolutionary change occurs at the beginning of symbolic thought (sixth stage). The child is able to imitate a situation that occurred at a previous time. Piaget calls this *deferred imitation*. As he says, "the child is no longer dependent on the actual action . . . and becomes capable of imitating internally." This is one of the examples Piaget gave of deferred imitation—imitation produced from a remembered model.

> When Jacqueline was a year and four months old, she was visited by a little boy a year and six months old. In the course of the afternoon he got into a terrible temper. He screamed as he tried to get out of a playpen and pushed it backwards, stamping his feet. Jacqueline stood watching him in amazement, never having witnessed such a scene before. The next day, she herself screamed in her playpen and tried to move it, stamping her foot lightly several times in succession (Piaget, 1962, p. 63).

Jacqueline represented the temper tantrum in her mind to the extent that she could reproduce it herself at a later time. As her father said, "The imitation of the whole scene was striking." This accomplishment is indeed a major step beyond merely perceiving and imitating. It is the beginning of symbolic or representational thought. Deferred imitation as a first step toward symbolic thought frees the child's mind from dependence on the "here and now" and allows for a more flexible adaptation to the world.

Piaget called the next major period in the development of cognitive functioning the "preoperational" period. This period, which starts at about the age of two and ends around seven, will be discussed in later chapters. Piaget points out, however, that sensorimotor cognition does not stop when a child reaches the second birthday; much of the behavior associated with it continues long afterward.

Piaget also recognizes that the development of each new stage is gradual and that the age of its appearance varies from child to child, depending on environment as well as on the child's own potential for cognitive growth. It is not surprising, then, to find other researchers suggesting, on the basis of various data, that some abilities begin to take shape long before the age with which they are commonly associated. Some researchers think that children may begin to form hypotheses before they are a year old. Kagan (1972) cites a number of studies, such as one which showed that older infants experienced a greater degree of deceleration in heart rate than younger infants when confronted with discrepant stimuli—in this case meaningless speechlike sounds after several repetitions of a meaningful phrase. Such deceleration in heart rate is known to occur when active mental work is going on, and Kagan suggests that the older infants are actively working on the sounds, trying out possible explanations for the discrepancy.

The point at which certain cognitive abilities develop may be an issue; however it is essential to Piaget's theory that the stages always occur in the same order. This may not have much practical importance in infancy and toddlerhood, when cognitive development is very rapid, but it can make a crucial difference in planning curricula during the school years. Pupils may skip grades, but they cannot skip a stage of development, and instructors can take advantage of this knowledge by adapting their materials and methods to the way the child learns at each age.

Cognition and Thought

It would seem that the modes of cognition—remembering, imagining, and reasoning—are abilities that develop as a person makes the transition to symbolic thought. Yet Piaget describes the infant's earliest mental activities as cognitive processes, although he does not believe that symbolic thought begins until about age two. How can there be cognition before there is some form of symbolic thought—some means by which children can represent to themselves what it is that they know?

As Piaget sees it, children's cognition before they develop the capacity for symbolic thought is entirely on the sensorimotor level. Every mental process is a response to some present physical stimulation, either from outside—holding a toy, being fed, or tickled—or from inside—hunger or a need for the physical contact supplied by cuddling. We can understand Piaget's position more clearly if we look for a moment at the biological principles involved in cognition.

Biological scientists do not yet understand all of the brain's workings, but they have traced some general patterns. There are certain areas of the

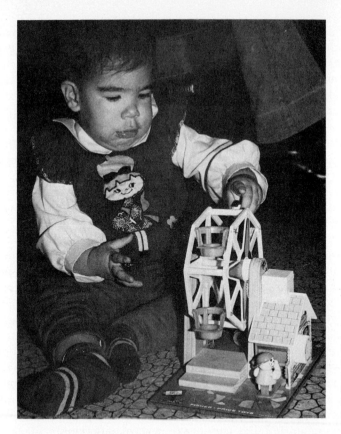

According to Piaget, children's cognition occurs entirely on the sensorimotor level before they develop the capacity for symbolic thought.

brain where incoming sensory impulses are received, sorted, and coordinated. Other areas store the huge amount of information received. Cognition might be described as the process by which the brain registers and files all this information. But although the brain apparently takes in and stores great quantities of information, only a small fraction of this is ever readily available to our immediate consciousness. The rest stays with us and is added to continuously throughout our lives, but we cannot "think" about it.

LANGUAGE

Before the end of the first year children have begun to understand words and to try to use them. They already understand a good deal more language than they can produce, and through prelinguistic sounds and gestures have become effective communicators with their parents (Harding & Golinkoff, 1979). During the second year, however, the gap between comprehension and performance begins to narrow, but it will never be fully closed—we always continue to understand more words than we use. For example, by the age of two the average toddler understands 200 words or so, but speaking vocabulary still lags behind by a wide margin.

It seems almost as if the knowledge of words brings with it a magical control over the environment. One observer (Fraiberg, 1959) notes that children's mastery of the expression "bye-bye" very often coincides with much easier acceptance of their parents' departures. Similarly, acquisition of the phrase "night-night" seems to make the nightly ordeal of having to go to bed a little more bearable.

A somewhat similar control of consequences through words can be observed in the toddler happily scribbling on the nursery wall to the accompaniment of rhythmic head-shaking and the incantation of "no-no, no-no." Out of such rote repetition there gradually emerges a better understanding of the meaning behind the words. A few weeks later the toddler may again approach the wall, with crayons, utter "no-no," and sadly turn away.

Language Acquisition

When we think of learning a language, our thoughts may run to vocabulary tests, conjugating French verbs, or listening to Italian tapes in the language lab. For infants or toddlers language learning is both simpler and more complex. It is simpler because they are relating each new word directly to an experienced object, action, or quality—not to a word in another language *about* that action, or quality. It is more complex because they are not merely learning a new language, they are learning "language" itself. They are learning the grammar of Spanish, Ute, or English, but at the same time they are learning something far more fundamental—the "rule-ness" of grammar itself. We call this unique process **language acquisition**.

Acquiring language transforms the child's world in many ways. Having a verbal label to attach to an experience makes that experience easier to remember and easier to deal with. In fact, one reason most of us fail to remember much of what happened to us in our earliest years may be that we had not learned to use such verbal labels. We had nothing to file away in our memories as a coded symbol of the experience.

One of the things forgotten from that early period is just how we ourselves learned to use language. In Chapter 3 we noted that a number of universal factors have been found to operate in children's language acquisition. Studies (Brown, 1970; Slobin, 1973; and Ervin-Tripp, 1973) further indicate that the stages children go through while progressing from baby talk to adult communication are roughly identical, regardless of native tongue, socioeconomic class, and ethnic background. In addition, it seems that children everywhere talk about the same things while undergoing these developmental stages. They all speak of objects and situations; they make demands; they use mostly nouns and verbs; they talk *to* themselves a great deal but never *about* themselves or their relationship with others.

One-Word Utterances

For the first few months after they begin using language, children's utterances generally consist of single words most of which are concrete nouns and verbs

As children acquire language, they relate each new word directly to what they are experiencing. At about eighteen months, a child may begin to combine two words, such as "see kitty."

(Moskowitz, 1978). But these are not used merely for single-word purposes; children employ them to express what an adult would express by whole sentences. "Dada" may be only a verbal "pointing at" Daddy right there in the living room, but it may also, in other circumstances, mean "Where's Daddy?" or "Daddy's coming." The toddler may say "Cup!" and mean "See my cup!" or "I want a cup of milk, not this nasty old spinach," or "That thing there in the big window looks just like my cup at home." Such speech, in which one word functions as a whole sentence, is called *holophrastic* speech.

What children are thinking when they use such speech is another question, and the experts disagree as to the answer (see Dale, 1976). Some, pointing out that children at this stage can understand simple sentences, maintain that the child is actually thinking of something like a full sentence but does not have the vocabulary to produce it. Others doubt this or simply say that we do not have enough evidence to draw conclusions. What we do know, though, is that as soon as children move into the next stage, they begin to put words together in a primitive, but definitely structured, sentencelike way.

Two-Word Sentences

At around eighteen months the infant emerges from the stage in which a single word stands for a whole sentence. Now two words are used in combination to convey meaning. The sequence of the words is that of adult speech, but the intermediate words are missing. The infant is evidently trying to imitate adult language, but at this stage of cognitive development cannot yet reproduce it completely or accurately.

One researcher (Braine, 1963) who observed the emergence of two-word sentences in his own children has divided this embryonic grammar into two classes of words: *pivots* (or operators) and *X words*. Pivots are words that are singled out for constant repetition in any number of combinations; then, after a time, a particular pivot seems to have been practiced enough and is replaced by a new one. X words are all other words at the child's command. They do not occur as often or persistently as pivots, nor are they necessarily part of a combination. Pivots are always used in combination and are always used in the same position, either initial or final.

The researcher's son Gregory provided an example of pivots and X words in action. His third word combination happened to be "see hat," which was followed by "see sock," "see horsie," and "see boy." "See" was the first word in most of his early word combinations. Other general pivot favorites are "my," "pretty," "allgone," and "more." The word "more" can have especially wide applications, such as "more Grampa?" on meeting the second set of grandparents.

As the above examples indicate, most pivots are not nouns, whereas most X words are nouns. In the next phase of two-word sentence construction X words become more important, and an increasing number of the two-word units consist of nouns in both first and second position, such as "Daddy office."

Researchers often refer to these short sentences as *telegraphic speech*. In telegraphic speech the child uses a "stripped-down" form of the language. Such words as "the," "a," "for," "to"—all the articles, modifiers, and prepositions, in fact—are disregarded. A two-word sentence, together with the variety of intonations that the toddler has learned to use comfortably, can carry a surprising amount of meaning. By age two most children are fluent in these two-word sentences; multiword sentences, however, do not usually come until a little later.

Complete Sentences

Beyond this point in the child's linguistic development there is no single accepted theory. Experts are sharply divided as to what accounts for the development of the ability to form complete, grammatical sentences. One researcher (Slobin, 1968) sees the explanation in a combination of reinforcement, expansion, and imitation. For example, the sound of the starting car centers the toddler's attention on his father's usual morning departure. He says, "Daddy office." His mother nods smiling (reinforcement) and replies, "Yes, Daddy has gone to the office" (expansion). The same situation is likely to occur again the next morning and the next; and with each repetition of this playful sequence associated with his mother's smiling face, the child comes closer to the realization that the idea "Daddy office" should be expressed as

A toddler's two-word sentence can take on many shades of meaning with the aid of intonations and gestures.

"Daddy has gone to the office." Since he loves to imitate her, he will shortly switch from his version to hers.

A very different view is expressed by other psycholinguists. One investigator (Brown, 1966), on the basis of his own longitudinal studies, points out that what parents reinforce is not grammatical accuracy but factual accuracy. For example, when one child said, "Mamma isn't a boy. He is a girl," the answer was "That's right." The child used the wrong pronoun but mother knew what she meant, and what she meant was true. (Brown, 1966). Brown argues that children acquire correct grammar quite early despite lack of reinforcement—indeed, parents often seem rather to reinforce the errors of repeating their offspring's "cute" mistakes.

Language and Grammar

The concept of grammatical speech is the very cornerstone of language learning. Without it we might know the meanings of any number of words, but we could not put them together to form meaningful utterances beyond the very simplest level. The rules of **grammar** and **syntax** govern the ways in which the parts of language are put together to create meaningful sentences.

We are all in the habit of using reasonable grammatical speech, and we can usually tell whether a speaker is using correct or incorrect grammar. We can pick up the grammatical signals that tell us that a significant word is being used quite differently in the following two sentences:

> This is the season for softshell crabs.
> Ignore him; he crabs like that all the time.

But just because we usually take grammar for granted, few of us have a clear idea of precisely what it involves.

The basic sound components of any language are **phonemes**. The English language uses about forty-five different phonemes. Examples are the "b," "e," and "d" of "bed." If we change one phoneme, we get a different word— "red," for example, or "bad." The phonemes of a language are the contrasting units that allow us to tell the difference in meaning between one utterance and another. They are analogous to, but not identical with, the sounds associated with the letters of the alphabet.

To make a language phonemes must be arranged into larger units called **morphemes.** A morpheme is the smallest part of a word that conveys meaning, and it cannot be further subdivided without destroying meaning. Thus, some morphemes are in effect words ("bed," "work"); these are called *free morphemes* because they can be used by themselves. However, if we add anything to alter their meaning in any way, we create words consisting of two morphemes rather than one ("beds," "worked"). Because these endings are not meaningful unless combined with a free morpheme, they are called *bound morphemes.*

Children's initial words are free morphemes; then, as they progress to longer sentences, they also learn to make use of the bound morphemes to give their speech more precision. They begin to differentiate "cup" and "cups," "walk" and "walked," "Daddy" and "Daddy's," according to the rules that govern such usage in the language of the people they hear. Long before children ever hear of nouns and verbs, plurals, tenses, and modifiers, they begin to develop a sense of practical, working grammar.

The linguist Noam Chomsky has given special attention to the grammar of English and other languages. Chomsky (1957) has pointed out that language seems to function on two different levels. In any language, a sentence can be assigned a *deep structure* and a *surface structure.* For example, compare these sentence pairs:

> The mother holds the baby.
> The baby is held by the mother.
>
> Jack does not like crying babies.
> Jack does not like diapering babies.

In this sample the sentences in the first pair have very different surface structures, but they share an identical deep structure; they "mean" the same thing. On the other hand, the sentences in the second pair, which have nearly identical surface structures, have very different deep structures and hence different meaning.

The deep structure of a sentence—what we would usually think of as the "idea" of the sentence—is translated, or transformed, into surface structure (a grammatical string of words) by applying a set of rules. Chomsky calls these rules transformational rules, and his theory is called a theory of *transformational grammar*. Although we use these rules constantly, we rarely if ever express them formally. Nevertheless, they are part of the intellectual equipment of every person who speaks a language. Thus, what the toddler learns in language acquisition is vocabulary plus syntax—the units of language plus the rules for making, recognizing, and understanding any grammatical sentence.

Theories of Language Learning

How do we learn to speak grammatically? Every theory that has been advanced to explain language acquisition has been severely criticized. The question of

As children use longer sentences, they begin to develop a sense of grammar, which gives their speech more precision.

language learning is fiercely debated today, with almost every conceivable position finding its champion; data from anthropology, biology, psychology, linguistics, and even mathematics are cited as evidence for each theory. We will not try to choose between them but simply set forth the main lines of reasoning.

One group of researchers, following what is commonly called the *empiricist* approach, emphasizes reinforcement and imitation in language acquisition. The empiricist position is closely associated with the behaviorist learning theories of psychologists C. L. Hull and B. F. Skinner. In *Verbal Behavior* (1957) Skinner tried to explain all language as simply a special form of behavior that could be accounted for entirely in terms of stimulus and response. As the title suggests, language is to be regarded as essentially a set of habits that the child learns in adaptation to outside circumstances. Language originates as behavior aimed at obtaining food, comfort, and other things needed, and it never loses this basic character no matter how elaborate it becomes. However, this is where the theory runs into trouble: how children can make up sentences they have never heard before (as all children do) is difficult to explain by the empiricist approach.

One empiricist (Mowrer, 1960) has introduced the concept of *mediation* in an effort to bridge the gap between simple conditioning and the creative use of language. Mediation is a rather complicated concept to explain in full, but in a general sense it says that when there is some behavioral element common to two situations, what is learned in one situation may be transferred to the other, even without any specific conditioning. Usually this is understood to mean two concrete situations, such as two maze-learning problems for a rat; however, it is quite possible that one of the "situations" could involve language rather than a concrete action. According to this modification of the empiricist theory it is by mediation that we understand the symbolic significance of words and sentences and use them freely and expressively.

Many psychologists vigorously oppose the empiricist viewpoint. Followers of Freud, Piaget, and Erikson, for example, point out that Hull and Skinner used animals as subjects for most of their experiments, and they question how a theory derived from such experiments can be applied to human behavior. They hold that human thought and learning are too complex and subtle to be completely explained by reinforcement theory, even if it is modified by bringing in supplementary concepts such as mediation.

Noam Chomsky, whose theory of transformational grammar we discussed in the previous section, has prompted many researchers to focus their attention on how the child acquires linguistic *rules*. Are humans born with a natural, innate tendency to acquire language—a "language-acquisition device"? If so, what processes activate the tendency and expand the child's linguistic capability? Here we come to Chomsky's most radical contribution to the theory of language learning: his belief that the infant has a basic sense of grammar. According to Chomsky (1968), this sense of grammar is innate and is present in children long before they begin to make any visible use of it.

This so-called *rationalist* approach of Chomsky and others questions the ability of empiricist theory to explain language development. This position is also referred to as *nativist* because of its claim that the ability to learn and use language is innate, or native, to the human brain. Support for the nativist position comes from many sources. One theorist (Miller, 1964) points out that "the magnitude of the learning task and the speed with which children accomplish it [are] impressive arguments that children must be naturally endowed with a remarkable predisposition for language learning." Another theorist (Lenneberg, 1964a) has listed some biological facts which suggest that language ability may have evolved as a uniquely human trait. For example, children of all cultures learn language at about the same age and tend to learn it in similar ways. Our tendency to learn language is so strong that many learn it despite blindness or deafness. In addition, a number of "language universals" have been dicovered independently by different linguists (Chomsky, 1957; Greenberg, 1963). As one rationalist (Lenneberg, 1964) has said, "although language families are so different, one from the other, that we cannot find any historical connection between them, every language, without exception, is based on the same universal principles of semantics, syntax, and phonology."

The conclusion of the nativists is that these universal principles are built right into the human brain in the form of what Chomsky calls an "innate schema." This allows children to hear and absorb language as it is spoken by themselves and others and to sort out the bits and pieces of speech into a formal system, even without explicit instruction. Speakers may never even be conscious that they are speaking a language according to a set of rules but, according to Chomsky, "It seems plain that language acquisition is based on the child's discovery of what from a formal point of view is a deep and abstract theory—a generative grammar of his language...." This theory has an advantage over the empiricist view in that it takes into account the fact that normal language use is creative, innovative, and appropriate to its social context (Chomsky, 1965). According to the nativist view, it is the mastery of grammar that makes these qualities possible, and the basic rules of grammar exist in the brain before language is learned, waiting to be activated by learning and experience.

A number of researchers (Berko, 1958; Brown & Fraser, 1963; Ervin, 1964) have accepted the major aspects of nativist theory but have remolded it in important ways. The result is what is called the *rule-learning* approach, which attempts to modify nativism in a way that accepts the importance of imitation, maturation, and comprehension. These researchers point out that, ironically, the correct use of language by children is not good evidence that they are using (or understanding) grammar; they may say "I saw it" rather than "I seed it" because they have been taught to say that particular sentence correctly or because they are imitating an adult. Brown and Fraser suggest that the best evidence that children are using a grammar to produce sentences is the occurrence of systematic *errors* in their speech:

> So long as a child speaks correctly, it is possible that he says only what he has heard. In general we cannot know what the total input has been and so cannot

Humans appear to be born with a natural, innate tendency to acquire language. Linguists theorize that toddlers also have a "sense of grammar" which is applied to the language of their culture.

eliminate the possibility of an exact model for each sentence that is put out. However, when a small boy says, "I digged in the yard" or "I saw some sheeps" or "Johnny hurt hisself," it is unlikely that he is imitating.

These researchers tried to determine the actual, as opposed to the ideal, grammatical rules used by young children by observing children's systematic errors and their use of made-up words. They concluded that quite early in their language learning children infer general grammatical rules from the language around them. The first rules are simple, forming a "provisional grammar" that is actually a simplification of adult grammar. The children then apply these rules to all cases, *regularizing* irregular forms to fit the pattern they think should apply to all language. Gradually, with age, maturation, and experience, the child's grammar becomes more detailed and complete and finally becomes quite similar to adult grammar.

Language and Thought

Reformers recognize that to change people's attitudes we often have to change their use of language. The women's movement, believing that traditional at-

Talking Apes

The origins of spoken language go back about 40,000 years. Verbal communication and the conceptual apparatus for conscious reasoning that accompanies it are usually considered unique to the human species. Since 1966, however, nonhuman primates—usually chimpanzees—have been communicating effectively with their trainers. It was in that year that R. Allen and Beatrice Gardner, animal behaviorists, succeeded in teaching a female chimpanzee, Washoe, to "speak" American Sign Language, or Ameslan, the primary language of the deaf in North America. Five years later Washoe had a vocabulary of 160 words and was sent with her assistant trainer, Dr. Roger Fouts, to the University of Oklahoma, where she became one of the first "fellows" of the Institute for Primate Studies. Here and at other centers interspecies communication is still being studied—and practiced.

The "languages" that the primate subjects at various centers are being taught are principally of two types: American Sign Language (ASL) and Yerkish. The latter is a picture language printed on a sort of electric typewriter. Chimps learn to punch the appropriate keys to signal their needs and also to read messages that researchers type on another keyboard. Yerkish is so-called because it was invented at the Yerkes Primate Center in Atlanta, where Duane Rumbaugh leads the chimpanzee-communication project. Dialogues in Yerkish have lasted as long as thirty minutes. American Sign Language is the more common of the two primate communication media. Since 1972 Francine Patterson has been working intensively at Stanford University with a gorilla named Koko. Patterson has taught Koko much as one teaches handicapped children, by putting their hands through motions that signify a word till the meaning is learned. The gorilla now uses more than 250 signs in one hour and responds to spoken words also. Koko can put words together in grammatically and syntactically correct order and can use words to signal her understanding of sameness and difference. She can use "if . . . then" constructions and can express moods, desires, and anticipation of future events. While playing, she signals to herself or her dolls, and she seems to have an awareness of herself that extends to her mirror image.

These and other feats of interspecies communication, such as successful programs in communication with dolphins, have prompted linguists, psychologists, and animal behaviorists to re-evaluate the traditional views of language. With this often disturbing and revolutionary data in hand, scientists are asking the age-old questions in new ways. What is language? Is it only speech, and is it unique to human beings? What made language come into being in the first place, and why is what we call "verbal communication" apparently the province of human beings alone? The answers are not in yet, but theorists have already arrived at some important, though hotly disputed hypotheses.

Language is more than speech, for it involves such complex intellectual processes as the ability to receive as well as to send messages, the capacity to transform visual stimuli into auditory ones, and the comprehension and manipulation of units of sound and of meaning (Linden, 1975). Tone and gesture are important parts of language, and speech is only one part of communication—a process that is practiced by animals (Midgeley, 1978). Chimps, after all, do learn to communicate with one another and with people. In fact, the only reason they don't speak in the conventional sense may be that they don't have sufficient control of their larynxes (Midgeley, 1978). Some theorists believe that spoken language came into being partly as a response to emergency and became the province of human beings because they were the fittest, in the Darwinian sense, to practice it (Linden, 1975).

Many theorists feel that people need to relearn the fact that we too are part of nature; we smell, feel, and move as animals do, and we may communicate in many of the same ways they do (Linden, 1975). There may even be direct connections between animal communication and human language (Midgeley, quoting Noam Chomsky) which, once discovered, will change our views of the nature of language and cognition forever.

titudes are tied to traditional terminology, works to change words, urging people to use such terms as "businessperson," "chairperson," and "Ms." in place of "businessman," "chairman," and "Miss/Mrs." The new usage is intended to redefine sex roles and thereby to hasten social progress. The use of new words to shape people's ideas about the roles of women and blacks in our society may owe something to a theory developed by two linguists: Edward Sapir and Benjamin Lee Whorf. The Sapir-Whorf hypothesis maintains that the grammatical structure of our language and the vocabulary we are taught determine the way we think.

After studying the languages of two very different cultures, the Hopi Indians and the Jivaro of South America, Whorf (1956) concluded that the language we use shapes our thinking and behavior. Before people can make sense of the millions of ideas and sensory experiences they are presented with daily, they must have some way of putting them in categories. It is one's culture that provides the categories. For instance, the English language has the category *bird*, which covers all kinds of birds. Some South American Indian languages lack the term *bird* but have words for specific kinds of birds. Eskimos have different words to describe different varieties of snow, whereas a typical New Yorker might see all snow as the same. Whorf said that every language contains concepts embodied in words and word patterns that are peculiarly its own, and this produces a special world view. According to his hypothesis, language determines the ways we think about such fundamental aspects of the world as time and space or cause and effect. Thus, as children learn their own language, they learn the world view of their society.

Whorf's hypothesis has been a fertile stimulus to further study of the relationship between language and culture. Does thought change language? Or does language change thought? Think of "moonwalk," "ecology," and "détente," which have become part of our vocabulary. In each case the idea came first, but the word, once in circulation, helps shape our further thinking.

Jean Piaget stands in opposition to the idea that language defines thought. Piaget writes, "Language is not enough to explain thought, because the structures that characterize thought have their roots in action and in sensor-motor mechanisms that are deeper than linguistics" (in Dale, 1976, p. 237). Thus, it is action that shapes thought; language is but the reflection of thought.

Lev Vygotsky (1962) also would agree with Piaget that thought does not derive from language, but his theory follows a different path. He postulates that thought and speech have different roots; that in every child there is both a preintellectual stage and prelinguistic stage; and that these two lines of development proceed independently of each other until the child is about two years old. At this time these two lines meet; thought becomes verbal and speech rational.

SUMMARY

▶ Toddlers grow more slowly than the young infant, but still rapidly. Their face and body proportions are beginning to change; the skeleton continues to harden; the nervous system, especially the brain, is maturing faster than any other part of toddlers.

▶ Motor skills depend on both learning and maturation. Children cannot perform any skill for which they are not physiologically ready, but they are eager to perform as soon as they are ready. Most children can stand alone by one year and walk alone a month or so later. By two they can run and jump, climb stairs, and manipulate crayons, book pages, and eating implements with some success.

▶ Sensory capacities are well developed in toddlers; their understanding of what they perceive must now grow by organization and learning. They need plenty of sensory stimulation and freedom to explore and experiment with the environment.

▶ Learning is the process by which a person acquires or modifies a pattern of behavior. What people learn depends not only on the stimulus but on the perceptual-motor abilities and the past experience of the learner. Much human learning takes place by imitation of others' actions.

▶ Conditioning is an important mode of learning. In classical conditioning the subject learns to associate a neutral stimulus (conditioned) with one that automatically evokes a certain response (unconditioned); the neutral stimulus thus comes to evoke the response. In operant conditioning the subject learns that performing a certain action will bring a predictable positive or negative reinforcement, and thus learns to perform or avoid the action accordingly.

▶ Punishment is one means of socialization and the control of children's behavior. The most effective punishment is verbal, delivered in a soft voice, accompanied by a short rationale, and administered by an affectionate and nurturant person. Physical punishment is always to be avoided because of deleterious side effects.

▶ In the fifth stage of the sensorimotor period—that of tertiary circular reactions—toddlers are interested in exploring novel situations and trying new ways of doing things. In the sixth and final stage they make the shift to the beginnings of symbolic thought. They become able to imagine what is not directly present and thus to envision a solution or plan a course of action, rather than working entirely by trial and error.

▶ During the second year the child begins to acquire language—not only the sounds and meanings of individual words, but the grammatical structure that makes possible complex, meaningful sentences. Much of this knowledge seems to be gained by imitation. The typical child goes from holophrastic, one-word utterances to telegraphic, two-word sentences and then to complete sentences.

▶ Although all children evidently acquire a working sense of grammar, there are various theories about how they do so. The empiricist approach emphasizes imitation and reinforcement and in its strictest form seeks to explain all language learning in terms of conditioning. Mowrer adds the concept of mediation to explain the development of more sophisticated speech.

▶ The rationalist or nativist approach of Chomsky and others, in opposition to the empiricist position, posits an innate "language-acquisition device," an inborn readiness to acquire grammar and symbolic meaning. A modification of the nativist theory is the rule-learning approach, which accounts for children's tendency to make mistakes by overregularizing their grammar at an early stage in language learning.

▶ Just as the ways of thought current in a society influence the form of its language, so the language we learn influences what we can think and how. The Sapir-Whorf hypothesis, in fact, maintains that our language rather narrowly limits our world view.

FURTHER READINGS

Ault, R. L. *Children's cognitive development. Piaget's theory and the process approach.* New York: Oxford University Press, 1977.
This book describes and compares Piaget's contributions to knowledge of cognitive development and recent research on information processing in children.
Clarke-Stewart, K. A. Popular Primers for Parents. *American Psychologist*, 1978, 33, #4 Pp. 359–370.
This article describes the extent and characteristics of the audience for popular

child-care manuals. The author comments on why parents seek advice of experts and the shortcomings of that advice.

Dale, Philip S. *Language development: Structure and function* (2nd ed.). New York: Holt, Rinehart and Winston, 1976.

A survey of research and current thinking in the field. The author considers development of meaning, syntax, and sound; discusses the functions of language and its relation to cognitive development; and considers the effects of factors such as dialect differences, which can have such practical importance for teachers when children reach school age. Brief readings from the works of major writers in the field are included in many chapters.

de Villiers, Peter A., and de Villiers, Jill G. *Early language.* Cambridge, Mass.: Harvard University Press, 1979.

These experts in child language make use of delightful excerpts from childrens' speech as they describe the process by which children learn a language.

The Diagram Group. *The child's body: A parent's manual.* New York: Grosset & Dunlap, 1977.

A lavishly illustrated directory of the growth and development of the preadolescent body, including sections on prenatal and postnatal care and nutrition, and the acquisition of cognitive skills.

Elkind, David. *Children and adolescents: Interpretive essays on Jean Piaget.* New York: Oxford University Press, 1970.

Although Piaget has been studying the development of children's thinking for fifty years, it is only in the last decade or so that professionals in education and psychology have come to recognize the importance of his contributions. David Elkind worked with Piaget in Geneva, and in this book he explains the entire body of Piaget's work in a clear and absorbing fashion. He introduces the volume with a personal recollection of Piaget.

Howe, Michael. *Learning in infants and young children.* Stanford, Calif.: Stanford University Press, 1975.

The author of this book seeks to present an integrated view of learning and child development, contrary to the practice of many researchers in these two somewhat distinct fields. He stresses the need to consider the nature and progressively changing capacities of the learner, as well as the nature of the environmental stimulus to learning.

Rubin, Richard R., Fisher, John J., and Doering, Susan G. *Ages one and two: Your toddler.* New York: Collier Books, 1981.

This book provides a guide to toddler's growth and development. It also includes practical suggestions about how to toddler-proof your home and toys for toddlers.

Tanner, J. M. *Education and physical growth.* New York: International Universities Press, 1970.

This concise book gives a quick overview of physical development from birth to early adolescence. It discusses the principles of physical development, the course of growth, the development of the brain, and factors that affect growth. The information is up to date and presented in clear, nontechnical terms.

White, Burton, L. *The first three years of life.* Englewood Cliffs, N.J.: Prentice-Hall, 1975.

White presents practical suggestions to parents along with excellent descriptions of early development.

Chapter 5

❖❖❖❖❖❖

Social
Relationships

*B*y the time healthy children are a year old, they each have a well-developed sense of self and a growing awareness that there are a lot of people in the world who are others. They can distinguish between parents, brothers and sisters, and other people, and they are beginning to discover that not all these people act in the same way toward them, or expect them to act in the same way toward others. They are beginning, too, to find that certain things are expected of them—that Mommy and Daddy are pleased when they do some things, not so pleased when they do others. The world is looking bigger than it did, and it turns out to contain things and events that babies are not always able to cope with or control—things that are frightening or frustrating. In short, as children move out of infancy into toddlerhood, they more and more encounter a world that challenges their ability to grow, a world that is not entirely devoted to meeting their needs, and a world in which they must eventually learn to give as well as receive. But if the first months of life have taught babies to expect love and encouragement, they will reach out to the new challenges with energy and enthusiasm, despite the inevitable shocks and setbacks that go with living in an imperfect world.

ATTACHMENT AND SEPARATION

In Chapter 3 we saw the beginning of specific personal attachments, as infants become able to distinguish their parents from other people and to perceive them as especially safe and important. We saw, too, that this attachment almost immediately gives rise, in most children, to a certain fear of strangers—of people who are recognized as not-parents and therefore as unknown and unpredictable. Stranger fear usually fades toward the end of the first year, but an equally normal and common fear, also an outgrowth of attachment, lasts longer. This is **separation anxiety,** the fear of being left alone, out of reach of the persons who are the child's anchor of safety and familiarity.

At a certain stage of his development—usually about ten months—infants are apt to spend a fair amount of time pursuing mother, following her from room to room, keeping track of where she is and making sure she is available when they need her. So long as they are free to go to her, they can play and explore even an unfamiliar environment with little sign of concern. According to Sroufe (1979), the securely attached child—the child who has developed trust—uses the caregiver as a base for this exploration. The security of knowing the mother is there enables the child to develop a sense of autonomy.

But what happens if the caregiver disappears—if she leaves the room and the child cannot follow? In a study of one-year-olds in such a situation (Ainsworth & Bell, 1970) the children's distress was unmistakable. They tried everything they could to get back to Mother or bring her back to them. They cried and screamed, watched the door intently, went to it, banged on it, tried to open it. Some, giving up, simply sat and rocked unhappily on the floor, ignoring the toys they had been enjoying a moment before. (The separation lasted only about three minutes at most, and if the child was too seriously distressed, the mother returned sooner.) In another study (Coates, Anderson, & Hartup, 1972) children of ten, fourteen, and eighteen months of age were observed, first in the presence of the mother, then during a period of separation, and finally upon reunion with the mother. At all three ages the children cried most during the separation. After the mother returned, they touched her, looked at her, and sought to stay close to her much more frequently than before—almost as if to reassure themselves of her return. Similar results have been obtained with apes (Spencer-Booth & Hinde, 1966). The increase in such so-called attachment behavior is considered to be an indication of separation anxiety.

In a recent book (Ainsworth et al., 1978) a team of researchers, in the belief that attachment and separation anxiety are a normal part of development, reported in detail on three different patterns of attachment behavior. One pattern they found to be highly adaptive. These children, whom they termed group B, were *securely attached.* They could be readily separated from their caregivers to explore. When distressed by separation, these children actively looked for their caregiver, maintained contact until they were reassured, and then returned to play and explore. The group A children *avoided* their caretakers upon reunion. They ignored her or turned away. Group C (*resistant*) children were not particularly interested in exploration and could not settle down after the caregiver's return, mixing contact-seeking with such resistance as squirming and kicking. These patterns of behavior remained stable over a six-month period (Waters, 1978).

Parents are a toddler's anchor of security and familiarity. This little girl feels safe in her mother's arms.

What explanation can be given for these varying but stable patterns of attachment behavior? In a later study Sroufe and Waters (1977) posed problems for two-year-olds to solve. One of the problems was too hard for the children, requiring them to get help from their mothers. The securely attached group B children tackled the problem with enthusiasm and persistence, seeking their mothers' help and paying attention to her directions. More important, perhaps, was the behavior of the mothers of the group B children. They pitched right in, encouraging the child and offering more directions. The group C (resistant, difficult-to-settle) children fell apart completely in the face of the more difficult problem. Highly frustrated, they became increasingly angry and uncooperative, at the same time seeking more help from their mothers. The mothers gave more help, but the quality of their help got poorer and poorer. As for the group A avoidance children—they more or less gave up. They and their mothers were less involved in the problem-solving tasks and made little adjustment to the harder problems. In the follow-up studies of these children, at the age of five the securely attached children were described by their teachers as resourceful, self-reliant, curious, and exploring. The group A avoidance children were overcontrolled, and the group C resistant children were undercontrolled.

These studies show that security resides in the quality of the attachment between the parent and the child. For the mother or other caregiver the important time to give comfort and aid consistently is in the first two years of the child's life. Infants and toddlers need a warm, consistent, responsive caregiver. Toddlers need both the freedom to explore and the knowledge that there is always support and comfort available immediately should it be needed.

Long-Term Separation

The fear of separation persists throughout childhood, becoming acute during periods of family upset and insecurity. The fantasies and dramatic art of children often reveal separation anxieties, and a child may react strongly to the portrayal of separations in stories. One film critic claims that children are universally terrified when Dumbo and his mother are separated in the Disney film. Being left, lost, or abandoned is a recurring fear of childhood.

To some children, it really happens. The effects have been well documented in various studies, and especially by John Bowlby (1973), who has made a lifetime study of separation and attachment. Bowlby found that a child left in an institution typically responds with protest, then despair, and finally detachment—a loss of interest in forming or maintaining intimate contact with other people. For example, he describes the behavior of children during the first days of one separation study. The ten children in the study ranged in age from thirteen to thirty-two months, and were being temporarily placed in residential nurseries for reasons that did not involve rejection by their parents.

> When the moment came for the parent(s) to depart, crying or screaming was the rule. One child tried to follow her parents, demanding urgently where they were going, and finally had to be pushed back into the room by her mother. Another threw himself on the floor and refused to be comforted. Altogether eight of the children were crying loudly soon after their parents' departure. Bedtime was also an occasion for tears. The two who had not cried earlier screamed when put in a cot and could not be consoled. Some of the others whose initial crying had ceased broke into renewed sobs at bedtime. One little girl, who arrived in the evening and was put straight to bed, insisted on keeping her coat on, clung desperately to her doll, and cried at a frightening pitch. Again and again, having nodded off from sheer fatigue, she awoke screaming for Mummy.

At this early age, of course, the child has no way of knowing whether the separation will be long or short, or even permanent. If the separation continues, the child may regress for a while to earlier patterns of behavior. Bowlby noted that a breakdown in sphincter control was usual. On returning to the parents after days or weeks of separation, the child will usually show some signs of detachment, treating the parents like strangers. After a few hours or days the detachment usually wears off, and confidence seems to be re-established. But if a child is subjected to repeated or very prolonged separation during the first three years, the detachment may persist, in one form or another, for many years. Detached children may seem to get along comfortably with nurses, social workers, or other caretakers in their world. But they do so only at the cost of giving up serious emotional interest in anyone. They have been hurt too badly to risk attaching themselves again.

It seems that the effects of separation anxiety are especially serious in the second six months of life—that is, immediately after the first specific attachment has been made. One investigator found that infants transferred to foster homes after the age of seven months showed severe emotional disturbances or traumas (Yarrow, 1964). Children have difficulty withstanding or understanding the breaking up of the relationship that is the largest part of their world (Rutter, 1979).

SOCIALIZATION

> John (twenty-one months) had a friend over, Jerry. Today Jerry was kind of cranky; he just started completely bawling and he wouldn't stop. John kept coming up and handing Jerry toys, trying to cheer him up. He'd say things like, "Here, Jerry," and I said to John, "Jerry's sad; he doesn't feel good; he had a shot today." John would look at me with his eyebrows kind of wrinkled together, like he really understood that Jerry was crying because he was unhappy, not that he was just being a crybaby. He went over and rubbed Jerry's arm and said "Nice Jerry," and continued to give him toys. (A mother's account of altruism displayed by her child, quoted in Zahn-Waxler, Radke-Yarrow, & King, 1979).

John is showing concern for Jerry and acting in an altruistic fashion. He is becoming socialized into his family and his social group—a family, as represented by his mother, that seems to put a high value on altruism. Other families and other social groups may consider compassion for others a waste of time and energy or a luxury. However, John, not yet two years of age, is learning to conform to the expectations of the members of *his* family with *their* cultural values.

Toward the end of the first year the parent-child relationship begins to change. Children are able to move about the house, crawling, creeping, and then walking. They now have a will of their own. Their social opportunities are increased as they recognize an ever-growing number of faces. As children interact with others in their social circle, they begin to learn what is expected of them by others. They become engaged in the socialization process.

Socialization is the learning process that guides the growth of our social personalities; it is by means of socialization that we become reasonably acceptable and competent members of our society. Through socialization we acquire the discipline, the skills and knowledge, the tastes and ambitions, and the empathy for those around us that allow us to participate in the life of the family and, later, in the life of the larger community. It is not merely a matter of learning to avoid doing the things we are told not to do. It is a positive learning process. When children are learning to play patty-cake with mother—or discovering that aunts and uncles are grownups who belong to them in some special way, or are being praised for some piece of good behavior—they are being socialized as surely as when they learn to control their bowels or are scolded for hitting the child next door. They are beginning to learn the innumerable things they will eventually need to know in order to participate responsibly and naturally in the culture of their society.

In many important ways socialization continues throughout the course of a lifetime. But the learning process starts well before the infant is a year old. Parents and other caregivers are the earliest socializers and are a determining influence on an individual's development (Baumrind, 1978). In conversation and by example each social interaction children have with an adult will be a socializing influence. Increasingly children learn that they are no longer going to be allowed to play, cry, sleep, and eat purely according to their own wishes; they are going to have to take account of the demands of others—demands tempered by the values of the culture into which they were born.

It must be emphasized that socialization is not a one-way process. Children are active in socializing their parents. From the baby's first smile to the adolescent's bid for independence, children are countering the parent with their own values and attitudes. Furthermore, each child responds in a unique fashion to the socializing of the adults around him in the same way. Individual differences, too, are striking even among infants when their exploratory impulses are restricted by their caregivers (Kagan, 1979).

> One nine-month-old girl learned to indicate refusal on her part through the headshaking gesture soon followed by the words "no-no." ... She obeyed prohibitions, but not without protest. Having desisted from the forbidden act she turned on her mother and loudly jabbered at her in unmistakable protest, as it were, "talking back." On the occasions when scolding and/or spanking followed she responded with a stream of angry jargon, addressing mother thus from across the room (Escalona & Corman, 1971).

This little girl did not easily conform to her mother's wishes. She quite early developed a conscience that told her when she did wrong, but she often rebelled against that conscience and indulged in what her mother felt was socially inappropriate behavior.

From this example we can see that children are not passive recipients of adult influence. However resistant some children may be to some aspects of socialization, they are always active participants and partners in promoting their own social and emotional development (Parke, 1979a). In order to become socialized, to develop as competent members of their society, they have an awesome task to perform. Clausen (1968) has listed the goals of socialization as a set of responsibilities of parents and tasks for children (see table below). Each parental aim or activity becomes a task and achievement for the child.

As children grow, they learn certain standards of
behavior through the process of socialization.

In a give-and-take relationship with the adults in their lives children must
learn to develop trust, control their impulses, talk and walk, control their
bladder and bowel activity, develop a cognitive map of their social world, learn
right from wrong, learn to take the perspective of another person and to look
at themselves from another's perspective. Each of these tasks takes place in
an ongoing relationship with their caregivers and peers. The parental aims
and children's tasks in the table are seen as universal: parents and children
in every culture must engage in teaching and learning involved in socialization
in order to carry on the culture for another generation.

Autonomy

An early task in socialization for young children is to learn a degree of independence from their caretakers. When toddlers pick themselves up and walk,
however clumsily, they are freeing themselves from the need to be carried
around by someone else. This is a major step toward autonomy. Think of how
you felt when you came into possession of your own driver's license. It was
an emancipation. No longer were you dependent on the bus or on being

Outside of the home the toddler often discovers that older siblings can be depended on for aid.

driven by someone else. That must be how toddlers feel as they stagger for the first time from one chair to the next and then plop down again on their rump. They can do it themselves. They can get to a toy in the corner and walk by themselves to the easy chair, climb up, and look out the window. They are each their own person. Erikson calls this stage the crisis between autonomy and shame. Autonomy represents the will of children to be themselves. As they stand on their own two feet, children learn the meaning of "I," "me," and "mine."

We have autonomy when we are in a position to make our own choices—to stay where we are or go elsewhere, to do something or refrain from doing it. Erikson (1968, p. 109) points out that this is a time when a child is "apt both to hoard things and to throw them away; to cling to treasured objects and to throw them out of the windows of houses and vehicles." The formation of a healthy sense of autonomy is an extremely important factor in the toddler's development, according to Erikson. Toddlers exercise autonomy when they gain some control over their own bowels and bladder. Both to toddlers and to their parents this is an important milestone.

Control of the bowels and bladder comes to children gradually. So does the pleasure of autonomy. Toddlers find that they can choose to "hold on" or "let go" and that there are rewards and sensations associated with each

TYPES OF TASKS OF EARLY CHILDHOOD SOCIALIZATION IN THE FAMILY

Parental Aim or Activity	Child's Task or Achievement
1. Provision of nurturance and physical care	Acceptance of nurturance (development of trust)
2. Training and channeling of physiological needs in toilet training, weaning, provision of solid foods, etc.	Control of the expression of biological impulses; learning acceptable channels and times of gratification
3. Teaching and skill-training in language, perceptual skills, physical skills, self-care skills in order to facilitate care, insure safety, etc.	Learning to recognize objects and cues; language learning; learning to walk, negotiate obstacles, dress, feed self, etc.
4. Orienting the child to his immediate world of kin, neighborhood, community, and society, and to his own feelings	Developing a cognitive map of one's social world; learning to fit behavior to situational demands
5. Transmitting cultural and subcultural goals and values and motivating the child to accept them for his own	Developing a sense of right and wrong; developing goals and criteria for choices, investment of effort for the common good
6. Promoting interpersonal skills, motives, and modes of feeling and behaving in relation to others	Learning to take the perspective of another person; responding selectively to the expectations of others
7. Guiding, correcting, helping the child to formulate his own goals, plan his own activities	Achieving a measure of self-regulation and criteria for evaluating own performance

Source: J. Clausen, Perspectives on childhood socialization. In J. A. Clausen (Ed.) *Socialization and society.* Boston: Little, Brown, 1968, p. 141.

(Erikson, 1968). In elimination and in other ways as well the small human beings start to bring their bodies under their own control.

Most American children are expected to be toilet-trained between the ages of one and a half and two years. Children must reach a certain developmental level before they are physically able to control their anal and urethral sphincters, the muscles that restrain elimination. In bowel training they must learn to defecate over a toilet. To do this they must be able to relax anal sphincters at will. Bladder control, which comes later, requires similar abilities.

Since success in toilet-training depends on maturation, we would expect that an eighteen-month-old child would learn much faster than a nine-month-old, and in fact this is true. Postponing toilet-training, however, until the age of two greatly reduces bedwetting, and soiling, and constipation in late childhood (Brazelton, 1962; White, 1975)—problems that are sometimes associated with early or coercive training. However, some children may voluntarily learn much earlier if, for example, they have older siblings to observe, or if they feel particularly sensitive to being wet.

In toilet-training as in other areas of socialization it is usually the parent-child relationship that has the most influence on success. Strict, coercive training methods are much more likely to trigger emotional upset than milder methods. But even in cases of strict training warmth and affection on the part of the parent reduce the incidence of disturbances by more than half (Sears, Maccoby, & Levin, 1957). Early and overanxious training puts the child at a disadvantage and leads to increased "accidents," increased punishment, and undue emphasis on toilet matters.

Researchers recognize that the toilet-training experience is difficult to isolate from other socialization experiences. It appears that parents who are strict and early toilet-trainers are also likely to restrict their children in "messing" activities—eating, finger painting, sand play, and bath splashing. Such parents are also more likely to punish children, physically or otherwise, when standards of neatness or decorum are not met. Personality theorists beginning with Freud have associated severe toilet-training with an obsession for cleanliness and order, extreme thriftiness (or stinginess), punctuality, and neatness of dress. This is the classic description of the "anal personality," but there has not been any confirmation of Freud's theory by quantitative research.

At this very time, however, children find that their parents are encouraging them—or commanding them—to control their bowels, not only for their own pleasure but because the parents want them to. In many cases the parent-child relationship is very good, and the children do not feel that they have lost their autonomy. They can still make choices; they can choose of their own free will to please their parents and at the same time demonstrate their new abilities. Although it takes a while for their control to mature, these children's progress is steady, and conflict with their parents is slight.

In other cases the parents impose severe or early toilet-training as part of a generally restrictive relationship. Like all children, these youngsters would like to prove to themselves that they are equal to the task, but in doing so they would be conforming to their parents' wishes. Perhaps they would rather thwart them. If so, these children may rebel by refusing to exercise the required control over their own movements. Unfortunately, they defeat their own purposes with this tactic, for they deny themselves the growing sense of autonomy that accompanies control. These children are thus faced with what Erikson (1968) calls "a double rebellion and a double defeat." They cannot be sure of themselves.

Defeated children do have some options. They can attempt to assert their autonomy and control by eliminating willfully in situations not to their parents' liking. They can refuse to defecate when sent into the bathroom for that purpose. But their resolution weakens, and their control is not at first so developed as to allow them to be consistent in action, even if they are firm of purpose. With a sloppy record, they cannot help but doubt themselves. Nor are they immune to feelings of shame even when their "accidents" are on purpose. Thus doubt, shame, and "hateful self-insistence" may be the eventual results of severely restrictive toilet-training (Erikson, 1968).

Although the toilet-training experience is important in the early struggle for autonomy, many other kinds of experience figure in it as well. For example, when children show a natural desire to begin dressing themselves or using a spoon, unwanted adult help will reduce their sense of autonomy and fill

> ### *Erikson's Crises in Psychological Development*
>
> *BASIC TRUST VERSUS BASIC MISTRUST (FIRST YEAR OF LIFE)*
>
> *AUTONOMY VERSUS SHAME AND DOUBT (SECOND YEAR OF LIFE)*
> Toddlers develop muscular control, move about, and begin toilet-training. They need firmness as a protection against the potential anarchy of their own impulses. The sense of self-control (autonomy) learned at this stage leads to a lasting sense of goodwill and personal pride. A failure to achieve well-guided autonomy can lead to a pervasive sense of *shame* before the world and compulsive *doubt* of oneself and others.
>
> *INITIATIVE VERSUS GUILT (THE PRESCHOOL YEARS)*
>
> *INDUSTRY VERSUS INFERIORITY (MIDDLE CHILDHOOD)*
>
> *IDENTITY VERSUS ROLE CONFUSION (ADOLESCENCE)*
>
> *INTIMACY VERSUS ISOLATION (YOUNG ADULTHOOD)*
>
> *GENERATIVITY VERSUS STAGNATION (PRIME OF LIFE)*
>
> *EGO INTEGRITY VERSUS DESPAIR (OLD AGE)*

them with self-doubt. When they do fail, they must learn that failure is not utter disaster—that they can safely take a chance on trying again. These are lessons to be learned in all areas of childhood endeavor and to be reaffirmed throughout adult life.

Managing Troublesome Emotions

Parents rather easily attribute complex emotions to their young children. Attachment quickly becomes "love," the search for human stimulation may be termed "friendliness," and the cry for food or diaper change is sometimes seen as "crankiness" or "selfishness." In actuality, the emotional range of infants and toddlers is much more limited. Probably they can enjoy a state of simple contentment that cannot be reproduced in adult consciousness. Their major problems are centered in their physical needs and their need for stimulation. Nevertheless, children at this age do experience at least two emotional states that are socially important. They experience fear and anger at people and things. Learning how to express these emotions in an acceptable way is an important goal of socialization.

Fear

We have seen that two common fears in infancy and toddlerhood are the fear of strangers and a more general anxiety about being separated from parents. But children are subject to numerous other fears, and the objects of these

Children's eagerness to dress themselves is a demonstration of their increasing autonomy.

fears change as the child grows. Newborn infants are startled by falling and loud noises, but by little else. As they experience more of their environment and gain in perceptual and cognitive skills, they discover more things to fear. Perhaps a little girl has a painful encounter with a cat's claws, or is knocked down by an overeager large dog; perhaps she senses a parent's fear of thunder, or is snatched anxiously away from an intriguing spider on the patio. In all of these experiences she is learning that the environment can be dangerous. In short, most fears are learned.

Children's fears come and go, but most children experience similar types of fears at the same age. For toddlers the worst fears are associated with separation and change. Toddlers want their own mommy, daddy, spoon, chair, bed. They are profoundly conservative little people. The most daring toddlers feel content only if they can hold onto what they already know (Wolman, 1978). Yet, children's fears are a useful index to their development. As we have seen, fear of strangers appears to be a consequence of their first specific attachment, and its ending a sign that they have acquired a more inclusive schema of faces in general. A child who is afraid of cats but not of rabbits evidently can differentiate one small animal from another. Fear of a particular person implies recognition of that person.

Just as children learn to fear things, they can learn what not to fear. So long as adult reinforcement does not make the fears too intense, their natural impulse to explore and discover things will be of help. Parents can be of

CHILDREN'S FEARS

Don't
1. Don't ignore the child's fears; don't dismiss them.
2. Don't overprotect the child; avoid making him feel helpless and overdependent on you; don't pity him.
3. Don't reject the child. Don't threaten him with abandonment; don't make him feel lonely.
4. Don't ridicule the fearful child. Don't punish him for being afraid.
5. Don't force the child into a situation he fears.
6. Don't involve your child in your own fears.

Do
1. Build the child's faith in himself and his abilities.
2. Praise his achievements, no matter how small they are (but without exaggeration).
3. Make him feel that you will always love him and protect him whenever necessary.
4. Listen patiently to the child and show understanding for his fears; whenever possible, try to explain that there is nothing to be afraid of.
5. Set an example by rationally coping with dangers yourself.
6. Give the child the opportunity to overcome his fears actively.

Source: B. B. Wolman. *Children's fears.* New York: Grosset & Dunlap, 1978, p. 102.

assistance, both in overcoming fears and in preventing their development. They can prepare a child by play and stories for dealing with new situations that might, if met with unprepared, be overwhelming.

Children's fears should be taken seriously, never ridiculed or dismissed as silly or babyish. Perhaps if the caregiver can get the child to explain exactly

A helping hand can often overcome a toddler's fears.

what it is that is so frightening, the child can be reassured. The one thing *not* to do is force children into confronting a feared situation before they are ready to do so.

Aggression and Anger

In toddlerhood, aggressive behavior is generally expressed as anger in the form of the temper tantrum. Sometimes the tantrum is a by-product of other socialization processes—strict behavior expectations or other adult pressures that go against the child's abilities or temperament. Another major cause of trouble is loss of attention, sometimes coupled with feelings of jealousy.

The temper tantrum usually causes great alarm among parents. By adult standards, it is an impressive display. Children scream, kick, and throw themselves about in a wild fashion. They may even engage in self-hurting behavior—pulling their hair, biting their fingers, holding their breath, or banging their head on the floor. Parents can hardly ignore the outburst, especially since it so often happens in polite company. Yet most parents are fearful that giving children what they want or smothering them with immediate affection will only encourage further outbursts, with further concessions, in the future. Indeed, this seems to be the case.

A famous longitudinal study (Goodenough, 1931) found that mothers generally do give in as a way of ending temper outbursts. Mothers reported that they could most effectively quiet the child by giving him what he desired, by eliminating whatever was frustrating him, or simply by diverting his attention with new toys and activities. Also effective were ignoring the child or putting him in a room by himself. However, these strategies are likely to cause confusion and ambivalence in modern parents. They know that giving in may cause children to use anger and aggression as a means of achieving their ends throughout life. Yet they feel—perhaps unlike their own parents—that anger should not be bottled up or denied. This study concluded that the control of anger in children is best achieved when the child's behavior is viewed with "serenity and tolerance." Teaching the child appropriate expression of anger and control of aggression is one of the most difficult feats of socialization.

As children grow older, the parents' own example becomes critical. The most aggressive behavior is found in children who have observed frequent and violent outbursts in their parents. Children who are often spanked will quickly see the point of physical aggression. This is not to say that they will necessarily be full of the hostile impulses that provoke aggression. It appears to be parental inconsistency, rather than spanking as such, which leads to angry and aggressive behavior in children. According to some observers (Sears, Maccoby, & Levin, 1957), children are most likely to be aggressive when their parents disapprove of aggression but nevertheless use physical aggression as a punishment—for example, by spanking a child because he has hit another child. When parents are generally permissive, yet resort to physical punishment, this inconsistency will likewise produce aggression in children. Socialization away from aggressive behavior does not succeed when parents are arbitrary in their own actions and attitudes regarding physical punishment.

APPROACHES TO CHILD-REARING

Child-rearing practices usually do not change much from one generation to the next. New parents tend to bring up their children as they themselves were raised; the child-rearing patterns learned from their parents are, after all, the ones they know best. Despite their conscious wishes, many parents find themselves even repeating the same words and phrases their parents directed toward them as children (Faber & Mazlish, 1974).

Nevertheless, child-rearing attitudes do change, in part as a result of larger social changes. For example, it is not unusual today for new parents to be far more tolerant than grandparents of certain "messing" activities, such as emptying wastebaskets or slinging mud. (Does the wider availability of vacuum cleaners, automatic washers, and drip-dry clothing, as well as advances in child psychology, have something to do with this?) Today's parents may also be less anxious about toilet-training and masturbation; on the other hand, they will probably be more worried by tantrums and other emotional upsets. Their viewpoint is determined not only by their own childhood experiences but by their familiarity with the current psychological literature and the "experts." Furthermore, their own needs as individuals will necessarily reflect the numerous social changes that have occurred since they were children. In some areas the changes are quite significant. For example, the need for a second income as well as the attraction for many women of working outside the home, has never been so high as it is today. Faced with new challenges and new "experts," the emerging generation of parents develops its own style of child-rearing.

Changing Views

In the United States the earliest child-rearing philosophies were based on religion and morality. Colonial children were taught from infancy that reverence for their parents was analogous to reverence for God. The emphasis was on obedience, but the time was not so harsh as we might suppose. The Reverend Cotton Mather, having stated that "my word must be law," goes on to say that "I would never come to give a child a blow; except in case of obstinacy or some gross enormity. To be chased for a while out of my presence I would make to be looked upon as the sorest punishment in the family" (Calhoun, 1960). The goal of child-rearing for Mather and other colonial authorities was to produce a God-fearing child with "a mighty desire of being useful in the world." Parental example, particularly of the religious sort, was more important than disciplinary method.

Today in middle-class America, the goals of child-rearing are mostly psychological rather than religious. We wish for our children to be happy, well adjusted, and productive in the world. The first trend in psychological thought to have a strong effect on child-rearing in this country was behaviorism, founded by J. B. Watson in the 1920s. An assertive, controversial figure, Watson believed that the goal of the psychologist was to control and predict behavior through the manipulation of environmental stimuli. Watson's famous boast makes clear his position, even as it exaggerates it:

> Give me a dozen healthy infants, well formed, and my own special world to bring them up in, and I'll guarantee to take any one of them at random and train him to be any type of specialist I might select—a doctor, lawyer, artist, merchant, chief, and even a beggarman and thief, regardless of his talents, penchants, tendencies, abilities, vocation and of his ancestors.

Watson's regimen required that punishment follow any and all acts deemed undesirable by parent and educator; positive behaviors were rewarded. However, the child was not to be treated with affection. "Never hug them and kiss them," he wrote. "Never let them sit on your lap . . . Give them a pat on the head if they have made an extraordinary good job of a difficult task" (Watson, 1930). Children were not to suck their thumbs; metal mittens were provided for infants who did so. Infants were not to be picked up when they cried; it would reinforce undesirable behavior. The relationship between parents and children was reduced to punishment and reward—the carrot and the stick. Mothers, in particular, were threatened with unhappy, spoiled children if they ever indulged in their own feelings for closeness and tenderness toward their children. For parents as well as children life was mostly punishment. The rewards Watson held out for child-raisers seemed scarcely worth the trouble.

Watson's viewpoint has not entirely disappeared even today. A major force in modern psychology is B. F. Skinner, a behaviorist who believes that successful child-rearing is accomplished through operant conditioning, the consistent rewarding of desirable behavior. (This mode of learning was discussed in Chapter 4.) Skinner's rational application of learning theory is not designed to produce a "model child" in the old-fashioned sense, but rather a creative and socially valuable individual. Still, few parents consciously condition their children in the manner Skinner suggests, and almost none choose to raise them in the controlled environment of the "Skinner box," even though attractive models are available.

The behaviorists' viewpoint has been opposed by the followers of Sigmund Freud. When he began his work in psychiatry late in the 19th century, Freud was not initially concerned with child behavior. His patients were mostly adults, and much of his clinical writing is concerned with the causes of adult disturbances, both emotional and physical. But Freud found that he could neither understand nor treat his patients' emotional problems unless he could locate their origins in early childhood experience. He found that disturbances very often seemed to be caused by overly restrictive or punitive treatment on the part of parents. For example, he traced certain malfunctions of the intestinal tract to harsh toilet-training, and concluded that certain neurotic dependency patterns are associated with restrictive mothering.

Another important recent influence on child-rearing has come from psychologists and anthropologists whose cross-cultural studies have shown the limitations of universal theories of behavior. Anthropologist Margaret Mead

All alone in the world of grownups. Their behavior toward her will help to determine the kind of adult she will become.

(1928) showed that the sexual stresses felt by most American adolescents did not affect children in Samoa. Later, psychologist Karen Horney (1937) observed that the neurotic personality type she had treated in England differed from the one she encountered in the United States. A number of studies showed that the problems experienced by indivdiuals in one culture are often the result of the particular child-rearing and socialization customs of that culture. Mead's *Coming of Age in Samoa* voiced a common theme in suggesting that anxieties, in this case pubertal anxieties, were caused by our own attitudes rather than by any natural tendencies.

Probably the greatest influence on child-rearing for the last two generations has been Benjamin Spock. The children of the baby boom following World War II were raised "according to Spock." Even Erik Erikson (1968) quotes Spock's famous admonition to parents, "Trust yourself." Spock's (1976) major point is that, after all, babies are people too. Parents are urged to see situations from the baby's point of view, keeping in mind that a child is not a miniature adult. Spock taught child development, physical and emotional, to whole generations of parents. Don't push your children. Wait until they are ready. Don't expect more than a child is capable of. Most of Spock's book on baby care is devoted to practical and medical matters, reassuring to a mother who doesn't know what to do when her baby wakes up in the middle of the night with a mysterious ailment. Spock's friendly advice did indeed help parents to trust themselves.

A generation later Chaim Ginott's *Between Parent and Child* (1965) took Spock's sensible and relaxed message a step further. Where Spock advised parents to be firm yet kindly and loving, Ginott furnished specific instructions on how to do it. Ginott is interested in how parents and children talk to each other. His code of communication is based on "respect and skill. It requires that (a) the message preserve the child's as well as the parent's respect and (b) that statements of understanding precede statements of advice or instruction." Ginott gives this example, Bruce, age five, is making his first visit to kindergarten with his mother. He looks at the children's paintings hanging on the wall and asks in a loud voice, "Who made these ugly paintings?" His embarrassed mother scolds him, "It's not nice to call the pictures ugly when they are so pretty." The teacher, however, replied, "In here you don't have to paint pretty pictures. You can paint mean pictures if you feel like it." A big smile appeared on Bruce's face, for now he had the answer to his hidden question—what happens to a boy who doesn't paint so well? Ginott illustrated his book profusely with such examples. His principal message is that children need to be listened to as much for what they don't say as for what they do say. They may be unable or unwilling to voice their concerns, as was Bruce in the example. Ginott suggests that the adult should listen for that concern and then voice it. The teacher understood Bruce's problem. It's okay, she was saying, if you are not such a good painter. You don't have to be Michelangelo to get into this kindergarten.

Parenting

Behavior that is affectionate, nurturant, warm, and supportive, usually on the part of an adult toward a child, is often referred to as "mothering." The term "fathering," in contrast, is generally used in a strictly biological sense. To get around the verbal sexism of the old terminology, the term "parenting" has come into use. It reflects modern insights into parental roles, not only in recognizing that the father has a nurturant role to play, but also in suggesting that the roles of mother and father may not be so inherently dissimilar as tradition has seemed to imply.

The traditional assignment of warm and supportive behavior to the mother reflects a traditional attitude toward women. To some extent this attitude may be an honest reflection of an earlier social order. Mother was right there in the home, and the house and children were her chief concerns. Father had to deal with a larger world of business, or with the hard demands of nature on the farm; he was outside—authoritative and perhaps affectionate, but more remote. Today, though, old stereotypes about male reserve and female emotionalism are giving way to a new set of attitudes. It is no longer enough simply to be there; a parent—male or female—is expected to invest feelings and attention in the parent-child relationship.

The value of the term "parenting" is that it encourages us to take a more comprehensive view of the whole child-rearing process. "Mothering" is always needed—a child must feel cherished, valued, and often comforted. But good socialization requires us to treat the child sometimes with firmness and even, on rare occasions, with severity. If there is an art to being a good parent, perhaps it lies in this—finding a healthy balance between the different values that used to be thought of as "feminine" and "masculine." Both mothers and fathers need to have within themselves the capacity for firm authority and for tenderness and concern.

Discipline

People who work or live with children have always been interested in the process by which children learn to conform to the wishes and demands of adults. Social scientists speak of socialization, parents of discipline. The two are not entirely equivalent. Usually we use the word "discipline" to refer to the means by which children are made to obey. Socialization is a broader concept, implying not only obedience but the learning by children of the cultural values, attitudes, and beliefs of their elders. When the toddler is told not to touch a glass tray, this is an instance of discipline—a command plain and simple, and one to which neither the parent nor the child attaches much social importance. However, in complying with the "No, don't touch," a little girl is at the same time learning a more general social rule: to obey her parents and other adults. This rule is part of the broader process of socialization.

Observers of child-rearing methods have tended to dichotomize parenting styles in regard to discipline: parents were either authoritarian or permissive. Advocates of one style blamed proponents of the other for everything from teenage drug use and the teenage pregnancy rate (permissive) to race

The significance of the father's role in parenting has been redefined in recent years.

prejudice and family violence (authoritarian). The authoritarian parent is one who imposes control and discipline. The highest value for this parent is unquestioning obedience. The permissive parent allows children to make their own decisions as much as possible. The proponents of permissiveness feel that children have a natural tendency to fulfill their own potential—"left to itself, the child will learn all it needs to know and turn to conventionally approved behavior when and if it chooses to do so" (Baumrind, 1978). Critics have exaggerated both positions.

Baumrind (1978) suggests that the parent or educator need not choose between either permissive or authoritarian discipline. She advocates a third style she terms *authoritative.* The authoritative parent does not relinquish control; the authoritative parent "exerts firm control when the young child disobeys, but does not hem the child in with restrictions, recognizing the child's individual interests and special ways" (Baumrind, 1978). The authoritative parent praises a child's accomplishments, but also sets standards for future conduct. Such a parent uses reason as well as power in achieving discipline and competence in the child. Authoritative parents were identified through their children, who were deemed *socially competent* by Baumrind. The socially competent child is defined by such attributes as socially responsible, independent, achievement-oriented, and energetic.

Neglect and low involvement seem to be the most detrimental to children of all parental qualities (Rosenberg, 1965). Harsh, exploiting, and arbitrary behavior on the part of parents has been shown in many studies to be strongly associated with delinquency and other antisocial behavior (Hetherington, Stouwie, & Ridberg, 1971; Elkind, 1967a).

Actually, children thrive under each of the parental styles—authoritarian, permissive, and authoritative—if parents are consistent and considerate. Learning theory suggests that children learn best when rules are applied consistently. In infancy this is usually not so difficult. Many of the commands involve matters of safety; few parents are inconsistent when it comes to allowing a child to touch an electric burner. Safety rules seem to be learned more readily, with less stress, than other rules—probably because parents do not hesitate to impose them.

What, then, of children who "always" disobey? They too have learned the broad social rule that children obey adults. But for many of them this is the only rule that never changes. Take the case of Gary:

> Eighteen-month-old Gary, playing with pots and pans, is one day given great approval since his activity keeps him busy for two hours as his mother completes a task, while three days later he is scolded and spanked for the same behavior because his mother had just finished arranging the pots and pans and did not wish them disturbed. Six-year-old Gary is encouraged to eat his dinner watching television because it is so difficult to drag him away and, besides, if his attention is engaged he eats more since he is not mindful of the food. The same Gary, two weeks later, is scolded roundly for setting himself down in front of the television at dinner time because mother has suddenly decided that it is not proper to eat in front of the television (Thomas, Chess, & Birch, 1968).

In Gary's case discipline is inconsistent. Yet Gary's required social role *is* consistent: he is always supposed to obey. Although his parents may regret that he gets his own way so often, they fail to realize that doing so does not necessarily help him to develop self-control, social competence, or self-esteem. Like all children he believes that the world is, and should be, run by adults (if only for the sake of children). Misbehavior, even when reasonable under the circumstances, will make a young child feel guilty and insecure. As children develop a sense of autonomy, they will occasionally misbehave as a means of asserting their independence. Misbehavior may take the form of aggression, stubbornness, or casual disregard of parental rules. Common forms include refusing to go to bed, refusing to eat, and refusing to produce bowel movements at the right time. Parents differ greatly in their ways of punishing such misbehavior. Some temporarily withdraw affection; others

Misbehavior in the form of refusing to obey a parent can be an expression of a child's autonomy.

Parent Effectiveness Training

Frustrated in their perennial effort to get their children to obey, behave, consider the rights of others, accept responsibility—in a word, grow up civilized—parents from time to time adopt new philosophies of child-rearing and novel approaches to discipline. One currently popular method, evidently derived from the client-centered psychotherapeutics of Carl Rogers, has had widespread influence. Parent Effectiveness Training (PET), founded by psychologist Thomas Gordon, helps parents learn a new way of getting along with their children. Gordon claims it is useful even with infants and toddlers, but it is easier to describe in the verbal form it takes with older children and teenagers.

Parents who take the PET course learn first how to listen to their children. *Passive listening*, in which they simply make themselves available for the child to talk to, is one way. *Active listening*, in which they try to extract the unspoken message from the child's words, is more difficult. For example, children who barge into the kitchen demanding to know when dinner will be ready may not merely want to know what time they can expect to eat. They may be announcing that they're hungry. Or they may be saying they hope there will be time to go out and play for another hour or two. In active listening the parents decode the child's message and express their interpretation of it.

Another aspect of PET is concerned with how parents speak to children. Gordon says that instead of sending *You-messages* to children focusing on their faults and failings, parents should learn to send *I-messages.* Imagine a child who always leaves books, coat, tennis racquet, clarinet, and gym shoes in the entrance hall after school. Most parents would attack this behavior by saying, "You dumped your things in the hall again!" or "When will you ever learn to put your things away?" These all "tell" the child that he or she is sloppy, immature, and stubborn. In PET parents learn to express their own feelings instead of passing judgment on their children: or "I'm tired of picking things up all the time," or "I really feel uncomfortable having such an untidy entrance hall."

If the simple expression of sincere feeling fails to change the behavior that bothers them, Gordon says, parents should try to approach the situation as an exercise in problem-solving. Families usually solve problems by *authoritative* methods, in which parents win ("If you don't put your things away, you can't watch TV tonight!") or by *permissive* means, in which the kids win (the parents give up and either ignore the mess or put things away themselves).

In *no-lose conflict resolution* Gordon advises parents and kids to sit down and state the problem objectively. In this case the child's habit of dropping things in the hall makes the mother feel very uncomfortable. Having identified the problem, the family lists all the possible solutions: (1) things can continue as they are, (2) parents can pick everything up and put it away, (3) parents can pick everything up and hide or discard it, (4) children can leave things in the hall until they have had their after-school snack, and then put things away, or (5) parents can provide a basket or other receptacle in which things can be neatly left in the entrance hall until the child needs them elsewhere later.

In step three of "no-lose" problem-solving the family evaluates the possible solutions. All participants can veto any solutions they cannot live with. What they are after is a solution where nobody loses and everyone who owns the problem can live with it. A family member who neither leaves things around sloppily nor cares if others do is automatically excluded from this discussion. When the disputants decide how they will solve it, they agree on ways to implement the solution, and then drop the subject. No punishments or ultimata are included, as the solution is supposed to be agreeable to the people on both sides of the conflict. At some later time, a week or so afterward, perhaps, they gather again to evaluate how it has worked out.

One important element of the method is deciding who owns the problem. A child's success in school may not be the parents' problem. A parent's desire to keep the house immaculate may not be the child's problem. Once the ownership of the problem is established, the solution is often easy to arrive at. Listening actively to what the others are saying, learning to send "I-messages" and avoiding the accusatory, judgmental language of "you-messages," families find that many of the old conflicts disappear. The few that remain often yield relatively easily and peacefully to "no-lose" problem-solving.

Over a quarter of a million parents and teachers have taken the course in Parent Effectiveness Training. Some parents and child-care experts, however, feel the method goes too far. They say that parents must firmly set limits and insist on certain values and standards of behavior. As in many other aspects of human relations, the answer probably lies somewhere between the two extremes. If only for its stress on nonthreatening, nonjudgmental communication between parent and child, PET is certainly worth considering.

take away possessions and, later, privileges; still others resort to a swat on the backside. While there are advantages and disadvantages to each approach, the important thing again seems to be consistency.

Recognition of cognitive limitation is also important. Very young children have no concept of sharing and no concept of cheating. Punishing them for being selfish or for cheating will simply result in angry confusion. Again, young children react very strongly to verbal abuse. Children who are continually told that they are selfish, dirty, or lazy will in all probability accept the description rather than the disciplinary recommendation that is implied by it. In accepting the verbal stigma children show a deep tendency to identify with the parent— even at cost to themselves. A common sight in the nursery is that of a little girl chastising her doll with the words, *"Bad* baby, *bad* baby."

Children whose needs are anticipated and met in advance have their own problems at this age. Almost more than the child who has been punished or shamed for mistakes, and certainly more than the one who has been punished for deliberate misbehavior, such children have been denied the opportunity to learn how to satisfy their own needs and thus develop their sense of autonomy. When anything was wanted—or even before—Mommy brought it; when something needed doing, Daddy or big brother did it, instead of helping the child to figure out how to do it. Unable to exercise initiative by building competence and self-reliance, the child has only one way of showing power—making demands on others. Such children have in truth, been "spoiled." But, as parents of spoiled children know to their cost, giving in will not put an end to demands. It will only confirm them in the sense that this, and this alone, is the area in which they can be powerful, autonomous, and controlling.

CHILD ABUSE

A recent television commercial begins with the announcement, "Johnny was just beaten up by the biggest kid on the block—his father." It goes on to show photographs of a boy who has bruises and scars all over his head and body. The intent of the commercial is to raise community awareness of the widespread incidence of child abuse. When this issue first surfaced in the early 1960s, it was viewed as pathological behavior: "How could anybody in his right mind willfully hurt a child too small and too weak to defend itself?" Today the battered child as well as the battered wife is being viewed in the context of violence—violence in the family.

The traditions of family relationships in western culture foster violence in the family. The ancient Greeks practiced infanticide, although only baby girls were left to die. In Roman times a father could sell, sacrifice, mutilate, or kill his offspring (Bybee, 1979). The Old Testament contains this advice from Proverbs:

> He who spares the rod, hates his son, but he who loves him disciplines him diligently.

A recent study of child abuse (Gelles & Straus, 1979) points out that with the exception of the military and the police, there is no more violent social group than the American family. "A person is more likely to be hit or killed in his or her own home by another family member than anywhere else or by anyone else" (Gelles & Straus, 1979). Nearly one out of every four murder victims is killed by a member of his or her own family.

The dividing line between a disciplinary slap that most Americans would probably find acceptable and child abuse is a difficult one to draw both in the home and in the school. An eight-year-old in Rochester, New York, came home from school with black-and-blue marks on his arm. The child's buttocks were raw and bleeding. The boy's father, a county sheriff, called the police, who informed him that they had no right to proceed against anyone. The wounds had been inflicted by the principal, and the state law says that corporal punishment in the schools is legal except for the use of deadly force (Hechinger, 1980). Where, then, does this society draw the line between corporal punishment for disciplinary purposes and child abuse?

Definition of Child Abuse

Two researchers (Gelles & Straus, 1979) who undertook a national survey of family violence, defined child abuse as "an act carried out with the intention or perceived intention of physically hurting another person." Physical hurt can range from slight pain, as in a slap, to murder. These researchers did not draw a line between punishment and violence. They define *any* physical act with an intent to hurt as violence. As these authors point out, such an act as a slap performed outside the home or the school is legally defined as assault. Usually a definition of child abuse also includes malnourishment, failure to care for and protect a child, sexual assault, failure to clothe a child, and psychological abuse.

Incidence

Gelles and Straus interviewed a nationally representative sample of 2,143 married couples of whom 1,146 had one or more children aged three to seventeen. Since the incidents of child abuse were revealed by the individuals themselves, undoubtedly the figures are low. However, 58 percent of the respondents said they had used some form of physical violence to punish their children during the last year. The survey revealed that the age of their children is a factor in parents' behavior. Eighty-two percent of the parents of three- to nine-year-olds reported hitting their children. Approximately three in every hundred children had been kicked, bitten, or punched during the year, more than one child in a hundred had been beaten, and one child in a thousand had been threatened with a knife or a gun. The parents of nearly three children in a hundred had actually used a gun or a knife against the child at least once during the child's lifetime (Gelles & Straus, 1979).

The researchers expressed astonishment at these figures, elicited as they were from the testimony of the parents themselves. They were also surprised to discover that the extreme forms of parental violence were not one-time events but were likely to occur periodically to the same child. Gelles and Straus turned these figures into an index of the likelihood of a child being injured by one of the more extreme forms of violence. They estimated that between 1.4 and 1.9 million children in the United States were vulnerable to physical injury from their parents—and they felt these figures underestimated the true level of abuse.

Social Class

Most of the studies of child abuse have been concerned with the social and psychological characteristics of parents who abuse their children: "What kind of people would do such a thing?" Official figures pointed to lower-class problem families. However, such figures were discounted on the basis that members of such families were more likely to come to the attention of the police, welfare workers, or the public hospitals. It was felt that there was an equal proportion of child abuse hidden among the middle and professional classes. Gilles and Straus' national survey, however, showed that social class did make a difference in the probability of violence toward children—children from the lower class were more likely to be subjected to abuse.

Women are slightly more apt to use violence toward their children than men and slightly more apt to use abusive violence, that is, violence with a high probability of injury to the child. The targets of violence are slightly more likely to be boys rather than girls (Gelles & Straus, 1979).

Why Do They Do It?

When we ask the question why—why do these parents do it?—we find that a common theme that runs through the studies of child abuse is a psychological one. The authors of one study claim, "as infants and children, all of the [abusing] parents were deprived both of basic mothering and a deep sense of being cared for and cared about from the beginning of their lives" (Spinetta & Rigler, 1972). This statement could be interpreted to mean that all abused children will grow up to be abusing adults and that anyone who was not abused as a child will not abuse his or her own children. This is, of course, not true. However, violence is very likely to beget violence. Gelles and Straus found that respondents who reported that their own mothers had used physical violence more than twice a year had a rate of severe violence toward their children of 18.5 percent. This is not anything like 100 percent, but a much higher rate than those who did not share their experience. An instructive finding was that women who saw their mothers being abused by their fathers had a high rate (19 percent) of abusing their own children.

One explanation for the abused child turning into an abusing parent is concerned with learning. In many cases there seems to be an almost undiluted transfer of the violence learned as a child to that practiced as an adult. A child learns violence as a solution and an outcome when there is family conflict. The intense emotion that accompanies the witnessing of violence by a child enhances the learning process. The violent lessons of family conflict are not likely to be forgotten. Another explanation was suggested many years ago by Leonard Cottrell, Jr. (1942): an abused child growing up in a violent family may not have learned any alternative means for dealing with conflict but violence. His or her repertory of behavior may not include such facilitative skills as negotiation, reasoning, exchange of services, or humor. Such a person may know of no other way to deal with a child than to use physical force.

Isolation

One study (Fontana, 1973) suggests that parents who abuse their children have great difficulty in developing trust, a difficulty that is linked to isolation of parents from family and other social groups. Isolation has been used to explain violence toward children in a number of studies (Maden & Wrench, 1977; Smith, 1973). Higher rates of child abuse have been found in families where there are no ongoing relationships outside the home. Gelles and Straus found a higher incidence of violence in families that had lived in a neighborhood less than three years. Those who did not attend or belong to any organizations in the community have a much higher rate of child abuse than those who belonged to or attended at least one organization (Straus, 1979).

The child-abuse problem is complicated by guilt on the part of both parents and children. Few children, even in the preschool and school years, will appeal to outsiders for help. Any parent, even an abusive one, may be deeply loved by the child. And it hardly needs to be said that very few parents, even among those who believe in physical punishment, would consciously feel justified in doing their child serious harm.

Violence as a Social Norm

These social and psychological explanations help to identify those who are more likely to use violence toward their children, but they don't explain the high prevalence of violence in the American family. There are norms or rules in every society regarding moral conduct. When we think of violence in the family, we conjure up the picture shown on the television commercial mentioned at the beginning of this section—a bruised child with broken bones, burned, or slashed with a knife. Such evidence of violence is the tip of the iceberg. As Gelles and Straus say, "Most family violence does not become a matter of concern because it is 'normal violence.'" Normal violence occurs in accordance with the norms of rules in our culture.

What are the rules in regard to violence? Under what circumstances, if any, is violence acceptable? In many American families it is considered all right to hit another family member, child or spouse, if that person is doing "something wrong" and "won't listen to reason." Furthermore, in accordance with biblical teaching, some parents feel they are almost under obligation to use physical punishment to teach their children how to behave. One out of four couples think it is all right for a husband to beat his wife if there is a "good reason" (Stark & McEvoy, 1970). Good reasons vary from couple to couple. Good reasons for punishing a child with physical violence also vary from family to family. Some families tolerate a high level of violence. Gelles and Straus mention the "stitch rule." The "stitch rule" is a police phrase referring to the fact that at one time, among the police in various cities, no arrest would be made in family fights unless there was a wound requiring stitches. Today in most states violence against children must be reported by doctors and social workers. The "stitch" rule, in a sense, is still in effect in that unless there is injury done to a child that requires medical attention, violence seems to be tolerated.

CULTURE AND UPBRINGING

Parents bring up their children with the understanding that the child will at some point be delivered over to society. In Western cultures this means that he will go to school, join his local peer group, and eventually enter adult institutions such as the factory, office, church, and political party. But in other cultures children must take other directions and therefore receive different training. In the Yanomamö tribe, for example, children are trained to be self-assertive and physically aggressive; in others, such as the Hopi Indians, they are expected to merge their ambitions with those of the group. Even within a single culture differences among ethnic, religious, and cultural groups are evident.

Child-Rearing in Other Cultures

The study of child development is international in its subjects and in many of its assumptions. Piaget's studies were based on observations of Swiss chil-

❖❖

What Can We Do about Child Abuse?

Mary Smith, after weeks of daily screaming bouts with her four-year-old son Mark, found herself shaking him violently, about to bang his head against the kitchen counter. Trembling, she picked up the phone and called the Child Abuse Hotline. She was calmed down at the other end of the wire by a volunteer counselor, a woman who had herself abused her child. Mary has since learned in classes and counseling sessions to go into another room and cool off, to carry through any threats she makes so that Mark will believe her, and to balance discipline with loving "strokes." (By "strokes" is meant that she notes with pleasure when Mark is helpful, responds to him with affection, and praises and encourages his little enterprises.) At the end of their first scream-free day Mark observed, "This was a good day, wasn't it, Mommy? I love today" (Richard, 1978).

Today there are social agencies both public and private that deal with child abuse. Mary and Mark are among the thousands who have been helped. Because of the current concern about child abuse on a national scale, intervention in child-abuse cases is far more common than in the past. Intervention can come about by the efforts of the parents themselves, or the child if he or she is old enough, or by an outsider—a neighbor, teacher, policeman, doctor, or a separated parent. Many outsiders hesitate to meddle in another family's problem. However, the public is growing increasingly aware of the seriousness of the problem and more people are following their initial impulse to "do something." In many states physicians for years have been required by law to report suspected child-abuse cases. Now in New Jersey, for example, any person who suspects child abuse is required to report directly to the New Jersey Division of Youth and Family Services. Although the agency gives first consideration to protecting the child, every effort is made to keep the family together and help the parents to improve the situation at home (Tritremmel & Ferrara, 1977).

In many places a child-abuse hotline (in most phone books listed under "Child Abuse Hotline") is available to parents who are, as was Mary Smith, afraid of their own tendency to violence. As one counselor at a hotline center put it: "We all have tempers. But a parent who calls us can get rid of it over the phone instead of beating up his child." The counselors at the center are, for the most part, members of Parents Anonymous (also listed in most phone books), an organization patterned after Alcoholics Anonymous. By discussing their problems openly within the shelter of such an organization, many parents find they can get through times of crisis without turning to violence against their children.

What are the signs of child abuse? Abuse and neglect include: unexplained cuts, bruises, fractures, burns, and scars; sexual abuse or exploitation; lack of proper food and clothing; and the leaving of small children unsupervised. Battered children "endure life as if they are alone in a dangerous world, with no real hope of safety." In an institutional setting professionals find that when such children are being treated for an injury, for example, they appear fearful, quiet, with no reaction to pain nor the expectation of being comforted. When other children cry, the battered child becomes apprehensive, especially when an adult approaches the crying child. They do not react as do other children but display the control generally found in adults (Division of Youth and Family Services, 1976).

dren, and several of the attachment studies cited in this chapter were conducted with British children. But do the findings apply equally well to children
in other cultures, to Eskimo and Zulu as well as American children? Seeking
to answer this question, researchers have carried out many studies of the
relationship cultural differences have to different patterns of child care.

To date, no one has clearly shown that any particular feeding or toilet-
training method will have a predictable effect in every culture that practices
it. This is partly because any given child-rearing practice is closely integrated
with other practices. In one culture, for example, permissive feeding might be

In all cultures children are expected to conform to the values of their parents. Here
a Western Nigerian mother draws water in an earthen pot from a jungle pond.

❖◆❖

Child-Rearing in Different American Subcultures

The myth of the American melting pot has given way to something like a salad bowl in which various cultures are tossed together but retain some of their special flavor, with the values and norms of each culture passed on to the next generation through child-rearing. Researchers have only recently begun to make some objective studies of the child-rearing patterns that typify the Mexican-American, American-Indian, and black-American subcultures, and their preliminary findings point to some values that differ from the dominant Anglo-American culture.

Heller (1967) found that Mexican-American families usually include other people in addition to the parents and children. This web of kinship imposes obligations of mutual aid, respect, and affection, and it extends beyond blood ties to *compadres*—people who are not related but assume family obligations. The mother provides affection and exercises considerable control with the home. The father or oldest male wage earner is the authoritarian master of the extended family. He is the central figure of the Mexican-American value system. Boys are encouraged to emulate his physical strength, enterprise, courage, self-confidence, and skill. With female children, who are closely supervised and encouraged in domestic skills, the emphasis is on obedience, humility, politeness, and good manners.

Another researcher (Guinn, 1977) has provided a summary of attitudinal differences between Mexican-American and Anglo-American cultures in the following tabular form.

Mexican-American Values	Anglo-American Values
Being rather than doing	Doing rather than being
Limited stress on material	Material well-being
Present-time orientation	Future orientation
Simple patterns of work organization and group cooperation	Individual action and reaction
Central importance of the family; personal relations	Impersonal relations
Tradition	Change
Fatalism; accommodation to problems	Man's mastery over the universe

When discussing how children are brought up in American-Indian cultures, one must keep in mind that these are diverse tribal cultures with differences as well as similarities in their value patterns which have, to some extent, survived five hundred years of white middle-class pressure.

Two studies (Hilger 1951, 1972) involve the tribes of the Northwest, who fished and hunted, gathered food, and traded. Thus relying on nature, they developed a cooperative way of life in harmony with nature. With this went a religious observance of traditions and values, which children were taught by the elders of the tribe. Generosity, bravery, and stamina were highly valued and therefore praised in children; boasting, lying, rowdiness, and stinginess were frowned upon and discouraged by ridicule. Children were respected as individuals but were in general expected to be seen and not heard. Physical punishment was not used.

Zintz (1970) contrasted the value system of the Pueblo Indians of the Southwest with that of the Anglo-American culture:

Pueblo Indian Values	Anglo Values
Harmony with nature	Mastery over nature
Mythology	Scientific explanation
Present-time orientation	Future orientation
Satisfaction of present needs	Working to get ahead
Time as infinite	Efficient use of time
Following the ways of the old people	Climbing the ladder of success
Cooperation	Competition
Anonymity	Individuality
Submissiveness	Socially acceptable aggression
Humility	Striving to win
Sharing	Saving for the future

In a comparative study of black, Anglo, and Mexican-Americans who lived in the same working-class neighborhood (Bartz & Levine, 1978), black parent-child relationships were typified by high control, high support, and open communication. Black parents showed their love and involved their children in decision-making, but they also believed in strictness and expected their children to obey and achieve and to control their body functions and their emotions at an early age.

Similar conclusions were reached in a study by Durrett et al. (1975), which also distinguished Mexican-Americans from blacks and whites as being more protective and consistent in rewarding and punishing, less achievement-oriented, but demanding greater self-control with regard to crying or anger. It also noted that black mothers instilled fewer guilt feelings than Mexican or white American mothers.

Contrasting black working-class and black middle-class mothers (Staples, 1971), the latter were generally more responsive to children's emotional needs, less reliant on physical punishment, and more apt to use reasoning and rewards to achieve desired behaviors.

It is important that teachers of the children in the various minority groups understand the traditional values and child-rearing practices of the home in order to minimize conflicting demands and to find the most effective educational incentives (Bachtold & Rangel de Jackson, 1978; Gay, 1978).

part of an approach that also includes permissive toilet-training and easy tolerance of childhood sexuality and aggression. But in another culture the same degree of permissiveness may be associated with the opposite attitudes toward toilet-training and sexuality. In such a variety of settings it is very difficult to tell just which practice is causing what effect.

Cross-cultural studies of breast-feeding have shown that in most preliterate (nonreading) and traditional societies the mother nurses according to her perception of her baby's need. In many societies infants sleep with their mothers so that they may be fed and comforted during the night. The Mundugumor of New Guinea, however, nurse their children standing up and push them away abruptly as soon as the feeding can be terminated (Mead, 1949). The Marquesans of the South Pacific nurse their children irregularly and with many misgivings, because they feel that lengthy nursing causes misbehavior later in childhood (Whiting & Child, 1953).

Breast-feeding of all varieties seems to decline as a society becomes more sophisticated (Jelliffe, 1962). Here the role of technology is obvious: only with advanced knowledge of nutrition, sterilization, and so on can a substitute for breast milk be provided.

Studies of play behavior promise to reveal some interesting cultural differences in children. In one study (Finley & Layne, 1971) the play behavior of children from Cambridge Massachusetts, was compared with that of Mayan children from the Yucatan Peninsula. The investigators concluded that the American subjects were more active and manipulative in their approach to toys, whereas the Mayan children were passive, socially oriented, and more visual in their explorations.

Preliterate cultures are not the only subjects of cross-cultural study. Urie Bronfenbrenner, in his survey (1970) of child-rearing in Russia, has attempted to describe "the making of a new Soviet man." We saw in Chapter 3 some of the practices he found in use in Soviet day-care centers, aimed at stimulating the child's perceptual and cognitive development. Beyond this, he found that Russian infants are held in their caregivers' arms substantially more than American children. The Russian child also receives more kissing and cuddling and is much more likely to be breast-fed. However, the infants do not have as much freedom of movement as an American infant, and they are not allowed to stray far from adult eyes even when they are much older.

From birth Russian children are introduced to a variety of parenting figures in addition to their own mother. They are quite comfortable with strangers as they grow up. Of particular interest is Bronfenbrenner's description of the socialization process that comes into full play as children enter nursery school. Parental discipline is accomplished through withdrawal of love. Among peers, as at school, there is a strong and ideologically supported need for conformity and good behavior.

Child-rearing practices in China are of particular interest because China, with a population of over 800 million, is the largest nation in the world, and child-rearing innovations there constitute the largest "experiment" ever conducted. But in contrast to the Soviet system of child care, which is highly centralized, there is much diversity in China. The Chinese believe in self-reliance and in suiting training and education to the specific needs of the country's different regions.

Much of Chinese life, both urban and rural, is organized around the commune, which one observer (Sidel, 1972) characterizes as a "planned, self-contained community where you ... create a system of interdependence in which nearly all ... needs are met within the commune." The day-care needs of working mothers and the educational needs of infants and children are met by means of nurseries, kindergartens, and primary and middle schools.

As soon as the infant is about two months old, his mother takes it with her when she goes to work. She nurses it twice a day, but the rest of the time it stays in a "nursing room" until the age of about eighteen months. Then, especially in the cities, the baby will usually go to a nursery school. The nursing room may have from twenty-seven to sixty babies, ranging in age from two to eighteen months. The children are supervised by several women (the observer found fourteen in the sixty-child nursing room) drawn from the factory staff; the children call them "Auntie." At about a year to a year and a half toilet-training is begun, and all children seem to become trained without difficulty.

The multiple or shared mothering found in the Soviet system also seems to be common in China. The caregivers are permanent figures in the child's world, and all of them seem to be warm and giving; in fact they are chosen for these qualities, rather than on the basis of special training or credentials.

In the nursery school children early become accustomed to group activity. There are short lectures, "military" training, singing, and a certain amount of free play; the more active children are not restrained, but are encouraged to help the teacher. The observer reports that out of several hundred children she had seen, only three or four misbehaved. These were firmly but gently calmed by their elders; she never saw an adult become angry at a child.

Out of its particular situation and needs China has clearly created a system of child-rearing fundamentally different from our own. Family life, however, is still very important in China, and although children seen by the observer were calm and well-behaved, they were also alert, active, and social.

SUMMARY

▶ Separation anxiety is a normal outgrowth of young children's attachment to their parents. Most toddlers are distressed if separated from their parents, even briefly, but institutionalized children who have no strong attachment appear to suffer no such anxiety. The anxiety may result from a discrepant schema, or from the loss of stimulation and interaction when the parent leaves.

▶ Children separated from their parents for long periods at this age show protest, despair, and detachment; when reunited with the parents, they may take a long time to regain confidence and dare to renew the attachment.

▶ Socialization is the learning process by which we become acceptable members of our society. It includes not only discipline, but also the positive learning of values, appreciations, and expectations. When the parent-child relationship is good, the child wants to please and imitate the parent, and socialization usually proceeds rather smoothly.

▶ Toilet-training is an early element of socialization. It cannot take place until children reach the necessary degree of physical maturation. At about this time children begin to strive for individual autonomy, and they find pleasure in expressing it in this way. They also need to be allowed autonomy in regard to other skills and to be praised as they learn to exercise these skills.

▶ Small children have a limited range of emotions, but they do manifest fear and anger. Most fears are learned, thus can be unlearned with intelligent help from parents. Anger can be channeled to different objects, and expressed in different ways, according to what is approved by the society. In toddlers it often takes the form of tantrums, frequently resulting from frustration, fatigue, overstimulation, or loss of a parent's attention. The parents' own example is critical in teaching children how to handle their own anger.

▶ Views on child-rearing do change, but slowly. From the moral emphasis in colonial America we have moved to a more psychological concern. Important schools of thought in our century have been the behaviorism of Watson and Skinner and the psychoanalytic approach of Freud. Cross-cultural studies by Mead and others, however, have shown the cultural limitations of universal theories of behavior.

▶ Discipline is the various means by which a child is made to obey. For it to be successful parents must be consistent in their behavior and demands and must not use it to crush the child's autonomy.

▶ "Mothering" as a term is associated with the cultural notion that certain behaviors are natural only to women. Today, however, we are recognizing that both mother and father must be both nurturant and firm, and the term "parenting" has been introduced in reference to the entire parental role.

▶ Child abuse, usually by the parents, is a serious and growing social problem in the United States. Usually, abusive parents are those who were themselves abused as children. They are unable to cope with their own emotions and with the economic and other stresses of the environment.

Reporting centers and hotlines can help somewhat, by bringing cases to official attention and by helping parents to control their abusive tendencies.

FURTHER READINGS

Comer, James P., and Poussant, Alvin F. *Black child care*. New York: Pocket Books, 1975.
Raising a black child is different in many ways from raising a white child. The authors, both black psychiatrists, feel that growing up black in America raises problems for children and their parents. The book addresses the problems of race and serves as a practical reference for bringing up black children.

Davis, W. A., and Havighurst, R. J. *Father of the man: How your child gets his personality*. Boston: Houghton Mifflin, 1947.
A classic discussion of child development and child-rearing with an emphasis on class differences. Includes an appendix on social class differences in child-rearing practices. The approach is personal with interesting examples from case histories.

Erikson, Erik H. *Childhood and society* (2nd ed.). New York: Norton, 1963.
A well-known study of childhood from a psychoanalytic viewpoint, by one of the best-known authorities of our day. Erikson's understanding grows out of his clinical work with troubled children and his cross-cultural experiences with two American Indian tribes. In the last part of the book he considers the "evolution of identity" in several industrial societies. Although the Freudian categories he uses will not be acceptable to everyone, this is an interesting and provocative book.

Kempe, Ruth S., and Kempe, C. Henry. *Child abuse*. Cambridge, Mass.: Harvard University Press, 1978.
An excellent, up-to-date discussion of the subject, emphasizing the treatment and prevention of physical abuse.

Montessori, Maria. *The secret of childhood*. (B. Carter, trans.) New York: Longmans, 1936.
Sensitive account of the newborn and of early childhood by the founder of an important educational philosophy. The Montessori method emphasizes the necessity of treating children with dignity and respecting their individuality. A spiritual as well as scientific approach.

Park, R. D., and Collmer, C. W. Child abuse: An interdisciplinary analysis. In E. M. Hetherington (Ed.), *Review of Child Development Research*, vol. 5. Chicago: University of Chicago Press, 1975.
An up-to-date and comprehensive review of the phenomenon of child abuse.

Sidel, Ruth. *Women and child care in China: A firsthand report*. New York: Penguin, 1976.
An extended visit to China convinced Sidel that the traditional attitudes toward parenting and child-rearing are changing in that country. She compares the practices in Chinese nurseries and those in Israeli kibbutzim and in Russia. Illustrated.

Watson, J. B. *Behavior: An introduction to comparative psychology*. New York: Holt, Rinehart and Winston, 1967.
To find out what behaviorism is, read this book, because John B. Watson defined it, shaped it, promoted it, and coined its terminology. Stimulus and response, reward and punishment, and the entire mechanics of conditioned learning are laid out. (This book was originally published in 1914.)

Weintraub, M., and Lewis, M. The determinants of children's responses to separation. Monograph SRCD #172, 1977.

The determinants of two-year-old children's responses in unfamiliar settings to brief separations from their mothers is the focus of this monograph.

Zimbardo, Philip G., and Radl, Shirley L. *The shy child.* New York: McGraw-Hill, 1981.

A parents' guide to preventing and overcoming shyness from infancy to adulthood. This book is based on nine years of research on shyness. The authors deal with the cause of shyness and what can be done to cure it. They describe parenting style that builds the child's self-esteem.

Observational Activities
Part Two   Toddlerhood

Television Viewing Patterns and Response

We are told that, the average, six-month-old babies watch television an hour a day. By the time a child is two years old, he or she is spending about twenty-five hours a week in front of a television set.

Interview three mothers of children between the ages of eighteen and twenty-four months to find out about their child's television viewing habits and reactions. Ask them the following questions, and take notes on their answers:

1. What is your child's favorite television program?
2. What is your child's favorite television character?
3. What is your favorite television choice for your child?
4. How much TV does your child watch on a weekday? Saturday?
5. What percent of your child's television viewing involves what you would call adult programs?
6. What TV program incident or person was funny or amusing to your child?
7. What has been most frightening?
8. Do you watch TV with your child? How often, and what programs?
9. Do you set your child's viewing schedule?
10. What do you think your child has learned and is learning from TV?

Analyze your responses, and draw some tentative conclusions about children's viewing patterns and the parents' role in establishing viewing patterns. It might be interesting to pool data with your classmates.

The Young Child's Verbal and Nonverbal Communication

Toddlers are occasionally frustrated by their inability to get their message across to an adult. They know what they want to say but still have trouble communicating verbally. Observe a child (eighteen to twenty-four months of age) and adult pair in a public place for about fifteen minutes and record:

1. Attempts at verbal language by the child—actual words used by the child in trying to get a message across to an adult.
2. Nonverbal attempts to communicate—body language used by the child trying to get a response from an adult (pointing, tugging, climbing onto adult's lap, turning adult's head, etc.)
3. Adult anticipation of child's desires or requests before child fully communicates them either verbally or nonverbally.

Analyze your written notes by considering the following, and write a brief summary of your findings:

1. Which mode is predominant—verbal, nonverbal, or anticipatory?
2. How does the adult either encourage or discourage communication or development of verbal skill?
3. If there is evidence of the child's frustration at trying to communicate, what occasions it, and how does the adult respond to the child's frustrations?
4. How soon does the adult respond to the child's nonverbal request?
5. Does the adult ever misunderstand the child's request? Describe.

PART THREE

Preschool Years

Chapter 6

❖❖❖❖❖❖

Physical and Perceptual Development

Laurie is a competent three-year-old, scarcely recognizable as the two-and-a-half-year-old who used to insist on an exact repetition each day of the ritual of her bath and going to bed; who demanded that the same books be read at the same time; who could be swayed neither by argument nor punishment. Now she looks up and asks, "Do it dis way?" When Laurie engages her mother in conversation, she speaks so clearly that she can be understood by anyone, not just her parents. She asks questions about what she sees, hears, and smells and even about what she only remembers or imagines. She likes to hear stories about herself when she was a baby. Her attention span is steadily increasing, and she has learned to listen and likes to listen in order to learn from adults. She is beginning to play cooperatively with other children.

Laurie's newfound amiability and self-control have much of their basis in physical control. Now she walks erect and has better control of her legs and feet as she moves. Her running is more coordinated, and she is less likely to engage in the fall-and-recovery pattern of toddlerhood. She no longer holds out her arms as she moves but swings them as adults do. She can ride a tricycle. The small muscles of her hands and eyes are more under control

221

also. She can work her buttons and zippers and put on her shoes. In fact, she is pretty much able to dress herself and feed herself as well.

Physical development is the foundation of Laurie's progress. Her increasing size and strength enable her more and more to find her way without adult protection and guidance; the development of her central nervous system prepares her for great advances in understanding as well as mastery over her own body.

PHYSICAL GROWTH

At age three the average boy is a little over three feet (90 cm) tall and weighs over thirty pounds (13.5 kg); by age five he has grown to about forty-four inches (110 cm) and forty-three pounds (19.3 kg). There are individual variations, but girls tend to be slightly shorter and lighter than boys. Children who are big for their age at the beginning of the preschool years will probably still be big for their age at the end of the period. There is also some correlation between the height of preschool children and the height they will attain as adults, though there are exceptions: A child who is small at four or five may well develop into a larger-than-average adult. See Figure 6.1.

Boys and girls develop at about the same pace during the preschool years and through childhood until puberty. Girls usually reach half their adult height shortly before they are two years old. Most boys do not reach their halfway point until they are almost two and a half, but boys generally have more height to attain as adults. One of the most significant developmental differences between boys and girls is that boys have more muscle and girls more fatty tissue. In both sexes the infant fatty tissue is gradually replaced, but girls tend to retain it longer than boys (Breckenridge & Murphy, 1969).

Body proportions change dramatically in the preschool period. The trunk and legs grow rapidly, but cranial growth is not so fast as before. As a result, by age six the legs are about half the length of the body, a ratio that will remain constant for the rest of the child's life. In other words, the average six-year-old already has the body shape of an adult.

In the preschool child's growing skeleton cartilage turns into bone and existing bones grow larger and harder. By age three most children have a complete set of temporary teeth (also called milk teeth or deciduous teeth).

Muscular development accounts for most of the weight gained during the preschool years by both boys and girls. Because the large muscles develop more rapidly than the small ones, motor abilities progress from broad to precise. A two-year-old can, for example, build a tower of six or seven blocks and kick a large ball, but he cannot do many things a five-year-old can, such as cut with scissors, catch a small ball, copy letters, or hop on one foot. With time and practice the smaller muscles mature and the child performs increasingly complex motions requiring more and more precise coordination. The small muscles do not reach full maturity, however, until adolescence.

While the skeleton and muscles of the preschool child are developing, so is the nervous system. By age five the brain has reached 75 percent of its adult weight, and only a year later, 90 percent. It is also during the preschool years that *myelinization*—a sheathing of nerve fibers in the brain composed of a white insulating material called myelin—is completed. This sheathing helps speed transmission of nerve impulses, allowing for more precise and efficient control of motor actions. Myelinization is usually complete before a child starts first grade.

Many other physiological changes occur during the preschool years. Breathing becomes slower and deeper; the heart beats more slowly and steadily; and especially in boys, blood pressure increases. Thus, by age five most children are physically prepared for all the physical demands that will be placed on them in middle childhood.

Diet and Health

In normal, healthy children the genetic potential is helped toward fulfillment by healthful, invigorating environmental conditions. The quality of children's nutrition and health care strongly influences their development.

Unfortunately, a majority of children in the world today receive neither proper nutrition nor adequate medical attention. They do not get enough protein for building body cells, or enough vitamins and minerals for structural development, or enough carbohydrates for energy. The children of poverty-stricken areas in Africa, India, Pakistan, and South America are short and slight compared to other children (Meredith, 1968). When people are poor, they are usually malnourished. Chronic malnutrition—usually beginning before birth—can produce permanent physical deformities and mental incapacity. Furthermore, poorly fed children, even when their growth is not stunted, are more susceptible to infections of the eyes, ears, and respiratory system and are less able to combat their illnesses. They are less alert mentally and less active physically.

Illness early in life is a particularly serious problem among the poor in the United States because of nutritional deficiencies. Although each generation tends to produce larger, healthier babies than the generation before it, millions of children continue to suffer from respiratory illness, bad teeth, and other conditions related to inadequate diet. One survey (Schaefer & Johnson, 1969) showed that among children under six years old 12–16 percent suffer from vitamin C deficiency and about 30 percent from vitamin A deficiency. One-third of all American children have anemia severe enough to require medical attention.

Malnutrition can result from the consumption of "junk foods" that provide only "empty calories"—that is, refined carbohydrates. In a consumer culture it is difficult to keep a child from eating presweetened cereals, candy bars, and soft drinks. Day after day the child sees this kind of food recommended on television by favorite cartoon characters and TV personalities. Yet when junk foods make up a large part of the diet, the result may be nutritional deficiencies, often accompanied by obesity. It is not uncommon for a child today to be both overweight and undernourished.

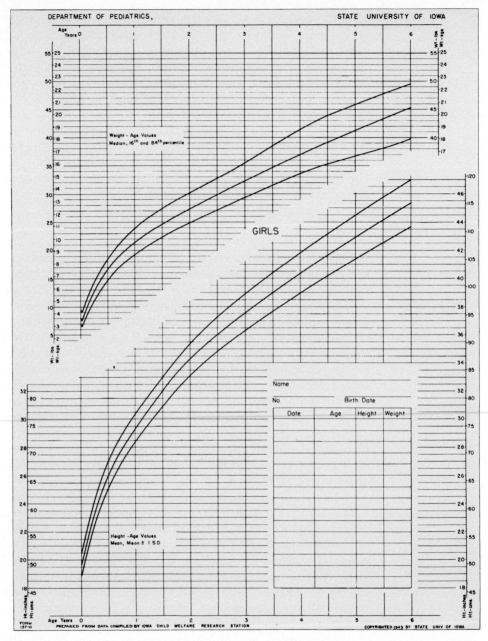

Figure 6.1 Iowa Growth Curves. The upper sets of curves show growth in height for girls (left page) and boys (right page) from birth to six years of age. Professionals use curves like these to compare the growth of an individual child with the average growth of children the same age.

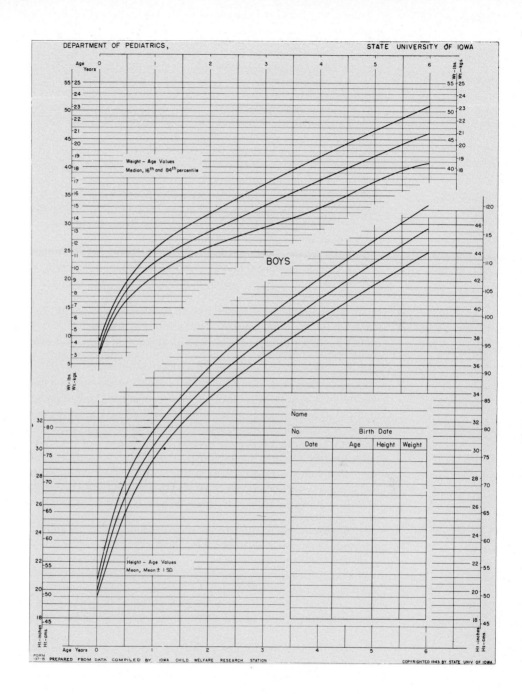

❖◆❖

Deprivation Dwarfism

Jonathan is three years old and in the hospital. Looking into his crib we see a very small, thin child—you might think he was just over one year old—legs sprawled, sucking his thumb and staring blankly ahead with sad, listless eyes. He looks as though he might be suffering from a disease or malnutrition, but in fact Jonathan is a victim of deprivation dwarfism. What has he been deprived of? His parents are middle-class Americans and he has been fed and sheltered like other middle-class children. He has no serious illness; he was not born with any physical defect. He has been deprived of only one thing: love. His parents didn't want a child, and when he was born they didn't hold him, talk to him, smile at him, or play with him. An adult may *say*, "I'm dying of loneliness," but a child can actually do it.

Researchers (Gardner, 1972) suggest that being deprived of affection almost always leads to emotional and physical disturbance in the child. The disturbance is registered at first in the higher, more developed brain centers. Then, it is theorized, these brain centers send messages to a more "primitive" part of the brain, the hypothalamus, which in turn regulates the pituitary gland, the "master gland" of the endocrine system. The pituitary is responsible for regulating the release of somatotrophin, the growth hormone that stimulates cells to reproduce. When children suffer from emotional deprivation, they produce much less growth hormone. The result is a boy like Jonathan.

Since there is a complicated chain of events between the brain functions and the release of growth hormone, researchers have had to devise sophisticated methods of determining exactly what part of the system is malfunctioning. For instance, a child who is born with a defective pituitary gland may fail to grow, but in that case the problem would be physiological, not emotional. Unfortunately, research suggests that many cases of dwarfism are caused by emotional deprivation. If a dwarfed child is removed from an inadequate home and placed in a situation where he or she receives stimulation and affection, the amount of growth hormone in the child's body rises remarkably, and he or she may begin to grow and develop normally.

Studies of the relationship between sleeping patterns and the release of growth hormone provide support for the hormone theory. Most growth hormone is released into the bloodstream during a stage of sleep when the higher brain centers are the least active. Victims of deprivation dwarfism have very irregular sleeping patterns. It seems possible that because of their emotional situation these children never reach this particular stage of sleep, for when they do return to normal growth, they also develop normal sleeping patterns (Shaywitz et al., 1971).

Deprivation dwarfism is an extreme example of how emotional environment can affect a child's physical growth. It can be isolated and studied by researchers because the affliction is so severe and its symptoms are so obvious. Some children, however, may exhibit less obvious symptoms of emotional deprivation. They may be small and weak but not dwarfed, or they may be sick often. Parents often think that these children simply have a "poor constitution." It may not occur to them to look for possible emotional causes. But there is evidence that even in adolescence emotional deprivation can affect physical well-being; a common problem among older children is malnutrition resulting from a loss of appetite. This condition usually arises when the child feels lonely and unwanted.

Thus, a positive, affectionate, loving environment is not just a luxury for children. Their physical development depends on it.

The federal government recently issued a set of dietary guidelines that recommends the selection of a variety of foods each day, particularly stressing the value of food high in complex carbohydrates—starch and fiber—found in such foods as beans, peas, nuts, seeds, fruits and vegetables, and whole grain breads and cereals. Ounce for ounce, carbohydrates are less fattening than fats and contain many essential vitamins and minerals in addition to calories (Brody, 1980). Children establish their eating preferences when they are very young and associate certain special foods with home and security. Many Americans are able to resist the appeal of junk foods and fancy desserts, showing their love and affection by serving healthy and nutritious foods to their children.

Physique and Personality

Many investigators have tried to establish a link between physique and personality. How convenient it would be if we could confidently describe someone's personality merely by classifying body type! So far, however, researchers have been frustrated by the tendency of most people to be exceptions to their categories. Nevertheless, the ingenuity of these researchers has provided some provocative ways of thinking about the relationship of physique to personality.

One widely known system of body typing was proposed by the psychologist W. H. Sheldon (1940). According to this system body types can be grouped into three broad categories: the soft and rounded *endomorph*, the well-muscled *mesomorph*, and the lean and slightly muscular *ectomorph*. Each of these body types is supposedly correlated with certain personality traits. The endomorph is supposed to be friendly and easygoing, the mesomorph bold and self-assertive, the ectomorph shy and socially restrained. Certainly these patterns can sometimes be found. President William Howard Taft, probably the roundest man who ever sat in the White House, was noted for his geniality; Muhammad Ali is well muscled and is equally bold and self-assertive. But how do we fit ectomorphs such as Peter Frampton or Jane Fonda into this scheme? Or the "endomorph" whose body type is a result of anxiety and overeating? Perhaps the answer is that somatotyping simply reflects social stereotypes: if you have a body like Santa Claus, you had better act jolly because people expect it. Actually, few people clearly belong in any one of the three categories. What personality could be predicted for a person who is a mesomorph above the waist and an ectomorph below?

The preschool years are characterized by the rapid growth of skeleton and muscles as well as increasing motor ability.

Physical *attractiveness* is also a potent factor in children's lives and hence on their developing personalities. This is the clear implication of a recent study of teacher's judgments. Seventy-six teachers were given identical psychological reports and asked how well they thought the child would probably do in academic and social pursuits. The teachers were also given photos of the child supposedly described in the report, but some of the photos showed an attractive child and others showed an unattractive one. The teachers systematically rated the attractive children more favorably (Ross & Salvia, 1975).

Locomotion and Manipulation

As children mature they discover that they can do many new things—run, jump, climb, balance themselves. The preschool years are marked by great advances in strength, speed, and coordination.

As children discover with delight that they can lift and move objects that defeated all their earlier efforts, their new muscular ability contributes much to a growing sense of self-confidence. There seems to be little difference in strength between boys and girl until around age six, and the lead that boys take from then on does not become pronounced until adolescence. Before adolescence most of the difference is probably a result of cultural attitudes: in our society boys are encouraged to develop their physical strength and most girls are not, so boys play strenuous games while girls spend more of their time in quiet play.

Competition becomes increasingly important for the preschool child during play particularly in terms of speed. Who can get to the other end of the supermarket aisle faster? Can Jane build a tower of blocks faster than Joan? Can Jim be the first to get to the top of the jungle gym? Because speed is largely a function of reaction time, children's success in such races depends on the speed of their responses. The sharpening of these responses is an important function of speed-oriented play.

Coordination

More complex than either strength or speed is coordination—the channeling of strength and speed into smooth, rhythmic, accurate movements. Consider these two actions: throwing a stone into a lake and throwing a ball to a person several yards away. Coordination—voluntary muscular control—makes the difference between them. The ability to judge time and distance and to relate them to muscular functions does not come easily to the preschool child, as it requires control of the small muscles.

The motor behavior of three-year-olds shows their increased control over their bodies. They delight in running, with sudden starts and stops. They turn corners rapidly and jump up and down with ease. Their coordination has developed sufficiently that they can stack as many as ten blocks before a collapse.

At age four most children can jump forward as well as jump straight up

The children copy different parts of their teacher's gesture. They have not yet developed control and coordination of the smaller muscles.

and down. They probably cannot yet throw a ball with much strength or accuracy, but they can swing their arms freely without any exaggerated movements of the torso.

By the time children are five or six they are capable of increasingly complex feats such as skipping, climbing, balancing, and throwing. Their coordination has matured to the point where their skills are recognized by other children, and their social life begins to involve rivalry and cooperation.

Manipulating Materials

Many of a child's efforts to learn about the world involve the manipulation of raw materials. Preschool children are eager to play with almost anything. They find excitement not only in paints, construction paper, and clay, but also in pipe cleaners, drinking straws, paper bags, toothpicks, and rubber bands. As their coordination develops, they become increasingly skillful in handling these materials. The three-year-old who can finger-paint and fold paper grows into a five-year-old who can paint with a brush and cut with scissors.

No matter what materials the child manipulates, mastery of them will develop in a similar sequence. Younger preschool children delight in investigating the materials themselves. Finger paints and modeling clay are sources of pure sensual pleasure as they are squished between the child's fingers; then they become interesting *things* to be manipulated in as many different ways as possible. The child explores the medium to become familiar with all of its potential for play, discovering and practicing the physical skills required to work with each new material. Given paints and a brush at this stage, children will lavish form and color in broad, abstract strokes across the paper. They show little interest in pictorial representation or in precision, but as they gain skill, they move fluidly through several different shapes, discovering what the material can do and what they can do with it.

Gradually preschool children develop a longer attention span, and their physical coordination and skills increase so that they have more control over their play materials. They are able to take the time needed to build a tall block tower that will stand on its own. Their paintings become representational and eventually may contain elaborate details, involving patience and planning for their execution. Pencil drawings lend themselves to representation even in the earlier stages of children's play, but as they become more skillful, their figures of people become more detailed and accurate. For example, the limbs are connected to the torso rather than to the head. The human face is by far the favorite subject of preschool drawings. Younger children carefully draw the eyes, nose, mouth, ears, and hair, but then indicate the rest of the body almost as an afterthought, rapidly sketching the arms and legs as stiff lines and the hands and feet as circles. Only later do details of clothing and background begin to appear. By age five most children have progressed beyond the rudimentary stick figures of their earlier efforts. However, their drawings still reflect their distinctive view of the world. Heads tend to be disproportionately large, and people tend to be larger than background objects.

The preschool period is a period of many exciting discoveries. As children become more and more aware of their expanding motor capabilities, they are spurred on to new levels of creativity and, ultimately, social interaction. The skills they develop as they compete during active play help determine their status in the eyes of others and, perhaps even more important, in their own eyes.

PERCEPTION

The study of perception is concerned with seeing, hearing, feeling, tasting, and smelling. Perception involves sensory input plus the initial categories and interpretations automatically given by the mind. During the preschool years initial perceptions usually trigger a chain of complex mental processes aimed either at problem-solving or at acquiring a fuller understanding of the situation. It is true that some perceptual awareness seems to be innate—depth perception, for example. But in the preschool years children's perceptions become finer, sharper, and more reliable. They begin to understand more clearly what pleases them, what hurts them, and why. They begin to see the world more nearly as adults do, and this maturing perception makes them more and more a part of that world.

Attention

Attention is not an ability but a quality of mental life that can be focused or shifted to some extent by conscious effort. Usually, however, it is habitual or immediate—it turns to the objects that elicit it.

Each of us is constantly aware of the many sights, sounds, and smells of the environment. It is impossible to heed all of these things all the time, so we respond more intensely to some of them than to others, according to our own individual needs and interests. This selective response is one aspect of **attention.** There is probably less difference between the attention of infants and that of preschoolers than many people might suppose. Infants are much more aware of details of the world around them than we give them credit for.

Burton White (1975) in his study of infants and young children noted that children from ages two to three spend about 14 percent of their waking time staring in a steady fashion. He says there is no good explanation for why children spend so much time staring (at age one 20 percent of a child's time is spent in steady staring), but he suspects that children are gaining information by means of their vision. After age three children spend less time staring (about 6 percent) and more time looking and listening (about 12 percent).

Part and Whole

An important aspect of the development of attention is the cognitive process of perceiving an object both in its entirety and in its component parts. Imagine a small girl whose mother takes her to a department store in a large suburban shopping center. As the girl stops for a moment to look up at a display of toys, her mother might disappear around a corner. What happens then? For a two- or three-year-old the experience might be terrifying—in the many-aisled store, with piped-in music and hundreds of strange people shopping, she may feel herself completely lost. She looks for Mommy, but all the women look alike to her at a distance. She may run from one shopper to another, growing more and more panicky. When she finally does find Mommy, it may be several hours before the fright wears off.

For a five-year-old getting lost in the same place may be only slightly alarming—or even enjoyable. This may be partly because she has been through it before—she knows her way around. But more important, she knows how to look for Mommy. She knows that Mommy is a tallish woman with short brown hair and a green overcoat, so she does not run to women who look somewhat different. She may remember what she and Mommy were shopping for and go to that part of the store where they are most likely to find each other. She will probably also be able to recognize her mother (and other people as well) not only by their features and clothing, but also by their characteristic gestures or ways of walking. What makes the difference is the older girl's ability to see both parts and wholes. She has learned to recognize the details of things and people that are important to her and to use them to find her way around in a confusing situation. She now has the ability to focus on details and, at the same time, to see how they fit into the overall situation.

The realization of how the parts relate to the whole is an important step in the cognitive development of small children.

There are two basic theories that try to explain how this ability develops. Some theorists suggest that we first make sense of a whole person, place, or thing and only later pick up the finer details. Other theorists see the process the other way around. According to them, we learn to recognize parts or qualities of things first, and later we add up these bits so that we can recognize the larger wholes. In any case the process is aided in the preschool period by the learning of concepts that bring the details together into a meaningful picture. For example, a certain picture might be described by a three-year-old as "lots of books in rows," whereas a five-year-old might say, "That's a library." The sight of a group of hard-hatted men operating huge machines and swinging steel beams on a city street might be meaningless to a three-year-old, but at age five that child might say knowingly, "The men are putting up a building."

Younger children characterize what they can of an object, preferably the whole if they recognize it, and if not, then an outstanding part. The ability to attend to both the whole and the parts at the same time—known as *perceptual integration*—develops with age (Elkind, Koegler & Go, 1964). The development of language, which gives the child concepts of collective wholes—a library, for example—also plays a critical role not only in the reporting of perception, but in the original perception itself (Flavell, 1963).

Attention Span

We all know people—children and adults—who can grasp very easily the essence of a situation or problem, but whose attention wanders as soon as the initial novelty wears off. The length of time we can focus our attention on a given object or task is called our **attention span.** Attention is sustained longer as perceptual abilities grow and concepts and skills develop.

Three characteristics of an object or event seem to determine whether a child will give it sustained attention. The first is rapid change. A flashing light, for example, will hold one's attention longer than a steady light. The second is novelty. Children trying pistachio ice cream for the first time will pay special attention to its taste and color because they are different (but not too different) from the ice cream they are used to. The third characteristic, which seems to become important after children are about nine to twelve months old, is harder to describe: basically, it is that children will give increasing attention to relatively familiar objects, such as a cartoon, that suggest ideas for them to play with. Here such objects elicit sustained attention because they cause children to use their minds actively, and the activity may be pleasurable in itself.

Children may be capable of quite sustained attention at a very early age. A one-year-old may play at a single task for fifteen minutes or longer. But attention span increases during the preschool years. This change seems to be linked to development in other areas—general intelligence, improved memory and analytical skills, the ability to ignore distractions, and probably most important, increased motivation. It is the motivation to spend a long time on a single task that enables children to do well at anything they may try, from reading to turning somersaults.

Discrimination

Discrimination is the ability to "tell the difference" between two objects. Children learn to discriminate among objects through their own observations and experiences. For example, it makes little difference to children whether a glass on the table is on their right or their left; all they care about is whether they can reach it and whether it has milk in it. Thus, they may learn to discriminate between near and far and full and empty more quickly than between left and right.

Daily life requires the ability to make many other distinctions, most of which must be learned by experience. A boy burned by a stove may at first stay away from the stove whether it is hot or cold; later he must learn that it was the heat, not the stove, that burned him. There are also discriminations to be made in the social sphere. At age three most children may not grasp the difference between "mine" and "yours," but sooner or later guidance from others—maybe in the form of playground quarrels—will pound the message home.

Because their experience is more limited, younger children generally require more clues than older children do to recognize objects and tell them apart. A three-year-old, for example, may require a great deal of detail to recognize a picture that a six-year-old can readily identify from a sketch or outline. Research suggests that it is only from about the fourth year on that children learn to distinguish things on the basis of form, size, orientation, or even color (Inhelder & Piaget, 1964).

Long before they can discriminate among graphic symbols, infants learn to differentiate between facial expressions. Mother's pleasure or anger, for example, are evident to them from the way she smiles or the way she creases her brow. There is some evidence (Pick et al., 1972) that we learn very early in life to see a downward-curving line as representing a disapproving mouth and to see an upward-curving line as representing a smile.

Discrimination involves the ability to recognize the distinctive features of similar but nonidentical things. One researcher (Gibson, 1963) has studied the development of this ability through the use of letterlike forms, or graphemes, a standard tool for studying perceptual development in children. By varying the distinctive features of each grapheme, she hoped to learn about the development of discrimination in youngsters. Working with a group of 160 children aged four to eight, she showed each child a set of twelve standard figures, one at a time. Then each child was shown a set of variations on the standard figures. The variations involved the curving of straight lines; the rotating, tilting, or reversing of the figures; and the closing or breaking of contours. The children were asked to choose the variant that exactly matched the standard. (In many cases no exact match was possible.) The number and the kinds of errors the children made were then counted and analyzed according to age group.

The experiment showed which errors are most characteristic of children at each age. Errors in closure (for example "O" and "C") were rare even among the youngest children. On the other hand, errors involving the slanting of previously unslanted lines were common even among the oldest children.

Marked differences were observed between the responses of four- and five-year-old subjects. The older children were consistently more successful in distinguishing certain transformations: line to curve (the change from "U" to "V"), rotation ("M" to "W"), and reversal ("d" to "b"). A broad range of individual differences was observed with all age groups, but it seems clear that, in general, different types of perceptual ability tend to appear only at particular ages, partly as a result of inner development and partly as a function of experience.

The Letters of the Alphabet

The ability to recognize the letters of our own alphabet and distinguish one letter from another is a most important kind of discrimination because it forms the basis for reading. Most children begin to learn their own alphabet late in the preschool years, at about five or five and a half. That, of course, is the age when most children start school. It would be a mistake, however, to think that going to school is the only way children learn the alphabet. Before they attend school, they have already learned a great deal about the alphabet from magazines, books, signs, and television. At first the letters look like so many interchangeable shapes. Then, rather suddenly, the letters begin to form a pattern—the children begin to discriminate the elements of their own written language. They start school at this time and learn to read; because they are ready to learn.

Researchers (Keislar, Hsieh, & Bhasin, 1972) have shown that this is true in many societies besides our own. They reasoned that if an important part of alphabet learning occurs before formal schooling begins, then children who were nearing school age should be able to distinguish between letters (and even words) written in their own alphabet better than letters and words written in a different, unfamiliar alphabet. They tested 153 children, boys and girls, in Taiwan, India, and the United States. The children, all preschoolers, were divided into three age groups and tested to see how well they discriminated characters in Chinese, Hindi, and Roman alphabets (English is written in the Roman alphabet).

The results of the study were fairly consistent from one society to the next. The two younger age groups could not discriminate reliably between characters printed in any language; the American children, for example, could not tell a "b" from a "w" any better than they could tell two Chinese characters apart. The oldest group, however, aged five to five and a half, did significantly better. The Indian children did best in Hindi, the Chinese children did best

Children's ability to discriminate one letter from another is the foundation on which their ability to read will be based.

in Chinese, and the Americans did best in the Roman alphabet, even though none of these children had been taught to read in school.

How can we explain this? Part of the answer is that growing preschoolers develop a new discriminatory ability that allows them to tell one letter from another. To that extent, learning to read depends on such internal developments as maturation of the brain. A lot of it is social, however. Some children who watch "Sesame Street" on television can identify letters when they are only three years old.

Reading Readiness

"Don't teach your child to read" is the admonition educators have been giving to parents for the past fifty years in the belief that teaching children to read is best left to professionals. We now know (Durkin, 1966; Smethurst, 1975) that some preschoolers are ready to read. When, then, should children be taught to read—in first grade, kindergarten, preschool? How should they be taught— by phonetics or by word recognition? As we might guess, there is no one right answer for all children. Children differ, as we have seen, in their rates of development, their early experience, and their genetic potential. So we can expect that they will be ready to read at different times and that some will learn best by one method, some by another.

Reading readiness is both developmental and experiential. Since reading calls for many small, rapid eye movements, the child must have control of the fine muscles of the eye. As we noted before, control of the fine muscles develops later than control of the large muscles. Furthermore, the child must be able to perceive the sometimes minute differences between one letter and another. As we have seen in Gibson's experiment, such perceptual abilities are not yet present in most preschool children. Most of Gibson's four-year-olds had trouble seeing such differences, whereas most of her eight-year-olds perceived them quite easily. On this ground alone we might suspect that the average four-year-old is not yet ready to read. Attention span, memory, and classification ability also enter into the total readiness picture.

Then there is the experiential factor. Perhaps the most important element here is spoken language. Children who have learned to communicate fluently in speech will almost always have an easier time with reading than those who have not. However, reading is different from speaking because it is a more abstract process that is harder to grasp (Vygotsky, 1962).

Some actual indicators of a child's readiness to read are acquisition of the following fundamental skills:

1. Naming capital letters
2. Naming lowercase letters
3. Associating the appropriate speech sounds with these letters
4. Combining these sounds to form short words, such as "man," "pin," "hot"
5. Recognizing some common words at sight, such as "the," "are," "some," "said" (Smethurst, 1975)

Some preschoolers show that they are eager to start reading. They enjoy looking at books and magazines, delight in being read to, and ask the names of letters and printed words. But if children do not show such eagerness and do not have the fundamental skills, parents should not push them to read. This can produce frustration for parents and children alike.

From research on reading (Durkin, 1966) we know that many children under five can be taught to read by nonprofessional teachers outside the school and that early readers do at least as well in school, and often better, than other children do.

Some reading specialists contend that learning to read is natural (Goodman & Goodman, 1980). In a literate society children must be able to read to become full-fledged members of the society. Surrounded as they are by print in the form of signs, advertisements, newspapers, and magazines, children are motivated to learn to read by the necessity for doing so.

But what of the millions of children in urban America who have not been talked to, read to, and encouraged to communicate, investigate, and explore, who do not have a rich fund of background knowledge and are not motivated to read? When will they be ready to read? In many school systems they will be expected to learn to read at the same pace as the others. Starting out behind, they will fall further and further back until they drop out of school, virtually illiterate, at sixteen or even thirteen or fourteen.

SUMMARY

▶ The body proportions of preschool children begin to approximate the adult form, and their nervous systems mature. By age five the brain is 75 percent of its adult weight; myelinization of the nerve fibers is completed, permitting speedy transmission of nerve impulses.

▶ Proper nutrition and health care are crucial to normal development. Poverty-stricken children often lack adequate nutrients and medical care and, as a result, may not develop to their full intellectual and physical potential. American children at all economic levels consume "junk foods" that endanger their development by filling them up without providing essential nutrients.

▶ Theories that propose a link between body type and personality have proved unconvincing. However, physical development may influence personality; the better-developed child may become a leader, while the less-developed child may become timid and withdrawn.

▶ Great advances in strength, speed, and coordination occur in the preschool years, and the child becomes increasingly skillful in handling tools and materials. This development helps a child to acquire status among playmates and a good self-image.

▶ In young preschool children the ability to perceive the parts and the whole of an object at the same time is somewhat limited; older preschoolers learn to focus on details and fit them into the overall situation. They also make use of unifying concepts, for which language is very helpful.

▶ Discrimination is the recognition of distinctive features in similar but non-identical things, such as the letters of the alphabet. The development of discrimination in children depends not only on maturation of the brain but on experience with the things to be discriminated.

FURTHER READINGS

Bower, T. G. R. *The perceptual world of the child.* Cambridge, Mass.: Harvard University Press, 1977.
This brief, highly readable book covers the major aspects of perceptual development.

Chukovsky, Kornei. *From two to five.* Berkeley: University of California Press, 1968.
Observations by a Soviet poet and writer of children's books on the development of thought processes and the acquisition of language. Chukovsky says young children need fairy tales and that they use fantasy to come to terms with the real world. Also, that children have a natural creativity in language use that can be stifled or encouraged, depending on the response of adults.

McWilliams, Margaret. *Nutrition for the growing years.* New York: Wiley, 1967.
A nutritionist discusses suitable diets for each stage of development and explains why eating patterns change. The book has an interesting chapter on how to teach nutrition to nursery school children, at the same time teaching them something about color and form. Height and weight tables are included.

Smith, L. *The children's doctor.* Englewood Cliffs, N.J.: Prentice-Hall, 1969.
Smith is a medical doctor who has had a popular television series. In this book he offers pediatric advice based on the patterns of development. The book emphasizes that children cannot learn until their neuromuscular mechanism is mature enough and clearly shows the relationship of physical development to activities and skills. An entire chapter is devoted to the hypermotor child.

Sparkman, Brandon, and Carmichael, Ann. *Blueprint for a brighter child.* New York: McGraw-Hill, 1973.
A small but explicit book that describes child development and tells how to bring out intelligence. Among other things the authors, who pioneered a preschool program in the South, tell why some toys are better than others for making children think. They also suggest simple games to teach the preschooler basic mathematical and verbal skills.

Chapter 7

❖❖❖❖❖❖

Cognition and Language

By age two children already understand a lot about what is going on around them. They know their families and a large number of other people, and they usually know what to expect from all of them. They have begun to understand and use language, and their memories may be surprisingly good. But they are only beginning to *organize* their perceptions. Over the next few years they will become reasoning and reasonable beings as they learn to think *about* events and people, time and space.

COGNITIVE DEVELOPMENT

Piaget regards the development of intelligence as an interaction between an individual's maturation and his or her social and physical environment. When Piaget began his work, most psychologists subscribed to the view that a complete explanation of cognition could be found in the response of the organism to its environment. Piaget, on the other hand, emphasized the developmental aspects of cognition—cognition as a continuous interaction between the active and developing intelligence of children and their ever-changing environments. Unlike many researchers Piaget was not especially concerned with individual differences in intelligence. He was not interested in investigating the question of why one child is more clever than another, but focused on intellectual processes that, he believed, would prove to be common to all children.

Cognitive development, according to Piaget, takes place by means of two processes: *organization*, in which one psychological structure is integrated with another, and *adaptation*, in which psychological structures are modified in the course of interactions with the environment. As we saw in Chapter 3, adaptation consists of assimilation and accommodation, two complementary processes that are present in every act of cognition. Individuals assimilate each new experience to what they already know, and at the same time accommodate or modify what they know to take the new experience into account.

Assimilation and accommodation are the same at all ages, though the matters they deal with may become more complex as the child matures. Preschool children who hear thunder for the first time may think that someone has slammed a door loudly in the next room. Their previous experience with loud noises forms a loud noise schema: the new experience has been *assimilated* to the preexisting schema. On second thought, however, the children may realize that the thunder was too loud to have been caused by someone in the house. Probably they will hear the thunder again and then begin to readjust all their ideas of loud noises and where they come from. Now, instead of fitting the new experience into the old categories, they revise their categories (schemas) to *accommodate* the new experience.

Piaget recognizes that development in our cognitive life occurs bit by bit, and that higher-order specialization occurs sooner in some people's lives than in others'. Nevertheless, he believes that we do achieve certain capabilities at more or less definite times (though we have long been building up to them) and that we then stay at that stage until we are ready to move up to the next. Although different people advance to the next stage at different times in their lives, Piaget maintains that the sequence of stages is the same for everybody. The period from birth to about two years is, as we have seen, the sensorimotor period. From age two until age seven, the child's cognition is what Piaget calls "preoperational." The preoperational period begins with the first appearance of symbolic representation—the symbolic function.

Symbolic Function

While on vacation a little girl asked questions about the mechanism of the bells in a church steeple. One morning she appeared at her father's desk, stiff as a ramrod, and made a deafening noise. "You're bothering me," he said to her, "Can't you see I'm working?"

"Don't talk to me," replied the little girl, "I'm a church."

Piaget tells this story to illustrate the symbolic function. The ability to represent something by means of language, a mental image, or by a symbolic gesture is called by Piaget the *symbolic function*. The image of the bells and the church are recalled as this little girl symbolically relives her experience.

The development from the immediacy of the sensorimotor period in which children can think only in terms of the here and now to the symbolism of the preoperational period is a gradual one. Piaget sees several steps along the way: deferred imitation, symbolic play, drawing, the mental image, and finally language (Piaget & Inhelder, 1969).

Deferred Imitation

Direct imitation of gestures prefigures the symbolic function. One little boy without even looking would throw his right hand into the air, index finger pointed skyward, to signify his awareness that a plane was flying overhead. The gestures accompany the presence of the object. Deferred imitation, as for example, Jacqueline's portrayal of the temper tantrum of her visitor of the day before, described in Chapter 4, marks the entry of the symbolic function. The object need no longer be present; the child's own gesture serves as a symbol instead.

Symbolic Play

In response to her son's, "What do you mean 'go out and play?' " a frantic mother replied, "Well, just go out and do whatever it is you do when you're having too much fun to come in to dinner" (Garvey, 1977). For parents play is something children do when they are not eating, sleeping, or watching television. For Piaget play is an activity in which children are not being pressured to adapt to reality; children may manipulate reality to serve their own purposes. Piaget makes a distinction between *symbols*, signifiers of the child's own choosing, and *signs*, signifiers given to the child by society. In play children may structure their own symbols, their own world, and their own roles in it. The little girl who was a noisy church is also recalled by Piaget in this example: at lunchtime the child saw a plucked duck on the kitchen table, and it made a deep impression on her. The next evening she was found lying on the sofa so still the family thought she was sick. At first she remained silent, then, after anxious questioning, she said, in a faraway voice, "I'm a dead duck" (Piaget & Inhelder, 1969).

Symbolic play is similar to the dream in its use by children. The child saying "no, no" to her doll or pretending to be a dead duck is often working out conflicts she has encountered in the real world. In fact, in experiments and in therapy a child is often presented with dolls and other play materials and asked to play. The world of play, like the world of dreams, lacks rational cause and effect, logic, and the reality of the world outside. Symbolic play is important for children; in a Piagetian sense, it gives them a space in which to assimilate the real world to their own understanding of it.

Drawing

Children's drawings, too, are used by experimenters and therapists to gain insight into the mental world of a child. For Piaget, drawing is a step midway between symbolic play and the mental image—midway because at first children's drawings are not purposeful. Children will draw first and then decide what the picture represents. The meaning of the picture is discovered in the act of making it. The stage of mental imagery is reached when the drawing represents, not the reality of classical perspective, but a reality in which the artist draws attributes of an object that the artist knows that object to possess. A profile may have two eyes, potatoes will be shown underground, and the wheels on the far side of a bus will be shown. Drawing parts of an object that are not visible from the vantage point of the viewer is called *transparency*. It is as if one could see through objects. Much of world art has been drawn in this fashion—the attributes of people and objects being more important to many artists than a "realistic" representation.

At age seven or eight children can draw in perspective, with nearer objects being larger and objects in the background smaller. An important acquisition for children is the ability to see the same scene from several points of view. At nine or ten children can draw an object not only as they see it, but as it would be seen by someone on the opposite side of the object and by someone to their right or left.

Mental Images

Gradually deferred imitation gives way to the pure mental image. A boy who turns to represent a closing door may begin to swing his arm. Still later his hand waves as a remnant of his previous imitation. Finally, the imitation be-

Drawings are the expressions of mental images that children hold. The meaning of the pictures is discovered in the act of making them.

comes internalized. The symbolic function has matured when imitation takes the form of the pure mental image.

The study of the child's mental imagery is difficult because images are necessarily private. They can be externalized only in simulated form. The most direct means of examining mental imagery is to ask people to describe their own images verbally. It is difficult enough for most of us to describe the objects we have before our eyes, let alone the images we have in our minds. This difficulty is magnified many times in the case of children because of their limited language ability.

A second approach to the study of mental imagery is the analysis of drawings. This method shares some of the drawbacks of the linguistic approach. Few children—indeed, few adults—can draw well.

A third approach involves the child's selection of a drawing from a collection assembled by the experimenter. However, the drawings from which the child must choose may be no more than rough approximations of his own actual images.

As none of these approaches alone can give the researcher an accurate notion of the child's mental images, they are used in combination. One experiment, for example, was designed to test the development of kinetic imagery—that is, objects in motion. First, some children were shown a pair of stacked blocks. The top block was subsequently displaced in such a way as to overhang the bottom block. After a while the top block was returned to its original position. The children were then asked to draw the blocks as they had appeared in the displaced position. They were also shown an assortment of drawings and asked to select from these drawings the one that correctly pictured the blocks when they were displaced. As a control, the children were also asked to draw the displaced blocks while looking at them.

The pictures drawn and selected by the children suggested a general awareness of movement, but no distinct image of its exact nature. The child seems to form a general impression of a changing situation but cannot analyze its specific details.

During the preschool years, and in fact up to about age seven, children's imagery is quite static. They can represent both the beginning and end states of an object that is being transformed but not the actual transformation itself. We will see that this static quality of "stay-putness" is one of the characteristics of the preoperational period.

Language

The acquisition of language is the final phase in the transition from sensorimotor to preoperational thinking. Piaget believes that the development of the symbolic function must precede language—that is, the mental image "mother" must be in the toddler's head before he can say "mama." He is matching his mental image to the sounds he is making.

Language permits children to communicate their mental images to another person. As much as one person's mental image of "mother" may differ

❖❖❖

Children's Drawings

Why do children draw the way they do? So asks psychologist Jacqueline Goodnow (1977), who argues that children's drawings often suggest general aspects of development and skill. Characteristics of children's art which may appear whimsical and irrational are actually expressions of the way children understand and order their observations of the world. Drawings reflect how children think, what they perceive to be important, and how well they understand the relationships between objects.

The sequence in which children draw the parts of their pictures is an important factor in how the finished drawing will look. It also reflects how the child focuses on the subject. Most preschoolers start their drawings of a human figure with a circle. Some then complete each part of the figure, including the details, "as they go along": first face details, then the trunk complete with arms, followed by legs with feet. Other children draw the major body parts, working from top to bottom, and then return to the top to work on details such as hair and arms. Their strategy is to "go back to finish." How does each strategy influence the look of the finished drawing? In the first instance, children become so involved with finishing details that they may leave out, or forget to make room for, some major body parts, such as arms. In the second instance, children have become adept at dealing with the figure as a whole and have postponed the enjoyment of completing the details.

Often children do not have a well-developed sense of how parts of a picture stand in relation to other parts of the composition. For instance, once they have discovered that the horizontal represents the ground, they prefer to place objects such as houses at a 90 degree angle to the ground. However, chimneys are usually drawn at a 90 degree angle to the roofline, without reference to the ground horizontal. Thus, children do not generally relate all of the parts of the drawing to the same reference point. They see each part individually and do not necessarily connect the pieces to the whole composition.

Another characteristic of children's drawing is that each object in the picture must have its own well-defined, separate space. Children have a strong sense of the discrete wholeness of each object in the picture. For example, when they are given a picture of a rectangle with two circles underneath and asked to put the other two wheels on the train, many children will come up with ingenious solutions. Some will place two small wheels between the circles already drawn. Some will place two wheels on top of the box. Some will draw a little more train to make more room. The children are following their own rule of allowing each part its own space. Therefore, almost none will draw wheels overlapping, as they would actually appear.

For the same reason, children may leave off important parts of a figure, finding, for example, that after drawing a massive head of hair on the head of a human figure, there is no space left to draw in the arms. The resulting hairy, armless creature provides us with another clue into the minds of children and the rules and patterns which characterize their thinking.

from another, we do, nevertheless, communicate with one another by means of spoken symbols that represent our mental images. Piaget calls language "the essential instrument of social adaptation" (Piaget & Inhelder, 1969).

Characteristics of Preoperational Thought

The preoperational period of cognitive development begins at about two years of age and characterizes a child's mental development until he is about seven years old. The symbolic representation that characterizes preoperational thought differs from the sensorimotor intelligence of infancy in several fundamental ways. First, representational thought is faster and more flexible. Unlike sensorimotor intelligence, which can link actions and perceptions one at a time but cannot achieve a cohesive overview, representational thought can grasp many events at once. For example, a boy may enjoy sailing a toy boat. Representational thought allows him to think about sailing it in the bathtub, in a mud puddle, or in a pond. He can consider which of these his mother will allow and where he would be most likely to meet his friends. Representational thought helps him to decide where he wants to sail his boat on this particular occasion.

Second, representational thought is not limited to goals of concrete action. Children at this stage are capable of reflection and of reexamining their knowledge; they can contemplate as well as act. The young sailor can remember that the last time he sailed a boat in a mud puddle it got stuck, and then when he sailed in the pond, he lost it.

Third, representational thought enables children to deal with numbers and such qualities as size. By thinking with symbols they can extend their scope beyond themselves and the concrete objects they encounter every day. The sailor's boat may have one mast and one sail, and although he may never have seen a boat with more, his understanding of number enables him to conceive of a boat with three—or, in principle, six or twelve—masts and any number of sails per mast.

Finally, representational thought can be codified and, most important, socialized; that is, we can translate our thoughts into forms that can be communicated to other individuals. Whereas sensorimotor intelligence is private and unshareable, the child at the preoperational stage can sail his boat with a friend, and the two of them can imagine together that one is the captain and the other the mate. The enriched intelligence and imagination of the preoperational stage can make even private play into a representation of shared social experience.

Egocentrism

Although the changes that announce preconceptual thought signal a leap forward in cognitive development, the thinking of the preschool child is far from mature. One of Piaget's central themes in describing the preoperational stage is **egocentrism,** the self-centered quality of the preschool child's thought and behavior. Piaget is assigning no moral values when he used the term *egocentrism.* He means only that children at this stage cannot take into account the point of view of others—only their own. For example, when Charlotte talks to you, she seems to expect you to know everything she knows. If you join her in a game, she has her own rules. If your ideas conflict with Charlotte's, she doesn't pay them any attention. She cannot understand your point of view or even that you may have one different from hers. She has not yet discovered how independent and different other people are.

Egocentric children often use language just for practice in communication with themselves. *Egocentric speech,* according to Piaget, is speech uttered either when the child is alone or in the presence of others and had no aim to communicate. The child will make no attempt even to assure that anyone is listening (Piaget, 1926b). When most adults talk to others, they try to take into consideration the extent to which they think the other is familiar with the topic under consideration. Children in the egocentric phase cannot do this because they are not yet able to take another's point of view.

Piaget also found that children in the egocentric stage are much more concerned with the material outcome of an event than with the intention of the actor. Such children have a stern sense of justice; if you break one of their toys by mistake, they won't forgive you just because it was an accident. According to Piaget children are unable to put themselves in the place of the actor, to empathize with the other's feelings.

However, there is evidence, based on more recent studies, that the egocentric child is not necessarily as lacking in empathy as Piaget supposed. Studies in altruism among young children show that even two-year-olds un-

Piaget's Periods of Cognitive Development

SENSORIMOTOR PERIOD (BIRTH TO 24 MONTHS)

PREOPERATIONAL PERIOD (2 TO 7 YEARS)

Coordinates schemata, engages in symbolic thinking, and makes novel responses. However, cognition has four limitations:

Centration: focuses attention on one aspect of a situation and disregards the rest. Unable to take two dimensions into account at the same time (e.g., size and number) and thus cannot understand the relation between them. Inconsistent in conservation of continuous qualities such as length, quantity, weight, and volume.

Focuses on static aspects of reality. Cannot follow or fully understand dynamic features.

Thought is irreversible. Cannot understand how something may change and then return to its original condition.

PERIOD OF CONCRETE OPERATIONS (7 TO 11 YEARS)

PERIOD OF FORMAL OPERATIONS (11 YEARS ON)

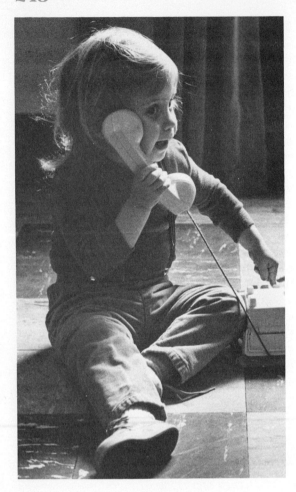

Children in the egocentric stage are not able to take the point of view of others into account, and often speak even when no one is listening.

derstand when another child is hurt or upset (Zahn-Waxler, Radke-Yarrow, & King, 1979). Preschoolers often talk and listen to each other carefully and sympathetically. They also play in cooperation with each other and may consider others' intentions when judging them.

Sociologist Carol Joffe (1973) observed children in a San Francisco Bay area nursery school and found that they have social selves and that they interact within a social system that bears a surprising resemblance to that of adults. She says that children seek to define themselves socially in terms of their common expectations and assumptions about status, property, and personal conduct. They communicate with each other within a coherent, mutually understood, social system.

Children in a social setting learn a system of rules and norms that they try to enforce among themselves, according to Joffe. Hitting a playmate on the head with a shovel is an extreme form of behavior control; the aggressor is using force in an attempt to coerce another. More common is the verbal "You can't do that" with which children establish themselves as distinct social beings with power over others in their social network. Joffe's observations indicate that, far from being presocial or egocentric, small children interact with each other in significant social ways.

It is interesting that Piaget himself observed that social interaction is the principal factor in **decentration**—the decline of egocentrism (egocentrism meaning, literally, "centering on oneself"). In their contact with others, especially their contemporaries, children must increasingly defend their own opinions and view of the world against contrary views and opinions (Flavell, 1963). Social and intellectual conflict, then, forces a child to take the point of view of others into account (Looft, 1972).

Another important component of preoperational thought is the process called centration. **Centration** is the child's tendency to center attention on a single feature of an object or situation. According to Piaget, the preschool child frequently errs in judgment because of an inability to balance the various features of a situation. For example, a child may insist that a tall, thin glass holds more water than a short, wide one even after observing the contents of one being transferred to the other. Here the child is centering on the height of the liquid in the glass and ignoring the glass's width.

In addition to being influenced by egocentrism and centration, preoperational thought is usually **static.** Preschool children are concerned more with states than with transformations, so they may be incapable of taking the in-between steps into account. As we have noted they can focus on the beginning and the end of a process—for example, the changing of a ball of clay into a long, thin snake—but find it extremely difficult to conceptualize the intermediate stages of the transformation.

Preoperational thought also tends to be irreversible. Preschool children cannot retrace their steps to reexamine a conclusion they have already formed. They tend to behave as though thoughts are as irreversible in the mind as physical events are in time. Most children at this stage of development cannot understand how liquid, transferred from a tall, thin container to a short, wide one and then back again, can regain its original appearance. They cannot readily conceive of the possibility that anything may return to a previous condition.

These, then, are the characteristic features of preoperational thought: it is egocentric, centers on one aspect of an object or situation, is static and irreversible. None of these features are unique to the preoperational stage; sometimes our thoughts may show one or more of these features even much later in life. Egocentrism, in particular, seems to return as a characteristic of old age (Looft, 1972). During the preschool years, however, these features are interdependent and mutually reinforcing. Taken together, they make preoperational thought distinctive.

Reasoning

Efforts at reasoning to a conclusion may take a number of different forms during the preschool period. The most fundamental form is that based on *memory of past events.* A child who is bathed every day after dinner may see its mother filling the bathtub at that time and think: "Mommy is filling the tub; it must be for my bath."

A second type of reasoning—or, more accurately, nonreasoning—characteristic of the preschool period is the *adoption of personal preference as evidence for matters of fact.* Michael may want to play outside even though it is raining. His mother's objection that he will get wet makes no impression on him; he may actually believe that because he wants to go out he will not get wet. In an adult we might call this wishful thinking, but in preschoolers it is another form of egocentrism. They have not yet realized that facts can be quite independent of their strongest desires.

In our society adult reasoning is based on two logical processes: we reason from general rules to particular instances, or we start with the particular facts and use them to formulate general rules. These processes are called *deduction* and *induction,* respectively. It is typical of preschoolers that they resort to a third, invalid logic called *transduction.* The preschooler may assume two particular events are connected just because they occur together. He does not know how to fit chance and coincidence into his system of reasoning.

Toward the end of the preschool period children grow more flexible in their reasoning. Their thoughts become less centered and more reversible. Slowly, they develop the ability to balance one feature of an event with another and to understand the various transformations that are involved. When they can consistently apply these elements of logical thinking to their reasoning processes, the stage of preoperational thought has come to an end and children gradually enter the next stage, the period of concrete operations.

CONCEPTS

Although preschool children have left the infantile period far behind, they have a picture of the world that differs widely from the one they will have just a few years later. To understand the child's world in this period, it is necessary to learn how children understand—and in what ways they fail to understand—the basic concepts of time, space, quantity, and relation.

Time

The concept of time is difficult for preschool children to grasp. Having had little past that they can remember, they have only a scanty basis for conceptualizing notions of past, present, and future. Generally, children seem to exhibit a clearer understanding of "yesterday" and "today" than of "tomorrow."

The concept of time is closely related to those of motion and speed. Because children have had little experience in dealing with distance and velocity, they tend to confuse time with distance. A four-year-old boy is taken for two drives lasting about the same time but to different destinations and

Preschool children find time and distance difficult to conceptualize. They would be likely to think that a ten-minute ride across town with many stops covers more distance than a ten-minute highway ride at top speed.

is told that on the second trip he went farther than on the first. He may then conclude that actually the second trip must have lasted longer.

If on a third trip the car stops frequently for gas or food, the boy may be convinced that this trip was the longest, although there was no real difference in elapsed time. Here we can see that his centration on stopping points is very important to his estimation of time; his inability to decenter prevents him from taking certain elements into account, such as the speed of the car.

Recent studies show that preoperational children understand time in terms of *succession* from one point to another sooner than they do *duration* or length of time. In one study the children explained that something took longer because of the order of beginnings and endings; that is they explained duration in terms of succession of events (Levin, Israel, & Darom, 1978). In a similar study of children's concepts of time and speed children were found to believe that greater speed implies a longer duration of time, or as the researcher noted, "more is more" (Levin, 1977).

Space

As adults we are very much concerned with spatial orientation: indeed, we use a great variety of words to describe relations in space. "Up" and "down," "left" and "right," "under" and "over," "here" and "there," "in" and "out" help us to achieve a clear conception of how things are situated in space. To what extent do children understand the spaces in which they themselves are situated—the spaces they live in? In 1948 Tolman coined the phrase "cognitive maps" to refer to the ways in which humans and rats understand the layout of their environments. Young children tend to have a knowledge of an environment in terms of routes from one point to another. They can represent the space in terms of specific routes but do not have a mental picture of the whole; they can't show the relationship of points on one familiar route to those on another in the same environment (Hazen, Lockman, & Pick, 1978). Children under five have difficulty in identifying what is on the other side of a wall separating rooms in their own homes (Pick, 1972). The tendency to centrate, the irreversibility of thought processes, and the inability to concentrate on transformational states all make it extremely difficult for children to make mature judgments concerning the measurement of space.

Quantity

An adult's concept of quantity generally rests on two fundamental concepts: *conservation* and *one-to-one correspondence.* These concepts are not generally used consciously, but they account for our ability to make sense of a world in which it is often important to make accurate estimates of quantity under conditions that may be confusing or misleading.

Conservation

Conservation is defined by Piaget as the understanding that certain properties remain invariant despite any transformations to which they might be subject. Conservation of quantity, for example, means the understanding that a certain amount of water will remain the same regardless of the shapes of the containers that hold it.

In preschool children the concept of conservation of quantity is as yet poorly developed. The tests used by Piaget and his followers to investigate it often involved presenting children with two identical beakers filled with identical amounts of water, or asking children to examine or handle identical balls of clay. Then, as the child watched, the shape of the container holding the water or the shape of the clay was changed; the water might be poured from a short, wide beaker into a tall narrow one, or the ball of clay might be rolled into a narrow sausage shape. A child who consistently recognizes that the changes in shape do not change the quantity of clay or water involved has learned the concept of conservation of quantity.

Before the age of about five or six most children are unable to understand that shape does not change quantity. In Piaget's experiments with water, for example, four-year-olds will usually concentrate on the height of the water in the beaker and not take the width of the beaker into their calculations: being unable to decenter, they will not understand that the quantity of water has not changed. By the age of five or six the ability to conserve has begun to develop; it is well established by about age seven. It is interesting to notice that conservation of different properties develops at different ages. At age six Sara may have a sure grasp of conservation of quantity; at the same time she will almost certainly not be able to conserve weight or volume, because these concepts do not develop until several years later.

One-to-One Correspondence

Another aspect of quantity is number, and this is where the concept of one-to-one correspondence is important. Given a number of objects, an adult can construct a second set with the same number simply by counting. If the given set contains six members, for example, we simply take six other objects to create the second set. Even if we were unable to count, however, we could still create a second set by matching up the new objects with the originals one by one.

As adults we take it for granted that quantities are not altered by physical arrangement. Ten pennies remain ten pennies whether they are in a line, in a circle, or in a pocket. Neither this concept—known as *conservation of numbers*—nor that of *one-to-one correspondence* is at all obvious to the preschool child, who is unable to compensate for the effect of density on length. Later in their development children may consider either length *or* density, but it is not until the end of the preoperational stage that they can consider both factors simultaneously and then divorce these spatial elements from the concept of number. Preschool children may attend to number rather than length, however, when the quantities involved are extremely small.

The ability to count does not necessarily indicate a mature concept of quantity. Children may count equal numbers of objects in two arrays and still deny numerical equality. In Figure 7.1, for example, children who can count may insist that the top row contains more pennies than the bottom row even though they agree that each contains five; they are attending only to the length of the row, not the density. Learning the principle of one-to-one correspondence is an important step toward mastery of conservation of quantity (Russac, 1978).

Relation

The ability to conceive of relations is one that begins to develop in infancy. Infants can discriminate between objects and, to some degree, differentiate levels of intensity. For example, they perceive that one sound is louder than another or that one object is larger than another.

Figure 7.1 Which row has more pennies? The top row—as seen by preschoolers.

Piaget devised a number of experiments designed to test children's grasp of order among objects. One study involved the ordering of a series of different-sized sticks. The child was given ten sticks and told to arrange them in ascending order—that is, to put the smallest stick first, the next smallest second, and so forth.

The youngest group tested (ages four to five) offered a variety of unsuccessful solutions to the problem. Some created an entirely random arrangement. Others began correctly and then continued at random. An interesting approach attempted by some children was to select any stick at random to start and then to line up the sticks in such a way that the top of each stick extended slightly above the top of the preceding stick, but without regard to the bottoms.

This solution—focusing on the tops of the sticks and ignoring the bottoms—exemplifies the inability of young children to center on more than one aspect of a situation at the same time. Although five- and six-year-olds were considerably more successful, they too experienced much difficulty, proceeding in a manner that might best be characterized as trial and error. It is not until after the preschool years that children consistently exhibit the ability to devise a logical plan of action in order to solve such problems.

Piaget (1968) has suggested that preoperational children also have difficulty in dealing with *transitive relations*. Having been told, for example, that "Mary is taller than Susan" and "Susan is taller than Beth," preschool children seem unable to infer that Mary is therefore taller than Beth. Other researchers, however, have found evidence that this form of reasoning may develop as early as four years of age (Bryant & Trabasso, 1971; Trabasso, 1977).

Classification

One of the most important cognitive functions to develop during the preschool years is that of classification. The ability to organize objects and ideas into useful categories is a fundamental prerequisite for mature reasoning.

Classes have four fundamental properties. First, they may be *mutually exclusive*. No figure, for example, can belong both to the class of circles and to the class of squares. Second, a class can be determined by its *intension*—that is, by the common characteristic shared by all its members. Third, a class can be determined by its *extension*—that is, by the list of all its members. And fourth, *intension must define extension*; we should be able to name the members of a class if we know the characteristic that they have in common.

In order to test preschool children's ability to classify, experimenters present the children with an assortment of objects and then request that they group the ones that go together. Young children rarely complete this task in a consistent way.

Some of them create entirely random "classes." For example, they group red circles with blue triangles and green squares. Others begin to form classes on one principle and then abandon it in favor of some other principle. For example, a child may assemble a red triangle, a green triangle, and a blue triangle and then switch over to a blue circle, a blue square, and then, perhaps to a red square. Although children perceive similarity of attributes, they are not yet able to concentrate throughout on a single attribute. Children also have difficulty in applying the notions of "all" and "some," which are necessary for purposes of classification.

As the prechool years near their end, children begin to group objects successfully and to exhibit the ability to subdivide groups into consistent components as well; however, the five- or six-year-old who accomplishes this task may still fail to understand fully the true nature of classification. Some concepts, such as color, are established early, but the development of mature conceptual capabilities is not complete until after the preschool period.

Concepts and Imaginative Play

In our discussion of symbolic play it was noted that Piaget took seriously what adults call "play." The connotations carried by the word "play" for adults are in opposition to those of "work." However, professional observers, as well as others who spend time with children, can scarcely help noticing that children work hard and intently when they play. Play is business for children. Taking this idea a step further, a number of researchers in recent years have linked play with cognitive development. Do children develop competence by means of imaginative play in such areas of cognition as conservation and the ability to take the perspective of the other? In other words, does imaginative play in some way help children to think and to reason?

In an interesting study Golumb and Cornelius (1977) hypothesized that coaching children in imaginative play would improve their cognitive abilities. Chosen as subjects were children four to four and a half years old, all nonconserving—that is, the children were not able to understand that a fixed quantity of something (water, for example) remained constant regardless of the shape or dimension of its container. The researchers designed an experiment in which some children were coached in imaginative play. For comparison, another group participated with an adult in constructive play with puzzles, etc. In the experimental condition the researcher initiated an imaginary situation and participated fully in the game of pretend. But then, suddenly, the experimenter would stop the action and question the pretense. For example, a child was asked to pick a "kitten" from an array of objects. After the game was well under way, the experimenter would naively point to the sponge or whatever represented the kitten and say, "but this is not a kitten, it's a sponge." The child was forced to explain both the pretense and the real world.

The theory underlying this strategy is as follows. Children who are nonconserving also don't understand that transformations are reversible—that is, that a piece of playdough transformed from a ball into an elongated sausage shape can be transformed back into its original condition as a ball. Nonconserving children, as we noted in a previous section, understand only the beginning state "ball" and the ending state "sausage." But children understand the game of pretend and know what is real and what is not. They will not, for example, eat a piece of clay that they are pretending is a piece of cake, and they can readily stop the game and become themselves again if their mothers call or they have to go to the bathroom. The researchers reasoned that if children were forced to explain what is pretense and what is real, they might realize that processes are reversible and thus gain the ability to understand conservation of quantity.

Golumb and Cornelius's experiment proved successful. A statistically significant number of the experimental group compared to the control group could explain Piaget's beaker and water problem after only four coaching sessions. Although two other researchers (Guthrie & Hudson, 1979) were not able to replicate Golumb and Cornelius's findings, a number of studies have shown the link between imaginative play and cognitive development (Burns & Brainerd, 1979; Rosen, 1974). In an experiment similar to that of Golumb and Cornelius, children coached in imaginative play were able to make cognitive gains in social-role conservation (understanding the reversibility of such family roles as mother and daughter, brother and sister), kinship relations, and also increase their levels of imaginativeness in free play (Fink, 1976). Play, it seems, is important not only in its symbolic form, as Piaget reasoned, enabling children to assimilate and organize their experiences, but also as these experiments show, is important to children's intellectual growth.

LANGUAGE

One of the most fascinating aspects of human development is the acquisition of language. Psychologists and linguists—and psycholinguists, whose studies include aspects of both fields—have devoted a great deal of attention to examining the relative importance of heredity, environment, and training in the development of language. How is the essentially nonverbal infant transformed into an active member of the adult language community in the span of only a few years?

The study of language development in the twentieth century has been characterized by several shifts in emphasis. The diary studies conducted in the early part of the century, in which linguists or psychologists recorded the development of their own children, were soon abandoned because they were unavoidably biased. Then psychologists began to study patterns of language development in a wide cross section of children. Their studies concentrated on such matters as the frequency with which certain words occur, the parts of speech used, and the average sentence length typical of children's utterances at various ages.

Eventually it became apparent, however, that these studies tended to create a static picture of language development. In stressing certain milestones of development—for example, that children produce their first sentences between the ages of two and three—early researchers tended to overlook the transformational elements of language development. The transition from two-word utterances to three-word sentences, for example, is characterized not only by a difference in sentence length but by significant changes in the child's understanding of syntax and grammatical rules as well. In the 1950s researchers began to work with smaller groups of children in order to discover not what *form* language takes but what children *know* about language at various stages of development. This approach was subsequently replaced by the effort to formulate a rule system that would account for the child's structuring and use of language.

Most recently the emphasis has shifted from the description of language development to its explanation. Psycholinguists are attempting not only to define the grammatical rules by which early speech is governed, but to examine the relation of those rules to the child's understanding of language meaning and functions. In this way the study of language is more closely integrated into the study of cognitive development as a whole.

Word Meaning

Children impose their own meaning on words according to private and individual rules. For example, in one study the relationship between word order and the ability of young children to understand simple commands was examined (Wetstone & Friedlander, 1973). The experimenters discovered that very young children generally respond to commands such as "Give to ball the Mommy" as readily as they do to "Give the ball to Mommy." Older children, with a better understanding of language, find it hard to understand the scrambled sentence. The young children apparently respond to familiar verbal clues, not to details of syntax and grammatical structure. They utilize the parts of a sentence they understand and ignore the rest.

Developmental psychologists have been especially interested in the acquisition of terms of comparison and relation. This is important because it is only when children have mastered such terms that researchers can ask them questions to learn how they perceive relationships.

Children appear to use and understand comparative terms such as *more*, *big*, and *long* before they are able to grasp their opposites, *less*, *little*, and *short*. Researchers (Donaldson & Balfour, 1968) who have studied three- and four-year-olds have found that they have a clear understanding of the concepts "more" and "same" but have not yet learned how to use the words that signify those concepts. For instance, when one child said "more," she consistently meant "more." However, when she said "less," she also meant "more." A three-year-old who describes two things as "different" might well mean that they were the same. It is clear, then, that we cannot analyze children's word meanings according to most conventional adult standards. Our understanding of these rules ultimately depends less on cataloging individual statements than on studying the relationship between language and thought.

Toward Communication

From his observations of children at play Piaget concluded that during the preoperational stage speech serves two distinct functions. It may be noncommunicative—*egocentric*, in Piaget's phrase—or it may be communicative. Egocentric speech is an essentially private exercise, but it shades gradually into communicative or *social speech*.

In the early preschool years, children find it difficult to see the world through the eyes of others, and thus they do not realize that a particular effort is necessary to make their speech really communicative. Because adults often try very hard to understand a child's speech, there may be little pressure on the child to adjust his language to meet the needs of others.

Eventually, as other children begin to challenge his egocentrism with their own, social pressures demand the development of more effective modes of communication and force the child to convert much of his private thought into language, thus drawing him out of his egocentrism. Piaget conceives of cognitive development as broadly following a path from the nonsocial, nonverbal thought of the infant to the socially expressed thought of the school-age child, with the egocentric stage of the preschool child in between.

The Russian psychologist L. S. Vygotsky agrees with Piaget that egocentric speech is not successful as communication, but rejects Piaget's belief that children do not particularly try to be communicative. Vygotsky's own studies of children at play revealed a close relationship between their egocentric speech and their nonverbal activities. He describes the case of the child who, in the process of drawing a streetcar, broke the point of his pencil. "It's broken," he said aloud and, taking up another pencil, began to draw a *broken* streetcar as he continued to speak aloud about the change (Vygotsky, 1962).

Vygotsky believes that the egocentric speech of the preoperational stage differs only in form from the more developed speech of older children. Egocentric speech, he suggests, should not be considered a fundamentally distinct type of language use but a transition from vocal to inner speech. When older children, after solving a problem silently, are asked to describe their thoughts, they generally reveal the same process that the preschool child expresses aloud. In Vygotsky's view inner speech serves the same function in adults as egocentric speech does in children.

Although Vygotsky argues that children's speech is intended to communicate from the start, other researchers have noted that younger children are considerably poorer than older children at both sending effective messages and interpreting the messages of others effectively (Asher, 1976; Asher & Olden, 1976). Performance in both areas improves with age. In these studies there was no difference between children's ability to communicate effectively and their ability to appraise accurately the messages of others. Children who were poor communicators were poor interpreters. In addition, it was found that young children who sent ineffective messages were no better at interpreting their own, possibly idiosyncratic or egocentric messages, than they were at interpreting the messages of others.

Preschoolers' speech is egocentric and often fragmented; little attempt is made to make it easily understood.

IQ TESTS FOR PRESCHOOLERS

IQ tests given in the preschool period are more reliable—that is, more likely to yield similar scores from one time to the next—than tests given in infancy. IQ is still more variable, however, than it will be after age six. The scores of some individuals vary more widely in IQ tests than others. The preschoolers who seem to have the most constant IQ scores are those with subnormal intelligence.

The most widely used intelligence test for preschool children is the Stanford-Binet test. It consists of a series of subtests that range from very easy to very difficult. A typical item for two-year-olds, for example, is the building of a block tower; three-year-olds are asked to identify the parts of the body, and four-year-olds to identify certain pictures and extract information from them.

The directions for taking the Stanford-Binet test are given orally, and the tasks required depend increasingly on vocabulary. It would be possible, therefore, for some children to fail a subtest merely because they could not understand the directions or express their thoughts, not because the substance of the test was beyond them. Furthermore, the language used in the Stanford-Binet test comes from middle-class usage, and the test has long been recognized to have a middle-class bias. This means that it is less reliable in testing children who are not from the middle class.

Another difficulty with the Stanford-Binet test is that it is designed to measure a general level of intelligence, not the particular elements or aspects that comprise intelligence. Conceivably, therefore, a child could be brilliant in some ways and yet get an average score on the test. These limitations will be discussed more fully in Chapter 10.

The Denver Developmental Screening Test is another test used to identify children from ages two to six years with delayed development or retardation (Buros, 1972). It is a quick and easy test to administer and does not require extensive training on the part of the examiner. This test also has been criticized as being biased in respect to minority group children.

What are some of the factors that influence performance on IQ tests? Apparently maternal IQ and educational background are not directly relevant, but certain circumstances of family life are of tremendous importance. Children from families that not only emphasize language development and academic achievement but also provide materials in the home for general learning usually get higher IQ scores than children from families that do not do these things (Scott & Smith, 1972).

DAY CARE AND DEVELOPMENT

Bronfenbrenner, the well-known child psychologist, has pointed out that we know much more about children than about the environments in which they live (Bronfenbrenner, 1979). Certainly, within the last few years parents and social scientists have become aware of how little they know about an increasingly common environment for young children—the day-care center. As of 1978 approximately 2.5 million infants and toddlers and 3.7 million preschoolers were enrolled in day care on a full- or part-time basis, and the number has grown since then. These children experience daily separation from the mother (or parenting figure) and enter the world of caregivers, peers, communal toys. In some cases they remain in the day-care setting for six or seven hours—a long time for a young child.

There are three main types of day care in the United States today (Belsky, Steinberg, & Walker, 1981). The most familiar is *center day care.* The center may be a community center; the common area of a housing project; a church basement; or a facility that is part of a larger education institution, such as a university. Center day care usually serves more than twelve children. A second type of care, *family day care*, is provided in private homes by experienced parents (who in some states must be licensed to give care). Group size is

Day care takes many forms, including in-home care, in which a sitter comes to the child's home; family day care, in which experienced parents take in several children; and center day care.

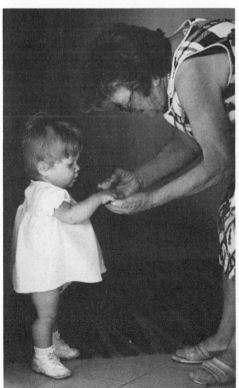

Television: An Influential Teacher

In the thirty years since the advent of commercial television parents, educators, researchers, and advertisers have tried to gauge its effect on children. Studies have long shown that the average child spends more time in front of the television set than in the classroom (Schramm, Lyle, & Parker, 1961), and that preschoolers may spend one-third of their waking hours watching TV (Stein & Friedrich, 1972). What are the effects of program content and presentation on children? It is becoming evident that television can be an influential teacher. Will the results be, as some critics suggest, a decline in social and cognitive abilities and a lack of imagination? Or will the effects be to increase children's awareness, to expose them to a wide range of experiences, to speed development, as supporters contend?

Psychologists have not found definitive answers to these questions. The information collected so far suggests that TV viewing by children does influence both learning and behavior. This can be beneficial. A study (Ball & Bogatz, 1970) of cognitive development of children who watch "Sesame Street" concluded that "three- to five-year-old youngsters from a variety of backgrounds acquired simple and complex cognitive skills as a result of watching 'Sesame Street.' Those who watched the most gained the most." Another study (Coates, Pusser & Goodman, 1976) found that positive reinforcement and social contact with others increased after exposure to certain TV programming, notably "Mister Rogers' Neighborhood." These studies would tend to support the notion of TV as a teacher of cognitive and social skills.

Critics respond with questions about the effects of violence and commercials. What are children learning from that sort of programming? Studies report that viewing violent programming, even cartoons, led to an increase in aggressive behavior (Stein & Friedrich, 1976). Moreover, children who had initially tested high in aggression sought out violent programming and responded to it with even greater aggression. Even between two essentially nonviolent programs, "Sesame Street" and "Mister Rogers' Neighborhood," the effect of negative behavior on children is noticeable. A study showed children who had initially scored low on punishment behavior (such as verbal criticism and negative physical contact, hitting, etc.) showed an increase in such behavior after viewing "Sesame Street" but not after exposure to "Mister Rogers' Neighborhood." Content analysis of the "Sesame Street" material showed characters reinforcing one another 740 times, punishing one another 213 times. The ratio for "Mister Rogers' Neighborhood" was 1,224 to 67 (Coates & Pusser, 1975). This suggests that small gradations of behavior are noticed by children and incorporated into their own behavior, as a result of exposure to TV programming.

With regard to commercials, a correlation has been found between the number of hours of commercial television watched and the number of attempts made to influence purchasing in a supermarket (Galst & White, 1976). Children who showed a preference for commercials, as compared with programming, and who watched the most TV were more likely to try to get their parent to buy products in proportion to the amount of advertising time the products received. This finding suggests that children are deeply influenced by commercials.

The debate goes on, and the facts are not all in. It seems clear that children are influenced by television. Parents and others responsible for the well-being of children would be well advised to exercise some discretion and control over the amount and type of TV programming children are exposed to.

limited by federal regulation to six children. The third and least visible form of day care is *in-home care*, or baby-sitting in the child's home. Of all types of day care family day care is the most widely utilized. More than twice as many children were in family day care as in center day care in 1978 (Office of the Assistant for Planning and Evaluation, 1978). Most child-development research, however, has been conducted on center day care populations, and specifically in university-based programs.

Differences between the Day-Care and Home-Care Environments

With growing numbers of children entering day care, it is hardly surprising that parents, psychologists, and educators have become concerned about the potential effects of day care on development.

What is surprising is how little we know about what children experience in day care *as compared to what they experience at home.* There is a general expectation among parents that day care will provide new opportunities for peer interaction, resulting in better (or more highly developed) play. This appears to be so. However, one recent study of eighteen-month-old children found some unexpected differences in the care provided in home and day-care environments (Rubenstein & Howe, 1979). Caregivers in the community-based day-care center initiated *more* tactile contact (fondling, patting, etc.) than mothers at home. They were *more* likely to initiate play or sharing of toys with infants. Mothers, on the other hand, were more likely to restrict an infant's activity, especially the exploration of objects not designed as toys. Mothers were also more likely to interrupt the infant and offer explicit play instructions. There was, it turned out, more crying at home and more smiling in day care. In verbal exchanges and responses to infant's touching mothers and caregivers did not differ significantly. However, mothers who talked to their infants at home were more likely to be rewarded with a responsive, interested infant than were caregivers in day care. Rubenstein and Howe's study points out numerous differences between the ways in which infants are cared for in home and day-care environments. Undoubtedly further observation of children in varied day-care settings will enable psychologists to better describe and compare the environments in which our youngest children spend their time.

Effects of Day Care

The developmental effects of day care have been more systematically observed than have the environments themselves. For example, researchers have studied the effect of day care on the mother-child bond and on the child's cognitive and social development. As we shall see, the results are sometimes contradictory. And they are necessarily incomplete, if only because day care and the community that supports it continue to evolve and change. However, the general picture is encouraging.

Most studies have found, for example, that day care does *not* disrupt the child's emotional bond to the mother (Belsky & Steinberg, 1978). In the most comprehensive study to date day-care and home-care children between the ages of thirty months and three and one-half years did not differ in their attachment behaviors (Kagan et al., 1976). Responses to separation (as demonstrated in a laboratory setting) were strikingly similar in the two groups. Moreover, day-care and home-care children both expressed strong preference for their mothers when placed in a stressful laboratory situation with other adults present. For day-care children the caregiver is clearly preferred over an adult stranger. Ricciuti (1974) found that the infant develops a "discriminatory attachment-like relationship" to the caregiver, but this does not supersede or replace the emotional bond with the mother.

Cognitive Development

The effect of day care on cognitive development is somewhat more complicated. For most children the day-care experience has neither beneficial nor adverse effects on intelligence, as measured by standardized tests. However, for children thought to be at "high risk" intellectually—mainly children of poor or poorly educated parents—day care may prevent the decline in intelligence scores that tends to occur for these children after the age of eighteen months. In one study a home-care "control" group of high-risk children showed a decline from 104 to 86 in mental development (on a subscale of the Bayley Infant tests), while those enrolled in a university-based day-care program retained a "stable" score near 104 (Ramey & Smith, 1976). Typically, results like this tend to "wash out"; however, a follow-up study found similar differences when the children were between two and three years old.

These and other results with disadvantaged children must be interpreted with some care. Most involve children in university-based, "cognitive-enrichment" day-care programs that are simply not representative of day care in the United States. Some researchers argue that the benefits to the disadvantaged are *not* limited to those enrolled in high-quality programs (Golden et al., 1978), but the results are far from clear. Moreover, it is possible that at least some of the differences in test scores can be attributed to the day-care child's greater experience in test-taking and greater ease with unfamiliar adults (Ramey & Smith, 1976). Finally, there is no real information on the effect of day care on intellectual abilities that are not measured by standardized tests.

While the effects of the "enriched environment" of the day-care experience has yet to be proven beneficial or adverse to children's development, research suggests that day care might prevent a decline in the intelligence scores of disadvantaged preschoolers.

Social Development

In the area of social development we confront some of the most frequently cited goals and expectations about day care. No matter what a day-care program is like, it does bring welcome new opportunities for the child to play with peers. Many studies show that day-care children are more peer-oriented than home-care children, especially at ages under eighteen months. Just as parents anticipate, they play at a higher developmental level than home-care children. (The difference, though, tends to disappear when children who know each other play at home—Rubenstein & Howe, 1979.) Day-care children do interact more with peers—in both positive and negative ways (Belsky & Steinberg, 1979). They share more, but they fight more, too. In fact they may fight a great deal. Aggressiveness, impulsivity, egocentrism, and less tolerance for frustration, failure, and interruption are characteristics that are more frequently encountered in children in full-time day care (Belsky & Steinberg, 1978). Decreased cooperation with adults (and later with the education system) is also a more likely outcome for day-care than for home-care children. These differences may result from the day-care experience. For example, we might hypothesize that day-care children have less tolerance for failure or interruption because they have not (like home-care children) been restricted much in the home. However, it is also possible that the characteristics of day-care children are a function of socialization values—that they are conveyed or reinforced by American society in general, rather than by day care per se.

Difficulties in Interpreting Current Research

The recent research on day care has proven useful to parents, social scientists, and the makers of social policy. Few parents, for example, can remain unaf-

The National Day-Care Study

As most day-care research is careful to point out, generalizations are difficult. The quality of day care varies from center to center. There are day-care centers in which children are helped by competent teachers to acquire new cognitive and social skills, and there are centers where very little meaningful interaction occurs.

Parents and policymakers have begun to ask: What makes the difference? What are the critical characteristics associated with a high-quality day-care experience?

In 1974 the federal government commissioned the National Day-Care Study to answer these questions. Over four years the study group observed and tested thousands of children and gathered detailed information on centers in three urban sites (Atlanta, Detroit, and Seattle). Because the government has found itself increasingly involved in the funding of day-care services, the study was concerned with both quality and cost. Essentially it sought to determine if new day-care regulations might allow the government to buy better care without spending a great deal more money.

Much of the study dealt with composition of the day-care class—the group size and caretaker/child ratio. The most important finding was that smaller groups were consistently associated with better care, more socially active children, and higher gains on two developmental tests (Ruopp et al., 1979). In preschool groups of fourteen or fewer children, caregivers engaged in more active play with children, and children in turn showed more cooperation and initiative. When group size was larger than eighteen, children were "watched" rather than stimulated. Aimless wandering and other evidence of noninvolvement were more often observed. Reducing group size, the study found, affects cost only slightly. Smaller groups thus represent a relatively inexpensive way of improving the quality of day care within existing budgets.

Increasing the caregiver/child ratio, in the other hand, tends to raise costs significantly. Fortunately the study found that the actual ratio of caregivers to children—assuming it fell between 1:5 and 1:10—did not affect quality so critically. In a preschool group of fourteen or fewer children, which was the best option identified by the study, the ratio should be at least 1:7. For infants and toddlers the recommendations were more stringent: group size should be between eight and twelve children, with a ratio of one caregiver for every four children in attendance. The study found that most programs providing federally funded day care conform to these recommendations. Many other centers do not. Perhaps as many as 60 percent of day-care centers not servicing publicly funded children fall short of what the study identified as the best option in class composition.

A second factor investigated by the National Day-Care Study was the qualification of caregivers and staff. It appears that caregivers who have received either training or education in fields related to young children deliver better care, with somewhat superior developmental effects for children (Ruopp et al., 1979). The number of years of formal education and the attainment of a degree were not systematically associated with high-quality care. Nor were the number of years of experience in the day-care center. This finding led the study group to recommend a specialized program of child-related education and training for day-care workers. It was noted that caregivers with the recommended training do not receive higher wages than other caregivers. (The wages, over all, are low.) Thus restricting the hiring of caregivers to those with the recommended training would not significantly drive up costs.

The National Day-Care Study puts before policymakers the results of large-scale research on day care. The findings will undoubtedly help shape, regulate, and fund the day-care programs of the 1980s.

---

fected by the lack of evidence for the much-feared disruption of the mother-child bond. However, day care is a relatively new institution in the United States, and much of the evidence is yet to be presented. To date there have been no comprehensive longitudinal studies of the effect of day care in this country. Most studies can describe only immediate, and possibly temporary, effects. Few studies have observed the same children before and after day care (Roopnarine & Lamb, 1978). Then, too, many of the early and influential studies were based on populations in nonrepresentative day-care centers, usually those sponsored by universities with research interests. At least in the early 1970s many day-care centers—perhaps as many as half—were only "fair" or "poor" in quality (Keyserling, 1972). It appears that both the quality of com-

A recent study found that smaller group size is consistent with better quality care, resulting in more socially active children and higher gains on developmental tests.

munity-based day care and the breadth of research has improved since that time.

A related point is that psychologists have not conducted sufficient re-search to determine whether or not the effects they measure are "program-specific" or unique to a particular day-care setting. They speak of the diffi-culties of using observations from one day-care center as a basis for assertions about day care in general (Macrae & Herbert-Jackson, 1975).

Within the next few years more and more young children are expected to enter community-based day care, and more research on day care will be conducted. Researchers are becoming increasingly interested in the effect of day care on the child's larger environment—on the family and the community. They have come to realize that it is not the child alone who is participating in the day-care experience. They are asking such questions as, How does day care affect the mother's attachment to her child? The mother's and child's relationship to the father? What effect does the increasing availability of day care have on work environment? On elementary school environments? Should children in day care be grouped with their age-mates only? Or should groups include older and younger children? Or other members of the community, for example, high school students or elderly adults? Perhaps most important, researchers are considering the development of supportive links between day-care and home and community environments. They are investigating the ways in which parents can become involved in day care and, conversely, the ways in which day care can involve parents in adult friendships and other helping networks that are known to assist families in the stressful task of child-rearing (Belsky & Steinberg, 1979). The results of these efforts will not only increase our knowledge of day care, they will also help clarify our goals for children and the values we attach to childhood.

❖❖

SUMMARY

▶ According to Piaget children in the sensorimotor period think in the here and now. Gradually children are able to symbolize by means of gestures, deferred imitation, and symbolic play; then, finally, they are able to use a mental image or language to stand for an object or an action. The ability to symbolize, the symbolic function, represents the beginning of the pre-operational period.

▶ Children in the preoperational period have limited reasoning power. Pre-operational thought is characterized by egocentrism (a child is unable to take the view of the other) and centration (a child tends to center on only one aspect of an object or situation). It is static and irreversible.

Children in the preoperational period do not understand the principle of conservation—that a quantity of a substance remains the same regardless of its shape or the shape of the container that holds it. Children in this stage tend to equate time and distance and to conceptualize distance in terms of routes or beginnings and ends. Play for children is serious business. Play enhances intellectual development.

▶   Psycholinguists are attempting to discover the grammatical rules that children use as they first learn to talk. Piaget believes that children do not intend to communicate with the egocentric speech characteristic of the preschool period, whereas Vygotsky thinks that they mean to do so but fail.

▶   The Stanford-Binet IQ test is the most widely used IQ test for preschoolers, though it relies heavily on the understanding and use of language and tests for general rather than particular abilities. Moreover, socioeconomic factors and individual motivation affect test scores.

▶   Day care is an increasingly common environment for infants, toddlers, and preschoolers in the United States. There are three main forms of day care: center day care, family day care, and in-home day care. Research on the effects of day care has focused mainly on center day care.

FURTHER READINGS

Anastasi, Anne. *Psychological testing.* New York: Macmillan, 1976.
Anastasi evaluates all kinds of psychological tests and discusses the interpretation of test scores. She discusses the origin, nature, and use of these tests and considers the social implications of testing in general.

Broman, S. S., Nichols, P. L., and Kennedy, W. A. *Preschool IQ: Prenatal and early development correlates.* Hillsdale, N.J.: Lawrence Erlbaum Associates, 1975.
This book summarizes the literature on preschool intelligence in order to sort out the relationship between early childhood variables and preschool IQ.

Evans, E. D. *Contemporary influences in early childhood education* (2nd ed.). New York: Holt, Rinehart and Winston, 1975.
An overview of early childhood education as it is practiced in the United States. Evans analyzes major developments and influences from the traditional school to the open classroom for young children aged three to six.

Galinsky, E., and Hooks, W. H. *The new extended family: Day care that works.* Boston: Houghton Mifflin, 1977.
An interesting description of some of the best day care in the United States.

Roby, Pamela. *Child care, who cares?* New York: Basic Books, 1973.
A collection of articles on child-care policies for infants and young children. Designed as a handbook of issues that underlie the impetus to child care as a basic right, the book surveys the history of child care and its implementation here and abroad.

Singer, Dorothy G., and Revenson, Tracy A. *How a child thinks: A Piaget primer.* New York: New American Library, 1978.
A clear summary of Piaget's ideas, with example and some ideas about modern applications.

Chapter 8

❖❖❖❖❖❖❖

Personality and Society

*P*ersonality—passive and cooperative or aggressive and disruptive—is the pattern of behavior and thought that characterizes individuals and remains relatively stable throughout their lives. It is that particular complex of emotional responses that differentiates one person from another and makes up an important part of an individual's identity. The study of personality is concerned with the development of individual differences.

The development of personality begins at or before birth, but the preschool years are the time when certain personality patterns become observable and more stable. We become conscious of our identity; infantile dependency is replaced by new patterns of social relations; aggression becomes more focused and is channeled into more socially acceptable forms. Moral behavior becomes possible as preschoolers begin to accept rules and the role of authority in their lives. New forms of social relationships, new methods of coping, new perceptions of reality are tested by means of fantasy, play, and humor. The patterns of trust or fear, compassion or selfishness that are learned at home are gradually extended to the outer world.

In the process of developing relationships with others, we begin to establish some notion of our own identity. For most adults, the outlines of a personal identity are fairly well drawn; people are partly what their jobs, interests, ideas, and relations to family and friends make them. Preschool children, however, lack many of these determinants, and as their egocentric views of the world clash with reality, they each begin to realize that they are distinct persons, different from the other people in their lives. They must learn to look at things in a way that will make sense not only to themselves, but to those around them. Primary in the makeup of a person's identity is one's gender role—a little boy's sense of himself as masculine, a little girl's identity as feminine.

SEX, GENDER, AND SELF

Jane, even as a very little girl, was not very active physically; she was interested in people, verbal, more likely to use her small muscles in activity. David was aggressive, active, strong, involved in gross motor activities, fascinated by forbidden behavior. Is it accidental that the traits of femininity and masculinity are exemplified in these children? Are babies born with a predisposition toward the traits they will display as children and then adults? Or are they encouraged to act out the sexual scripts of their society in their social experiences? Are babies infinitely plastic, capable of playing gender roles in any number of ways, or is it more than coincidental that in most societies the scripts for men call for strength, self-reliance, and achievement, and those for women emphasize nurturance, adaptability, and obedience (Barry, Bacon, & Child, 1972)?

Sex Differences

Despite the changing attitudes toward traditional sex roles among a large segment of American society today, it is still a social blunder to mistake a child's sex in front of her—or his—parents. But differences in appearance between boys and girls at the preschool level are so slight that most of them must be communicated deliberately by means of dress or hairstyle. Nevertheless, boys can differ markedly in their behavior from girls almost from birth. Furthermore, studies (Seavy, Katz, & Zalk, 1975; Sidorowitz & Lunney, 1980) show that parents, teachers, and other adults behave differently toward baby boys than they do toward baby girls and continue to do so as children get older. What, if any, are the intellectual and behavioral differences between the sexes that are due to biology or to socialization?

Aggression

The principal behavioral difference between males and females that shows up in study after study is the much greater aggressiveness of males (Maccoby & Jacklin, 1974). Aggression seems to be partly biological in origin. Male infants are heavier than females even at birth, with heavier musculature, even though they are less well developed than females. Evidence of aggressiveness also comes from studies of primates. For example, Harlow (1962) observed that young male monkeys engaged in much more rough-and-tumble play than

Preschool boys' behavior differs markedly from that of preschool girls. Studies have indicated that the aggressive behavior in boys is partly biological in origin.

females. Moreover, subsequent research has shown that when a pregnant monkey is given injections of male hormone immediately before she gives birth, her female offspring will be unusually aggressive in play and other respects (Young, Goy, & Phoenix, 1964).

Numerous studies have found that teachers and peers of boys from five to fourteen rate boys as more aggressive, noisy, and negative than girls of the same age. Similarly, several studies (Bach, 1945; Bandura, 1961, 1973) have shown that after observing aggressive behavior, boys exhibit more physical aggression than girls, although both sexes are on a par in terms of verbal aggression. The tendency for boys to be more aggressive than girls is also reflected in the caseloads of the courts and child-guidance clinics, where about three or four times as many boys as girls are referred (Elkind, 1971). In playtime activities boys are observed to engage in more rough-and-tumble play than girls. Although the evidence points to the greater aggressiveness of boys, it has been suggested that boys express their aggression overtly, whereas girls are more concerned about their aggressive tendencies and thus are more likely to inhibit their expression (Brodzinsky, Messer, & Tew, 1979).

Other Sex Differences

Aside from aggression, what psychological differences between boys and girls can actually be supported by research? This question has been answered by investigators Maccoby and Jacklin (1974) who reviewed hundreds of studies of sex differences. There is no evidence, these investigators concluded, to support the belief that girls are more "social" than boys. Neither does it seem to be true that girls are more "suggestible" than boys, whether "suggestibility" means likeliness to imitate other people or susceptibility to persuasion. Other unfounded beliefs are that girls have lower self-esteem; that girls are better at rote learning and simple repetitive tasks, boys at higher-level cognitive tasks; that boys are more "analytic"; and that girls are auditory, boys visual. Interestingly, it is also untrue that girls are less motivated to achieve than boys. In fact, girls seem to strive for achievement harder than boys, unless the boys are challenged by appeals to ego or by competition. It is probably true that girls' verbal abilities mature somewhat more rapidly than boys' though the difference is hard to detect until about age eleven. Research also seems to support the beliefs that boys excel in visual-spatial ability and in mathematical ability (Maccoby & Jacklin, 1974).

Science seems to support the view that sex differences, apart from reproductive functions, are minimal except for the greater aggression of males, their greater physical strength and taller and heavier bodies, and male superiority in some mathematical and visual-spatial abilities. Since our sex marks our personality to a greater degree than any other personal characteristic, we might well wonder at the different social roles that are, for the most part, assigned to each sex, especially in modern industrial society in which there is no longer a great need for physical strength and physical aggression. More relevant to the issues of child development is this question: How do little babies with apparently few differences beyond their reproductive organs take up the vastly different social roles of men and women? Closely related to that of how little boys become men and little girls become women is this question: How are women induced to take the subservient role at every level of society?

Gender Roles

Suppose a baby was born with ambiguous external sex organs so that it was not clear whether it was a boy or a girl. Would such a baby be able to achieve a stable sexual identity? Would it make a difference if the child was arbitrarily assigned a sex and brought up accordingly? If so—that is, if such a baby was brought up as a girl, for example, and as she matured felt herself to be a woman and behaved like a woman—then it could be said that socialization plays a vital part in the learning of gender roles and the establishing of gender identity. (It may seem curious that we speak of gender rather than sex, but there is a good reason; sex is biological, whereas gender is social. Gender depends on how the individual is viewed by himself or herself and by others. Gender identification is expressed in behavior that is learned rather than inherited. In some cases such as clothing, hairstyle, and gestures, the distinction between learned and inherited can be made readily. In other cases, such as male aggression, it may not be so easy to disentangle the inherited from the learned.)

Biology and Socialization

That biology is strongly modified by socialization and the learning process is demonstrated by a series of studies by Money and associates (Money & Ehrhardt, 1972). These researchers studied many cases in which children with ambiguous external genitalia were raised as one gender although their internal reproductive organs were of the other. For example, a genetic female whose genitalia looked masculine might be raised as a boy or a genetic male might be raised as a girl. The research of Money and his associates showed that the gender assigned to a child, and the child-rearing style accorded that sex, appear to be the overriding factor in establishing gender role, gender behavior, and gender identity. If a child is brought up a girl, her self-concept will be that she is female, and she will behave as females do. And the same holds true, of course, for males.

Money found that there is a critical period in reassigning sex to a child. Reassignment must take place before the child is two to three years old. For example, biological males with ambiguous external genitalia surgically corrected to females can be successfully reared as females. But if the change is made after the child is two to three years old, the person will have difficulty in establishing a stable and unambiguous gender identity.

Should little girls be encouraged to play with dolls? Child development specialists are researching the effects of gender-related toys on gender-appropriate behavior.

Infant Socialization

The studies of Money and his associates suggest that the reactions of others to our sex, rather than biological determinants, are important in the formation and corroboration of one's gender identity. To determine whether people react differently to babies according to their sex, two researchers (Condry & Condry, 1976) showed a videotape of a nine-month-old to 204 subjects. The videotape showed the infant reacting to a teddy bear, a jack-in-the-box, a doll, and a buzzer. Half of the subjects were informed that the infant was a "girl," half that it was a "boy." There were three interesting findings. First, the male subjects reported a greater difference in the infant's behavior according to whether the child was labeled "boy" or "girl." Thus, it may be that fathers expect to see greater differences between the behavior of boys and girls and react accordingly. Second, the infant as a "boy" was seen as more active and potent. This would support the traditional sexual stereotypes. And third, in an ambiguous situation as in the infant's reaction to the jack-in-the-box, the infant as a "boy" was seen as angry and the infant as a "girl" was seen as fearful. This suggests that when a situation is unclear, sexual stereotypes may take over.

As we have just seen, socialization for sex-appropriate behavior begins long before a child can talk. Even at birth the announcements and gifts are pink for girls, blue for boys. More important are the parents' styles of inter- action with their infants. Mothers are more likely to breast-feed girls. There is also evidence that mothers of girls spend more time touching their infants and interacting with them visually and vocally (Goldberg & Lewis, 1969). And the little girls reciprocate this attention: "When the children were six months old, mothers touched, talked to, and handled their daughters more than their sons, and when they were thirteen months old, girls touched and talked to their mothers more than boys did." Mothers encourage infant boys more than girls to engage in such gross motor activities as walking, climbing, and crawl- ing (Smith & Lloyd, 1978).

Preschool Socialization

The conclusions of the studies mentioned above were, for the most part, based on experimental evidence. Much of the research on the actual observed be- havior of parents toward infants according to their sex seems contradictory. Perhaps this is because, as Michael Lamb (1976) points out, infants tend to be treated simply as "babies" rather than "baby boys" or "baby girls." After the first year parents and others tend to encourage sex-appropriate behavior. In one study (Fagot, 1978) interactions between parents and their two-year-old children were observed in their own homes in a systematic fashion. In certain categories parents behaved quite differently toward their male or female off- spring. For example, girls asked for help three times more frequently than boys did. Yet parents were more likely to respond positively to the requests from girls; they responded negatively to boys' requests for help. Although parents were not aware they were doing this, such behavior rewards girls for being dependent and punishes boys. Girls were more likely to receive a negative reaction when they manipulated objects; boys a positive one. Girls were more likely to be criticized for such gross motor activities as running, jumping, and climbing. Girls were given positive responses for watching television and dancing. Boys were more likely to be left alone. In effect, boys are allowed to learn about the physical world with less chance of criticism; girls are given more feedback for interacting with the parent.

Boys are handled and played with more roughly (Maccoby & Jacklin, 1974). Boys receive both more praise and more punishment. Socialization pressure, or the pressure to conform to sex-appropriate expectations, is more intense for boys. There is more latitude for girls, at least while they are growing up. The tomboy is acceptable; the sissy is not. Girls may wear boys' clothing— T shirts, jeans, and sneakers. Boys may never wear a dress or a hair ribbon. Asked by one researcher (Lansky, 1967) how they would react if their son wanted to play with a cosmetic kit, parents said they would be strongly opposed. But if their daughter wanted to play with a toy gun, the same parents said they would not particularly mind. One researcher suggested that the basic developmental task of girls is learning how not to be a baby; that of boys is learning how not to be a girl (W. Emmerich, 1959).

Becoming a Boy or a Girl

Socialization is a two-way street. Children are not just creatures of their parents' making. They are active participants in the formation of their own individual identities and their own concept of sex roles. They do not merely respond and imitate, they explore and think in their own way.

Children's notions of gender are rarely based on genital differences or other biological characteristics. They differentiate the sexes by means of clothing, speech, and hairstyle. Inasmuch as gender seems to depend on superficial characteristics, the preschool child may believe it can be altered merely by changing external features—if a boy dresses and behaves like a girl, he becomes one. Many children also believe that gender can change with age; a four-year-old boy may say he wants to grow up to be a mommy. It is not until the age of five or six that most children are convinced that sexual identity is not determined just by behavior and appearance.

In a recent study (Kuhn, Nash, & Brucken, 1978) two- and three-year-olds were asked about masculine and feminine behavior. There was not necessarily agreement among the little boys and girls as to appropriate gender behavior. However, both boys and girls believed that girls like to play with dolls, help their mothers, talk a lot, say "I need some help," and never hit. The little boys believed that little girls cry, are slow, say "You hurt my feelings" and "You're not letting me have my turn." Girls (but not boys) believe that girls like to give kisses, never fight, and look nice. Both girls and boys believe that boys like to play with cars, like to help their father, and say "I can hit you." Girls (but not boys) believe that boys like to climb trees and fight. Boys (but not girls) believe that boys work hard, are naughty, and can make you cry. It is interesting to note the attributes that were nonstereotyped by these little children. Both boys and girls believe that both sexes like to play ball, play house, build towers, run fast, but do not like to work; that they are strong, not scared, going to hit, messy, dirty, smart, and quiet; that they will never give up and that they say "I can't do it" and "I love you." The children with a stronger sense of gender stereotypes were also those who perceived their sex to be permanent and irreversible.

Theories of Gender Identification

Essentially, theories of gender identification fall into three approaches: *biological theories* stress the part physiology plays in determining sexual differences; *social learning theory* emphasizes learning by observation, imitation, and the socialization processes; *cognitive development theory* emphasizes self-labeling and the cognitive organization of gender information.

Biological Theory

Theories based on biology emphasize the genetic and hormonal aspects of sex differences. The presence or absence of the various sex hormones is the major determinant of physical sexual processes throughout the lifespan. The questions put to such theories by social scientists concern the extent to which behavior according to sex, other than that involved in reproduction, is influenced by biological factors. As we have seen already Maccoby and Jacklin (1974) believe that sex differences in aggression are due in part to biology.

Social Learning

Closely related to behaviorist learning theories of reward and punishment is the theory of *social* or *observational learning, modeling,* and *imitation.* Ac-

Children differentiate between boys and girls by such characteristics as clothing, speech, and hairstyles.

cording to social learning theory, children are conditioned to appropriate gender roles by the praise or criticism, reward or punishment, of their parents, peers, and other representatives of society. But more important in social learning theory is the idea that the children don't have to be directly rewarded. They learn appropriate gender roles by observing the rewards and punishments meted out to others. Other members of society serve as models for appropriate behavior, and their behavior is imitated by the child.

Bandura and Walters (1963) have shown that models who are powerful and have control over resources are more readily imitated than less powerful models. To a great extent children's concepts of sex stereotypes are based on their own observations of adult society both in real life and in books, television, and movies. Rigid as their thinking is, it is clear to children at an early age that men assume the aggressive roles in our culture. Women are cast as housewives and schoolteachers; men play the role of soldier, policeman, athlete, and politician. Furthermore, children tend to equate physical size and strength with power and social prestige. Because he is usually larger and stronger, Daddy is assumed to be smarter and to wield more authority than Mommy. Modeling the powerful figure, however, readily explains the development of masculinity but not of femininity. (Social learning theory as it relates to the development of gender roles is described more fully in Chapter 9.)

Cognitive Development

Kohlberg's (1966) theory explaining the adoption of gender roles is an extension of Piaget's theory of cognitive development. Kohlberg is interested in why a boy chooses to model himself on the masculine model and a girl on the feminine model—a response to Bandura's social learning theory. Children at about the age of six, Kohlberg explains, achieve gender conservation; they now understand that their biological sex is irreversible—they will always remain male or female. At this point they not only identify with their own sex, but they come to hold those things associated with their own sex to be valuable. Thus, boys will seek out male models to imitate, girls will seek out female models.

In addition, children at this age are concerned with rule-making. From their personal experience they form their own rules with which to judge gender behavior. These rules tend to be oversimplified and exaggerated. But as children develop intellectually, they become less rigid and allow more latitude in gender behavior.

There are several problems with Kohlberg's cognitive theory. Children identify with and imitate their own sex models at an earlier age than six years; children must establish their gender identity by the age of three, according to Money and Ehrhardt (1972). Also, many girls, particularly tomboys, do not seek out female models but model themselves after males. Yet they successfully develop stable female gender identities at a later date.

As we have seen in the more general theories of child development, each theory explains one aspect of the development process. None explains every question that can be raised. However, we have come a long way from explanations that ony serve to justify existing attitudes. Thus, opposing theories force us to sharpen our wits and send us back to the empirical evidence for new insights.

EMOTIONAL DEVELOPMENT

The preschool years are a time of dramatic and sometimes painful change. The preschooler's growing awareness and abilities start to bring demands and responsibilities. It becomes important to deal with some surprising new problems: Who am I? Am I a boy or a girl, and what difference does it make? When can I show anger, and when must I control it? How much do I need others, and to what extent can I go it alone? What should I be afraid of, and how should I manage fear?

We meet these problems in a particularly acute way in the preschool period, but we do not settle them. We keep on dealing with them all our lives, and though the circumstances and relationships change as we mature, the patterns of meeting these problems that are laid down in the preschool years tend to abide. They form the core of that hard-to-define something that we call personality.

Dependency

None of us is an entirely independent individual. To some degree everyone is dependent. We rely on others for information, support, and emotional comfort. Our *dependency* varies with the extent to which we rely on others. As adults, we recognize that dependency is a give-and-take process. We are glad to receive nurturance, but we recognize that sometimes we must nurture others in return. Young children's dependent behavior is not nearly so reciprocal. They expect to be nurtured, but they are unaware of the necessity of giving something in return.

Dependent behavior in children takes the forms of affection-seeking and instrumental help-seeking. *Affection-seeking* dependency can be seen in the demand, "Look at me!" Children are extremely pleased to be noticed and praised. *Instrumental help-seeking*, on the other hand, involves dependency in performing some new or difficult task. A little girl building a sand castle at the beach may ask for help from her mother. In this kind of situation the child's need for dependency is satisfied in two ways; she gets "practical" help in her play, and at the same time the adult's willingness to help reassures the child that Mommy cares for her.

Dependency and Self-Image

Preschoolers' concepts of themselves are difficult to understand and even harder to analyze because these children's language skills are not very strong and their view of the world is still egocentric. They may, therefore, have a

Preschoolers seek nurturance and affection from adults.

complex and subtle system of views and perceptions but be unable to express them. It has become clear, however, that a child's independence and self-confidence, not only in the preschool years but in later life, are closely related to the way in which the parents deal with this early dependency. As parents, we try to protect our children from danger and frustration while simultaneously trying to prepare them to face danger and frustration on their own. The greatest challenge of parenthood is to strike a proper balance between too much and too little protectiveness.

Despite popular notions to the contrary studies suggest that children who are regularly punished for dependent behavior or are punished for ordinary offenses by being deprived of love or attention tend to grow up to be more dependent than children whose early dependent behavior is indulged. In other words, children who are not offered the nurturance they need when young may continue to seek it as they grow older. Children who do not find sufficient nurturance at home often turn to the nursery teacher or to other children.

Overly protective parents who encourage dependency and offer assistance where it is not needed may also be harming their children. In later life the children may be slow to learn how to help themselves and may rely excessively on other people for help just as their undernurtured playmates do. One investigator (Baumrind, 1971) found that the children of parents who were warm and understanding, but at the same time self-confident, directing, and demanding, tended themselves to be self-confident, outgoing, purposeful, and self-controlled in a nursery school test. On the other hand, the children of indulgent, permissive parents—parents who encouraged dependency and failed to let their children know, clearly and consistently, what was expected of them—tended to be aimless in their behavior and to lack self-reliance.

Initiative versus Guilt

In his now classic work *Childhood and Society* (1963) psychoanalyst Erik Erikson theorized that preschool children experience a developmental crisis as they become less dependent, a conflict between what Erikson terms *initiative* and *guilt*. As children grow physically and their intellectual capabilities mature, they develop an increasing sense of their own power—their ability to make things happen. They become more and more able to control their physical environment as they gain mastery over their own bodies; begin to understand that other people have different motivations and perceptions from their own; and they delight in their own ability to figure things out. This growth supports what Erikson calls initiative.

> There is in every child at every stage a new miracle of vigorous unfolding, which constitutes a new hope and a new responsibility for all. Such is the sense and the pervading quality of initiative. The criteria for all these senses and qualities are the same; a crisis, more or less beset with fumbling and fear, is resolved, in that the child suddenly seems to "grow together" both in his person and in his body. He appears "more himself," more loving, relaxed, and brighter in his judgment, more activated and activating. He is in free possession of a surplus of energy which permits him to forget failures quickly and to approach what seems desirable (even if it also seems uncertain and even dangerous) with undiminished and more accurate direction (Erikson, 1963).

At this stage children are ready and eager to learn and work cooperatively with others to achieve their goals. They learn to plan realistically, and they are willing to accept the guidance of teachers and other adults. It is at this stage, according to Erikson, that the child's energy is directed "toward the possible and the tangible, which permits the dreams of early childhood to be attached to the goals of an active adult life."

The danger of this stage is that children's newfound energy will lead them to act, or wish to act, in ways that will make them feel guilty. Along with this great sense of power comes an increasing awareness of the requirements that limit behavior. Donald feels angry at his little sister and realizes that he would like to push her out of her high chair, which he knows he is able to do. But he also realizes that pushing his sister would bring punishment from his mother. He cannot always do what he wants.

Both the adults and the other children in Donald's world require him to develop self-control and some responsibility for what he does. As children grow in the ability to observe themselves, they are expected to control themselves—and they become able to punish themselves with guilt if they fail to fulfill that expectation. On the one hand, children at this stage are experiencing themselves as more powerful than ever before; on the other hand, they are beginning to realize that they must control their own behavior and that they will feel guilty if they fail to do so. "The child indulges in fantasies of being a giant and a tiger, but in his dreams he runs in terror for dear life...." (Erikson, 1963).

If this crisis is handled well, children learn to function in ways that will allow them to use their initiative constructively. They will take pleasure in their own increasing power, and become better able to cooperate with and accept help from others. They will find ways to use their energy and capabilities in a strong, solid way that will allow them to get some of what they want without violating their developing sense of right behavior.

Less happily, some children may be unable to find the balance between initiative and guilt. Their own desire for control and mastery may come into conflict with a wish for the acceptance and support of others or with the dictates of a developing conscience. This conflict may lead them to overcontrol themselves, to close off their energy to satisfy the requirements of obedience or to avoid guilt. They may become resentful of those who require control of them or even of their own sense of inner control. If the conflict is not resolved, such children may grow into adults who feel that the only way they can get what they want is at the cost of doing something that they believe is wrong— or, alternatively, that the only way they can do what is right is to deny themselves the things that they want.

Aggression

In recent years there has been a very active and noisy debate about the nature and origin of aggression in human behavior. In our society aggression is not always considered an undesirable form of behavior. In fact, a person who is unable to act aggressively when it is appropriate may be ineffective and frustrated. Each of us, child and adult alike, must act to promote our own self-

---

Erikson's Crises in Psychosocial Development

BASIC TRUST VERSUS BASIC MISTRUST (FIRST YEAR OF LIFE)

AUTONOMY VERSUS SHAME AND DOUBT (SECOND YEAR OF LIFE)

 INITIATIVE VERSUS GUILT (THE PRESCHOOL YEARS)

These children have a boundless supply of energy, and they learn skills and information quickly and avidly. They concentrate on successes rather than failures, and do things for the simple pleasure of activity. But their new physical and mental strength encourages ambitions that may turn out to be beyond their abilities or forbidden by their parents. Unless they can come to terms with these limitations, they may be troubled by guilt.

INDUSTRY VERSUS INFERIORITY (MIDDLE CHILDHOOD)

IDENTITY VERSUS ROLE CONFUSION (ADOLESCENCE)

INTIMACY VERSUS ISOLATION (YOUNG ADULTHOOD)

GENERATIVITY VERSUS STAGNATION (PRIME OF LIFE)

EGO INTEGRITY VERSUS DESPAIR (OLD AGE)

interest, and when this can only be done at the expense of someone else, it may be called aggression. This aggression can be purely instrumental or it can be hostile. When Joey pushes Peggy in order to get her away from the toy fire engine he wants to play with, he is engaging in *instrumental* aggression. That is, his aggressive act—the pushing—is directed toward the attainment of a basically nonaggressive goal—playing with the fire engine. But if, having gotten her away from the toy, he continues pushing and hitting her, his purpose must be to hurt her. This is *hostile* aggression.

Frustration-Aggression Hypothesis

The question, you might object, is not what *causes* hostile aggression, but what *provokes* it. And the answer, in a word, is frustration. Preschoolers have more than their share of occasions to feel frustrated. Several times a day they may want something and cannot get it, try to do something and fail, suffer affronts to their dignity and invasions of their privacy. Even their own inner conflicts, such as those between initiative and guilt, can be terribly frustrating.

The obvious thing to do when we are frustrated is to remove the cause of frustration. Failing this, we may try to get even. And when it is impossible to get even with the actual cause of our frustration, we may take it out wherever we can. Teased by her older brother all day, for example, a child may treat her younger brother to a dose of hostile aggression.

If aggression is simply a reaction to frustration, then punishment would not do much, in the long run, to deter it. The boy who is punished by his father may see the father's behavior as another form of aggression. Far from having a corrective result, the punishment may serve as a model for further aggression on the part of the boy. Also, the girl who anticipates punishment for aggressive behavior that she feels is justified may have her frustration intensified when she inhibits herself. The inhibition of aggression may lead to the heightening of frustration and ultimately to an intensification of aggressive behavior. However, hostile aggression can be minimized by diverting it into healthy, nondestructive outlets such as physical activity.

But can all hostile aggression be accounted for as a reaction to frustration? Some theorists believe that humans also have a hostile instinct. They say, however, that this instinct only gives us a *predisposition* toward aggressive behavior. It also takes early experience—"training" in aggression—before we will actually behave aggressively. For that matter aggression can also be seen as a form of behavior that is learned through practice, reinforcement, and imitation even without the instinct.

It is impossible to decide among these views without further research to provide more conclusive data. In the meantime we can learn how aggression actually manifests itself in preschoolers.

Aggression in Preschool Children

Most research on the aggressive behavior of preschool children has been based either on observations made under test conditions in nursery schools and day-care centers or on the (frequently biased) reports of mothers. A boy's pattern of aggression at home may differ significantly from his behavior under laboratory conditions. Nevertheless, it is possible to make a number of useful generalizations about aggression in preschoolers.

During toddlerhood aggressive behavior usually takes the form of temper tantrums. They generally occur in reaction to emotional states such as frustration, overstimulation, or loss of attention. As the child matures, behavior is increasingly influenced by interaction with other children and adults. Most aggression during the preschool period is triggered by the social conflicts that arise in the course of cooperative play; yet despite the increase in provocation, physically aggressive behavior generally decreases with age. In most cases this decline of physical aggression is accompanied by an increase in verbal aggression. Hitting may be replaced by name-calling, and in time children learn to be as much hurt by names as by sticks and stones.

The decline of physical aggression during the preschool period may be a reflection of the change in parental disciplinary techniques during these years. Generally, parents start to deal with aggression in a more authoritative manner. In the belief that toddlers cannot very well understand verbal prohibitions, parents may ignore their outbursts of temper, try to divert their attention, or simply use force to quell aggression. As children grow older they are scolded, threatened, or deprived of privileges as a punishment for misbehavior. The increased use of verbal controls by parents may serve as a model for children's choice of verbal rather than physical aggression in the preschool years.

Is the pattern of aggression displayed during the preschool years relevant to future behavioral development? Long-range studies indicate that it is, especially for boys (Olweus, 1979). Researchers (Kagan & Moss, 1962) have found that patterns of aggressive behavior in children three to six years old gave surprisingly good indications of the kinds of behavior the children would show as adolescents and, to some extent, as adults. Children who were dominant, competitive, and indirectly aggressive to their peers tended to be especially competitive as adults. Childhood aggressiveness, then, may not be a transient phase. On the contrary, it may last, although in a different form, throughout the individual's entire lifetime.

Fear and Anxiety

Generally people are afraid of that which is unknown or incomprehensible to them. For young children the category of things incomprehensible is an uncomfortably large one.

Because infants perceive the whole world on an essentially sensorimotor level, their fears may be readily relieved by removing the immediate cause. But as children grow older, they encounter many new and frightening situations, and they are no longer so easily comforted. Now they come to rely more heavily on nurturance and comfort from mother and other trusted adults. A critical characteristic of the maturing process is the expanding ability and need to find comfort socially, in one's parents and peers, and ultimately in oneself.

Social stress is a primary source of fear for the preschool child. Not knowing how to act in a new social situation, many of these children are easily frightened by exposure to unfamiliar people and places. Shyness and silent withdrawal are common responses. This may not be serious if it occurs only occasionally, but a child may need support and encouragement from the parents in such situations. Without such help, shyness may develop to the point where the child is seriously hampered in social relationships, developing a fear of the unfamiliar that can remain for many years.

Fears may also be learned through conditioning and reinforcement. Children may acquire fears through exposure to frightening films or television shows. For example, they may be afraid to get a haircut after seeing a film in which the barber is portrayed as a killer. More directly, children may acquire fears on the basis of their own experience. Having once been stung by a bee, the child may run in terror from any buzzing insect. Other common "irrational" fears among preschoolers are fear of the dark, fear of being washed down the drain in the bathtub, and fear of being flushed down the toilet.

Some of children's most terrifying fears originate in their own imaginations. From year to year preschoolers develop a more and more powerful capacity to conjure up vivid scenes and situations. They use imagination to entertain ideas that they would not enact in reality and to vent their aggression privately. They also use it to invent fearsome perils. At bedtime a shadow on the ceiling may become a ravening beast; a dark corner may conceal nameless horrors. It is important for parents to take these fears seriously because they are very real to the child even if their causes are not.

The nature of children's fears changes as they grow older. In one study (Bauer, 1976), the researcher encouraged children in kindergarten, second grade, and sixth grade to talk about their fears and to draw a picture of them. The kindergartners were most afraid of monsters and ghosts, not because they might be physically injured, but because they were ugly—frightening to look at. The fear that they might be physically injured had not yet occurred to most of the kindergartners. The sixth graders, on the other hand, more realistically, were afraid of physical danger and of bodily harm to themselves or their parents. Thus, as children get older, they are less likely to have fears with imaginary themes, but more likely to express realistic fears of danger or bodily injury.

Ultimately, fear is a highly individualized response. One child's nightmare may be another child's joke. In general, children gradually become less expressive of their fears, and their responses to frightening objects become more constructive as they grow older. Most children, even those with intense fears, manage to overcome them in two years time; younger children tend to lose their fears much more rapidly than do older children (Graziano, De Giovanni, & Garcia, 1979). Eventually children work out ways to overcome irrational fears and to manage those that have some basis in fact.

Altruism and Moral Development

One of the most important human abilities is telling right from wrong. "Moral development," "conscience," and "ethics" are all terms we use to denote our efforts to deal fairly with others. Preschool children's training and experience gradually teach them which actions are considered acceptable by other people and which are not. They learn that doing certain things may lead to punishment.

Ethical behavior, however, consists of more than avoiding punishment by behaving properly. In a fuller sense it means understanding that the needs of others are as valid as our own. If you find a stranger's wallet and return it because you think you may have been seen picking it up, you are behaving prudently. If you return it out of consideration for the owner, you are acting ethically. This distinction, obvious enough to adults, is seen only gradually by the preschooler.

Altruism is moral behavior that involves a concern for the welfare of others. Rather than moral rectitude, altruistic acts are acts of kindness requiring an empathy for the situation and feelings of others. Altruism is the opposite of egocentricity. According to Piaget, moral development and the development of altruism, like all phases of human growth, occur in a series of stages. In view of the egocentricity of the preschool child Piaget doubts that children below the age of seven are capable of empathizing with others to the degree required for truly ethical behavior. He suggests that preschool children cannot be taught ethics but can only be trained to behave properly.

As we have seen in Chapter 7, later research has taken issue with Piaget's interpretation of the behavior of preschool children as entirely egocentric:

> Observations of young children interacting suggest that preschool youngsters are not only aware that other people have feelings but also actively try to understand the feelings they observe. The 2½ year old who holds out a toy to a crying child certainly appears to be demonstrating an awareness that the other youngster is experiencing unhappy feelings (Borke, 1971).

This study suggests that from the age of three, children may be aware that other people have feelings and that these feelings vary according to the situation in which the person finds himself. The researcher notes, however, that children are able to recognize happiness and fear in others more readily than they can recognize sadness or anger. No difference was observed between boys and girls, but older children demonstrated much more empathetic capability than younger ones. This general trend for social sensitivity to increase with age supports Piaget's thesis that egocentricity declines gradually toward the end of preschool years, even if children begin to show some capacity for empathy a few years sooner than he thought.

It is children's increasing social awareness that largely accounts for their early manifestations of sympathy, conscience, and generosity during the preschool period. As they become more conscious of the needs and concerns of others, they begin to desire the satisfaction of others' needs as well as their own, and their behavior shows a growing capacity for sharing and compas-

Studies indicate that children begin to understand the feelings of others at a fairly early age.

sion. In an experiment designed to study generosity in children researchers (Rutherford & Mussen, 1968) observed that generosity is closely linked to other moral characteristics such as cooperation, altruism, lack of interpersonal aggression, and sympathy. They further suggested that these aspects of moral development are closely linked to the child's perception of the same-sex parent as warm, affectionate, and nurturant.

Altruistic behavior of preschoolers is related not only to the affection and nurturance they receive from their parents, but also to the parents' disciplinary style (Hoffman, 1979). Parents who discipline children by pointing out the harmful consequences of their behavior to others are fostering moral development. This disciplinary style teaches children to understand how their behavior is related to the well-being of others. Since children at this early age are disciplined from five to six times an hour (Wright, 1967), this becomes a compelling message, aiding the internalization of moral standards. On the other hand, parents who regularly discipline a child with physical punishment and the deprivation of privileges foster a morality based on fear. Such power-assertive techniques do not teach the empathy for others that encourages such prosocial behavior as helping, sharing, and comforting.

The proposition that preschoolers are capable of a higher order of moral behavior than Piaget thought has also been suggested by studies of the child's conception of social justice. In an experiment designed to study leniency toward cheating, researchers (Ross & Ross, 1968) tested the attitudes of preschool children both before and after they were allowed to cheat successfully at a given task. They found that children who cheated became more tolerant of cheating in others, while those who did not cheat became more severely critical of cheaters. Even at a very early age, apparently, learning to obey the rules involves expecting others to obey them as well.

It appears that children have a fairly conventional notion of social justice by the end of the preschool period. One study (Irwin & Moore, 1971) suggests that young children understand that returning a stolen toy is more meaningful than merely apologizing for having stolen it. They were not only able to make the fundamental distinction between right and wrong, but they also recognized that in order to right a wrong it may not be enough just to say "I'm sorry."

Although these studies take Piaget's work as their starting point, they challenge his description of the preschooler as an amoral being who behaves properly only in response to adult authority. On the contrary, they have found that preschoolers are well on the way to internalizing and understanding basic moral considerations.

PLAY AND FANTASY

> Two boys, both twenty months, are playing together. Each stands on opposite sides of a coffee table. First boy slaps his hands vigorously and repeatedly on the table. Second boy joins in the banging. First boy ducks down below the table. After a pause, second boy stoops down in a version of peek-a-boo. They spot one another and laugh. First boy stands up and starts banging the table again. Second boy does the same. The sequence is repeated about eight or ten times. Each time the banging gets louder, lasts less time before the boys go under the table, and laughter comes earlier. Finally, the boys are noisily ducking under the table almost simultaneously and rather wildly (Kaplan, 1980).

The boys are playing, and with each other. The first thing the average observer would notice is that they are having fun. Lois Murphy (1972) says that "play is most fun and most playful when it is spontaneous, evolving from an integration of impulse and ideas and providing expression, release, sometimes climax, often mastery, with a degree of exhilaration and refreshment. Good play leaves one feeling good, happy, and alive." Watching television is not play, it is a passive occupation. When children are playing, they are active, in control—masters of a situation of their own invention. Play has been defined as behavior performed for its own sake, dominated and controlled by the player (Weisler & McCall, 1976). Play is likely to occur only in a familiar atmosphere—one in which the organism feels safe and is neither tired nor hungry.

Children and monkeys that are deprived of affection and playful interaction with their mothers are not able to play. Harlow's baby monkeys, reared on a mechanical mother, could not play with their peers. Lois Murphy (1972) points out that some extremely poor children do not play with words or

Fairy Tales

Malevolent giants, evil stepmothers, wolves who eat children, wicked witches—
these are some of the stock characters in fairy tales. The situations of the main
characters are no less frightening: a little girl locked in a high tower, another
child put to sleep forever, parents die at the beginning of the story or cast their
children out of their homes. Many parents might prefer to protect their children
from fairy tales, feeling that they should only be exposed to heroes who strive to
be good, villains who learn to see the error of their ways, and situations that are
realistic and pose challenges that can be easily met with the proper
determination and effort. Bruno Bettelheim, in *The Uses of Enchantment: The
Meaning and Importance of Fairy Tales* (1977), contends that fairy tales are not
only harmless to children but offer great positive values.

Bettelheim argues that today, as in times past, the most important and also
the most difficult task in raising children is helping them to find a meaning in
life. The deepest meanings in life are rooted in moral behavior. But children do
not learn by being preached at or exhorted to be good. Morality and virtue are
learned in more subtle ways—by implication and by examples set forth in a
simple and uncomplicated fashion. Nowhere in literature better than in fairy tales
can children find good and evil personified—the villain is uncompromisingly
wicked, and the hero is pure goodness.

Just as the people in fairy tales are personifications of one dominant
characteristic, the plots, too, are stripped of nonessential detail. A fairy tale
presents a basic human dilemma at a level that reaches a child. The story begins
with the death of a parent, or, as in Hansel and Gretel, the children are
abandoned. But as the characters overcome such calamities, the child may
discover that life's meaning is in the struggle. Cinderella's mother died at her
birth, and she was assigned the most menial place in her stepmother's
household. There she behaved morally and with good cheer—the passive
struggle—and finally achieved the prince and happiness in life. In Jack and the
Beanstalk, Jack must take the initiative. He climbs the beanstalk, pits himself
against the giant three times, and each time is able to bring back a means to
support himself and his mother.

Even young children can understand that elements of a story have more
than one meaning. One five-year-old listened to his mother read about Jack and
said, "There aren't really such things as giants, are there?" Before his mother
could respond, he went on, "But there are such things as grownups, and they're
like giants." Thus the fairy tale helps the child vicariously to win in a struggle
with adults.

Children identify not only with the hero but with the cunning witches and
wicked stepmothers. Each may represent one side of a child's nature. When the
hero vanquishes the villain, children can recognize that it is possible to overcome
their own bad feelings of anger, selfishness, and the desire to hit someone.
Having access intellectually to the different plots and characters of fairy tales
thereby enriches children's experience and provides substance for their fantasies.
Out of fantasy comes the strength to deal with the troubling events and issues in
their own lives.

materials like middle-class children. They don't organize toys or solve problems with blocks; they don't participate with other children using toys for props in elaborate games of play. And they don't have fun. Murphy observes that a child deprived of early affection and play with its mother remains at the sensorimotor stage, playing with water or sand, without goals, running around without a purpose.

Social Play

That play contains an element of fun is undeniable; fun and the lifting of the usual social constraints set play apart from the rest of a child's waking time. In control of the situation, then, the child feels safe enough to experiment with social encounters. A child can test the social rules in play where the consequences are minimized and explore the ways in which people get along with one another. Children approach their peers and learn to play with them in a sequence that stretches over a number of years, interacting with and paralleling their cognitive and emotional growth.

Early Play

The earliest form of social play may start almost as soon as the baby is born. Mothers, fathers, grandparents, and many others coo at babies, wave rattles at them, sing nursery rhymes, and bounce them and hold them up in the air. The baby responds at first by smiling and later by screaming with delight. The baby does not initiate this play, but there is no doubt that it is play and that it is social. Later the infant will play peekaboo and pat-a-cake.

A six- or seven-month-old baby, terrified of strange adults, will be completely absorbed and fascinated by other children. Like dogs that always recognize other dogs no matter how big or small, smooth or furry, the older infant can always distinguish other children, including teen-agers, from adults. Even by the age of ten months one child's play will be highly influenced by that of another child (Eckerman & Whatley, 1977).

Types of Play

The sequences in the development of social play are generally as follows: solitary play, parallel play, associative play, and cooperative play. At first in *solitary* play children play with their toys alone, but within earshot of their mothers. At school they will play independently without reference to what any of the other children are doing. Later, in *parallel* play, they play within sight and earshot of another child, perhaps playing with a similar toy but in their own way. In the early phases of peer interaction children seem to be more engrossed in objects than in each other (Mueller & Lucas, 1975). The next type is called *associative* play, in which two or three children use the same equipment and participate in the same games, but each in his own way. Then gradually children begin to participate in *cooperative* play—they share playthings, organize games, make friends. Cooperative play reflects children's

Most of the children in this sandbox are engaged in associative play, using the same toys but playing independently. The few who are playing together are participating in cooperative play.

growing capacity to accept and respond to ideas and actions that are not originally their own.

These categories of play have been observed in the nursery school situation in a developmental sequence, but all forms of play may continue through the lifespan. Skiers, for example, may go off on their own, find their own hill, and practice turns *(solitary)*. Or a skier may choose to follow another skier down a trail *(parallel)*. Some skiers like to ski as a group, keeping together as they descend the hill, but not in any organized way *(associative)*. Finally, are the skiers who race all following the same rules and participating in an organized way *(cooperative)*?

Playmates

Perhaps the most significant advance preschool children make in their relationship to their peers is the establishment of personal one-to-one friendships. Three-year-olds acquire various playmates, but at this early age their egocentricity prevents them from seeing much importance in the differences between playmates. Soon, however, they begin to have preferences: one may be too

Developmental Views of Friendship

As early as the fourth century B.C. Aristotle, the Greek philosopher, theorized about friendship. There are three kinds of friendship, according to Aristotle: One chooses friends for their usefulness, for amusement and pleasure, and, finally, for their virtue—friends, admiration and respect for one another. Can Aristotle's types of friendship be applied to children? Is there a developmental sequence in choosing and maintaining friendships?

In two related studies (Bigelow & La Gaipa, 1975; Bigelow, 1977) children were asked what they expected from their best friends. The younger children's responses were egocentric and materialistic (a friend plays with you and gives you help), corresponding to Aristotle's first two types. By eighth grade the responses tended toward a more socially supportive orientation (friends are loyal and can be trusted to help with problems), implying a certain intimacy. Aristotle's highest type of friendship, admiration for another's virtuous characteristics, does not seem to form a basis for friendship among Americans, even adults (Reisman & Schorr, 1978).

To what extent are children capable of initiating and sustaining intimate relationships based on sharing as well as mutual emotional support? Recently two researchers (Selman & Selman, 1979) worked out a developmental theory of friendship based on open-ended, semistructured interviews with 250 people aged three to forty-five. The researchers identified five stages in children's ability to make and sustain friendship.

The first stage, from ages three to seven, is called Stage 0 because it cannot properly be called friendship. Called by the authors Momentary Playmateship, in this stage friends are valued for their material and physical attributes and their proximity. "He is my friend." "Why?" "He has a giant Superman doll and a real swing set."

Stage 1, from ages four to nine, is labeled One-Way Assistance, in which the "friend" does what you want. "She is not my friend anymore." "Why?" "She wouldn't go with me when I wanted her to."

Stage 2, from ages six to twelve, is called Two-Way Fair-Weather Cooperation. In this stage, as the name suggests, the child is beginning to understand reciprocity. However, the basic function is still at the stage of Aristotle's utility.

Stage 3, from nine to fifteen, is characterized as an Intimate, Mutually Shared Relationship. Children's friendship is a collaboration with others for sharing and mutual interests. Friends divulge secrets, agreements, and plans and help each other to solve personal problems. But friendship at this stage is viewed as an exclusive and rather possessive connection.

Stage 4, the highest stage, is one in which the adolescent or adult is aware that people have many needs. As one child put it, "One thing about a good friendship is that it's a real commitment, a risk you have to take. You have to be able to support and trust and give, but you have to be able to let go, too" (Selman & Selman, 1979).

Having created this developmental model of friendship, the authors are using it to assess the level of friendship of children who are having difficulties making friends with other children. They are developing strategies based on the stages to help children who are far behind their peers in the social skills needed to make and keep friends.

passive to have much fun with; another may be a bully. The children who are the most fun to play with are soon singled out as special friends, though the relationship may not be sustained or consistent yet because very young preschoolers respond strongly to feelings that change from moment to moment.

Preschool children usually choose friends they perceive as being similar to themselves. For this reason a child's close friends are usually of the same sex and age as the child. The establishment of personal friendships marks an important step in the child's awareness of other people as distinct and unique individuals.

Fantasy

A five-year-old girl and her three-year-old brother rushed into the kitchen and demanded real sponges and real water and Ajax in order to clean the doll's carriage and toy car. After rubbing away for some time, the little girl announced, "Now we will play." Somewhat surprised, her mother asked, "Haven't you been playing all along?" No, according to the little girl, they had been working. "Play is only when you pretend" (Millar, 1974).

The Function of Fantasy

Pretend and games of make-believe are at their height in children from the ages of eighteen months until about eight years. Fantasying is rarely the time-wasting pastime it was once believed to be. By means of fantasy children can explore their feelings and emotions in much the same way that they explore their physical space. Ellen can hit her stuffed dog instead of her baby brother, feel bad, soothe the dog, kiss it, and put it to bed—experimenting with her different feelings toward her brother. Repetition lessens the impact of frightening or exciting events. After losing her mother in the supermarket, a little girl can play at being lost, always finding her mother again until the experience becomes no longer frightening. Millar suggests that a rich fantasy life enables children to sit still and wait in boring situations. Or some children may use fantasy to try to make sense out of something they have encountered that is puzzling. They try out each solution by acting it out (Millar, 1974). Perhaps the best explanation for the use of fantasy is that of Piaget. By exploring, pretending, repeating, and classifying events, verbal expressions and their own emotions, Piaget sees children as assimilating new experiences into a cognitive framework. Thus, children's make-believe is a clue to the way they experience the world.

Stages in the Use of Fantasy

Early fantasy often involves a substitution (symbolic play) in which one object or situation is used to stand for another. A spoon held to the ear while the child talks gibberish is a telephone. The newspaper is held upside-down and "read." The child needs to look like what he is pretending to be—big like his daddy, or blue like the sky. The focus is on physical appearance.

Later the substitute object is no longer needed. Action will substitute for the object. Children will sit on a chair and "steer" the car; they will flap their

Piaget has theorized that fantasizing is the means by which children assimilate new experiences into their cognitive framework.

arms as if they were wings; they will throw an imaginary ball. Next a single scene will be enacted. A child may take a teddy bear for a ride in the chair after he has been out in his stroller (Chaillé, 1978).

Sociodramatic play may follow the re-enactment of single events. Such play involves the cooperative playacting of a group of children. A chair or a radio becomes a spaceship as a group of children enact a trip to the moon. With older children sociodramatic play may continue for days.

In the final stage of fantasy neither objects, actions, nor the dramatic acting out of scenes are needed. The game of pretend takes place in the head; it is "pure" imagination (Chaillé, 1978). At this stage anything is possible. There are no restraints. We can pretend we are famous—a movie star or President of the United States. We can feed the hungry, steal from the rich, and rescue maidens.

Fantasy and Reality

Children, as we have seen in Chapter 7 are perfectly capable of distinguishing between substitutes and the real thing. They will not try to eat a cardboard cake. Children will not use just any object as a substitute for the real thing; the context is important. They would not use wooden animals for building blocks in one experiment, for example, but were willing to use hard clay and pebbles. When the animals were sawn in half, they were accepted. Adults are not permitted to intrude in a game of make-believe as themselves, but are readily accepted if they join in the make-believe (Millar, 1974).

Children do not so easily distinguish between real characters and such fantasy characters as a witch, a dragon, or Big Bird. They don't seem to use the category of pretend or make-believe to apply to such adult fantasies as mermaids and Mickey Mouse, although with age, helped by their greater knowledge of the world, their ability to make such distinctions improves (Morison & Gardner, 1978).

Sex Differences

Several sex differences have been observed in the pattern of fantasies reported by children. Generally boys' fantasies involve more action and aggression and incorporate a greater number of objects, judging at least from their own reports. The fantasies described by girls, on the other hand, are more detailed and passive and are more often concerned with human relations. But these patterns conform suspiciously to culturally reinforced notions of masculinity and femininity. A girl who has a fantasy involving violence or aggression may be afraid she will be criticized if she expresses such thoughts. A recent study (Cramer & Bryson, 1973) suggests that preschool girls and boys do not differ much in the content of their fantasies, although later, in the early school years, girls do begin to fantasize less about aggression.

Imaginary Companions

Preschool children commonly adopt imaginary companions. They may assume any form, human or animal, male or female, and may bear any relationship to the child. The companion, for example, may be an amiable friend or an outlet for the child's aggression and hostility. It has been observed that girls are generally more apt to have imaginary playmates than boys and that creative and outgoing children are more apt to have them—or at least talk about them—than more introverted children. The imaginary companion is also more prevalent among firstborn and only children.

The imaginary companion usually disappears as the child becomes more involved with real playmates. In the absence of other children, however, the imaginary companion may serve a valuable function for the young child.

> One of the many crucial components in socialization and personality development is social interaction with siblings and peers. In the absence of such interactions [later] social interaction with age-mates may be greatly reduced. Some of the necessary developmental experiences can be provided through the vehicle

of an imaginary companion. With this companion, the child can practice and develop social and language skills which might otherwise develop more slowly (Manosevitz, Prentice, & Wilson, 1973).

Humor

As preschoolers develop a rich fantasy life, they also begin to develop a sense of humor. Several theories have been proposed to explain the origin of humor. The most important is Freud's, which was first published in 1916. The core of his theory is that the pleasure we take in humor is based on its ability to relieve us of psychic strain. A serious, threatening situation is suddenly "disarmed"; the stress disappears, and our laughter expresses our relief.

For a preschooler who is undergoing a great deal of frustration and anxiety, fantasy and humor can be important releases. Of course, in many cases laughter is much more than just a mechanism that serves to relieve stress, but it can perform the valuable function of a safety valve during the difficult preschool years.

Because children's thinking does not always follow the logic of adult thought, their jokes may fail to make adults laugh. Humor is generally based on incongruity; that is, we laugh at things that turn out differently from what we expected or that do not fit into a framework of normality. But children have very much their own sense of what is normal.

What do preschool children laugh at? Studies suggest that they laugh most in response to ongoing physical activities: tickling, teasing, romping. Preschoolers are also more likely to laugh if they realize the situation they are in is socially unacceptable. They are fond of telling long and rambling jokes—sometimes memorized and sometimes improvised—which usually fail to end in any sort of recognizable punch line. Young children take delight in the humor of facial expressions and pratfalls, gradually developing a more sophisticated appreciation of verbal humor as they mature.

Children delight not only in hearing and reciting riddles and nursery rhymes but in listening to and singing songs as well. Early in the preschool period children develop the ability to make up simple songs that often give useful insights into their thoughts and feelings at the time. Humorous ideas may also be expressed through dance. Most children are quick to respond to rhythm and music, using their bodies freely for self-expression without the inhibitions felt by many adults (McGhee, 1979).

SUMMARY

▶ Personality is that particular complex of emotional responses that differentiates one person from another. It is an important component of a person's identity. Gender is a prime determinant of a person's identity.

▶ Although few psychological and intellectual differences between the sexes can systematically be found, studies consistently show that males are more aggressive physically than females.

▶ Appropriate gender-roles are learned. Development of appropriate gender behavior is encouraged by socialization processes. Starting almost from birth little girls are treated differently from little boys in respect to dependent behavior, gross motor activity, and exploration. Three major approaches that explain the development of appropriate gender identity and behavior are biological theories, social learning, and Kohlberg's theory of cognitive development.

▶ Dependent behavior may be shown in seeking affection, attention, and help in doing things. Studies suggest that children whose early dependency needs are reasonably indulged tend to grow into less dependent adults than those who are deprived of love or attention. However, overprotective parents may prevent the child from becoming self-reliant.

▶ Erikson theorized that preschool children experience a developmental crisis of initiative versus guilt. These children take initiative as they become aware of their own powers, but this may lead to guilt when their thoughts or actions are what they have learned to call bad.

▶ Frustration provokes aggression. Physically aggressive behavior generally decreases with age, with verbal aggression replacing it. Patterns of aggression evident in the preschool years may continue in later life.

▶ Although Piaget suggested that preschool children, being egocentric, cannot understand moral values, other investigators have found evidence that preschoolers do become aware of the feelings of others. The development of such altruistic behavior as generosity and cooperation is closely linked to the child's perception of warmth and affection in the parent of the same sex.

▶ Play is fun—performed for its own sake, dominated and controlled by the player. Social play develops from a progression: solitary play, parallel play, associative play, and cooperative play.

▶ Fantasy helps children to assimilate chunks of reality into their individual frames of reference. Some children adopt imaginary companions.

FURTHER READINGS

Bjorklund, Gail. *Planning for play: A developmental approach.* Columbus, Ohio: Merrill, 1978.
    An instructional approach to play as an integral part of development.
Damon, William, *The social world of the child.* San Francisco, Calif.: Jossey-Bass, 1977.
    In this well-written book, Damon draws on his own research into children's understanding of social encounters at different stages in their development. He explores and compares the quality of children's reasoning in a number of areas, including rules, manners, and sex role conventions.

Edge, David (Ed.). *The formative years: How children become members of their society.* **New York: Schocken, 1970.**

Several essays by various child-development specialists discuss such topics as early socialization, security and anxiety, ability and social class, and the importance of language in socialization.

Fraiberg, Selma. *The magic years.* **New York: Scribner's, 1968.**

Fraiberg shows the reader, from inside the preschool child's mind, what the world is like to children and how they try to deal with it.

Garvey, Catherine, *Play.* **Cambridge, Mass.: Harvard University Press, 1977.**

This delightful book describes different forms of play, showing how children learn and develop socially in the process of playing. It also quotes the children themselves.

Glick, J., and Clark-Stewart, K. A. (Eds.). *The development of social understanding.* **New York: Gardner Press, 1979.**

In light of new data on children's interactive abilities, these articles reassess such topics as moral development and how children react to strangers. Although written for academics, most of these articles are not difficult to understand.

Le Shan, Eda J. *How to survive parenthood.* **New York: Random House, 1965.**

Just because traits such as jealousy and aggression are considered "normal" behavior by psychologists is no reason for parents not to step in when such feelings make children behave in antisocial ways, this child psychologist advises. The book consists of down-to-earth discussions about dealing with children.

Maccoby, E. E., and Jacklin, C. N. *The psychology of sex differences.* **Stanford, Calif.: Stanford University Press, 1974.**

This comprehensive survey has become a standard reference on sex differences. It includes a tremendous amount of research on intellect, achievement, and socialization.

Observational Activities
Part Three Preschool Years

Number-Object Correspondence

Many children have been taught to count to ten and can do so before they realize that there is a correspondence between number and object. For example, you may put ten blocks on a table and ask a child to count them. Most children will count correctly and point to the blocks as they count, but may only have pointed to six of the blocks by the time they have counted aloud to ten.

Arrange to observe in a preschool class where you have access to three children between the ages of three and four. Have the teacher help you identify three children who can count from one to ten without hesitation. Then arrange ten objects (pencils, blocks, raisins) on a table and ask each child, in turn, to count them for you. Write down how they go about it. You will want to consider:

1. Does the child demonstrate an understanding of number-object correspondence by touching an object for each number said?
2. Does the child touch each object only once, and are all objects touched by the time he/she finishes counting?

Be sure to identify each child by age and sex. You may decide to pool data with other class members to see if you can develop answers to such questions as:

1. Is there an age above which children understand number-object correspondence?
2. Is there a sex difference apparent?
3. Are there characteristics that differentiate successful from unsuccessful performers?

Sex Stereotyping

Sex stereotyping begins almost at birth and is unwittingly reinforced by adults and the media to which the child is exposed. Preschool teachers and parents are increasingly alert to the problem of sex stereotyping.

Observe a group of preschoolers in a free-play situation (child-care center or playground) for half an hour. Select, in advance, several sex-specific objects: a doll, a truck, a hammer, for example. Note down each instance of a child playing with a sex-specific object and the sex of that child playing with the object. Then analyze your notes and draw some tentative conclusions. Some of the points you might consider are:

1. How many boys played with the traditionally male-oriented object?
2. How many girls played with that same object?
3. Was there a difference in time spent with the object by boys and girls?
4. Did the teacher seem to have a role in encouraging the cross-sex play situation? (If you have explained your observation focus to the teacher in advance, you will not get a true measure of teacher intervention. It is best if you simply tell the teacher you want to observe for half an hour without spelling out the details of your observation.)

PART FOUR

Middle Childhood

Chapter 9

❖❖❖❖❖❖❖

Growth and Personality

*B*y the time Alice started grade school, she had formed a distinct personality; it began to develop before she was born and will continue to change until she dies. In the elementary schoolchild like Alice we sense— sometimes quite suddenly—a complete person. School-age children have characteristic ways of behaving that we recognize as distinctly their own and that we can predict to some extent if we know them well.

Each individual personality develops under the influence of countless major and minor factors. We can even say, in a broad sort of way, what these influences are. The strongest factor in the development of personality is undoubtedly the child's individual social history. Most of a child's learning is from social experiences, and although these experiences are sometimes supervised by parents and teachers, more often they occur in spontaneous family or neighborhood settings. No two children have exactly the same social history, even if they are twins who do everything together.

A second kind of factor that influences personality is cultural. Everything from music, television, and incidental remarks overheard but hardly understood by the child to deliberate modeling and training works as a subtle encouragement for the child to embody the typical or ideal personality of the culture. Third, there is the particular situation—the elements of place and time that bring out some personality traits and leave others in reserve. And finally, there are the factors involved in biological makeup: height, growth rate, temperament, and appearance. Genetic heritage provides the potential for these features.

As one researcher (Mussen, 1973) put it, these four types of factors are "interwoven—operating, interacting, and affecting personality development concurrently." Together they have formed a distinct personality for each of the children entering grade school, and will continue to do so as they grow.

PHYSICAL DEVELOPMENT

A child's growth rate and physique are not entirely the result of genetic inheritance. They are also affected by diet, by health care, and by physical exercise. These influences then affect personality through a child's growth rate and physique. Without minimizing the importance of social and cultural factors, researchers are recognizing more and more that physical development has a strong influence on a child's personality. One researcher (Tanner, 1962) put it this way:

> All the skills, aptitudes, and emotions of the growing child are rooted in or, conditioned by his bodily structure. Behind each stage of learning lies the development of essential cell assemblies in the brain; behind each social interaction lies a body image conditioned by the facts of size and [other features]....How fast a child grows and what type of body structure he has can exert a crucial influence on the development of his personality. The child's sense of identity is strongly linked to his physical appearance and ability.

Physical Appearance

The rate of growth in the elementary school years is not as spectacular as it is in infancy or adolescence, although some children do experience a small burst of growth between the ages of six and eight. As children grow, their trunk tends to become slimmer, their chest broader, and their arms and legs longer and thinner. At the same time the size of the head gradually approaches the adult proportion of one-seventh to one-eighth of total height. Permanent teeth appear, making the bottom part of the face look "heavier." Toward the end of middle childhood youngsters may look as though parts of their body are out of proportion, and indeed some parts do grow faster than others, causing even the most normal children to feel self-conscious or worried about their bodies.

Physique and Personality

The body is a particularly important instrument of the school-age child's success. Size and body build are key factors in achievement at sports and other play activities, and a large portion of children's prestige comes from their physical ability. Of course size has no direct influence on academic achievement, but it does seem to have some indirect effect. It has been shown, for example, that from the age of six physically large children average higher

Children's sense of identity is linked to their physical appearance and abilities.

scores on tests of mental ability than do smaller children (Scottish Council, 1953; Tanner, 1962). This correlation of height and intelligence persists into adulthood but gradually diminishes (Tanner, 1966).

The relation between body build and personality has been summarized in these words:

> Small, poorly coordinated, and relatively weak children are inclined to be timid, fearful, passive, and generally worried. In contrast, tall, strong, energetic, well-coordinated children of the same age are playful, self-expressive, talkative, productive, and creative (Mussen, 1973).

It should be emphasized that these personality traits are not the immediate and direct result of genetic endowment. That is, physical attributes affect a child's aptitudes and interests and the way others react, all of which in turn influence a child's personality.

For example, adults and classmates tend to treat small, thin children as though they were delicate, dependent, and incompetent. Such children's limited ability at sports will further reinforce this attitude and a lack of self-confidence among them. The result may be that they avoid sports and other

❖❖

Secular Growth Trends

"Secular growth trends" is the term which biologists who study human beings use to describe the drifts, tendencies, or general directions of human physical growth which are found in large samples of populations throughout the world. To calibrate secular growth trends biologists weigh and measure defined groups—usually national ones—over a period which should extend to several decades. The findings are then recorded and graphed (Roche, 1979). Secular growth is measured in weight, length, proportions of limbs, changes in craniofacial structure, changes in body fat, and changes in rates of maturation. Such variables as weight and length at birth, puberty, and adulthood may be taken into account. Maturity is calculated by skeletal development; in women, by menarche (menstruation), and in men, by the breaking of the voice.

Over the past fifty to one hundred years, the rates of growth during childhood, which are also associated with rates of maturation, have increased in all developed countries but not in many other countries. This increase appears to have ceased, particularly in the upper socioeconomic strata, in some countries such as Japan, the United States of America, Norway, and England. In other countries it continues, and in some it has declined and become a trend of decreasing growth.

Statures of children have increased a great deal in recent decades. British children of both sexes have increased in stature about .3 cm per decade at six years of age, .7 cm at nine years, and 1.1 cm at twelve years of age. In Australia childhood stature (without regard for age trend) has increased about 1.5 cm per decade. In the United States the stature of boys has increased about 2 cm per decade until the age of fifteen years, after which the trend is smaller (in adults, it is about 3 cm in eighty years). This adult stature increase trend in the United States continued until about 1965 (Roche, 1979). It was also accompanied by changes in body proportion and age of maturation. Measurements of select groups of fathers and sons showed that the sons were not only taller but also leggier—especially in thigh length—than their fathers. Daughters in the United States were both heavier and taller than their mothers, but the length increased more in the trunk than in the leg (Roche, 1979). Increasing stature has been accompanied by a trend toward lower age of maturity. The age of menarche has decreased notably. Trends in the United States and Europe show almost straight line decreases from 1840 to 1960, but in some countries, such as Norway and England, this trend seems to have stopped. Age of menopause, on the other hand, seems to have remained stable since Classical times. Maturation ages of boys seem to have decreased in some countries.

Although no one is certain what the causes of secular growth trends are, they are generally believed to be both environmental and genetic in origin. Secular growth trends cannot be explained by one single cause but there is, for example, some apparent relationship between crop production, urbanization, family size, and mortality. This relationship does not clearly indicate cause. One cause which seems likely to affect these changes is improved health and better care during childhood. Genetic factors, altered by such events as a change in immigration and marriage patterns, may also be important, as may changes in socioeconomic status, eating patterns, and environmental stress (Malina, 1979).

And the implications? Without a clear-cut understanding of the underlying causes it is difficult to suggest effective steps to maximize growth and health in every sphere. However, it is clear that the reproductive span has increased and that some populations are maturing earlier. This latter fact suggests the importance of teaching sex education earlier. The trend to earlier maturation suggests the importance of reviewing parent-child relationships in cultures affected. The evidence provided by secular growth trends recorded over the last fifty to one hundred years may affect such diverse issues as medical research, educational planning, furniture design, nutritional planning, and industrial or ecological practices (Malina, 1979). Many other and more striking implications will undoubtedly emerge as the study of secular growth trends continues and we begin to understand how social, physical, medical, and economic factors alter the course of human condition.

forms of competition altogether, thereby perpetuating physical frailty and the responses it elicits. In time these children develop the personality character-istics that people expect of them because of their size. On the other hand, adults and classmates will tend to regard tall, muscular children as compe-tent; this competence at games will foster further success, and in this way such children will be encouraged to develop outgoing traits.

Obesity is another physical characteristic that carries a negative stereo-type. It has long been known that young children have negative attitudes toward obesity. Even overweight children express such attitudes (Lerner & Korn, 1972). In a recent experiment (Young & Avdze, 1979) the researchers wondered if the behavior of an obese child would mitigate the negative image caused by his obesity. The results showed first that the child of average weight is very much preferred to the obese child, and the obedient child is preferred to the disobedient child. However, an obese child who was shown to be obe-dient was preferred to the normal-weight child who was disobedient. Thus, a child's behavior can override the negative force of obesity, but only if the behavior is "good."

Good behavior, unfortunately, will not completely solve the social stigma of a child's obesity. Another researcher (Sallade, 1973), using a self-concept scale, found that obese children in the third, fourth, and fifth grades had poorer self-concepts than average-weight children. If children express their negative attitudes toward their obese peers (and it is beyond a doubt that they do), the results may have profound consequences for the social adjustment of obese children.

Health

The average child has fewer illnesses during middle childhood than either before or afterward, and most of the illness is accounted for by the common cold. However, when children start school they go to more places and meet more people than before—and thus are exposed to more new diseases. This is the time for the so-called childhood diseases: mumps, measles, chickenpox, whooping cough, and the like.

At one time people felt that everyone was going to get these diseases sooner or later, and since having had them then usually makes one immune, or partly immune, to a second attack of the same disease, it seemed better to have them in childhood and get them over with. But we now know that these diseases can have serious complications and aftereffects. Whooping cough, for instance, can develop into pneumonia; measles can lead to deafness or brain damage; chickenpox can produce the usually fatal brain infection known as Reye's syndrome. Besides, vaccines have been developed for most of these diseases, and so there is no need to expose children to these risks. Still, many parents do not have their children immunized against all the diseases for which immunization is available, and the result is unnecessary sickness and sometimes even permanent damage, as in the case of polio.

One widespread health problem for which there is as yet no vaccine is dental caries, or tooth decay. In one study fully 93 percent of the children in a poor city neighborhood were found to be suffering from some degree of tooth decay (Myers et al., 1968). Levels for middle-class children are not so high, but tooth decay is undoubtedly a major health problem among all school-age children in the United States, closely related to poor eating habits. Researchers have now established that caries is caused, at least for the most part, by a specific bacterium call *Streptococcus mutans.* This knowledge may lead to a vaccine in the not-too-distant future.

Diet

Seeing to it that their children are getting an adequate and healthy diet becomes a problem for parents who no longer have complete control over what their children eat. School-age children may spend their lunch money on soft drinks and potato chips from the school vending machines or their allowance on candy bars after school. Making an attractive as well as nutritious lunch for children to take to school may not solve the problem; there is no guarantee that it will be eaten. To make matters worse, friends at school may suddenly decide that all vegetables are "yucky" and that no self-respecting ten-year-old should ever be caught eating a poached egg. So if good food habits have not been established earlier, it will be hard to introduce them now.

This is unfortunate, since school-age children are growing, and the quality of their diet has a good deal to do with the quality of their growth. Growing children need more protein, pound for pound, than adults do because new cells are composed mostly of proteins. Meat, fish, eggs, milk, cheese, and other dairy products all provide high-quality, *complete* proteins. The protein in beans, nuts, whole grain cereals, and other vegetable foods are *incomplete*— that is, each of these foods do not contain all twenty of the amino acids found in complete protein foods. However, the high-protein vegetable foods can be combined to provide all the amino acids found in complete proteins. Vegetable protein has several advantages: it poses no cholesterol problem for those children who tend to be high in blood cholesterol, and it provides necessary roughage or fiber to aid the digestive processes.

Good nutrition is particularly important for school-age children. Unfortunately, they may lose interest in meals because of outside snacks.

Mineral requirements are also high at this time. Calcium and phosphorus are needed for bone growth, and iron for blood. Vitamins are always needed as well. This calls for balanced diets that include milk, fresh fruits and vegetables, whole-grain breads and cereals—in short, all the things children are apt to neglect if they are left to the mercies of TV commercials and their own notions about after-school snacks.

In fact, snacking can be one of the chief factors in an inadequate diet at this age. Active children probably need between-meal snacks, but some of them seem to live on nothing else. Some youngsters get up late and have no time for a proper breakfast, so they swallow a slice of white toast and jelly and then run out the door. At lunchtime they are in a hurry to join their friends on the playground, so they buy a package of doughnuts and a can of soda. They come home from school hungry and make a peanut butter and jelly sandwich to eat in front of the TV. By suppertime they are starved, but friends are waiting outside with a soccer ball, so they gobble half a hamburger and a plateful of instant mashed potatoes, swallow a glass of milk in two gulps, mutter " 'Scuse me," and run off before their parents can muster their forces to insist on at least a token helping of green beans. No wonder some children end up in bed with a cold or down at the dentist's office with three new cavities!

How parents get such children to eat properly depends a good deal on the particular circumstances. Children are old enough now to understand *why* they should eat this or that, so explanation and reasoning are likely to work better than threats or nagging. Good nutrition and poor nutrition can be discussed in school. For example, a class could examine the evidence that artificial colors and preservatives in processed foods may contribute to hyperactivity in children. And the schools could practice what they preach by serving attractive lunches of good nutritional quality in their cafeterias.

Accidents

Unlike illness, accidents are particularly common during middle childhood. Children in these years are active, inquisitive, and daring. They do not yet have enough experience to warn them of all the dangers in the things they want to do. This is the age for swimming, racing, climbing trees, roller-skating or skateboarding in the street, building campfires in vacant lots. It is also the age for falling out of trees, breaking through thin ice, and getting hit by cars.

The problem is to guard children against danger without stifling their natural adventurousness and curiosity. Rather than overprotect or simply threaten punishment, it is better to teach commonsense safety rules and see that each child understands why they are important.

Maturation

The wide differences in size that often distress adolescents are not so prevalent among school-age children. We grow fairly evenly through middle childhood, until by the age of eleven most boys have attained about 85 percent of their mature height. However, around this time with the girls' adolescent growth spurt, which begins two years earlier than the boys', many girls will be taller than boys in the same classroom. Though born lighter, girls will have become as heavy as boys by the age of about eight, and heavier by the age of nine or ten. It is not until the age of about fourteen that the overall size of males again exceeds that of females.

Many of the small, underdeveloped children in the classroom are only growing at an entirely normal but relatively slow rate of maturation. Some of them will keep their thin, lanky physiques as adults, but many others will grow up to be taller and stronger than most of their peers.

Environment and Growth

Researchers have found a definite correlation between height and economic class. Children from higher income homes grow taller and, in some countries, mature earlier. It is likely that variation in nutrition and patterns of exercise and sleep account for part of this difference. However, there is also strong evidence that a pattern of social mobility tends to push tall people upward and short people downward on the social scale (Scott et al., 1956; Thompson, 1959), reinforcing the genetic pattern of short individuals from low-income homes.

Physical growth can also be inhibited by severe psychological stress in the home. A study (Powell, Brasel, & Blizzard, 1967) of children originally thought to be stunted by disorders of the pituitary gland reported that the children's growth accelerated as soon as they came to the convalescent hospital, although no growth hormones were given them. At home, the children

Active sports and risk-taking are common during middle childhood. So are accidents. Children may underestimate dangers and overestimate their ability to cope with them.

had been subjected to stress caused by marital discord, promiscuity, alcoholism, and physical abuse. The stunting of their growth was not due to a lack of food, however. Far from being starved, they gorged themselves at the table—and at garbage cans and the cat's dish. They stole food from the neighbors and drank water from the toilet bowl. This behavior disappeared in the hospital, and the children rapidly caught up to their normal growth level. Psychological stress does not commonly result in this disorder—the brothers and sisters of the children reported in this study were nearly normal in size— but even a low incidence of this pattern illustrates the potential effect of psychological factors on physical growth.

SELF-AWARENESS

As sociologist George H. Mead (1934) has noted, the self consists of both the "I" (the one who acts) and the "me" (the one who is the object of an action). We can say that children between the ages of eight and twelve start to define "what makes me me." In the process they may become more aware of their own emotions and exhibit them in new ways. For example, fears that in the

❖❖❖

Teaching the Hyperactive Child

Nervously tapping his pencil on his desk, seven-year-old Stanley is unable to concentrate on the worksheet the teacher has given him. He fidgets in his seat, swings his legs, snaps his fingers. As the other children in the class become annoyed, Stanley taps his pencil more loudly and shakes his head from side to side, imitating a drummer in a rock band. The teacher asks Stanley to stop it, but he jumps out of his seat and dances around the room. Singing out his drum solo, he spins and leaps ahead of the teacher and rips the pictures off the bulletin board like a human tornado. Finally captured by the frantic teacher, Stanley falls to the floor and throws a screaming, thrashing temper tantrum.

Stanley is not crazy. He is an unhappy victim of hyperactivity, a behavior disorder characterized by an abnormally high level of impulsive, uncontrollable activity. Hyperactivity afflicts an estimated 5 percent of the elementary school population, most of them boys (Ross & Ross, 1976). Hyperactive children have a short attention span, are easily distracted and quickly frustrated. They have great difficulty sitting still long enough to eat a meal or complete a class assignment. Hyperactivity by itself does not directly impair intellectual functioning, but most hyperactive children cannot concentrate long enough to do well in school. This leads to a poor self-concept and a lack of confidence. Hyperactive children also tend to be aggressive and domineering with their peers, which cripples their social development.

To make matters still worse for them and everyone around them, hyperactive children are especially susceptible to temper tantrums, and their tantrums are longer and more violent than those of normal children. They are often light sleepers who fall asleep late at night and rise early in the morning. They have a predilection for getting into things, making them prone to poisonings and household accidents.

What causes this disturbing disorder? No single agent or event has been shown to account for every case, but scientists have suggested several possible explanations. An important area of ongoing investigation is the possibility of minimal brain damage that may be the result of prenatal or perinatal trauma (Denckla, 1978). Inheritance cannot be ruled out as a factor, for one study (Morrison & Stewart, 1973) found that hyperactive children tend to have hyperactive parents. Another investigator, Bruno Bettelheim (1973) believes that certain children have a natural tendency toward hyperactivity which is brought out by environmental stresses. Environmental factors including the lead used in some house paints, food additives including synthetic food colorings (Feingold, 1975), and X rays produced by standard fluorescent lights can induce hyperactivity in some children.

When the cause of a child's hyperactivity cannot be identified and/or removed, drug treatments ranging from caffeine to methyphenidate (Ritalin) are prescribed. Due to developmental differences in children's nervous systems these drugs, which are actually stimulants, often tend to help reduce children's activity level and allow them to focus on tasks and to control their impulses. The use of these drugs is very controversial, as little is known about their long-range effects (Sroufe, 1975). Dosages have to be carefully monitored and adjusted because individual physiological differences can produce a variety of side effects; mild drowsiness, constant sleeping, loss of appetite, long staring spells. For these reasons most doctors insist that drug treatments only be used in conjunction with some other environmental adjustments for monitoring and controlling behavior.

past were expressed primarily through actions such as crying or running may now be channeled into anxiety.

At the same time that children begin to understand what makes them who they are, they also develop an understanding of what makes others who they are. Through the self-awareness that arises from interactions with other people children become more sensitive to their own attitudes about others—they may seek out those who are similar to themselves and shun those they perceive as different—and, likewise, they become more sensitive to the attitudes of peers and adults toward them. They also become more aware of the forms of social behavior that win popularity, and they may adopt some of the traits that seem to win approval for others.

Self-Esteem

With their new self-awareness at this age children invariably compare themselves to their peers. As they judge others—and often children pass harsh judgment on their peers—they find that others are judging them, too. Although children's self-esteem is essentially their judgment of their own abilities, influence, and popularity, this self-judgment is highly tempered by others. Children's self-judgments, their self-esteem or lack of it, comes to resemble evaluations of them made by significant others in their lives (Sullivan, 1953). Their degree of self-esteem will affect their behavior by limiting or extending the range of things they will attempt, whether in academic tasks, sports, or friendships. Low self-esteem tends to make children less original and more imitative, whereas high self-esteem brings out initiative and independent judgment.

In comparing children of high and low self-esteem one researcher (Coopersmith, 1967) discovered that those with high self-esteem were able to devote more time to others and to external activities because they were less preoccupied with themselves. High self-esteem children asserted themselves even at the risk of disapproval, showed initiative, were confident of their own judgments and capabilities, and took leadership roles. On the other hand, low self-esteem children withdrew rather than face disapproval, tended to be quiet and unobtrusive, did not participate in groups, and were filled with self-doubts about their own judgments and capabilities.

This same study notes a correlation between child-rearing and self-esteem. Parents of children with high self-esteem usually possessed a high degree of self-esteem themselves, and further, they tended to be reasonable and fair in disciplining their children. Parents of children with low self-esteem

Middle childhood is a time of increased self-awareness, of recognizing and defining one's own emotions and personality.

tended to have low self-esteem and tended to alternate erratically between harsh and permissive treatment.

Children's self-regard may also be related to the closeness of the child-parent relationship. The findings in a recent study (Dickstein & Posner, 1978) showed that high self-esteem was not only highly correlated to closeness between children and their parents, but that the close relationships were between sons and fathers and daughters and mothers. This does not necessarily mean that being close to your children will give them a positive self-concept, but it does show that one of the characteristics of high self-esteem in school-age children is a good relationship with their same sex parent.

Another characteristic of children with high self-esteem is a close relationship with a friend. As children talk openly with each other, preadolescents realize that they share many of the same feelings and ideas with their friends. A boy begins, "perhaps for the first time in his life, to appreciate the common humanity of people" (Mannarino, 1978). By sharing troubles, children can find they are not unique and can begin to resolve some of their uncertainties. As children realize that their friends like them, they can allow themselves to like themselves, too.

Industry versus Inferiority

The developmental crisis of middle childhood, according to Erik Erikson, is centered in the growing need for children to use their abilities in ways that will be satisfying to them and acceptable to society. Erikson calls this *industry versus inferiority*; it is an extension of the preschool conflict between initiative and guilt. In middle childhood children develop a strong sense of industry unless they are hampered by a sense of inferiority. It is at school that the child learns to be a worker and to earn recognition by producing things, mastering the use of tools, and working with other people:

> The child must forget past hopes and wishes, while his exuberant imagination is tamed and harnessed to the laws of impersonal things—even the three Rs. . . . He develops a sense of industry—i.e., he adjusts himself to the inorganic laws of the tool world. He can become an eager and absorbed unit of a productive situation. To bring a productive situation to completion is an aim which gradually supersedes the whims and wishes of play (Erikson, 1963).

During this period of development children learn the fundamentals of technology—in Western culture, the basic tools of literacy and mathematics that will make later specialization possible. Further, children internalize the production ethic, learning to value work and cooperation. It is their acceptance of these values, and their acquisition of skills at work and cooperation, that will make them productive members of society. "This," Erikson writes (1963), "is socially a most decisive stage: since industry involves doing things beside and with others, a first sense of division of labor and of differential opportunity, that is, a sense of the *technological* ethos of a culture, develops at this time."

Ideally, children will develop a sense of industry as one strong component of their personality. However, they face two basic dangers: on the one hand, some may overreact and value utilitarianism too much: "If he accepts work as his only obligation," Erikson says, "and 'what works' as his only criterion of worthwhileness, he may become the conformist and thoughtless slave of his technology and of those who are in a position to exploit it."

On the other hand—and this is the countertheme of this stage of childhood—children may develop a sense of inferiority that impedes their ability to acquire the necessary sense of industry. "The child's danger, at this stage, lies in a sense of inadequacy and inferiority. If he despairs of his tools and skills or of his status among his tool partners, he may be discouraged from identification with them and with a section of the tool world" (Erikson, 1963). Such feelings, the result either of a child's not really being prepared for the school experience or of problems encountered at school, may bring about regression to behavior more appropriate to an earlier age.

GENDER-ROLE DEVELOPMENT

By the time children are of school age, they have already learned the concepts of male and female and have begun to display attitudes and behavior appropriate to their own sex. Once children leave the relatively closed environment of their families to enter the larger world of school, they begin to broaden their knowledge of gender roles, adopting the stereotypes of masculinity and femininity that are dominant in their society. Despite all the efforts in recent years to equalize the power and prestige of the male and female roles, changing deeply held attitudes is a slow process. Our own traditions still teach, for example, that boys should be tough and aggressive, girls polite and submissive; that athletic skill is a male trait, and cooking still a female trait.

Social Learning and Modeling

Regardless of the genetic and hormonal differences between male and female, it is clear that gender-role stereotypes are learned. Children learn sex roles by observation and continue to display them because they are reinforced by social approval and a need for cognitive consistency. Observing these roles not only in their parents but in other adults and peers as well, children pick them up by a process known as *social learning*.

The theory of social learning takes the idea of conditioning and reinforcement and carries it a stage further. In operant conditioning, as we saw in Chapter 4, a person receives positive or negative reinforcement as a consequence of some action, and so either repeats the behavior (in case of positive reinforcement) or changes it (in the case of negative). Social learning theorists point out that reinforcement does not have to be something that happens to us personally. It can also be something we see happening to someone else. In such a case the observed person functions as a model. For instance, suppose Billy sees Warren nailing boards together to make a box, and then sees the teacher come over and praise Warren. If Billy likes the teacher and already thinks well of Warren, he may try making a box himself.

But what if, on a class trip, he sees Jimmy fingering the yarn in a store's needlework department, and then sees Joe and Pete come up and hoot derisively, "Hey, look at Jimmy! He thinks he's a girl!" The chances are that Billy will henceforth stay away from yarn and knitting supplies. He will not have to learn the lesson by suffering any such embarrassing experience himself. By observing how Jimmy's behavior was punished, he has learned something useful for his own behavior. For this reason social learning is sometimes called *observational learning*. It enables us to learn appropriate social attitudes and behavior much faster than would be possible if we had to depend entirely on our own direct experiences. The models for observational learning can be TV characters, even cartoon ones.

Observational learning is not limited to behavior. It can also teach emotions. If Ginny observes that her big sister is afraid to go off the diving board, she may learn to be afraid too, even though she herself has never belly-flopped or gotten water up her nose trying it. Similarly, Billy will not only avoid the knitting department; he will squirm with shame at the very notion of going there. In this way social learning leads children to set up standards for judging their own behavior. Reinforcement is no longer entirely external. The child's own self-approval or self-blame is also a powerful reward or deterrent (Masters & Mokros, 1974).

How do you think these boys' peers would react to their taking ballet lessons? Boys have traditionally been taught to be tough and aggressive, although in recent years male and female roles have become less defined.

This is not to say that children are helpless to resist social influences. If all the influences press in one direction, resistance is difficult; but usually there are a variety of different influences. For example, Ginny may scorn her sister's "sissy" attitude and risk her neck following the boys off the high-dive platform, whether she is afraid or not. She has chosen to govern her behavior by the boys' reinforcement of her courage rather than by her family's reinforcement of her fear. (Meanwhile, of course, the boys know from their own social learning experience how embarrassing it would be to let a girl outdo them in courage. They will probably be lucky if the lifeguard comes along before someone gets hurt.)

Fathers' Influence on Gender Roles

In gender-role development the evidence points to fathers as having the more important influence, not only in fostering a male self-concept in boys, but femininity in girls. Mothers do contribute to their daughters' adoption of the

❖❖

Erikson's Crises in Psychosocial Development

BASIC TRUST VERSUS BASIC MISTRUST (FIRST YEAR OF LIFE)

AUTONOMY VERSUS SHAME AND DOUBT (SECOND YEAR OF LIFE)

INITIATIVE VERSUS GUILT (THE PRESCHOOL YEARS)

INDUSTRY VERSUS INFERIORITY (MIDDLE CHILDHOOD)

Building on the previously developed trust, autonomy, and initiative, children can achieve a sense of industry. In school they learn the basic tools of literacy and cooperation that will enable them to become productive members of society. They learn the satisfaction of persisting at a task until it is completed, and of using their skills to perform according to their own and others' expectations. The dangers of this period are twofold: on the one hand, children may learn to value achievement in work above all else, alienating their peers by excessively competitive behavior. On the other hand, they may feel unable to perform the tasks required of them and develop a sense of inferiority that prevents them from trying.

IDENTITY VERSUS ROLE CONFUSION (ADOLESCENCE)

INTIMACY VERSUS ISOLATION (YOUNG ADULTHOOD)

GENERATIVITY VERSUS STAGNATION (PRIME OF LIFE)

EGO INTEGRITY VERSUS DESPAIR (OLD AGE)

feminine role but have little influence on the masculinity of their sons. In a survey of research on the influence of the father in the gender-role development of both boys and girls David Lynn (1974) concludes that the father's role is paramount. Most studies, he says, "support the position that the father, in his instrumental function of launching his children into society, is more concerned than the mother with enhancing his boy's masculinity and his girl's femininity." However, the direct concern of the father may not be the salient factor. Perhaps it is the power associated with the masculine role; children may perceive the father as a more important person than the mother and be more affected by any paternal intervention in their lives.

Important characteristics of the father who is successful in developing appropriate gender-role identification seem to be not only the highly masculine traits of decisiveness and dominance, but also nurturance and warmth. For example, highly masculine boys are more likely to have fathers who are firm and decisive in setting limits and dispensing both rewards and punishments. Such fathers play an active role in the discipline of their sons (Hetherington, 1965). However, discipline by fathers fosters a strong masculine identity in their sons only when it is accompanied by fairness, support, and warmth. Warmth on the part of both parents fosters femininity in their daugh-

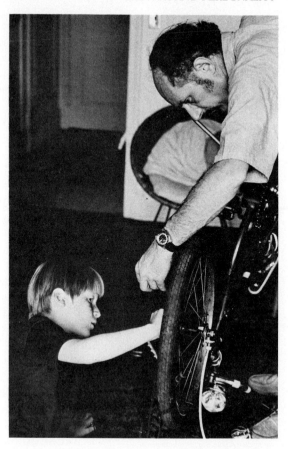

Not only the traits of decisiveness and dominance, but also nurturance and warmth, help to ensure a successful father-son relationship.

ters. Highly masculine sons perceive their fathers, but not their mothers, as warmer and more nurturant than do boys lower in masculinity (Hetherington, 1965). The dominant but not domineering father, confident in his masculine role, can afford to show such so-called feminine traits as nurturance and warmth to his children. In so doing he not only displays the power inherent in the masculine role, but the attractive attributes of the feminine role—a double spellbinder for children.

Father's Absence

The importance of the father to the gender-role development of children shows up most forcefully in homes in which the father is not present at all. Today, with a divorce in almost one in every three or four families, this is no longer a hypothetical situation. Although in a small number of cases the father brings up the children, mostly it is the father, however reluctantly, who leaves the children to the mother to raise.

Hetherington has been particularly interested in the gender-role development of children in families in which the father is absent. First of all, she points out that although there are drawbacks to raising children in a one-parent family, there is strong evidence for the greater disadvantage of raising children in an intact family characterized by constant fighting and perhaps physical, emotional, or sexual child abuse. Remarriage is not a satisfactory solution in all cases either. Studies indicate that friction, competition, and hostility between a child and a stepparent are frequent, especially among adolescents (Hetherington & Parke, 1975).

Permanent separation from the father due to death, divorce, war, or a lack of interest on the part of the father has a deleterious effect on normal gender-role development as well as cognitive development and the development of self-control among boys (Hetherington & Deur, 1971). Preadolescent boys, particularly, in the absence of their fathers, suffer from a disruption of gender-role development. Indeed, poor intellectual performance and academic achievement and a lack of self-control seem to increase through the school years. For boys with absent fathers other masculine models, especially older brothers, can help to take the place of the father.

The age of the child at the time of the separation from the father is an important variable in gender-role development. In a study by Hetherington (1966) boys who were six years or older at the time the father left home, did not differ in masculinity from boys from intact homes. Boys who were younger than six at the time of separation were rated as more dependent, less assertive, and observed to engage less in rough-and-tumble athletic activity.

The lack of a father in the home is thought to cause a more difficult problem in the development of gender identity in boys than in girls. Boys have no role model directly available to them as they are growing up. Adolescent girls without fathers seem to encounter problems of relating well to males and of forming stable heterosexual relationships later on. This is especially acute for girls if they do not grow up with a brother (Hetherington, 1972). Thus, we gain insight into the importance of fathers in the development of gender identity by studying families without fathers. Surprising though it may be, these studies show that children may need their fathers as much as, if not far more than, their mothers to learn their adult roles as men and women.

PERSONALITY PROBLEMS

Psychologically speaking, normal children are those whose behavior is in harmony with their environment and with themselves. But even perfectly normal children experience problems in growing up. Temporary personality problems may in fact be a sign that a child is facing up to new situations at home and at school. It is only when problem behavior becomes severe that a child can be said to be "disturbed" or neurotic. According to one estimate (Vaughan, 1961), only about 10 percent of all children have severe enough personality problems to require professional treatment. Often, a wise parent or teacher may be able to help a child learn to deal with a problem.

Fear and Anxiety

Fear is a natural response to real or imagined danger. Schoolchildren find many things in their environment that they cannot understand or control and that they may perceive as threatening. Precocious children may be afraid of things that their peers have not yet learned to see as dangerous (Holmes, 1935), but some children develop unwarranted fears, such as the fear of dogs or fear of crossing the street.

What causes a child's particular fears? Psychologists, regardless of orientation, tend to agree that fears are mostly learned. Sometimes children's fears result from their experience of real dangers. Sometimes fears are taught to them, perhaps unconsciously, by their parents, siblings, or playmates. Sometimes, as in fear of storms, fears result from a child's misunderstanding of situations.

Typically, during the elementary-school years, the child may develop a fear of the supernatural, of accidents, school failure, or ridicule. Children's experience will determine their fears: a child from a low-income home tends to fear the physical dangers associated with poverty, such as lack of food or shelter, while the middle-class child is more afraid of such threats as academic failure (Angelino et al., 1956).

Anxiety, like fear, is a response to a felt danger, which may or may not be real. However, anxiety is usually not directed toward a specific object or situation. In fact, anxious children often do not know exactly what is worrying them. Outwardly they may only seem nervous; their anxiety is mostly indirect or internal. Though preschool children show anxiety by a generalized excitement, elementary school children may develop specific symptoms: insomnia, headaches, stomachaches, or tics, such as repeated blinking or yawning.

Anxiety in children is quite common. Many children are apprehensive in new situations but are able to deal with them after the initial anxiety. Sometimes the child's own fantasies about a situation create fear. But only the child with excessive or habitually chronic anxiety should be viewed as having a personality problem.

Conflict

One major source of anxiety is conflict—that is, the struggle between two or more desires or emotions that cannot be satisfied. Psychologists distinguish three basic types of conflict. The boy who likes pie and cake equally, but must choose only one, faces *approach–approach* conflict. In contrast, the girl who must go to a piano lesson she hates, or refuse and get a spanking, experiences *avoidance–avoidance* conflict. The most frequent and most difficult to deal with is *approach–avoidance* conflict, as in the case of the child who wants to ride on a merry-go-round but is afraid of falling off.

Children who have serious anxiety problems probably often find themselves in situations that allow no relief. For example, a child who lives with a tyrannical grandmother may have a strong desire to fight back and at the same time fear standing up to her because she is stronger. Such children may want to hit her and at the same time think they are evil just for wanting to do so. They may not learn to express either fear or anger directly and may develop some of the more extreme types of anxiety.

Phobias and Other Problems

Children who say they dislike lakes, streams, and swimming pools, and feel anxious whenever they see one, can be said to fear water. But children who are constantly anxious that they might drown and do not want to leave home because they fear this possibility, have a **phobia**. A phobia is a severe and excessive fear aroused by a particular object or situation and characterized by an extreme desire to avoid the object.

A relatively common phobia of school-age children is, of course, *school phobia*. School phobia upsets most parents and teachers more than any other because it can disrupt the whole pattern of a child's life. It is characterized by a refusal to go to school, anxiety at school and at the thought of school, and usually by physical complaints, such as stomachaches or sore throats. These physical symptoms are caused by the child's anxiety, not by a virus. School phobia is equally common in boys and girls. Although it seems to be more frequent among higher socioeconomic groups (Hersov, 1960), it is likely that when school phobia occurs in low-income groups it tends to be labeled truancy and is treated in a more authoritarian manner (Milman, 1966). However, one researcher (Davidson, 1961) has pointed out a distinction: "while the truant runs away from school, the school phobic runs back to his home."

Obsessions and Compulsions

An obsession is a persistent preoccupation—an idea a child cannot get out of his or her head. Many obsessions begin as phobias. Children with a dog phobia may find that taking great pains to avoid dogs still does not reduce their anxiety. They may begin to think about dogs all the time, worrying constantly that they will meet one, that it will attack, and that they will not be able to escape.

Obsessions tend to be either precautionary or repugnant. The precautionary ones may involve cleanliness or health; the repugnant ones tend to involve such fantasies as hurting someone or doing something bad. Children's obsessions are a kind of self-torture and usually help them avoid their feelings of guilt.

When children can no longer control their anxiety through their thoughts and fantasies and instead begin to do something, their obsessions become *compulsions*—repetitive and ritualisticlike acts. Children obsessed with neatness, for example, may straighten the objects in their rooms several times a day. It is an irrational action that children feel compelled to perform over and over again.

But the adult should not be too quick to diagnose a compulsion as abnormal. Even normal children, particularly seven- and eight-year-olds, exhibit some compulsive behavior. The common childhood game, "Step on a crack, break your mother's back," which involves compulsively avoiding sidewalk cracks, is one example of such behavior. Rules, ceremonies, and rituals are essential elements of all games, and children's games, particularly the ones they play when they are eight years old, usually involve many rules.

How can you tell if a child's compulsion is normal or abnormal? As one researcher (Kessler, 1972) puts it, the "common compulsions are like games which the child enjoys playing by himself or with others, and he has no feeling of inner coercion. In the pathological form, the compulsion is unique to the child, and he derives no pleasure or social benefits from it."

Hysteria

Like phobias, obsessions, and compulsions, hysterical symptoms develop in children who have strong anxiety responses. Hysterical symptoms tend to fall into two groups: most common are tics, such as a constant clearing of the throat, or constant blinking. Studying 487 elementary schoolchildren, researchers (Lapouse & Monk, 1968) found that 12 percent of the children had unusual movements, twitching or jerking. Less common is loss of a function, as in deafness or muteness that is not caused by any physical reason. Cases of hysteria are believed to be far less frequent today than in former times, when there were stronger cultural restrictions on direct expression of anxiety.

Regression

Behaving in a manner more suitable to a younger age is called **regression.** The five-year-old girl who reverts to wetting her pants just like her baby brother may be attempting to reclaim the parental affection she sees lavished on the baby. Her regression is evidence that she cannot think of another way of gaining attention that she has lost. Regression is one way children deal with the tensions of frustration, but it is usually not the most desirable way, since it temporarily prevents them from learning more mature methods of coping with the problem.

Depression

Recently psychotherapists have begun to diagnose many cases of such childhood emotional disorders as regression, hostile acting out, delinquency, school phobias, and psychosomatic illness as due to an underlying *depression* (Albin, 1981; Toolan, 1978). Children do not express their depression as adults do. At different stages in their development and at different age levels children will show depression differently. Childhood depression seems to be a reaction to loss, either of an object or of a state of well-being. Early loss of the mother has a devastating effect on young children (Bradley, 1979; Bowlby, 1973). Infants and young children may fail to develop and remain emotionally at their stage of development at the time of the loss. School-age children often react with anger and hostility toward persons they feel have betrayed them (usually their parents). Although their anger may mask their painful feelings of loss, the hostile behavior of depressed children may antagonize parents and teachers, compounding the child's problems even further. Sometimes children turn the anger against themselves, causing them to feel evil. Such children have a very poor sense of self-esteem. Some children become suicidal; indeed, the rate of suicide among children and adolescents is on the increase, becoming a major cause of death among children.

Perhaps labeling symptoms in a new way does not break any new ground. The most important advantage in naming as "depression" such well-known emotional problems as school phobia and hostility is to focus the attention of the parents and the helping professions on the essential tragic aspects of children's problems. Although children manifest hostile, aggressive, and other forms of behavior that are difficult to manage, the cause is often sadness, despair, and a profound lack of a sense of self-worth. The challenge of parents and child-oriented professionals is to restore to such children a sense of well-being—the will to live.

Childhood Psychosis

As we have just seen, during middle childhood children begin to develop a sense of their own identity and the world around them and to form relationships with people outside the family. But some children follow a very different path. Their relationships with others may be severely impaired, even nonexistent; they may have almost no sense of self-identity; they may be unable to talk or understand others; they may be intolerant of any change in the world around them. When these symptoms (or a number of others) appear in severe form, psychologists describe the condition as a schizophrenic syndrome, or more generally, **childhood psychosis.** This condition, or rather set of conditions, is hard to define with any precision. The psychoses are a broad group of disorders, and their exact clinical dimensions have not yet been determined.

Some researchers have suggested that the major cause of psychosis is the parents' failure to give these children the attention they need, physically or emotionally. Other researchers have tried to trace childhood psychosis to metabolic or biochemical malfunctions, to brain damage, or even to genetic causes. There is some evidence to support all of these theories, but so far each theory has been able to account for only some of the cases.

In a review of the literature on childhood psychosis one researcher (Goldfarb, 1970) singled out nine signs of severe emotional disturbance. We have already noted some: severe impairment of emotional relationships, an apparent unawareness of personal identity, inability to learn or to use language, and an abnormal resistance to changes in the environment. The other signs listed in the review are obsessive preoccupation with particular objects; abnormal perception of stimuli; acute and excessive anxiety, especially in situations that should not be frightening; distorted patterns of movement, such as rigid immobility or hyperactivity; and a history of serious mental retardation.

No single one of these symptoms is a sure sign of emotional disturbance.

When children become psychotic, their sense of self-identity is almost nonexistent and they are intolerant of any change in the world around them.

What clinicians look for is a pattern in which a number of the symptoms appear together and in severe form. "Unawareness of personal identity," for example, does not mean simply an occasional lapse back into self-forgetfulness. Instead, it might refer to children's abnormal behavior toward themselves, examining parts of the body as though it belonged to someone else, or even mutilating themselves.

Psychosis often takes the form of schizophrenia or autism, two disorders that are themselves not clearly defined. **Schizophrenia** is a rather general term for disturbances that have detachment from reality at their core; the symptoms may include regression to an earlier stage of development, bizarre behavior, apathy, and destructive rages. **Autism** is a near-total withdrawal that occurs when the child can achieve a feeling of safety only by shutting out the world. In mild cases autistic children can avoid contact or interaction with others; they rarely look at people, and when they do, their gaze does not indicate normal attention. More severe symptoms are extreme isolation, refusal to hear or speak to others, virtually no interest in people (although the child may be fascinated by an object), and obsessive insistence that nothing in the environment be changed. The autistic child typically begins to show some of these symptoms from the earliest days of life.

Treatment of psychotic children is usually geared toward minimizing symptoms in order to help them live as normal a life as possible. Therapy, often centered around play, is designed to teach these children to express their feelings freely and, by building their self-respect, ultimately to improve their social functioning. In some cases therapy has succeeded in improving social behavior, but it is rarely able to reverse fundamental deficiencies in intellect, perception, and language.

SUMMARY

▶ Physical development and appearance affect the child's aptitudes, interests, popularity, and personality development. School-age children are less susceptible to illness than preschoolers are, but they are more prone to bad eating habits and to accidents. Physical characteristics influence a child's self-concept.

▶ Children's sense of self-worth comes to resemble the evaluations of them made by significant others in their lives.

▶ Erikson theorized that in middle childhood the individual undergoes the crisis of industry versus inferiority. In this crisis children will develop a strong sense of industry unless they are hampered by a sense of inferiority.

▶ Gender-role stereotypes are adapted by the process of social learning. Fathers are especially important in the development of appropriate gender-role attitudes and behavior for both boys and girls.

▶ Fears are learned, whether they are warranted or not, and may result from experience or teaching. Conflict is a major source of anxiety. The three basic types of conflict are *approach–approach, avoidance–avoidance, and approach–avoidance.*

▶ Phobias can result from the child's own experience, or they can be transmitted by models such as parents, siblings, and peers. Phobias may lead to obsessions, and obsessions may lead to compulsions. Normal children exhibit some compulsive behavior. Abnormal compulsion involves a loss of control and can involve highly complicated ritual. Hysterical symptoms arising out of strong anxieties may take the form of repeated physical responses, such as facial tics or apparent illness. Regression is another means of dealing with frustration.

▶ Such childhood problems as failure to thrive, failure to learn, hostility, aggression, school phobias, and somatic illness are now thought to be symptoms of depression. Depression is caused in children by a sense of loss and characterized by a lack of self-esteem. Some depressed children are suicidal.

▶ Schizophrenia and autism are two forms of childhood psychosis. It is not known whether the causes of childhood psychosis are environmental, biochemical, or genetic. Therapy for it is very difficult.

FURTHER READINGS

Bettelheim, Bruno. *Dialogues with mothers*. New York: Free Press, 1962.
In Bettelheim's opinion theories do not have much practical value when parents run into trouble with children. He recommends a careful investigation into each troublesome circumstance to find out why children react as they do. The quality of daily interactions between parent and child is an all-important influence on personality development, he writes.

Briggs, Dorothy C. *Your child's self-esteem: The key to his life*. Garden City, N.Y.: Doubleday, 1970.
Briggs writes that a negative self-concept is the root cause of misbehavior, that "the key to inner peace and happiness is high self-esteem, for it lies behind successful involvement with others."

Lederman, Janet. *Anger and the rocking chair: Gestalt awareness with children*. New York: McGraw-Hill, 1969.
A personal account of Gestalt methods used with "disturbed" children in an elementary school classroom. This readable book is intended to teach or suggest to others ways of giving troubled children a sense of themselves. Photographs depict classroom situations.

Lynn, David B. *The father: His role in child development*. Monterey, Calif.: Brooks/ Cole, 1974.
Today more and more children are being brought up without fathers in the home, while in other families fathers are taking a larger part in child-rearing than before. What will this mean for the children and for society in general? Lynn seeks answers through examination of the father in history and in other cultures and through a survey of studies on the father in modern society.

Renshaw, D.C. *The hyperactive child*. Boston: Little, Brown, 1974.
A well-researched, comprehensive account of the pathology of the hyperactive child. Renshaw includes an extensive definition of hyperactivity, its medical treatment and management, and its prevention.

Chapter 10

❖❖❖❖❖❖

Learning and Cognition

*O*ne day Susan was speaking like the ten-year-old she was; a week later, she sounded like an adult. Susan's vocabulary had grown, her tone had gained authority, she read everything she could get her hands on. "Her mind is fully developed," her mother decided. "All she needs now is more information." If Susan continued to follow this pattern typical of grade school children her age, she would gain more than information in the coming months and years. She would also undergo some fundamental changes. Her ability to think in abstract terms would advance. She would begin to perceive some highly complex aspects of the environment and would become more efficient at remembering what she learned. Partly as a result of this cognitive development, she would also become a more effective problem-solver, both in daily life and in school.

PROBLEM-SOLVING

We begin to do things on purpose in infancy, and this can be regarded as solving problems in that most deliberate actions have to overcome some resistance or obstacle. We do not begin to solve problems in a thoughtful way, however, until we can imagine a possible solution without putting it instantly into effect. Most of us acquire this ability at about two years of age, and then we improve rapidly; by the time we are in elementary school we can apply some ingenious solutions to the problems we face.

In order to examine the different ways in which our problem-solving abilities improve, psychologists have identified a number of separate steps that we usually take toward the solution of any problem. The main steps are perception, memory, and applying hypotheses. In the first step, perception, children perceive an event—that is, they become aware of a situation that involves some kind of problem to solve. Their perceptions provide them with different kinds of information: the way different objects in the situation look, for example, and the way they are related to one another. In the next step, memory, children draw forth data from memory that will help them to deal with the new situation. For example, they may try to remember past experiences that were in some way similar to the present one and might, therefore, offer clues to solving the new problem. Finally, children consider the different ways in which the problem might be solved, choose among them, and then act upon their choice.

Whatever the outcome of this process—whether the problem is solved to a child's satisfaction or requires new thought and appraisal—the child will store away some information that he has derived from experience and later use this information in other situations. As children grow, their problems will undoubtedly multiply; even play activity will involve more numerous and difficult problems and decisions. But as they progress through middle childhood, their ability to solve these multitudinous problems will increase. They will arrive at solutions through increasingly complex forms of memory and the application of a growing body of hypotheses.

Memory

Human memory works very much like the memory unit of a computer, except that some information in the human memory may be irretrievable (although most psychologists believe it can never be deleted). Sometimes we wish to hold information only momentarily, for temporary use; for example, we may remember a telephone number only for the length of time needed to dial it. On such occasions our memory is deliberately short. The information is entered in a temporary storage unit of the mind known as *short-term memory*. Though "memorized," this information will not be available to us for use in the future—not because it has been deleted, but simply because it has not been filed in the proper area of the mind. The area that stores information for permanent use is called *long-term memory*; the ability to retrieve information from this storage area is known as *recall*.

In the middle years of childhood we become more capable of recalling information from long-term memory. Moreover, a child at this age is capable of making a conscious (or unconscious) effort to retain short-term memories long enough for them to be transferred into the long-term reserve. Ten-year-old children have much better recall than children of four because they can shift information into long-term memory and have more efficient devices for retrieval.

The older children's greater facility with classification gives them a distinct edge over younger children in remembering information (Rossi, 1966). Classification of information is a basic skill for independent thinking and problem-solving, and facilitates both short-term and long-term memory. In an experiment with memorization strategies (Neimark et al., 1971) children from first to sixth grades were shown sets of pictures related to four categories: animals, furniture, clothing, and transportation. But the children were not told that all the pictures belonged to these classes. They were given three minutes to look at the pictures displayed at random on a table and to arrange them in any way that would help them remember the pictured objects. Children in the first to third grades, with the exception of a few third graders, showed no inclination to classify the pictures, but an increasing tendency to arrange pictures by category was found among children in grades four through six. Furthermore, the more proficient the children were in organizing pictures into classes, the more successful they were in remembering the pictures during the recall period.

The ability to remember develops gradually and seems to be linked to cognitive development in general (Piaget & Inhelder, 1973). As people mature, they pass through various stages of cognitive growth during which different cognitive faculties develop. These include the ability to perceive the relationships of objects to each other and to themselves, the ability to categorize objects, and the ability to decide what objects or pieces of information are important. These cognitive skills affect peoples' abilities to remember objects and events in various ways: from the contexts in which they occur, from the relations of objects or events to one another, and from the knowledge of which objects are important to remember and the strategies that are most effective for remembering them (Liben, 1977).

Two processes that seem to play in important role in remembering and learning are *metamemory* and *metacognition*. *Metamemory*, which is one part or aspect of *metacognition*, is conscious or intuitive knowledge about memory. It seems to affect both how well we remember and the techniques we employ in memorization process (Wellman, 1978). *Metamemory* includes such kinds of information as our knowledge about how good we are at memorizing, what kinds of information we remember best, and what techniques we might employ to remember different kinds of information.

As children develop, their knowledge of memory and their ability to understand the elements of memory and their interaction grow. Although metamemory is considered an important part of cognition, its development in children is not fully understood. We do know that metamemory is one portion of a larger cognitive process called *metacognition*, which is the conscious knowledge we have about factors and beliefs involved in the learning process.

Metacognition is the faculty that provides information about such matters as how fast we learn, whether our parents are good at math, what a

Children pass through a series of stages of cognitive growth that enables them to perceive relationships of objects to each other and to themselves, and to categorize those objects.

particular learning *task* requires of us, and what *strategy* we should employ to learn the material involved in that task. All of these parts of metacognition are known as *metacognitive knowledge.* However, metacognition also includes *metacognitive experiences,* which are the conscious experiences that either accompany or are related to learning and knowing. If you feel confusion when you are trying to learn a mass of details, or if you suddenly realize that you don't understand something a teacher is saying, you are undergoing a metacognitive experience. Metacognitive experiences affect your metacognitive knowledge. That is, if you know from experience that you are confused by details, you may expend extra effort to develop strategies that will simplify learning tasks involving details (Flavell, 1979).

Applying Hypotheses

The final step in problem-solving is the assessment of possible solutions (hypotheses) and the application of one or more of them to the problem situation. As children grow older, the greater amount of information they have about many things will tell them when additional information is needed in order to reach a correct answer. They can also apply more than one rule in solving a problem. The teacher says to Mary, "If I give you ten apples and you give one to Jane and one to Tommy, how many apples will you have left?" Mary applies two rules: first, one plus one equals two; and second, two from ten equals eight. So she answers: "I still have eight apples."

If Mary's hearing had been faulty and she thought the teacher said two instead of ten, she would have given a wrong answer. If she had heard correctly but recalled the problem incorrectly, she would still have given a wrong answer. She needs both correct perception and correct recollection before she can arrive at correct solutions or reasonable alternatives for decision-making.

As Mary grows older, she will improve her hypothesis-testing abilities because her memory techniques have become more refined. She will be able to recall which hypotheses did not work under similar conditions (Kemler, 1978). Because she need not retest unworkable hypotheses, she will be able to focus her attention on forming more productive ones. This new skill will assist her in making decisions more rapidly and efficiently.

COGNITIVE STYLES

Patterns of thought and behavior that influence learning and problem-solving techniques are known as "cognitive styles." A *cognitive style* is an individual "manner and form of cognitive performance" (Sigel & Brodzinsky, 1977) and reflects that individual's personality or preference, not his or her ability or intelligence. For example, when Jane looks at three different kinds of buildings, she thinks of what each might be used for, whereas Susan, looking at the same three buildings, notes only their ages and architectural styles. Both girls are equally logical and intelligent. Their responses to the buildings, however, reflect differences in style or manner of analysis. Jane is a functionalist. She focuses primarily on the uses to which the buildings may be put. Susan, on the other hand, is more of a detail, "nuts and bolts", analyzer. She likes to categorize things into their component parts. Both approaches are legitimate, although clearly different; and they reflect different styles of learning.

Theorists have studied the developmental aspects of three different cognitive styles, which they call *field-dependence/field-independence*, *reflection-impulsivity*, and *categorization* styles. The cognitive style known as field-dependence/field-independence is defined by an individual's ability to consider an event or object separately from the context in which it occurs or appears. That context is called the *field*. Highly field-independent persons will have little difficulty in considering an object or event separately from its field, and so, for example, they can easily find the central motif in an elaborate design or place themselves parallel to the wall of a room in which the floor is crooked. There are obvious relations between this cognitive style and social behavior. Field-dependent people are usually more sociable (Witkin & Goodenough, 1977). Patterns of child-rearing have been cited as one of the possible origins of field-dependence/independence (Dyk & Witkin, 1965).

Cognitive styles are patterns of thought and behavior that influence learning and problem-solving. Each child might use a different approach to solve the puzzle of the "cat's cradle."

The cognitive style known as *reflection-impulsivity* (R-I) refers to the tendency of the person to pause and reflect on the quality of his answer in problem-solving situations involving moderate to high response uncertainty (Messer, 1976). Impulsive children tend to respond with the first answer that "pops into their heads", and as a result, they are frequently incorrect. Reflective children are more careful and detailed in their initial analysis of problems, and therefore are more likely to be correct. Research indicates a tendency for children to become more reflective with increasing age, at least through the early adolescent years. As children gain cognitive maturity, especially after the age of eleven, they are better able to answer quickly and yet still retain a high degree of accuracy (Salkind & Nelson, 1980). The reflection-impulsivity pattern has been linked to many areas of problem-solving, academic achievement, and socioemotional behavior, usually with the outcome that reflective children perform more adaptively than impulsive children. Research indicates, however, that the impulsive pattern can be altered somewhat by training; that is, it is possible to teach children to become more reflective (Messer, 1976). Although the origin of the reflection-impulsivity style is unknown, one current hypothesis that has received some support is that reflective children are more anxious than impulsive children about making mistakes. Fear of failure leads to a slowing down of response and a more careful analysis of the problem, which in turn is likely to lead to increased accuracy. (Kagan & Kogan, 1970). Reflective children are not, however, more intelligent than impulsive children.

Categorization styles are the types of groupings by means of which a person classifies or arranges stimuli. Several people presented with the same objects will justify grouping them according to different criteria. For example, one may say that a needle, a tack, and a pin belong together "because they are all straight." Another may say, "They are all used to connect two objects." Categorization styles have been subdivided into three types. A *descriptive-analytic* style concentrates on a single obvious detail common to all the objects. ("They are all straight.") The *relational-contextual* approach seizes on a common theme or function. ("They are all used to connect two objects.") A *categorical-inferential* style focuses on the class of the objects (tools, fasteners, studs, etc.). As they develop cognitively, children tend to become somewhat more *descriptive-analytical* and less *relational-contextual* (Sigel & Brodzinsky, 1977).

Each cognitive style has its advantages and disadvantages. Fast responders are often less accurate than slow ones. However, fast responders can be better at solving complex problems that have no single answer because they can consider more aspects of the problem and more solutions to it than slow responders, who can get bogged down in testing out each solution (Rollins & Genser, 1977). Field-dependent people may be less independent as thinkers, but they are more socially skilled and can make better use of social situations in the educational setting (Witkin et al., 1977).

STANDARDIZED TESTING

Among the more important problems children have to solve are the contrived ones in tests. And probably the most intimidating kind of test is the thick, expensively printed variety known as the standardized test. The Scholastic Aptitude Test is the most universally taken, but many students must survive numerous other standardized tests through elementary and high school to demonstrate their reading level and mathematical ability. IQ tests, which are supposed to measure general intelligence rather than some specific ability or achievement, are also standardized throughout the United States.

Some educators say they need standardized tests because education in the United States is not carried out under a uniform system for all parts of the country but is run by autonomous local school boards. Without an SAT score how can an admission officer at the University of Arizona know that an applicant from the Bronx, N.Y., learned anything in high school, though his grades may be good? How can the taxpayers of Moorhead, Minn., know that their teachers are doing a good job unless they can prove that sixth graders in Moorhead can read at least as well as sixth graders throughout the country?

Yet the National Education Association has called for an end to standardized testing because the association believes the results are too often misleading and unfair. Some pupils, the association suggests, have a special ability for taking tests, while other pupils lack it; and the tests measure this ability rather than academic achievement. The pupils who lack this ability, moreover, are usually those who suffer the brunt of unfairness in many other respects as well: namely, blacks and members of other minorities.

No doubt a good teacher can judge a pupil's academic achievement more accurately than any standardized test. But not every teacher is a good teacher. One student, for example, had mediocre high school grades but got a good college board score and went on to earn a master's degree. Most students, he told a reporter, "have a tendency to learn the teacher rather than the subject," but he never managed "to get that skill together." He believes the test gave colleges another basis on which to judge him (Dionne, 1977).

Intelligence Quotient

The most controversial of standardized tests are IQ tests. IQ standards for intelligence quotient. Most tests of general academic ability include tables for converting raw scores into intelligence quotients. Terman set the pattern for calculating IQ as a ratio because he thought the score reflected present ability and potential. Thus, IQ was calculated by dividing a person's mental age by chronological age and multiplying by 100, as symbolized by the following equation:

$$IQ = \frac{MA}{CA} \times 100$$

Mental age was determined by the number of items of increasing difficulty passed on the test. The major problem with ratio IQ is that it assumes continuous mental growth. That is, a child's mental age in successive years would form an ascending straight line. This linear growth obviously is not true through adulthood. Wechsler introduced the deviation IQ as an alternative to the ratio IQ. The deviation IQ reports children's standing compared to others of their age. The deviation IQ is used for reporting both child and adult IQs.

The first IQ test was devised by French psychologist Alfred Binet in the early 1900s to identify pupils in the Paris public schools who needed special therapeutic training before they could benefit from ordinary instruction. Binet believed the special training would raise the IQ of children who had initially obtained low scores on the test.

But when Binet's test was adapted for American use by Lewis M. Terman, it came to be regarded as a measure of a fixed quality, "innate intelligence."

The Gifted

A tormented mother bought new goblets, being about to give a family dinner. When she had set the table, she sighed deeply and calling her eight-year-old daughter in, said, "Look, Jennie, we have new goblets. The flowers on them are etched into the glass. I don't know how etching is done, so don't ask. Don't ask where goblets came from in the *first place* or who *named* them goblets, for I don't know. These came from Wanamakers. They cost 50 cents each. The reason I did not buy colored ones is they do not go with all our dishes. These were delivered today. Now run along and get ready for dinner."

At dinner all went smoothly and Jennie was seen but not heard for quite a while. But in a pause her voice was raised, clear and insistent, "Mother, where are all our *old* goblets *now?*" (Hollingworth, 1939).

Jennie is gifted. Her curiosity, while sometimes irritating to others, sparks learning and becomes the essence of investigation and creativity. But she may be restless, inattentive, and impatient with details that require rote learning or drill. Our society depends on its gifted individuals. However, they are often the most neglected group of exceptional children in school.

There has been much controversy over establishing a definition of giftedness. In 1972 the U.S. Commissioner of Education, Sidney P. Marland, defined gifted children as those who display "high performance" in one or more of the following areas:

1. General intellectual ability
2. Specific academic aptitude
3. Creative and productive thinking ability
4. Leadership ability
5. Ability in the visual or performing arts
6. Psychomotor ability (Marland, 1972)

Marland's definition attempted to expand the concept of giftedness beyond high IQ and superior academic achievement. J. J. Gallagher (1975) stressed that creativity as well as divergent and evaluative thinking skills are largely untapped by IQ tests, and that these areas play an important part in giftedness. However, since IQ and academic achievement are the only two areas that can be measured with any degree of accuracy, these remain the principal criteria of giftedness.

J. P. Guilford (1965, 1967) proposed a model of intelligence that included creative talents and conceptual thinking not formerly measured by traditional intelligence tests. He called his model the "three faces of intellect"—content (type of information that the intellect operates on); products (forms that result from intellectual operations on different content); and operations (cognitive processes or intellectual actions). While Guilford's model has not been widely used in special education of the gifted, it, too, has pointed up how traditional IQ tests lack divergent thinking tasks and hence neglect creative talents (Guilford and Hoepfner, 1971). Among the forms of divergent thinking Guilford stresses as major components of intellect are: fluency; flexibility; originality; penetration (ability to perceive beyond the superficial); and redefinition (ability to perceive utility beyond the routine practice).

Procedures for organizing, administering, and implementing programs for the gifted are still closely related to the traditional statistical view of giftedness, thus being limited to those students with high IQ and high academic achievement. Current educational programs for the gifted fall into three general categories; acceleration; ability grouping; and enrichment. Acceleration refers to plans that are designed to move the gifted student through the school program at a faster rate. This may be accomplished through early school admission, grade-skipping, curriculum compression, and early college admission. Ability grouping is the process by which gifted children are placed in self-contained groups, classes, or even special schools in order to receive more concentrated instruction. And finally, enrichment focuses on providing the gifted with more advanced educational experiences without separating them from nongifted peers.

In other words, IQ was thought to be determined mainly by genetic inheritance and therefore essentially unchangeable.

Since then the question of whether or not heredity contributes anything to differences in intellectual performance has become deeply mixed up with racism and politics. But Nobel laureate P. W. Medawar, considering the scientific evidence alone, concludes that it would be going too far to deny that heredity has any influence on intelligence at all. At the same time, however, Medawar states that the idea of innate intelligence betrays a "deep-seated misunderstanding of genetics" (Medawar, 1977).

Another question raised by IQ tests is whether anything as complex as intelligence can be summed up in a single number. Actually, what we call general intelligence is compounded of several more or less different elements. One such element is *grasp:* how much a person's mind can take in, and how fast. Another element is the ability to see implications. Yet another is the ability to see analogies and distinctions—and there are many more, probably varying widely in the same individual. "One number," Medawar believes, "will not do for all these" (Medawar, 1977).

Looking back over the storms of debate raised by IQ testing, we may wish that Alfred Binet, instead of calling his test an intelligence test, had called it a predictor of academic success. After all, that and nothing more is what he hoped it would do. And how well does an IQ score predict academic success? It gives some idea, but only a rough one. The correlation between IQ and academic success is about the same as that between height and weight (Houts, 1977). In other words, there are almost as many people with low IQ scores and high academic success, or vice versa, as there are people who are short yet heavy or tall but light.

READING

Our culture takes reading for granted, a skill everyone is expected to possess. Its value lies not only in practical application but in the access it provides to the wider world. Through reading, a person can find out what is happening

Do IQ tests indicate a person's intelligence? Researchers question whether intelligence can be summed up in a single number.

in Washington or Moscow, Mexico or Tanzania. One can learn what spots on the sun may have to do with tomorrow's weather and what a Japanese court lady thought about love centuries ago. True, one can learn some of these things in other ways, such as by listening to the radio or watching TV. But radio and TV programs are available only when a station happens to air them, and they contain only a limited amount of information on a few subjects. Books are there whenever they are wanted, and they contain far more information. Thus it is hardly surprising that reading, and learning to read, are regarded as of primary importance when children start school.

Methods of Teaching Reading

There are two basic ways to go about teaching children to read. In the *phonetic* method the child learns the sounds of letters and basic letter groups such as "ch," and then learns to analyze (sound out) words in terms of these letter-sounds. In the *word-recognition* method the child learns to recognize whole words as single units, without analyzing them into their parts. At present, most schools teach by some form of the phonetic method, which seems to be the more successful way for most children.

One major advantage of the phonetic approach is that it equips children with a technique for figuring out new words on their own. Once they have learned the sound of "m," for instance, and the difference between "at" and "ate," they can make a pretty good stab at "mat" and "mate" even if they have never seen these words in writing before. Word-recognition readers may eventually figure out how to do the same thing, but it will probably take them a lot longer, and some children never do manage it. However, some children appear to learn better by word recognition. Perhaps they happen to be very visually oriented, or perhaps their ability to classify and analyze is not equal to that of other children their age.

Reading Disorders

Among the total elementary school population in the United States an estimated 15 to 20 percent of the children are retarded readers—those who read at the level expected for students a grade or more below their own (Bond & Tinker, 1973). Among the many factors that may cause reading retardation are slow maturation; low intelligence; physical conditions such as fatigue, malnutrition, or chronic illness; undetected problems in hearing or vision; psychological and social problems, the fact that English is not spoken at home, a minor neurological malfunction. Because a reading disorder is caused by several factors, not just one, teachers and psychologists use several tests to identify a pattern of causes.

Causes of Reading Disorders

Some children of normal intelligence may start as slow readers simply because their neurological development has not caught up with their mental age; when it does, such children will be able to read at grade level. But difficulty in learning to read may make a child feel like a born loser, and such a self-concept may be a source of problems throughout life. Early reading difficulties create frustration and a sense of inadequacy that hamper a child's further efforts to learn. A large percentage of high school dropouts have had severe reading disabilities that have contributed to repeated academic failures and a sense of hopelessness.

Observant teachers often find clues to the causes of reading difficulties in the behavior of their students. Noticing that a boy brings his book too close to his face, and loses his place frequently, a teacher may guess that this student has poor eyesight and recommend an eye examination. If a girl does not seem to hear unless she is looking directly at the teacher, her poor classroom performance may be related to a hearing problem. Hyperactive or highly impulsive behavior may suggest that a child has an endocrine disturbance.

Reading difficulties may also be related to emotional disturbances, though it is often difficult to determine whether a reading problem is the cause or the result of such problems. A child's confusion, fear of competition, and low self-opinion may act as blocks to learning. If Jody's mother calls him stupid each time he does something wrong at home, he will come to school with a self-concept of stupidity that will be evident in his classroom performance.

Children in low-income families often live in an overcrowded and tension-filled environment where not only their emotional but also their physiological needs are rarely satisfied. These youngsters may be so malnourished and deprived of sleep that they do not have the energy to concentrate in school. Where both parents have to work at tiring, mind-deadening jobs to support the family, they seldom have the energy to read stories to their children or even to talk with them. This is unfortunate, because these are means by which children develop perception and memory.

There are a number of children from all backgrounds who cannot read, or who read with great difficulty, and yet for whom none of the above factors is the major cause of the disorder. These children have a learning disability. A great deal of research is being done in this area, and it is becoming possible to teach children with learning disabilities to read.

Diagnosis and Remedies

Judy, David, and Michael are in the same third-grade class. Their teacher, Ms. Timmons, has noticed that all three appear to have difficulties in reading. She gives the whole class the Stanford Achievement Test and finds that Judy, David, and Michael read on the level of first graders. This indicates severe reading retardation, but it does not tell her the reasons for it.

She next gathers information about each of the children and looks for patterns. Judy and David are nine years old, but Michael is only eight. He entered the first grade when he was five. While Judy and David have above-average IQ scores, Michael's is below average. The teacher calls Michael's parents and discovers that they do not speak English. At this point the teacher has made a *general diagnosis*. However, since Michael comes from a different cultural or linguistic background, his teacher may want to consider whether his IQ score accurately reflects his intelligence. In this case she may give him further tests before designing a remedial program for him.

Michael is younger than his classmates, comes from a different language background, and has difficulty in mastering the nuances of spoken English. Reading is naturally especially difficult for him, and he cannot be expected to have developed the skills necessary for reading at a third-grade level. The teacher may want to design either a bilingual or a special tutoring program for him. She will start Michael on a developmental reading program at his present level, pacing it to his abilities and maturational readiness. She will also stress language skills, listening and speaking, and sound discrimination.

Now, why are Judy and David having problems? The teacher moves to the next level of diagnosis, *analytical reading diagnosis*. She may use one or more of several reading tests.

Catching a reading disorder—such as one caused by poor eyesight—early can prevent the frustration and sense of inadequacy that can hamper a child's efforts to learn.

In testing Judy the teacher finds that she can read words she knows even when she is only allowed a quick look at the word, but will not attempt to sound the word out no matter how much time she is allowed to look at it. This finding indicates that Judy has a *sight vocabulary*, but is unable to use phonetics. The next question is why. The teacher gives Judy further tests to determine whether she can hear the different sounds in similar words and whether she can blend sounds she has heard separately into words. It turns out that Judy can do all these things very well.

As a final test the teacher shows Judy some nonsense words made up of common sounds, and she is unable to pronounce them even if she can see the separate parts of the words. For example, one word on the test is "trock." Judy cannot even begin to pronounce it, so the teacher shows her only "tr." Judy is still unable to pronounce the sound even though she has just read the word "train" after seeing it for only half a second.

At this point the teacher decides that she can prepare a remedial plan for Judy with no further testing. The remedial program will focus on a structured, developmental approach to phonetics. At the same time she encourages Judy to enlarge her sight vocabulary.

David's performance on the reading test is different from Judy's. He is very nervous and does not always pay attention to instructions. When he is unable to do a task, he becomes very upset. He can read some words when he is allowed all the time he wants, but when allowed only half a second he freezes and is unable to respond. David has particular trouble blending sounds into words and hearing differences in the sounds of similar words. He is, however, able to pronounce some of the nonsense words that Judy had so much trouble with. The teacher concludes that David has some limited knowledge of phonetics and some sight vocabulary, but that his response to the test calls for closer examination. She carries the diagnosis to the third level, *case-study diagnosis.*

At this level she needs the help of specialists in different fields. David is sent to a speech therapist to have his hearing tested. The therapist finds that David's ability to hear sounds is normal, but his abilities in blending and discriminating sounds are lower than what would be expected of a child his age. This is an indication of general neurological immaturity, so David is sent to a neurologist, who finds that he is neurologically immature. The neurologist suggests that it is probably a temporary problem, but warns that David should be watched closely for signs of development. If they do not appear within a year, learning disability might be present.

David is also sent to a clinical social worker, who interviews him and his parents. David's parents pressure him to do better. Disappointed by his performance, they have decided that he is lazy or stupid. David has felt guilty, angry, and confused. He has come to hate school and reading because he fails. His parents' and his own attitudes make him hate himself for his failure.

Now the teacher can construct a remedial program for David designed to match his maturational level. With goals he can meet, David will be able to succeed and see his progress. The teacher includes exercises particularly in auditory discrimination, that might accelerate David's maturation in specific areas important to reading. David's ability in phonetics and his sight-word vocabulary are areas of relative strength that the teacher will use to help him with his weaknesses.

LEARNING DISABILITIES

For many years teachers and diagnosticians were baffled by children who could not read even though none of the usual causes of reading retardation could be found. Often these children were considered mentally retarded, though they could do some things very well. Sometimes they were simply termed "unteachable." Then in 1937 psychologist Samuel Orton discovered that many younger children tend to reverse or rotate letters of the alphabet. For example, they confuse "b" with "d" and "p" with "q." He found other children whose writing at first appears to be nonsense but in reality is *mirror writing:* it is quite normal when read in a mirror (Figure 10.1).

More important, however, Orton found that most children who by the age of eight or nine still tend to reverse letters or write mirror style have an

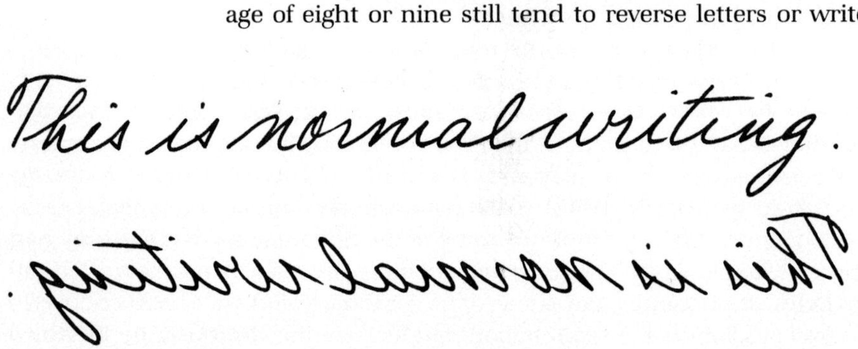

This is normal writing.

Figure 10.1 Mirror writing. For some children it is more natural to write the mirrored way.

unusual neurological trait. In most people one side of the brain is dominant over the other. The right side of our brain controls most of the left side of our bodies; the left side of our brain controls the right side of our bodies—and most of us are either right-sided or left-sided. Right-sided people not only use their right hand best, but the right eye leads their left eye, and they favor the right foot. People who have **cross-dominance**, however, may use their right hand best, but their left eye may lead their right eye. Some people do not have any fixed dominance at all—that is, there is an equal chance that they may use either side (Orton, 1937). There is some controversy now over the role of dominance patterns in learning disorders, but all psychologists agree that Orton made an important contribution by connecting learning disorders to neurological patterns. It is now generally accepted that learning disabilities are caused by one kind of neurological malfunction or another, though we cannot yet pinpoint the source of each type of malfunction because the nervous system is so complex.

There are a great many different learning disabilities. Some children, for example, cannot organize what they see. Some cannot remember what they hear; others cannot make associations between letters and sounds or apply such simple concepts as "same" and "different"; and as we just saw, some read and write backward. There are also many theories, diagnostic techniques, and programs currently being used to help children with learning disabilities. Most of the theories are based on the idea that children must go through specific developmental stages to gain certain abilities, and that learning-disabled children have not gone through the proper sequence because of some neurological problem. For example, one program (Fernald, 1943) teaches children to read through feeling and hearing a word as well as seeing it in writing. The children trace the word before they write it on their own so that the integration of all the things they feel and perceive is fixed before they actually produce the word. Later they read the word they have written, and it is always a word of their own choice. Users of all these techniques report some success with children who have learning disabilities, but there is no objective evidence that any one technique is better than another. In some cases the child improves seemingly for no reason; or he learns to compensate.

STAGE OF CONCRETE OPERATIONS

In Jean Piaget's theory of cognitive development the period from roughly two to seven years is called the preoperational period. It is followed by the *period of concrete operations*, which extends to approximately the age of eleven.

In the preoperational phase, children's thinking is still limited in a number of ways. We saw in Chapter 7 that although they can go beyond what their senses perceive, they usually cannot reverse a mental operation. This was illustrated by the experiment in which children were asked to arrange a bunch of sticks in order of size, smallest to largest. Preoperational children could not do this task. Slightly older children almost at the stage of concrete operations

Piaget's Periods of Cognitive Development

SENSORIMOTOR PERIOD (BIRTH TO 24 MONTHS)

PREOPERATIONAL PERIOD (2 TO 7 YEARS)

PERIOD OF CONCRETE OPERATIONS (7 TO 11 YEARS)

Children classify concrete objects by category and begin to understand the relations among categories. They do not, however, think of the categories as abstract or formal entities, but still consider them just groups of concrete objects. Four major accomplishments include:

Decentration: become able to focus attention on more than one aspect of a situation at a time.

Consistently conserve such qualities as length, quantity, and weight.

Begin to grasp changes in objects or situations throughout the entire dynamic sequence, not just the static beginning and end points.

Thinking becomes reversible. Able to conceive that the effects of some action or transformation may be reversed by a subsequent action.

PERIOD OF FORMAL OPERATIONS (11 YEARS ON)

succeeded, but only by trial and error. After the age of seven years, however, the children used a systematic approach. They first found the smallest stick, then looked through the pile for the next smallest, and so on. What these children were able to do, and the less advanced children were not, was to reverse the direction of their thinking: they looked for the stick that was *bigger* than the previous one but *smaller* than the remaining ones (Piaget, 1970b).

Another limitation in preoperational children is their lack of awareness of the principle of conservation. For example, when a quantity of water is poured from a tall, narrow glass to a wide glass, it reaches a lower level in the wide beaker, but the youngsters in the concrete-operational stage are not fooled. They realize that the amount of water remains the same—is conserved—even though the shape of the container has been changed.

Decentration

Both reversibility and conservation—qualities of thought that make their appearance with the attainment of the concrete operational stage—involve the ability to shift the focus of attention from one part of the situation to another. With the stick problem, children can say that stick A is smaller than stick B, and therefore stick B is *bigger* than stick A. They can switch from "smaller than" to "bigger than" and back, and can see that this relationship is relative. In the conservation-of-liquid quantity problem they can shift their attention from height alone to both height and width in relation to each other. Piaget calls this ability to shift one's attention *decentration*.

This ability to decenter actually begins before the period of concrete operations, but as the child progresses, it becomes more and more general and is applied to increasingly complex problems. In the area of conservation, for example, the child first masters conservation of number. Twelve beads remain twelve beads whether they are placed in a straight line, a circle, or a heap. The child is able to decenter from the configuration of the beads and to see that their number remains constant. Conservation of weight—the realization that equal weights remain equal despite changes in appearance such as shape and number—is a more complex sort of judgment. It does not appear until two or three years after the beginning of the concrete-operational stage. Conservation of volume does not appear until even later, and problems involving transformation of the physical state of objects (for example, the dissolving of sugar in water) make the appearance last. Decentration also figures significantly in relationships of part to whole. The concrete-operational child can, for example, see that ten blue beads and five red beads make fifteen beads and that there are more beads together than there are beads of either color. The child includes both kinds of beads in the class of beads and can reason simultaneously about the class and each of its subgroups. Preoperational children, on the other hand, would have trouble saying that there are more beads than there are blue beads because they could not easily decenter from the fact that there are more blue than red ones. Not only do such children lack a firm grasp of the concept of class, but their thinking is not reversible: they applied the term *more* to the blue beads the first time, and they continue to do so.

Another way in which the thought of children in the concrete-operational stage differs from that of children in the preoperational stage is in the older children's ability to grasp the *transformations* that change an object from one state to another. They can have an overall mental picture of a sequence of events, such as an inning of a baseball game, that involves past, present, and future; and they can describe this sequence of events without having to perform them. Preoperational children, by contrast, have trouble describing sequences. They need to act them out because they are centered in the present.

A concrete-operational child is also better able to understand how physical objects can go through a series of changes. One experiment (Inhelder, Sinclair, & Bovet, 1974) has demonstrated this fact quite clearly. Children were shown transparent jars of different shapes that were arranged on top of each other and emptied through spouts in their bottoms. The children observed the liquid fall from one jar to the next until it reached the bottom jars, which were identical in shape to the top jars but different from the jars in between (see Figure 10.2). It was found that from this display a majority of the preoperational children did not learn anything about conservation of quantity, whereas most concrete-operational children did. The experiment demonstrated that the preoperational children could not coordinate a series of perceptions—in this case the liquid in each of three jars. In other words, they could not decenter from a static condition to a process.

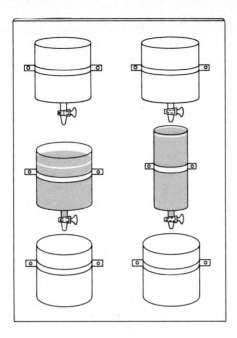

Figure 10.2 Demonstration of conservation of liquid quantity. As the water is released from one container to the next, a
child at the stage of concrete operations
can see that its volume remains the same
regardless of the container's shape.

A major cognitive gain made by school-age children is that their thinking
becomes *reversible.* They begin to see how one action can actually negate its
opposite, and how one action can make up for the effects of another even
though the two actions are not opposites. This relationship is known as *com-
pensation.*

Measurement

Even very young children three or four years of age have some numerical
abilities that they can apply to simple measuring tasks under the right conditions (Gelman & Gallistel, 1978). When they reach school age, children have
a more quantitative attitude toward things, and are readier to measure things,
than are preschool children. In middle childhood we learn how to do many
things with numbers. As Flavell (1977) points out, it is during this period that
we become able to estimate, without counting, small sets of objects. Also,
Flavell continues, the child

> learns to *count,* both accurately (no objects missed or counted twice) and to task
> specifications (e.g., count out exactly 10 objects from a set of 16). He knows the
> relation between the *ordinal* (*n*th) and the *cardinal* (*n*) aspects of number. For
> instance, he knows that if he has just counted the *fifth* object in a series, then
> there are exactly *five* objects counted out so far. He can read printed *numerals*
> as well as comprehend spoken numbers. He knows that two sets formed by
> putting elements in one-one *correspondence* are numerically equal, and that
> correspondences can be used to divide and multiply sets. He can *compare set
> sizes,* correctly interpreting and using comparative terms ("more than," "less

than," "equals"). He can distinguish set transformations that are *relevant* to number (addition or subtraction of elements) from those that are numerically *irrelevant* (e.g., spacing out the elements), and he knows that any addition of elements to a set can be reversed or annulled by an equivalent subtraction (Flavell, 1977).

SOCIAL COGNITION

Another crucial implication of centration and decentration is its relation to the child's egocentricity. According to Piaget's theory the sensorimotor child and the preoperational child tend to view everything in the world in relation to themselves—that is, in relation to their momentary state (including felt needs and interests). They cannot decenter from themselves in order to take the viewpoint of other people, as concrete operational children can.

Taking the viewpoint of others is closely related to the comprehension and use of social-relational terms. For a boy to understand that he is his brother's brother, for example, or his mother's son, he must grasp the nature of reciprocal relationships. This, in turn, implies the mastery of reversibility in thinking, which is an achievement of concrete operational thought. Obviously, the development of the ability to decenter from oneself and take the role of others has important consequences for the child's ability to understand the feelings of others and function socially. Hence, cognitive growth facilitates the development of social behavior and morality.

Knowledge about social relationships and reactions is called *social cognition.* It may be generally described as awareness and understanding of how other people think, feel, and see things (i.e., have a point of view), what they intend, and how to describe other people. Social cognitive skills (which are developmental) are primitive in the preoperational child, but some three- and four-year olds can assume another person's visual perspective in a familiar environment (Shantz, 1975).

Preschoolers usually describe other people physically, judgmentally, and in terms of their relations to them. Since they cannot conceive that someone else has thoughts different from theirs, they cannot comprehend or predict thoughts of other people. Social understanding and interaction are limited by the inability to decenter (Forbes, 1978).

Between the ages of three and six children begin to recognize that there are differences between themselves and others. They still cannot always identify the differences and are likely to persist in the earlier belief that their own goals and those of other people are the same.

In the next phase of development (ages six to ten) children understand and even infer differences between their feelings and thoughts and those of others. They also realize that others can have contradictory thoughts and feelings. At seven Susan will probably know that her friend can be both pleased and sad that she is going to camp. She will also grasp some of the relations between circumstances and behavior and will be able to judge others by their intentions instead of merely by the outcome of their acts.

During middle childhood, children develop an understanding of how other people think and feel.

  Susan (and her peers) will begin to understand the thoughts and feelings of people in situations unfamiliar to her (Forbes, 1978). She is likely to describe people in terms of their thoughts and feelings. When they are about eleven, Susan and her cousin Robert will probably be able to engage in mutual role-taking. That is, they will be able to put themselves in another person's position while simultaneously arriving at and maintaining their own (Shantz, 1975).

  In adolescence social cognition expands to include the larger world (Damon, 1977). Adolescents realize that they and others are parts of the larger social system. They now understand that the social system shapes people's thoughts and feelings through formative influences such as the past and the social milieu in which a person was reared.

  Although understanding the thoughts, feelings, and intentions of others is obviously linked to social development, just how this development occurs is still not understood (Shantz, 1975). Some theorists believe that environment influences the development of a child's social cognition. Others emphasize the importance of: modeling, imitation, and exposure to a variety of social experiences (Shantz, 1975; Damon, 1977).

Social cognition seems to affect peer acceptance (Ladd & Oden, 1979), self-definition (Damon, 1977), and learning through interaction. It follows a developmental pattern, and its appearance is revealed in increasingly sophisticated social information gathering, observation, and communication (Turiel, 1978). Although social cognition and morality are not identical, they are closely related to one another (Turiel, in press).

MORAL DEVELOPMENT

Piaget has conducted extensive studies of the attitudes children have toward rules. He found that, from about the age of five, children begin to feel that obedience, duty, and rule-keeping are of great importance. He also noted that a sense of personal judgment and choice—that is, a sense of justice—develops as children mature (Piaget, 1965).

At the earliest stage that Piaget tested—children from ages two to about five—there is little concern for rules. Children in this age group who are involved in playing a game of marbles, for example, have slight interest in "winning" the game, but are more concerned with exploring by themselves the muscular control they can achieve by manipulating the marbles, in various ways. At the approach of the fifth year Piaget's children began observing the rules of the game as played by older children, trying to imitate the older children's behavior but without a sense of commitment or cooperative agreement on how the game should be played.

From about the age of five to nine or ten children tend to regard the rules as sacred and unchangeable, the only guidelines to proper and acceptable behavior. During this period they perceive the world in terms of *moral realism*, in which the rules are considered to come from the same authoritative sources as natural laws. Just as children of this age come to understand that touching a hot oven will burn them or that scattering toys around the house will make Mommy and Daddy angry, so they come to think that any variation in the rules of the game of marbles must inevitably bring bad results.

One six-year-old boy told Piaget that the idea of the marbles game and its rules "just came into peoples' hands," and that "Daddies show little boys how to play." When pressed to acknowledge that the rules might be changed, the boy admitted it, but said he did not know how to change them. To the six-year-old a game had to be played in a certain way. Asked why, he replied, "Because God didn't teach them [any other way]." The likelihood of punishment resulting from the detection of a lie by an adult is often what constitutes its seriousness. In the eyes of a child at this stage a mistake that brings punishment is worse than a harmless lie that goes undetected.

With full teams and equipment, the rules of baseball are "official." But when a few children are hitting flies, or playing catch, they may play by any rules they agree on.

Between the ages of five and ten role-taking becomes an increasingly important factor in a child's moral growth. In one study (Ambron & Irwin, 1974) two Piagetian dimensions of moral judgment—intentionality (the motive of an individual) and restitution (punishment that provides for restoration of damage)—were correlated with three dimensions of role-taking—perceptual (the ability to take the visual perspective of another), cognitive (the ability to take into account another person's knowledge), and affective (the ability to empathize with another's emotions). Kindergarten children and second graders were used as subjects. The study clearly indicated developmental differences between five-year-olds and seven-year-olds. The seven-year-olds not only got higher scores on cognitive and affective role-taking than the five-year-olds, but they were also better able to consider the motives of others.

The shift from blind acceptance of authority and rules to reciprocal understanding becomes even more evident in the next few years. Piaget found that by the age of about ten the child's moral development begins to enter a more mature phase, in which the reverence for rules yields to a "morality of cooperation"—that is, a growing awareness that both oneself and others have reciprocal needs and rights. The older child learns that there is a difference between a natural rule, such as the fact that one will be burned by touching a hot iron, and a rule in a game.

At this stage children modify the rules of a game of marbles in many ways, provided that all the players agree on the changes. Children are developing a sense of justice, and they can appreciate the viewpoints and wishes of others and realize that others can also understand and value theirs. At first deviation from the accepted rules may be regarded as not playing fair. But once everyone in the group agrees on what is fair, a new rule is established. When Piaget asked an eleven-year-old, "Did your father play the way you showed me, or differently?" he received the answer, "Oh, I don't know. It may have been a different game. It changes. It still changes quite often." By the age of twelve Piaget's subjects were generally adjusted to the idea that any game rules would be fair if all the players accepted them.

Since Piaget opened the study of moral judgment in children more than thirty years ago, many investigators have explored the reasoning a person uses when confronted with a hypothetical moral conflict. Lawrence Kohlberg, one of the most active and influential of these investigators, has come to the conclusion that a moral sense is not acquired simply through the acceptance of society's rules as taught by precept, punishment, or identification with respected figures. He found that it also involves an internal, personal series of changes in social attitudes. He diagrammed this series of successive changes in three levels, each with its own characteristics. Each level must be achieved and assimilated before the child can progress to the next level. When the moral reasoning characteristic of one level proves inadequate for coping with the person's moral problems, the person begins to strive toward the next level.

Kohlberg (1963, 1964) uses doll play and stories about moral dilemmas to elicit reactions from children at different levels of development. Each dilemma consists of a story in which disobedience to a rule or an adult resulted in either reward or punishment. One such story involved a boy who was told by his mother to stay in the house and watch the baby while she went to the store. As soon as the mother left, the boy ran outside and played. The mother, upon returning, gave the disobedient boy some candy. Four-year-olds tended to disregard the boy's disobedience because the act brought a reward. Seven-year-olds, however, expressed feelings of conflict because they sensed an injustice in rewarding bad behavior—they could conceive of the reward being offered but in general felt that disobedience would necessarily lead to punishment, and therefore the story was unrealistic. Kohlberg finds in this a correspondence to the moral realism of Piaget's younger children.

The conflict in thinking that arises at this level of moral development is illustrated by one child's reaction to the following story. Joe was promised by his father that if he earned fifty dollars by himself he could go to camp. Later, however, Joe's father wanted the money and asked Joe to give it to him. Joe lied, saying he had only earned ten dollars. He gave his father the ten dollars and kept the rest for himself. Joe then told his younger brother what he had done.

The question asked about the story was this: "Should the younger brother tell his father what Joe did?" A ten-year-old answered, "In one way it would be right to tell on his brother or his father might get mad and spank him. In another way it would be right to keep quiet or his brother might beat him up."

These responses illustrate Kohlberg's Level I of moral development—an approach to morality that focuses primarily on anticipated rewards or pun-

Kohlberg's Levels of Moral Development

LEVEL I: PRECONVENTIONAL MORALITY (EARLY MIDDLE CHILDHOOD)[a]

At this level children make moral judgments solely on the basis of anticipated punishment and reward—a good or right act is one that is rewarded. **Stage 1 morality** focuses on the power and possessions of those in authority and on the necessity for the weak to please the strong in order to avoid punishment. You do what you do in order to avoid displeasing those who have power over you.

Stage 2 morality focuses on the pleasure motive: you do what you do in order to get what you want from others. There is a sense of fair exchange based on purely pragmatic values and of noninterference in the affairs or values of others.

LEVEL II: CONVENTIONAL MORALITY (LATE MIDDLE CHILDHOOD)[b]

At this level right behavior is that which is accepted, approved, and praised by other people who are seen as being in positions of authority. Children seek to avoid guilt by behaving in ways that will be approved by the social conventions of their culture.

Stage 3 morality focuses on the approval of those immediately involved in judging one's behavior. Justice at this stage is seen as reciprocity or equality between individuals.

Stage 4 morality has been called "law and order" morality. Here the focus is on obeying the rules for their own sake. Justice is seen as the reciprocity between each individual and the social system. Societal order is very important in making judgments at this stage.

LEVEL III: POSTCONVENTIONAL MORALITY (ADOLESCENCE)

[a]*Kohlberg found that about 95 percent of all moral judgments made by seven-year-olds are at this level.*
[b]*Kohlberg (1963, 1964) found that about 40 percent of all moral judgments made by ten-year-olds are at this level.*

ishments. At Level II Kohlberg found a tendency to accept a stereotyped view of what makes a good person. This was not the "goody-goody" behavior that is meant only to win the approval of others and escape blame, but rather the emergence of an admiration for those who perform a role properly and who like and help other people. There was also an awareness of the need for authority to make society function in a just manner. Kohlberg asked a thirteen-year-old boy what he thought about President Eisenhower. The boy's comment was, "President Eisenhower has done a good job and worked so hard he got a heart attack and put himself in the grave, just about, to help the people."

Another boy, asked what he would think if he were Joe's younger brother in the dilemma described above, said, "If my father finds out later, he won't trust me. My brother wouldn't either, but I wouldn't have a *conscience* that he [my brother] didn't."

Kohlberg interprets this statement as equating "conscience" with an avoidance of disapproval by authorities but not by peers. Later, the same boy stated, "I try to do things for my parents, they've always done things for you. I try to do everything my mother says, I try to please her. Like she wants me to be a doctor and I want to, too, and she's helping me get up there." In this instance the boy is not expressing fear of disapproval by his superiors but an identification of his own wishes with theirs and an effort to anticipate their desires.

Kohlberg is acknowledged as a major figure in the study of moral development, and his work has inspired many important and interesting studies. However, certain reservations have been expressed about some of his sampling techniques and conclusions. For example, his sample population was restricted to small numbers of white, middle-class males, so that it was not generally representative. In a review and evaluation of his approach Kurtines and Greif (1974) suggest that while there may be trends in moral development, there is insufficient data to support "an invariant developmental sequence" consisting of six specific stages. Furthermore, recent investigations have suggested that for children to reach Kohlberg's various moral stages, they must have matured in many areas besides moral ones. Moral development is probably contingent on far more than background and upbringing and seems to be related to cognitive development of many kinds. Finally, it should be noted that failure to respond to Kohlberg's dilemmas does not necessarily indicate low morality, nor are people's behavior and their response necessarily correlated with one another. That is, people who answer a Kohlberg dilemma on a higher level may behave as if they were on a lower level, and people who answer on a lower level may behave as if they were on a higher one.

SUMMARY

▶ In middle childhood problem-solving ability improves as children become more capable of recalling information from long-term memory and of deliberately retaining memories in long-term reserve. Also, they remember more information by being able to classify it. In applying hypotheses impulsive children make more mistakes than reflective children because they do not pause to think things through.

▶ Standardized tests of every variety have been called misleading and unfair, but none more so than IQ tests. Some people suppose IQ tests measure innate intelligence, but this is not true. In fact, it is not really meaningful to try to give a single number of anything so complex as human intelligence.

▶ Some people respond impulsively to questions, and some pause to reflect before answering. Impulsivity and reflectiveness indicate personality, not intelligence, and are individual ways of responding to and processing information. These latter two activities are called cognitive styles. Other types of cognitive style include the way a person classifies objects or events and the way someone responds to environmental stimuli. Each style has many advantages and disadvantages that should be taken into account when an individual is confronted with any type of learning task.

▶ Many possible factors may cause children to be retarded readers. Often a teacher can identify the cause of an individual child's reading problem by means of a general diagnosis. Causes that are not revealed by a general diagnosis can be pinpointed with special tests, and once the cause is found, the teacher can start a remedial program.

▶ Learning disabilities, unlike most of the conditions that result in retarded reading and other difficulties in school, are caused by neurological malfunctions. These disabilities may represent areas of difficulty in an otherwise intelligent person. Special techniques to help children with learning disabilities have had encouraging results.

▶ At about age seven most children enter what Piaget calls the period of concrete operations. At this level of cognitive development they are able to understand the reversibility of actions, to conserve quantities, and to decenter from the immediate situation and from themselves.

▶ Piaget found that younger children tend to regard rules as fixed and eternal, like natural laws. Later they begin to realize that rules can be made up and changed if everyone concerned agrees. They also become more adept at taking the viewpoint of others.

▶ As children mature, their ability to understand other people's motives and points of view develops by stages. This social cognition is important in their definitions of themselves, their capacity to comprehend the motives and ideas of other people from different backgrounds and cultures, and their moral development. Until children reach adolescence, they are usually unable to perceive the relationships between people's behaviors and the cultures, histories, or immediate circumstances that influence them.

▶ Kohlberg has outlined a series of stages that most children pass through as they improve their moral understanding. Youngsters prefer the highest stage they can comprehend because it is broader and more consistent than the one below it, but they may not be able as yet to apply it to every moral dilemma that they confront.

FURTHER READINGS

Cohen, Dorothy H. *The learning child.* **New York: Vintage, 1973.**

Both the school and the outside world have much to teach a child, and as agencies for learning both have perils as well as satisfactions. Among the specific problems discussed by Cohen are reading and writing skills and innovations in education.

Dechant, Emerald. *Improving the teaching of reading.* **Englewood Cliffs, N.J.: Prentice-Hall, 1974.**

Second edition of a comprehensive book on reading development, causes of reading disabilities, and remedial approaches.

Englemann, Siegfried, and Englemann, Therese. *Preventing failure in the primary grades.* **New York: Simon & Schuster, 1969.**

A child's mind closes to learning when school is a confusing place where he or she experiences failure. The Englemanns offer a program to help children who have failed to learn basic reading and arithmetic skills.

Farnham-Diggory, S. *Learning disabilities.* **Cambridge, Mass.: Harvard University Press, 1978.**

Presents up-to-date information on a variety of learning disabilities, with particular focus on diagnosis and treatment approaches.

Ginsburg, Herbert. *The myth of the deprived child.* **Englewood Cliffs, N.J.: Prentice-Hall, 1972.**

An interesting discussion of IQ testing in the context of social class. Ginsburg argues that the tests do not accurately measure true differences.

Simon, Sidney B., Kirschenbaum, H. (eds.). *Readings in values clarification.* **Minneapolis: Winston, 1973.**

Urie Bronfenbrenner, Lawrence Kohlberg, Carl Rogers, and others contribute individual articles on the problem of values. They address such questions as "How do we know what our values are?" and "How do people's values change as they grow up?"

Weiss, H. G. *Home is a learning place: A parents' guide to learning disabilities.* **Boston: Little, Brown, 1977.**

The first half of this book deals with the possible causes and diverse symptoms of learning disability, and the frustration and tension it arouses in both parent and child. The second half depicts the stages in which children develop essential skills, and describes ways to encourage such skills to avoid later complications.

Chapter 11

❖❖❖❖❖❖

Home, Peers, and School

Nathan can hardly wait for summer. He has already found some boards to use for a roof on the tree hut, and Mr. and Mrs. Cooper—the parents of Steve, his best friend next door—have promised to take him canoeing with them in July. Of course he and Steve will sleep out again this year. One night last year they stayed awake and counted twenty-six shooting stars!

As the Coopers have evidently recognized, Nathan and Steve are inseparable. This close friendship is something new in their development: during the first few years of elementary school both boys had several playmates and got along with them well enough, but now they seem to have chosen each other as blood brothers. It is the first time anyone has meant almost as much to either boy as he means to himself.

The ability to get along with people outside of the family—peers and teachers, for example—is a major developmental accomplishment. During the middle childhood years children must make a place for themselves in the world of friendship and commitment. Success and failure in these endeavors will affect children for the rest of their lives.

THE HOME

Nathan and Steve are among the fortunate children growing up in stable, loving families. Not every child has that opportunity. A rapidly changing urbanized and industrial society has disrupted traditional family life for better or for worse. More than half of all American families—from the migrant worker to the corporate executive—move every five years. For a small child a move of even a few blocks away can prove to be traumatic because proximity is such an important factor in the choice of playmates. Although death is a less frequent cause for family breakups than formerly, one in every three families will be destroyed by divorce (Glazer, 1978). A significant portion of divorced parents remarry; nevertheless, it has been estimated that between 40 and 50 percent of American children will spend about six years of their childhood in a single-parent home (Keniston, 1978). Finally, a basic change has taken place in the occupation of women: half the mothers of school-aged children in intact families and over a third of the mothers of preschool children are working outside the home. Moving, divorce, and working mothers are major changes in American home life—not all necessarily the worse for children. Secure, happy children learn to make new friends, a characteristic that will stand them in good stead as they progress from elementary school to junior high to high school, go off to college, and change jobs as adults. Children in homes where only bitterness and hate are expressed by the parents toward each other may find a greater peace of mind when parents finally separate and divorce. As for children of working mothers, we will see that if mothers like their work, such children will develop a competence and independence greater than that of children whose mothers stay at home.

Autonomy and Control

If Nathan finds Steve confident and trusting, it is probably because the Coopers are warm, affectionate people—not only toward Steve but toward each other as well. Unfortunately, the opposite is also likely to hold true: when parents are hostile to their children much of the time, the children begin to feel and act as if they were among enemies everywhere. They grow afraid to approach others in hope of finding a friend. Soon they stop trying to gain love and try only for what they know how to get—hostile attention. They actually work at being mean and annoying to parents and siblings, and to peers and teachers as well. In middle childhood, as the approval of teachers and peers becomes more important to them than ever before, their fear of others can lead such children into a vicious circle of hostility, isolation, and rejection.

By contrast, children who feel loved at home are not afraid to seek the esteem of teachers and playmates. They feel equal to the tasks that they must perform in order to win the approval of others. They develop a sense of industry in school and a capability for cooperation with peers.

Internal Control and Discipline

One particularly notable feature of children's personality that is closely related to warmth or hostility in the home is the extent of their internal control over how they act. Lack of internal control over behavior has been closely associated with parental rejection and punitiveness (Bronfenbrenner, 1961). A strong

The family remains the most important social influence on a school-age child.

correlation has also been found between aggression on the part of the child and parental rejection and punitiveness (McCord, McCord, & Howard, 1961).

There are a number of explanations for why severe punitiveness on the part of parents leads to a lack of control in the child. One explanation is that such children feel that everyone in their lives is potentially hostile, learn hostility as the normal way to get along in the world. Another theory (Bandura & Walters, 1963a) is that children tend to imitate their parents. Thus, if a parent shows direct physical aggression in punishing a child, the child will tend to adopt this aggressive behavior when dealing with peers or siblings. Furthermore, physical punishment and verbal abuse may make children sensitive to occasions for punishment, without teaching them what to do and what not to do in the absence of the punishing parent (Aronfreed, 1968).

Withdrawal of parental affection, on the other hand, produces an internal feeling of anxiety in children even when the parent is not physically present.

Children are motivated to change their behavior to reduce their anxiety and win back the parent's love. However, withdrawal of love or the threat of it is as much an assault on a child's self-esteem as physical punishment is an assault on a child's body. Such children are not learning self-control or being socialized toward desirable behavior; they are learning how to try to keep their parents' love. If children feel unloved by their parents in the first place, however, a withdrawal of the parent's affection will be nothing new; it will not be likely to teach them to control their behavior.

The emotional climate of the home also influences the degree of **autonomy** accorded children—that is, what sorts of matters they are allowed to decide for themselves. Parents can react to their children's growing ability to manage by themselves by giving them all the freedom they need, or they can stifle the children with too much control. By the age of eight years, for example, most children are able to decide for themselves what they should wear; they eat well and have considerable ability with personal hygiene and grooming (Gesell & Ilg, 1949). They may need occasional advice or reminders, but generally they are able to look out for themselves in these respects. When children are babied by their parents, however, they may not learn to do these things as rapidly as other children do; and if the parents insist on keeping a close watch over them and never allow them to try things for themselves and make mistakes, they may fail to develop a sense of independence and personal responsibility. If parents never let their children struggle for anything but always give them whatever they want, the children may have little reason to believe that what they do makes a difference in the world. They may never blame themselves for hurting a playmate or cheating in school (Bronfenbrenner, 1961).

As we have seen in Chapter 10, school-age children have a great respect for rules. For toddlers and preschool children the rules must be laid down by parents: never run in the street; you don't have to eat supper but you must finish your milk. By the time children have started school, they are capable of working out some of these rules with their parents. Thus, rules and the accompanying penalties can be arrived at in a democratic fashion. As children grow older, their participation in making and amending family rules can increase, but parents maintain the ultimate authority. However, the greater the participation of the entire family in rule-making and the perception by all that the rules are fair, the more likely the force of the rule over the child. Rules about diet (no candy or soft drinks), television watching (only before supper), going out in the evening (only on no-school nights), having children for supper (once a week for each child in the family), chores (set up a schedule), straighten rooms (before any TV) help to keep down arguments over specifics. But more important, rules offer guidelines for children; and set limits and encourage responsibility.

Social Learning

An interesting experiment in the development of autonomy and control and social learning is quite unrelated to modes of discipline and parental inter-

When a child learns to feel competent and self-confident within the family, it carries over into life outside the home.

vention. A team of researchers (Toner, Moore, & Ashley, 1978), having discovered that children show self-discipline after watching self-discipline modeled by another child on television, wondered what the effect might be on a child who was the model. They found that children who served as models in resisting the temptation to play with forbidden toys were able to refrain from playing with forbidden toys to a much greater extent than the children in the control group who did not serve as models. Apparently children learn control in many ways. Giving children responsibilities they can fulfill will usually instill in them a sense of maturity.

Fathers

If the 1950s was the "togetherness" decade, in which magazine articles and advertising emphasized the family that did things together, the 1980s may well be the decade of the reemergence of the father in family life. Two national trends seem to have focused on father power. The women's movement, as a part of its consciousness-raising, pointed to the unfairness of gender roles in the traditional paternalistic family: the mother carried almost the total burden of bringing up the children; the father, cold and distant, was too absorbed in work or other activities outside the home really to know his children. He was totally responsible for the economic support of the family. The other trend, the rising cost of living coming at a time when women are eager to find paying work or to embark on a career, has forced women in ever-increasing numbers out of the home and into the workplace. The result is that fathers also have to do their share to keep the household running—shopping, cooking, and taking care of children. The response of many fathers is a joyful affirmation of fatherhood. "It was the most incredible, wonderful, terrifically joyful, sexual, sensual, loving, time of our lives," wrote actor Donald Sutherland (1974) about the birth of his first child. Many men are discovering an added dimension to their lives as they participate in taking care of their own children.

The Twentieth-Century Nuclear Family

The nuclear family was an adaptation to city life, and as the family changed, the role of the father changed with it. Now the father left the family each day to work. The wife stayed home and took care of the children and kept house. He brought home the paycheck as his contribution to family life. Until recently it was the rare father who helped with child care or housework. Is this father superfluous to children's development? Not at all. Traditional fathers are socializing agents; they bring the values of the larger society into the home, preparing children, particularly their sons, to take their places in adult society. As the person who controls the family resources, the father exerts more force as the disciplinarian of last resort, backing up the mother in this role. (See Chapter 8 for a discussion of the influence of fathers in the development of gender behavior and identity.)

Michael Lamb (1979) suggests that the mother and father complement each other to such an extent that it is difficult to identify and quantify the unique influence of the father on his children. The father's role is redundant in an area in which redundancy—overlapping and reinforcing the mother's role—gives a greater assurance of success in this long-term task of bringing up children. Just as important to the welfare of the child is the indirect influence of the father in giving emotional support, encouragement, and appreciation to his wife in her performance as a mother. "An intimate relationship in which the mother is valued and cherished contributes to her feelings of self-esteem, happiness, and competence which influence her relationship with her children" (Hetherington, 1979).

The Nonstereotyped Father

The word is not yet in on the influence on children of the father who witnesses their birth, changes their diapers, cooks for the family, chauffeurs, shops, and generally shares household and child-care tasks with his wife. Today on the streets, in supermarkets, libraries and parks, outside schools, fathers are seen alone with their children. It is a new and refreshing combination. Some researchers are raising questions about the development of appropriate gender identity in the children of such men. Benjamin Spock in his book *Raising Your*

Child in a Difficult Time urges fathers to take an equal share in raising their children, not only to ease mothers' burdens but to show that they recognize the importance and worthiness of child care. One male researcher (DeFrain, 1978) says that "the benefits of childrearing are too great to be the sole possession of mothers."

Fathers with Working Wives

Most of the research on working women has centered on the mother-child relationship and on the question of what toll is paid by children whose mothers work outside the home. The father yet again becomes a nonentity in the family situation. However, the attitudes of the father toward working women, toward his own job, and toward child-rearing and his own family may be even more important than the attitudes and behavior of his working wife. Men bring to their marriages ideas about family life and the roles that they and their wives will play in their family. What combination of attitudes toward work and family priorities of husbands of wives who work makes for a happy marriage and a happy environment for children? One study of English husbands and their working wives (Bailyn, 1972) found that couples in which the primary life interest of the husband was his career while the wife's career was also important to her, are not happy. The most successful pattern that emerged was one in which the husband finds satisfaction in his work, has high ambitions, shares the household and child-rearing responsibilities with his wife, and has a high income. In addition, an inference can be made from the findings that it is not chiefly the success with which a working mother integrates her family and her work that makes for a successful marriage and, therefore, an environment for successful child-rearing; the key variable is whether the husband shares in family responsibilities and is happy with his own work.

Divorce

Once upon a time, at least in storybooks, every child had two parents who were married to each other, loved each other, and stayed together while the children grew to adulthood. In the United States today, however, an increasing number of families are not following the old scenario. One in every three marriages ends in divorce, and to repeat the startling statistic already mentioned: between 40 and 50 percent of American children born since 1970 will spend about six years in a single-parent family.

It was once believed that children were always better off if their parents stayed together no matter how much tension and conflict there was in the home, but few professionals today would agree with that. The general feeling now is that, while divorce is always upsetting to the child, the alternative is likely to be more stressful. No child can help being hurt by living for months or years in a home where parents are constantly fighting or icily ignoring each other, perhaps using the child as a weapon in their battles.

Working mothers, feeling the need to "compensate" for time taken away from their families, often spend more time in positive interaction with their children than nonworking mothers.

Nonetheless, divorce is hard on children, just as it is on their parents, and for some of the same reasons. There is the emotional turmoil that always, in some measure, precedes the divorce. There are usually problems of living in a home with only one parent afterward and often, later, the problems of building a relationship with a new stepparent.

And the divorce itself is a problem, for under ordinary circumstances the family is the most basic, rock-bottom point of stability in children's lives. It is the framework within which they have lived since birth, the central core of their world. Even the self-identity of each child is defined in relation to the family. Thus, when the family breaks up, the very foundations of their world are knocked loose. Like a person caught in an earthquake, they find the earth itself shaking under their feet.

Sequences in a Divorce

Rather than viewing a divorce as a single event in a child's life, it is more helpful to see it from the child's point of view as a sequence of experiences (Hetherington, 1979). The transition may start with the child living in a family situation marked by discord and hostility. The actual break for children occurs

Working Mothers

Today the mother who is at home when the children come in after school is almost the exception. The working mother is the norm. Lois Hoffman (1979) recently reviewed the status of working mothers and found that all is well with children whose mothers work outside the home.

Infancy is the most controversial time for a mother to work. Burton White (1975), Selma Fraiberg (1977), and others stress the importance of the mother to the infant. The first two years of life are so important, they say, in terms of attachment and cognitive and emotional development that the mother should make every effort to stay home with her child. Hoffman, on the other hand, makes a case for the working mother. The studies, she says, show that infants need reciprocal interaction, verbal stimulation, visual experience, and reward contingencies. Most infants of working mothers, she points out, are cared for in their own homes. There is no reason why the caregiver must be the mother. As for attachment, there is also no evidence that multiple attachments interfere with the attachment of baby to mother.

As children get older and reach nursery school age, the picture is clearer. Gold and her colleagues (1979) compared four-year-old, middle-class children whose mothers had worked since they were born, to equivalent children of nonworking mothers. The children of the working mothers showed a better social adjustment. Studies of school-age children are even stronger in their affirmation of working mothers. Children of working mothers are more likely to share in household responsibilities, giving them an opportunity to develop a sense of responsibility, independence, and competence. Working mothers, especially in working-class homes and one-parent families, are more likely to have rules that encourage consistency in discipline and set limits (Hoffman, 1974).

The benefits to adolescents of a mother who works are the strongest of all. Recent studies show that working mothers of adolescents are more apt to encourage independence in their offspring. In one study (Gold & Andres, 1978), adolescents with mothers who worked showed a significant difference in their sense of self-worth, social adjustment, and a feeling of belonging, as compared to adolescents whose mothers were not employed outside the home. The pattern for girls is especially clear. The adolescent daughters of women who worked are more outgoing, independent, active, highly motivated, have a higher academic achievement, and score higher on scales of personality and social adjustment.

Having a working mother, according to the research, then, is salutory for children. However, a caution is in order. Children need and are entitled to adequate parenting, whether it be performed by a mother, father, grandmother, or hired helper. Furthermore, working does not automatically confer superior characteristics on the child of the working mother. Those advantages to children of mothers who work outside the home that show up in the research are, for the most part, a direct result of the active efforts of working parents to compensate for the mothering denied their children because of their commitments outside the home.

Although most children can cope with the immediate crisis of divorce, feelings of anger, fear, depression, and guilt must be dealt with.

when they find themselves living with just one parent. In only 10 percent of the cases will it be with the father. The likelihood is that the children will be living with a distraught mother trying to cope simultaneously with a drastically reduced income, with problems of finding work if she doesn't have a job, and with the responsibility of the sole care of her children. The children at this point are experiencing their own sense of loss. Most respond with anger, fear, depression, and guilt. It is usually not until after the first year that the distress following divorce eases and a sense of well-being begins to emerge for the child. "Almost all children experience the transition of divorce as painful" (Hetherington, 1979). Later, perhaps five years later, the child will probably have to accommodate to a stepparent.

Most children can cope with the immediate crisis of divorce. Their long-term response depends on such variables as the age and sex of the child, past experiences, temperament, plus the success with which the parent they live with copes with their individual problems. Not only are poor families more likely to divorce, but the divorce will probably bring a greater hardship for the children. Although the standard of living in middle-class families is likely to be much lower after a divorce, if a mother wants to work and makes adequate provisions for the care of her children, the long-term effects will be positive for both her and her children.

During the crisis period surrounding a divorce the children are frequently dragged into the conflict between the two parents. Each parent may try to enlist the child's loyalties in an attempt to form a hostile alliance against the other parent. Most children want to keep both their parents, but conflict offers an opportunity for a child to play one parent against the other (Tessman, 1978). In the year following a divorce children, especially boys, evidence more problems than do children in those intact families characterized by fighting and hostility.

Not only do young children have only a hazy idea of what is happening, but they are more directly dependent on the parents, and so they will respond differently from older children. They may distort the situation in their own minds. It is not unlikely that young children will blame themselves for the divorce, just as they often blame themselves for the death of a parent. They may feel that it was something they did—an act of disobedience or misbehavior—that caused the parents to divorce. Young children may exaggerate the likelihood of a reconciliation as well as the feeling that they will be abandoned.

Fathers

Although fathers tend to see as much if not more of their children immediately following the divorce, most divorced fathers rapidly tend to see less and less of their children. Fathers are more likely to keep up their relationships with sons than with daughters. The best adjustments of children tend to be associated with frequent visits with a father who is readily accessible to his children. "A mutually supportive relationship and involvement of the father with the child is the most effective support system for divorced women in their parenting and for their children" (Hetherington, 1979). For parents embroiled in the emotional turmoil of a divorce to reach an agreement concerning the raising of their children might seem like an impossible task, but many couples are able to put the welfare of their children above their own differences.

Today there is a very small (one percent of all family living arrangements) but growing trend toward joint custody in which husband and wife, though divorced, share the responsibility for their children (Roman & Haddad, 1978). In some cases the arrangement is half a week with one parent and half with the other, or one whole week with one parent and one with the other. Obviously, the parents must live in the same school district and, more important, must be involved with one another perhaps more than they would like in the mutual day-to-day planning for their child. In view of the prevalence of divorce it may be that joint custody, by maintaining the family structure in reorganized form, resolves such problems as the banishing of the father, the heavy burden placed on the mother, and especially gives children their birthright of two parents who love them and place the highest priority on their welfare.

Stepfamilies

Almost as big an adjustment for a child as divorce is a parent's remarriage. Suddenly the child finds herself with a "mother" who is not her real mother, or a "father" who is not her real father. A whole new relationship has to be built with this person, this stepparent who has walked into her life.

Stepmothers in fairy tales are always like Cinderella's, wicked and cruel. In real life, of course, stepparents are generally decent human beings who really want to love their new spouse's children, and to be loved by them. With understanding and patience they are likely to succeed. But they do face some problems on the way.

Some of these problems are on the child's side. In the breakup of her real parents' marriage, she has lost something sure and dependable, and her basic trust in others may have been shaken. Therefore she may be afraid to invest very much of herself in a new relationship. Whether she expresses the thought to herself or not, she may feel, "I loved Daddy, and he went away. If I love Tom, maybe he'll go away too, and I'll get hurt all over again."

At the same time, the child may resent having to share her real parent with a comparative stranger. Most particularly, she may resent any exercise of authority by the stepparent. "You're not the one to tell me what to do!" she may shout, or "This isn't your house, it's Mommy's!" when her stepfather tells her to take her feet off the coffee table or pick up her toys.

For an older child, sexual feelings may complicate the picture. A stepfather may be felt as a boy's rival for the mother's affection; a girl may unconsciously be attracted to her stepfather more as a man than as a parent. A stepmother may excite the same feelings in reverse. And the stepparent may feel the same way about the child. If the newly created family is to survive, such feelings must, of course, be resisted. But the feelings themselves do not show that anyone is evil or perverted. It is simply that, whereas true parents and their children learn from the start not to perceive each other in sexual (rather than gender) terms, there has been no such conditioning for steprelatives.

Death in the Family

Death is extremely difficult for children to understand. Some schoolchildren who still use preoperational modes of thought think that a dead person or animal can be brought back to life. In middle childhood children may be concerned about their parents dying. One eight-year-old asked her father, after they had experienced a near-accident in the car, "Daddy, if you get killed, who will take me home?"

Comprehending Death

Three stages in the full comprehension of death as adults view it were identified in a recent study (Kane, 1979). All of the children from ages three to twelve recognized death as a concept. In the youngest stage children tend to see death as a particular position—that is, lying down. Their thinking about death is both egocentric and magical. Thus, they can, they think, make someone dead by their behavior, their wish, or by a label ("he's dead"). In the second stage, beginning at ages seven and eight, death is specific and concrete. Death implies dysfunction. The dead can neither eat nor speak. Older children

An adult's explanation of death to children should be truthful to prevent misconceptions.

are more subtle: the dead cannot smell flowers, dream, or know they are dead. By age ten, in the third stage, death becomes a definition. Inactivity, dysfunctionality, and insensitivity characterize death. "Responsiveness is not just a characteristic of life, it is a requirement" (Kane, 1979).

Telling Children

Most adults fear death and are uncomfortable in its presence. They may react by trying to shield a child from the hard facts of death. Adults may find themselves unable to handle the questions children ask when a loved one dies. Answers such as "Daddy's gone away" only lead to additional questions: "Where did Daddy go? Why did he have to leave?" It is also a mistake to explain it in terms of sleep. Children who are told that dying is like going to sleep may fear that they too may not wake up if they go to sleep. Adults should make it clear that death, unlike sleep, is permanent and irrevocable. It is advisable that the explanation be truthful, but it need not be complete. Parents can also promise further explanations when a child is older if the conversation becomes bizarre or macabre.

Adults who must explain death to a child, particularly the death of a person close to the child, must confront their own feelings first. "Only if they are prepared to explore their own feelings and anxieties can they help a child to cope with separation, loss, and death" (Parness, 1975).

It is not uncommon for children to blame themselves for the death of a parent. Unable to understand what has happened, many children wonder if it was something they did wrong that made the parent go away. Alternatively, some may transfer their feelings of guilt to the surviving parent: Why didn't Mommy make Daddy stay? Why didn't Mommy die instead? Who will be next? Me?

Mourning

Several studies have shown that, in general, children who have lost a parent are more likely to experience difficulties than those who have not. One study

(Brown, 1961) found that children who lost either a mother or a father between the ages of five and fourteen had a much greater chance of becoming depressive later in life than those who had both parents. An explanation for such correlations has been proposed by John Bowlby (1967) in an article on childhood mourning. According to Bowlby a child is less capable of dealing with the loss of a parent than an older person might be. Normally, whenever we experience the loss of a loved one, we go through a mourning period in which we try to recover the lost person and feel angry at the lost person for leaving us. Then, finally, the mourning process runs its course, and we face up to the reality of the loss. Children, too, should not be denied their right to mourn. They may express mourning by regressing in their behavior to more childish ways, by showing a clinging dependency, or by repressing their feelings altogether. Or they may not go through the whole process because the feelings are too severe. Instead, they either repress the feelings or displace them on other objects.

Probably the most important factor in a child's adjustment to the death of a parent is the attitude and emotional response to the surviving parent. Children's confusion can only be intensified when, for example, their mother pretends during the day that everything is all right, but cries herself to sleep at night. The parent who does not openly share grief does the child a disservice. By isolating children the survivor deprives them of the parent whom they so desperately need at this time.

Single-Parent Families

The general public as well as the helping professions tend to view the single-parent family as somehow deviant, even pathological. Yet the so-called normal family of husband, wife, and children accounts for only 45 percent of American families (Sussman cited in Schorr & Moen, 1979). Single-parent families and husbands and wives without children each account for 15 percent of family arrangements. Other statistics show that the number of divorced women heading families tripled from 1960 to 1975 and that the number of children living in one-parent families increased 60 percent between 1970 and 1980.

In addition to divorced men and women, single-parent families are headed by widowed men and women and unmarried mothers. Widowed women receive social-security benefits for their children and tend to be better off financially than the other groups. The unmarried mothers, most of whom are very young and have few marketable skills, tend to have the most serious financial difficulties. A problem for women who head single-parent families is the fact that at every level of work women are paid only 60 percent of what men are paid (U.S. Department of Labor, 1976). With divorce the standard of living of a female-headed family is reduced. The income of those few men who head single-parent families is twice as high as their female counterparts. Yet both single mothers and single fathers report feelings of success and satisfaction about parenting. Women, even though they have less money than before their divorce, feel they are better off financially because they have control over the family income (Schorr & Moen, 1979).

Unmarried Mothers

Not only are more children today going through the experience of losing a parent, but more are growing up without ever having had more than one—to live with, at any rate. Formerly most people took it for granted that unmarried mothers would give up their children for adoption, but today more and more are choosing to keep them. Some are even deliberately seeking to have children without marrying. Also, more and more single women and men are adopting children.

How is the child affected by having only one parent? The answer seems to depend on the parent's motivation for remaining single. One study (Klein, 1973) found that women who become pregnant outside of marriage and decide to bear and keep their children often are motivated by their own unresolved psychological problems. When this is the case, they are likely to find that parenthood only complicates their problems. A pregnancy that results from a need for love, a desire to be punished, or competition with one's mother can only lead to disaster for both the new mother and the child. At the same time there are single women who are psychologically mature and can handle the many problems of parenthood outside of marriage. These women probably have as likely a chance of being good mothers as married women do.

Child Care

On a practical level, of course, single parenthood usually means that someone else—a relative, housekeeper, or day-care center—must be found to care for the child while the parent works. Despite the public image that children of working parents spend the bulk of their time in overcrowded institutional settings, the facts are otherwise. About 90 percent of children are likely to be cared for by relatives, neighbors, or friends. Single parents prefer to leave their children in an informal setting. "A modern view regards substitute care as a supplement to maternal care rather than as a substitute for it" (Schorr & Moen, 1979). Actually, for the child to spend time outside the home on a regular basis may be a broadening influence, easing the too intense bond that might be created between a child and a single parent. However, as we have seen with working women who are married, the most successful arrangements are those in which the father shares in child-care responsibilities, again pointing to the advantages of joint custody in divorce settlements.

The most difficult aspect of the single-parent arrangement is the lack of someone else to carry the burden, at least once in a while. The single parent must juggle work, housekeeping, and time with his or her children—creating an enormous strain. Lacking, too, is the emotional support provided by a spouse. Such parents may feel a sense of isolation without adult company. Feelings of rejection and depression are only too readily transmitted to children. Such feelings can become a major problem for single parents.

Children in Single-Parent Families

The absence of a parent, for whatever reason, creates a special family situation and may have important consequences for a child's social adjustment. If the home has been broken by death or marital discord, the child may, as we have seen, feel isolated, rejected, or abandoned. On the other hand, if there has been a relatively amicable divorce, the child will probably maintain contact with both parents, and any sense of dislocation will be less severe.

How is a child's personality development affected by growing up without parents of both sexes? Some studies have shown that boys without fathers at home have trouble establishing a secure masculine identity of their own and relating to women in later life. They seem more likely to become delinquents. However, most of these studies did not take sufficient account of the reason for the father's absence, the financial and social status of the family, and other conditions that would probably contribute to a boy's emotional growth (Biller, 1970).

But these problems are not inevitable. A mature parent who is secure in his or her own identity can supply many of the qualities ordinarily associated with the other parent. Just as a man can be tender and nurturant without losing his masculinity, so a woman can be authoritative and challenging without becoming unpleasantly mannish. After all, many children in two-parent homes do not have a really satisfactory relationship with both parents. Thus it seems reasonable to suppose that healthy childhood development depends not so much on how many parents a child has as on the quality of the family relationship.

One thing that can be helpful to the child in a single-parent family is the chance for close relationships with adults of the other sex outside the family. For this reason the growing trend toward male teachers in kindergarten and the primary grades may be very valuable. A warm, friendly, admired male teacher can serve as an excellent role model for a six- or seven-year-old who has no father at home.

Social Networks

An important resource for both single parents and children is the informal social network of relatives, neighbors, and friends of which they may form a part (Cochran & Brassard, 1979). In our description of the friendship of Steve and Nathan in the introduction to this chapter we can see a social network and its advantages in action. Each of the boys has access to relationships outside the family. In a divorce situation such friendships as well as the relationship established between the boys and each others' parents become a source of emotional support. For single parents social networks can provide material support as well. Single parents can share child care, personal problems, information about jobs and housing, and leisure time. The availability of support from friends, neighbors, and relatives was found to be positively related to the mother's effectiveness in interacting with her preschool child (Hetherington, cited in Cochran & Brassard, 1979). Friendly adults play with children in a different manner from parents and make a child familiar with a broader range of patterns of interactions. Within the black community extensive social networks serve as a primary source of child-care arrangements and become a major source of stability for the economically disadvantaged black family.

The quality of the relationship between parent and child may be more important than the presence of both parents.

Adoption

What happens to the children their parents do not want? Not long ago many were sheltered in orphanages, given a little education, and trained to earn their living in domestic service or other low-paid labor. If they were overlooked by the institutional arrangements (or evaded them), they might roam the streets, sleeping in abandoned buildings, begging, stealing, fighting, and scrounging for the necessities of life. Even today every major city has such "wild children," and where poverty is severe there may be many of them. It was partly the vast increase in the numbers of homeless children in Europe after World War I that led to the modern attitude toward adoption.

Adoption itself, of course, has been practiced at least from the time when Moses was adopted by Pharaoh's daughter. But until fairly recently it served mainly the interests of the adopters. If a man had no sons, for example, he might adopt a neighbor's boy to carry on his family name and inherit his property. Only in the last century or so has adoption also been used to give a normal family life to a child who would not have it otherwise.

Most adoptive parents today would say that they wanted a son or daughter both for their own sake and for the child's. Some couples want children but cannot have them naturally; others start with the idea of helping unfortunate children, such as the handicapped or the orphaned. Whatever the adoptive parents say about their motives, the institution handling the adoption takes great pains to ensure the child's welfare.

The majority of adoptions are handled through state and private agencies. The agency matches available children and would-be parents, checking carefully on background, health, and general suitability. It also sees that the legal formalities are fulfilled. One can adopt a child through a private lawyer or even by direct arrangement with the natural mother or other guardian, but this not only risks legal trouble but also the possibility that some birth defect or congenital disease has been overlooked.

Siblings

Brothers and sisters, whether natural or adopted, are the child's first peers. Children learn much from interactions with their siblings and from observation of their parents' responses to the siblings' behavior. Often they generalize this information to their relationships with teachers and schoolmates.

In many families, large ones especially, siblings are classified by the family into distinct types. One child in the family, according to some researchers (Bossard and Boll, 1960), may be identified as the responsible child, "the one that is looked up to, the one that assumes direction or supervision of the other siblings, or renders service to them." The researchers have also found seven other types frequently reported by siblings themselves. The responsible child is usually the first-born sibling; the second-born is often labeled the popular or social one. The eldest having claimed the position of power and responsibility, the second-born often tries to gain recognition through likability. Another type is the social butterfly, who tries to gain recognition outside the family. This sibling may be third, fourth, or fifth in birth order. The fourth type (but not necessarily the fourth-born) is the serious sort, who tries to gain recognition through doing well in school. The fifth type is the asocial or even stubbornly antisocial one, who withdraws from competition in the family. This child may spend a lot of time away from home and refuse to participate in family activities; unlike the social butterfly, however, this child does not necessarily seek recognition outside the family. The sixth type of sibling also withdraws from the family but in a different way: instead of absenting themselves physically, these children simply avoid the responsibilities that all the others accept. They will be reluctant to clean up around the house and at

❖❖

What Should Adopted Children Know

All authorities agree that adopted children should be informed that they are adopted. However, the time of the first "telling" and what should be told have been suggested only in the most general terms, accompanied by the caution that the matter should not then be hidden away but discussed from time to time as appropriate. Most experts suggest telling children at an early age, around two or three, but no later than four years of age (Mech, 1973). Recent research calls attention to the fact that preschoolers scarcely understand the concepts involved in adoption (Brodzinsky et al., 1981a, 1981b). They have only the dimmest understanding of the birth process itself, let alone what might be involved in adoption. And only by early to middle adolescence do individuals understand the motives for adoption and the legal processes involved. The authors of this study stress that the content of discussion about adoption should take into account children's intellectual capacities.

In many cases adopted children will eventually want to know something about their natural parents. Adoptive parents should not be hurt when this happens. The child is probably not rejecting their love and care but he simply needs to know who he is, biologically as well as culturally, to help establish an independent identity.

In view of the fact that adopted children are seen proportionately more than other children by psychotherapists, it has been recommended that both adopted children and their adoptive parents be permitted, if they so desire, to try to make contact with the biological parents of the child (Derdeyn, 1979). Adoptive parents sometimes fantasize about the behavior and personalities of the biological parents of their child. Children, even more so, are likely to spin fantasies about their biological parents. For example, a twelve-year-old girl in a bitter fight with her adopted parents thought she would fare better with her biological mother. Visitation may provide means for the child and the adoptive parents to test their fantasies against reality. For adopted children it also provides that sense of continuity with their own past that they may feel is missing. However, the courts tend to be reluctant to open the sealed records involved in adoption. Some countries, however, have a policy of open records once the child has reached legal age. In the United States a few states also allow children of legal age to obtain information about their biological parents.

The policy of sealed records in adoption cases serves to protect the parents and the adopted child from a change of heart on the part of the biological parents. The biological mother, for example, might demand to have her child back. It also makes the arrangement a more permanent one psychologically for the adoptive parents: they cannot change their minds either. The children, too, may more readily accept their adopted parents when there is no possibility of any others. Rather than the mystery involved in completely sealed records, an alternative arrangement might be that cultural and medical information concerning the biological parents be made available to adopted children when they reach maturity. Another arrangement might be the registration of biological parents and adopted children. When an adopted child reaches maturity, the records would be made available if all three parties want to make contact with each other—the child, the adopted parents, and the biological parents (Sorosky, Baran, & Pannor, 1979).

The nature of the relationship between siblings is a permanent one—they belong to each other, and in time of need they will be there.

times will not even hear when requests are made of them. The seventh type is the one who is chronically ill, has physical defects, or is a hypochondriac. Often these children learn to utilize their physical problems as a means of getting favor or attention.

In contrast to the sibling, only children do not need to compete with other children for parental recognition. However, they are more dependent on their parents for recognition than are children with brothers or sisters. Like first-born children, only children are achievers and tend to have high self-esteem. There is more to sibling influence than just birth order (Sutton-Smith & Rosenberg, 1970). In order to assess the influence of being a sibling on a person's development, it is also necessary to take account of the sex of all concerned and of the number of years separating one sibling from the next. A consistent finding is that first-born girls tend to be affiliative in stressful situations; that is, they will seek to be with other people in the face of a frightening or ambiguous task (Schachter, 1959; Kushnir, 1978).

Sibling Relationships

In any family with more than one child squabbles, teasing, and serious hitting between siblings may be a constant state of affairs. When an older, larger child takes it out on a younger, smaller sibling, parents may become uncomfortable and even outraged. Although sibling rivalry is usually considered natural, it doesn't occur in all families and all cultures. Parents should intervene, but in what way? Certainly, for the much older and much larger parent to pick on the offending child will not change the situation. Lillian Katz (1979) suggests that parents stop a fight immediately in whatever way they can. Then they can look at the possible causes and deal with them. Rivalry is usually caused by a scarcity—be it affection, praise, recognition. A parent might regularly spend a little time alone with a child who seems to feel neglected, in his favorite pastime. Treating each child in the same fashion may be equitable but not effective. Different children need different kinds of attention. When a child says really nasty things about a sibling, it may be the time to remind children that brothers and sisters are permanent, even if not chosen, lifetime companions. They belong to each other. And in time of need they will be there to help.

THE PEER GROUP

Many types of peer groups form during middle childhood. In school groups are chosen for various activities; out of school neighborhood groups roam the streets and coalesce in rumpus rooms and backyards. Formally organized groups are brought together for Little League, Scouts, and dancing, art, and music lessons.

But whether the groups are formal or informal, most of them are composed of members of the same sex, particularly when children are six to ten years old. Boys' groups tease girls' groups, and girls' groups pointedly ignore boys' groups. Sometimes a group of boys make war on a group of girls. Perhaps children at this stage are making sure of their sex-role identities by rejecting the opposite sex and engaging only in activities that they see as typical for their own sex. Whether this polarization will continue in force if sexual stereotypes break down in our culture cannot be foreseen.

Informal peer groups in middle childhood, boys' and girls' alike, often have leaders, a code of their own, and a set of values and norms. As a group, the peer group differs from the family in several interesting ways. The family, for example, has institutional authority—that is, society at large and even the law courts recognize the obligations of members of their families—whereas the peer group does not. In the family, moreover, there is a wide difference in the power of various members, much more than that between a peer group leader and the lowliest member. Another contrast is that family membership is obligatory, peer group membership voluntary. And finally, the emotional investments in a family are few but highly intense; in a peer group emotional investments are usually more numerous and less intense.

Group Norms

What happens when two groups of boys are formed at summer camp by putting them in separate living quarters? In only five days each group takes a name and establishes a code of behavior and a system of punishment. The boys in the two groups may share some activities, but friendships will develop only within the living quarters (Sherif & Sherif, 1953). Such patterns can be studied with considerable precision when the investigators use *sociometry*— a technique for plotting mutual attractions and rejections in a group.

Norms spring up rapidly in groups of school-age children because they are making major gains in their ability to understand rules. They realize that they are not simply "there"—handed down by tradition or adult authority— but that people make rules and can change them if they wish. Because it is a new discovery, it is exciting for children to develop their own rules in co-operation with their peers.

The development of norms seems to be stimulated by other factors as well. In the experiment known as Robber's Cave (Sherif et al., 1961) twenty-two fifth-grade boys were divided into two groups at camp, but neither group knew of the other's presence. Norms did develop in each group, but they multiplied and became much stronger after the groups' "accidentally" discovered each other. Perhaps peer groups establish norms in order to create an identity for the group members and distinguish them from outsiders. This explanation might also apply to the exclusiveness of boys' and girls' groups.

Solidarity against Grownups

One of the most obvious features of peer groups in middle childhood is their independence from adults. The extent to which children will resist adult values and authority varies a great deal. One extreme is that of the gang, a peer group in which the norms of the group stand in opposition to adult authority and call for pranks or illegal and dangerous acts. Members are often required, sometimes as an initiation, to engage in misconduct, and if they refuse to do so, they are ostracized.

In some instances youngsters are forced into a gang and threatened with harm if they try to stay out. Once they are in, however, they gain a feeling of protection, even of security and identity (Alexander, 1964). Whether or not preadolescents join a gang depends, of course, on many factors. One is the extent to which they identify with their parents and other adults. Children who have strong connections with groups may have the inner strength to resist the pressures of the gang. If they come from a home that is inadequate in some way, however, or if they live in a dangerous, gang-ridden neighborhood, the pressures from peers will probably be harder to resist.

Fortunately, gang behavior is the exception rather than the rule for most preadolescents. Extreme resistance to adult authority is not typical of most youngsters. Studies have shown that conformity to peer influences in six- to eight-year-olds were actually positively correlated with conformity to adult influence as well (Crandall et al., 1958). The influence of peers, according to a recent study (Bixenstine, DeCorte, & Bixenstine, 1978), increases greatly through eighth grade, especially in regard to antisocial behavior. But this is not accompanied by a decrease in parental influence, especially of the mother. This would indicate that a sort of general conformity may make children susceptible to both peer and adult influence. Apparently children in grade school are able to keep their world outside the home separate from their world of home and parents—perhaps, as Berndt (1979) suggests, by not discussing their friends with their parents. However, the children who are most influenced by their parents are best able to resist their friends' pressure toward antisocial behavior.

Another study (Harris & Tseng, 1957) surveyed children of a wide range of ages and found generally positive attitudes toward both peers and adults. The study also discovered a slight decrease in positive attitudes toward parents during middle childhood, which might be the result of increased peer identification or of seeing parents more realistically, not as superhuman beings. Other researchers (Witryol & Calkins, 1958) have found an increase from fourth- to fifth-grade age groups in children's agreement with dares or challenges to adult authority. From the research done so far, therefore, it would be difficult to draw conclusions about the extent to which peer groups in middle childhood form alliances against adults.

Status in the Group

Status is the relative standing of an individual in a group—the dimension of peer acceptance or rejection and peer approval or disapproval. Those who are highly accepted and approved by their peers are said to have high status, and those with low acceptance and approval are said to have low status.

Not surprisingly, studies have found that children who like their peers are liked by them. Acceptance was found to be associated with friendliness and an outgoing character (Bonney & Powell, 1953), with kindness as perceived by others (Smith, 1950), and with lack of withdrawal (Winder & Rau, 1962). Another study (Campbell & Yarrow, 1961) showed that popular children tended to be more sensitive to others' motives than did unpopular children. The popular children were able to make complicated inferences about why various peers did certain things. Leaders especially were found to be very attuned to others' feelings and actions. Although high sociability is generally associated with acceptance, at least one study (Elkins, 1958) indicates that for twelve- to fifteen-year-olds, low sociability is not a usual reason for rejection by peers. High-status or dominant children are more likely to imitate other children and be imitated (Abramovitch & Grusec, 1978). A possible explanation given by the researchers is that higher-status children with greater social skills may understand that imitation is a form of flattery and ingratiation. On the other hand a lower-status child tends to imitate the more popular children because they may be seen as reliable sources of information for what is appropriate and interesting behavior. Boys imitate and are imitated more than girls.

Another factor in acceptance is children's correct perception of their own status. Research (Goslin, 1962) has found that unpopular children show a wider discrepancy between their self-ratings and the ratings given to them by others in the group. These children also differed from the group in their rating of others. Thus, it would seem that sensitivity to status within the group does have a relation to popularity.

One possible explanation of why sensitivity to status brings popularity is that a child who is sensitive to many aspects of other people, including their status, can easily take their roles and thus will be well liked. Children who are less skilled at role-taking would be less liked and would interact less with peers.

If it is true that role-taking, which is largely a cognitive ability, is associated with peer acceptance, then other cognitive traits might also be related to popularity. Many studies have been made of the relationship between popularity and IQ, and almost all of them found a positive relationship between the two.

Socialization and Peers

The process of socialization of children that begins in the home with parents and siblings is carried on by peers. Within the peer group the child learns what is acceptable to others and what is not. Social learning plays an important part in socialization. The example of other children in subtle ways influences children to conform to group values. In one study of social learning (Toner, Parke, & Yussen, 1978) second- and third-grade boys watched a child on television resist the temptation to play with attractive but forbidden toys. The children who were exposed to the model were themselves able to resist playing with forbidden toys to a significantly greater degree than the children in the control situation who did not observe the televised model. By observing another child conform to a rule ("Do not touch the toys on that table"), children were better able to exert self-control and conform to the same rule.

Many studies have been made of the ways in which peer groups influence their members and of the ways in which the members are prone to influence. A classic study (Berenda, 1950) that measured the extent to which children of different ages conform to false judgments when pressure is exerted on them by peers found that they conform most often when the pressure is exerted by peers whom they believe to be very competent.

Other studies (McConnell, 1963; Bixenstine, DeCorte, & Bixenstine, 1978) have supported the theory that conformity is at its highest during middle childhood. One explanation for such findings is provided by the theory of Piaget, who maintains that in the middle years children become much better at grasping rules and taking the role of the other. They can step outside their own limited viewpoint, see many aspects of a situation including the views of others, and try out various solutions to a problem. These developments make a child more susceptible to outside influence. This may change in the adolescent years, when because of greater experience and a better mental grasp, an individual becomes freer to range through many theoretical possibilities. Situational factors, including suggestion by peers, may have less influence then.

Among the other variables that have been studied in connection with conformity are IQ, sex, and such group factors as the size of the group exerting pressure and the perceived competence and attractiveness of the group or person influencing the individual. No significant correlations between IQ and

Peer group influence is especially strong during middle childhood. Children must learn when to conform to social rules and when to pursue their own goals.

conformity have been found for children in the middle years. This finding conflicts with the widely held common-sense belief that more intelligent children are necessarily more independent than less intelligent children. On the variable of sex, it has been found in some studies that girls in middle childhood are more conforming than boys (Iscoe et al., 1963). However, boys are more influenced by their peers in regard to antisocial situations.

With respect to the variable of group size a study (Hare, 1953) has shown that members of a group tend to form a consensus more easily when the group is small. On the question of the status or attractiveness of the source of influence a researcher (Gelfand, 1962) found that children are more conforming to peers whom they perceive as being more competent than themselves. Another study (Harvey & Rutherford, 1957) established that children who found themselves agreeing with low-status peers and disagreeing with high-status peers tended to shift their opinions more often than children who agreed with high-status peers and disagreed with low-status peers.

Friendship

As with Steve and Nathan at the opening of this chapter, middle childhood is a time when children form their first close friendships. For the first time they discover that there is another person in the world quite like themselves with the same interests, the same problems with family and school, the same

A formal peer group whose norms are imposed by adults. In this group, clothes, band instruments, and style of marching are all rigidly controlled.

values, attitudes, and opinions. On what basis are friendships made? Age and sex are important in middle childhood, and so is proximity—living in the same neighborhood. The school is an important setting for friendship. In a study that upsets our preconceptions about the desirability of small classes it is suggested that large classes facilitate the formation of friendships (Hallinan, 1979). Children in large classes have more best friends, but there were fewer cross-sex and cross-racial friendships in large classes. One reason for the greater number of friendships in large classes is the larger number of children from whom to choose friends and the greater likelihood of children finding compatible friends. Proximity is another reason: children may be assigned a seat near someone whom they would not have thought of as a friend.

We might ask, for example, whether status influences children in their choice of close friends. One study (Sells & Roff, 1967) found no significant correlation of the status of the choosers and the chosen, but another study (Tagiuri, Kogan, & Long, 1958), this one of boys in a private school, found that in choices of roommates there was a similarity in status between chooser and chosen. Are friends made on the basis of similar personalities, or do opposites attract? One investigation (Davitz, 1955) showed that children see the person they choose for a friend as having the same characteristics that they believe themselves to have. However, when similarity was independently assessed, the person children liked most was not really more similar to them than the person they liked least. Such a finding would lead to the suggestion that children do not choose friends on the grounds of similarity, they perceive others as similar because they are friends.

Racial Awareness and Prejudice

Children may be quite conscious of racial differences without being prejudiced. The awareness of racial differences begins as early as age four, regardless of whether the children are reared in an integrated or a segregated environment. The development of racial prejudice—the feeling that one race is inferior or superior—depends on many factors.

Racial prejudice in the home, even if unspoken, has an undoubted effect on the child. If white parents shun blacks or members of other minorities at school events or public meetings, it will not escape their children. Some psychiatrists (Poussaint & Comer, 1972) recommend that parents be honest with their children about any racist feelings they might have and discuss them openly. In this way parents may become better aware of their own attitudes, and children will be able to think about them rationally.

Another source of prejudice in children is exposure to racism in the attitudes of other children, adults other than their parents, and books, magazines, and newspapers. It is impossible to shield children from these influences, but parents can deal with them by talking about them openly as the child comes across them.

As long as racial prejudice exists in many children, we should try to understand its effects. According to several studies (Clark & Clark, 1947; Morland, 1958) black children's race awareness is accompanied by preference for the white race and ambivalence toward their own race. With the rise of movements for blacks and other minority groups, it is to be hoped that self-disparagement on the part of members of these groups may be decreasing. Since the original study by the Clarks there have been several contradictory studies (Banks, 1976; Gregor & McPherson, 1966; Harris & Braun, 1971). At the very least these social movements have provided more positive attitudes for minority children toward themselves. To the extent that their homes and schools foster racial pride, it seems that minority children may be able to feel better about themselves and their racial heritage.

THE SCHOOL

Children who have spent most of their time within the family find themselves in a very different setting when they start school. In the family the ratio of adults to children is usually about one to one or two, whereas in the classroom it is about one to twenty-five. School and family differ in composition, too: the classroom adult is usually a woman, while the family has one woman and one man. The classroom children are all the same age; in the family the children are different ages. The duration of a class at school is about nine months, where family relationships (at least for the children) are lifelong. The basis of acceptance in school is performance; the family usually accepts the child "as is." Finally, the school setting is by nature public, while the family setting is private.

Everyone knows that the function of school is to transmit skills that the future citizens will find valuable. But what many people do not realize is that school, like most other large institutions, serves a variety of other functions as well. For example, school also channels or selects some children for preferential rewards in society and deselects others. And all the while school serves a custodial function: it keeps children off the street and out of the labor market.

Perhaps more important than any of these functions, however, is the school's function as an agent of socialization. At home children learn their parents' values, which may be idiosyncratic or representative of some culture other than the dominant culture. School provides a corrective to these parental values, or at least a rival set of values that the children know they must recognize if not accept. This is most useful, of course, to immigrant children, who might otherwise have difficulty understanding the values of the dominant culture. But all children, native no less than immigrant, need to learn the norms and behavior approved by society at large, and school is a particularly good place to do so. First, much of the subject matter of classroom instruction has a socializing effect in one way or another. And second, school provides powerful adult models (the teachers) and peer models for emulation.

School has an enormous influence on children's personality in other ways as well. It can show them the need for discipline and give them the joy of accomplishment. Unfortunately, it can also shake some children's self-confidence and give them an inferior image of themselves. There are many variables that affect success or failure in schooling, and a great deal has been written about each of them. Two factors that are currently under intense discussion are teaching methods and the personalities of teachers.

Teaching Methods

One broad approach to directing teaching methods regards the teacher as a *facilitator*—that is, the teacher does not attempt to teach strictly defined lessons or bits of knowledge but rather tries to provide the students with materials and methods with which they can learn at their own rate and according to their own interests. A good description of this type of teaching is found in Herbert Kohl's *36 Children* (1967). Instead of teaching his whole sixth-grade class lessons in reading and math, Kohl brought in lots of books, art materials, and play materials, then spent his time trying to establish an atmosphere in which the children were free to explore the objects and their own fantasies as well. Under his warm encouragement they soon developed various projects of their own and made remarkable progress in language and thinking abilities.

John Holt, author of *How Children Learn* (1970), also subscribes to a version of this method, particularly with very young children. He maintains that children can be easily hurt and discouraged when they come up against something they do not know and cannot figure out. If the teacher does not try to force the children to learn but just lets them experiment with books or materials on their own, they will eventually acquire the basic learning skills and a taste for knowledge as well. This will happen, Holt believes, because children are naturally curious. What the teacher must do is be available to help when a child asks for help, and get out of the way at other times. Holt cautions that getting out of children's way does not mean neglecting them or ignoring their request for information or help. He observes that if children repeatedly fail to get a response from the people in their world, they will soon stop trying—that is, they will stop asking questions and, in effect, give up on learning. Thus, the task of the teacher is not to obstruct the child's own learning pattern, but to be there when needed.

Another school of thought about teaching methods takes its cue from the theory of Piaget. This approach assumes that children can master a particular skill only when they have reached the appropriate stage of cognitive development. A course of instruction should be carefully planned, therefore, to suit children at each stage of cognitive development. Learning can thus proceed with a minimum of frustration. This approach does not necessarily conflict with the open-classroom approach advocated by Kohl, inasmuch as both let children proceed on their own and at their own rate. In the Piagetian approach, however, the situation is more carefully structured in order to increase the child's chances of successful learning.

Of course, either tendency—structure or lack of it—can be taken to extremes. As Erikson (1968) points out, teachers can make the school a miniature version of an oppressive and comfortless adulthood, full of duties for the child, organized to the last detail, and clocked to the last second. Children in this situation may learn a sense of duty, but they learn it because it is imposed on

Close one-to-one friendships are likely to develop for the first time during middle childhood.

Teacher Expectations and Pupil Performance

It's only natural for teachers to expect some of their pupils to do better than others. And it is inevitable that in some cases teachers will begin to form their expectations before they even see the pupils. For example, one teacher may know that his class is the "slow group" in the grade, or he may have heard that a certain pupil's mother is on welfare. On the other end of the scale, another teacher may expect a lot of a pupil because she got a high score on an achievement test last year or because she comes from a wealthy family.

Investigators (Rist, 1970; Wilson, 1963) have shown that teachers do hold up lower standards of achievement for lower-income children. This low expectation may work upon the children as a self-fulfilling prophecy—that is, teachers may communicate their high or low expectations to the children by treating them differently. Researchers (Firestone & Brody, 1975; Rowe, 1974) have found that teachers will not expose children for whom they have low expectations to as much material as they do the children from whom they expect better work. It was also found that teachers spend less time with the "low" group in their class.

But can a child's academic performance actually be improved by raising the teacher's expectations? This question was investigated in a public elementary school fictitiously named Oak School (Rosenthal & Jacobson, 1968). First the researchers gave all the pupils a simple test of verbal and reasoning abilities. The Oak School teachers, however, were told that this test was a very sophisticated index designed to identify children who were about to "bloom"—to go through an intellectual "growth spurt."

Then the teachers were told which of their pupils had been predicted by the test to "bloom" in the coming months. Actually, the names of the "bloomers" had been selected at random; the test had nothing to do with it. About one pupil in every five was named as being a "bloomer."

Eight months later the investigators gave all the children in the Oak School the same test of verbal and reasoning abilities. The test showed that as a group, the "bloomers" had made significantly greater gains than had the other pupils. Evidently the teachers' expectations of their success helped improve the performance of the "bloomers" more than the school average.

---

them from the outside. They learn it to please authority, not to please themselves.

The other extreme is freedom carried to the point of chaos. As the children are told only to do what they want, they receive no direction and are left confused amid all the choices.

SUMMARY

▶ The traditional stability of the home has been shaken in recent years by the prevalence of divorce, the frequency of family relocations, and the large number of mothers who work outside the home. The attitude of parents toward their child affects the child's behavior toward others. Loving parents produce loving children; hostile parents, hostile children. Correlations have been found between punitiveness and rejection by parents and lack of internal controls and aggression in children.

▶ Fathers are now playing a much larger part in their children's lives than formerly. In the homes of children with working mothers, fathers are helping out with child care and household chores as well as supporting their wives emotionally. One in every three families is disrupted by divorce, a situation emotionally disturbing to children. Studies show, however, that children are worse off in a home in which the parents are unable to get along with each other. Death is a difficult concept for children. Nevertheless, children should not be shielded from the knowledge of a death in their own family. They should be encouraged to express their feelings of grief.

▶ An increasingly prevalent family arrangement is the single-parent family. Single mothers have a far more difficult time economically than single fathers. Social networks, the social groups to which the family belongs, are an important resource for single-parent families for child care, job opportunities, and economic and emotional support. Adoption is another arrangement to which some children must adapt. Children should be told they have been adopted—the discussion continuing on a more mature level according to the child's cognitive capacity. Interactions with siblings affect the way children relate to schoolmates and teachers. Children tend to adopt a pattern of behavior that will gain them their share of attention from parents and siblings.

▶ Peer groups in middle childhood are usually composed of members of the same sex. Norms arise rapidly in any new peer group, partly because the members are at an age to understand and make rules and partly because they want their group to be distinct from other groups. Peer-group behavior is influenced by the size of the group and the nature of its activity. Status in the group depends on the degree of acceptance by other members. Factors in acceptance are friendliness, an outgoing personality, and the child's perception of his own status.

▶ One approach to teaching sees the teacher as facilitator in an atmosphere where children are free to make their own explorations, whereas a more structured approach aims to increase the child's chances for success. Regardless of approach, regard for the child's self-esteem is essential in a teacher.

FURTHER READINGS

Biller, Henry, and Dennis, Meredith. *Father power.* **Garden City, N.Y.: Anchor, 1975.**
This book for fathers urges greater participation by men in raising their children and tells how to become actively involved. A special section discusses divorced and single fathers, and stepfathers.

Gardner, R. A. *The boys and girls book about divorce.* **New York: Bantam, 1971.**
Written for the children of divorced parents by a psychiatrist, this book deals with such issues as anger and divided loyalties.

Ginott, Haim. *Between parent and child.* **New York: Macmillan, 1968.**
Ginott's understanding of preadolescent and adolescent problems won him wide respect as a clinical psychologist. Here, with many examples, he shows how adults unconsciously damage self-esteem, undermine integrity, and create hostility.

Golding, William. *Lord of the flies.* **New York: Coward McCann, 1962.**
A powerful novel about the influence of peer-group conformity on preadolescents. English schoolboys stranded on an uninhabited island become savages under the control of a bullying leader as they turn against the dissenting loner who is the tragic hero of the book.

Hoffman, L., and Nye, F. *Working mothers.* **San Francisco: Jossey-Bass, 1974.**
These articles based on research deal with the mother working outside the home and the effects of her working on herself and her family.

Holt, John. *How children fail.* **New York: Pitman, 1968.**
Holt maintains that few schools meet children's needs. He writes that children fall short of their learning potential when they are afraid of displeasing adults, bored, or confused, and describes the ways that they use to meet or to escape demands made on them by adults in school.

Jencks, Christopher. *Inequality: A reassessment of family and schooling in America.* **New York: Harper & Row, 1973.**
Jencks and associates at the Center for Educational Policy Research who contributed to this book arrive at the conclusion that educational reform cannot bring about economic or social equality. Their research suggests that children are more influenced by the family and the street than by the school. Jencks recommends a long-term restructuring of the entire social system.

Keniston, Kenneth, and The Carnegie Council on Children. *All our children.* **New York: Harcourt Brace Jovanovich, 1978.**
This book discusses the contemporary family, the strains upon it, and the relationship of the child and family to society.

McNamara, Joan. *The adoption adviser.* **New York: Hawthorn, 1975.**
McNamara provides detailed information on the adoption opportunities offered by the government, the legal procedures involved, and the complex problems of reaching a decision to adopt and choose the right child.

Rutter, Michael, et al. *Fifteen thousand hours.* **Cambridge, Mass.: Harvard University Press, 1979.**
Do schools make a difference? This team of researchers, comparing several schools serving London's "disadvantaged" youth, found that they do. An interesting and optimistic study.

Observational Activities
Part Four   Middle Childhood

Assessing a Child's Cognitive Ability

Middle childhood is a time for making friends and spending time with those friends. The child is free to move around the neighborhood without a parent and relate to peers independently. Inevitably a child selects some children to spend more time with than others, and friendships are made. The reasons for selecting one person over another may include:

1.   Similarity of interests
2.   Same age or sex or class in school
3.   Families are friends and spend time together
4.   Proximity of homes

Go to a shopping center or playground where children are interacting freely with a minimum of adult supervision and interference. Select four children (two boys and two girls) to interview. Ask them individually:

1.   Do you have a best friend?
2.   What is the thing you and your friend enjoy doing together most?
3.   What do you like to do that your friend doesn't like to do?
4.   Is your friend the same age as you? Is your friend in the same grade at school? In the same school?
5.   Where does your friend live—how many blocks away from your house?
6.   How often do you and your friend get together? Every day? Once a week?
7.   Do you have other friends you spend time with outside school?
8.   What do you enjoy with your other friends that is different from what you enjoy with your best friend?
9.   What does it mean to have a best friend?

On the basis of your interviews discuss the characteristics of "best friends" as differentiated from other friends.

Definition of Family

Family can be defined in many ways. In some homes there is a mother, children, and no father. In other situations there is a mother with her children, her second husband and his children, and their children. Sometimes an older person—grandparent or aunt—lives with the family. Do a class analysis of the kinds of families represented by class members. Work together as a class to develop a form for each class member to fill in (no names need be used in completing the form). Get information on each class member's family *when that class member was a preschooler*. The kinds of things to include are:

1.   Number and relationship (to child) of adults living in the home
2.   Number and relationship (to child) of children living in the home

You may have to pick a specific age—age four, for example—because the data probably varied from year to year in many homes as siblings were born. Tabulate the data on the board, with several class members working at the front of the room. When all the data have been entered on the board, work as a class to define "family" in such a way that all the situations represented within your class are covered.

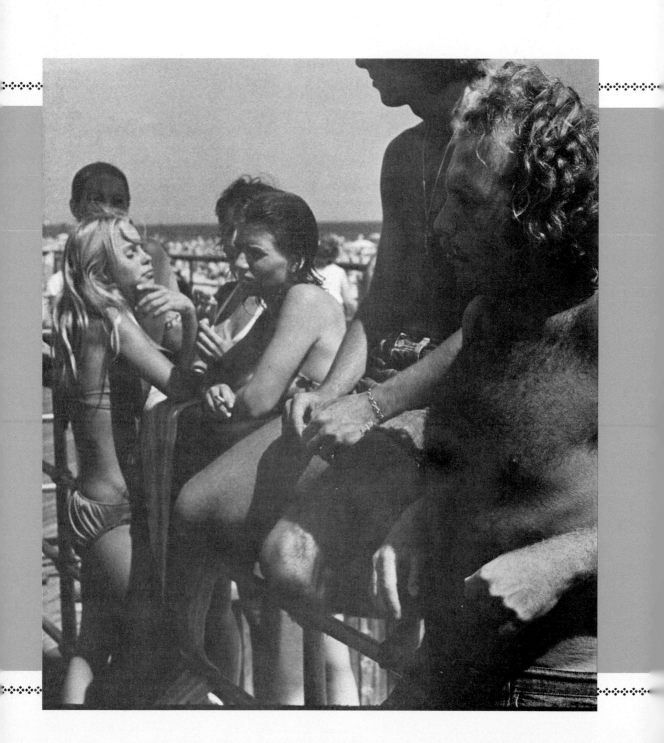

PART FIVE

Adolescence

Chapter 12

❖❖❖❖❖❖

Growing into Adulthood

Adolescence is the bridge between childhood and adulthood. The sex organs mature, secondary sex characteristics appear, and height and weight increase dramatically. At the same time the person's mode of reasoning changes, allowing new alternatives to be considered and making everyday reality and the status quo only one set of alternatives from among infinite possibilities. These physical and intellectual changes set the major developmental tasks of this stage of life, including the forging of an identity and the integration of sexual impulses into the person's social behavior.

The framework for individual development in the adolescent period varies from place to place. An adolescent in the rural West does not make the same transition to adulthood as an adolescent growing up in Boston or New York. There are even wider differences between industrial and nonindustrial countries. For example, in nonindustrial societies people usually marry earlier than do people in industrialized societies, making the period of transition much shorter.

There are, of course, some changes that take place in every person beyond the tenth birthday no matter where he or she grows up. Other changes seem to be at least as much social as they are biological, and it is sometimes difficult to draw a clear line between the two aspects. The onset of adolescence in every culture, however, is heralded by certain physical and sexual changes.

PHYSICAL AND SEXUAL DEVELOPMENT

Some people confuse the terms "adolescence" and "puberty." *Adolescence* can be roughly defined as the period from the onset of puberty to adulthood. *Puberty* is the shorter period of adolescence during which an individual reaches sexual maturity. Puberty lasts from two to four years and is marked by great physical and psychological changes: Children's bodies become capable of functioning sexually, and their attitudes and behavior become more mature.

But the outward signs of the development of sex organs and a mature body type are not the first physical changes in adolescence. Many months before those outward signs become visible, the body is changing in unseen ways, particularly in its hormonal makeup. This prepares the way for sexual maturity and the ability to procreate.

Physical Growth

Human beings grow most rapidly at two times during their lives: before they are six months old and then again during adolescence. The second period of accelerated growth, often called the *adolescent growth spurt*, usually lasts from two to three years (Barnes, 1975).

Adolescents grow both in height and in weight, with the increase in height occurring first. As they gain weight, the amount and distribution of fat in their bodies changes, and the proportion of bone and muscle tissue increases. During puberty the final 20 to 25 percent of growth in (ideal) height is achieved, as is the final 50 percent increase in weight (Barnes, 1975).

In girls the adolescent growth spurt usually begins between the ages of nine and eleven and reaches a peak at an average of twelve and a half years. Then growth slows down and usually ceases completely between the ages of fifteen and eighteen. The growth spurt in boys generally begins about two years later than it does in girls and lasts for a longer time. It begins between the ages of eleven and fourteen, reaches a peak at about age fifteen, and slowly declines until the age of twenty or twenty-one (Roche & Davila, 1972; Roche, 1979). During the period of maximum growth girls grow about three and a half inches (8.75 cm) in one year and put on about eleven pounds (4.95 kg). Boys grow four to five inches (10 to 12.5 cm) a year and gain twelve to fourteen pounds (5.4 to 6.3 kg).

Changes in body proportion accompany the changes in height and weight. The trunk widens in the hips and shoulders, and the waistline drops. Boys tend to broaden mostly in the shoulders, girls in the hips. One of the earliest changes in both boys and girls is the addition of a layer of subcutaneous (under the skin) fat in the hips and legs. This fat soon disappears in the boys but remains with the girls. The additional height gained in adolescence is primarily the result of increased length of the trunk, not the legs. At first, however, the neck, arms, and legs grow more rapidly than the trunk, and this gives the young adolescent an awkward, disproportionate appearance.

Hands and feet have a growth spurt about a year before the arms and legs, and they add to the young adolescent's ungainly figure. The hands, feet, and head are the first body parts to reach their mature size.

Head circumference increases by less than one inch (2.5 cm) during adolescence, but the face changes markedly. It grows first in length, with the upper part changing before the lower part. As the face lengthens, it becomes broader as well, and the nose and chin become more prominent. Boys' faces generally become more angular, girls' faces more oval.

Heredity and nutrition influence the timing of the adolescent growth spurt in several ways, one of the most important being their effect on the secretion of hormones by the endocrine glands. A growth hormone released by the pituitary gland is primarily responsible for the rapid growth at the beginning of adolescence. The thyroid gland aids in this development by releasing larger amounts of the hormones that permit the conversion of food into tissues and energy. The gonads—the ovaries in the female and the testes in the male—are stimulated by hormones secreted by the adrenal glands and the pituitary. It is the gonads that bring about sexual development, and they play an important role in stimulating the physical development that occurs before the visible signs of puberty appear.

Puberty

The first menstruation is often considered the beginning of puberty in the girl, but even before it can occur the sex organs have to develop and the

Adolescence is characterized by dramatic changes in height, weight, and body proportions.

secondary sex characteristics—the nongenital physical features that distinguish men from women—will begin to appear. In the boy semen, pubic hair, a lower voice, and growth of the penis and testes are often taken as signs of the onset of puberty, but about one to two years before the outward signs appear, the gonads begin secreting androgen in boys and estrogen in girls. These hormones initiate the striking physical and mental changes of adolescence.

Puberty can be divided into three stages. In the *prepubescent* stage the secondary sex characteristics begin to develop, but the reproductive organs do not yet function. In the *pubescent* stage the secondary sex characteristics continue to develop and the reproductive organs become capable of producing ova and sperm. In the *postpubescent* stage the secondary sex characteristics are well developed and the sex organs are capable of adult functioning. The great majority of American girls have their first menstruation—an event known as **menarche**—between the ages of eleven and fifteen. In the United States the mean age is 12.7 years (Zacharias et al., 1970). Puberty for boys seems more subject to variation.

Primary Sex Characteristics

The male testes are present at birth, but are only about 10 percent of their mature size. They grow rapidly during the first year or two of puberty, then grow more slowly, not reaching mature size until the age of twenty or twenty-one.

Shortly after the testes begin to develop, the penis starts to grow in length, and the seminal ducts and the prostate gland enlarge. Though the penis is capable of erection by means of contact from birth, only during adolescence does it begin to erect spontaneously or in response to sexually provocative sights, sounds, or thoughts.

The female's uterus, fallopian tubes, and vagina grow rapidly through puberty. The ovaries grow during puberty, too, and though they begin to function about midway through the period, they do not reach full adult size until the age of twenty or twenty-one. The ovaries produce ova and secrete the hormones needed for pregnancy, menstruation, and the development of the secondary sex characteristics. Following menarche, menstruation may come at irregular intervals at first. For six months to a year or more ovulation may not always occur.

Secondary Sex Characteristics

The secondary sex characteristics—breasts, body hair, voice change—are not directly related to reproduction. The secondary sex characteristic that first develops in boys is sparse patches of light-colored, straight pubic hair. This hair takes on its characteristically dark, curly appearance after a year or two. Axillary (underarm) and facial hair begin to appear when the pubic hair has almost fully grown in. Like the pubic hair, this hair at first is light-colored, fine, and sparse. As for facial hair, few boys find that they need to shave before they are sixteen or seventeen. Hair also appears on the arms, legs, and shoulders, and later on the chest. Body hair continues to develop for some time, often into adulthood. The amount and density of hair is determined by heredity.

Peoples' skin becomes coarser and thicker during puberty, and the pores enlarge. The *sebaceous*, or fatty, glands in the skin become active at this time and produce an oily secretion, as persons suffering from acne know all too well. The sweat glands in the armpits begin to function even before the axillary hair appears, and the amount and odor of perspiration increase.

Perhaps the most noticeable change in boys is the deepening of the voice. Usually by the time a boy is thirteen, his voice has become husky. Only later, at about age sixteen or seventeen, does it begin to crack. This may last for a year or two, until the voice change is complete. The voice change occurs because the male hormones cause the larynx to enlarge and the vocal cords to lengthen. Later in adolescence the male voice drops an octave or more in pitch, increases in volume, and develops a more even tonal quality.

Girls' secondary sex characteristics generally develop in the same sequence as boys'. The first indication of approaching sexual maturity in a girl is change in the shape and size of her hips, which grow wider and rounder. This development is caused in part by enlargement of the pelvic bone and in part by the thickening of the fat that lies under the skin.

Soon after a girl's hips start to develop, her breasts begin to grow. The first stage of breast development is the bud stage, in which the nipple elevates slightly and the surrounding areola becomes fuller. This occurs at an average age of ten or eleven. Before the menarche there is an increase in the amount of fat underlying the nipple and the areola, and the breast rises in a conical shape. After menarche the breasts become larger and rounder with the development of the mammary glands. The extent of all these changes varies with the individual.

Changing Growth Patterns

Children in widely separated parts of the world seem to be reaching puberty earlier than their parents did, and growing taller and heavier as well (Roche, 1979). For example, records show that in the United States, a young man will, on the average, be one inch (2.5 cm) taller and ten pounds (4.5 kg) heavier than his father. A young woman will probably be almost an inch (2.5 cm) taller than her mother and two pounds (.9 kg) heavier, and will reach menarche ten months earlier than her mother did. Today's adolescents are also reaching full adult height earlier than their ancestors did. A century ago boys did not reach full height until age twenty-three or twenty-four, but now an adolescent boy stops growing around the age of twenty. At the turn of the century girls reached full height at the age of eighteen, whereas the modern girl stops growing at age seventeen. Evidence of this increase in size can be seen in the clothing and furnishings of past generations. A modern family would find the furniture of a house in colonial Williamsburg far too small. The armor worn by medieval warriors would cramp a modern boy of twelve. The first colonists who settled in Jamestown were, on the average, less than five feet (150 cm) tall.

In addition to growing bigger in height and weight recent generations

❖❖❖

Rites of Passage

At the age of thirteen Jewish boys all over the world participate in the ceremony of *bar mitzvah* and announce to the world, "Today I am a man." From this day on they are eligible to participate in the rituals of the adult religious community. In most Western groups, however, a lad of thirteen is still considered very much a child.

In fact there is no clearly defined line that separates children from adults in secular American society, though the physical changes of puberty mark the biological end of childhood. Most people would agree that shaving and menstruating are things done by adults and not by children. Getting a driver's license, graduating from high school or college, embarking on a career, and moving out of the family home are all steps that contribute to the achievement of adult status in our society; yet the end of adolescence is never clearly defined. We even hear some people accused of prolonging their adolescence indefinitely.

In most non-Western societies the entrance into adulthood is unmistakably defined. At a specified age individuals must participate in a ritual or series of rituals that qualify them to assume an adult role in their society. Anthropologists refer to the procedure whereby a child becomes an adult member of a culture as *rites of passage*, or puberty rites.

Although the original meaning and function of ancient puberty rites are shrouded into the mists of time, we do know something about the role of these rites in surviving nonliterate societies. The rites generally entail familiarizing the pubescent male with the secret traditions and folkways of society. Often they involve mutilation of the body, most especially the sexual organs. By initiating the young man into adult society, the elders secure their own position of power, unite the tribe, and ensure the continuation of traditional social behavior.

In some societies the rites continue throughout most of the individual's adult life. Among the Karadjeri of Australia, for example, initiation is an extremely complex and drawn-out affair that begins at puberty and ends only when the man finally achieves the status of an elder.

Initiation begins for the Karadjeri youth when he is covered with human blood at the age of twelve. Two weeks later, after a hole has been bored through his nasal septum and a feather has been inserted, he achieves the status of *nimanu*. After the passage of a year or two the *nimanu* is ready to undergo his first major puberty ritual, an elaborate circumcision ceremony that lasts for several days. At the conclusion of this ritual—after much singing, dancing, self-mutilation, weeping, throwing of boomerangs, drinking of blood, and, ultimately, the circumcision itself—the young man becomes *miangu*. It is not until after another year or two that the *miangu* undergoes subincision, the ritual slitting of the urethra. This ritual, during which blood from the young man's wound is used to draw designs on his back, confers upon the youth the status of *djamununggur*.

In the years that follow the young Karadjeri continues to participate in a series of rituals that serve to elevate his status gradually in the community. By eating particular foods, reciting certain words, and wearing special garments, he slowly becomes familiar with the traditions and sacred objects known to the elders. Initiation culminates several years after marriage, when the man is permitted to participate at a feast where he is shown the *primal*, inscribed wooden boards that are the tribe's most sacred objects. Even after a man has participated in this feast, his prestige continues to grow throughout his life until he eventually achieves the status of an elder.

The elaborate rituals of the Karadjeri are closely linked to the tribe's ancient history. Each of the initiation customs harks back to the legend of the Bagadjimbiri, the mythical superhuman race from whom the Karadjeri trace their ancestry. Throughout his initiation, the young man gains more and more insight into the history and customs of his people and their ancestors.

Recently, some psychoanalysts have proposed that male puberty rites reflect a fundamental envy by men of the sexual organs and functions of women. Because they do not menstruate, adolescent boys do not experience any clear-cut proof of their sexual maturity. It has been suggested that mutilation of the genitals, stopping up the anus, and other common puberty rituals are symbolic expressions of the male's desire to share in the procreative power of the female.

also develop earlier than their ancestors did, so that puberty begins at a younger age. This is not a recent phenomenon, nor is it confined to the United States. Children in such diverse areas of the world as China, New Zealand, Italy, and Poland are reaching maturity earlier, and the trend seems to be operating in all populations of these countries. Many studies in recent years have used menarche as the criterion for tracing this trend. In Scandinavia, England, and America the age at menarche has been getting steadily earlier at the rate of one-third to one-half year per decade, and it is continuing to arrive earlier.

With these physical changes has come a correspondingly earlier age of social and intellectual maturity. Sometimes parents do not realize that when they were adolescents they may have been less mature—physically as well as socially—than their children are at the same chronological age. Failure to recognize changes in growth patterns (as well as individual variations in development) has led to what Lipsitz calls "the myth of chronological age":

> To think about all the ages that an adolescent juggles—biological, social, emotional, intellectual and academic—makes a mockery of chronological age... To be told that someone is 13 is to be told just about nothing except perhaps grade level in school (Lipsitz, 1979).

No one factor can be singled out as having caused these changes in physical growth. Among the factors usually mentioned are improved diet, immunization, and better general health care; and increased mobility resulting in intermarriage between formerly isolated communities and a more vigorous "hybrid" stock (Muuss, 1970).

Varying Rates of Development

Within any age group of adolescents one can observe significant variations in physical maturity, as well as concomitant variations in areas of emotional and intellectual development. As Lipsitz explains:

In many cultures, elaborate rituals celebrate the passage to maturity.

The fact is that there is no more variable group that we can deal with than adolescents, especially young adolescents. . . . Because of this extreme variability, there can be a six-year-span in biological development between a quickly developing girl and a slowly developing boy, and here I am only talking about biological age.

Early-maturing boys are taller, heavier, and more muscular than their age-mates. They tend to excel at sports, achieve popularity, and become leaders in student government and extracurricular activities. Early-maturing boys also tend to be more interested in girls and gain the advantage of acquiring social graces early. In adult life they are likely to be more successful socially and vocationally and to be more conventional in career and life-style choices.

Early-maturing girls are faced with the problem that few other girls and almost no boys are as tall and well developed as they are. Friends may avoid them simply because they are bigger. Early-maturing girls tend to date older boys until their age group catches up with them.

Late-maturing boys are smaller and less well developed than almost everyone in their age group. They may lack interest in dating, and when they do become interested in girls, they often lack social graces or are rebuffed by the prettiest and most popular girls. Late-maturing boys tend to participate in extracurricular activities such as band, chess club, or the school newspaper, where their lack of physical maturity is not a drawback. In adult life they tend to be insightful, independent, and less conventionally successful. Little has been written about late-maturing girls, perhaps because they still mature before many of the boys. Late-maturing girls do not face the problems that confront late-maturing boys, but they may be at some social disadvantage if they are less attractive to boys than other girls are.

The observations offered above should be viewed as very general ones. Moreover, it must be emphasized that rates of growth in various areas of

Some girls will develop sooner than others even though they are the same age.

development are not synchronized (Lipsitz, 1979). For example, a young woman who becomes physically mature more rapidly than her age-mates may still be a child emotionally and socially.

Sexual Behavior

American society has succeeded in limiting the sexual activity of the adolescent by various means, the most important of which is the double standard. Some sexual activity has been acceptable in boys but many people have thought that girls should restrict their sexual activity to marriage. Indeed, a study by the Project on Human Sexual Development found that parents seem twice as likely to condone premarital sex for their male children as for their female children (*Time*, 1978). The same study showed that while the discussion of sexual matters in our culture would seem to be much more open in this time of "sexual liberation," 85–95 percent of the 1,400 (mostly young) parents questioned claimed never to have discussed any aspect of sexual behavior with their children.

There has always been some discrepancy between what parents approve and what their children do, especially in connection with sexual behavior. At a time when traditional sexual values are being called into question, this discrepancy may be widening because the parents themselves may be questioning their own sexual mores. Parents may be less comfortable laying down the old rules than in previous generations even though they may be emotionally committed to traditional sexual values.

It is difficult to gather reliable data about sexual behavior in any culture where so many contradictory attitudes prevail. The first systematic studies of sexual behavior were the Kinsey reports, published in 1948 and 1953. Kinsey found that at least 70 percent of the male population had had sexual intercourse at least once by age twenty. About half of all women who were married by age thirty had had premarital sexual intercourse, but only 21 percent had experienced coitus at twenty. A review of some of the research on human sexuality (Gordon & Scales, 1977), presenting a "composite picture" of more recent studies on sexual behavior, indicates that about seven million males and four million females experience intercourse as teenagers; about 55 percent of women have had intercourse by age nineteen; and that, according to a national survey, about one in five fifteen-year-olds have experienced intercourse.

Such statistics were summed up in a recent article (Fox, 1979) on adolescent sexual behavior:

> More teenagers are sexually active, more are active with a greater number of partners and with increasing coital frequency, and more teenagers are initiating their sexual activity at increasingly younger ages (p. 21).

It was suggested that this behavioral pattern partly accounts for the continued high rate of adolescent pregnancy, despite the increased use of contraceptives.

According to Gordon and Scales (1977), of the Institute for Family Research and Education, many young people may be pressured into early and unprotective intercourse partly by the "myth of the normal outlet":

> Some years ago, young people (especially girls) who had "premarital" intercourse were worried that they might not be "normal." Now the concerned question is "Am I normal if I wait for marriage?" Some years ago, desire for more than one sexual relationship at a time was considered aberrant. Now it is easy to second-guess a desire for exclusive monogamy as suggesting that one lacks sexual "liberation" (p. 101).

In the opinion of the two researchers young people need a broader program of formal sex education—one that goes beyond discussions of sexual anatomy and quantitative statistics—in order for them to express their sexuality in a responsible way:

> Sex education ... should inform people of the wide range of sexual behavior which is normal, teach them about contraception, and help them connect their understanding of sex with feelings and relationships with others (p. 101).

Other researchers also suggest that sex education programs should encourage the involvement of parents. A review of the rather limited research on the family's role in adolescent sexual behavior (Fox, 1979) indicates that very few children receive direct instruction from their parents on sexual matters. When direct instruction does occur, it is usually from mother to daughter and, less frequently, mother to son. In the studies examined, "the most notable

Many adolescents today are more open about their sexual behavior than they have been in the past.

aspect about the father is his almost complete absence as a source of sex education for his children" (p. 22). The research suggests that when parent-child communication does occur, it appears to restrict the frequency and nature of adolescent sexual involvement, though the reasons behind this influence have yet to be clearly understood. It was also noted that mother-daughter communication was associated with more effective use of contraceptives.

Homosexuality

The first reliable data on homosexual behavior came from the research of Kinsey and his colleagues (Kinsey et al., 1948, 1953). Their studies showed that a surprisingly large number of people had had some homosexual experience during their lives—about 37 percent of males and 19 percent of females. For most of the males and about half of the females these experiences had begun during adolescence. But it was also found that most of these people were not exclusively homosexual. Many of them had both homosexual and heterosexual contacts during the same general period of time, and felt comfortable in both. Also, many who engaged in homosexual activity in adolescence or early adult life gave it up later on. Most of them were never identified as homosexuals by their heterosexual friends or co-workers.

Teen-Age VD

"Today's teen-ager," says Dr. Murray Kappelman (1977), "now accepts sex as a natural biological, *integral* aspect of everyday life," not a furtive, guilt-ridden secret. In spite of their apparent precocity, however, many teen-agers are quite naive when it comes to venereal disease. Many believe that the Pill, the diaphragm, and the intrauterine device (IUD) protect against syphilis and gonorrhea as well as against pregnancy. And many believe that "nice" people don't get or transmit VD. The fact is that anyone who has sexual intercourse can catch and transmit venereal disease. And the fact is that of all of the methods of contraception, only the condom may act as a barrier to disease.

The inevitable consequence of all this is a VD epidemic. Of all the infectious diseases, only the common cold occurs with greater frequency. In one recent study the highest incidence of VD occurred in the group between the ages of twenty and twenty-four. Next came the fifteen-to-nineteen-year-old group, with 10 percent of all youngsters between the ages of thirteen and nineteen having had a venereal disease at some time. About 11 percent of females and 12 percent of males sixteen to nineteen years of age have had VD, and the figures show a significant upward trend. In fact, people under age 25 make up about half of all reported cases of VD (Katchadourian, 1977).

Other facts about these diseases are as alarming as their statistics. Untreated syphilis can lead to brain damage, severe heart disease, and death. Gonorrhea untreated may lead to blindness and sterility. Both can damage unborn children if a pregnant woman's disease goes undiagnosed and untreated. Yet both syphilis and gonorrhea are relatively easy to cure if treatment is begun early and continued adequately. And both are preventable.

What can be done? Physicians, public health officials, and educators say that there must be more public education. VD should be discussed at home, in school, and in the media as a group of communicable diseases, not as a moral or ethical issue. Crisis-information centers and hotlines should be readily available and adequately publicized. Diagnostic and treatment centers should be set up in such ways that the privacy of the individual is protected without impeding the case-finding and contact-tracing needed to control the spread of infection. They also recommend the use of the condom as a method of birth control.

As in other problems of adolescence, the understanding and trust gained when adults and teen-agers work together with patience and tolerance can go a long way toward helping young people grow up healthy. As Dr. Kappelman says, "Venereal disease presents a physical and sometimes an emotional or psychological problem for both the victim and the parents." By confronting the problem together in an atmosphere of understanding and mutual respect, adults and teen-agers may achieve the double success of overcoming the disease and strengthening the relationships that facilitate the process of coming of age.

Since these early studies the social profile of homosexuality has changed. Part of the reason is that many gay men and lesbian women from all strata of society have become more open about their sexual orientation. In the past individuals have tended to disguise or deny this orientation, because of guilt, fear of social ostracism, and fear of discrimination in school, housing, and employment. Today civil rights activism and scientific research appear to be challenging religious and cultural traditions, which have viewed homosexuality as immoral and unnatural, and the long-held psychiatric stance, which has viewed homosexuality as an illness. In 1973, for example, the American Psychiatric Association published its majority decision no longer to classify homosexuality as an emotional disorder or pathological condition.

There are many people, however, who continue to condemn homosexuality and who are determinedly opposed to its legalization. They are convinced of two things: that homosexual behavior is simply wrong, and that if it becomes legally and socially acceptable, young people will be pressured into adopting it.

The first concern is, finally, a moral one, and cannot be settled by social science alone. As to the second, it would be easier to predict if we knew more about what really causes homosexuality. According to some theories people who become homosexuals have a predisposition, a sort of sexual confusion, that is established in early childhood and can never really be changed. One suggestion is that the typical homosexual male had a strong, dominating mother and a weak father. If these theories are correct, then no amount of later exposure to other people's behavior is going to make homosexuals out of youngsters who lack the predisposition. But if occasional homosexual inclinations were as common as Kinsey's data seem to show, then perhaps people could be influenced by what goes on around them in adolescence to choose either a homosexual or a heterosexual orientation for themselves, or something in between.

In this connection a study of adolescent sexuality (Sorensen, 1973) came up with some interesting findings. Many of the young people studied were sympathetic to others who engaged in homosexual activity, even if they did not do it themselves. Generally they felt that love was what mattered—that if the partners really loved each other, and homosexual activity helped them express their love, then it was all right. Yet many of these same young people did not approve of homosexuality in itself and said they had no intention of trying it. They simply did not wish to condemn those who were different.

Sex clinician John Money states flatly that a few exposures to homosexuality in early adolescence cannot turn a youngster into a permanent homosexual. "The worst a homosexual experience can do," he writes,

> is to whet a dormant appetite that had already been created in childhood. For proof there are the societies that prescribe a period of homosexuality for adolescent boys as a standard part of the growing-up process. Examples are the Batak people of Lake Toba in northern Sumatra and until recently the Marind Amin people of southern New Guinea. In these cultures, which have endured successfully for centuries, the homosexual period is followed by heterosexual marriage (Money & Tucker, 1975).

One unfortunate result of all the attention currently being paid to homosexuality is that many adolescents are wondering if they might have homosexual tendencies. Most of them, of course, do not, but they worry anyway, sometimes quite excruciatingly. In some cases adolescents may confuse their

Teen-Age Pregnancy

In present-day America about a million teen-agers a year find themselves pregnant, and for girls this has become the most common reason for dropping out of school. Among women over twenty the birthrate has declined steadily over the last decade, but among teen-agers it rose 75 percent between 1961 and 1974. By 1975 America had the fourth highest teen-age birthrate in the world. That year more than 600,000 teen-age girls became mothers. Of these, 227,270 were between the ages of fifteen and seventeen, and 12,642 were in the ten to fourteen age group (Yarrow, 1979).

Before the advent of effective female contraceptives, the fear of pregnancy was a powerful deterrent to premarital sex. Then the invention and general availability of the Pill and other devices led to a marked increase of sexual activity among teen-agers as well as society as a whole. Nonetheless, two-thirds of the teen-agers who became pregnant did so by accident, and half of all sexually active teen-agers questioned admitted that they never use contraceptives (Castleman, 1977). Their explanations for failing to use them are various.

Some believed they would not become pregnant unless they wanted to, or were in love with their partner, or had sexual intercourse very often. Some misunderstood how fertility relates to the menstrual cycle. Some who understood the situation correctly would have liked to get themselves put on the Pill or fitted with a diaphragm or an IUD by a clinic or a physician, but were afraid of what their parents might do if they found out. Finally, there were those to whom it seemed calculating and unromantic to prepare themselves for intercourse in advance, and those who imagined that pregnancies only happened to other people (Population Institute, 1978).

The babies of teen-age mothers have twice the normal chance of being born prematurely or with low birth weight, neurological defects, or birth injuries; they run two or three times the normal risk of dying in infancy. The younger the mother, the greater the risk. Teen-age mothers themselves are 60 percent more likely than women in their twenties to suffer complications or death during pregnancy or delivery, with hemorrhage, miscarriage, toxemia, and anemia as the most frequent causes.

Attitudes toward relinquishing an illegitimate child have undergone a complete change in the last decade. Whereas the majority of unmarried teen-agers used to give up their babies for adoption, only one out of ten does so today (Planned Parenthood, 1976).

Roughly one-third of all teen-age mothers are married at the time their baby is born. But the likelihood of these marriages breaking up within six years is three times greater than it is for older couples. Due to their relative lack of education and to their own immaturity, teen-age couples often cannot meet the economic pressures and the parental responsibilities of raising a child, and many of them neglect or mistreat their children.

Despite increases in sexual activity, adolescents are still largely unknowledgeable about the various methods of birth control. This has led to a dramatic rise in the rate of teen-age pregnancies.

sexual orientation with their approximation to a sexual stereotype. Sexual orientation is a question of who in fact arouses one sexually—a member of the same sex or a member of the opposite sex. Sexual stereotypes, on the other hand, are ideas of what a typical male or female is like. Thus, one can be powerfully oriented (that is, attracted) to the opposite sex and yet be quite different from the cultural stereotype for one's sex in several other respects.

To help relieve their self-doubts, teen-agers can take advantage of the fact that sexual stereotypes in the United States are becoming much roomier and more tolerant. "Real men" no longer have to be athletic, competitive, and unemotional; "real women" can be strong, ambitious, independent, and assertive. The traditional stereotypes kept men from learning how to cook dinner or take care of children and kept women from making a living or making repairs around the house. But now adults of both sexes need to be able to do everything, and it appears that they are happier and healthier when they do (Bem, 1975).

COGNITIVE DEVELOPMENT

One of the major achievements of early adolescence is the attainment of what Piaget calls formal operational thought (Inhelder & Piaget, 1958). Before adolescence children are largely concerned with the here and now, with what is apparent to their senses and with problems that can be solved by trial and error. During adolescence most people grow much better able to deal with problems on an abstract level, to form hypotheses, and to reason from propositions that are contrary to fact.

Formal Operations

It is not until the **period of formal operations**—the stage of cognitive development that is reached between the ages of eleven and fifteen—that a person can think flexibly enough about the world to consider abstract universals such as freedom and justice, and to grasp their intrinsic qualities. Children develop the ability to generalize before the age of eleven, but they are not yet ready to understand abstract characteristics such as congruence and mass. By the age of fifteen most individuals can operate with these abstract concepts. They can also begin to think and operate on the level of theory, rather than being constrained by the observable facts or the apparent reality of a situation.

These abilities are manifested in a number of areas, such as the realm of problem solving and scientific reasoning. In one of Piaget's experiments, for example, subjects were shown an object hanging from a string. This pendulum could be modified by changing several factors: length of the string, weight of the object, height at which the pendulum was released, and force with which it was pushed. Subjects were asked to find out which of the above factors determines how rapidly the pendulum swings. (The experimenter knew, of course, that length of string was the key factor and that testing any one variable would necessitate controlling all others if accurate results were to be obtained.)

The concrete operational children began their experiments by physically manipulating the various factors that could influence rate of swinging. They were more analytic and systematic in their approach than preoperational children and they made careful and objective observations of what happened. But their inferences could at best only be partially correct since they had not planned for any sort of control, nor were they capable of extrapolating beyond directly observable results. In one case a child compared a pendulum made with a long string and a heavy weight with one that had a short string and a light weight. The child concluded that *both* weight and length were important. A truly scientific approach would have entailed using the same length of string for both pendulums, the same height, and the same force, while varying only the weight.

When working at their peak capacity, formal operational adolescents would (and did) use just this sort of scientific approach. Moreover, they do not simply plunge into the experiment, nor is their thinking bound by immediately observable results. Adolescents first consider all of the several possibilities, or hypotheses, about what makes the pendulum swing faster. They are able to imagine that one or some combination of factors is involved; and they can deduce what *might* occur if one or another possibility were tested. Thus, before even starting an experiment, they work out a detailed plan or design for systematically testing each alternative.

By the age of fifteen most of us can operate with these abstract concepts. We can also arrive at several possible conclusions when given a hypothesis, whereas a child would see only the obvious conclusion. A child shown a picture of a car wrecked in an accident, for example, may simply conclude

Adolescents have the ability to conceive of ideas outside the realm of their own experience.

that the car went into a skid and hit a tree. An adolescent can propose several possible causes for the accident—faulty brakes, wet road, or drowsy driver.

The thinking of adolescents, unlike that of younger individuals, involves the ability to conceive of terms outside the realm of their own experience and the information given. The adolescent can also deal with propositions that are contrary to fact, can deal with the possible as well as the real. No longer bound by actual occurrences and data from the sensory world, adolescents can jump from proposition to proposition and from hypothesis to hypothesis and gain greater insight into many ideas and theories. Their interest in theoretical problems not related to everyday life and their ability to hypothesize new solutions increase throughout adolescence.

The adolescent also develops a more mature notion of time—the ability to conceive the distant future concretely and to set realistic long-term goals. With this conception comes a new, sometimes poignant awareness that oneself and others are caught up in the ongoing process of growth, aging, and death.

Piaget also found that the individual's ability to deal with symbols develops significantly during the stage of formal operations. One becomes able

Piaget's Periods of Cognitive Development

SENSORIMOTOR PERIOD (BIRTH TO 24 MONTHS)

PREOPERATIONAL PERIOD (2 TO 7 YEARS)

PERIOD OF CONCRETE OPERATIONS (7 TO 11 YEARS)

PERIOD OF FORMAL OPERATIONS (11 YEARS ON)

Realizes that classes are not only groups of concrete objects but may also be conceived of—and operated on in thought—as abstract or formal entities. Four major categories include:

Imagines several alternative explanations of the same phenomenon.
Operates with propositions that are contrary to fact.
Operates with symbols that stand for nothing in the individual's own experience, but have an abstract definition.
Operates with symbols of symbols. Understands metaphor.

to understand political cartoons and metaphors for the first time, and can use symbols for other symbols, as in algebra.

The adolescent's increased freedom in forming hypotheses often creates problems in making decisions. He or she sees not one but many alternatives, and this leads to doubt about his or her judgment. It often leads to external conflict, too, especially with parents and other authority figures (Weiner, 1977). Adolescents challenge adult decisions, demanding to know the reasoning behind the decisions but also wanting to present the virtues of their opinions and the opinions of their peers. They are not likely to accept a decision without questions and some debate, and are also likely to challenge religious and social values.

Interest in theoretical ideas also leads adolescents to construct ideal families, societies, and religions. As a formal operational thinker, the adolescent is freed from the bonds of personal experience and present time to explore ideas, ideals, roles, beliefs, theories, commitments, and all sorts of possibilities at the level of thought (Neimark, 1975). They see that there are alternatives to the way things are presently done, and they want to find ways to end human suffering and poverty, social inequity, and false belief. Utopian solutions to the world's problems—planned communities, Eastern religions, and new forms of consciousness—find many adherents in the adolescent group.

Adolescents caught up in idealism often place their ideals before family values. They may be outraged to find adults indulging in a few "harmless" or "pragmatic" vices while recommending virtue to young people, or practicing discrimination while invoking justice. The adolescents who take offense at such hypocrisy may rebel against the social structure in an intellectual sense, but usually they have no means to carry out the remedies they conceive. As they approach adult roles and responsibilities, such as undertaking a real job, adolescents' idealized structures are usually modified by the reality of existing conditions: "the weight of the world gradually transforms adolescent flights of fancy into adult anxieties" (Neimark, 1975, p. 587).

It should be noted that several researchers regard the work of Piaget and Inhelder only as "a good first approximation" for studying the level of development beyond concrete operations. As Neimark (1975) points out, studies of older adolescents and adults in Western cultures show that formal operations is not attained by all individuals. Also, some people attain it only in certain areas of expertise. Even Piaget (1972) notes that different individuals may attain formal operations at different ages, and the manner and age at which it is displayed may depend on aptitude and experience. In reviewing cross-cultural and other research, Neimark claims that there is still a need for more comprehensive studies and more objective experiments to ascertain the components of formal operational thought and to determine how variables such as class, culture, sex, IQ, education, and training affect the course of formal operations development.

Postconventional Morality

The ability to reason abstractly and conceptualize alternatives increases the range of adolescents' moral judgments. They may become aware of potential conflicts among socially acceptable standards and between individual rights and social standards or laws. In terms of Lawrence Kohlberg's levels of moral development the criteria of stage 4 ("law and order" morality) cannot resolve these conflicts; adolescents may recognize that society's rules can be mutually inconsistent and that the rules can be used to violate individual rights. If they recognize the inadequacy of stage 4, they will reach for the next level of moral development, the level that Kohlberg calls **postconventional** morality.

At the level of postconventional morality the individual defines moral values and principles apart from the authority of the groups or persons holding these principles, and apart from his or her own identity with these groups. At this level people control their own decisions internally; that is, they base their decisions on their own evaluation and standards of what is right, rather than by conforming to social pressures and expectations.

The postconventional level is divided into two distinct stages: the social-contract orientation and the universal-principle orientation. In the social-contract orientation (Kohlberg's stage 5) moral action is judged in terms of individual rights and in terms of policies that have been wittingly agreed to by the whole society. The person at this stage believes that if a law is inequitable, it must be changed in a democratic and constitutional manner and in accordance with social utility, not by breaking a law.

The universal-ethical-principle orientation (Kohlberg's stage 6) recognizes right as defined by the individual conscience in accordance with self-

Kohlberg's Levels of Moral Development

LEVEL I: PRECONVENTIONAL MORALITY (EARLY MIDDLE CHILDHOOD)

LEVEL II: CONVENTIONAL MORALITY (LATE MIDDLE CHILDHOOD)

LEVEL III: POSTCONVENTIONAL MORALITY (ADOLESCENCE)[a]

At this level people make choices on the basis of principles that they have thought through, accepted, and internalized. Right behavior is the behavior that conforms to these principles, regardless of immediate social praise or blame.

Stage 5 morality focuses on the social contract and on basic human rights that do not need to be earned. The "law and order" emphasis of Stage 4 gives way to a concern for the creation of good laws, rules that will maximize the welfare of the individual.

Stage 6 morality rests upon individual conscience. Right behavior produces a feeling of being right with oneself; people can obey the law and still feel guilty if they violated their own principles. The rights of humanity independent of rules of civil society are acknowledged, and human beings are seen as ends in themselves. At this stage the individual has achieved the capacity for principled reasoning and is thus morally mature.

[a]Kohlberg found that about 28 percent of all moral judgments made by sixteen-year-olds are at this level.

chosen ethical principles. These principles are abstract, and they include justice, the equality of human rights, and respect for the dignity of human beings as individual persons.

An individual may act at one level in most situations but at another level in other situations. People usually at the postconventional level slide back to the conventional level when their support of individual rights conflicts with rules formulated by an authority figure. For example, a person may be morally opposed to racial discrimination and yet may fail to uphold the rights of another when such an action would lead to a confrontation with authority. Such backsliding is not unusual during a period when an individual's values and beliefs are in a stage of reformation. Though an individual may backslide and then regain the highest level, Kohlberg believes that progress always takes place in the same sequence of levels. Some people, according to Kohlberg, never reach the final stage of postconventional morality.

Value Systems

As adolescents try to throw off their dependency on parents and other authorities, they may be attracted to ideologies that seem to offer some order and authority to replace those they have rejected. The ideologies that most appeal to them tend to be rigid and authoritarian—predictable systems that

Adolescents sometimes experiment with values which differ from those of their parents.

impose a framework in which adolescents can work out the details of their lives. It is important to adolescents to know where they stand and with the help of an inflexible system of values, they can be certain of their own positions. Gradually, however, as adolescents become more confident of their own judgment, rigid systems are usually replaced by looser, more flexible points of view.

But does the adolescent progress as far as is potentially possible in developing individual values? One observer (Friedenberg, 1959) believes that pressures for conformity with peers overwhelm the adolescent and prevent the full development of his or her own values. Another study (Sorensen, 1973) found that 86 percent of all adolescents felt that they did have their own personal values, though not so many were satisfied with the way they were putting them to use. An important part of the task, as Robert Kastenbaum suggests, is to integrate one's preferred values into an overall system.

> Adolescence is usually the time during which the developing person begins seriously to create his life perspective. He has had many of the elements previously but now, for the first time, he also has the intellectual equipment to forge these elements into a perspective—and the psychosocial readiness to venture forth as his own self. Children have their notions—but it is adolescents who have ideologies (Kastenbaum, 1969).

Sorensen (1973) believes that a particularly difficult problem for young people is that adults seem determined to view and define them in terms of what they do—their educational success, their job plans, their participation in organized activities—whereas adolescents are struggling to view and define themselves in terms of what they are, or at least in terms of the person they want to be. He says, "Substantial dissonance exists in the minds of many adolescents between being and doing, with young people drifting without decision about what they want to do, in order to be sure of being what they want to be."

Political Awareness

Relatively few adolescents ever become actively involved in political move-ments. Even at the height of the period of demonstrations in the 1960s a study (Allport, 1968) found that most college students seldom worried about national welfare or the fate of mankind. What they were really concerned with was obtaining a rich, full life for themselves.

The political attitudes of adolescents have been correlated with their cognitive and moral development in a study (Adelson & O'Neil, 1966) that asked subjects to respond to a hypothetical situation in which 1,000 people become dissatisfied with their government and go to an island to form a new government. Thirteen-year-olds found it hard to imagine what consequences such an action might have at all, and fifteen-year-olds could not easily outline the community that might evolve or think of the services that the new gov-ernment might provide for its citizens. Many also tended to be intolerant of civil liberties and to favor an authoritarian form of government. After the age of fifteen the subjects of the study were able to perceive that law (not raw power) could promote the general good and produce social and moral bene-fits. They were able to understand the idea of an implicit "social contract" between the citizens and the state, and they recognized both the individual's right to freedom and the necessity for restraints on actions that infringe the rights of others or threaten social order.

A later study by Adelson (1972) also supports the idea of a developmental trend in political attitudes. Younger adolescents tended to personalize issues of political philosophy. Older adolescents tended to evaluate the overall effects of events, ideas, and actions on society as a whole.

Psychologist Kenneth Keniston has suggested that political issues may serve as catalysts for moral development. He says:

> Physical maturation may make possible the development of postconventional morality, but it obviously does not ensure it. And the pressures of socialization may in many instances militate against the development of a principled morality that can place the individual in conflict with his socializing environment—for example, with college administrators, with political parties, with the police. . . (Keniston, 1971)

Keniston believes that major events in the political life of the nation, such as the Vietnam War or Watergate, are the stimulus for moral development that otherwise might never take place.

If Keniston is correct, then there may be reason to worry about the amount and kind of political socialization that takes place in the school. A number of studies have confirmed that most adolescents have little or no understanding of the way our government works; nor do they understand our fundamental liberties, for in response to opinion polls they consistently take positions against freedom of speech and freedom of religion. Moreover, as Robert Hess (1968) has pointed out, the political socialization that does take place is aimed at reinforcing the concept of obedience to authority—specifi-cally school authority, of course, but governmental authority as well. Such socialization does not encourage efforts to arrive at one's own moral principles.

The difficulty which young, politically inexperienced, adolescents have in understanding our political system is well documented in recent research by Roberta Sigel (1979; Sigel & Hoskin, 1981). Using an open-ended interview procedure Sigel sought to determine what high school seniors comprehend about democracy—"What is it that makes any country a democracy?" She found that although most students had some notion about the meaning of democracy it was restricted primarily to simple, slogan-like themes related to individual freedom. Only 16 percent of the 992 students interviewed displayed a sophisticated understanding of this concept—that is, they were able to delineate multiple characteristics of a democratic society and explain how these characteristics interrelated.

Many researchers have focused on the role of the family in the political development of the young, since the family influences the formation of values and attitudes toward authority figures before the child enters school. A survey of the field of political socialization (Niemi & Sobieszck, 1977) indicates that between the 1950s and 1960s the influence of the family appears to have diminished, though studies have found that in general the political attitudes of children do not differ significantly from those of parents. Also noted is the fact that mothers have apparently become as important as fathers in the transmission of political values and views.

An overall conclusion made in the survey is that in recent years "more amorphous factors" than school or family—for example, peers, specific political events and the media—have emerged as important sources of political information and/or as agents of political development and activism. These factors increase the *potential* for differences between generations.

SUMMARY

▶ Even before the sex organs show an outward change, hormonal changes are preparing the body for adulthood. Soon a dramatic change takes place in height, weight, and body proportions known as the adolescent growth spurt. There are always variations in physical, emotional, and intellectual development within any adolescent age group.

▶ Puberty is the period during which an individual reaches sexual maturity, which is not necessarily synchronous with other areas of development. In the prepubescent stage secondary sex characteristics begin to develop. In the pubescent stage the reproductive organs begin producing ova or sperm. In the postpubescent stage the sex organs become fully capable of adult functioning. Spontaneous erection in the male in response to sights, sounds, and thoughts first occurs during adolescence. The appearance of breasts and menstruation in girls, body hair in both sexes, and voice change in boys herald sexual maturity.

▶ Traditional American values require that adolescents postpone sexual intercourse until after marriage, although this prohibition is more strictly applied to girls than to boys. The reality is that increasing numbers of adolescents are sexually active at increasingly younger ages. The family appears to play a limited role in adolescent sexual education.

▶ The ability to deal with abstractions and to reason deductively develops during what Piaget calls the stage of formal operations, between the ages of eleven and fifteen. The ability of individuals to consider many alternatives leads them to question their own ideas and to challenge authority figures and traditional beliefs.

▶ Changes in cognitive development facilitate changes in moral judgment. According to Kohlberg, the highest stage of moral development, postconventional morality, is characterized by reasoning in accordance with self-chosen ethical principles.

▶ The formation of a value system and political attitudes appears to follow a developmental trend. The influence of parents in these areas seems to have diminished, while the media, peers, and specific political events have emerged as important factors.

FURTHER READINGS

Caprio, Frank S., and Caprio, Frank B. *Parents and teenagers.* New York: Citadel, 1968.

This book by a psychologist and his son is directed at both adolescents and parents. The first part, for parents, deals with such matters as improving communication, attitudes toward dating, and the use of the family car. The second half advises teen-agers on dealing with problem parents, developing confidence, and coping with sex, among other things.

Comfort, Alex, and Comfort, Jane. *The facts of love: Living, loving and growing up.* New York: Ballantine Books, 1979.

This is a book for young people about their emerging sexual feeling. It deals with all aspects of human sexuality in an honest and positive way.

Grinder, Robert E. (ed.). *Studies in adolescence: A book of readings in adolescent development* (3rd ed.). New York: Macmillan, 1975.

The absent father, adolescents in the work force, and other contemporary issues are discussed in this anthology. The contributions are written from the standpoints of psychology, medicine, sociology, and other disciplines.

Hass, Aaron. *Teenage sexuality.* New York: Macmillan, 1979.

This study of the current sexual attitudes and behavior of teen-agers is based on hundreds of questionnaires and interviews. It lets teens speak for themselves on such topics as their romantic expectations, fantasies, ideas about various sexual behaviors, and about the double standard.

Keniston, Kenneth. *The uncommitted.* New York: Harcourt, 1965.

In one of the most discussed books of the sixties Keniston examines the alienation of American youth. What he has to say about tensions created by social change, the shattering of traditional social values, and noncommitment as a way of life is still relevant.

Semmens, James P., and Krantz, K. E. (eds.). *The adolescent experience.* New York: Macmillan, 1970.

A handbook designed for adults who counsel youth. Comprehensive discussions by many contributors of the sexual and social development of adolescents, reproductive physiology and anatomy, problems of sexual identity, and sociomedical aspects of adolescent behavior, including pregnancy, abortion, venereal disease, and drug use.

Chapter 13

❖❖❖❖❖❖

The Meaning of Identity

There are millions of real, flesh-and-blood people who happen to be teen-aged, but "adolescence" is more like a state of mind. Society expects the adolescent to exhibit a whole repertoire of behavior in areas ranging from sexuality to musical taste. Society also expects adolescence to be a time of stress and confusion—and more often than not it is, both for the adolescents and their parents. These expectations go a long way toward producing the "typical" behavior we associate with this period of life.

The power of social expectation in creating the state of adolescence has been well documented through studies of other cultures. Perhaps the most famous is anthropologist Margaret Mead's *Coming of Age in Samoa*. Living with the Samoans in 1925, Mead found that the tension, stress, and rebellion that Western people associated with the period of adolescence did not exist there. Growing up in a society of peaceful conformity, the young Samoans moved from childhood to adulthood smoothly and easily. Mead concluded that "adolescence is not necessarily a time of stress and strain, but that cultural conditions make it so" (Mead, 1928).

Even within our own society in a very limited span of time we can see how social expectations of teen-agers have changed. Reading today any of the books or articles written ten years ago, full of pronouncements about the young people of the late 1960s, one gets the nostalgic feeling of learning about a quaint but vanished race. Obviously, American teen-agers themselves could not have changed so drastically in one short decade—but the social role of "teen-ager" certainly has.

Sociologist Robert C. Sorensen has commented on the resentment sometimes generated by the demands of the social role of "adolescent":

> Many young people object to the proposition that they must be "adolescents." They know they are young, have limitations, and need family support. But they bridle at a formally defined "adolescence" which carries with it obligations to engage in specific types of work and play—obligations that society imposes on adolescents. Despite reservations many have about whether they are prepared to be adults, young people resent being labeled collectively: each seeks his own identity as a human being rather than as a member of a group whose image and lifestyle he often feels society arbitrarily defines (Sorensen, 1973).

In an industrial society, with its many opportunities and its great variety of adult roles, individuals are obliged to form for themselves a stable, coherent identity that they and others can be comfortable with. In adolescence one faces more urgently than ever before the questions that define us as persons: Who am I? What do I care about? What do I want to do with my life? Throughout the crises and changes of adulthood—marriage, parenthood, a new job, separation from one's children, old age—people have to rework their own notions of identity. The identity that is formed in adolescence is a dynamic, mobile construction that will change and grow as the person does.

Erik Erikson (1968) calls this stage of development the period of identity versus identity diffusion, and believes that in this period the individual must overcome four conflicts. They are (1) task identification versus a sense of futility, (2) anticipation of roles versus role inhibitions, (3) will to be oneself versus self-doubt, and (4) mutual recognition versus autistic isolation.

Erikson theorizes that identity formation consists of two stages. In the first stage individuals seek an answer to the question "Who am I?" Uncomfortable with their physical and sexual development and unsure of the judgment and social role, adolescents become preoccupied with who they really are and what they appear to be in the eyes of others. Often they adopt the tactic of emulating heroes and committing their faith to ideals. In the service of these ideals they believe they could prove themselves trustworthy. Young people also cling to these ideals in the hope that the ideals will prove constant while they themselves are undergoing the rapid changes of adolescence. Some individuals, however, fear the finality of making commitments; they may express their fear and need for faith by making a great point of cynical mistrust.

At this stage of identity formation conformity to the peer group may be intense. Adolescents may identify so completely with the heroes of the peer group that they seem to lose their own emerging identity. By trying out various characteristics on peers and observing the reaction elicited, adolescents hope to clarify their own idea of themselves. Somewhat intimidated by the many possibilities of the future and the conflicting values offered by society, adolescents often temporarily identify with stereotyped peer group values, thus gaining time to sort out their own values and aspirations. They may switch abruptly from utter devotion to someone or something to a complete abandonment of their commitment. The individual must test the extremes, Erikson believes, before he or she can settle on a steady course.

The adolescent's identity is affected by prior and continuing experiences and identifications but is not simply the sum of these influences. The process of identity formation requires "the capacity to synthesize successive identifications into a coherent, consistent, and unique whole" (Conger, 1978, p. 134). When the process of identity formation at this stage is completed, Erikson (1959) concludes, the individual will be "confident that he possesses an inner sameness and continuity that are matched by the sameness and continuity of his meaning for others." Then one enters the second stage, which Erikson calls the stage of intimacy. Intimacy is the capacity to commit oneself to someone or something and develop the ethical strength to abide by such commitments, even when they require painful sacrifice and compromise. Many people achieve this stage for the first time before they are out of school; others live through it in their twenties or enter it later in their adult lives.

Erikson's Crises in Psychosocial Development

BASIC TRUST VERSUS BASIC MISTRUST (FIRST YEAR OF LIFE)

AUTONOMY VERSUS SHAME AND DOUBT (SECOND YEAR OF LIFE)

INITIATIVE VERSUS GUILT (THE PRESCHOOL YEARS)

INDUSTRY VERSUS INFERIORITY (MIDDLE CHILDHOOD)

IDENTITY VERSUS ROLE DIFFUSION (ADOLESCENCE)

Adolescents are in a period of questioning that comes with their rapid physical growth and sexual maturation at a time when they have established a first level of competence in the world of tools. The chief concerns of adolescents are to establish their identity and to find a career commitment. Role diffusion may threaten among adolescents who feel ambivalent about their identity. As a result, adolescents may experience anxiety and feel incapable of making decisions or choosing roles. To compensate, an adolescent may become completely committed to some fashionable hero or ideal. Another reaction is to seek temporary relief in young love, where the adolescents seek to define their own identity through a close relationship with a peer.

INTIMACY VERSUS ISOLATION (YOUNG ADULTHOOD)

GENERATIVITY VERSUS STAGNATION (PRIME OF LIFE)

EGO INTEGRITY VERSUS DESPAIR (OLD AGE)

Adolescents may conform to the peer group so completely that they may seem to lose their own emerging identity.

ADOLESCENT EGOCENTRISM

As children develop, they slowly overcome various forms of egocentrism (Inhelder & Piaget, 1958; Piaget, 1950). In infancy egocentrism is expressed by the child's incapacity to distinguish reality from his or her own point of view and immediate experiences. In fact infants do not even know they have a point of view. But by adolescence, during the stage of formal operations, individuals become able to think and reason not only about their own thoughts but about those of others as well. However, it is at this point, according to David Elkind (1967a), that a new form of egocentrism emerges. Adolescents, searching to know who they are, become very self-absorbed. They indeed take into account the thoughts of others, but they assume these thoughts are all directed toward themselves. Specifically, egocentrism at this stage means that adolescents believe that other people are as preoccupied with their behavior and appearance as they themselves are.

Thus, unlike younger children, adolescents are constantly evaluating themselves and measuring themselves in terms of other people's reactions. Teen-agers anticipate that others will be immediately aware of and as critical of those things they find wrong about the way they look or act. Similarly, they expect others to be as cognizant of and concerned with those things they find attractive or appealing—even some slight gesture or personal mannerism. Thus, for example, when parents express a negative reaction to behavior the adolescent finds attractive, the adolescent is surprised or confused.

Adolescents, then, are in a personal "fish bowl" and are continually positing an *imaginary audience*, as Elkind says, before whom they perform. It is imaginary because actually the adolescents are probably not the focus of attention, though their overly developed self-consciousness leads them to think they are. When young people meet, each one is playing to the audience and is at the same time an audience for the others. This testing of images takes the place of substantial interpersonal communication.

Together with the imaginary audience, many adolescents begin developing what Elkind calls the *personal fable*, an ongoing, private, and imaginary story, often full of exaggerations, in which they themselves play the leading role. As part of the personal fable, adolescents come to believe that their thoughts and feelings are unique—that they are the only ones ever to experience such euphoria or anguish. This belief in one's own specialness is often tied in with a sense of immortality, a feeling the writer Joseph Conrad eloquently expressed in the story "Youth":

> I remember my youth and the feeling that will never come back anymore—the feeling that I could last for ever, outlast the sea, the earth, and all men.

According to Elkind the imaginary audience provides a way of testing reality and one's self-concept. In time adolescents begin to perceive that there is a difference between their concerns and anticipations and the real concerns of others. This usually happens when the stage of formal operations has been established (about the age of fifteen or sixteen). At this time adolescents can begin to develop true relationships, in which they find that others share many of the same pains and pleasures. The extreme self-interestedness associated with the personal fable is thus slowly, though probably never completely, overcome. Elkind suggests that Erikson's "intimacy" (1959) serves as the replacement for the personal fable.

INDEPENDENCE FROM THE FAMILY

One necessary step in achieving an integrated identity is the gradual loosening of ties to the family. The difficulty of this step depends in large measure on the nature of the parent-child relationship previously established. Much that has been written about "the generation gap" grossly overstates the problem. According to a Harris poll taken in 1971 that asked adolescents to describe their relationships with their parents, 57 percent said they got along fine with their parents and enjoyed their company. About 35 percent said that they were fond of their parents but had trouble communicating with them, and most of these felt the communication problem was "both our faults." Only a very small group—4 percent—said they did not enjoy spending time with their parents. And perhaps more surprisingly, 75 percent of the respondents said they were in general agreement with their parents' ideals.

Often tied to the assumption of differences and conflicts between generations is the notion that ideas and ideals are passed only from the older to the new generation. A review of research literature (Bengtson & Troll, 1978), however suggests that the values and attitudes of youth may actually exert some influence on parental behavior and viewpoints. In some such cases the children may serve as a connection to the "larger world" and the prevailing social and cultural mood of the times.

Yet this is not to say that generational conflict is purely a myth, either from the parents' or adolescents' viewpoint. One study involving midteens suggests that the sources of rebellion may include a lack of sufficient freedom to make one's own decisions in areas including clothing, hairstyle, and choice of friends; a desire to provoke greater parental interest and concern ("to get my parents to pay attention to me"); and a feeling of being overcriticized. Interestingly, most of the teens questioned did not want absolute freedom in decision making, but, rather, preferred their parents to be interested and actively involved in their lives (Clemens & Rust, 1979).

The degree of conflict between adolescents and parents can vary. Adolescents who have internalized many of the values of a traditional family, for example, show a greater acceptance of parental control than other adolescents. Authoritative parents who show a willingness to distribute family power as the child matures appear to have more effective interactions with their children than parents who are overly permissive or authoritarian (Baumrind, 1978). Adolescent difficulties in school, social relationships, and other areas appear to occur more frequently in families in which there is "parental hostility, rejection, or neglect" (Conger, 1977).

Some adolescents may push too hard against authority. Some parents may react arbitrarily or coercively to the changing needs of their child, thus fostering conflict. There may also be pressures from the outside world, such as school, which make the situation worse. The developing sexuality of the adolescent may also add to problems in the relationship with the family. Difficulties inevitably arise because the child becomes a sexually mature person while still living within the family structure. The adolescent must find a way out of this situation, a socially acceptable means to satisfy emerging adult needs.

The overriding task of adolescence, then, is to achieve autonomy. Adolescent autonomy develops in three areas: emotions, behavior, and values (Douvan & Adelson, 1966). Emotional autonomy occurs when people have resolved their infantile attachments to parents, when they have someone outside the home to satisfy some of their needs for affection and intimacy. Behavioral autonomy comes gradually as people are given, or demand and win,

Teen-agers feel that they are continually on display. As a result, they constantly evaluate and measure themselves in terms of other people's reactions.

the right to make decisions about personal behavior—about everything from whether they can wear jeans to a party to which college they will attend and what vocation they will choose. Value autonomy occurs when people have constructed their own set of values—a sense of right and wrong, a commitment or lack of it to a given religious tradition, and so on—that are not simply borrowed from or reactions against those of their parents but developed out of their own inner sense of themselves. Many people continue to struggle for value autonomy long after they have left their parents' homes. A young mother, for example, may find herself scolding her child in exactly the same tone of voice that her mother used years before—and suddenly realize that her value system is still very much a reflection of her mother's in spite of the fact that intellectually she might defend values that are altogether different.

PEERS AND SOCIETY

At the same time that adolescents are loosening the family ties, they are also building a greater identification with others of the same age group—evolving a sense of belonging to a generation. The results of Sorensen's 1972 study show this trend very clearly. Sixty-eight percent of his sample said they believe that their own personal values are shared by most adolescents. Moreover, 58 percent of all adolescents identified themselves with others of their own age rather than with others of their own race, religion, community, or sex. According to Sorensen, "They think of themselves primarily as being members of their own generation and look upon their youth as the main factor that differentiates them from other segments of the American population" (Sorensen, 1973).

The Society of Adolescents

Parents and the mass media have had much to say about the "youth culture" or the "adolescent subculture." Does such an adolescent society exist? Have adults merely created a convenient stereotype as a means of explaining adolescent behavior?

Insofar as adolescents organize certain features of American culture and make them specifically their own—haircuts, clothing, music, and the like—it is true that they have created their own society. But this separation is not necessarily a revolt against institutions or norms. It is more often just the way adolescents articulate their own needs and create a context in which to work out mutual problems.

In nonindustrialized cultures adolescents usually do not separate into a distinct group with an identity and values that differ from the society as a whole. Instead, adolescents in these cultures are permitted to participate to some extent in the society of adults. In Samoa, for example, adolescent girls are admitted to the *Aualama*, the organization of untitled women, and boys join the *Aumaga*, the organization of untitled men. The ceremonial life of the village centers around these groups, and much of the work in them is allotted to the young unmarried members (Mead, 1928).

In the United States adolescent society focuses on the school. The high school is usually the first place that adolescents are massed together in a large enough group to create their own social world. School is the place where the adolescents spend most of their time, in classes and extracurricular activities. In their environment they create a miniworld in which to seek answers to many of the conflicts that mark this period, the search for self-identity and values in particular. Experiences are shared, common problems are discussed, and individual achievement is measured.

Adolescents often prefer the company of their peers to that of their family, but it should not be forgotten that this can also be true of children and adults. The social milieu of adolescents is a large one. They mix socially not only with their many acquaintances but also with relative strangers. Thus, adolescent society in our culture serves as a bridge to the adult world, where adolescents will be confronted with the wide variety of colleagues and occupations of our mobile society. The peer interaction involved in extracurricular activities also mirrors the procedures by which organizations operate in the adult world. Student government and other activities create power hierarchies, and the adolescent learns how to deal with them.

Authority in many adolescent organizations, however, tends to be lateral rather than vertical. That is, adolescents tend to diffuse authority among group

A pleasant personality and physical attractiveness often determine popularity and admission to a clique.

members and are reluctant to assume positions of authority over their peers. They see their interrelationships more as a brotherhood than a vertical power arrangement.

Adolescent society differs from adult society in other ways, too, but these differences are mainly superficial. For example, adolescent society thrives on fads, distinctive modes of dress, and slang. Feeling that they are not fully accepted as individuals in adult society, they create a group identity that gives them a sense of belonging to the larger world. Despite these shows of distinctiveness, however, researchers (Bandura, 1964) have shown that normal adolescents do not differ significantly in moral attitudes from their parents. In most cases they conform to parental standards of achievement and vocational preferences.

Composition of the Peer Group

In the prepubescent period children band together in same-sex groups. In a year or so, as interest in the opposite sex increases, same-sex groups, or cliques, usually develop informal associations with a clique of the opposite sex. Individual dating is initiated by the leaders of the clique.

The clique provides a setting for intimate personal relationships that formerly were found primarily in the family. Clique members are bound together by geographic propinquity, education, heterosexual interest, degree of social and personal maturity, and similar social backgrounds as well as by mutual interests and similar academic orientation. There is usually little cutting across social class lines in clique membership.

Around the clique is the larger and less rigidly defined *crowd.* The crowd is held together by its orientation to the future, the social background of its members, and their personality types. In later adolescence the crowd disappears and is replaced by cliques of couples going steady.

In addition to belonging to crowds and cliques, adolescents usually have one or two close friends. Friendships are based on more intimate and intense feelings than clique relationships. Interaction is more open and honest and less self-conscious, and there is less role-playing to gain social acceptance. The individual hesitates less about showing his or her doubts, anxieties, and resentments. Friendships are usually based on similar social backgrounds, interests, and personality types. Friendships between widely different personality types are rare.

Popularity

Membership in the clique and the crowd is determined by popularity, and popularity may be enhanced by membership in the "right" clique. Lack of popularity (peer-group approval) can be excruciatingly painful. Knowing who you are involves knowing what others think of you. Though parental interest and involvement appear to be extremely important in the development of self-esteem (Rosenberg, 1965), the perceptions and reactions of peer-group members also strongly affect how adolescents perceive themselves.

Certain kinds of clothes, posters, and music are used by adolescents to set themselves apart from adult society.

One researcher (Ringness, 1967) found that possession of a pleasing personality was the most crucial factor in achieving popularity. Another study, however, found that physical attractiveness is the most important factor, at least for those adolescents who are perceived as highly attractive or unattractive in physical appearance (Cavior & Dokecki, 1973). The same study suggests that for those adolescents of average attractiveness a reciprocal effect may occur: attractiveness generates popularity; then popularity enhances the perception of attractiveness. The standards for physical attractiveness appear to be based on cultural definitions, which are acquired at an early age (Cavior & Lombardi, 1973; Cross & Cross, 1971).

Athletic prowess, scholarship, knowledge of popular culture, and other attributes may supplement personality qualities and attractiveness in achieving popularity, but in themselves they are not sufficient for peer acceptance. Many studies (Bonney, 1946; Tryon, 1939) have tried to identify the components that constitute a pleasing personality. Among the components they identified were: liking other people; being tolerant, flexible, and sympathetic; being lively, cheerful, good-natured, and possessed of a sense of humor; acting naturally and being self-confident without being conceited; possessing initiative and drive; and planning for group activities.

Some personality types seem more likely than others to be rejected. Those who are ill at ease and lack self-confidence may try to disguise their discomfort by aggressiveness or conceit. Being timid, nervous, or withdrawn alienates other people, as does making excessive demands for attention. Youngsters who were popular in childhood generally continue to be popular in adolescence, in part because they began adolescence with a relatively stable self-concept.

Conformity

Strictly speaking, conformity is simply following the norms of one's family, society, or peer group. This is not always so easy as it sounds, however, because these various norms sometimes conflict with one another. Ultimately, the individual must choose among them and adopt only the ones that are personally suitable. Children learn the norms by the age of eleven or twelve. Then in adolescence they begin to evaluate these norms in relationship to themselves and their evolving value system.

Researchers (Costanzo & Shaw, 1966) have used Piagetian cognitive development theory to measure the degree of conformity in adolescence. They found that with the onset of pubescence the person becomes aware of rules and relies on them for patterns of behavior. At the formal operational stage of development individuals are uncertain of their own values and judgments, and when they are in doubt, they may follow the behavior patterns and values of their peer group. However, it is also during approximately this same period in cognitive development that the adolescent becomes increasingly able to oppose the pressure exerted by the peer group (Costanzo, 1970).

Some studies of adolescent conformity tend to stress the importance of peer pressure on the choices an adolescent makes. But other research implies that parents as well as peers exert an influence that varies with the situation or issue at hand. One such investigation (Emmerich, 1978), which involved two age levels (ninth- and twelfth-graders) as well as both sexes, also suggests that, in addition to the situation, the age and sex of the adolescent may determine the relative influence of parents or peers. The study found that ninth-grade boys relied on parental advice and opinion more than either the older boys or the younger (ninth-grade) girls did. This seems to support the idea of a developmental trend in conformity and also seems to reflect the fact that girls mature more rapidly than boys.

The degree of conformity at any particular stage may vary with the situation. For example, people show an increased tendency to conform in threatening situations. One study recruited sixty-four college girls for an experiment that was said to involve painful shocks. Before the experiment was performed, the girls sought information from others to help them evaluate their emotions and opinions, and in the experiment they tended to conform to the group opinion. The implications of this study can be extended to normal adolescent behavior: perhaps adolescents develop solidarity with their peers as a means of coping with the threatening adult world. Under constant threat of the dire consequences of dropping out of school, getting poor grades, and the like, adolescents may feel that the safest thing to do is to follow the group (Ramsey, 1967). On the other hand, strongly conforming to peer norms may reflect the sudden absence of parental control or support which the child had relied on in the earlier years (Baumrind, 1978). Rather than seeing a coercive adult world, some adolescents may perceive an uncaring one, which allows them to flounder through feelings of insecurity and stress.

ETHNIC AND RACIAL ISSUES

An important aspect of identity for adolescents is awareness of ethnic or racial origins—"roots." Adolescence is the time when people take a stand, or adopt an attitude, toward being black, Jewish, "Chicano," Irish-Catholic, Italian-American, and so on. In seeking independence from parents, adolescents are often in the position of deciding whether or not to incorporate parents' ethnic customs and tastes into their own life-style. Are they to accept their roots as a positive and necessary part of their emerging identity; or are they to resist parents' customs in the interests of a new, enlightened self?

Erikson, in discussing his own admittedly drawn-out identity crisis, notes that settling on an ethnic identity was a large part of the problem (Coles, 1970). Erikson was a Dane raised among Germans; his mother had both a rabbi and a church historian-pastor among her ancestors. Though raised in the home of a Jewish stepfather, Erikson was referred to as Gentile by his childhood friends. These various identifications contributed to a prolonged and fruitful identity crisis. Ultimately it led him to observe the role of ethnic or racial issues in the identity crises of both ordinary and great men. For example, Erikson associates Mahatma Gandhi's identity crisis with his realization that

Ethnic pride is an important factor in minority teen-agers' search for self-definition and identity, and eases the transition into a productive adulthood.

in South Africa he belonged to the class of people who were called "coolies" or "coloureds" (Erikson, 1959). From that point on, he worked for, led, and identified with the subjugated Indians of his own country. Similarly, many young people in the United States develop a new sense of racial identity as a result of having been the victims of racial discrimination—of having been denied entrance to a club, for example. The same kinds of incidents may affect members of the dominant culture. Thus, Robert Coles, the child psychiatrist and author, discovered important aspects of himself only after seeing racial violence in which white men like himself were the apparent aggressors (Wilkes, 1978). The awakening of ethnic or racial identification may occur at any point in adulthood. But very often it occurs in adolescence, or in the period of youth which precedes full adulthood.

In American high schools, particularly in racially mixed urban settings, adolescents may seek to define themselves, and differentiate themselves from others, on the basis of ethnicity. One phenomenon that has helped is the recent rediscovery of ethnic pride. This pride has been an important factor in the shaping of today's culture. It is also becoming important in the individual's search for self-definition and identity, especially during the adolescent years. For example, a summary of cross-ethnic research (Smith, 1979) indicates that the self-concept of black students is on par with that of white students, contrary to the negative self-concept so often associated with young blacks in the past. The reason offered for this change toward a positive self-image is that black youths have been affected by the civil rights movement and a new awareness of black culture—history, art, fashions—that allows blacks to take pride in their racial heritage and achievement. Similar racial and ethnic pride movements among Hispanics and Native Americans may do much to give adolescents in these minority subcultures a more secure identity and to ease the transition into functioning and productive adulthood.

PROBLEM BEHAVIOR

Except for dropping out of school, most of the asocial behavior and mental health problems exhibited by adolescents are not the exclusive domain of that age group. Certainly adolescents have no monopoly on drug abuse and alcoholism, and such problems as depression, schizophrenia, and obesity cut across all age levels. Child psychologists and other social scientists disagree about whether these problems have specific characteristics when they originate in adolescence, but most agree that the developmental crises of adolescence—the physical and psychological upheavals that young people go through during this period—make teen-agers more susceptible to some of these disorders than they might be at other times of life.

Some of the problems that may cause serious concern also occur to a lesser degree without becoming serious conditions or long-term pathological syndromes. Obesity, for example, is not uncommon in adolescence, but it is usually transient and not severe. Like many adults, teen-agers have periods of depression; wide swings of mood are considered normal in adolescence. At some point many teen-agers in the United States experiment with drugs or alcohol and are little the worse for it. Unfortunately, however, in a few cases these problems become chronic (permanent) or entail severe psychological effects or social implications.

Disorders

The adolescent is subject to nearly all of the mental and emotional upsets and social maladjustments that the adult is. These run the gamut from neuroses (anxiety, phobias, obsessions, and compulsions) to psychoses such as schizophrenia. Many youngsters troubled by psychiatric disorders do poorly academically and drop out of school. Some turn to drugs; others act out their problems through asocial behavior. Unless detected and treated, psychiatric

Despite a lifetime of hearing antismoking propaganda, teen-agers continue to adopt the habit and flaunt it as a badge of maturity.

disorders during the adolescent years will continue into adulthood and can impair normal psychic functioning throughout a person's life.

Schizophrenia

Schizophrenia is a complicated psychosis characterized by a pronounced inability to relate to one's environment. Contrasting systems of behavior are typical of schizophrenic behavior. On the one hand, schizophrenics are inactive, seem indifferent to the world around and are frequently lost in reverie; on the other, they can be hypersensitive and subject to emotional outbreaks and manifestations of anxiety, panic, and profound depression. When severe, schizophrenia may permanently impair personality development, social adjustment, and mental function, usually requiring that the patient be institutionalized. But there are also mild forms. Remission of symptoms and sometimes even a complete cure are possible.

Psychiatrists are becoming increasingly aware of schizophrenic behavior in teen-agers. The problem of diagnosing this disorder in adolescence is that the usual ego changes that occur during puberty resemble those of early schizophrenia. The schizophrenic adolescent becomes increasingly seclusive, has disconcerting fluctuations in mood, is edgy, is sometimes lost in fantasy, is sometimes aggressive with siblings and impertinent to parents, and fluctuates between deep depression and euphoric exultation. All of these behavior patterns can occur in normal adolescents. The difference seems to be that healthy adolescents remain in touch with reality. Their behavior is only selectively disturbed (they may, for example, display difficult or defiant behavior at home or at school, but adjust well elsewhere), whereas the behavior of the schizophrenic is more or less uninfluenced by time and place.

Depression

Melancholy and dejection are common during adolescence. Sometimes, however, they become so severe as to require professional attention. One very severe form of this disorder is known as *manic-depressive* psychosis; it is characterized by drastic mood swings from elation to depression. These changes in mood may be either random or cyclical, and they are often accompanied by delusions or hallucinations. In manic periods a person is elated or irritable, very talkative, disconnected in thinking, and physically active. People in depressive periods may be melancholy, mentally and physically retarded, inhibited, apathetic, convinced of their own worthlessness, unable to sleep, and preoccupied with suicide.

As with the symptoms of schizophrenia, it is sometimes difficult to distinguish normal shifts in mood from abnormal ones. True manic-depressive reactions are rare before fifteen years of age.

One researcher into this problem (Toolan, 1962) believes that the most accurate way to describe depressive illness in adolescents is in terms of a set of symptoms that add up to depressed behavior. Chief among these symptoms are boredom and restlessness, fatigue, hypochondriasis (imaginary ill health), preoccupation with the body, and difficulty in concentrating. Depressed teen-agers may have a devalued self-image, which frequently leads to antisocial behavior that only produces further depression and guilt and reinforces their belief that they are bad, ugly, or inferior.

Psychotherapy seems to be the chief tool for treating the condition in teen-agers. Antidepressant drugs, which are often administered to depressed adults with good results, seem to be less effective with adolescents. The depressed teen-ager is usually eager to obtain help and frequently responds quite well to therapy.

Teen Suicide

In the United States the number of suicides among fifteen- to twenty-four-year-olds almost tripled in the years between 1955 to 1975. In 1978 suicide was the third leading cause of death in that age group. Among ten- to fourteen-year-olds the rate has risen almost as rapidly, though the actual number of individuals involved is rather small (Frederick, 1978).

Many reasons have been offered to explain these statistics. Some claim that adolescence is typically a time of special anxiety and frustration, which can trigger impulsive acts of suicide. While certain researchers (e.g., Weiner,

❖❖❖

A Report Card for Marihuana

With any drug that is deliberately introduced into the body, one must ask what harmful side effects it can have either immediately or in the long run. Concerning marihuana, both questions have been under continuing study. The following data are taken from *Marihuana and Health* (1980), the Eighth Annual Report to the U.S. Congress from the Secretary of Health, Education, and Welfare.

Millions have taken marihuana as a "recreational" drug because it usually induces a sense of relaxed well-being, a subjective increase in perception, and often an altered awareness of space and time. But negative psychological reactions do occur. In 1978 they resulted in more than 10,000 visits to hospital emergency rooms by marihuana smokers exhibiting transitory paranoia and acute anxiety, symptoms that appeared to be dose-related. Also, marihuana has frequently aggravated the condition of people who suffer from depressions or other emotional disturbances, and it is known to trigger latent severe disorders such as schizophrenia (Treffert, 1978).

The body's immediate, measurable responses to inhaling marihuana include a slight contraction of the pupils and reddening of the eyes, a greatly increased heart rate (which is dangerous for people with heart ailments), and decreased reaction time. While the intoxication lasts, it impairs certain functions, especially the processing of new information and its transfer from short-term to long-term memory; it also diminishes the ability to judge and respond to new situations. This makes drivers under the influence of marihuana a menace to themselves as well as others because they take too long to respond to unexpected events, and the greater the demands of the situation, the less they can cope. Additional dangers are that the impairment may last for several hours after the "high" has passed, and that any simultaneous consumption of alcohol multiplies the impairment, rather than merely adding to it.

With regard to learning activities, it has been amply proven that materials and concepts studied in an undrugged state are significantly better understood (Klonoff, Low & Marcus, 1973; Clark, Hughes & Nakashima, 1970) and remembered than those studied while "high" (Tinklenberg & Darley, 1975). With regard to social and intellectual pursuits, there is some concern that their development may be impeded by frequent use of marihuana, since it gives teen-agers the option of artificial relaxation as an alternative to learning how to deal with difficulties and frustrations.

What damage long-term use of marihuana may do has not as yet been established, largely because its use in Western society is of recent origin, and data from elsewhere are few and unscientific. Furthermore, deliberate and controlled experiments can be conducted only on animals, not on humans. The reliance one can place on studies that have failed to find evidence of lasting damage is therefore limited, and it is further reduced by one important factor: there has been a great increase in the potency of "street" marihuana over the last five years. In 1975 the psychoactive ingredient THC (delta-9-tetrahydrocannabinol) found in confiscated samples rarely exceeded 1 percent, while it was commonly 5 percent in 1979; and so-called hash oil, a marihuana extract that was not available a decade ago, averages 15 to 20 percent THC, and may contain as much as 28 percent. Since higher dosages create greater immediate impairment and disorientation than lower doses, they may also cause significant long-term damage.

1977) suggest that emotional crisis and stress are not the norm in adolescence, today's competition for getting good grades, good jobs, and the "good life" may be exerting increasing pressures on young people. As Dr. Bruce L. Danto, the president of the American Association of Suicidology, notes:

> Kids feel confused and frightened about the future. If you go to school, it doesn't mean you'll get a job. If you get a job, it may not be a meaningful one. If you get married, it may not last (*U.S. News & World Report*, 1978).

Also implicated in suicide is the quality of family life. Divorce (which is disrupting families at a soaring rate) or the death of a parent, for example, make adolescents feel insecure or abandoned. Excessive pressures from parents to succeed can contribute to a distorted self-image and loss of esteem, even if the child "fails" in minor ways. Some studies, like those involving suicidal adolescents from multiple foster home placements, indicate that continuity of care is perhaps even more important than the quality of family life (Glaser, 1978).

"Danger signals" of impending suicide may include rapid changes in behavior or mood; sudden loss of appetite; new or increased drug or alcohol use; long-lasting depression; oversleeping or the inability to sleep. All such warnings should be investigated. In severe cases hospitalization and medication may be required. In nearly all cases some form of psychotherapy has been shown to be important.

Eating Disturbances

Being overweight or underweight may appear to be strictly physical problems, but in adolescence in particular these condition sometimes either result from or lead to emotional disturbance. One study of adolescents categorized as "overweight," "underweight," or "average" in physique refers to the considerable body of evidence correlating appearance with self-esteem (Hendry & Gillies, 1978). Self-concept and self-perception are partly shaped by body concept, which in turn is influenced by the reactions and expectations associated with different body builds. Early on, children perceive the ideal body images transmitted by the culture and begin to judge their own physiques on the basis of feedback from others. "The fat child, like the thin, learns that the playground gives rewards to the mesomorph, not to him" (Allport, 1961). Both the overweight and underweight child's self-concept is thus vulnerable to injury or distortion. In adolescence the problem may be especially acute, since it is a time when each person's identity is coming into focus.

The physiological factors that may influence abnormal body weight include (1) dietary habits and underexercise, (2) genetic predisposition, (3) excessive number of fat cells acquired in early childhood—rarely, (4) hormonal imbalance. Obesity may occur purely as a result of any of these conditions, but it is frequently seen in people having emotional problems as well (Stults, 1977).

The list of psychological factors that might be involved in obesity could be almost endless, but one writer on the subject (Bruch, 1961; 1973) feels that there is a more basic underlying reason for eating disturbances. She believes that the fundamental problem of serious over- or underweight people is an inability to recognize one's own bodily needs—essentially, an inability to differentiate hunger from satiety—and that this incapacity stems from a child's earliest eating experiences.

> If . . . a mother's reaction [to her child's hunger] is continuously inappropriate, be it neglectful, oversolicitous, inhibiting, or indiscriminately permissive, the outcome for the child will be a perplexing confusion. When he is older he will not be able to discriminate between being hungry and being sated, or suffering from some other discomfort (Bruch, 1961).

Included in Bruch's studies of eating disorders is a condition that chiefly affects adolescent girls, *anorexia nervosa*. One of the few psychiatric disorders that can result in death, anorexia is characterized by the voluntary restriction of food intake, resulting in chronic undernutrition. Whereas most underweight adolescents may desire to have an average body build and may feel self-conscious about their appearance, anorexics pursue thinness with a vengeance.

The typical anorexic may start out being slightly overweight—more commonly, she simply fears becoming "fat"—and so begins to reduce food intake drastically and to exercise frantically. Anorexics deny all feelings of hunger, yet they are always preoccupied with food. They may eat ravenously from time to time, only to remove the food through enemas, self-induced vomiting, or diuretics. Eventually the anorexic's psychological and physiological functions become distorted. She has great difficulty sleeping and may become supersensitive to sound, light, temperature, and pain. Hyperactivity often masks a feeling of exhaustion, though anorexics will deny such fatigue. They will also deny that their emaciated appearance is abnormal. In fact, they usually continue to perceive themselves as being overweight. These symptoms are often accompanied by increasing social isolation and a fierce preoccupation with school studies.

Though once considered a rare phenomenon, anorexia has become much more common in the past twenty years. The cause of the disorder is not absolutely clear. Among females there appears to be a correlation with a delay in the beginning of menstruation or with the arrest of menstruation if the disorder is already under way (Unger, 1979). Bruch (1977) associates anorexia with an almost delusionary body concept and an overdemanding family situation. The families are usually financially and socially successful, and the parents project an image of marital happiness. Yet this image often masks serious dissatisfaction that the child feels expected to resolve or ameliorate.

According to Bruch, early diagnosis of anorexia and an integrated treatment program are very important. In chronic anorexia hospitalization and the use of intravenous feeding may also be necessary.

Delinquency

An earlier discussion in this chapter of teen-age rebelliousness mainly focused on the normal conflicts that can arise with changes in the adolescent's cognitive development and his or her need to establish a more independent status and a personal identity. Adolescent "acting out," however, can go well beyond a mere resistance to parental values or child-rearing techniques and conflicts with parents over such issues as style of dress or sexual behavior. In these cases the adolescent's behavior is construed as antisocial and may be of concern not only to the individual family but also to the society as a whole.

The term "juvenile delinquency," which was widely used in the 1950s and 1960s, is heard less frequently today. This is not, however, because delinquent behavior has abated in recent years; rather, it is because we now tend to place antisocial teen-age behavior in more concrete categories. These range from illicit drug use and violations for which adults would not be subject to legal action (such as truancy) to acts that violate the property rights or physical well-being of others and which if they were committed by an adult, would be considered crimes. Today the overall trend is to treat teen-agers more like adults (Ramsey, 1967) and to deal with individual problems in a specific way. A seemingly parallel trend is the increasing reluctance of law-enforcement officers to mediate family quarrels or personal conflicts in the parent-child relationship.

Some studies view the home environment or family as a major determinant of antisocial adolescent behavior. Negative outcomes in adolescence have been related to overly permissive or overly harsh and authoritarian attitudes and behavior of parents (Baumrind, 1978). However, others suggest that while the family plays some role in delinquency, the causal link is far from clear or direct. In other words it is not simply a case of malfunctioning families producing delinquent adolescents.

A recent investigation (Johnstone, 1978) found that the highest correlations between the family and delinquency were in the areas of drug use and "status violations," such as truancy or other such breaking of school rules. Peer influence was related most strongly to status violations, drug use, and property offenses, such as vandalism and shoplifting. However, violent acts, such as fighting or using a weapon, and criminal delinquency—serious violations of the law, such as burglary—were most significantly correlated not with peer or family influences but rather with community poverty and external pressures, including high unemployment or a high crime rate. The study goes on to suggest that problems in family relationships may have a stronger, more direct effect on adolescents growing up in "more stable and affluent social settings" than on those adolescents growing up in an oppressive and hostile external environment. In the latter case the external environment "may well overshadow negative influences from the home" (pp. 311–12).

VOCATIONAL CHOICE

One of the most difficult and potentially frustrating tasks of adolescence is the choice of a career. In the distant past vocational "choice" was really a matter of social dictate. A craftsman's son had few alternatives but to assume his father's trade; a peasant's son could only aspire to vocations that were appropriate to his social class; and women had no socially approved options

Teen-Age Drinking

About 60 percent of the American teen-agers polled in 1978 claimed to have used alcoholic beverages during their high school years. "Used" meant anything from a single drink, or a taste of someone else's drink, to fairly regular weekend beer parties (DHEW, 1979).

Opinions are divided on the dangers or advantages of letting teen-agers and children become acquainted with alcohol. Those in favor point out that few alcohol problems are found among Italians, Spaniards, Chinese, Lebanese, or orthodox Jews, who are traditionally exposed to wine or beer early in life as part of family meals and celebrations. For them drinking is therefore no proof of adulthood, and it is not regarded as either a virtue or a vice, or as the prime focus of any occasion; and while abstinence is considered socially acceptable, excessive drinking or drunkenness is not.

For teen-agers in this country, with its various prohibitions and its general mystique about drinking, alcohol acquires all sorts of connotations beyond being a pleasant accompaniment to meals and conversation. It often becomes a symbol of independence, adulthood, virility, or defiance; and in as much as these have to be demonstrated to oneself or to others, they provide incentives for an immoderate use of alcohol. This may lead to drunkenness in the first place, and to alcoholism in the long run.

The alarm with which many people and organizations here view an early acquaintance with alcohol can be seen in a fact sheet on alcoholism by an affiliate of the National Council on Alcoholism (NYCA, 1978). Most of its cited statistics concern the various kinds of havoc alcoholism causes in our society, but it also cites the statistical increase of 48 percent in the number of teen-agers who had their first drink before they had reached seventh grade.

In a Gallup Youth Survey of 1,069 teen-agers conducted in May 1977, 34 percent listed drugs and alcohol as the greatest problems they faced. In a follow-up survey two months later, 29 percent gave peer pressure as the teen-agers' reason for drug and alcohol abuse, while 26 percent attributed it to the wish to escape from the pressure of life and society (*Parents*, 1979). An estimated million teen-agers drink too much (*Human Behavior*, 1978), and girls are beginning to drink as much as boys, according to the National Council on Alcoholism (1978). For those teen-agers with drinking problems who seek help, group therapy and individual counseling is available in most cities. Alcoholics Anonymous helps people of all ages, including an increasing percentage of teen-agers.

Driving under the influence of alcohol kills about 8,000 teen-agers a year, and disfigures a further 40,000, some of them because they have misconceptions about alcoholic drinks. They don't know that a twelve-ounce can of beer—the most popular drink with teen-agers—contains just as much ethyl alcohol as the average cocktail or the average glass of wine, and that a blood alcohol content of 0.5 percent is the safety limit for a driver. Someone weighing 100 lbs. reaches that limit with 1½ drinks taken within two hours before driving; someone weighing 120 pounds, reaches it after two drinks; and someone weighing 180 pounds, after three drinks (U.S. Dept. of Transportation, 1975).

Alcohol is often a symbol of independence, adulthood, or defiance for teen-agers in this country.

beyond the roles of household manager, wife, and mother. In nearly all cases personal needs and desires were subordinated to the demands of a rigidly structured society.

Today both men and women have, potentially speaking, a wider margin of freedom in the choice of careers. Yet various factors may make the job choice difficult and may impose limitations on one's actual range of choices. Those without sufficient education or training—dropouts, for example—will probably be limited to certain jobs, no matter what career they may wish for. Adolescents from economically or socially disadvantaged homes may not even be aware of the full range of career possibilities for they lack or have limited interactions with role models outside their primary relationships, and so they may unwittingly limit their aspirations (Laska & Micklin, 1979). Women and other minorities are still affected by discrimination in the job market, though the situation has improved somewhat in the past decade. Women also continue to be influenced by negative self-perceptions and, as one study indicates, by "internalized sex role stereotypes that evidence a clear male bias" (Hanes, Prawat, & Grissom, 1979). These influences can affect the choice of occupation.

Background of the Choice
The world of work is first delineated by the family. Parents provide the first models of what workers do and how one feels about work. The socioeconomic level of the family still largely determines the vocational aspirations and attitudes of the child because ideas about the kinds of work open to the child

Parents provide the first models of what they do and how they feel about work.

and notions of the emotional significance of a person's job are determined to a large extent by family and friends. It is usual for the children of professionals to enter the professions, for example, and for parents who are unemployed or underemployed to pass these difficulties on to their children both by example and because of the economic realities of their lives.

Making a vocational choice is a long and complex process, and the factors that influence it are developed through much of an individual's life. In one study of the developmental process involved in making a career choice, the researcher (Havighurst, 1964) developed a pattern of decision making that parallels Erikson's psychosocial tasks. Notice that the development process envisioned here takes about thirty-five years and represents a major thread in the growth from early childhood into adulthood:

Age 5–10   The child identifies with the worker. His concept of working is part of his ego ideal.

Age 10–15   The person develops basic working habits and learns how to use his time and energy in order to complete tasks.

> Age 15–25   The person gains a worker identity by choosing a vocation and preparing for it.
>
> Age 25–40   The person becomes productive by perfecting the skills of his chosen vocation.

Another study (Ginzberg, 1951) of the processes involved in a child's decisions about work divides it up into three developmental stages, the first of which begins early in childhood. In the fantasy stage, up to about age eleven, children assume that they can enter any career. Their thinking about the work they want to do is purely subjective, unrelated to the realities of the work itself or to their own abilities to perform the work. The second stage, called the tentative period, includes children from age eleven to seventeen. In this stage they gradually become aware of the fact that certain qualifications are required for certain kinds of work and that these correlate with personal qualities and abilities. They develop a more realistic idea of what is involved in doing various kinds of work and come to understand that there are training requirements for specific jobs. An important realization of this period is the understanding that personal values influence vocational decisions.

In the third stage, called the realistic choice period, people begin to devise a workable plan for a career choice. This plan requires a synthesis of subjective and objective considerations, bringing together what people want to do and what it is possible for them to do within the limitations of their abilities, economic situation, and interests. Three phases are involved in this planning: (1) exploration, in which the people attempt to find out more about specific job areas through discussions with counselors, and through work-related experiences (a job after school, for example); (2) crystallization, in which people prepare to commit themselves to a vocational choice; and (3) specification, in which people select a particular occupation.

In the Ginzberg study the sample of women was too small to make a generalization. But other research provides evidence that career decisions and self-realization through work may be a more complicated problem for women. A recent study (Rosen & Aneshensel, 1978) points to the fact that there are significant sex differences in occupational attainment—women, in general, hold lower-status jobs. The researchers argue that while discrimination plays an extremely important role in this work profile, restrictions against women begin well before they enter the labor force. Their study suggests that sex differences in occupational attainment partly reflect the impact of traditional sex-role socialization, which strongly influences the expectations of adolescents.

> Sex role socialization does more than incline individuals to choose occupations traditionally assigned to their sex: it also fosters needs, values, and skills that cause some women not to enter the labor force at all, and others to do so intermittently. For traditional sex role socialization places more emphasis on achievement and occupational success in the rearing of boys than girls (p. 165).

The expectations and aspirations of adolescents are shaped not only in the home and school, but also to some extent by the very fact that the labor force continues to reflect sex segregation.

Now, more than ever before, adolescents are resisting sex-role expectations and turning to role models that challenge the existing sex-differentiated status structure, as exemplified by this workshop in engineering for high school girls.

Vocational Counseling

The complexity and increasing rate of change in today's job market makes the work of the vocational counselor both more important and more difficult than ever before. Many jobs are unappealing to youth, and many more unknown to them. In an era of extensive specialization not even a guidance counselor will know all the types of jobs that are available. Furthermore, new job categories open up continually, while others become obsolete. An adolescent, therefore, is faced not only with determining whether he or she will still be interested in a particular profession years after making the choice, but also whether that particular job has a viable future.

In an effort to help the adolescent make a career decision some high schools offer a course in vocational planning. Students also take aptitude tests that are administered and evaluated by trained vocational psychologists in many high schools and universities. These tests give at least some indication of a student's fundamental abilities and skills (mechanical, spatial, conceptual, and so on) and often disclose interests the student may not have been previously aware of.

Perhaps most helpful to adolescents are the individual counseling programs offered by many schools, church youth clubs, and government agencies. However, the need for these programs—especially among low-income adolescents who receive little or no guidance from their own families—often exceeds their availability. There simply are not enough counselors providing the time and quality of guidance that many young people require. A partial solution to the problem of time and limited facilities is group career orientation. Lectures on vocational opportunities and planning that are offered by universities, the armed services, corporation representatives, and independent service groups cannot possibly equal the value of individual counseling, but they can at least stimulate interest, broaden the person's understanding of the job market, and provide a realistic conception of the training and skills needed in various fields. Some group career workshops and lecturers are specifically geared to the vocational problems of women. They often try to provide encouragement, along with much useful information, to adolescents who are planning careers, to women who wish to change careers, and to women who are entering the job market for the first time.

SUMMARY

▶ According to Erikson adolescence is the period in which the individual must establish an integrated identity or remain troubled by identity confusion. This period has two stages. In the first stage the person seeks an answer to the question "Who am I?" and often tries to find it in conformity to the peer group. In the second stage the person tries to form and abide by a strong commitment.

▶ In order to establish their own identity people must become independent of their family. They must find other ways to meet their material and emotional needs, must make their own decisions about how to behave, and must work out their own values.

▶ Popularity with peers is tremendously important to the adolescent, but the pursuit of popularity can lead to conformity and a failure to work out one's own values. Some degree of conformity with peers is normal and indeed unavoidable, because working out personal values takes time, and meanwhile one needs some guide to action.

▶ Adolescents are prone to many of the same social and psychological problems as adults, including drug abuse and crime. Young offenders are responsible for a disproportionate amount of the crime in the United States.

▶ Because most young people have such a wide variety of vocational choices, the decision is often difficult, though guidance counseling and publications on various vocations can be a great help. Sexual stereotyping imposes vocational limitations on women and deprives them of much encouragement that men usually get.

FURTHER READINGS

Chapin, William. *Wasted: The story of my son's drug addiction*. New York: McGraw-Hill, 1972.
A father's account of drug abuse by a middle-class youth and the family's struggle to understand and deal with it. Mark Chapin started smoking marihuana at fourteen and moved on to LSD and amphetamines. He was in a mental hospital when the book was written.

Kett, Joseph F. *Rites of passage: Adolescence in America, 1790 to the present.* **New York: Basic Books, 1977.**

Compared to other countries, America has lacked rites of passage from childhood to adulthood, and that is part of the story Kett tells as he describes the experience of young Americans over nearly two centuries. Carefully researched, skillfully organized, and written in lively prose.

Klein, Norma. *It's OK if you don't love me.* **New York: Dial, 1977.**

Seventeen-year-old Jody, free-wheeling native New Yorker, has already been through two fathers and one father-figure. Then she meets Lyle, midwesterner and eighteen-year-old virgin. This novel tells what first love was like in the 1970s.

Le Shan, Eda J. *The conspiracy against childhood.* **New York: Atheneum, 1967.**

Decrying the demand for "ever-accelerated learning at an ever-earlier age," this prominent child psychologist charges that children are being forced into premature adulthood. In trying to stuff them with knowledge, we are neglecting to develop them into whole human beings, she asserts.

Schreiber, D. *Profile of the school dropout.* **New York: Random House, 1967.**

Every year almost a million youths drop out of school into a world where jobs are limited for the unskilled and uneducated. In this symposium of educators, school administrators, and psychologists the emphasis is on society's failures and on the problems and possibilities of American education. Contributors include Paul Goodman, Bruno Bettelheim, and Martin Deutsch.

Twiford, R., and Carson, P. *The adolescent passage: Transition from child to adult.* **Englewood Cliffs, N.J.: Prentice-Hall, 1980.**

This nontechnical book gives a complete overview of adolescent psychological development.

Willings, S. B. *Hassling.* **Boston: Little, Brown, 1970.**

This book about adolescent rebellion against society reports events in a high school in Palo Alto, Calif., from 1967–1969. Dissent, demonstrations, and confrontations arose over the Vietnam War, race relations, the draft, drugs, and student power.

Observational Activities
Part Five Adolescence

Teen-Agers' Values

According to Margaret Mead children in contemporary American society cannot learn useful behavior and values from their parents because the fast pace of change has made their elders' beliefs and practices obsolete in their own time. Ask four teen-agers—two boys and two girls—to define their own values. Interview each individually so that their replies will not influence one another. Ask them:

1. What are the three things that you feel are essential for happiness as an adult?
2. What are the three things that you think are most important to your parents for their happiness?
3. What are the three things that you think your parents would want for you as an adult?
4. What are the three things that are most important in your life right now?
5. What do you think you will be doing in the year 2000?
6. What do you think your family would like you to be doing in the year 2000?

Analyze the values reflected in the answers you get. It might be interesting for you to answer these same questions yourself and compare your answers with those of teen-agers several years younger than you are. You might also want to spend some class time comparing and analyzing responses others in your class got in their interviews.

Problems of Adolescence

For the first time in their lives adolescents begin to be aware of, and have to cope with, problems we usually associate with the adult world. Develop a questionnaire for five teen-agers to complete anonymously. Select fifteen- to sixteen-year-old boys and/or girls; be sure to ask them to give their age and sex on the forms. You might give them a stamped, self-addressed envelope to help them protect their identity. Your questionnaire might look something like this:

Adolescents often face problems and decisions that can affect their whole lives as adults. Please number the following problem areas from most important (put a number 1 in front of the one you think is most important to you personally) to least important (number 10):

—— sex before marriage	—— getting into college
—— drinking alcoholic beverages	—— keeping my weight where it should be
—— smoking	—— teen-age pregnancy
—— choosing a career	—— feeling depressed
—— taking drugs	—— staying out of trouble at home and at school

When you have collected the data, you may want to analyze your results together.

PART SIX

Young Adulthood

Chapter 14

❖❖❖❖❖❖❖

Physical, Cognitive, and Personality Development

M any people begin to consider themselves grown-up at about the time they graduate from high school. They are more or less physically full grown by then although they may put on another inch or two in height, and they are sexually mature. But to a greater extent than the earlier developmental periods, adulthood is defined in terms of social status rather than age or physical maturation. Thus young adulthood is marked by the taking on of social roles. Being adult means being no longer a child, a teen-ager, a student, but an engineer, a husband or wife, a parent.

Researchers mark off the period of young adulthood differently. In part this is because the study of adulthood as a developmental period is so new that a consensus has not yet been reached. But the definition varies also because the social roles of postadolescents are so varied. Some twenty-year-olds are students involved in exams and "relationships," but others already are parents—budgeting their income and bringing up their children. Some men and women enter the job market immediately after high school graduation, whereas others, such as developmental psychologists, do not undertake full-time employment until the age of twenty-seven or twenty-eight. For these reasons the early adult period is usually defined in terms of tasks accomplished and roles assumed, rather than in terms of age.

In early adulthood people usually form serious personal commitments, marry, start their families, and take their place in the world of work. During this period people define their relationship to society through love, work, and play. Adults are people who are in charge of their own lives; they earn their own keep. They make the decisions, both important and petty, about their own lives independent of other people's dictates, and accept the responsibility and consequences for these decisions. The number of years that people take to accomplish this varies—and for many people the break between adolescence and adulthood is less a moment in time than it is a long and gradual process.

YOUTH: AN OPTIONAL PERIOD

We have no trouble perceiving as "adult" the eighteen-year-old married woman who has a child *and* a part-time job. She has already undertaken some of the tasks and responsibilities of adulthood. But what about the so-called "eternal adolescent" who is in a state of moratorium or indecision well into his twenties or thirties? How do we classify the twenty-five-year-old student who is dependent on the support of his parents and the evaluation of his professors; or the thirty-one-year-old community activist who has graduated from adolescent street life, only now to explore and challenge the system. Individuals assume adult roles on very different schedules.

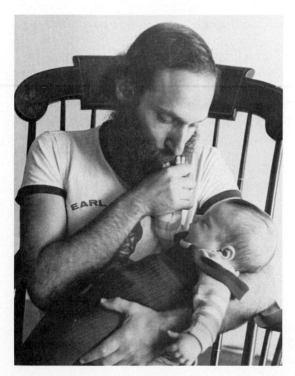

Early adulthood is usually defined in terms of tasks accomplished and roles assumed, such as husband and parent, rather than in terms of age alone.

The concept of *youth* has been introduced to deal with the postadolescent period of life that sometimes precedes adulthood (Keniston, 1970). Those young people who take a long time to "settle down" are said to have entered an optional period of development called "youth." This period stretches from the point at which the person is legally an adult (generally at eighteen) to the point at which he actually undertakes adult work and family roles. For example, a man may be legally an adult when he is old enough to vote, drive, drink, and join the armed forces, and yet not consider himself "grown-up" until he can support himself and a family some five to ten years later.

Historically, youth, like adolescence, is a rather new period of life. Unlike adolescence, however, which can be defined both biologically and socially, the youth period is exclusively a social phenomenon, which has emerged in response to several cultural factors (Kimmel, 1974). One factor is the rise of technology. The rate of technological change and increasing societal complexity require extended preparation on the part of young adults before they can become effective workers or professionals. Never before has graduate study been so acceptable, or seemed so necessary. And never before has it seemed so difficult for the nonspecialist to find entry into the world of work. The result for many young people is a period of moratorium—youth—corresponding to the college and graduate school years, though often including travel, self-study, "dropping out," and other exploratory behavior.

The period of youth is also related to the wider range of available options in life-styles and social roles. At no other time have people had such a diversity of choice in the way they live their lives. Furthermore, the responsibility for the choice increasingly rests on the shoulders of the individual making the choice rather than other family members or the traditions of society. Yet the diversity of choices and the individual responsibility for the decision tend to prolong the period before a specific choice is made.

The kinds of developments associated with youth are well summarized in the experience of a woman from California, in her sophomore year of college:

> During the year four significant things happened; first, I became reacquainted with an old high school friend and because of that year Karen and I remain the closest of friends. Second, I became panicky about the future and decided that I should become a nurse. Third, I was admitted to the honors program which gave the first unstructured classes that I'd ever had and with professors who talked about "the life of the mind"; such a world of the mind was pretty new to me and at that time it presented an alternate style to the extreme practicality that I had always known. Fourth, I took my first philosophy course, which introduced me not only to existentialism but also to Oriental religion; I also took courses which gave me my first contact with art and serious music, areas which were unknown in my home (Goethals & Klos, 1976).

Youths may reject such conventional ideas as "settling down." Especially if a person enjoys a prolonged youth, he may demonstrate what Keniston calls a "refusal of socialization" (Keniston, 1970). For example, a man may decide, after self-analysis, that the nine-to-five work pattern he has been taught

Youth is a period of moratorium, a time that often includes travel, self-study, "dropping out," and other exploratory behavior.

to respect is for him inappropriate; that rural life or entrepreneurial crafts-manship makes more sense. Often there is a sudden awareness of a lack of fit between the emerging "self" and the enduring "system." There is also, for most young adults, a new need to forge intimate relationships outside the family, and perhaps outside traditional forms. Finally, there is a need to make commitments to moral, political, or religious ideologies on the basis of the person's own rather than his parents' experiences.

Because youth is a new and optional period of life, we have not fully integrated it into our understanding of early adulthood. It is enough to say that during the uncharted period between adolescence and middle adult-hood, certain psychosocial developments occur. As we describe these devel-opments, we shall refer to a period of early adulthood, with the understanding that in some lives it is appropriate to identify a more tentative, exploratory period of youth within this period.

PHYSICAL DEVELOPMENT

Although psychologists tend to describe and define early adulthood in terms of *psychosocial developments* such as entrance into college or marriage, this period does have its special physical characteristics. During early adulthood—the twenties and early thirties—the individual is at the peak of life biologically and physiologically. Not all systems of the body peak simultaneously, however; nor do all systems peak during this period. Each system of the body has its own unique pattern and rate of development. Early adulthood is characterized both by biological maturation and decline. Yet when we consider the body as a whole, it is clear that this period is one of optimal biological functioning.

During early adulthood most people reach their full height, women around seventeen, and men, somewhat later, around twenty-one (Roche & Davila, 1972; Roche, 1979). Peak physical strength usually follows the attainment of mature stature, but is not achieved until the middle to late twenties. Thereafter, physical strength declines gradually—approximately 10 percent between ages thirty and sixty (Troll, 1975). The capacity for vigorous activity requiring not only strength but speed, coordination, and endurance also is greatest during this age period. Most Olympic and professional athletes are in this age group. One study found that all of those competing in short-distance running, jumping, or hurdling—sports that demand high agility and speed—were between eighteen and thirty (Tanner, 1964).

A number of sensory and neural functions also are at optimal levels during young adulthood. Visual acuity and hearing are most acute around twenty, the former remaining relatively constant into the middle adult years, while the latter showing a very gradual loss over the same period of time. In addition, full brain weight and mature brain-wave patterns are achieved during early adulthood.

Young adults are the healthiest individuals in our society. In fact, they are much more likely to die from violent causes—accidents, suicide, or hom-

Modern dance is a vigorous activity requiring the speed, strength, coordination, and endurance that is greatest during early adulthood.

icide—than from diseases (Fuchs, 1974). Still, some of the health problems of later life are discernible in this age group. For example, blood cholesterol—a significant contributor of cardiovascular disease—increases from the age of twenty-one.

Optimal biological functioning has important implications for the personal, social, and occupational adjustment of young adults. Indeed, in the occupations that rely on physical and sensory abilities early adulthood is considered the prime of life. A construction worker or foot soldier, for example, may be said to be in his occupational prime at twenty or twenty-five, and past it at forty. For some individuals there is no drop in measurable performance. Such musicians as Artur Rubinstein and Pablo Casals and artists such as Picasso and Titian were still at the height of their powers in their mid-eighties, with little dimunition even as they approached their nineties.

For women, reproductive capacity is also at its peak during young adulthood. Biologically speaking, the best age for a woman to become pregnant for the first time is in her twenties. This is because the organs and physiological systems involved in reproduction are better developed and coordinated during young adulthood than either earlier or later in life. During young adulthood, women are more likely to produce fertilizable eggs; their hormone cycle related to reproduction is more regular; and their uterine and pelvic environment is more conducive for sustaining a pregnancy and facilitating a safe delivery. Though many women comfortably bear children during the teen-age years or into the early forties, fertility is not as high; delivery is sometimes more difficult; and there is a greater incidence of defects in the infants during these periods than in the twenties.

Except in rare cases of disease, disfigurement, or abnormal growth, physical development usually is taken for granted by young adults. It is in middle adulthood that signs of *aging* begin to generate concern, and physical skills begin to be measured against past performance. In other words, the optimal physical characteristics of early adulthood tend to be noticed only in retrospect during the middle and elderly years of life.

COGNITIVE DEVELOPMENT

Like physical skills, certain intellectual abilities also appear to peak during the early adult years. Research indicates that tasks requiring quick response time, short-term memory, or the ability to perceive complex relations, are performed most efficiently during the late teens and early twenties. Certain creative skills, particularly those involving the development of unique or original ideas or products, also reach their highest level during young adulthood. Most other abilities, however, continue to develop beyond this age period. Intellectual skills related to verbal ability and social knowledge, for example, show increases well into the fifties (Horn, 1970). These are skills that improve with education and experience. The question of adult development and decline in intellectual areas, however, is complicated by methodological problems. As we shall see in Chapters 16 and 18, the high performance of young adults and the relatively low performance of middle-age and elderly adults on IQ tests, may well be a result or "artifact" of the cross-sectional research design.

In the broader area of intellectual functioning some developments in early adulthood have been tentatively identified by Piaget and others. Originally, Piaget's scheme of cognitive development ended in adolescence, with the period of formal operations (the period characterized by hypothetical reasoning and abstract thought). Piaget stated that this stage was reached between the ages of twelve and fifteen, and indeed for many people, including his original subjects, it is. However, in more recent writings (Piaget, 1972) he has suggested that the period of formal operations may not develop or become consolidated until late adolescence or young adulthood (ages fifteen to twenty), and that it may be expressed more narrowly than was first supposed. For example, an adult may demonstrate hypothetical reasoning in his particular field of specialization, but not in other fields. Thus an auto mechanic may show highly developed reasoning as he isolates the cause of a malfunctioning car, yet may be unable to apply the same logical skills to problems in an experimental or unrelated situation. Evidence has shown that not everyone can use formal thought to generalize from one field to another (DeLisi & Standt, 1980). In early adulthood people develop specialized interests and career commitments. Different cognitive structures, mental processes as yet unidentified, may be involved in organizing different fields of activity; or it may be that cognitive structures common to all individuals are applied differently by those in different fields.

What are some of the factors that determine the variability in development and expression of formal operational thought? Undoubtedly, cultural factors, such as the technological level of the society, play a crucial role. Societies with advanced technologies are more in need of individuals capable of high-level abstract thought. Consequently, such societies are likely to provide avenues for the development and eventual expression of this type of thought. One such avenue is education. Research indicates a positive relationship between the number of years of schooling and an understanding of volume conservation (Papalia, 1972). However, the educational content, for example, the kind of science training—genetics rather than astronomy—does not appear to affect the development of abstract thought. Another factor related to formal thought is intelligence level. As one might expect, people who are more intelligent are more likely to develop and use formal operations.

It has been widely demonstrated (Arlin, 1975) that not all adults, perhaps no more than half, ever reach the cognitive level of formal operations. The adults who do not reach this level tend to fall into certain groups such as the aged (Papalia, 1972), the less well-educated members of other cultures (Goodnow, 1962; Graves, 1972), especially non-Western ones (Dasen, 1972) and for some measures, women (Elkind, 1961, 1962; Leskow and Smock, 1970). It has been suggested (Neimark, 1981) that it may not be that these people are unable to reason logically according to Piaget's concept of formal operations, but that the tests themselves do not allow everyone to display their competency

Premenstrual Blues: Real or Imagined?

It is commonly believed by most people that women suffer from adverse premenstrual symptoms. Scientific studies corroborating this belief have produced findings that show that women in the period from three to six days before the onset of menstruation are more likely to be irritable, depressed, to gain weight, change their eating habits, retain water, and have tender or sore breasts. The phrase "premenstrual blues" began to show up in advertising copy as long ago as 1931 when a researcher gave the name "premenstrual tension" to a set of symptoms that women are supposed to experience before every menstruation. When it became known that estrogen (one of the female sex hormones) was at a low level during the premenstrual period, premenstrual tension was said to be due to these low estrogen levels. Furthermore, ovulation, when estrogen is at the highest level, has been associated with positive moods such as self-confidence, high self-esteem, and good feelings about the world. Thus the symptoms associated with the menstrual cycle have been said to be due to women's physiological makeup.

Recently a number of studies have questioned the concept of a negative premenstrual syndrome caused entirely by physical factors. Diane Ruble at Princeton University conducted a study of premenstrual symptoms in which the women who were the subjects in the experiment were duped into thinking that they were either premenstrual or intermenstrual—halfway in their cycle from the onset of menstruation—when in fact they were all about six days from the time of their monthly period (Ruble, 1977). Ruble hypothesized that the women who thought they were premenstrual would be more likely to experience premenstrual symptoms than those who thought they were not premenstrual.

The women in the first phase of the experiment were hooked up to a large oscilloscope which, they were told, would be able to determine in which part of their menstrual cycle they were. On a random basis they were then told they were premenstrual, intermenstrual, or were told nothing (the control group). They were then administered the Menstrual Distress Questionnaire developed by R. H. Moos. The "premenstrual" group scored significantly higher than the "intermenstrual" group in three of the four predicted symptoms: water retention, pain, and change in eating habits. An unanticipated variable, sexual arousal, also reached statistical significance.

Commenting on these findings, Ruble said that the results did not suggest "that women never experience pain or water retention, nor that such symptoms never accompany the premenstrual phase." Rather, the findings seemed to indicate that women, because of cultural attitudes, associate such symptoms with the premenstrual phase so that they tend to look for such symptoms when they are premenstrual as well as to think they are premenstrual if they experience these symptoms.

Other researchers have noted the extent to which other than physiological factors affect a woman's menstrual cycle. For example, women living together in a college dormitory had menstrual cycles that corresponded more closely as the college year went on. Doctors have long known that stress may delay or precipitate the onset of menstruation. Many women in concentration camps in World War II ceased menstruating; this might have been due to the near-starvation conditions in the camps.

Cultural factors also play an important part in women's perception of symptoms during the premenstrual period. In many societies and religions the menstruating woman is held to be unclean. Even today many couples in the United States do not have sexual intercourse when the woman is menstruating. In one study (Paige, 1973) it was found that most Jews and Catholics would never have intercourse while the wife was menstruating as compared to less than half of the Protestants interviewed. Protestant women did not experience much fluctuation in anxiety level, whereas the Catholics interviewed showed extreme variation.

Attitudes toward premenstrual symptoms have serious repercussions in society. Premenstrual symptoms can be used as an excuse for discriminatory hiring practices. They also offer an easy handle for patronizing and excusing: "Oh, she'll come around. It's her time of the month, you know." Most women develop coping routines if they experience monthly pain or negative feelings, such as keeping busy or making time for a little extra sleep to combat fatigue. But some researchers have found that more than 50 percent of women do not experience any symptoms at all (Rees, 1953).

equally. In particular, Neimark suggests that cognitive style affects performance. For example, people who are field-independent—that is, those who can dissemble information from a broader context to solve a problem—do well on such tests. However, people who are judged to be field-dependent, that is, those who have difficulty recognizing and isolating what is relevant to a particular problem containing other information, do poorly. Another testing factor is ambiguous instructions. The researcher, Neimark advises, should make clear not only what is wanted but should pose problems that include familiar objects and situations. Certainly, she concludes, there is a qualitative difference between child thought and adult thought. We should be able to devise tests and testing methods that reflect that difference to a greater extent than is being done at present.

Beyond Formal Operations

Although Piaget believed that the highest level of intellectual development was reached with the attainment of formal operations, other researchers have attempted to define levels of cognitive processes beyond this stage. Arlin (1975;1977), for example, has identified a fifth stage of cognitive development termed *problem-finding*, which focuses on the ability of the individual to generate new and relevant questions about the world. In problem-finding a person poses new problems rather than just attending to old ones. Or a problem-finder might discover new ways of looking at old problems in order to make new solutions possible. Arlin believes that problem-finding might be the process that links Piagetian cognitive structures to creativity. Arlin's data suggest that formal operations is a necessary, but not sufficient, condition for problem-finding. However, others have questioned the validity of this fifth stage both on empirical and logical grounds (Commons & Richards, 1978; Fakouri, 1976).

❖◆❖

Piaget's Periods of Cognitive Development

SENSORIMOTOR PERIOD (BIRTH TO 24 MONTHS)

PREOPERATIONAL PERIOD (2 TO 7 YEARS)

PERIOD OF CONCRETE OPERATIONS (7 TO 11 YEARS)

PERIOD OF FORMAL OPERATIONS (ADOLESCENCE)

 PERIOD OF CONSOLIDATION AND STABILIZATION OF FORMAL OPERATIONS (YOUTH AND EARLY ADULTHOOD)

Individuals who have attained the level of formal operations become more accustomed to operating at that level, particularly in those content areas which are related to occupational or academic specialties.

A second suggestion for an additional adult cognitive form of thought comes from the work of Klaus Riegel (1973b; 1975). According to Riegel, adult thought is characterized by a *dialectical process*—that is, a recognition and acceptance of, and even a desire for, conflict or contradiction. Riegel criticizes the notion that formal operational thought—the highest stage in Piaget's theory—is seen as the most mature form of thinking. He is especially critical of the notion that mature thought seeks equilibrium—a tensionless state where "everything fits together." According to Riegel, mature thought does not seek balance or a lack of tension, but intellectual crisis. The mature mind needs constant stimulation. It welcomes the apparent contradiction that accompanies two or more opposing viewpoints, for this is the foodstuff that fosters the growth of intellect.

Riegel notes that dialectical thinking can occur in any one of Piaget's stages, although the content of the dialectical process is much less complex at lower stages. The preschooler, for example, at first attributes absolute qualities to characteristics such as "big," "small," "heavy," "light." A person is either big or small, heavy or light. Later on, however, children become aware of a conflict with respect to these qualities. An older brother is big when compared to oneself, but at the same time, he is small when compared to Dad. How can a person be both big and small? The young child resolves this apparent contradiction by recognizing that certain characteristics have a relative quality—that is, they can be understood only in a particular context, or in relation to something else. This resolution not only solves the immediate problem for the child—understanding how someone can be both big and small at the same time—but also provides the child with the cognitive ingredients necessary to view the world in a broader, more sophisticated sense.

Youths and young adults, like preschoolers, according to Riegel, engage the world through a dialectical process although at a much higher level. The contradictions that are confronted are more often on the level of abstract ideas. Mature adults struggle with conflict in their lives in such areas as morality, ethics, politics, religion, and the meaning of life. And yet they do not necessarily need to resolve the contradictions they confront. According to Riegel, in maturity " . . . the individual accepts these contradictions as a basic property of thought and creativity" (Riegel, 1973b).

Riegel has suggested that dialectical thought may be a different type rather than a higher-order level of reasoning. Other researchers, however, argue that dialectical thought constitutes a true postformal operational stage of development (Basseches, 1980). To date, there is no agreement among researchers on the existence or possible nature of an adult cognitive stage beyond formal operations and yet the search for one continues. In large part this reflects certain limitations in Piaget's theory, specifically his exclusive focus on logical thought. Researchers have long recognized the problems of applying Piaget's theory to nonlogical areas of reasoning such as moral/ethical and esthetic thought. To the extent that research continues to yield data on adult cognition that do not fit well within Piaget's framework, there will be further attempts to identify and investigate postformal levels of reasoning.

MORAL DEVELOPMENT

Many young people are directly concerned with an area of development closely related to cognition; that is, moral development, or the development of a personal value system. It appears that a given logical ability is necessary before a person can reason at a given moral level (Kohlberg, 1973). For example, one has to have reached the formal operational level of cognition before one can engage in principled or postconventional reasoning. However, the higher levels of moral development seem to require more than cognitive development. They require certain kinds of personal experiences. For example, leaving home and entering a college environment typically exposes one to conflicting values, to emotional choices, and to new perceptions of self. Many college students react with skeptical relativism, a position that what is right is merely relative and depends on the person, his needs and circumstances, and so on. This position reflects the student's new awareness of the diversity in values and people. As students consolidate their identity they achieve a higher level of moral judgment. They may proceed to the social contract orientation of Kohlberg's stage 5 and possibly to the universal ethical principled orientation of Kohlberg's stage 6.

In the discussion of the two stages of the postconventional level in Chapter 12, it was noted that only 23 percent of all moral judgments made by sixteen-year-olds were at this level. Subsequent research suggests that the college experience is critical to these stages of moral development. For example, in one study none of the subjects who went directly into adult occupations, bypassing the stage we have called "youth," showed development to Kohlberg's highest moral stage (Kohlberg & Kramer, 1969). Other studies suggest that educational attainment is not the critical factor; that adult-life ex-

The college experience typically exposes one to conflicting values, to emotional choices, and to new perceptions of self, which promotes a higher level of moral judgment.

periences enable people who have not been to college to "catch up" to their more educated peers (Papalia & Bielby, 1974).

Recently, Kohlberg's theory, particularly the adult stages at the level of postconventional morality, has come under attack (Murphy & Gilligan, 1980). Most researchers accept the first two levels, but in research tests, according to Murphy and Gilligan, too many people show retrogression back to an earlier stage rather than development to a higher one. This lack of fit between the stages of Kohlberg's theory and test results prompted Murphy and Gilligan to call for a revision of the adult aspects of the theory. In particular, whereas Kohlberg and others believe that formal operations is a sufficient cognitive foundation for the development of postconventional morality, Murphy and Gilligan argue that a more advanced form of reasoning underlies adult post-conventional moral thought. The shift from adolescence to young adulthood, according to these authors, is accompanied by a shift in the way in which formal thought is applied within moral domains. Adolescents use formal logic in an *absolutistic* way when dealing with moral/ethical issues, whereas adults, because of their greater experience with moral conflict and choice, are more inclined to appreciate the "gray" areas of life—that is, to recognize and accept multiple perspectives in moral situations. Thus, according to Murphy and Gilligan, the absolutism of adolescent logic gives way to a more *relativistic*

Kohlberg's Levels of Moral Development

LEVEL I: PRECONVENTIONAL MORALITY (EARLY MIDDLE CHILDHOOD)

LEVEL II: CONVENTIONAL MORALITY (LATE MIDDLE CHILDHOOD)

LEVEL III: POSTCONVENTIONAL MORALITY (LATE ADOLESCENCE OR EARLY ADULTHOOD)

It is at this stage that the individual determines "right" and "wrong" on the basis of personal, internalized standards rather than societal standards.

Stage 5 morality emphasizes the regulation of just and moral laws which are not primarily concerned with law and order (as in Stage 4), but with others' individual rights and freedoms.[a]

Stage 6 morality is not attained by most people. It is a state in which the individual determines "right" and "wrong" solely on the basis of his conscience. If the person obeys the law yet violates his own principles, he feels guilty.[a]

[a]According to Kohlberg, these stages are not attained by the majority of adults.

approach to moral dilemmas during young adulthood. For example, when asked whether his moral beliefs had changed since he entered college, one person in Murphy and Gilligan's study answered that as a result of

> experiences in trying to get [my beliefs] into practice [I have become] more considerate, taking into account other people's feelings and other people's lives and how you as a person affect their lives. And seeing whether your effect is a good effect or a bad effect. And before, I didn't really care about that too much. My first responsibility was mainly to myself, and the other just went along (Murphy & Gilligan, 1980).

Although controversy continues to surround the nature of Kohlberg's advanced moral stages, it is generally agreed that while postconventional morality may begin to develop during late adolescence, it is not until adulthood, when people have finally attained the freedom to make their own life choices and have begun to assume responsibility for others, that this higher form of moral thought is established. According to Kohlberg (1973), "while cognitive awareness of principles develops in adolescence, commitment to their ethical use develops only in adulthood." It is then that people make serious commitments—to themselves, to others, to ideas and ideologies.

PERSONALITY AND ADJUSTMENT

Early adulthood is the fullest, most individualistic, and at the same time, loneliest period of life (Havighurst, 1974). During this time tremendous pressures are brought to bear on individuals to "make a constructive place" for themselves in society. And yet the support systems available for any person to accomplish this goal are few indeed. Havighurst has suggested that, with the exception of the elderly, young adults receive less educative support to accomplish their *developmental tasks*—the prescriptions, obligations, and responsibilities thought to be related to healthy adjustment—than any other age group.

Growth Trends in Adjustment

Youth and young adults often find themselves searching for meaning in their lives. Having tackled the basic issue of identity in adolescence and it is hoped, having achieved some, if only temporary, resolution about self-definition, the young adult is often preoccupied with the expansion of self into society, that is, with finding new avenues of self-exploration in interpersonal and societal contexts. Youth and young adults seek growth and expansion—they abhor the status quo (Keniston, 1970). This emphasis on movement, change, and transformation is expressed in several psychological and behavioral domains. One useful framework for understanding these changes has been presented by White (1975), who identified five *growth trends* commonly found during this period.

Stabilization of Ego Identity

Ego identity—one's feelings about oneself—is less influenced by momentary or transient experiences during this period than at any time in the past. One's ego cannot be destroyed as it might have been ten years earlier by being called a coward, for example, especially if one is quite certain it is not true. As a result of greater commitment to social roles and to other human beings, the young adult begins to develop a relatively stable, consistent, and clearly defined sense of self. In particular, deciding on and working in one's occupational role, if the role is a congenial one, helps a person to define him- or herself.

Freeing of Personal Relationships

Also, young adults are less tied to their own desires and fantasies than are adolescents. This allows them to develop interpersonal relationships that are truly responsive to another person's unique characteristics and needs. The freeing of personal relationships from one's own anxieties and absorption in oneself is facilitated by a more stable sense of self-assurance. Until the individual knows who he or she really is, it is difficult to relate freely and openly with others.

Deepening of Interests

During this period there is greater engagement in specific areas of interest. Unlike the child and the adolescent, whose involvements are often short-lived, young adults show true commitment and a deepening of interests, whether in academia, occupation, hobbies, sports, or personal relationships. Further,

Early adulthood is the fullest, most individual-istic, and at the same time, loneliest period of life.

because of their increased interests and deeper involvement, young adults, more than younger people, usually gain more from their activities both in terms of skills learned and satisfaction received.

Humanizing of Values

Young adults also display an increasing awareness of the human meaning of values and the ways in which they function in society. Morality and ethics are no longer viewed as inflexible or absolute rules, but rather are seen in a more personal, humanistic light, based to a greater extent on life experiences.

Expansion of Caring

A person's concern for the welfare of others expands during youth and early adulthood. There is movement toward increasing empathy, not just with the specific individuals that one encounters, but with common humanity. In essence, this is a generalized extension of the self to the more unfortunate in our society—to the poor, the oppressed minorities, the ill.

These growth trends, outlined by White, represent only *potentials* for change. During youth and young adulthood people may show some movement along these dimensions, but do not necessarily fulfill all these goals. In fact, it is probable that these growth trends represent ideals achieved only by a few individuals in our society. But regardless of the degree to which they are achieved, the trends do represent the most important personal tasks or challenges confronting the young adult—tasks that are bound up inextricably with the person's socioemotional adjustment during this period of life.

SEQUENCING OF LIFE EVENTS

We have noted that youth and young adulthood are the times when people begin to adopt adult roles—worker, spouse, parent, community activist, and so on. And we have noted that people differ in the ages at which these roles are adopted—one person may marry at eighteen, another may choose to wait until thirty. The *order* in which people choose to do things also varies during this period. In the past, fairly rigid custom prescribed that a young man should first finish his education and military service, then get a job; only after these steps were taken was he expected to marry and have children. Young women, in contrast, were expected to marry and bear children soon after high school— if their education even reached this far. Over the past few decades, however, the timing and order of life events have become less clear-cut for both sexes. Education for men, and especially women, is being completed much later than in the past. Women are entering the work force in greater numbers and are setting their sights on higher career goals than ever before. People are having fewer children and more couples are actually choosing to not have children. Do these deviations from the customary order of life events in the young-adult period make a difference in people's lives?

One researcher (Hogan, 1978) examined the order of completing school-ing, taking a first job, and marrying among 33,500 men born between 1921 and 1950. Most men, it was found, followed the expected order of life events described above, although there were socioeconomic and ethnic differences in this regard. For example, Caucasian males were less likely to follow the expected pattern because they completed their education much later than other groups of men. Furthermore, black men were more likely to marry, and Hispanic men were more likely to work, prior to finishing their education. For men who deviated from the usual order of life events there was a higher rate of marital separation and divorce. Marital disruption was 17 percent higher among those who married before getting their first job and 29 percent higher among those who married before finishing school.

The effects of early and delayed childbirth have been the most frequently studied aspects of deviation from expected life events among women. Re-searchers have found that 10 percent of the women questioned became preg-nant before finishing high school and 40 percent of the live births to these women occurred before marriage (Green & Polleigen, 1977). One consequence of the disruption in life events for these teen-age women was that 80 percent of those who gave birth to a child did not finish high school. Furthermore, it appeared that women whose education is interrupted by childbirth at any age, in general, do not make up the educational deficit later in their lives (Moore & Waite, 1977). Other research has found that if a woman marries after becoming pregnant and before school is completed, she is likely to have a greater number of children—and to have them closer together in time—and her marriage is two to three times more likely to end in divorce. At the other extreme, women who postpone their first pregnancy until after their educa-tion is completed and after they have been married a year or two, are more likely to work before the birth of their first child and to expect and get more help from their husbands (Presser, 1978; Scanzoni, 1975).

The order of adopting adult roles thus makes a difference in the sub-sequent life of the person. To a certain extent this is because of the disapproval most people encounter when they do not do what they are expected to do.

There is no great rejoicing in a family whose unmarried daughter has just had a baby; a school dropout can scarcely expect festivities such as attend a graduation when he fails to finish school. Individuals who deviate in life events, too, are likely to become distressed if their life-styles do not follow the course they expected. They also suffer because social institutions do not offer the same support systems to those whose lives deviate from expected norms. Yet societal response to people whose life events are ordered differently than the majority appears to be changing in a more flexible direction. This change in attitude appears to be tied to various social movements such as the rise of technology, the demand for greater education, and the women's movement. Given the continuation of this social trend, we speculate that adopting adult roles in an atypical order probably will have a less negative impact on people in the future.

IDENTITY

In youth and early adulthood the individual begins to stabilize his identity. Especially if he goes to college, he is likely to find himself changing the identity he forged in adolescence (Waterman, Geary, & Waterman, 1974). He may reexamine many of his values and self-images as a result of challenges during his freshman year. He will probably experience a new form of identity crisis. Whereas the adolescent asks, "Who am I?", the young adult tends to ask "Where am I going?—and with whom?" Youth or early adulthood is the period in which a person tackles the question of how he is to find his place in society. He begins to establish his own life-style, and to make commitments, more often than not in the belief that decisions are irreversible (Sheehy, 1976)—which of course they are not.

Identity Statuses in Young Adulthood

As we noted in Chapter 13, Erikson (1968) described the identity crisis confronting adolescents as ego identity—the achievement of a relatively consistent sense of self—versus identity diffusion, the feeling of a diffuse sense of self resulting from being overwhelmed by role possibilities. However, Marcia (1966) has suggested that the resolution of the identity crisis in young adulthood is more complex than the description offered by Erikson. Marcia has identified two factors as critical to the resolution of identity in young adulthood: (1) the existence of a personal crisis in such areas as occupation, religion, or politics, and (2) the person's degree of commitment to issues in these areas.

Combining these two factors, crisis and commitment, Marcia created four resolutions of the identity crisis that he termed *identity statuses. Identity achievers* are individuals who have experienced crises in occupational, religious, and political areas, and have reached a personal decision or commitment which may or may not agree with parental desires and viewpoints. Such a commitment must be based on the experience of a true decision-making process, and not be simply a reflection of parental wishes. In contrast, individuals who are characterized by *identity foreclosure*, while also making lifestyle and value decisions, do so in a way that precludes crisis and personal-value commitment. These individuals give in to parental desires and points of view either out of emotional or financial pressure, fear of disapproval, or feelings of inadequacy and incompetence. For example, consider the young man who enters the family business because "it is expected of him." Marcia believes that although such individuals may appear to have strong ideological and career commitments, they actually lack a strong ego identity because they have avoided personal confrontation and crisis in these areas.

Individuals categorized as in *moratorium* or as being *identity diffuse*, unlike identity achievers and foreclosures, show no evidence of commitment. On the contrary, they are indecisive about life decisions and values. Individuals in moratorium, in contrast with identity-diffuse individuals, are, however, at the height of crisis about these issues. They are struggling to achieve a degree of consistency about who they are and where they are going. Identity-diffuse individuals appear less concerned or preoccupied with these issues; not only are they uncommitted to specific life-styles or values, but they also show no evidence of personal crisis in respect to these issues.

MARCIA'S ADULT IDENTITY STATUSES

	Crisis	No Crisis
Commitment	Identity Achievers	Foreclosure
No Commitment	Moratorium	Identity Diffuse

What relationship do these identity statuses have to personality and socioemotional adjustment in early adulthood? To summarize just some of the findings, identity achievers usually are high in self-esteem, independence, moral reasoning, and low in anxiety. Individuals in moratorium are quite similar to identity achievers, but because they are still in crisis, show higher levels of anxiety and conformity to external pressure. Young adults who have foreclosed identities show greater rigidity and submissiveness to authority. Foreclosed men tend to be conventional in morality, and lack insight about themselves. Finally, identity-diffuse individuals show evidence of low self-esteem and high anxiety. For example, identity-diffuse women are more likely to choose easy college majors (Matteson, 1975; Whitbourne & Weinstock, 1979).

In a follow-up study six years later with thirty of his original subjects, Marcia modified his concept of identity statuses. "The problem with identity statuses is that they have a static quality and identity is never static, not even for the most rigid Foreclosure [a person in the foreclosure status] who must somehow accommodate himself to each new life cycle issue . . . A Foreclosure

Personal crises in areas such as commitment to a political position contribute to resolution of identity.

[should be seen as] coming from someplace and going to someplace" (Marcia, 1976, p. 153). Thus it is clear that as people enter into adulthood they show considerable variation in identity development, which in turn is reflected in differences in personality and adjustment. Adult identity must be thought of as a process—an ever-changing aspect of the human being that is responsible to, and reflects the unique experiences of one's life.

INTIMACY

From the very beginning of life, intimacy—physical and emotional—is critical to development. Infants and their mothers, the little leaguer and his dad, the junior high school girl and her best girl friend are examples of intimate relationships that occur in the course of development. In the early adult period, however, a new kind of intimacy becomes possible. This is the intimacy freely chosen by two equal persons who have worked through the adolescent crises and know basically who they are.

Erikson theorized that the ability to become intimate with another—the central psychosocial task for the young adult in his theoretical model—awaits the resolution of the identity crisis. Researchers who have undertaken to measure ego identity and intimacy variables, have largely substantiated this hypothesis. It is only after one achieves a sense of identity that it becomes safe to risk fusing this identity with that of another person.

Psychological Androgyny

"Why can't a woman be more like a man?" Perhaps she can: One of the important consequences of the resurgence of the women's movement in the past decade has been a reevaluation of sex-role stereotypes. Feminists and others have attacked the traditional assumption that a psychologically healthy individual must necessarily have a well-defined masculine or feminine sexual identity.

In an eye-opening study, a group of researchers demonstrated that such stereotyped feminine characteristics as dependency, expressiveness, obedience, and passivity were considered unhealthy by a group of psychoanalysts (Broverman et al., 1970), saying in essence that mental health experts regard the stereotyped women as psychologically ill. A number of studies have found a high correlation between masculinity and self-esteem and adjustment (Leahy & Eiter, 1980; Spence et al., 1975). That is to say, a masculine male represents robust mental health; a feminine female, poor mental health. Now, however, it is argued that no matter how well adjusted the male with masculine characteristics may be, the strong, silent, innerdirected masculine man may not represent the best adaptation to today's society. Perhaps it is possible, even desirable, for a person to be androgynous—that is, to possess both masculine and feminine personality traits.

Advocates of psychological androgyny suggest that people who adhere strictly to a particular sex role not only cut themselves off from a whole range of valuable experiences, but may be a detriment to others. For example, the man who cannot communicate with his children or his fellow workers, who cannot empathize with the situations of others, who demands and gives only on his own terms, may only stifle those around him. Suppose such a person was empathetic, a good and understanding listener, and a source of support in addition to strength, courage, and integrity, then he would combine the best of the so-called masculine and feminine traits into an androgynous personality. The feminine woman who is also assertive, self-reliant, and confident combines a different set of characteristics to exemplify the androgynous person.

The androgynous person is not one who is locked into a particular sexual self-image; he or she is free to accept or reject activities on their merits rather than their gender associations—free to become a doctor, a machinist, a house painter, a jockey, a police officer, or a parent.

In recent years a number of psychological researchers, notably Sandra L. Bem of Cornell University, have attempted to test these hypotheses empirically. Bem devised a self-rating procedure which measured the degree to which young adults possessed both masculine and feminine characteristics. Subjects were typed masculine (i.e., scoring high on traits judged to be masculine—such as ambition, forcefulness, and self-reliance; and low on those judged feminine—gentleness, warmth, loyalty); feminine (low on masculine, high on feminine); androgynous (high on both masculine and feminine); or undifferentiated (low on both masculine and feminine). Bem then conducted a series of experiments that introduced subjects into situations designed to elicit either distinctly masculine or distinctly feminine response. For example, one feminine-oriented experiment involved the interaction of a subject with an infant.

As we might guess, masculine-typed subjects responded significantly better in masculine situations than in feminine situations, whereas the reverse held true for feminine-typed subjects. (There were no significant differences between the performances of masculine-typed men and masculine-typed women, or between those of feminine-typed women and feminine-typed men.)

Androgynous subjects, on the other hand, responded well in both masculine and feminine situations. This seems to bear out the theory that androgynous individuals are open to a wider range of experiences than sex-typed individuals.

Psychological androgyny is not a new concept. In every society there have been perceptive people who have realized that roles assigned to the respective sexes are arbitrary and, in many respects, debilitating. But in the past there always existed compelling social and economic reasons for adhering to strict sex-role patterns. In today's highly mobile society this may no longer be the case. Dr. Bem writes, "In a society where rigid sex-role differentiation has already outlived its utility, perhaps the androgynous person will come to define a more human standard of psychological health" (Bem, 1976).

Intimacy and Attachment

What are the origins of adult intimacy? What factors are important for determining the capacity of the adult to form warm, reciprocal, and enduring physical and emotional relationships with others? According to some developmental psychologists, the foundation of adult intimacy can be traced to the early attachment bonds between infants and other human beings, particularly their parents (Troll & Smith, 1976). For some individuals, these early socio-emotional relationships produce a sense of security, trust, and the desire to be close to others; other individuals become frustrated and insecure, providing the seeds for later problems in forming mature relationships based on respect and mutuality.

Attachment is a lifelong process influencing the frequency and quality of all interpersonal relationships—both sexual and nonsexual. Some researchers have even suggested that when we become attached to groups, ideas, or objects, the critical factor in all of these examples is a strong emotional involvement (Kalish & Knudtson, 1976).

While attachment is a pervasive and enduring process throughout life, the nature and object of our attachments change with age. In earlier chapters we have noted examples of attachment among family members and peers and the emergence of tentative, heterosexual attachments in adolescence. In young adulthood new forms of attachment develop—to spouse, children, job. These attachments, some of which are quite strong and others weak, are the bonds of adult life—the bonds by which people find meaning in their lives.

The willingness to care for the other as much as one cares for oneself underscores the intimacy of early adulthood.

Sexual Intimacy

Before the resolution of the identity crisis, attempts at sexual intimacy are usually of the searching, self-serving kind in which something is given or someone is reassured. Both partners are afraid of losing themselves of course because they do not have a strong sense of self to begin with.

By contrast, the intimacy of early adulthood is characterized by *mutuality:* ideally, one cares for the other person as much as one cares for oneself. Mutuality entails the willingness to make sacrifices and compromises. And it involves mature sexual functioning—genital love. Genital love, as defined by Erikson, involves the choice of a partner with whom one is willing to regulate the cycles of procreation, recreation, and work. In other words, it affects the entire composition of life in this period and later.

Naturally, researchers have been interested in determining when young people achieve mature sexual intimacy, and what variables affect the outcome. It does seem that the potential for mature sexuality occurs for most people in young adulthood rather than during adolescence. Although a major 1973 study indicates that 52 percent of all teen-agers have had sexual intercourse, only 15 percent report sexual relations with one special person at a time (Sorenson, 1973). In early adulthood there is a major shift from masturbation and sexual fantasy and casual sexual encounters to regular sexual intimacy with one other person.

Erikson's Crises in Psychosocial Development

BASIC TRUST VERSUS BASIC MISTRUST (FIRST YEAR OF LIFE)

AUTONOMY VERSUS SHAME AND DOUBT (SECOND YEAR OF LIFE)

INITIATIVE VERSUS GUILT (THE PRESCHOOL YEARS)

INDUSTRY VERSUS INFERIORITY (MIDDLE CHILDHOOD)

IDENTITY VERSUS ROLE CONFUSION (ADOLESCENCE)

 INTIMACY VERSUS ISOLATION (EARLY ADULTHOOD)

> The young adult, having emerged from the identity crisis, seeks to fuse his identity with that of another human being. He has developed the ethical strength to make commitments—to causes, to friends, and to sexual partners. It is in this stage that true *genitality* and *mutuality* develop; with a loved partner, the individual looks forward to the responsibilities of adulthood. If the young person avoids intimate relationships out of fear that they will threaten the emerging identity, isolation and self-absorption will result.

 GENERATIVITY VERSUS STAGNATION (MIDDLE ADULTHOOD)

> The young adult typically *begins* to express the crisis of generativity in decisions and feelings about parenthood.

EGO INTEGRITY VERSUS DESPAIR (OLD AGE)

Although most people begin to establish sexual relationships in early adulthood, there is great variation in the intimacy which is thereby achieved. Sexual union can be the all-encompassing development described by Erikson; or, reduced to its most common denominator, it may become "the joining of separate almost disembodied anatomical parts" (Masters & Johnson, 1975). It appears that the outcome of the identity crisis, and the resulting strength of the ego, influence the quality of sexual intimacy.

In one recent study, for example, college students who scored high on ego identity were found to score high on intimacy as well. These students were able to share worries, and express anger as well as affection toward their partners (Orlofsky, Marcia, & Lesser, 1973). On the other hand, students who scored low on identity measures were shown to have developed alternatives to intimacy: "stereotyped" relationships, or relationships characterized as "pseudointimacy."

In stereotyped relationships, the partner is treated more or less as an object, and the person seeks not intimacy, but sex for its own sake. In pseudointimate relationships the commitment is usually more permanent. The couple look and behave like partners but the relationship is largely based on convenience. For example, a woman may need a man because he provides status; the man may need her because she provides certain housekeeping services. On the emotional level, the couple hardly communicates. A typical statement of the pseudointimate partner is: "She meets my needs and doesn't make demands on me, so why should I complain?"

The opposite of intimacy in Erikson's model is *isolation*. Some young people isolate themselves from close relationships with others. In some cases this is an indication of emotional disturbance. For example, a man may have been so psychologically damaged by a parent's having abandoned him that he is unable to engage in satisfactory interpersonal relationships. In another case, a woman may be in a moratorium state. Problems involved in breaking free of parents or choosing a career may leave her with little energy or desire to get involved with another person.

Nonsexual Intimacy

Intimacy in heterosexual love relationships is not the only kind of intimacy that is first achieved in early adulthood. New relationships with peers and elders become possible in response to what White calls the "freeing of relationships" from childhood expectations (R. W. White, 1975). Adults are no longer perceived in terms of parental stereotypes, but are appreciated as people in their own right. "For the first time," says a returning college student, "I was able to talk to my mother and my older brother as if they were real people—or friends."

"Psychological apprenticeships" to older people may be formed during this period (Keniston, 1970). At work or in college and graduate school *mentors*—teachers, advisers, or "parental figures" who may be eight to fifteen years older than the young person—become important (Levinson et al., 1977). Finally, the quality of friendship changes. Whereas adolescents tend to choose friends who remind them of themselves or what they want to be, young adults choose people for their own sakes; that is, they respect individual differences (Vaillant, 1977).

SUMMARY

▶ Early adulthood is a time of greater diversity than earlier stages. Some young adults are students, some are already parents, some hold jobs, some live with their parents, some live alone. Because many positions in modern society require extended preparation, young adults may stay in school or live at home until their late twenties. *Youth* is the term used to cover the time between age eighteen and that time when individuals adopt adult commitments, identities, and life-styles.

▶ In early adulthood people are at their biological and physiological peak in terms of speed, coordination, strength, endurance, and health. For women, early adulthood, biologically speaking, is the best time to bear children. The ability to perform cognitive tasks that require quick response time, short-term memory, and perception in complex relations is at its sharpest.

▶ Recent work suggests that Piaget's period of formal operations (the period characterized by hypothetical reasoning and abstract thought) may not develop until late adolescence, and is expressed more narrowly than was first supposed. Some investigators have speculated on the existence of a cognitive stage beyond formal operations, although research evidence supporting its existence is still not compelling. Moral development requires both cognitive development and personal experience. Experience during the "youth" stage and the outcome of identity issues may influence moral values.

▶ Early adulthood is a time of personal growth. White postulates five major growth trends during this period: stabilization of ego identity; freeing of personal relationships; deepening of interests; humanizing of values; expansion of caring.

▶ Youth and young adults begin to adopt the roles associated with maturity—worker, lover, spouse, parent, and so on. The timing and order of adopting these roles varies considerably from one person to another, which in turn makes a difference in the subsequent life of the individual.

▶ A major question for young adults is how they are to relate to society—where do they fit in, and what roles will they adopt? These are issues that are closely tied to the stabilization of ego identity. Research by Marcia and his colleagues suggests that there are four separate identity statuses in young adulthood—identity achiever, identity foreclosure, moratorium, and identity diffuse—and each is associated with different patterns of psychosocial adjustment.

▶ Once people have established their own identities, a new kind of intimacy becomes possible, an adult intimacy based on mutuality. In Erikson's models, the opposite of intimacy is isolation. People may isolate themselves from close friendships and contacts, either because of some emotional disturbance or because they are in a "moratorium" state. Intimacy in nonsexual as well as sexual relationships can be fully realized at this time; parental stereotypes are discarded, mentors may become important, and friends come to be cherished for their own sakes.

FURTHER READINGS

Goldberg, H. *The hazards of being male: Surviving the myth of masculine privilege.* New York: Signet, 1976.

A discussion of the heavy emotional price—including death—that men pay for the denial of feeling and repressing emotions.

Milgram, J. I., and Sciarra, D. *Childhood revisited.* New York: Macmillan, 1974.

Famous people recollect their youth. Selections are taken from the autobiographies of Chet Huntley, Joan Baez, Upton Sinclair, Jean-Paul Sartre, Charlie Chaplin, and others.

Rich, A. *Of woman born: Motherhood as experience and institution.* New York: Norton, 1978.

Rich demonstrates that the sources of male and female personalities can be traced to the experience and institution of motherhood.

Troll, L. E. *Early and middle adulthood.* Monterey, Calif.: Brooks/Cole Publishing Co., Inc., 1975.

In Chapters two and three of this text, Troll provides a complete examination of physical and intellectual development in early and middle adulthood.

White, R. W. *Lives in progress.* New York: Holt, Rinehart and Winston, 1966.

Three extensive case histories supplement White's coverage of adult personality development. The book covers the various growth trends at work during young adulthood.

Yankelovich, D. *The new morality: A profile of American youth in the 70's.* New York: McGraw-Hill, 1974.

Yankelovich, a public-opinion expert, compares a survey of young people polled in 1967 with one in 1972. One of his findings was that although the teenagers of the seventies still rated interesting work highly, they had become more concerned about money and security.

Chapter 15

❖❖❖❖❖❖

Family and Occupational Development

Freud once was asked what a normal adult should be able to do well. He replied, "To love and to work" (quoted by Erikson, 1968). Young adulthood is a time when people make commitments in personal relationships and work. New roles are adopted—lover, spouse, parent, worker—and are incorporated into the developing self. By taking these roles people not only attain personal growth, but they bind themselves to other human beings, becoming adult members of society. Kenneth Keniston speaks of young adulthood as a time when people expand into society. That expansion takes place as we marry, establish our families, and find our places in the work world.

MARRIAGE

Marriage is not, like intimacy, a psychosocial achievement; it is a social and legal status. There are laws that regulate behavior in marriage. For example, despite a wedding ceremony, a couple are not legally bound to one another in marriage if the marriage is not consummated, that is until they engage in sexual intercourse. Thus does the state reach into the sanctity of the home; laws regulate the responsibilities of both the husband and the wife.

Social norms, the unwritten rules that govern society, very much influence the age at which people marry. According to a study in the sixties, social expectations were so strong that most young people were conscious of being "early," "late," or "on time" with respect to marriage (Neugarten et al., 1965). These perceptions were an influence on behavior. For example, a middle-aged woman confessed that she married upon graduation because "at the time it was the thing to do." Another woman became terribly depressed because she was not married by thirty—the easy deadline she had set herself years before. Under similar social pressures, a man may feel the need to be married at a particular point in his career; to do so is to be perceived as socially acceptable, responsible, and heterosexual.

These pressures undoubtedly still exist among many social groups. However, there is a greater tolerance today for later marriages. Women who are advancing in their careers may want to postpone marriage and men may want to establish themselves firmly by their performance on the job. A greater acceptance of cohabitation has made it possible for many people to live together, putting off marriage until they feel more sure of themselves and of their choice of a legal partner.

The pressure on young adults to get married also seems to be lessening. For example, although four-fifths of all respondents in a research survey con-

Marriage is predicated by new personal relationships and the expansion into society; it confers both a social and legal status.

An increasing number of men and women are choosing to remain single longer, postponing the responsibilities of child-rearing until their mid-to late thirties.

ducted in 1957 indicated that it was wrong to not marry, the corresponding figure for a similar sample of respondents in 1976 was only one-quarter (Douvan, 1978). Marriage today, or at least the traditional early marriage, appears to be but one of several possible life-style choices. Although most young adults still choose to get married, an increasing number of men and women are making the choice to remain single, or to postpone marriage until their late twenties or thirties.

Mate Selection

One of the most obvious problems to be faced in regard to marriage is the choice of a partner. The field seems large enough; there are millions of unattached people in the world. But realistically, the range of selection for each person is limited. All the while one is seeing, meeting, and going out with potential partners, a selective screening process is taking place. In the end, people seem to choose their mates from a narrow group of others who are much like themselves.

There are three factors which influence the mate-selection process: physical attractiveness, propinquity, and endogamy. Physical attractiveness has been found to be the best predictor of mutual liking between new acquaintances. In a study at the University of Minnesota, male and female freshmen were matched randomly at a dance. Four student ushers secretly evaluated the attractiveness of each student. Results showed that the higher the attractiveness rating, the greater the liking, and the more the subject expressed a desire to see the person again. The correlation between attractiveness and liking was even higher when the rating was done by the subjects themselves (Walster et al., 1966). Later in establishing a relationship, personality traits and other characteristics gain more prominence—and may even weaken the effects of physical attraction (Mathes, 1975).

Propinquity means nearness. People are more likely to choose a mate from among those who live or work nearby, if only because they are more likely to meet such people. In a study of married couples, Clarke (1952) found that slightly more than half of the couples he studied lived within sixteen blocks of each other while dating.

Endogamy refers to the general practice of choosing a mate from within one's own social group. Marriage choices in the United States tend to be endogamous. Thus people will tend to choose a partner who is of the same race and ethnic group, the same religion, the same social class, of roughly the same age, the same level of education, and whose values and world view are similar.

Some endogamy factors are stronger than others. Judging by the scarcity of interracial marriages, race would seem to be the single most powerful of the endogamous factors in mate selection. Religion is still important: over 90 percent of Protestants marry other Protestants; over 90 percent of Jews marry other Jews; and over 75 percent of Catholics marry other Catholics (Carter & Glick, 1970). And social class exerts a strong influence. However, when people marry outside their own class, men tend to marry women of lower social class, while women tend to marry men of higher class.

The factors involved in mate selection have been listed and defined, and the word "love" has not yet been mentioned. Most Americans would take the position that love is and should be the major factor in choosing a husband or wife. To marry someone for money or connections or family background would not be approved by many in our society. Yet this is a relatively recent attitude. Formerly in Western society, and even today in many parts of the world, the heads of families choose marriage partners for the young people. Marriage is seen as a public matter, joining families as well as individuals. A family makes sure that their son or daughter marries someone of the appropriate class, religion, education, and financial standing. Now that these barriers have fallen, many twentieth-century Americans choose to fall in love with the same sort of person their families would have selected for them anyway.

Courtship

Traditionally, mate selection begins with casual dating, which leads to going "steady," becoming engaged, and finally getting married. And yet it is obvious that not all couples who casually date move on to the other phases of courtship. Becoming a "serious" couple is a process that is dependent upon many factors. Lewis (1973), for example, has speculated that couple formation is related to six factors, including:

People tend to choose marriage partners from among persons who share their own interests and values.

1. the couple's perception that they have much in common, particularly shared values and interests and a similar sociocultural background.
2. the couple's achievement of rapport: they are able to talk easily together; they think highly of each other; are satisfied with the relationship; and are validated in their conception of themselves by their partner's approval.
3. the couple's achievement of openness by having disclosed their secret thoughts and fears to one another.
4. the couple's ability to understand each other's perspective: they can successfully take the role of the other.
5. the couple's ability to fit their roles and needs together.
6. the couple's achievement of dyadic crystallization; that is, they speak of themselves as "we" not "I." Their commitment is made; they function as a couple; and feel an identity as a couple.

Subsequent research undertaken by Lewis has largely substantiated the claim that couples who score high on these dimensions are more likely to remain together longer. Furthermore, Lewis noted that couple formation and development also is more likely to be successful if the two are perceived as a couple by others.

MARITAL ADJUSTMENT

The tasks confronting the newly married couple are numerous and important. These include learning how to manage conflict, that is, to fight without being destructive; coming to some understanding about the getting and spending of money; developing workable relationships with parents and other relatives;

and preparing for parenthood or, on the other hand, deciding against it. These areas of marital adjustment have long been the subject of discussion in popular as well as professional journals. Newer issues have arisen in the areas of sexual commitment and role expectations.

Sexual Adjustment and Fidelity

Apart from decisions about the nature of engagement and marriage ceremonies (decisions which may be difficult indeed), a major issue faced by the married couple is the nature of sexual adjustment and commitment. Premarital sex is, by now, common: fully 80 percent of women between the ages of eighteen and twenty-four are not virgins when they marry (Hunt, 1974). This represents a substantial increase in the incidence of premarital sex for women over the past few decades (Bell & Coughey, 1980). Nevertheless, newly married couples, even with the more flexible sexual attitudes of today, face sexual adjustments.

Sex, like other social behavior, is learned. But people come to the sex act weighted down with all kinds of psychological and emotional baggage. They have ideas as to how they should feel and how they should behave. Some people feel that if they are in love, satisfying sex will just follow naturally. But they may have to discard some of their strongly held notions. Individuals have to discover in practice what causes sexual arousal for them, what acts they are comfortable with, and then be able to coordinate their preferences with those of their partners. The issue of what constitutes permissible sexual technique may arise as partners gain experience with each other. New contraceptive planning may be called for.

Even if the couple have lived together before marriage and have worked out some of these issues, a new issue arises: marital fidelity. Are the partners to be faithful to one another in the traditional sense or are casual sexual encounters or even extramarital affairs to be tolerated, in theory or in practice?

Despite the change in attitude in recent years toward premarital sexual activity, there is little change in regard to extramarital sex. From 80 to 90 percent of the couples interviewed by Hunt (1974) found extramarital sex unacceptable, although young people are unwilling to say it is wrong under all circumstances (Athanasiou et al., 1970), or should never be forgiven. There is some feeling that extramarital sex may be "OK" if both partners agree to it: if it is part of the initial marriage contract or understanding. What is unacceptable is deception, because this compromises intimacy and usually requires lying and other sneaky behavior. Nevertheless, 50 percent of all married men eventually commit adultery and so do some 25 percent of married women by the time they are fifty-four years of age and in only one of five marriages do the spouses know about it (Hunt, 1974).

Although movies and novels might lead one to suspect that extramarital sex is more exciting and more satisfying than sex within marriage, this may not be the case. According to Hunt (1974), 53 percent of married women almost always reach orgasm with their husbands, but only 39 percent do so in extramarital coitus. Or to look at the figures another way, only 7 percent of women never reach orgasm with their husbands, but such is the case with 35 percent of women in extramarital sex. There is a similar finding with husbands: two-thirds of married men said that coitus with their wives was very pleasurable; less than one-half of the husbands who had extramarital sex rated it so highly. Such findings seem to corroborate the notion that sex is learned behavior and that a sexual adjustment satisfying to both partners requires love and commitment, time, and practice.

Role Adjustment

When two people marry, each assumes a new social role—that of "husband" or "wife." The wife usually assumes a new name, whether or not she chooses to use it in other than legal contexts. Although the social expectations for married and unmarried women may not be as different as they were in the previous century—when matrons wore somber colors and stayed as a group apart during social gatherings—today's newly married woman is still conscious of some changes in social status. Regardless of the degree to which a couple share in the furnishing, decoration, and maintenance of their abode, the wife is expected to manage her new home as she did not, for example, formerly manage her own apartment. Her husband, on the other hand, despite any career commitments on the part of his wife, is generally expected to think more seriously about his financial responsibilities than before and to avoid flighty career decisions.

Within any marriage two individuals must integrate their roles. If, say, the husband insists on playing the dominant role, the wife can hardly remain independent without causing a conflict. Both cannot be self-assertive, but both can learn to compromise. Describing their marriage as a partnership does not resolve these issues. To become partners they must create role patterns which permit the sharing of decisions. And they must determine the more practical problems of who does what. Resolving these issues may require personal change. One study of marital adjustment showed significant changes in married people for traits such as dominance and self-acceptance; no such changes appeared in a control group of unmarried people (Vincent, 1964).

The tendency has been for women to make the greater role adjustment. Newly married women often exchange the status of student or career woman for the status of housewife and mother (Barry, 1970). This transition may result in less marital satisfaction for the wife than for the husband. Married women have been shown to have more psychological problems than either married men or single women (Bernard, 1972). On the other hand, marriage is good for the husband. As compared to single men, married men live longer, are healthier, and report they are happier than single men. Most research also indicates that husbands are less likely than wives to become disenchanted with the relationship with the passing of years (Veroff & Feld, 1970). Furthermore, if the husband becomes unhappy, it seems to affect the marriage relationship more deeply than does the unhappiness of the wife (Tharp, 1963).

Sex Therapy

The assumption on which the practice of sex therapy is based is that inadequacy in sexual performance is an illness that, with the proper treatment, can be cured. Masters and Johnson, the most prominent popularizers of sexual inadequacy as an illness, have identified the symptoms in men as premature ejaculation and impotence (failure to achieve erection), and for women as orgasmic dysfunction (inability to reach orgasm), vaginismus (an involuntary spasm of the vagina that prevents penetration), and dyspareunia (painful coitus).

In some cases an inability to function sexually can occur as a result of such chronic debilitating diseases as cancer, degenerative diseases, severe infections, or disorders of the renal, cardiovascular, and pulmonary systems. Cirrhosis of the liver, hepatitis, hypothyroidism, and diabetes are other diseases that affect sexual functioning. Another, perhaps more common cause for sexual inadequacy, is the use of alcohol and drugs such as barbiturates and narcotics (heroin, morphine, codeine, and methadone). The use of any drug should always be suspected in a case of sexual malfunctioning. Recently a diagnostic procedure has been developed to detect organically caused impotence. Since all healthy men have erections in their sleep about every hour and a half that last from 20 to 40 minutes, and such erections can be detected in a sleep laboratory, the lack of such erections would clearly indicate an organic cause.

In the great majority of cases of sexual dysfunctioning there are no identifiable organic causes. Rather, sexual inadequacy seems to be due to emotional, cultural, or interpersonal factors. In such cases sex therapy is considered appropriate. Masters and Johnson are the first to have worked out a treatment and have based their therapy on the medical model. They do not seek the root causes for sexual inadequacy in the personal history of their clients, but treat the symptoms directly. They endeavor to create a nonjudgmental atmosphere and to teach, not techniques, but attitudes toward enjoying sex as a mutually gratifying activity for the two people involved. They treat only partners (married or otherwise) or single men for whom they provide a surrogate partner. The therapy costs several thousand dollars and lasts two weeks, during which time the couple learn to relax and enjoy touching and "pleasuring" each other. Masters and Johnson claim a success rate as high as 100 percent for women who claimed to suffer from vaginismus to only 40 percent for impotent men.

Thomas Szasz, a psychiatrist and critic, objects to the medical model of sexual dysfunction and, in particular, Masters and Johnson's promotion of sex therapy as a treatment. Under the guise of dysfunction, disorder, and disease, according to Szasz, Masters and Johnson have become the authorities on sexual health, providing definitions and symptoms in regard to the sex act. Szasz compares sexuality to eating. Some men, he notes, may complete the sex act quickly ("premature ejaculation"), just as some people bolt down a hamburger and french fries in three minutes flat (Szasz, 1980).

Standards and attitudes concerning sexual behavior differ from time to time and place to place, and in every society they have been a cause for social control. Szasz points to masturbation as a case in point. For two centuries masturbation was defined by the leading physicians of the day as a most serious illness, leading even to death. Now sex therapists look on masturbation as not only the most permissible outlet of all, but the best means, particularly for women, to learn to recognize what is most pleasurable sexually for them. In another example, Szasz notes that the early Christian ascetic regarded sexual desire as a curse: abstinence was the ideal. For some people abstinence is still the ideal. Surely, Szasz argues, we do not want to let doctors make these decisions for us.

In sum, each person's sex life is intimate and private. Each individual must find his or her own personal way to express sexual desire and find sexual release. The mantle of medical authority is scarcely needed for people to learn that sex is a primary urge; that although it is based on natural body processes, all people must learn, perhaps over a period of many years, how best to achieve enjoyment for themselves and their partners. Szasz points out that from time immemorial a most successful way to learn how to enjoy the sex act was to be taught by a more experienced person—essentially the heart of the new sex therapy. Szasz argues that, of course, people should learn, in whatever way seems appropriate, to engage in sexual activity, but it is to perpetrate a falsehood to coach people in the sex act and call it "sex therapy."

Today social expectations regarding roles in marriage are more flexible. In a recent media poll, for example, only 27 percent of people between eighteen and twenty-nine preferred the traditional marriage roles over the new shared roles in marriage, as compared to 59 percent in their parents' generation (Meislin, 1977). In addition, Bahr (1973) reported that husbands of working wives perform significantly more household tasks than husbands of nonworking wives. Women feel more justified in asking husbands to help with housework and child care when they themselves are working. And yet other research that compared the work activity of husbands and wives around the house found that husbands spend a much shorter time actually engaged in household tasks than wives (one and a half hours as compared to five hours a day), and that wives generally are responsible for, and perform, most of the household and child-care tasks, as well as meal preparation (Walker, 1970). Husbands in turn spend their time on masculine-oriented tasks such as washing the car and fixing things, which occur less frequently than the tasks wives are responsible for.

Work Roles and Marital Roles

Especially significant for the young couple in the 1980s are issues involving sex roles and work roles. When both partners work outside the home, as is increasingly the case in early marriage, the traditional pattern of male dominance may be compromised. Typically, the woman who chooses to be a homemaker is less assertive, more oriented toward nurturance and self-sacrifice. The married working woman, on the other hand, appears to be unconventional, competitive, and not at all self-sacrificing (Birnbaum, 1971). Burke and Weir found that homemakers showed greater tendency toward passivity than working wives; but husbands of homemakers were more dominant than the

Social expectations regarding roles in marriage are more flexible today, with greater numbers of married women pursuing careers outside the home.

husbands of working women (Burke & Weir, 1976a). When marital satisfaction is measured, working wives appear to be more satisfied and to perform more effectively than wives who do not work outside the home. However, Burke and Weir found that husbands of working wives tend to be more dissatisfied; they report greater job pressures, more worries; and they seem to have poorer physical and mental health (Burke & Weir, 1976b).

On the positive side, husbands of working wives reported greater agreement with their wives over important issues (such as friends and sexual relations) and were more likely to solve disagreements in an egalitarian manner. A subsequent study by Booth (1977) refuted Burke and Weir's findings. Booth found that husbands whose wives were employed evidenced no more signs of stress and marital discord than did husbands whose wives were full-time homemakers. If anything, Booth concluded, husbands of working women were happier and under less stress. They more often reported their wives as "loving" and "not more critical than she used to be." And they showed less psychiatric impairment. According to Booth, when stress does appear it is likely to be the result of a transition period. Wives entering the labor force and working women who became homemakers showed signs of stress.

For some young married couples a special problem is that of relating marital roles to work roles. It has become much more common for a man to report to a woman supervisor, and for women and men to compete for promotion. Yet at home, different roles may be required. A wife may find that her husband feels threatened by her assertiveness in financial matters—though this is the very trait for which she has been well rewarded by male supervisors on the job. Or she may discover that growing success or commitment to a job is unwelcome. One woman reported:

> In theory my husband was the type of guy who said you should go out and work, but in practice he was somebody who didn't like it emotionally. As long as I was in a clerical position we got along fine. The problems started when I moved up the ladder. I'm not alone in this. I recently attended a seminar for women in management. Every woman there was either divorced or never married (Dullea, 1977).

Personality Factors in Marital Adjustment

The newly married couple not only has to adjust to new roles—those of a husband and a wife—but also to one another. Every person has a unique personality that influences the way he or she will approach and adjust to new situations—including marriage. Some personality characteristics enable an individual to adapt well to marriage and to build a stronger relationship, whereas, others do not. Characteristics such as emotional maturity, self-control, willingness to engage in self-disclosure, ability to demonstrate affection and consideration for others, and the ability to handle frustration and anger combined with high self-esteem and flexibility all have been linked to marital satisfaction (Stinnet & Walters, 1977). So too has the ability to communicate openly and honestly with one's spouse.

Interestingly, many studies indicate that at the beginning of marriage—at least traditional marriage—it is the husband's personality traits rather than the wife's that are more strongly related to later marital happiness (Barry, 1970). Among the important factors are the husband's "stable male identity" which is, in turn, related to the happiness of his parents' marriage, and to his close attachment to his father. High socioeconomic status and educational level in the husband are also correlated with marital success.

Perhaps most important in traditional marriages are the eyes of the beholder; that is, the wife's perception of the husband's maturity and role enactment. The higher the wife rates her husband on emotional maturity, and the closer he seems to come, in her eyes, to fulfilling the culturally prescribed role of husband, the happier the marriage. However, in light of the increasing equality between the sexes, and the movement away from traditional marriages, one may question whether this pattern will continue to exist in the future.

DIVORCE

When a couple marry, they pledge to love, honor, and cherish one another until they die. But many people are unable to fulfill that pledge. The stresses and strains that are common in marriage often lead to separation and divorce. In fact, nearly one out of three of all couples who marry today can be expected to divorce. Most of these divorces will occur in early adulthood and within the first seven years of marriage. About 18 percent will occur in the first two years of marriage (Love, 1976).

The typical divorced person is between thirty and thirty-three when divorce becomes final, lives in a city, and has at least one child (Hunt & Hunt, 1977). The divorce rate is higher among the poor, the working class, and the poorly educated (Glick, 1975). Geographically, divorce is more common in the West. A California demographic study, for example, yielded the following data: Every married man in that state will marry an average of one and two-thirds times, and every woman can expect to spend six and one-half years as a divorcee (Schoen & Nelson, 1974).

Nobody knows for certain what accounts for all these divorces, apart from the increased social acceptance of divorce itself. However, it is clear that divorcing people tend to have married early (Glick & Norton, 1971). For example, people who got married in their teens show quite a high probability of divorce. Those married in their late twenties show consistently lower probabilities.

Early marriage does not really explain divorce because the majority of teen-age marriages do survive. However, the tendency for early marriages to end in divorce and for marriages generally to break down in the early years does suggest an underlying developmental issue. The partners may not have emerged fully from the identity crisis of adolescence That is, one or both may not have succeeded in becoming emotionally free from parents, or in making a commitment to his or her own values or occupation. Not having done so makes it difficult to establish a relationship, based on mutuality, with another person.

The process leading to divorce differs for each couple. Hunt and Hunt (1977) identify three common scenarios. For a relatively few couples, the marriage simply fades like an old photograph—that is, without conflict or awareness. Any chance happening—a job offer in another town, a passing flirtation—is enough to bring the relationship to a quiet end. In the second scenario, separation and divorce come as a shock to one of the partners:

> A woman who is happily in love with her husband finds a love note in his pocket. A man who is proud of his serene, smoothly running marriage comes home to find his wife strangely glum: she asks him to sit down, tells him she must leave to find some happiness in her life before it is too late (Hunt & Hunt, 1977).

In such relationships, one person is entirely ignorant of the other's feelings, much less, activities; in retrospect, no intimacy seems to have existed. Perhaps most common are divorces undertaken only after prolonged and agonizing conflict. In this scenario, both partners realize that divorce is likely, but wait months or even years to take the final steps.

Naturally, reactions to divorce depend on the nature of the process that preceded it. The happy wife who comes home to find a note taped to the refrigerator will react with shock; the wife who has been locked in self-destructive conflict with her husband for five years will react with relief. There is much evidence, though, that both will suffer a great deal of pain, and will need time to "mourn" the relationship. Some people, however, are never able to adjust to the divorce. They react to the breakup of their marriage with profound depression and anguish, in some cases, to the extent of contemplating suicide.

The divorced person will also encounter an identity crisis in the course of building a new life-style (Wiseman, 1975). For example, the woman who married young may have tied her identity to that of her husband—to her married status. Now she has the new status of divorcee, and possibly single parent. She will need to establish a career identity, or at least find a job. And she will need to resolve issues of sexual identity. The search for sexual identity is expressed, for example, in the often observed "candy store" phase, in which the divorced person samples a variety of sexual experiences with people toward whom she feels little emotional commitment. The reworking of identity is also observed in the avoidance of relationships, in a refusal to socialize, and a preference for crying into one's pillow or one's drink. Such a divorced person is temporarily unwilling to risk personal intimacy although this is what may ultimately be desired.

At the same time that the individual is resolving her identity crisis and experimenting with sexual intimacy, she is confronting a host of practical problems. For most young couples divorce brings financial distress and a lowering of the standard of living, perhaps by as much as 25 percent. If there are children, new parental relationships must be developed. This is especially true for the father, who does not usually have primary responsibility for child care.

Most divorced people eventually remarry. About one quarter do so within the year; within three years, one-half are remarried; within nine years, three-quarters (Glick & Norton, 1971). Men tend to remarry sooner than women. Though divorce rates are higher for second marriages, the majority of those who marry again remain married. For many, divorce is seen as a growth experience by means of which they are able to find not only a new and more suitable partner, but a greater awareness of themselves—what they need and what they have to give to a relationship.

NONMARITAL LIFE-STYLES

A great deal has been written in recent years about such alternatives to marriage as living in a commune, having a child and bringing it up without a spouse, or the adoption of a child by a single person. In the end few people opt for these alternatives.

Almost all Americans marry at least once. Yet nonmarital life-styles become important for many people as a temporary condition between marriages as a result of divorce or the death of a spouse; as a permanent condition by choice or by default; or in the form of cohabitation before or after a marriage. For the young adult both cohabitation without marriage or the life-style of the single person provide life satisfactions, problems, and developmental possibilities that are only now beginning to be studied.

Cohabitation

An increasingly common life-style is cohabitation in which an unmarried couple live together and maintain a sexual relationship. Living together may come about as a result of a dating relationship. In many cases the couple do not make a deliberate decision to live together; they gradually drift into the relationship (Macklin, 1974). "The relationship may grow in time to become something more, but in the meantime it is to be enjoyed and experienced because it is pleasurable in and of itself" (Macklin, 1974, p. 59). Other relationships constitute a "trial" marriage during which each partner works at emotional commitment, but with the security (and insecurity) of knowing that one or the other can pack up and leave. Some couples live together for unromantic reasons. They may share living quarters for financial or other reasons and subsequently develop a sexual relationship. And in still other cases a couple may live together because they cannot legally marry; for example, because they are of the same sex or because one or both may be married to another person.

No one knows for certain how many young unmarried couples live together. Recent estimtes, however, place the figure between 1.75 and 2 million people (Glick & Norton, 1977; Yllo, 1978)—nearly double of what it was in 1970. This figure represents slightly over 4 percent of all couple households in the U.S. A random sample of males between the ages of twenty and thirty found that the stereotype of the liberal-minded, cohabitating college couple may be misleading. Living together was more common among blacks than whites, and more common among high school dropouts than high school or college graduates (Clayton & Voss, 1977).

Still, living together is fairly common in the college population. In a national survey of students in human relations courses, 23 percent of women and 34 percent of men reported having lived with a member of the opposite sex to whom they were not married (Bower & Christopherson, 1977). Nearly all students expected that their parents would disapprove of the arrangement; and nearly all (96 percent) said that they wanted to marry some day. They were, however, less certain than other respondents that they wanted to marry before the age of twenty-five. This led researchers to conclude that living together did not represent an alternative to marriage so much as a postponement of it. Other research suggests that premarital cohabitation has little impact, either positively or negatively, on subsequent mate selection, sex roles in marriages, or marital success in general (Jacques & Chason, 1979; Newcomb, 1979). Males are more willing than females to enter into a long-term cohabitation relationship, as well as most alternative forms of marital and family life. They were more reluctant, however, to take part in marriages characterized by a reversal of the traditional male-female roles (Strong, 1978).

Single (Never Married) Life-Style

Although twenty-five may be the age by which many young people plan to be married, about 33 percent of all men and 22 percent of all women find themselves single on their twenty-fifth birthday. At thirty, the percentages are approximately 15 percent and 7 percent, for men and women, respectively (Quindlen, 1977). A significant number of people in our society live much of their early adulthood as singles.

Single people tend to live in, or be drawn to, urban centers where opportunities for employment and social interaction are high. They tend to associate with other singles, and to be concerned with establishing relationships that meet the need for intimacy. This means, of course, that singles are interested in meeting and dating prospective mates and partners. To this end, they utilize certain social institutions: graduate or adult education courses, creative arts workshops, travel resorts, tennis courts, church groups, therapy groups, laundromats, coffee shops, discos, and singles bars. It appears too, that single people develop networks of friends who provide emotional support similar to that afforded by a family during illness or other crises. Indeed, it may be that the well-adjusted single enjoys richer friendships—friendships characterized by greater age and ethnic diversity—than do married couples in the same age range.

Relatively little research has been done on the developmental consequences of single life-styles. However, it has been reported that single women generally show greater mental health, in that they suffer from fewer neurotic or antisocial tendencies, than do married women or single men (Bernard, 1972; Gurin, Veroff, & Feld, 1960). Single men, on the other hand, belie the stereotype of the carefree bachelor. Statistically, compared to married men, single men are more likely to be poor and to suffer from mental and physical problems; are more likely to be criminals (75 percent of criminals are single or divorced men); and are four times more likely to commit suicide than young married men (Gilder, 1974).

PARENTING

One of the most powerful drives in living things is the drive to preserve the species: to establish and care for a new generation. In the course of life almost every human being becomes, through choice or chance, a father or a mother. Nearly 95 percent of all women in the United States and 90 percent of all couples have at least one child. Of all women who marry, perhaps one in twenty—and no more than one in ten—has no children (Pohlman, 1970; Veevers, 1973). Only about half are childless by choice. It would seem that even today, in an age of contraception and controversial motherhood, most couples and many single women have children. The desire to remain childless is influenced by educational level. Women with more education are less likely to want children. Only 6.9 percent of women between eighteen and thirty-four who have not graduated from high school expect to remain childless; the corresponding figures for high school graduates, and women with one or more years of college, is 8.5 and 14.4 percent respectively (U.S. Bureau of the Census, 1977).

In Erikson's model of development, parenthood emerges in response to the crisis of generativity. Erikson sees the desire to care for others as an important commitment to the past as well as to the future: "Fate as well as the life lived so far decide whom and what one is committed to take care of so as to assure the next generation's life and strength" (Erikson, 1976). Erikson recognizes, however, that some people, because of misfortune or genuine gifts in other directions, achieve generativity through means other than parenthood, through work or through meaningful interaction with parents and children.

On the other hand, merely wanting or having children does not amount to true generativity. Some people are unable to develop as parents due to difficulties experienced at earlier dates of development. For example, couples who have not developed the capacity for mutuality and sacrifice in their relationships, are often unprepared for children. Instead of caring for a new generation, they may indulge themselves as if they were their own or one another's only child (Erikson, 1963).

Fertility Motivation

"Should we have a baby?" is an important question for most young married couples. Researchers in fertility motivation—the reasons for having or not having children—have studied the factors that influence the decision. They have found that the value of children to parents differs, and the reasons for having children differ too. Because there is now virtually fail-proof contraception, as well as increased availability of abortion, fertility motivation has come in for lively discussion.

One tendency has been to speak of parenting as if it were an occupation for which one may or may not apply. Thus a woman might say, "Some people are good at parenting, but my husband and I are good at writing books" (a claim made by a writer in the area of the psychology of women). In the cost-benefit approach, on the other hand, the gratifications provided by children are weighted against other career and life-style decisions. This approach to understanding parenting assumes that for some people the growth in education and career opportunities, particularly for women, will make having children less pleasurable or desirable, and less necessary for personal development. Indeed, when highly educated subjects were found to report fewer gratifications from their infants than subjects with less education, researchers hypothesized that this was because they had alternative means of personal fulfillment (Russell, 1974). Still, the satisfaction provided by a career does not prevent most career-oriented women from having at least one child. Involvement in work serves mainly to postpone childbearing or limit the number of children in a family; it is usually not an alternative to having children.

The financial expense of having children can come as quite a shock to unsuspecting first-time parents.

BENEFITS AND COSTS OF HAVING CHILDREN

| | Percentage of persons who gave this response | | | |
| | Parents | | Nonparents | |
	Women	Men	Women	Men
BENEFITS				
To promote love and family ties	66	60	64	52
To create fun and enjoyment	60	55	41	34
To give life meaning and enrichment	35	33	33	31
To give adult status	22	19	14	9
For achievement and creativity	11	10	13	20
COSTS				
Loss of freedom	53	49	56	45
Financial cost	40	45	54	54
Concern for child health	20	20	20	24
Unpleasantness of child-rearing	10	9	6	8
Concern for the state of the world	6	8	12	12
Interference with mother's work	6	1	9	0
Number of Subjects	1,259	356	310	100

This data was adapted from results reported for a nationally representative sample of married women aged 16–40 and a subsample of their husbands (Hoffman, 1979b).

What motivates couples to make the transition to parenthood? One factor usually cited is social pressure, particularly pressure from prospective grandparents. Other factors include a delight in children for their own sakes; a desire for the emotional comfort which children may provide in old age; a desire for heirs to whom one can bequeath the resources, ideas, and tastes acquired over a lifetime; and a sense that one's work may not be all there is to life—that children may be needed to "make it all worthwhile." Those who decide to have children in their thirties tend to mention feelings about their own mortality and the need for something that will outlive them.

Other motives for having children tend to be viewed less positively. Caseworkers placing children with a couple for adoption would be critical of such motives as having a child to improve their marriage, or to prevent it from deteriorating altogether. Some persons want a child as an escape from boredom ("something to do"), or from an unsatisfactory job. Some see a child as a form of social status. Finally, some women, either single or unhappily married, want a child because in the absence of adult intimacy they need someone with whom to form a genuine attachment.

The transition to parenthood also involves recognition of the costs of having children. The toll on the couple in terms of loss of freedom and financial expense can come as quite a shock to unsuspecting, first-time parents. While most young couples are aware of and accept these costs, for other people, children represent too great a restriction on their lives, and hence a decision is made to remain childless.

It should be noted that even with the widespread use of contraceptives, couples do have children without having been consciously motivated to do so. Perhaps as many as two-thirds of all births are unplanned, though not necessarily unwelcome (Kenkel, 1966).

Parenting as a Developmental Process

For a woman, pregnancy itself may be developmentally significant in that it makes use of what Erikson calls the "productive inner space" which is symbolically and biologically at the center of feminine fulfillment (Erikson, 1968). For both parents, having a baby has significance in that it revives the earlier developmental conflicts through which they themselves have passed. Benedek, a psychoanalyst, believes that the mother retains memory traces of infancy—of having been fed and cuddled; she relives the pains and pleasures of her own infancy as she tends her baby; moreover, her motherliness is derived from her early and basic identification with her own mother (Benedek, 1959). More recently, Dinnerstein (1976) has suggested that these feelings about parenthood would be quite different if fathers played a larger role in nurturing their children. The parenting experience is an integrating one, and it continues to be so. One middle-aged woman said: "It is as if there are two mirrors held at particular angles: I see part of myself in my mother who is growing old and part of her in me. In the other mirror I see part of myself in

The unfamiliar status of parenthood encourages new mothers to seek out the companionship and advice of those who have gone through the same role adjustments.

my daughter. I have had some dramatic insights just from looking into those mirrors" (Neugarten, 1964).

During the young adult years the parent must come to terms with the stress and anticipation of pregnancy; the absolute dependency of the infant; and the growing autonomy and rivalry of the preschool child. This can involve new learning as well as parental self-control. For example, tantrum behavior in the two-year-old or rebellion in the preschooler may force the parent to recognize the anger she dislikes or fears within herself. Yet she cannot express her anger as the child does. ("I am weak from held-in rage. How shall I learn to absorb the violence and make explicit only the caring?" wrote Adrienne Rich, poet and mother, in her journal.) As the child develops, different conflicts and growth opportunities are reactivated in the parent.

Adjustment to Parenthood

With the birth of the child, the couple become parents and the heads of a new nuclear family. They begin the process of socializing the infant and are, in turn, socialized by him. That is, parents teach the child eating and toilet habits, and sex-role behavior. At the same time, they learn such things as how to speak to their baby, how to keep him comfortable, how to make him smile, how to relate in new ways to his grandparents.

The transition to parenthood has been described as a crisis point in the life of the couple, requiring adjustments for which they are often not prepared (Rossi, 1968). Part of the problem is that society does little to prepare people for parenthood, either before or after the child arrives. Furthermore, the transition to parenthood is an abrupt one. One day the couple are by themselves, and the next day they have "another mouth to feed"—a human being for whom they are responsible.

Parenthood disrupts the two-person pattern of the married couple and frequently interrupts the career of the wife. The arrival of an infant restricts the parents' activities outside the home, as well as their privacy within. Communication of feelings and ideas is sharply curtailed. Indeed, one researcher found that young parents talk to one another about half as much as newly married couples—and then they tend to talk about the child (Schulz, 1972).

Overall, the evidence suggests that marital satisfaction decreases with the advent of the first child, although it often increases again in later stages of family life, particularly after the departure of children from the home (Alpert & Richardson, 1980; Lewis & Spanier, 1979; Schram, 1979). Still, the drop in marital quality does not occur for all couples. Hoffman and Mavis (1978) reported that if children are planned and desired, they can strengthen rather than weaken the marital relationship.

The new status of parenthood necessarily leads to new relationships between the couple and society. New mothers seek out other new mothers for companionship and advice. Many show increased pleasure in the company of their own mothers and aunts. Parenthood also brings renewed contact with institutions that may have been ignored during single life and early marriage. As the child progresses through the preschool years, parents begin evaluating the parks and libraries and especially the schools of their neighborhoods. For some this leads to community activism, perhaps on behalf of better playground maintenance or in opposition to salacious advertising and violence on television. For others, dissatisfaction with the neighborhood can lead to great changes in life-style. A move from city to suburb, for example, will have considerable effect on a family's consumption and commuting patterns.

A couple's relationship to religious institutions may also change. Home rituals, such as the saying of grace before eating or lighting of candles, may be resumed "for the child's sake." It is not unusual even for agnostic couples to affiliate with a church in order to provide a religious education for their children (Cox, 1970).

Finally, the role of parent may result in a stronger identification with existing social structures. One father (and professor of philosophy and religion) put it this way: "When my own sense of identity was that of a son, I expected great perfection from my father. Now that I am a father, I have undergone a psychic shift. Blame upon institutions, upon authorities, upon those who fail in their responsibilities have a new claim on my sympathies"

(Novak, 1976). To be a father or a mother is to recognize human imperfection and to have a stake in improving and maintaining what exists.

Working Mothers

Another significant issue confronting the young couple is integrating work roles and parent roles. This is especially true for women. In 1978 approximately 42 percent of women with husbands present and children under six worked, or were looking for work outside the home; 58 percent of those with children between ages six and seventeen were in this category. Of those women previously married, 60 percent with children under six, and 73 percent with children between six and seventeen, were in the labor force (U.S. Bureau of Labor Statistics, 1978).

Working mothers of children under the age of six are one of the fastest growing groups in the labor market. In fact, it is projected that by 1990 slightly over 55 percent of this group will be working—an increase of 13 percent over the 1978 figures (R. E. Smith, 1979). This represents a major change in maternal employment patterns and family life.

A woman's decision to work when her children are young is often a difficult one to make. Research suggests that one of the factors associated with the decision is the woman's perception of the effects of separation from the infant. Hock (1978) found that women who planned to return to work following childbirth and had done so, felt less infant distress at separation, were less anxious about the separation, and were more trusting of others to care for their infant than were nonworking women. In contrast, women who had not planned to return to work following childbirth, but who subsequently changed their minds, were more anxious about separation from their infants than nonworking mothers (Hock, Christman, & Hock, 1980).

It is clear that the reasons or motivation for working following childbirth play a major role in the subsequent adjustment of the mother and, in turn, the rest of the family. When work is viewed as an avenue of self-expression and development, women are much more likely to be successful in integrating occupational and family roles than in situations when women work primarily for financial reasons. Similarly, when adequate substitute child care and other support systems are available to the woman, the integration of work and parental roles is that much smoother. Yet some women not only must work to help suport their families, but they cannot afford, or do not have available, the kind of support that they need to meet adequately the day-to-day household responsibilities—child care, cleaning, shopping, cooking, and so on. For these women, the period of early adulthood is often marked by task overload, and accompanying feelings of frustration and despair.

The Family Life Cycle

With the birth of the first child and the establishment of a new nuclear family, it becomes appropriate to speak of the *family life cycle*. The cycle actually begins, of course, with marriage; it ends with the stages of bereavement of the surviving spouse. The number of stages varies according to the theorist.

Duvall's eight stages, with approximate number of years for each stage, appear in Figure 15.1. Since the average mother sends her youngest child to school when she is between thirty and thirty-five, we can say that the early adult period generally corresponds to stages 1 to 3 in Duvall's scheme. This varies for individual couples, of course. A couple who postpone, having children may spend six or seven years, instead of the predicted two, in stage 1, and this will affect the rest of the cycle; for example, the "empty nest to retirement" stage will be shorter. However, Duvall's model fails to take into account the considerable proportion of people who divorce or are widowed, who remarry, or those who have a second family. Many of these people will spend some years as single parents or may bring up children not their own.

It is worth noting too that although we tend to picture families as young adults with young children (the kind of group attractively portrayed in advertisements), the amount of time spent in the first three stages of family life is relatively small—no more than a dozen out of a total of perhaps fifty years (Duvall, 1977). Almost half of the family life cycle occurs after the children are gone. Thus, adjustments worked out in the young adult period are not necessarily appropriate for later periods.

A family's financial resources do not necessarily match their needs throughout the family life cycle. Families with children, stages 2 to 5, are in the greatest need of money for such things as food, medical bills, clothing, and sizable housing accommodations. Although many mothers of preschool children are in the work force, many others remain home. Fathers of small children are still far below their full earning potential. Thus with the mother not earning money and the father's earnings fairly low, the family income is at its lowest during a time of greatest need. Later, when the father's earnings are at a peak and the mother is also at work, there is less need for the money. As we shall see in Chapter 17, the combination of a more comfortable financial position and the children out of the home makes stage 7 the happiest time in the family cycle since the early days in stage 1.

OCCUPATIONAL DEVELOPMENT

A large part of a person's identity—and about forty years of his life—are bound up with work. For men, the question "Who are you?" has traditionally been expressed in the question "What do you do?" Today women, too, are expected to be able to answer this question. "I am an English instructor, a programmer, a hospital administrator."

Early adulthood is the period in which people are expected to make decisions about what kind of work they want to do. They define their relationship to society by narrowing their occupational choices and finding their first job. In the mid-1960s in the middle class the consensus was that twenty

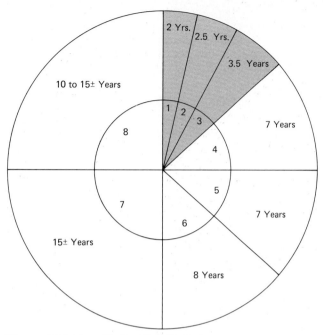

Figure 15.1 Duvall's Family Life Cycle

By Length of Time in Each of Eight Stages
1. Married couples (without children).
2. Childbearing families (oldest child, birth–30 months).
3. Families with preschool children (oldest child 30 months–6 years).
4. Families with schoolchildren (oldest child 6–13 years).
5. Families with teen-agers (oldest child 13–20 years).
6. Families launching young adults (first child gone to last child leaving home).
7. Middle-aged parents (empty nest to retirement).
8. Aging family members (retirement to death of both spouses).

Source: Based upon data from the U.S. Bureau of the Census and from the National Center for Health Statistics, Washington, D.C. Adapted from E. M. Duvall. *Marriage and family development* (5th ed.) Philadelphia: J. B. Lippincott, 1977, p. 148. Copyright 1977. Reprinted by permission of the publisher, J. B. Lippincott Company.

to twenty-two was the best age to finish one's education and go to work; between the ages of twenty-four and twenty-six such a person was expected to settle on a career (Neugarten, Moore, & Lowe, 1965). Today with increased acceptance of postcollege training or a few years of moratorium time for finding oneself, a person may be twenty-five or thirty before being expected to do fulltime work. Moreover, people from different social classes have differing views as to the time when a person should have "settled down" in an occupation. Nevertheless, men and women are expected to make an occupational commitment, or the educational choices that lead to one, during their twenties.

Stages in Occupational Development and Self-Concept

It is usually during the early adult years that the individual takes a first serious full-time job. In many cases, this job represents an implementation of the person's self-concept: for example, the person who believes that she has the qualities of a nurse actually becomes a nurse. Research, using trait description checklists, has in fact shown that there is a high correlation between people's self-concept and occupational stereotypes or images to which they aspire (Holland, 1973).

For most people career choice is not a one-shot decision made in early adulthood. The life cycle imposes different tasks at different periods of life; consequently, people develop and change in respect to their vocations. It has been suggested (Super, 1957; 1963) that there are five stages of occupational development: (1) *crystallization* of one's ideas about work (14–18 years); (2) *specification* of a particular occupational preference and the beginning of job training (18–21 years); (3) *implementation* of training and entry into first job (21–24 years); (4) *stabilization* or becoming established in a particular field (25–35 years); and (5) *consolidation and advancement* within a field or on the job (35 years and on). Super has also noted that as people go through these stages of vocational development there is continual updating and implementing of self-concept. As we know, self-concept changes. Thus, the research scientist becomes the director of the Research and Development divison of a chemical company, gradually moving from meticulous solitary work to the supervision and management of a large number of people. This change may coincide with other developmental events, for example, a broadening of family responsibilities, and the management of a larger household. By the same token, a woman may undertake a new vocational identity as her household responsibilities shrink, becoming an officer in a bank rather than a part-time customer service representative.

Other researchers (Levinson et al., 1976) whose sample consisted of forty men in four different occupations from blue-collar worker to novelist, did not project such a straight line in occupational development as suggested by Super. Levinson's stages include more tentative exploration and several crisis periods of reassessment. He said that it is a cruel myth to believe that at the end of adolescence you choose your career, settle down, and continue this way more or less indefinitely.

In early adulthood, a stage Levinson calls *Getting into the Adult World*, the young man tries to settle on an occupation or an occupational direction in line with his own interests and his sense of his own identity. He explores the possibilities in the work world and at the same time tries to match what he finds with his sense of his own potential. His task is to build a *life structure*, forging a link between the work world and his own identity. This is a period of provisional choices. From the ages of about twenty-eight to thirty-two many men experience a *transitional period*—a crisis of reassessment. For every choice made, parts of the self are ignored. These aspects of the self come to the surface and must be dealt with. For example, a man who has gone into the manufacturing business with his father may not want to settle for just making money—he may want to have a try at writing a play. He stays home for eighteen months, completes the play, and then finds a new career as an advertising copywriter and account executive. Some people find the right combination of career and identity and make a deeper commitment. Levinson's observations led him to hypothesize that if a significant start is not made by the age of thirty-four, chances are small that a man will find a satisfactory life structure with an occupation consistent with his identity and interests.

Sometime in his early thirties a man *Settles Down*. This is a period of deeper commitment to work and to family. The individual makes and pursues long-range plans and goals. Although he feels autonomous in his work he may, in fact, be subject to many restrictions imposed by higher-ups or by the rules under which he works. This may push him into the next stage.

Becoming Your Own Man may occur from the late thirties to early forties. At this time a man wants desperately to have society affirm him in his work role—to be made manager or foreman or head of his department. This period comes to an end with another crisis, the *Midlife Transition* around forty to forty-five. Whether or not a man achieves the recognition he feels he deserves, he may go through a period of reassessment. "Is this after all what I want? Am I the kind of person who is a manager (or who failed to become a manager)?" The man must make peace with himself or drastically change his life structure. Great personal growth can result from the midlife transition.

Since the men in Levinson's sample have not yet lived through middle adulthood, the stages are not yet complete. But growth and change are seen as characteristic of occupational development, as well as of other aspects of a man's life.

Unfortunately, Levinson did not include women in his sample. A woman's occupational development, if we define occupation as work outside the home, is more directly affected by her family roles as mother and wife and is also undoubtedly different and shows much more variability than Super's stages of adult occupational development.

For some people the need to distinguish themselves in early adulthood is very intense: "If you haven't made it by thirty or thirty-five ..." the saying goes. In a longitudinal study of promising men, this period was characterized by hard work, conformity, and little self-reflection (Vaillant, 1977). An increasing number of younger women are also following the pattern described.

Occupational commitment and achievement also is linked to the establishment of *mentor-protegé relationships* on the job (Levinson, 1976). A mentor is someone usually older and with greater job-related experience and power, who takes an interest in the newly recruited young person. The mentor teaches the protegé job-related procedures, makes recommendations for promotions, and generally guides and shapes the development of the protegé within the company. It is fairly common that occupational success is tied to a relationship with an older, wiser, and more powerful colleague. Relationships with mentors last on the average about four years. A part of Becoming Your Own Man in Levinson's model of development is the severing or gradual

Women in Male-Dominated Occupations

During World War II men went off to war and women of all ages built airplanes, trucks, and machinery. Rosie the riveter was a popular stereotype. There was no question but that Rosie was a good riveter and she earned a riveter's wages. But after the men returned, Rosie was no longer so welcome in the well-paying, blue-collar occupations. She has never been welcome in the highly paid professions such as doctor or lawyer. The image much of the public has of such occupations as doctor, lawyer, or machinist includes knowledge, skill, special competence, and one other attribute: the practitioner is always male. It is, in good part, just because of this image of the competent worker as male, reinforced by the media, that men are able to dominate the professions and other occupations. Even staunch feminists may find themselves startled when confronted by a female veterinarian, a female appliance repairman, or a female bank vice-president.

Women in male-dominated occupations appear deviant to many. They don't conform to the image. This in itself puts a strain on the woman. For example, behavior that would seem suitable in a man may be interpreted as unfit in a woman. According to a woman attorney, "When a male attorney gets into a heated discussion over a point of law, he is a dynamic ball of fire. Should a woman get equally excited, she is overwrought, easily agitated, and taking the matter personally" (Dinerman, 1969, in Patterson & Engelberg, 1978). Another psychological difficulty is the common identification of the woman in a male-dominated profession as unfeminine. A woman may consciously or unconsciously be troubled by the prospect of success in her field because competence in a male-dominated occupation conflicts with her own image of herself as a woman. Matina Horner (1969) found that women were much more likely than men to be troubled by the prospect of success in a male profession.

Despite these difficulties, many more women are entering medical school and law school today than there were just ten years ago—almost a quarter of the students now are women as compared to 5 percent or less in the recent past. Since the male image of the doctor or lawyer can best be changed by the presence of more women, is the image likely to change? Unfortunately, once admitted to practice, women find themselves again stereotyped within the professions. Women doctors are more likely than men to become pediatricians, considered by many a less prestigious specialty, than surgeon or heart specialist. Women lawyers are often shunted into domestic law and estates and trusts (Patterson & Engelberg, 1978).

According to one study (Burlin, 1976), young women now entering the job market would like the freedom to work in fields other than teaching, nursing, office work, and social work. When asked to choose an ideal occupation—one they would pursue if they lived in a society that offered unlimited possibilities—high school girls more frequently chose innovative (male-dominated) occupations than those traditionally associated with women.

What are some of the characteristics of women who actually choose to work in the male-dominated professions? Sandra Tangri found that women in the male-dominated professions do not reject the core female roles of wife and mother, but they do expect to have fewer children than the more traditional woman. They do not think of themselves as masculine women. Tangri found no evidence that women go into traditionally masculine fields because they cannot attract men; they have as many men friends and romantic attachments as the more traditional women. These women are, however, more autonomous, more personally ambitious, and more committed to their careers than women who choose the traditional feminine occupations (Tangri, 1975).

There is another side to the coin. Women in male-dominated professions often express doubts about their ability to succeed, worry about such questions of identity as "Who am I?", and feel that they must always be acting rather than being themselves. Such women need support—recognition from a faculty member or from women friends. Most important, according to Tangri, is a tolerant or supportive boyfriend or husband who, at one and the same time, confirms their identity as women and encourages their career in a male-dominated field.

termination of the mentor-protegé relationship. A former protegé may at this time become a mentor and adopt a protegé himself.

Interestingly, research suggests that same-sex mentors or role models are more effective than cross-sex role models in influencing career-related attitudes and productivity (Basow & Howe, 1980; Goldstein, 1979). This finding is particularly important for career-oriented women, given the relatively low number of females in upper management. One limiting factor in the advancement of women within business may be that they have not had available to them the most effective role models to emulate. And, indeed, Levinson suggests that "the absence of mentors may be associated with various kinds of developmental impairments." This in and of itself constitutes an important reason for companies to bring more women into higher level positions.

Career Choice and Sex Role Identity

One aspect of identity involved in career choice is *sex role.* People entering their twenties today find that entrance into many occupations is determined less by sex than it used to be. Women who had assumed that they would enter a feminine "caring" profession, such as teaching, nursing, or social work, are being encouraged by popular spokespersons, as well as the Equal Opportunity Act, to reconsider their options. For some young women this has meant taking the risk of expressing abilities and life-styles believed by the parental generation to be masculine. Women have become mine workers, engineers, corporate managers, and ministers—not always, however, without some social and interpersonal stresses. A mother may caution her "manager" daughter that success may stand in the way of personal fulfillment in marriage. Or her male coworkers may harass a female steelworker on the job, making it difficult for her to do her work. Or a woman herself, after years of stereotypic socialization, may find these new career options contrary to the self-concept she has already developed, and therefore anxiety producing, even though they pay far better than the traditional feminine occupations.

Research has indicated that women in male-dominated professions tend to be more autonomous,
more personally ambitious, and more committed to
their careers than women in more traditional feminine occupations.

With more than half of all women over sixteen in full-time work, it has
become more common for women to define or identify themselves in terms
of the work they do outside the home. This applies to the middle class as well
as the welfare mother.

Every able-bodied man is expected to work or, if unemployed, to seek
work, until he reaches retirement age. But the extent to which a man puts his
job above family and community status may be changing. A survey of managers in large corporations found that even in this high-achieving group, there
was a growing reluctance among younger subjects to uproot their families for
the sake of a promotion. There was also more openness with respect to the
possibility of second careers, suggesting that identity was less rigidly tied to
the job or the company than in earlier samples (Williams, 1977). A related
phenomenon is the tendency of men to prefer jobs that leave them time "to
be a father." Whereas the young woman says she will not be "just" a housewife
and mother, more and more young men are saying that they do not want to
become "just" a corporate vice-president.

SUMMARY

▶ Marriage is an institution with both social and legal status. The age at
which people marry and the way they marry are influenced by social
norms. Some of the factors affecting the courtship process are physical

attractiveness, propinquity, similarity in background and values, achievement of rapport, mutual self-disclosure, role-taking ability, the fitting together of roles and needs, and the mutual commitment to each other as a couple.

▶ The newly married couple must learn to deal maturely with conflict and to make adjustments in areas dealing with money, sex, relatives, and the possibility of children. Adjusting to their new roles as husband and wife usually requires some personal change. Most young people today prefer a marital relationship of shared responsibilities. When both partners work, there seems to be more satisfaction in the marriage.

▶ Among couples who marry today nearly one in three can be expected to divorce. Most divorces occur within the first seven years of marriage. After a divorce people seem to need time to rework their lives and identities. Whereas most divorced people make adequate adjustments to their new status, and eventually remarry, many have a very difficult time adjusting to divorce.

▶ Most Americans marry at least once, yet "living together" is an increasingly common arrangement. The couple cohabits and maintains a sexual relationship that has no legal status, except in cases where it can be classified as common-law marriage. Other people remain single throughout much or all of their young adulthood. Women who remain single exhibit better mental health and fewer neurotic tendencies than married women or single men.

▶ In Erikson's model of development, parenthood emerges in response to the crisis of generativity. However, some people choose to express this generativity through their work. In either case, it represents a commitment to the past and to the future.

▶ The reasons for having (or alternately not having) children vary from one couple to the next. And yet each couple experiences similar kinds of adjustment problems associated with parenthood. The arrival of the infant restricts parental activities, as well as privacy, imposes a financial burden on the family, and often interrupts the career of the wife. Research indicates that marital satisfaction decreases with the advent of the first child, although it often increases again in later stages of family life. However, if the children are wanted and planned for, they can strengthen the marriage.

▶ For many people, identity is bound up with the work they do. In early adulthood a person is expected to discover his "field," if not by actually taking a job, then at least by taking the first steps toward a commitment to a particular career.

▶ Initial job choice is influenced by many factors including one's self-concept and sex role identity. People entering the work force today find that
entrance into many occupations is less sex-determined than it once was.
This is having a significant impact on career development in women.

FURTHER READINGS

Bach, George, and Wyden, Peter. *The intimate enemy: How to fight fair in love and marriage.* **New York: Morrow, 1969.**
This book demonstrates how the act of fighting between loved ones can be constructive instead of destructive if partners agree to rules set forth in this book.

Beyer, Eugenia Hepworth. *Parents as partners in education.* **St. Louis: Mosby, 1981.**
This text is designed to help parents and school personnel work together effectively.

Callahan, Sidney Cornelia. *Parenting: Principles and politics of parenthood.* **Baltimore: Penguin Books, 1974.**
A sensible, articulate book on the rights and responsibilities of parents and children, based on the author's own experience as well as the theories and observations of R. D. Laing, Erik Erikson, Jean Piaget, and Haim Ginott.

Dinnerstein, Dorothy. *The mermaid and the minotaur: Sexual arrangements and human-malaise.* **New York: Harper & Row, 1976.**
Dinnerstein urges the reader to examine and perhaps relinquish his or her gender arrangements in the household. Why is it that women are traditionally the child rearers and men the child supporters? Dinnerstein attempts to answer this question in light of evolutionary theory, anthropological evidence, folklore, and recent psychological and biological studies.

Green, Maureen. *Fathering.* **New York: McGraw-Hill, 1976.**
A discussion of the changes which the traditional role of the father has undergone. Green deals with the father's role in other cultures, the relationship between fathers and children, divorced fathers, and the future of the father's role.

Hall, Francine S., and Hall, Douglas T. *The two-career couple.* **Reading, Mass.: Addison Wesley, 1979.**
New research, common-sense advice, interviews, and questionnaires on such topics as competition, transfers, managing the home and family, sex, and splitting up.

Murdock, Carol Vejvoda. *Single parents are people too!* **New York: Butterick, 1980.**
A timely account of the single parent life-style. The book emphasizes the need for social support.

Observational Activities

Part Six Young Adulthood

The Value of Children to Young Adults

In the past two decades, with the rise of the women's movement and the increase in dual career families, the decision of whether or not to have children has become a very important issue. More and more couples are consciously weighing both the costs and benefits of raising children before committing themselves to a decision concerning parenthood.

Interview five to ten young married couples about the value of children in their lives. Ask each couple:
1. What do you think are the benefits of having children?
2. What are the drawbacks?
3. What factors determined your decision to plan for parenthood early in your marital life, or to postpone it?
4. How did career planning and development influence your decision concerning parenthood?
5. If you are parents, describe the changes in your lives that followed the birth of your child.

After interviewing several couples compare the responses you received with those of your classmates. What are the major benefits and costs of parenthood for today's young couples? How many couples plan to remain childless? What factors appear to be important in this decision? How do you interpret the data on the costs and benefits of parenthood in light of the changes that have taken place in society over the past few decades?

Shared Roles in Marriage

In the past, when a man and woman married, each had a reasonably clear idea of the responsibilities and roles each would assume. The husband "provided" for the family and assumed those roles requiring leadership, strength, and technical knowledge. In turn, the wife's primary responsibilities centered on domestic activities and raising the children. The expectations that young adults bring to marriage today, however, may be quite different. Traditional marital roles no longer seem so clear-cut.

Interview several young couples who have been married for a year or two about the roles and responsibilities that each partner assumes. Ask each partner:
1. To what extent do you have your own specific roles and responsibilities?
2. Do these roles correspond to traditional sex-role expectations?
3. To what extent are marital roles shared?
4. In what areas of your marriage, if any, have traditional, sex-related roles prevailed?
5. What factors in your life as a couple influence the assumption of marital roles?

From the data collected by you and your classmates does it appear to be true that traditional marital roles are breaking down? If so, what factors seem to be influencing this process the most? Can you speculate on the impact of a "shared roles" marriage on children's socioemotional and personality development?

PART SEVEN

Middle Adulthood

Chapter 16

❖❖❖❖❖❖

Physical, Cognitive, and Personality Development

Middle-aged people are not young; neither are they old. They have left behind the vigor of youth, but have not yet wound down to the gentler rhythms of old age. They may be expected to live as many years as they have lived so far. In this day of increased longevity, the average person is statistically at midlife in the late thirties: the life expectancy of the 37-year-old American is thirty-seven more years.

But for most people middle age lies somewhat further along the life span. For example, in a classic study, Neugarten and her colleagues found that a middle-class sample defined a middle-aged man or woman as between the ages of forty and fifty (Neugarten, Moore, & Lowe, 1965). Older people may have different perceptions. In one study more than half of those between sixty and sixty-nine classified themselves as young or middle-aged (Busse, Jeffers, & Christ, 1970).

Attitudes toward middle adulthood are continually revised in response to the lengthening of the life span. In the advertising language, middle age has recently acquired a younger image. A woman in her mid-fifties today may well have parents who are alive and active. Those parents, at fifty-five, were the senior citizens of their day. But they were not—as their daughter is—discovering new freedoms, new jobs, and new definitions of womanhood and sexuality. Probably they considered themselves middle-aged as soon as they took up the well-defined responsibilities of marriage and job. In one study of middle-aged and older grandparents, a large majority of the subjects described themselves as "more youthful than my parents were at my age" (Neugarten & Weinstein, 1964).

When does a person define himself as middle-aged? Boundary dates, such as forty or forty-five, do not seem to be significant. Chronological age, writes Neugarten, is "no longer the positive marker it was earlier in life, when to become older means to become bigger, more attractive, or more important; neither is it the positive marker it becomes in old age, when each additional year increases one's distinction" (Neugarten, 1967).

A person tends to perceive himself as middle-aged in response to signs of physical aging, as well as events that occur in family and work contexts. The most sobering indication of aging comes with the death of one's parents. In a single moment, suddenly one has become the older generation. Having adolescent or young adult children is also a sure indication that one is not young—there *is* a younger generation. More telling is the birth of a grandchild, the third generation. Similarly, gaining seniority in the company or being asked to supervise a young trainee may result in the awareness of middle age. Research has shown that women tend to perceive middle age in terms of family events. Even unmarried women are conscious of arriving at an age at which they would have had children (or do have nieces and nephews) that make one old enough to be middle-aged. Men, on the other hand, usually take their cues from work and economic status (Neugarten, 1967). For the purposes of definition, we will consider the years forty to sixty as the time of middle adulthood.

PHYSICAL DEVELOPMENT

The peak of physical development is reached in early adulthood; decline begins, gradually, in the fourth decade of life. For example, height begins to decrease very slightly between forty-five and fifty. The only part of the skeleton that continues to grow in later life is the head and face (Marshall, 1964). Muscular size and strength decrease and the ability to do hard physical labor steadily falls. People accustomed to physical work will continue to be productive in late middle age; but as one fifty-eight-year-old sanitation worker put it, "to me the alleys are getting longer and the cans larger. Getting old" (Terkel, 1972).

The most obvious signs of physical aging, however, are those that are open to the inspection of others—that are manifested on the exterior of the body. In middle age, the skin loses some of its elasticity, resulting in facial lines as well as looseness and flabbiness in other parts of the body. For many people there is a redistribution of weight leading to a noticeable midsection paunch. Hair begins to thin out at this time, and often turns gray.

With increasing age there is a noticeable reduction in breathing effi-

People's attitudes toward the middle years has changed as a consequence of the increasing life span. Middle age has recently acquired a younger image.

ciency; the person is more easily winded when running or climbing. The heart, too, must work harder to achieve less. This is especially true of people who are overweight or have atherosclerosis, a degenerative condition involving thickening and hardening of the artery walls. The problems of obesity and cardiovascular disease become more common in late middle age.

Changes in the sensory systems are also marked. There is a sharp decline in visual acuity, although this problem is almost always correctable with glasses. The size of the pupil becomes smaller around age fifty, resulting in less light entering the eye. This means that the person may need brighter lighting to see adequately. At this time problems with depth perception, recovery from glare, and adaptation to darkness also are observable (Troll, 1975). The most common auditory problem associated with increasing age is *presbycusis*—a progressive loss of hearing, especially for tones of high frequency, caused by degenerative changes in the auditory system. This condition more often affects men than women (Corso, 1977). Under ordinary circumstances, however, hearing loss has little impact on the day-to-day life of the middle-aged or older adult. Some loss of taste, smell, and sensitivity to touch also occurs in the late forties and fifties but is not generally noticed by the individual until later in life.

The nervous system undergoes changes which, under ordinary circumstances have a minimal affect on behavior, perception, and intelligence during middle age. Brain weight decreases after age twenty, gradually at first, and more rapidly in later life. However, studies involving electroencephalograms (EEGs), which record the electrical activity of the brain, show little difference between healthy young and old people in many instances (Bromley, 1974). Simple reflex time (the hammer-on-the-knee reflex, for example) remains about the same from twenty to eighty years (Hugin, Norris, & Shock, 1960). Reactions to complex stimuli involving more complex transmission of impulses, however, become slower. There also seems to be a slowing of conductivity in the peripheral nerves and across synapses, which may result in a generalized slowing down of bodily functions and processes (Timiras, 1972).

In middle adulthood people gradually find themselves less able to contend with physical and emotional stress. They cannot bear cold as well as formerly, and may begin planning to retire to a warmer climate. Extreme heat is also handled less efficiently. Gastrointestinal complaints become more common. The middle-aged businessman, for example, finds that he cannot eat a rich late meal without feeling the effects the next day; and he recalls that this was not always the case.

Although the middle years bring a gradual decline in physical functioning from the peak reached in the twenties, the human organism does not experience a sudden reversal from growth to deterioration. Even in early life, both processes are taking place. For example, since nerve cells do not multiply after the first year of life, their number consequently declines. Because of the overabundance of such cells, the loss is insignificant.

The heart (cardiovascular) diseases of middle age are also the result of cumulative rather than sudden conditions. For the average person, cardiac output (as measured in a state of rest) begins to decline not in middle age but at age nineteen, at about the rate of one percent a year (DeVries, 1975); perhaps at age fifty a problem is noticed. Similarly, some medical authorities claim that the first lesions of atherosclerosis are laid down in the first years of life (Timiras, 1972). Midlife, then, is not a sharp turning point; it simply marks the point at which the balance begins to shift, gradually and inevitably, from growth to decline.

If the physical changes that appear in middle adulthood seem depressing (and to some middle-aged people they do), it is worth noting that they usually do not represent disabilities to members of our society. Physical exertion and stamina are no longer required for survival in modern society. Few jobs today require the sensory acuity or quick reaction time that was required of our ancestral hunters or footsoldiers.

Some writers go so far as to refer to middle age as the prime of life, whereas the term was once reserved for the twenties or thirties. This reflects a recognition that the gradual decline in physical capacities in middle adulthood does not compromise the individual's effectiveness in society. Physical strength is not an important asset; experience, judgment, and seniority give the middle-aged person power in social and work relationships.

Factors Related to Health and Aging

It has been long recognized, and more recently documented, that an individual's rate of physical decline is partly determined by *heredity*. There are families whose members seem to be particularly long-lived. Insurance companies and other actuarial accounts show that a person whose same-sex parent suffered a condition such as cardiovascular disease or breast cancer is at risk by virtue of heredity. Striking similarities have also been found in the aging patterns of identical twins. Even photographs reveal the similarity of smile and facial wrinkles from one generation to the next. How well the organism wears, and which diseases it is vulnerable to, are partly influenced by the original genetic endowment.

But aging is not merely a biological process. Many *environmental factors* are involved. For example, a recent study has shown that a series of life changes—death of a spouse, divorce, change of job or residence—may be so stressful as to result in rapid aging or increased vulnerability to conditions ranging in seriousness from warts to leukemia (Rahe, Mahan, & Arthur, 1970). Moreover, statistics show that married people, especially men, tend to live longer than their unmarried cohorts; that white middle-class people live longer than poor white or minority-group members in our culture; that certain Russian peasants who live in cohesive social structures live longer and more vigorous lives than certain urban American populations. An absence of role conflict, the presence of social support systems, and a more regular pattern of life are presumed to lengthen the life span by reducing the stresses to which the person must adjust.

HEALTH AND NUTRITION TIPS

The extent to which we can defeat the inexorable decline in energy and succumb to the aging process is strongly influenced by our personal habits—the minutiae of our daily lives. We will live longer and be in better health if we realize that we should take as good care of our bodies as we do of our cars and clothes. In a nine-year study (Belloc & Breslow, 1977) seven personal habits were shown to be deleterious to health and longevity.

1. smoking cigarettes
2. drinking immoderately
3. sleeping less than seven hours a night (and to a lesser degree, more than nine)
4. failing to eat breakfast
5. weighing too much (and to a lesser degree, too little)
6. failing to exercise on a regular basis
7. eating between meals

The mortality rate of men who practiced four or more of these habits was four times higher than those who had none of them; among women the death rate was doubled. Although people in lower economic circumstances are known to have higher mortality rates and poorer health, the same relationship between the above personal habits and death and poor health was observed within each income and educational category. Moderate alcohol consumption, one or two drinks per sitting, was positively associated with good health; teetotalers had slightly higher death rates. A complete lack of

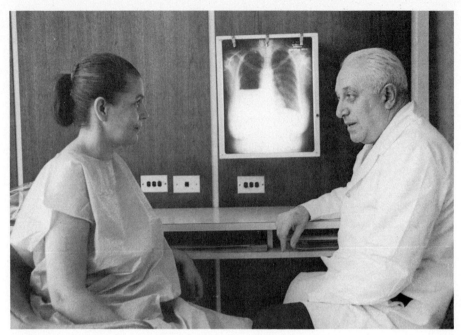

Experience, judgment, and seniority give this middle-aged doctor power and respect in social and work relationships.

exercise doubled the death rate for both men and women, but there was no difference shown between moderately active and very active people. Even a little exercise kept people healthier than no exercise at all.

A proper diet may be more important than all the other health habits mentioned above. Not only should we eat only at meal times but we should choose our calories carefully. According to the Surgeon General's report on diet and disease, 1979, similar to the Surgeon General's report on smoking in 1964, the typical American diet is too high in fats, sugar, cholesterol, and salt, and too low in fiber.

Scientists have estimated that as many as half of human cancers are diet related. A high intake of fats is associated with cancers of the breast and colon and may promote the growth of other cancers as well, according to Dr. Arthur Upton, director of the National Cancer Institute (Brody, 1979). The risk of colon cancer is reduced by eating fiber, which is found in whole grains (bran) and cereals, and fresh fruit and vegetables.

Dr. Robert Good, president and director of the Sloan-Kettering Cancer Center in New York City, goes further. He advocates cutting your daily food intake by about one-third to prevent cancer and the diseases associated with aging. In studies at the center, laboratory mice with a life expectancy of five to seven months have lived up to three years on a restrictive low-calorie, low-fat diet. "The decline in the immune system that normally occurs in aging just didn't occur in animals on the restrictive diet," Good said (Brody, 1979).

How then should we plan our meals?

- Eat about 30 to 40 percent less of the 2,500 to 3,000 calories daily in the average American diet.

- Maintain a balanced diet of fresh fruits and vegetables, skinned chicken, veal, and fish; a diet low in starches, sugar, and salt. Eat more grains, nuts, and legumes.

- Avoid bacon and pork products, lunch meats, mayonnaise, and all prepared foods.

- Do not eat food with preservatives such as nitrites, nitrates, BHA and BHT, saccharine, and other chemicals. (A good rule of thumb is, don't eat it if you can't pronounce it.)

- Cut out butter, creams, chocolates, and prepared snacks (high in sugar and salt).

A low-calorie, well-balanced diet is recommended not just for the middle aged, but for everyone. You'll stay healthier and feel better mentally as well as physically.

Type A Behavior: A Factor in Heart Disease

Whereas the leading causes of death for young adults are accidents and suicide, during middle adulthood the major causes are cardiovascular diseases and cancer. Nearly 40 percent of deaths in this age group are due to heart disease, of which 80 percent of the victims are men (U.S. Department of Health, Education & Welfare, 1978). Cardiovascular diseases have been associated with heredity, diet (particularly foods high in cholesterol and fat), smoking, over-

The impatience reflected by these commuters is characteristic of Type A behavior.

weight, and lack of exercise. However, 50 percent of all heart disease victims could not be linked to any of the known causal factors. Recently scientists have identified a pattern called Type A behavior as one missing link and a major cause of heart disease.

Type A people are characterized by a chronic sense of time urgency and an excessive competitive drive. They are restless and harried human beings, exhibiting undue irritation and impatience with delay. They move, walk, and eat rapidly and often attempt to accomplish two tasks simultaneously. Compulsive in their acquisition and quest for "numbers," Type A people measure their self-worth by the pace of status enhancement. Highly motivated and competitive, they possess an aggressive drive that may evolve into a free-floating hostility. A simple conversation or sporting event, for example, can become a hostile struggle. The Type B person, in contrast, is the direct opposite of the Type A person—relaxed, unhurried, and nonaggressive (Friedman & Rosenman, 1974).

The causative link between Type A behavior and heart disease is based on a number of findings, including (a) the presence of Type A behavior patterns in those individuals already afflicted with coronary heart disease, (b) the extreme vulnerability of Type A persons to the disease—Type A behavior is associated with at least twice the occurrence of heart disease as Type B behavior (Jenkins, Rosenman, & Zyzanski, 1974), (c) the identification of coronary biochemical abnormalities in Type A persons, and most importantly (d) successful experiments in which Type A behavior was induced, and following which coronary biochemical derangements were found. Other research suggests that Type A people may ignore physical symptoms. In turn, this may actually contribute to the risk of heart disease by preventing them from seeking medical attention or altering their behavior to reduce tension (Mathews & Brunson, 1979; Weidner & Mathews, 1978). Interestingly, although the stereotype of the Type A person is the hard-driven, compulsive male executive, research evidence suggests that women who exhibit this behavior pattern are also at greater risk of heart disease (Eisdorfer & Wilkie, 1977).

Life Stresses

Another health-related factor for middle-aged adults that has received increased attention is general life stress. Theorell and Rahe (1974), for example, have noted a positive relationship between the incidence of heart attacks and the number and type of such major changes in the person's life as death of a spouse, divorce, loss of job, or retirement. And yet many people experience stressful life events without subsequently becoming ill. What differentiates the "adapters" from the "nonadapters"? Kobasa (1979) studied two groups of middle- to upper-level executives who had experienced comparable high levels of stressful events in the previous three years of their lives. One group suffered the stress without falling ill, whereas the other group reported a variety of illnesses following the stressful events. The findings from the Kobasa study indicate that executives who adapted to the life stresses, in comparison to

Obesity and lack of exercise are bad health-related habits that tax the body's cardiovascular system.

those who did not, had a clearer sense of their own values, goals, and capacities, and a stronger commitment and belief in themselves. They adopted a more vigorous attitude toward the environment and sought active, as opposed to passive, involvement with it. They were better able to evaluate the life changes in a meaningful way, and incorporate them into a general life plan. And they also were more likely to display an internal locus of control—a belief that they could handle life events and, to some extent, control them. Kobasa used the term *hardy personality* to characterize individuals who are more successful in adjusting to life stresses.

The Climacteric and Menopause

One aspect of aging that has been carefully studied is the effect on behavior of the decrease in the production of gonadal hormones. These are the sexual hormones, estrogens and testosterones, produced, respectively, by the ovaries and testes. Although the pituitary continues to send strong messages to the gonads, and although the adrenals, thyroid, and pancreas continue to function as before, the gonads simply become less productive in the middle years.

Midlife Pregnancy

"My mother had my brother when she was forty-two years old. It was an easy birth without drugs. My grandmother had her sixth child at the same age. My best friend's mother also had her last child at forty-two. So I was in no hurry. It never occurred to me to worry about being a 'high risk' simply because I was over thirty" (Brewer, 1978). According to Ian Morrison (1975) "the label 'high risk' in a modern obstetrical context applies to the fetus." With careful prenatal care and a nutritious diet, there is no longer a greater risk to the life of an elderly (defined by doctors as over thirty-five) pregnant woman than to a younger woman. The risks involve the infant. There is a greater likelihood of stillbirth or a neonatal (within the first month of life) death; there is a greater likelihood that the fetus will be smaller over the nine-month period, resulting in a greater chance of miscarriage, stillbirth, or premature birth; and there is a greater chance of neonatal morbidity, that is, that the infant will have central nervous system problems or respiratory problems related to the birth itself.

If these statistics seem alarming, it is important to bear in mind two considerations:

1. The rates are still low. The mortality rate for infants of elderly mothers, for example, is still only 47 per thousand births—more than twice the national infant mortality rate but an unlikely event for any individual mother.

2. Such statistics based on age combine the birthing experience of two different groups of women. First is the elderly mother who has had more than one child (multiparous) who is likely to be poor, not in good health, and perhaps malnourished during her pregnancy. This woman has a poor chance of having a healthy baby in midlife. The woman who is having her first child (primagravida) is more likely to be middle class and in excellent health. This woman will seek out the best care for herself and should have no problems. General health is a better predictor of the outcome of pregnancy than age. As Gail Brewer says, "It is necessary for each individual to know as much as possible about her own situation, physically, emotionally, and socially before she can decide whether pregnancy would be a high risk for her."

The incidence of Down's syndrome (mongolism) is definitely related to age. The chances—one in a thousand at age thirty—rise to one in a hundred at age forty-five. It is possible to determine whether the baby will be born with Down's syndrome by a procedure called *amniocentesis*. A sample of the amniotic fluid is obtained and analyzed for genetic abnormalities. It is usually recommended that women over forty undergo the procedure. If Down's syndrome is present, the parents may choose abortion.

One other statistic that climbs for elderly mothers is the rate of delivery by cesarean section, a surgical procedure. One explanation is the greater readiness of obstetricians to perform cesareans on older mothers. It is generally accepted by obstetricians that a cesarean will prevent many of the complications that might arise during the delivery of a child by an older woman. Rather than judge each case on its own merits, some obstetricians prefer to be safe and remove the infant surgically.

The emotional readiness of a middle-aged woman to give birth and bring up a child is as important to a successful outcome as her physical readiness. One woman was quoted as saying, "The pleasure of having your first child at forty is immense. My enthusiasm for getting pregnant was due to a feeling of readiness mentally as well as physically" (Brewer, 1978). Clearly the advantage of a midlife pregnancy is the maturity a woman and her husband can bring to the pregnancy experience. An older woman knows herself better, has had a greater depth of experience in the world, and can handle any problems that arise more wisely and with greater strength. She should not be threatened by the idea that at thirty-five or forty she is too old to bear and rear children of her own.

The term "climacteric" is used to describe the changes in the reproductive and sex organs.

For women, the late thirties or early forties mark the beginning of a decline in estrogen and progesterone levels. The decrease in estrogen levels eventually lead to the *menopause*, the cessation of the menses when women stop menstruating and can no longer bear children. The cessation of menstruation may take place over a period of from two to five years. The decline in estrogen levels results in the thinning of the vaginal walls, a slowing down of the vaginal lubrication response, cessation of ovulation and menstruation, and a shrinking of the ovaries and uterus.

At about the age of fifty men experience a decline in testosterone more gradual than that of women. The decline in testosterone levels results in a slight decrease in the number of healthy, active sperm and in the size of the testicles; a reduction in the force of ejaculation and the volume of fluid ejaculated; and an enlarging of the prostate gland (Weg, 1975). Middle-aged males also find that they require more time to achieve an erection, and a longer period between erections than they did in adolescence and young adulthood. On the other hand, erections can usually be maintained for longer periods of time by the middle-aged male.

The way in which these changes are experienced somewhat parallels adolescent developments. Women experience a clear beginning to "womanhood" in the first menstruation (menarche) but for the first year or so, the menstrual cycle may be anovulatory, which means that the young girl may be infertile or only irregularly fertile. During the climacteric, women again experience relatively clear signs of change in the menopause. Twelve consecutive months without menstruating is experienced on the average at fifty years of age (Weideger, 1976), though there is wide individual variation. Again, like the adolescent girl, the older woman is irregularly fertile; she may be anovulatory one cycle, and may be surprised to find herself pregnant the next. Neither change is experienced primarily in terms of sexual performance; that is, a woman can participate in and enjoy sexual intercourse no matter what her fertility status.

For men, unlike women, there is no one biological event that initiates manhood. Similarly, there is nothing like the menopause, no striking biological development, that marks the climacteric. Fertility is not an issue, since most men are fertile throughout life. Just as the coming of manhood tends to be defined in terms of desire and performance (the first nocturnal emission, the first intercourse), so the climacteric, if experienced at all, is felt as a falling off of desire (less frequent spontaneous erections) or performance (impotence anxiety). Many men are unaware of physical changes, as opposed to changes in life circumstances. Seldom does a man consult a doctor about the climacteric; indeed, unlike most women, he does not have an ongoing relationship with a physician who is especially concerned with reproductive functions.

A number of unpleasant symptoms have been associated with menopause, including profuse sweating, "hot flashes," dizziness, headaches, irritability, depression, insomnia, and weight gain. Approximately 30 percent of all menopausal women seek medical attention for one or more of these symptoms (Weideger, 1976.) Physicians ascribed these symptoms to a hormone imbalance, and have treated them in the past biochemically—usually with estrogens. Recently, however, medical studies have shown a strong relationship between the incidence of cancer of the endometrium (the lining of the uterus) and the use of estrogen in treating the symptoms of menopausal and postmenopausal women (Smith et al., 1975).

Some women have strongly objected to the medical-model approach to menopause, which stereotypes this biological state as a disease. Goodman (1980) reminds us that menopause refers to the cessation of menstruation which sometimes, but certainly not always, is accompanied by unpleasant physical symptoms. She found that these same symptoms are often present in premenopausal women. In fact, the only difference Goodman found in her research between menopausal and premenopausal women, after adjusting for age differences between the groups, was that the former more often had surgery related to female disorders. No difference was found for the incidence of sweating, headaches, nervous tension, and other "common menopausal symptoms."

Only a small percentage of women have symptoms so severe that they are prohibited from going about their daily routine (Neugarten et al., 1963). And yet the stereotype remains, often contributing, and unnecessarily so, to midlife adjustment.

Some men also report a sudden increase in insomnia, irritability, headaches, and other "menopausal" symptoms in middle life. This has led to speculation as to whether there is a "male menopause." Strictly speaking, there is not. Naturally, there are cases of testicular insufficiency (just as there are cases of thyroid insufficiency or adrenal insufficiency). However, such cases are insignificant in number (Hess, Roth, & Kaminsky, 1955). The use of the word "menopause" to explain or describe male irritability in middle life is instructive mainly in that it shows us the way in which the physiological term has come to be used. Menopause for women (and now for men) explains away an assortment of emotional upsets and psychosomatic complaints that are associated with middle age itself.

COGNITIVE DEVELOPMENT

Until fairly recently, it was assumed that intelligence, like muscular strength or height, was fully developed by late adolescence or the early twenties. This assumption recognizes the physical basis of intelligence—that is, its neurological foundation. More recent work has suggested that although some aspects of intelligence may grow only until young adulthood, intellectual development continues into later adulthood. Continued development occurs in those intellectual or cognitive abilities that are influenced by the accumulation of the experiences of life, for example, verbal skills, social knowledge, and moral judgments.

Intelligence Scores

The intelligence quotient (IQ) has long been the measure of intelligence in school-age children. Standardized intelligence tests measuring IQ have also been given to large adult populations, as for example, to army recruits. When different age groups are tested in a cross-sectional design, that is, testing all ages at one time, age-related patterns emerge. These patterns are naturally of interest to psychologists studying intelligence over the life span.

In an early large-scale administration of a standardized intelligence test, Jones and Conrad (1933) discovered that individuals about twenty years of age scored higher than middle-aged and older adults; this was interpreted to mean that intelligence began a long decline at age twenty. In more recent cross-sectional studies of adult intelligence, the average peak of performance seems to occur between twenty-five and thirty-five (Schaie, 1975). Middle-aged and older people do less well on these tests than younger adults.

A problem with the cross-sectional design is that we cannot assume that the differences between age groups are the results of aging. Younger subjects may score higher than middle-aged subjects not because they are more intelligent, but because of such variables as more formal education, better nutrition, and greater childhood exposure to television. Just as important is the greater experience that most younger people have with the standardized testing situation. The higher scores, then, may represent *generation* or *cohort effects* as opposed to (or in addition to) effects of age. (A further discussion of cohort effects will be found in the section in this chapter on personality development.)

In order to minimize generation effects, longitudinal studies have been conducted. In these studies the same individuals are tested and retested at different points in their life span. Using this approach, little or no decline has been found in middle age. In fact, two major studies showed that middle-aged adults performed better than they had as young adults (Bayley & Oden, 1955; Nisbet, 1957)—though this increase may have been a reflection of the highly select, intellectually superior sample of subjects. The longitudinal studies have their own biases, however. For one thing, it is the highly motivated and healthier individual who remains in the study (which may continue for twenty, thirty, or even forty years). The results then may reflect intelligence as it operates in the more vital and thoughtful individual. A second point is that the longitudinal studies may be affected by changes in environment. For example, if testing were to become much more common during a given decade, all respondents tested after that time might do better, on the basis of their experience in the testing situation, than they had done twenty years earlier. Similarly, being given the same or similar tests repeatedly over a period of time sensitizes people to the test-taking situation—that is, they learn how to take tests, and consequently may do better on later tests. In both cases, an increase in test scores would not just reflect aging. The best conclusion we can draw from the longitudinal studies is that the decline in intelligence during middle age is, if it exists at all, not universal. Birren (1974) and Birren, Woods, and Williams (1980) suggest that much of the age-related decline in intellectual functioning as it appears in the testing situation can be explained on the basis of speed of psychomotor response: as we get older, it takes longer for the central nervous system to process information. In test-taking situations, this slowing down of neurophysiological systems would certainly place the middle-aged and elderly adult at a disadvantage.

Fluid and Crystallized Abilities

In order to test intelligence, researchers must define what it is they are testing. Over the years the concept of intelligence has included a large number of factors such as verbal abilities, long- and short-term memory, reasoning abilities, general information, and quickness of response. Because of the need to distinguish between intelligence acquired as a result of education and absorption of one's culture, and intelligence acquired as a result of more "casual learning influences" (Horn & Donaldson, 1980), some researchers have proposed a model in which intelligence is divided into two patterns they call *fluid* and *crystallized* intelligence (Cattell, 1963; Horn, 1972; Horn & Cattell, 1966).

Crystallized intelligence is culturally derived, that is, it is a result of knowledge and of problem-solving techniques learned initially in school and more generally through socialization; it involves a knowledge of one's language and of the skills and technology of one's culture. Examples of crystallized intelligence include such abilities as vocabulary, general information, reasoning ability related to formal logic, and mechanical knowledge such as the use of tools and the understanding of mechanical principles. Crystallized intelligence is associated with the use of principles common to the culture in which one lives.

Fluid intelligence, on the other hand, is displayed by solving such problems as completing a series such as 3, 7, 11, 15,—and so on. Questions testing fluid intelligence aim to be culture free, tapping abilities that are more directly related to neurophysiological intactness. Fluid abilities are characterized by the use of personal strategies rather than those learned at school to solve problems. For example, in estimating the amount of cement needed for building a sidewalk, a person relying on fluid intelligence would use a personally derived system for making the estimate; the use of algebra might be used by a person using crystallized abilities. Fluid intelligence is more affected than crystallized intelligence by hereditary factors as well as by injury to the central nervous system.

What is the relevance of fluid and crystallized intelligence to aging? Fluid intelligence peaks between the ages of twenty and thirty and thereafter declines. Crystallized intelligence, on the other hand, increases as one gets older (Horn & Donaldson, 1980). Horn and Donaldson try to explain these differences by pointing to the learning process. If one is concentrating one's energies, the quality of learning is enhanced. These researchers point to the years from twenty to thirty as a period of great intensity in learning one's occupation as well as making sexual and marital adjustments. Thus one's fluid abilities are strained to the utmost in finding personal solutions to life's problems. At the same time one builds one's crystallized intelligence on the retention of what was learned during these years.

Logic and Morality

Until recently, there was little interest in the *logical* structure of adult thought. Changes in adult thinking beyond the adolescent years were believed to be of a quantitative sort, in which information was added to, or lost from, one's general knowledge with the passing of time. As we saw in Chapter 14, however, there has been a new interest in identifying structural changes in adult cognitive development. Additional stages, beyond formal operations have been suggested (Arlin, 1975; Basseches, 1980), and Piagetian-type skills (e.g., conservation, classification, seriation, perspective-taking, moral judgment, etc.) have been investigated across the life span (Hooper & Sheehan, 1977; Papalia & Bielby, 1974). Research indicates that logical concept development remains relatively stable from early to middle adulthood, although in certain areas, or under certain conditions, advances in cognition may be evident. One group of researchers found that *moral* judgments tend to rise to the highest average level in early middle age. And middle-aged people were found to be better able than other adults to see things from another person's perspective (Bielby & Papalia, 1975). Subjects referred to life experiences (such as responses to illness or conflicts with children) as having influenced their moral reasoning. Middle-aged people seem to be especially capable of thinking through an issue and reflecting on solutions to moral problems.

Creativity

While most researchers interested in intellectual functioning across the life span have focused on the skills and knowledge represented in standardized intelligence tests, or Piagetian-type measures, others have sought to examine the more creative aspects of human functioning. One researcher (Lehman,

The creativity of middle age is a more "sculpted" kind of creativity than that of youth, emerging from experience, revision, and interpretation.

1953) studied the quality of the creative work of recognized artists and scientists and found that his subjects made fewer high-quality creative contributions as they became older. Creative breakthroughs were more often the work of young adulthood; there was a falling off in the quality of creative productions in middle age. Another researcher Dennis (1966) studied productivity, that is, the number of contributions, regardless of quality, in males who had lived to eighty years of age. He found that artists, such as musicians and poets, reach their peak productivity earlier than scientists and scholars.

Scientists and scholars whose creative work involved extensive collection and evaluation of data as, for example, historians and geologists, were, however, especially productive in middle and late adulthood.

What factors might be related to the decline in creativity of artists from young adulthood through old age and the later productivity of scientists and scholars? One early explanation for a decline in creativity is the apparent decrease in intellectual functioning associated with age (Bromley, 1956). This, of course, makes the assumption that creativity and intelligence are highly correlated, and in fact, may be one and the same thing. But as we have seen, more recent work has shown that crystallized intelligence, the component that relies on learning based on one's cultural heritage, does not decline with age. Recently Alpaugh and Birren (1977) identified two variables that are related to a decline in the creative contributions of older people: *divergent thinking* and a *preference for complexity*. Divergent thinking includes the ability to think of many different ideas appropriate to a situation; originality; and the ability to change and transform ideas from one state to another. A preference for complexity of ideas has been equated with creativity itself (Barron, 1963; Helson, 1967). Alpaugh and Birren, working with a cross-sectional sample of subjects from twenty to eighty-three years of age, carefully controlled for education, found systematic declines in both variables with increasing age, whereas their measures for intelligence remained constant. They concluded, therefore, that in addition to declines in such factors as energy and vigor, declines in creative production across the life span—as related to cognitive processes—can be explained in terms of a decrease in divergent thinking and preference for complexity rather than any decline in intelligence per se.

Some observers speculate that different kinds of creativity are associated with different age groups in adulthood. For example, Jacques (1964) speaks of "hot-from-the-fire" creativity of young adulthood, and the "sculpted creativity" of midlife. During the early years the creative work is intense and spontaneous; the product seems to emerge as an effusion, ready-made. Einstein is a prototype. The creativity of middle age, on the other hand, is a slower, more "sculpted" kind of creativity. The content and quality of the work reflect an awareness of death and human destructiveness. Rather than effusion, one finds a "working through." Shakespeare and Dickens are prototypes. It appears that spontaneous hot-from-the-fire creativity peaks in early adulthood; but forms of creativity that require experience, revision, and interpretation either remain unchanged or increase in middle age.

PERSONALITY DEVELOPMENT

To some people, personality development in midlife seems improbable. Middle-aged people are said to be "set in their ways." Put more positively, they have achieved a welcome stability of personality. Middle-aged people are not the last to subscribe to this image. In one study (Gould, 1972) subjects in their early forties showed a striking increase in agreement with the position, "My personality is pretty well set." The same group tended to agree with statements such as "It is too late to make any major changes in my career," or "Life doesn't change much from year to year."

On the other hand, observation and the psychological literature suggest that middle age can be a period of extraordinary growth and change. The old saw, "life begins at forty," supports this position, as do many popular and scholarly descriptions of the midlife crisis. Indeed, many writers go so far as to compare the onset of middle adulthood with adolescence, coining the term *middlescence* to account for a troubled midlife passage, as well as its new social role (Fried, 1967). Middlescence is seen as an opportunity to carry forth the identity crisis of adolescence. It is a second chance to "do your own thing, sing your own song, to be deeply and truly yourself," in one middle-aged writer's popular statement (Le Shan, 1973). "Instinctual reawakening," "rebirth experience," "fresh vigor of human midlife," are a psychiatrist's words for the same phenomenon (Vaillant, 1977).

Personality Stability and Change

Having raised the issue of personality change in adult development, let us examine it more closely. The focus of the issue has to do with the affect of aging on personality. Do individuals show systematic changes in such aspects of personality as character structure, values, and beliefs as they move from young adulthood to midlife, and finally to old age? Or is personality relatively stable across the adult life span?

At first glance, it would appear that these questions would be easy to answer—simply measure some trait or cluster of traits at one age, say twenty, and then again at a later age, say forty. To the extent that personality is stable, one would expect people to remain the same over the twenty-year period— that is, the hostile-aggressive twenty-year-old should also be hostile-aggressive at forty; the warm, nurturant young adult should develop into a warm, nurturant middle-ager. If personality changes with increasing age, however, these patterns would not be expected—the hostile-aggressive or the warm, nurturant young adults would not be the same type of people at midlife as they were during early adulthood.

Unfortunately, the answer to the question of personality stability versus change is not so easily discerned. Personality is a very complex aspect of the individual and difficult to measure over time. Many theorists differentiate between genotypic and phenotypic continuity with respect to personality (Livson, 1973; Neugarten, 1977). *Genotypic continuity* refers to the stability of an underlying personality structure or pattern of traits—a structure that may be expressed, however, in different behaviors at different times. Thus, a hostile-aggressive person may be physically assertive and verbally caustic during young adulthood—directly confronting people, arguing constantly, and even occasionally getting into fights. That same person during middle age, however, may express hostility in more indirect, passive-aggressive ways, by repeatedly "forgetting" to invite a colleague to join the group at lunchtime, for example, or by "misplacing" an important report that the boss needs for a conference presentation. In this example, it is assumed that the basic structure or trait pattern of personality, that is, hostility, is stable over time—it is only the behaviors representative of hostility that have changed.

Phenotypic continuity, in contrast, refers to the degree of similarity in overt behavior at two different times. In the above example, phenotypic continuity would be low since the overt behaviors representing hostility have changed dramatically from early to middle adulthood. Thus, it should be clear that the lack of similarity in overt behavior from one time to another is not necessarily evidence of instability or change. Likewise, similarity in behavior

Middle age can be a period of extraordinary growth and change. A troubled midlife passage might account for sudden flare-ups of temper that accompany midlife crisis, or "middlescence."

does not necessarily imply continuity or stability. Two identical behaviors can be based on quite different underlying motives. The worker who offers help to a colleague may do so because of a genuine desire to assist others, *or* because he needs to inflate his own self-image by letting others know of their incompetence and inferiority in specific areas—a passive-aggressive "put down" of others.

As in measuring intelligence, there is the problem of distinguishing between differences that are due to *development* and those that are due to *cohort* or *generational* effects in investigating personality development. Changes due to development would be true for most people as they progressed through the life span. Generational effects would be observed only for a particular cohort of people who lived through a specific historical period— people who were members of the "now" generation of the sixties, or those who were young during World War II. Woodruff and Birren (1972) examined personality changes in adolescents tested in 1944, and then retested twenty-five years later when they were in middle-age. To examine cohort differences, the personality scores of the subjects also were compared to a set of scores of adolescents and youth tested in 1969. The researchers found that personality changes from adolescence to middle adulthood were small in compari-

son to the differences due to cohort experiences. The major differences between the adolescents tested in 1944 and those tested in 1969 were that the
former scored higher in self and social adjustment.

Putting aside these theoretical and methodological problems, the research evidence generally supports the assumption of personality stability in
adulthood. This is particularly true of those studies that have utilized longitudinal designs (Costa, McCrae, & Arenburg, 1980; Haan & Day, 1974; Leon et
al., 1979; Schaie & Parham, 1976; Woodruff & Birren, 1972). Some of the most
stable characteristics include values (aesthetic, religious, economic, social, and
political) and vocational interests. When cross-sectional designs are used, as
Neugarten (1977) notes, the findings are more complicated, with some but not
other studies reporting age differences in such personality characteristics as
rigidity, cautiousness, conservatism, self-concept, and life-satisfaction. However, most researchers agree that with increasing age there is a move from
extroversion to introversion—that is, the aging adult shows less preoccupation
with the outside world, and more preoccupation with the self.

In summary, adult personality development is not, generally speaking,
characterized by large and pervasive changes in beliefs, attitudes, and values.
The midlife crisis, if it is experienced at all, involves more of a reshaping and
reorganization of existing personality characteristics than a complete transformation of the person into a "new human being."

Developmental Tasks of Middle Adulthood

Although the evidence suggests that basic personality structure does not
change much during adulthood, certainly the developmental tasks confronting adults do. Moreover, some theorists have speculated that the way in which
people cope with life crises may well undergo some transformation as they
are confronted with the new tasks of middle adulthood.

In Erikson's psychosocial scheme, the central crisis for middle-aged
adults is the resolution of *generativity* versus *stagnation*. Erikson notes that
"evolution has made man a teaching as well as a learning animal, for dependency and maturity are reciprocal" (Erikson, 1968, p. 138). Generativity,
then, is primarily the concern for establishing and guiding the next generation.
For some individuals, generativity is expressed in the context of the family,
through loving and nurturing relationships with spouse and children. For
others, it is found in job productivity or as a mentor to younger workers—
guiding and helping them in their career development. Generativity is a person's link with the future—the means by which one can transcend one's own
mortality. The opposite of generativity in Erikson's theory is stagnation—a
feeling of personal impoverishment, boredom, and an excessive concern or
preoccupation with the self. Erikson points out that early invalidism can become the means for a permitted self-absorption.

The work of Robert Peck (1968) echoes some of the same themes found
in Erikson's theory. Peck outlines four major challenges or tasks for middle-
aged adults who are attempting to cope with the changes taking place both

A loving and nurturing relation with the family is important for people in their middle years. The developmental task of generativity underlies their concern for and guiding of the successive generation.

within and outside themselves. First, people must come to value wisdom over physical strength and attractiveness. They must acknowledge and accept the inevitable decline in physical areas, and rely more on experience, knowledge, and mental processes for life satisfaction. Second, they must redefine relationships with others. People, including spouses, should increasingly be viewed as individuals and companions—relationships, on the whole, becoming broader, more social, and less sexualized at this time. Three, middle-aged adults must also be able to demonstrate what Peck calls *cathected flexibility*— that is, the capacity to shift one's emotional investment to new people or activities. This capacity becomes especially important in middle-age because of the increased exposure to "breaks" in relationships during this time—parents die, children grow up and leave home, certain activities (such as vigorous athletics) may have to be put aside. To adjust to these changes, middle-aged people must be able to "let go" of relationships—with parents, children, a job—and then reinvest themselves in something new. Fourth, Peck suggests that successful adjustment to middle age also requires remaining mentally flexible and open to new experiences or ways of doing things. If people continue to rely on well-worn ideas or answers, they may become slaves to the past. Instead of controlling their lives, their lives may control them.

Erikson's Crises in Psychosocial Development

BASIC TRUST VERSUS BASIC MISTRUST (FIRST YEAR OF LIFE)

AUTONOMY VERSUS SHAME AND DOUBT (SECOND YEAR OF LIFE)

INITIATIVE VERSUS GUILT (THE PRESCHOOL YEARS)

INDUSTRY VERSUS INFERIORITY (MIDDLE CHILDHOOD)

IDENTITY VERSUS ROLE CONFUSION (ADOLESCENCE)

INTIMACY VERSUS ISOLATION (EARLY ADULTHOOD)

 GENERATIVITY VERSUS STAGNATION (MIDDLE ADULTHOOD)

Generativity, in the forms of productivity and creativity, is the focus of middle adulthood. At this point the individual becomes concerned with future generations; his care is expressed in raising children or contributing to his culture through work and other creative processes. The person who does not demonstrate this care for, or belief in, future generations, may succumb to stagnation, personal impoverishment, or excessive self-concern.

EGO INTEGRITY VERSUS DESPAIR (OLD AGE)

Another perspective of midlife challenges is offered by Havighurst (1974). He notes that developmental tasks arise from changes within the person, from societal pressures, and especially from pressures laid upon the person by his own values, standards, and aspirations. Middle age is a unique time of life. At no other point in the life span does the person have as much influence upon society. And yet it is also the time when society makes its greatest demands on the person. Middle-aged adults must cope with important tasks at home, for example, assisting teen-age children to become responsible, happy adults and maintaining a harmonious relationship with a spouse. They face pressures at work and must reach and maintain a satisfactory level of occupational performance. And at the same time they are asked by society to accept and fulfill their social and civic obligations and responsibilities. The middle-aged person, according to Havighurst, must also find new outlets for leisure time; outlets that reflect changes in body, interests, values, financial status, and family structure.

Although each of these theorists portrays the tasks of middle age in somewhat different ways, a common thread runs through their writings. Each sees middle age as a time of continued challenge for the individual—challenge that may require considerable adjustment in areas such as self, family relations, social interactions, career development, and leisure activity. And yet successful adjustment to the tasks of midlife, like all periods of development, is dependent upon many factors, and takes many forms. Middle-aged adults are not a homogenous group. Each person is a unique individual, with unique experiences—and each will adjust to the challenges of midlife in his or her own unique way. As one fifty-year-old schoolteacher recently said: "As I watched my father go through middle age, I saw a person I loved begin to fall apart. He lost interest in everything, became preoccupied with his health, and what he saw as a 'looming death.' He was no fun to be around. Now I'm at the point of my life that he once was and I still can't understand his reaction. Sure, it's no fun to get old. But I'm finding new interests all the time—new things to do. My job has become somewhat less important as I discover these interests. Many I can share with my husband; others are just for me. I don't feel that old and I just don't worry about getting older . . . life is just too short to be preoccupied with those kinds of thoughts. I'm middle-aged, I guess, but I feel good about where I'm at."

Psychological Reactions to Aging

In middle age, as in adolescence, people must come to terms with physical changes that affect their status in society, as well as their feelings about themselves.

While physical aging affects both sexes, women traditionally have felt its impact more severely. Sontag (1977) has written of the "double standard of aging," which refers to society's equating of womanliness and femininity with physical appearance. As she ages, and becomes more wrinkled and gray-haired, a woman's status in today's society may decline significantly. In contrast, the aging male is often cast in a more positive light—the gray hair is seen as distinguished; the wrinkled face as evidence of wisdom and character.

Middle age is a time when people may experience a new relationship to time. Life is seen in terms of time-left-to-live rather than time-from-birth (Neugarten, 1967). Goals and values are revised accordingly. Levinson (1978), for example, sees the forties as a period of midlife transition in which the person engages in serious introspection, reevaluating the self, and soul-searching for "what I really want." If he has attained "success," a man may find that it is not enough. If he has fallen short of his goals, he will begin to reconcile himself to his own limitations or perhaps to society's imperfections (the fact that hard work is not always rewarded, for example). In either case, the person may take the opportunity to establish new life goals and priorities, or to resurrect earlier interests that had been set aside—perhaps a redirection toward more "caring" activities; or a more active participation in the community. Midlife brings a renewed interest in friends and social activities for many people. Whereas the twenties and thirties can be a turning inward to the immediate family and/or the job, the forties and fifties can be a flowering of human relationships that come to be valued for their own sake (Gould, 1972). In sum, being able to care for and about people seems to have greater value, and accomplishment relatively less.

Psychological Reactions to Death

Signs of aging may bring a recognition of one's own mortality. Although this recognition is not unique to middle age, there is an increased concern with death during this period. For example, in one recent study, the greatest fear of death was expressed by those in the forty-five to fifty-four age group (Bengston, Arellar, & Ragan, 1977). Exactly when individuals become more conscious of life's finitude probably depends on events or accidents which befall them. Among the precipitating events described by Sheehy are the death or serious illness of a contemporary; the death of a parent; or an unanticipated brush with death for a person in the thirties or early forties (Sheehy, 1976). In some cases the awareness grows slowly. In others it comes like a blow, inducing panic, crying spells, or temporary breakdown. In later middle age, fears about death seem to be resolved; perhaps they are more openly acknowledged; perhaps more fully integrated into the understanding of one's own life.

The death of a close friend from natural causes is, for most people, a shock; the death of a parent is psychologically even more significant. This event causes the middle-aged person to revise his self-concept: he is now the oldest in his family—the next to go. In some individuals, the death of a parent is a final stage in the movement away from childhood. The person feels finally adult. Some people seem to inherit personality characteristics of the deceased, a father's authority or decisiveness, for example, along with his tool chest and patriarchal status. If there has been some yearning to be free of parental domination, a parent's death will cause conflicting feelings of guilt and liberation (Kastenbaum, 1977). It may also cause some middle-aged people to cling more tightly to children or to become more dependent on a spouse.

Middle age also is marked by many deathlike experiences (as well as by potential rebirth). According to Kastenbaum, it is a period in which "developmental death" seems to occur with greatest frequency. People may show themselves unwilling to age, to relinquish the young version of themselves. A classic example of this kind of failure occurs in the stage character of Willy Loman (*Death of a Salesman*). Willy does not understand that the salesman he was once (or thought he was) has "died" and must be replaced by an older man, with different self-image, virtues, and realities. Nor can Willy bring himself to discard the younger image of his son, the once-charmed football hero. The result is that the death of a salesman becomes the death of the man. Kastenbaum likens such a reaction to a refusal to bury the dead.

Analogies to death in midlife include the burial of the younger self that is implied in a change of self-image or career commitment. Related to this is the death of dreams—that is, youthful dreams. Even in the most successful lives, the awareness of time remaining means that some possibilities must be relinquished, some ambitions scrapped. "I don't plan on leaving any big footsteps behind," writes one man in his mid-fifties, "but I am becoming more insistent in my attempts to move the town to build a new hospital, support schools, and teach kids to sing." Another writes, "For good or evil I find myself with few hopes or ambitions for the future—but contented rather than in any way despairing" (Vaillant, 1977). People work out ways of living satisfactorily within their own time, place, budget, and energy restrictions. Perhaps they find that the world is less in need of change than once it was. Perhaps they are concerned not so much with finding the meaning of life as with keeping the meaning (Vaillant, 1977).

SUMMARY

▶ Middle age is accompanied by a gradual physical decline from the peak reached in the twenties. The individual does not experience a simple reverse from growth to deterioration; both processes have been taking place since early in life. As for the changes themselves, they do not represent disabilities in our society. Judgment, experience, and management ability have come to be valued more than physical strength.

▶ As people enter the middle years of life, concerns regarding physical health become more common. Cardiovascular diseases and cancer are the two leading causes of death during this time. Research indicates that emotional and personality factors—particularly *Type A behavior*—are major contributors to the health problems of middle-aged adults.

▶ One effect of aging is the *climacteric*—the changes in the reproductive and sexual organs that result from a decrease in the production of gonadal hormones. For women, the decline in estrogen and progesterone levels brings a clear signal of biological change: *menopause*. Menstruation gradually ceases over a period of a year or two. For men, the results of a decline in testosterone levels are less clear-cut.

▶ Cognitive development continues in middle age in abilities that are influenced by experience, such as verbal ability, social knowledge, and moral judgment. A decline in intellectual function through the middle years is found only in studies based on a cross-sectional design. Longitudinal research, in which the same people are measured more than one time in their life span, does not show decline in intelligence relative to age.

▶ Some theorists propose two components of intelligence. *Fluid abilities*, which are closely related to neurophysiological intactness, peak in early adulthood. *Crystallized abilities*, which are the result of acculturation, remain unchanged or even increase during middle age.

▶ Research suggests that logical concept development remains relatively stable through middle adulthood, although in certain areas increases in performance have been found.

▶ Both the quality and quantity of creative contributions, except for the productivity of scholars and scientists, declines in middle age. The decline in creativity across the life span appears to be related to decreases in divergent thinking and a preference for complexity.

▶ There are different views of personality development in midlife. Most theorists do agree, however, that middle age is a time of challenge for the individual—challenge that may require considerable adjustment in such areas as the self, family relations, social interactions, career development, and leisure activity. Erikson, for example, sees the midlife crisis as one of generativity—a concern for the next generation—versus stagnation—a sense of boredom and preoccupation with the self.

▶ It is difficult to determine whether adult personality is basically stable, or whether people undergo major personality changes across the life span. Some theorists have suggested that although the basic personality structure or trait pattern of the individual remains the same across the adult years, the behaviors representative of the underlying structure may well change. Most research, particularly those studies using longitudinal designs, support the assumption of personality stability in adulthood. Some of the most stable characteristics include values and vocational interests.

▶ In middle age, people typically become sensitive to their own mortality. Life is felt in terms of time-left-to-live rather than time-from-birth. Personal confrontation with illness, death, and the recognition of life's finitude often cause midlife adults to revise their values and to discard youthful dreams.

FURTHER READINGS

Barry, John R., and Wingrove, C. Ray (Eds.). *Let's learn about aging.* New York: Halsted, 1977.
A comprehensive collection of readings on the physiological, psychological, and social processes of aging. The list of authors includes both scholarly and popular writers of the past two decades.

Chew, Peter. *The inner world of the middle-aged man.* New York: Macmillan, 1976.
A compassionate and fascinating exploration of the changes occurring in the middle-aged man. Chew examines such aspects of the middle-aged crisis as impotence, employment difficulties, and the drive to recover lost youth. The book is based upon scores of interviews with businessmen, scientists, blue-collar workers, athletes, and religious men. Chew supports his excellent text with appropriate quotations from writers of the past.

Levinson, Daniel J. *The seasons of a man's life.* New York: Knopf, 1979.
Levinson outlines the developmental stages of a man's life. His theory is based on a ten-year study, and the book includes many case histories. Levinson's writing is poetic and readable.

Sheehy, G. *Passages: Predictable crises of adult life.* New York: Dutton, 1976.
Sheehy offers a highly readable account of the turmoils, struggles, and triumphs of every age stage past adolescence. Her writing is journalistic and engaging.

Chapter 17

❖❖❖❖❖❖

Family and Occupational Development

I f youth and young adulthood are times for sowing the seeds of adult life, then middle age is the time for reaping them. And as we saw in Chapter 16, middle age brings with it a sense of challenge. In Erikson's (1968) scheme, the psychosocial crisis at midlife is the challenge of generativity versus stagnation. Nowhere is this challenge better expressed than in the contexts of family and work life. In middle age there is a broadening of interests and a turning outward toward others. Having found their own place in society, mature adults reorient their energies toward the future—to the next generation. The issue of generativity, as we pointed out in Chapter 16, involves the need to teach and otherwise become responsible for the development of the next generation. Within the family middle-aged parents give encouragement and support as their offspring prepare to set out from home and make their own way. The middle-aged worker expresses generativity not only in managing people and policies, but in training and guiding one or several younger employees in so-called mentor relationships. Thus, the fruits of middle age, according to Erikson, are found primarily in relationships based upon generativity. Midlife identity also is tied to this issue, for it is through generative relationships that adults seek answers to the meaning of their lives—meanings that transcend the short time they have on this planet.

Yet not all adults are successful in achieving generativity. For some, family life is a constant source of irritation. Previous or ongoing emotional problems may prevent the person from engaging in supportive relationships with spouse, children, and friends. At work, too, some people are unable to interact effectively with others. A man may feel defeated because he has failed to achieve some earlier established career goal. A woman may become disillusioned because she believes her work or ideas are unappreciated by her superiors. For such people the midlife "harvest" may be sparse and if they are unable to reach out to others in their personal life, their lives may take on the hollow feeling of stagnation.

FAMILY LIFE

The nature of family life changes dramatically during middle age. Because most middle-aged adults married in their twenties and had their children soon thereafter, by the time they are in their early forties their oldest child may be out of high school. In a few more years their youngest and last child will be launched into society as an independent adult, leaving the middle-aged couple by themselves. In fact, Duvall (1977) notes that a couple spends fully one-half of the family life cycle living together alone after the children have grown up and departed.

Duvall's scheme, revealing as it is of the number of years that an older couple live alone together, does not take into account the increasing variety of individual differences in the timing of marriage, as well as the timing, number, and spacing of children (including the decision to remain childless). Whereas the stereotypical middle-aged couple, in their early forties, are getting ready to launch their first child into the adult world, other couples of the same age who married late or postponed pregnancy, may still be trying to cope with the conflicts and strains of adolescent, preadolescent, or even very young children. A small percentage of couples may even find themselves parents for the first time during middle age. The effects of divorce, living as a single parent, remarriage, and perhaps even establishing a second family also changes the number of years and the sequence of events in the family life cycle.

Each phase of the family life cycle not only is characterized by differences in family composition, but also by differences in role prescriptions and life responsibilities. The development of the husband and wife as a couple, and each one as an individual, depends to a great extent on the way in which midlife developmental tasks are undertaken and accomplished. For example, whereas some adults experience feelings of joy, pride, and even relief with the launching of children, for others it is a cause for depression—as if the very reason for one's existence now is gone.

Families with Adolescents

Much has been written about the turmoil that frequently occurs in families with adolescent children. Usually referred to as the "generation gap," this

Parents must maintain an effective base of communication between themselves and their teen-aged children, especially in supporting adolescents in their search for identity and in helping them to take their place in the world of adults.

turmoil centers around the conflict between parents and adolescents over the "giving" and "getting" of independence. Typically, we think of the problem in terms of parents attempting to maintain their authority and control over adolescents, who in turn are striving for autonomy and freedom. And yet it is often the case that it is the parents who push their children toward independence, and the adolescents who are reluctant to accept it. In most families, however, both parents and children show evidence of vascillation between "holding on" and "letting go."

During this stage of family life, a number of developmental tasks for parents becomes prominent, including supporting the adolescents in their search for identity, helping them with their emerging sexuality, and preparing them to take their place in the adult world. If parents are to accomplish these tasks, they must maintain an effective base of communication between themselves and their children. Yet this may be difficult because adolescents often perceive contradictions between what their parents say and what they do. For example, as most parents enter the middle adulthood period, their views about sexuality and related topics often become more conservative, at least as they apply to their developing sons and daughters. While they may profess to be "liberated," most parents of adolescents find it difficult to accept premarital intercourse for their own children. Moreover, as Wagner (1980) notes, "There is one word that describes parent-child adolescent communication about sexual issues—absent" (p. 298). The same probably can be said about the use of alcohol and drugs.

While the parenting of adolescents has been described as a period of conflict and strain, some researchers suggest that the extent of the conflict may not be as great as is usually assumed (Thurnher, Spence, & Lowenthal, 1974). The focus on the "generation gap" ignores the well-documented fact that among themselves adolescents differ in values every bit as much, if not more, than they differ from their parents. As Stevens-Long (1979) points out, most parents anticipate problems. Since the stereotype of adolescent/parent relationships is one of conflict, such expectations may bring about the very problems that are feared in a self-fulfilling prophecy.

Families with Adult Children

At some point in the family life cycle parents and children begin to "let go" of one another, at least to the extent of allowing the children—now legally adults—to become independent, self-reliant individuals. This stage of parenting, which almost always occurs in middle age, is a poorly researched phase of family life. For one thing, it is often referred to as the "postparental" period, as if the launching of children into the world relinquishes adults of all parental needs, responsibilities, and obligations. In reality people do not cease to be parents simply because their children no longer live with them; just as adults, regardless of age, are still their parents' children even though they may be married, have children of their own, and lead relatively autonomous lives.

The middle-age stage of parenting is a relatively recent development. Only two generations ago, life expectancies and fertility patterns were such that a typical couple survived thirty-one years of marriage, only two years beyond the time when their last child—let's say, their fifth child—might be expected to marry. And yet as we see in Duvall's chart (Fig. 17.1), today's middle-aged couple may expect to spend approximately one-quarter of the family cycle in the "empty nest" phase before retirement. What are the characteristics of this period of family life?

For one thing, as Troll, Miller, and Atchley (1979) point out, there are close ties between adult children and their parents. Young adult children frequently rely on their parents for financial help, for example, in contributing to the down payment for a house, for child care, and for emotional support. In turn, middle-aged parents also receive emotional satisfaction from their relationship with their adult children, as well as companionship, and a sense of achievement, that is, of having produced independent, responsible, and loving offspring who will carry on after they are gone—in other words, generativity. Middle-aged parents also share vicariously in the accomplishments of their adult children—at work, at home, and at play. They take pride in their daughter's graduation from medical school, and their son's promotion within the company; they share the joy of their children's marriages, and the birth of grandchildren. For some middle-aged adults, the success of their children becomes the avenue for fulfilling some of their own unmet needs and goals. The office manager, for example, who is a talented amateur musician may find personal satisfaction in her daughter's career as a successful professional

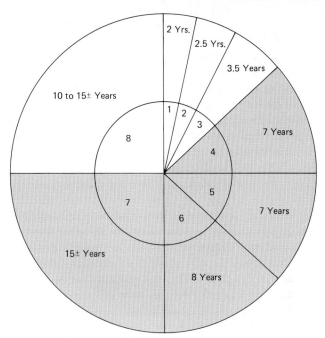

Figure 17.1 Duvall's Family Life Cycle

By Length of Time in Each of Eight Stages.
1. Married couples (without children).
2. Childbearing families (oldest child, birth–30 months).
3. Families with preschool children (oldest child 30 months–6 years).
4. Families with schoolchildren (oldest child 6–13 years).
5. Families with teen-agers (oldest child 13–20 years).
6. Families launching young adults (first child gone to last child leaving home).
7. Middle-aged parents (empty nest to retirement).
8. Aging family members (retirement to death of both spouses).

Source: Based upon data from the U.S. Bureau of the Census and from the National Center for Health Statistics, Washington, D.C. Adapted from E. M. Duvall. *Marriage and family development.* (5th ed.) Philadelphia: J. B. Lippincott, 1977, p. 148. Copyright 1977. Reprinted by permission of the publisher, J. B. Lippincott Company.

violinist. Thus, the relationship between middle-aged parents and adult children is one of interdependence—each relying on and needing the other for their own unique purposes and well-being.

Yet the empty-nest of family life is not without its problems. Some parents experience considerable stress when their children finally leave home for good. Bart (1970), who has studied midlife depression in women, notes that the transition to middle-age family life may be a difficult one for the traditional woman who has spent most of her time and energy on her children, and whose identity and self-esteem are closely tied to the role of motherhood. The "supermother," as she is sometimes called, ranks "helping children" as most important on her list of family and community activities; and she identifies "my children" as her most important accomplishment. When her children leave home she is deprived of her most important social role and activity. Understandably, she may feel depressed, useless, and unloved. This is the "empty nest" syndrome Bart identified among the depressed middle-aged women in her sample.

Until recently, little thought was given to the effects of the "empty nest" on fathers. Yet emerging evidence indicates that mothers are not the only ones who are upset by the departure of the children from the home. Lewis, Frenau, and Roberts (1979), for example, found that 22 percent of their sample of fathers reported considerable unhappiness over the departure of their last child from home. Furthermore, it was the older father, who had few children, who was more involved in nurturing relationships, and whose marriage showed evidence of problems, who was the most affected by the absence of children.

Although the "empty nest" has a negative connotation, research evidence suggests that many parents greet the departure of children with a sense of relief and psychological well-being (Harkins, 1978). This may be particularly true for working women because they are freed from the conflict of career versus raising children. As one fifty-two-year-old female executive commented: "I love my children, but God, how glad I am that they are out on their own. Suddenly I feel free . . . It's just me and my husband now . . . The funny thing is that the kids and I get along better now . . . I guess the strain of a career *and* managing a house full of kids can kind of get to you."

In recent years people, particularly women who are not in the work force, plan ahead in anticipation of the time when their children will be gone. Many women return to school (high school or college) to train or retrain for new careers. Many even begin this preparation soon after their youngest child is in nursery school. The largest number of women returning to school after the age of thirty-five, however, are in the fifty-year-old or older group (U.S. Department of Labor, 1977). These women are less likely to have been in the labor force than other groups returning to school. Some middle-class women are freed to pursue nonpaying work on a full-time basis such as volunteer hospital work, fund raising, or other community activities. Other older women, like Tillie Olsen or Grandma Moses, find that they finally have the free time to write, paint, spin and weave, or raise flowers and vegetables. For many couples, the midlife period of the family cycle brings increased privacy, and a rediscovery of each other, and of shared interests.

Relationships with Aged Parents

In middle adulthood many individuals are truly in the middle of the family structure—typically, between a parent and a child. Historically, this is a recent phenomenon, for only two generations ago, middle-aged adults usually were the oldest surviving members of the extended family—that is, their own parents were no longer living.

Today, many middle-aged adults assume important responsibilities toward the older generation—their parents. They provide emotional and physical support, and often assume financial responsibility for many aspects of their parents' lives. In fact, there is often a reversal of parent-child roles during this time, as middle-aged people become the providers and nurturers for their aging parents. Yet most research indicates that older parents do not want to be dependent upon their middle-aged children; on the contrary, they show a strong preference for remaining independent as long as possible (Yankelovich, Skelly, & White, 1977). Still, research indicates that contact between adult children and their aged parents is important and beneficial for old people's psychological well-being (Alpert & Richardson, 1980).

There are difficult decisions to be made by the children of aged parents. How long can you let old people live alone who are not in good mental or physical shape? Can you put your own mother or father in a nursing home, no matter how well-managed? The line between taking over and destroying old people's sense of their own independence and protecting them from physical harm is a delicate one to draw.

Today's middle-aged adults assume important responsibilities toward their parents by providing emotional, physical, and sometimes financial support for the older generation.

Grandparenthood

Although the stereotype of grandparents is that of gray-haired, wrinkled, and bespectacled old people whose favorite pastimes are sitting in a rocking chair, or baking cookies or cakes for the family, today this image is not appropriate (Troll, 1980). With the changes in fertility and mortality patterns, and the shift in population characteristics over the past century, becoming a grandparent is more of a middle-age than old-age event. First-time grandparents are likely to be healthy, working at full-time jobs, and living independent and active lives. In fact, a few middle-aged people find it difficult at first to accept the grandparent role—they may feel it casts a shadow of age on the youthful self-image they are maintaining.

Just as individuals differ in their personalities and styles of parenting, so too do they differ in their styles of grandparenting. In what has become a classic study, Neugarten and Weinstein (1964) identified five styles of inter-actions with grandchildren among middle-class grandparents in their fifties and sixties:

Not all grandparents fit the stereotype of the gray-haired, bespectacled old person whose favorite activity is sitting in a rocking chair.

1. Formal—shows interest in the grandchild and occasionally provides special gifts or services, such as baby sitting, but does not interfere in the raising of the child; leaves the parenting to the parents.
2. Fun-seeker—an informal, leisure orientation toward grandparenting; assumes the role of playmate, and expects mutually gratifying experiences with the grandchild.
3. Surrogate-parent—grandparent (almost always the grandmother) assumes the child-care responsibilities while the parents are working.
4. Reservoir of Family Wisdom—grandparent (usually the grandfather) adopts an authoritarian role in the family; all family members, including parents, are subordinate to him; he dispenses resources, knowledge, and advice to others.
5. Distant Figure—has little consistent relationship with the grandchild; visits on holidays or special occasions; adopts a benevolent but emotionally distant role.

Neugarten and Weinstein also noted that many grandparents experience a sense of biological renewal—a feeling of carrying on the family line—as well as a sense of emotional self-fulfillment in their new family role. In fact, the older mother may relive her pregnancy, delivery, and early mothering through her daughter's or daughter-in-law's early parenting experiences. The new grandfather, in turn, may realize that he has the time and interest for his grandchildren that he never had for his own children. Robertson (1977) reports that many people find grandparenting easier and preferable to parenting. It is not uncommon, in fact, to hear grandparents assure themselves that they are better grandparents than they were parents.

MARRIAGE

With the advent of the empty-nest stage of the family life cycle, the husband and wife enter into a new phase of married life. The absence of children from the home allows the couple to refocus their attention on the marital relationship. This is a time in which couples rediscover one another—and sometimes recognize the gulf that lies between them. And it is a time in which marital patterns are reexamined. Many couples are pleasantly surprised to find a strong, vibrant, and constructive relationship still existing after twenty or more years of marriage; for others, the harsh light of reality may reveal a weak, unexciting, and routinized pattern of existence, an almost total lack of communication, and a number of unsettled ancient grudges.

Marital Adjustment

One early and important study suggests that most couples become progressively disenchanted over the course of a marriage (Pineo, 1961). More recent studies, however, show an upturn in the later stages of married life. For both husbands and wives the stage when children are school age represents a low point, whereas the postchild and retirement stages are positively viewed (Rollins & Feldman, 1970; Schram, 1979). The launching period becomes a time of stress, but the dissatisfaction seems to be with children or with parenthood, rather than with marriage itself. Marital satisfaction returns to high levels in the postchild stage for most couples. Satisfaction with sex and companionship experiences rises nearly to the level of the early preparenthood years (Burr, 1970).

Marital Styles

We have discussed the stages in the family life cycle that are related to marital satisfaction, and yet we have not defined what we mean by this term. Just what constitutes a happy marriage? Is there some optimal form of marriage that all of us should be striving for?

It is obvious that people differ in their personalities, interests, needs, fantasies, and life goals. In turn, marital adjustment is, in part, determined by the kind of characteristics the husband and wife bring to the marriage relationship. But does marital happiness necessarily imply that the husband and wife share the *same* interests and needs? Certainly, some researchers believe so. In reviewing the research on this issue, Clore and Byrne (1977) concluded: "Marriage, and stable marriages in particular, are composed of people with similar personalities, attitudes, and other characteristics" (p. 548).

In contrast, other researchers have argued that marital adjustment is determined by *complementarity* in the relationship—the two individuals possess different and yet compatible traits. Winch (1974), for example, was interested in the complementarity of role playing. He chose two sets of complementary roles (dominance/submission and nurturance/receptiveness) to arrive at four types or styles of complementary relationships in marriage: (a) the Ibsenian relationship (named after the author of *A Doll's House*), characterized by a dominant, nurturant male and a submissive, receptive female; (b) the Thurberian relationship (named after James Thurber's view of male-female relationships), involving a nurturant, submissive male and a dominant, receptive female; (c) the master–servant girl relationship, in which a dominant, receptive male marries a submissive, nurturant female; and (d) the mother–son relationship, involving a submissive, receptive male and a dominant, nurturant female.

Most of the marriage and family research, to date, suggests that the complementarity theory is inadequate for explaining mate selection and adjustment in the early stages of marriage. Still, some investigators have speculated that the longer the couple remain together, the more likely the marriage relationship will be characterized by complementarity of roles.

Even if marital adjustment is linked to the couple's similarity in such areas as personality, interests, and values, this does not imply that adjusted or happy couples are all alike. In fact, there are many forms of marriage that can be considered successful—if success is defined in terms of personal satisfaction and marital stability. Cuber and Harroff (1965), in what has become

Involvement in each other's interests reflects the refocusing of the middle-aged couple's attention on the marital relationship.

a classic study, identified five different forms of marital success among upper-middle-class older couples. They are:

1. *conflict-habituated:* The marriage is characterized by considerable conflict and tension, which becomes a habitual but acceptable pattern. In fact, the consistency of arguing and bickering may even provide a sense of stability to the marriage.

2. *devitalized:* The couple believe that they love one another, and yet there is little zest or vitality to the marriage. Although they may appear disenchanted, they still view their marriage as a good one.

3. *passive-congenial:* The couple are content and comfortable with what they have. There is little effort, however, at improving or changing the marriage. Conflict is avoided if possible.

4. *vital:* The marriage is characterized as vibrant and exciting. The couple are highly involved with one another, particularly in areas related to family life—finances, child care, recreational and social activities.

5. *total:* Like the vital marriage, this one is characterized by a high degree of involvement between husband and wife, only to a greater and more complete extent. This relationship is rare.

Wife-beating: A Common Practice

Law-enforcement officials estimate that there are 28 million victims of wife-beating—women who are physicaly assaulted by their husbands. Research indicates that at least one-sixth of all married couples experience one "violent episode" every year. Studies show that up to 60 percent of all married women are subjected to physical violence by their husbands at some time during the marriage (FBI Law Enforcement Bulletin, 1978). One study showed that 20 percent of all husbands beat their wives "regularly" according to their own report—from daily to six times a year (Gelles & Straus, 1979).

For some people this is shocking news. But for too many women, it is a part of their experience. They have seen their mothers beaten or may have been beaten themselves. The United States is a violent society, although probably not any more so than many others; but why does one of the kinds of violence take the form of beating one's wife?

In the historical-legal approach we must note that up through the nineteenth century wives had the legal status of cows, slaves, or similar property. In addition the legal system had for centuries given husbands the "right of chastisement." Along with the wife's duties to her husband went his right to punish her for disobedience or other improper behavior. Under the doctrine of "coverture," in which a marriage makes two persons one—the one being the husband—married women lost a separate identity under the law. They could neither testify against their husbands nor sue. Thus in court, they had no redress against being beaten. By custom and by law, to be a wife was to expect to be beaten.

Wife-beating can be explained psychologically in the context of social learning and role theory. For example, people learn the approved roles of their own and the opposite sex. But in American society men play the dominant role. The laws are created and enforced by men. Furthermore, although ours is a violent culture, only one-half of the population is encouraged in violence, while the other half is encouraged to avoid and fear violence. So in the case of domestic violence, women are likely to be socially conditioned into the victim role and men into the aggressor role (Pagelow, 1979).

What about the victim? What kind of women find themselves victims of their husbands' beatings? Any woman may find herself in a battering situation and find it difficult to extricate herself from it. Despite the danger to herself and to her children, she may stay with her husband because of lack of financial resources, dependency, terror, for the sake of the children, and often because she has nowhere else to go.

It is fairly commonplace to blame the victim—the beaten wife. It is thought, even by some professional social workers and police officers, that many of these women provoke their husbands; or that they enjoy being beaten. Such ideas couldn't be further from the truth. One battered woman stated that "no one has to provoke a wife beater. He will strike out when he is ready, and for whatever reason he has at the moment. I may be his excuse but I have never been his reason" (quoted in Fleming, 1979). According to Lenore Walker (1979) battered women suffer from situationally imposed emotional problems due to their victimization. They do not choose to be battered because of some personality defect but develop emotional disturbances because of the battering.

What is being done about wife-beating? As of 1979, women, mostly volunteers, were operating 185 shelters and 138 other services for battered women, such as hotline telephone answering services and advocacy programs that help women to establish new lives for themselves and their children. In some communities the police have been made aware of the need for police protection for battered women although it is one of the most difficult matters for police to deal with. The courts are slowly becoming aware that wife-beating is a deadly crime of assault: 12.4 percent of all murders in the United States are of one spouse killing the other.

Of primary importance is a change in attitude toward women and violence. No woman should ever be made to feel that she must endure beating by her husband or boyfriend, that she deserves it, or that it is her fault. It is to be hoped that a change in public opinion will not only encourage wives to leave a violent domestic situation, but put wife-beating husbands on notice that being married to a woman does not imply permission to threaten her or to beat her.

The first three forms of marriage—conflict-habituated, devitalized, and passive-congenial—represent the more traditional or institutionalized types of marriage, in which the relationship between the husband and wife is based primarily on adaptation in the outside world. In contrast, the vital and total forms of marriage—often called companionate marriage—are focused primarily on the couple relationship. There is more emphasis on communication, self-disclosure, sharing, and the expression of love in this form of marriage than in traditional marriage. Interestingly, Reedy and Birren (1978) found that companionate marriage is most common among young adults and traditional marriage among older adults.

Midlife Sexuality

In the past, it was more or less assumed that middle-aged people did not approach sex with anything like the vigorous interest of the young. Be it due to fatigue, impotence, or declining beauty, the middle-aged person was thought to experience a falling off of desire: "You cannot call it love," says Hamlet to his mother, "for at your age/The heyday in the blood is tame, it's humble/And waits upon the judgment."

Today it is understood that Hamlet (and everyone else who believes one's parents to be past sexuality) was ill-informed. It is understood that everyone can be sexually alive; that with good health and good spirits, sexual activity can be carried on into the eighties. In particular, middle-aged women are thought to have strong sex drives. These changing attitudes and expectations should not obscure what appear to be the facts: sexuality is a vital part of the lives of middle-aged and older people, but frequency of sexual activity declines with advancing age.

To some extent, sexual expression in midlife (as in adolescence) is influenced by cultural expectations. Whether it is the increased willingness of middle-aged people to respond honestly to questions put by researchers on sex or the more relaxed attitudes toward sexual matters since the 1960s and 1970s, there seems to be greater and more varied sexual expression among the middle-aged since the 1949 *Kinsey Report*. The average frequency of marital intercourse for couples in all age groups increased from the time of Kinsey's sampling to Hunt's sampling (1974); the increase was proportionately greatest for people over fifty-five. Moreover, the thirty-five to forty-four age group was more active than the twenty-six to thirty-five age group a generation ago (Hunt & Hunt, 1975).

Nevertheless, there are differences between youthful and middle-aged sexuality. Some time between the ages of forty-six and fifty-five, the majority of men and women become aware of a decline in sexual interest and activity (Pfeiffer, Verwoerdt, & Davis, 1972). Although middle-aged men and women experience complete and satisfying sexual relationships, sexual response is usually slower, characterized by more leisurely and imaginative foreplay. The older male may require prolonged physical stimulation before he achieves erection (Kaplan, 1977). This may actually enhance the intimacy between partners.

In fact, there are a number of reasons that middle age brings new sexual satisfaction to some couples. For women there is reduced fear of pregnancy and, after fifty or fifty-five, little fear at all. Birth control can be safely ignored. With the launching of the children from the home, privacy increases, promoting sexual expression and the other forms of communication that enhance sexual response. Finally, there is cultural support, as never before, for pleasurable and guiltless sexuality among people of all ages.

Despite these seeming advantages, some middle-aged couples do experience problems in sexual image and performance. The natural slowing down of the responses may cause some apprehension in the older man; he fears he will not be able to perform adequately, and for that reason sometimes he cannot. It is widely recognized that most impotence in middle age is the result of anxiety or other psychological problems, rather than an effect of aging. The older husband may be bored, upset about financial or career decisions, or simply feeling the effects of overwork and alcohol. No matter what the cause, the result is fear of failure. Masters and Johnson (1966) observe that "once impotent under any circumstances, many males withdraw voluntarily from any coital activity rather than face the ego-shattering experience of repeated episodes of sexual inadequacy." Within marriage, according to one study, it is the man who is more often the partner who determines whether or not sexual relations continue (Pfeiffer, Verwoerdt, & Davis, 1972). The middle-aged wife will sometimes agree to a sexually impoverished marriage. Yet it is generally recognized that a woman can be orgasmic at any age, and that the experienced woman is more—not less—likely to reach orgasm than a younger woman.

Most current research suggests that cessation of intercourse is not necessarily a result of aging—that it is more often the result of social or psychological factors. "Presuming some continuity [of sexual expression]," says Masters, "the only thing a male or female needs for effective sexual function is a reasonably good state of health and an interested partner." To which Johnson amends, "an interest*ing* partner" (Tavris & Sadd, 1975). Generally, research has found that a stable, enjoyable sexual relationship in the earlier years is the best basis for continuing sexuality into middle (and old) age.

Midlife Divorce

Approximately one-third of all marriages end in divorce; approximately one-fourth of these divorces occur after fifteen years of marriage, and therefore involve middle-aged partners (Hunt & Hunt, 1975). The divorce of couples who have been married for twenty or twenty-five years was formerly uncommon; today nearly everyone knows at least one couple who have survived this life ordeal.

Divorce in midlife occurs in response to such stresses as differential growth of partners, midlife career crises, and extramarital affairs. Historical trends and expectations may also be at work. Many of today's middle-aged divorced people claim to have married without much thought at the socially prescribed time. They did what was expected. Now social attitudes have changed and these couples have an opportunity to make corrections. Indeed, it appears that in some social groups midlife divorce occurs with the same regularity as the earlier, conventional marriage: "Well, I look at it this way," said one middle-aged woman. "There was a year when it seemed everybody I knew, including me, was getting married, and now there's another year when it seems everybody I know, including me, is getting divorced" (Fried, 1967).

For many middle-aged couples, divorce is seen as a growth experience. Certainly some of the problems of the young divorced person are removed. The anguish of children, economic sacrifice, and disapproval of parents are not so threatening to the divorcing middle-aged couple. On the other hand, the couple have built up a more extensive household, and have made more investments and purchases together. There are joint checking and savings accounts; joint car ownership; and the deed for the house may be in both names. The couple have also developed a larger network of mutual friends, and these relationships may be strained upon separation.

Divorce at midlife, as earlier, is painful. It is typically followed by lone-liness, self-doubt, mood swings, and many practical adjustments in living. For example, the divorced woman may start to date at the time she begins to experience doubts about her attractiveness—and she is expected to consider sexual relations after a number of years of intimacy (or the painful lack of it) with one partner. Fear of sexual inadequacy may also inhibit the divorced middle-aged male from pursuing new relationships with female companions.

If midlife divorce is almost always followed by uncertainty and stress it is also usually followed by remarriage. Middle-aged men are more likely to remarry than women (Carter & Glick, 1970).

Remarriage in midlife is most often successful (Hunt & Hunt, 1975). Although the risk of divorce among remarried couples is higher than for first marriages, the majority of remarried people—particularly men—report that they are happier than they were in their first marriage. This generalization may hold especially well for midlife marriages, which are made between potentially more mature people and which are not plagued by custody and stepparent arrangements.

Widowhood

Widowhood is usually associated with old age, but approximately one-half of the women in the United States lose their husbands before the age of sixty (Troll, 1975). Women are outliving men in an ever-widening margin (Berardo, 1968), with the result that widowhood is beginning to be seen as an inevitable and almost universal phase of life—and one frequently associated with middle age.

Many of the problems of widowhood are related to the problems of later adulthood. (Indeed, a woman may define herself as "old"—as having entered the final stretches of life—after she loses her husband.) Among the problems unique to the middle-aged widow, however, is the fact that she may be the first, or one of the first, to lose her husband. Her friends are still married, and she may consequently come to think of herself as the fifth wheel at any social occasion. Friends may be insensitive—alternately exhorting her to socialize and then forgetting to invite her. She also tends to be less willing than the older woman to resign herself to life without masculine companionship and sexuality; yet she may be unable to meet single men (especially widowed men) who can understand her experience. Consequently, for many women widowhood can be an extremely lonely and alienated period of life.

In recent years there has been increased attention to the social and emotional problems of the bereaved wife. As a result, a number of programs have been developed that appear successful in alleviating the problems of these women. Some programs utilize "widow helpers," where women who have lost their own husbands are specially trained to help other bereaved women handle their grief and make adjustments to their changed life (Silverman, 1972). Other programs are like group therapy sessions and concentrate on self-help techniques, the use of "confidants," or consciousness-raising, as means for promoting emotional adjustment (C. J. Barrett, 1978). In addition to these programs, there are more opportunities today for older women—plus the fact that a woman's identity is not confined to being a wife—that may also reduce the widow's adjustment problems, though nothing necessarily lessens her grief.

Singlehood

Approximately 5 percent of all middle-aged adults in the United States are single people who have never been married. There is relatively little research on this group, and almost none on the positive aspects of its adjustment. But ordinary observation produces many examples of single people who, in the absence of immediate family obligations, have achieved an especially intense career commitment: obvious examples include the dedicated priest, schoolteacher, or charity worker.

Naturally, single, middle-aged people encounter special problems. They must accept the social identity of a single—spinster or bachelor—which even today carries some stigma. They must plan for a late adulthood that does not include support from, or involvement with, children—though, of course, they may be involved with other people's children. And they are less protected against illness or misfortune. For example, if they become mentally disturbed they are more likely to be hospitalized than are the married people, who may be cared for by their families.

The single, middle-aged person, however, is not usually a loner. Most single people develop close relationships with friends—single as well as married. And they often maintain close contact with their nuclear and extended family—particularly single women.

The motives for remaining single typically are somewhat different for males and females—with a major exception noted for male and female homosexuals, most of whom choose never to marry. Never-married women are better educated, come from higher socioeconomic groups, and are more achievement oriented than single men. Moreover, it appears that the older single woman has chosen not to marry rather than having never been asked (Havens, 1973). In contrast, Spreitzer and Riley (1974) report that successful, achievement-oriented men are the least likely to remain single.

OCCUPATIONAL DEVELOPMENT

In middle adulthood people have a new opportunity to become generative in their work. Generative midlife people produce goods, ideas, plans, and policies at a higher rate than they did earlier. They may also become generative in the sense of teaching what they know to others—usually younger people. In midcareer, for example, a person may train new workers; represent a union chapter; head up a department; lead a state government or a multinational corporation or the board of a community organization. The worker as well as the parent feels able to contribute something to the world to be inherited by coming-up generations. On the other hand, when people have no opportunity—or take no opportunity—to impart their skill, experience, or care to others, they may suffer from a sense of stagnation. They will feel alienated both from what they produce and from what they leave behind.

Occupational Advancement

In midlife, people are concerned with consolidating their position and advancing (Super, 1963). Advancement at this stage frequently means moving from in-depth involvement in a speciality to a managerial or supervisory function. For example, the assembly worker becomes a foreman; the research chemist becomes director of a unit.

Men and women show a striking difference in advancement in status and income with increasing age, with women lagging far behind especially in income. For the older woman discrimination at the work place becomes particularly evident as she fails to be promoted and be given salary increases, as well as responsibility, commensurate with that of her male counterpart. Between the ages of thirty-five and sixty-five, men's average yearly earnings are nearly double that of women (U.S. Department of Commerce, 1977). Furthermore, this sex difference in income is not completely accounted for by differences in occupation. N. S. Barrett (1979) notes that within all major occupational groups women's earnings are far below those of men.

In addition to sex what differentiates the individuals who advance within their respective companies from those who do not? In one twenty-year longitudinal study of AT&T executives, Bray and Howard (1978) found that men who rose higher in the corporation were more committed to the job, more interested in success, showed higher achievement motives, and were more forceful and dominant than their less successful colleagues. Interestingly, there was no difference between these groups in life satisfaction. It would therefore appear that occupational achievement is to a great extent tied to motivational and personality variables—and presumably to competence. Yet we must remember the harsh realities of the world—sexism, racial and ethnic discrimination, and even just plain favoritism are all factors in determining who gets the job opening or the higher salary.

Among the serious problems encountered by middle-aged workers are job obsolescence, unemployment, and age discrimination in hiring and job advancement. Not infrequently in our fast-paced society, the middle-aged person becomes obsolete as businesses strive to incorporate innovative technological changes into their production line. Computerized robots, for example, now do the assemblyline work in automotive plants that used to be done by many workers.

In only a few fields do middle-aged people become obsolete because of reduced physical powers (athletes) or changes in style (the "1940s journalist"). Generally, older workers are valued for their experience, judgment, and stability—qualities that enable them to make adjustments to changes in the work environment. Should they lose their job they may, nevertheless, find it difficult to obtain another. Sweetland (1978) has reviewed some of the factors working against the rehiring of older workers. They include: (a) unfavorable employer attitudes—"He's too old. We're a 'young' company"; (b) high salary and benefit demands in comparison to younger workers; (c) the reluctance of older workers to relocate or retrain themselves; (d) the employer's belief that hiring older workers represents an unwise investment in the absence of long-term career potential; and (e) less education and technological skill in comparison to younger workers. Regardless of the reasons, prolonged unemployment in midlife may cause serious loss of identity, status, and health, as well as loss of income.

Unemployment is a serious problem encountered by middle-aged workers. Should they lose their jobs, they might find it difficult to obtain others, due in part to job obsolescence and age discrimination in hiring and promoting.

Job Satisfaction

The midlife phase of the occupational cycle is often a time of "truth" for most people. As in many other contexts of life, both men and women become acutely aware of the time remaining to accomplish their goals. For those individuals who are within reach of achieving their goals, this period of occupational life is experienced as exciting, challenging, and rewarding. For others, however, the large gulf between aspirations and achievements may become a major factor in triggering a midlife crisis.

In middle age most people are seeking some assurance of job stability—seniority, for example. They are less likely than younger workers to leave their company. This may reflect the fact that older people generally take fewer risks than younger ones. But it also represents positive satisfaction with the work itself. The highest percentage of satisfied workers can be found in the over-forty categories. These workers are significantly more satisfied than young adults, not only with their jobs but with the monetary rewards and challenges they provide (Quinn, Staines, & McCullough, 1974). In fact, the bases of job satisfaction differ between younger and older workers—at least for white-collar workers. For the younger group, dissatisfaction with the job is likely to be tied to salary; for the older group, it is more likely to be related to the lack of challenge and the resources to get the job done. In contrast, for blue-collar

❖❖❖

Second Careers

"I had the feeling I was getting nowhere. I struggled all my life to make money and be a successful business executive. But when I got there I realized it wasn't at all what I wanted. It became boring and meaningless, and that's when I decided to get out. I sold my business and got a master's degree in social work. Now I'm working in a counseling center for college kids and have never been happier." This type of career change is typical of many people going through the midlife crisis. There seems to be an overwhelming fear that time is running out— a now-or-never feeling doing something important. Sometimes the change is made to pursue a dream that was put aside for a secure livelihood.

These midlife feelings seem to be largely responsible for the phenomenon of second careers. More and more people in their thirties and forties are changing their lives and attempting to find more satisfaction in their work lives.

Of course, other factors contribute to the growing trend of second careers. There is increasing acceptance of job-hoppers and career changers—it is no longer considered a sign of flightiness or immaturity to move from one job or one vocation to another. Another factor is the higher standard of living that has made it possible for potential career changers to take time out and live on their assets during the critical period of transition and readjustment. More people therefore feel the freedom and security to carry out a career change. The feminist movement is also responsible for career changes. Many homemakers are pursuing careers because of economic need and a desire to participate in the wider society outside the family (Sheehy, 1976).

workers, income level is an important factor in job satisfaction for both younger and older workers.

The reported satisfaction of most middle-aged workers does not mean that they are complacent. Midlife is a time when many workers are likely to reevaluate their career goals. One writer finds that an important task of this period is to set one's own milestones, in the absence of school or institutional guidelines (Mills, 1970). Another notes that at forty a person may fix on some key promotion or accomplishment that will magically affirm his worth to society. For example, he may set a deadline for becoming a full professor, or for writing a best seller (Levinson et al., 1977). Typically, the middle-aged worker begins to assert control over the path of advancement by seeking or turning down promotions or transfers and accepting the limitations of the self with respect to work (Mills, 1970). All of these are factors in the extent to which individuals are satisfied or dissatisfied with their work.

Integrating Work and Leisure

As people look ahead to retirement, the question of "what they will do with their time" becomes particularly relevant. During middle age, people often have more time for leisure activities, especially after the children are launched from the home. Integrating work, family, and leisure becomes an important goal for the midlife adult. Yet in our society, leisure is not given a very high priority in everyone's value hierarchy. In fact, many people are skeptical of those who seem to have too much time for hobbies, sports, or community work. According to Gordon, Gaitz, and Scott (1977), however, leisure activities often help to bridge role conflicts at different stages of the life cycle. Thus, people may use leisure activities to achieve goals or to satisfy needs not met in other aspects of their life—particularly on the job. The owner of a neighborhood gas station found an outlet for his sense of drama as a 32nd-degree Mason; a middle-aged medical social worker spends her winter weekends on the ski patrol and hikes in the summer.

The nature of leisure activity changes as one enters midlife. Between thirty and forty-four, leisure time is most often spent with the family. With the launching of children, however, more time is spent in personal expressive activities, in which the family is not included (Gordon, Gaitz, & Scott, 1977).

Finally, the question of leisure time also becomes important as plans begin for retirement. Individuals who are deeply involved with avocational pursuits may be eager to retire; those who "live for their work" may find retirement traumatic. Once again, leisure activities may help the person to deal with role changes—in this case, from worker to nonworker.

SUMMARY

▶ The composition of the family changes dramatically during middle age. After years of sharing their lives with their children, the middle-aged couple find themselves alone together. Before the children leave, the parents must deal with the conflicts encountered in raising adolescents. They must support adolescents in their search for identity, help them with their emerging sexuality, and prepare them to take their places in the adult world. Guiding their children is a part of the resolution of Erikson's crisis of generativity versus stagnation.

▶ For most parents the "empty nest" phase of the family life cycle signifies freedom and is experienced as a relief. But for some, both mothers and fathers, the absence of their children is difficult to bear—part of their reason for living is gone.

▶ Relations between middle-aged parents and their adult children are closer than is generally assumed. Each relies on the other for support and psychological well-being.

▶ In middle age a parent-child role reversal often occurs, with the middle-aged child caring for and supporting aging, dependent parents.

▶ Becoming a grandparent for the first time is more of a middle-age than old-age event. Just as there are styles of parenting, so too are there styles of grandparenting which people begin to adopt during this period.

▶ Most research suggests that marital adjustment is high during middle adulthood, particularly in the postchild phase of the family life cycle. When problems do arise they are often related to differential growth of partners, finances, sexual boredom, and work pressures.

▶ Contrary to many popular myths, people remain sexually active well into old age. While the frequency of sexual activity does decrease with advancing years, middle-agers today are more sexually active than most younger adults a generation ago. When impotence is encountered in middle age, it is almost always due to psychological rather than physiological causes.

▶ Successful marriages take many forms, from couples who are totally involved and committed to one another, to couples whose bickering and fighting form the basis for marital continuity. Although some investigators suggest that the longer a couple remain together, the more likely their relationship will be characterized by complementarity of roles, most research indicates that marital adjustment is linked to couple similarity in interests, attitudes, and personality.

▶ Midlife divorce is becoming a more common phenomenon, particularly as cultural attitudes toward marriage and divorce become more flexible. Divorce during middle age, as at any other time, is painful and is usually followed by loneliness, self-doubt, mood swings, and many practical adjustments in living. Most people who divorce in midlife do remarry, however; and these remarriages are usually successful.

▶ Approximately 50 percent of U.S. women lose their husbands before the age of sixty—thus, widowhood is often a middle-age event. Middle-aged widows must deal with such problems as meeting new male companions, starting up new sexual relationships, maintaining old friendships, and adjusting to reduced finances. A number of successful programs have been developed to help widows adjust to these problems.

▶ For many adults, generativity is achieved not only through family relations, but also on the job—by the development of ideas, products, plans, and by guiding others in their job development. In middle age, most people are concerned with consolidating their work position and advancing. Because of sex discrimination on the job women lag far behind men in occupational status and income. Research suggests that the most successful businessmen are achievement oriented, forceful, dominant, and committed to the job. Should the middle-aged worker lose his job, he is often faced with serious problems in getting hired by another company; many prejudices exist in the business world that work against the rehiring of middle-aged and older workers.

▶ Middle-aged people generally are the most satisfied workers; moreover among white-collar workers, satisfaction is less often tied to income than is true for younger or blue-collar workers. In midlife many workers re-evaluate career goals and try to accept the limitations of self with respect to work.

▶ In midlife, leisure activities are often pursued alone in contrast to the family-oriented activity of younger families. Such activities often help people to adapt to role changes and to find a satisfaction and interest that may be absent in work life.

FURTHER READINGS

Bernard, Jesse. *The future of marriage*. New York: Bantam Books, 1972.
Bernard discusses the differences between the "his" marriage and "her" marriage, and compares them to other life-styles, such as being single, divorced, or widowed. The mental health of each group is discussed and compared with that of others.

Boston Women's Health Collective. *Ourselves and our children*. New York: Random House, 1978.
This practical, informative book discusses decisions and conflicts in the role of parenting. The text examines parenting throughout the life span.

Fuchs, Estelle. *The second season: Life, love, and sex—women in the middle years*. Garden City, N. Y.: Doubleday, 1977.
This book deals primarily with the complex physiological, social, and psychological concerns of the middle-aged woman: sex, pregnancy, hysterectomy, menopause, divorce, widowhood.

Laing, R. D. *The politics of the family and other essays*. New York: Random House, 1971.
Laing questions some basic assumptions about interpersonal relationships among family members. He meticulously structures and examines the politics of the family, including the formulation of rules, and family scenarios.

MacPherson, Michael C. *The family years: A guide to positive parenting*. Minneapolis, Minn. Winston Press, 1981.
This is a practical book that addresses family issues such as limits and rules, conflicts and their resolution, and family conferences.

Schowalter, John E., and Anyan, Walter R. *The family handbook of adolescence*. New York: Alfred A. Knopf, 1981.
A highly straightforward reference book for adolescents and their parents. It is written from a medical point of view.

Stenizor, Bernard. *When parents divorce: A new approach to new relationships*. New York: Pantheon, 1969.
A practical and constructive book which focuses on how divorce affects the children. Stenizor describes how divorce seems to children, and discusses the child's anxiety and guilt. The book also explores how to help children understand without judging, and suggests ways to help them cope.

Observational Activities

Part Seven Middle Adulthood

Vocational Development

Vocational development takes many forms. Some people choose a job or career early in adulthood and stick with it through their entire working life. Others try a variety of jobs before settling into the particular one they believe is right for them. Still other people find that after many years of commitment to a job a sense of dissatisfaction or boredom has developed, thereby leading to a midlife vocational change.

Interview five to ten middle-aged working men and women about the nature of their vocational development. Ask each of them:

1. Describe your job history starting with your first full-time job.
2. How satisfied have you been with your job development?
3. Have you thought seriously about switching jobs recently?
4. What factors might influence your decision to change your job during this time of your life?

On the basis of the data collected speculate on the societal, situational, and personality factors that influence the course of one's working life. Are there differences in vocational development for men and women; for blue-collar versus white-collar workers? What factors might contribute to these differences?

How Old Is Old?

How old will you be when you start to "get old"? Perceptions of age, especially relative age such as young, middle-aged, and elderly, are based on many social and personal experiences. Some of these experiences are objective in nature, such as reaching legal voting age or the age of retirement; others are highly subjective, such as the satisfaction with life goals one has achieved, or the perception of time left to pursue those goals. Because people differ in their social and personal experiences, perceptions of the aging process also vary considerably among people.

Develop a short questionnaire with the purpose of ascertaining the perceptions people have about age. For example, you might ask: "At what age does a person stop being young? When is a person middle-aged? When is a person old?" Keeping track of such data as age and sex, and perhaps a rough estimate of social class (as shown by such indicators as employment and education), direct your questions to about forty people.

1. Tabulate your results.
2. What differences in perception of aging did you find for different age groups, males versus females, or social classes?
3. Do single adults view aging differently than married adults?
4. What factors seem to be most influential in a person's perception of aging?

Summarize your data and draw some conclusions. Finally, answer this question: "Is it really true (based on your findings) that you are as young or as old as you feel, or as you perceive yourself to be?"

PART EIGHT

Late Adulthood

Chapter 18

❖❖❖❖❖❖

Physical, Cognitive, and Personality Development

To the psychologist, the social planner, the politician, and even to themselves, older people have become controversial. The age at which people ought to retire is an economic issue. Nursing homes are a "scandal." The voting habits of the elderly are the subject of costly political surveys. Since older people as a group vote to a greater extent than other age groups, politicians want to know if they are conservative politically; if they like to be called "senior citizens"; and what issues are most important to them. In the academic environment, too, controversies emerge in the area of late adulthood. For example, some researchers find that the aging individual shows a steady and measurable decline in intellectual skill; others say that the intellectual decline of older people is a myth. Some find that successful aging involves disengagement from society; others actually use the extent of social involvement as an index of adjustment.

Even when we address ourselves to areas that seem not to be problematical, we find serious contradictions. For example old age brings measurable losses in sensory abilities. The older person sees less well, does poorly in color-matching and discrimination tests, cannot hear high tones as well as formerly, and may be less able to taste sugar and salt. It seems clear that sensory awareness of the world is dulled. And yet one psychologist reports that he has observed "increased awareness of the basic elements, the sensations of life" in older persons of all talents and backgrounds as they become free of daily routine (Butler, 1971). Another psychologist, Abraham Maslow, described his perceptions during the last years of life: "You get stabbed by things, by flowers, and by babies and by beautiful things.... Everything seems to look more beautiful, rather than less" (quoted in Puner, 1974).

The point is not that older people retain the sensory efficiency of the young. It is, rather, that the effects of even the most normal and verifiable processes of aging are difficult to interpret. It may be because of a lifetime of memories that an older person has a richer emotional response to sensory experiences. Or perhaps an awareness of the short time remaining enhances a moment of beauty or joy. Or it may be that sensory loss is experienced differently by different older people.

One reason that findings in late adulthood tend to be contradictory is that it is difficult to generalize about older people. One tends to view age as the great "leveler" that eradicates individual differences. But psychologists have found that differences between people may actually increase with years. Neugarten notes that as individuals age, the factors that influence their behavior are, if anything, more complex (Neugarten, 1973). If the present behavior of individuals must be understood in terms of their past experience, a long life will be more difficult to understand than a short one, an older person more complex than a younger one.

A final point is that old age is the one life stage that most researchers have not visited. That is, most research on the elderly is conducted by young or middle-aged adults who share many social misperceptions of older people and who may, for various reasons, fail to elicit their confidence. Whereas old people can (and frequently do) "reexperience" their youth, younger people have not experienced old age. Consequently, they may lack insight. Recognizing this, studies have been designed to enable young people to *pre*experience old age. For example, the young subject may be placed in an accelerated environment, so that he can experience the relative slowness of the older person (Kastenbaum, 1971). However, such "simulation" experiments can only touch upon isolated experiences of the old. In real-life situations, the young or middle-aged person seldom has reason to put himself in the position of the older person. The reverse may not be true. There are more older people who behave like the young than there are young people who behave like the old (Schonfield, 1974).

PHYSICAL DEVELOPMENT

As people age, they experience numerous structural and functional changes in the body—changes which, while not usually beginning in late adulthood, do have their most significant impact during this time. At the structural level, the most obvious changes are in appearance. The wrinkles and gray hair that

Possibly as a result of a lifetime of memories, an older person has a richer emotional response to sensory experiences.

began in middle age become more pronounced. Decreases in fat and muscle tissue result in inelastic skin that tends to hang in folds. Loss of hair—including scalp, axillary, and body hair—also is common with aging for both sexes. So too is an increase in "age spots"—irregular skin pigmentations—and loss of teeth (Rossman, 1977).

One of the most pronounced changes in physical appearance during the aging years is the postural stoop manifested by many older adults. As Stevens-Long (1979) points out, this characteristic slump, with head projected forward and lower limbs and hips flexed, is probably caused by years of poor posture that is now exacerbated by the shrinkage of muscles and tendons, increased calcification of ligaments, compression of spinal discs, and thinning of bone. Older people also show a decrease in height that is related to spinal disc compression and probably postural stoop as well. Rossman (1977), however, cautions that much of the decline in height in older people may be due to a cohort effect, since this decrease in stature with age is less evident in longitudinal studies (where cohort or generational effects are reduced) than in cross-sectional studies.

Another important structural change in the elderly is the deterioration of bone tissue. Chemical changes in bone results in a thinning and weakening of bony material, particularly in the long bones. These changes increase the older person's susceptibility to fracture; and they prolong the healing process when breaks do occur.

At the functional level, the older person experiences a number of losses. Most of these losses are less observable than the structural changes in appearance noted above. They are nevertheless extremely important for the older person's life adjustment. These changes are related to the biological intactness of the individual, and to every facet of a day-to-day psychological, social, or economic adaptation.

At the cellular level, the capacity for regeneration slows, and there is an increase in the potential for malfunctions. At the system level, there are marked reductions in organ efficiency. The cardiovascular (heart and blood vessels) system, in particular, manifests significant changes. The heart, like other muscles in the body, requires a longer time to contract, thereby increasing blood circulation time. Fatty concentrations (cholesterol) in the heart and arteries also reduces blood flow throughout the body; degeneration of the blood vessels leads to increased blood pressure (Kohn, 1977). Yet these changes, while most evident in later life, do not originate during this period. In fact, losses in cardiac output (the amount of blood the heart can pump through the body) are evident from early adulthood. Brandfonbrenner, Landowne, and Shock (1955), for example, found a linear drop-off in cardiac output at the rate of one percent per year in males aged nineteen to eighty-six.

Other organ systems also show reduced efficiency in late adulthood. Vital lung capacity decreases with age. Older people frequently report shortness of breath, particularly after mild exercise such as climbing stairs or raking the yard (Klocke, 1977). Changes in the gastrointestinal system, such as deterioration of the mucosa lining in the intestinal tract, and reduction of gastric juices, contribute to the frequent intestinal complaints of the elderly. Normal immune functions also decline with age, and in the elderly may be related to an increase incidence of cancer (Makinodan, 1977; Teller, 1972).

Nearly all the sensory systems show loss of efficiency in old age. In many cases, the loss is simply a continuation of the problems that arose in middle age, but at a more accelerated pace. For some people, however, new problems arise while old problems stabilize. In the area of vision, for example, changes in the lens that produced farsightedness in middle age now stabilize for the older person. On the other hand, new changes affecting the retina and nervous system result in decreased visual acuity and color vision for the aging adult (Fozard et al., 1977). Many older people also have considerable difficulty seeing in the dark—a situation that makes night driving particularly hazardous. In the aged, these changes also are exacerbated by the formation of cataracts—the most common disability of the aged eye—and glaucoma. Nearly 60 percent of the elderly suffer from cataracts and 1 to 3 percent from glaucoma (Crandall, 1980).

Probably the most usual sensory loss associated with aging is hearing. According to Corso (1977), 17 percent of people who are sixty-five or over show signs of advanced presbycusis—hearing loss due to degenerative changes in the auditory system. This loss is primarily restricted to high-frequency sounds, including many speech sounds. Many speakers try to compensate for the older person's auditory handicap by talking loudly, but increasing the volume of one's voice, or shouting, only serves to obscure the intelligible sounds for the older listener. To promote effective communication with the hard-of-hearing, one should actually lower one's voice, since this reduces voice pitch—the vocal quality that poses the most trouble for the aged.

There is some evidence that sense of taste and smell also decline with age, although researchers such as Engen (1977) point out that this sensory loss may be due primarily to some other pathological condition, or to such chronic habits as smoking. In any event, the older person who has trouble tasting and smelling things is quite likely to be less interested in food, thereby leading to nutritional problems—a serious issue for many individuals in later life.

If many of these changes suggest a pessimistic picture of late adulthood, it should be pointed out that except at advanced states—which usually occur only in very old age—these physical changes typically do not prevent normal life adjustment. Such modern technological improvements as better medical facilities, amplified telephones, hearing aids, and eyeglasses have helped the elderly to live quite comfortably despite the reduced efficiency of their bodies. Indeed, it is primarily under conditions of stress that the age-related losses appear to make a significant difference in the adjustment of older people (DeVries, 1975).

Health Factors in Late Adulthood

One of the most serious problems confronting the older person is increased susceptibility to disease. This is particularly true of chronic or long-term conditions. In contrast, the incidence of acute or temporary illness actually decreases with age.

Most people over sixty-five suffer from one or more chronic conditions. And yet, relatively few of these individuals are seriously restricted in their mobility. In fact, when all things are taken into consideration, it is clear that most older people are in reasonably good health. Only 4 to 5 percent of the elderly are in chronic care facilities, hospitals, mental institutions, or nursing homes. The remaining 95 to 96 percent of the aged live in the community and are able to "get around" despite their chronic conditions (Harris, 1978).

The prospect of illness is nevertheless a very real threat to the aging adult. Older individuals are less likely to "bounce back" from an illness; once admitted to the hospital, they are likely to stay longer than the younger person. They are also more likely to die from the illness (Harris, 1978). Even acute conditions, which are contracted less frequently by the elderly, generally are more serious at this time. Influenza, for example, can progress to pneumonia, and possibly death, for the aging adult.

The most common chronic conditions restricting activity in individuals sixty-five and over are heart disease, arthritis, hypertension, visual impairments, and orthopedic problems (Harris, 1978). Although all of these conditions take a significant toll on the aged some people find that the secondary effects, beyond the purely physical ones, are even more difficult to live with. The dependence on others that often accompanies these chronic conditions can be extremely frustrating, particularly for people who are used to "doing for themselves." As one seventy-eight-year-old woman said, "The pain I can bear. You can get used to that part. What really bothers me is not being able to care for myself ... I don't like being waited on ... The loss of dignity is something you can't imagine."

In addition to the conditions noted above, two categories of mental disorders have a significant impact on the aging adult—*functional disorders* and *organic brain syndromes.* The common feature of these two conditions is that they produce substantial cognitive and personality changes. Functional disorders are those for which there is no apparent physiological basis. Organic brain syndrome disorders are organically caused.

The most common functional disorders in the elderly include depression, paranoid reactions, hypochondriasis, and chronic anxiety (Butler & Lewis, 1977; Pfeiffer, 1977). Of these, depressive reactions are the most frequent and are characterized by extreme sadness, social withdrawal, inhibition, lowered self-esteem, pessimism, indecision, and occasionally, a slowing down of mental processes as well as physical movement. The suicide rate for the elderly, which is linked to depression, is higher than for any other age group—especially for white males. Moreover, when the older adult attempts suicide

Dependency on others can be extremely frustrating for elderly persons who have always done things for themselves.

there is roughly one chance in two that he will succeed, whereas the ratio is one in seven for young adults (Pfeiffer, 1977).

The two most common organic brain syndromes associated with aging are cerebral arteriosclerosis and senile dementia. Cerebral arteriosclerosis is related to increased arterial cholesterol levels—as the arteries "harden", blood flow to the brain is reduced and localized brain death occurs. Initially, mood or affect changes are noted, as well as increased irritability, fatigue, and head-aches. As the condition progresses, cognitive processes are affected, especially memory, abstraction ability, and assimilation of new information. The onset of this disease, which more often affects men than women, may occur as early as the mid-fifties.

Senile dementia, on the other hand, begins much later in life, usually in the mid-seventies, and is more often found in females than males—probably because women live longer than men. This condition is associated with diffuse or general brain loss of unknown origin. Over the course of the disease brain weight can reduce as much as 15 to 30 percent. Typical symptoms include errors in intellectual and social judgment, mood changes, memory impair-ment, spatial and temporal disorientation, general confusion, loosening of inhibitions, and deterioration of personal habits.

Both cerebral arteriosclerosis and senile dementia are chronic condi-tions; full recovery from them is not possible, although improvement can be obtained at times with proper medical treatment (Butler & Lewis, 1977; Pfeiffer, 1977).

Central Nervous System and Behavior

The effects of aging on the central nervous system have been well studied, especially by James Birren and his colleagues. On the average, older people are found to be slower to respond to stimuli than young people; this reflects a basic change in the speed with which the central nervous system processes information (Birren, 1974; Marsh & Thompson, 1977). Whereas young people appear to be quick or slow depending upon the demands of the situation, older people characteristically require more processing time. When rapid de-cisions or movements are called for—avoiding an oncoming bicycle, for ex-ample—the older person may be unable to make the appropriate dodge. In fact, older people are very prone to falls and other accidents that might be avoided by quick movements and readjustments. Using an electrical analogy, Birren refers to a generalized "brownout" in the nervous equipment.

The slowing down of the central nervous system appears to be significant in several areas. For instance, it may account for some of the difficulties older people experience in memory retrieval and learning. It may also explain some age-related differences in intelligence-testing situations in which speed is a factor. The slowing down of responses may even affect personality and ad-justment, undercutting the self-confidence with which older people manage themselves in a fast-paced urban environment—or in a fast-paced clinical interview. It may contribute to rigidity in behavior, or to the reduced risk-

Exercise and the Aged

In 1981 John Kelley ran his fiftieth Boston Marathon. He was seventy-three years old. One minute after the race his heart beat was 64. Although a twenty-six-mile race is not prescribed for people in their seventies, walking, jogging, running, and swimming are recommended not only for people in late adulthood, but for all men and women who live sedentary lives. Surprisingly, regular exercise improves mental abilities (Powell, 1974) as well as combatting the degeneration of the cardiovascular (heart and blood vessels) and pulmonary (lung and breathing) systems. Even after years of neglecting their bodies, people can make remarkable comebacks. One man who did not start jogging until he was sixty-seven holds fourteen field and track world records for his age category (Crandall, 1980).

To a large degree it has been found (Wessel & Van Huss, 1969) that the losses in physiological functioning of older people may be related as much to human inactivity—the modern sedentary life—as to age itself. Wessel and Van Huss coined the term hypokinetic disease (hypo = under, kinetic = motion) for the loss of function due to inactivity. To prove the point, Saltin and his colleagues (1968) confined a group of young athletes to bed for three weeks. Their maximal cardiac output declined by 26 percent, their maximal ventilatory capacity by 30 percent, and even the ratio of fat to active tissue declined by 1.5 percent (loss of active protoplasm, that is, a change in the ratio of protein to fat tissues being a phenomenon of aging). If the bodies of active young men in excellent physical condition can deteriorate to that extent in only three weeks, what must occur over the period of forty or fifty years of inactivity in the body of a seventy-four-year-old person?

DeVries, an exercise physiologist, points out that there are three causes for physiological losses in older people: the processes of aging itself, undetected incipient diseases, and hypokinetic disease. Of the three, hypokinetic disease is reversible. DeVries (1970) set up a vigorous exercise training regimen in a retirement community. One hundred and twelve volunteers, men aged fifty-two to eighty-seven (mean age sixty-nine and a half), exercised at calisthenics, jogging, and stretching or swimming for one hour three times a week. The most significant findings were related to oxygen transport capacity. Oxygen pulse and minute ventilation improved by 30 and 35 percent, respectively. There was a 20 percent gain in vital capacity. Significant improvement was found in the ratio of fat to protein, physical work capacity, and both systolic and diastolic blood pressure. A group of men with heart trouble were placed on a modified program of milder exercise and their improvement showed similar gains. In a subsequent study (Adams & DeVries, 1973) older women aged fifty-two to seventy-nine participated in a vigorous exercise program for three months and also showed significant improvement in physiological functioning.

In another experiment DeVries and Adams (1972) prescribed exercise for a group of elderly anxious patients. They were compared to a control group who were given a tranquilizer pill and a third group who were given a placebo. A single "dose" of mild exercise (15 minutes of walking) was significantly more effective as a tranquilizer than either the pill or the placebo. DeVries recommends that exercise not be overlooked when tranquilizers are prescribed for nervous patients, especially since there are no harmful side effects.

None of the experiments that prescribed vigorous exercise had any ill effects on the subjects. These subjects were tested before embarking on the exercise programs, however, as well as after. For elderly people who want to engage in more than vigorous walking in a regular exercise regimen, it is recommended that they consult a physician or a physical education expert. Furthermore, since it is the large muscles that influence heart and lung capacity as well as the other factors mentioned above, it is recommended that a personal exercise program consist of natural activities as walking, jogging, running (or a combination of these three), or swimming. For example, a thirty- to sixty-minute daily walk can bring about marked improvement in elderly men and women.

While running in a marathon is not prescribed for all people in their seventies, milder exercise on a regular basis is recommended for the maintenance of the cardiovascular and pulmonary systems.

taking that seems to be characteristic of older subjects. One study showed that older workers tended to leave jobs in which performance was paced by an external source, such as a machine or an assembly belt (Welford, 1958). A well-known researcher goes so far as to conclude that time limitations of any sort may be emotionally upsetting to an older person (Eisdorfer, 1968).

Although the slowing down of the nervous system normally affects many kinds of behavior, this fact is not related to the stereotype of the slow-paced, shuffling elder. The older person may take a split second too long to grab hold of the banister (and therefore fall); but will not necessarily take longer than a younger person to walk up the stairs and down the hallway. It is primarily in the redirection of movement in response to new information that impairment occurs (Welford, 1959). If an older person is accustomed to rapid and finely coordinated movement (if such movements do not represent new kinds of decisions), responses may be so quick as to astonish the unpracticed young. Artur Rubinstein, Vladimir Horowitz, Claudio Arrau, and Rudolf Serkin are examples of well-known pianists who continue in their late seventies, eighties, and nineties to interpret difficult compositions even at prestissimo tempos. With continued practice, the older person loses little; and what is lost in response time is somehow compensated for in experience. "Little problems in technique that one had before—suddenly you let the muscles alone and they solve them, so to speak," said one seventy-five-year-old pianist who performs as often as he ever did, but practices much less (Horowitz, 1978).

Although older people may be slower to respond to the timed stimuli of production line machinery, with continued practice the older person loses little, and what little is lost in response time is compensated for by experience and dexterity.

Theories of Aging

Although there is an increased vulnerability to such cardiovascular diseases as heart failure, atherosclerosis (clogging of the arteries), and hypertension and to cancer, it is not clear exactly what part age plays in these processes. Practically everyone who has studied the aging person has remarked upon the difficulty of isolating the effect of aging per se from the effects of disease, or the gradual degenerative changes that develop with the passage of time. For example, is atherosclerosis a disease, or a degenerative process that only becomes evident in older people? Is heart failure the result of a disease process or the effect of age alone (Timiras, 1972)?

There are a number of theories linking the loss of physiological function with the aging process. One is the theory of *cellular error*, in which aging and eventual death are explained as resulting from the accumulated effects of errors that occur in the sequence of the transfer of information at the cellular level. For example, information originally stored in the genetic code must be transformed into biochemical processes. With increased age, errors occur. As biochemical errors increase over time, cellular functioning deteriorates. Another theory, the *wear-and-tear* theory, compares the human organism to a machine and human cells to machine parts. For example, human cells wear out with prolonged use just as machine parts do. The gradual deterioration of vital organ cells eventually leads to physical loss and death. The *deprivation theory* holds that aging is due to the inadequate delivery of essential nutrients and oxygen to cells; this kind of deprivation may be related to certain disease

Many senior citizen centers provide hot meals for elderly persons, who, for such reasons as loneliness, poverty, or ignorance, may suffer from malnutrition.

states such as atherosclerosis. The cells begin to deteriorate under these deprived conditions and eventually die. In the *metabolic waste theory*, aging is attributed to the slow poisoning of the body by itself. According to this theory, there is a gradual buildup of the waste products of metabolism that interferes with normal cell functioning. In the *immunological theory*, the immune system of the individual gradually deteriorates with age and so cannot provide protection from foreign substances and mutant cells. This increases the chance of disease and cellular dysfunction. A variation of this theory is called the *autoimmune theory of aging:* as the immune system deteriorates, the body cannot tell the difference between normal and abnormal cells, and therefore destroys both. According to the *stress theory of aging*, any stress on the organism leaves a residual impairment. The accumulation of these minor impairments over long periods of time leads to a deterioration of the ability of the body to adapt, and eventually to death (Shock, 1977).

These are a few of the various theories of aging which exist; there are others. However, it is still unclear whether many of these processes described are causes of aging or the outcome of aging. For example, does the increased accumulation of metabolic waste in the cell cause a person to age, or is the accumulation the *result* of the aging process (Shock, 1977)?

It is equally difficult to know how much of an individual's declining function is related to age as opposed to changes in life-style. For example, malnutrition is common among the elderly, as a result of such factors as loneliness, poverty, and ignorance. Though evidence is far from complete, some researchers have linked problems in cardiac and thyroid function to nutritional deficiencies in the older person's diet (Bender, 1971; Caster, 1971). A more common observation is that physical activity declines with age, which in itself may contribute to reduced performance. In a study of women between the ages of twenty and sixty-nine, it was found that age-related losses in physiologic variables were more highly related to decreased activity level than to age itself (Wessel & Van Huss, 1969). Thus, it is difficult to determine which losses are due to aging and which to deconditioning and a less active life-style.

COGNITIVE DEVELOPMENT

It is commonly believed that people lose some of their mental abilities as they grow old. For example, older people are not expected to catch on to things so quickly or to remember so accurately. They are seldom characterized as "brainstormers" or initiators of ideas. A great deal of research has been conducted on intelligence and cognitive functions in later life, and the conclusions are controversial. What does seem clear is that the kind of large losses we sometimes imagine are by no means inevitable in the healthy older person.

Intelligence Scores

By far the most frequently studied component of intellectual functioning in the aged is their performance on standard IQ tests. As we noted in Chapter

16, considerable controversy exists about the apparent decline in intelligence during middle and late adulthood. Cross-sectional studies often report decreases in test performance beginning as early as the third decade of life, whereas longitudinal studies indicate relative stability in most intellectual functions through the fifth decade, after which a slow but progressive decline is noticeable. In addition, even when decreased test performance is observed, it is usually only in areas measuring psychomotor skills, perceptual-integration ability, memory, and inductive reasoning, as well as in areas emphasizing quickness of response. Social knowledge, verbal-conceptual ability, and arithmetic reasoning, among other skills, are little affected by the aging process per se (Botwinick, 1977).

If intellectual performance does decrease during late adulthood—even if only in select areas—it also appears to be true that the decrease is not experienced equally by all people. One interesting theory is that "age is kinder to the initially more able"—that is, subjects with high ability show less decline in old age than do subjects with low ability. Since higher abilities tend to be related to higher education levels (and higher income levels), it has also been suggested that well-educated individuals experience less, if any, decline. One twenty-year follow up of eighty-year-old subjects supports both these hypotheses—at least for a sample that included a wide range of abilities (Blum & Jarvik, 1975). The researchers suggest that mental activity throughout life, including the latter part of life, protects against intellectual decline.

This view finds support in the careers of well-known intellectuals who, having gained high levels of insight and achievement, sustained these levels through the eighth decade of life (Bertrand Russell, Sigmund Freud, Jean Piaget, and George Bernard Shaw are examples). There is also common-sense support for ability-related aging of intelligence. In the words of Ward Edwards: "If you are smart and manage to stay healthy, you'll also stay smart, although it may take you longer to demonstrate that fact at sixty-five than it did at twenty-five, and the print in which the questions are written may need to be larger" (Edwards, cited in Comfort, 1976).

Learning and Memory

Although it is often said that "you can't teach old dogs new tricks," this age-old adage certainly cannot be applied to people in late adulthood. Older people continue to take in new information and make appropriate life adjustments until the very end of their lives.

On the other hand, this doesn't imply that their learning performance is equal to that of younger adults. The accumulation of several decades of research on the elderly suggests that there are age-related decrements in the ability to acquire and remember information. The critical issue for psychologists, then, is not whether the elderly can learn, but under what conditions learning and memory are impaired for older people, and whether the elderly can be helped to overcome these learning obstacles.

One of the most important variables that has been studied in learning research is pacing—the amount of time the person is allowed to examine the stimulus and/or to make a response. It has often been thought that fast-paced conditions place the aging adult at a significant disadvantage; and that increasing inspection and response time would decrease the performance difference between younger and older adults, and possibly eliminate it altogether. In fact, research does indicate that learning in the elderly is adversely affected by fast-paced conditions. It also indicates that slow pacing and self-pacing improves the older person's performance. On the other hand, increased performance under self-paced conditions still does not equal the level of performance for younger adults (Arenberg & Robertson-Tschabo, 1977).

Other factors—besides pacing—may also contribute to the performance decrement of older adults in learning tasks. Carl Eisdorfer and his associates, for example, have suggested that the reason older people perform more poorly than younger people is because they are *physiologically overaroused,* that is, overly anxious and nervous—a condition that is known to interfere with the learning process. When elderly subjects have been administered drugs to lower autonomic nervous system arousal, performance has improved substantially—although still not to the level of younger subjects (Eisdorfer, 1968; Eisdorfer, Nowlin, & Wilkie, 1970). The meaningfulness of the material to be learned also influences the performance of older individuals. Hulicka (1967) found that many older subjects resent having to learn material that they cannot understand or that they find uninteresting. In fact, in her experiment, the vast majority of older adults refused to participate because the material was viewed as "nonsense." When one considers that many learning experiments employ nonsense syllables and other patently uninteresting and meaningless stimuli, one must begin to question just what the performance decrements of the elderly on these tasks represent: decreased ability or simply lack of interest and motivation?

Once information has been acquired it must somehow be stored, so that under appropriate conditions it can be retrieved and acted upon. Whether we are talking about a laboratory experiment involving nonsense words or a more realistic and meaningful problem situation such as trying to remember which grandchild's birthday falls on January 15th, it is obvious that the process of memory is involved. Researchers often differentiate between *primary* and *secondary* memory (Craik, 1977; Waugh & Norman, 1965). Primary memory refers to recall of information which is still being attended to "in one's mind"—short-term memory. Secondary memory, in contrast, refers to information that has been encoded but is no longer the focus of active or focused attention—long-term memory.

Most research suggests that primary memory capacity—the number of words, letters, or numbers a person can remember in correct order—does not usually decline with age (Craik, 1977; Hartley, Harker, & Walsh, 1980). In other words, both older and younger adults are capable of remembering the same *number* of items—but only under ideal or undemanding conditions! To the extent that the person is requested to reorganize the stimulus material (e.g., repeating the list backward), or divide attention between the "to be remembered list" and some other component of the task (Talland, 1965), the older adult, more than the younger, is likely to show performance decrements in primary memory.

With respect to secondary memory, the research is remarkably clear in showing that older people have significantly more problems in remembering material that is no longer being actively attended to or focused upon. Furthermore, this deficit has been linked to three distinct components of memory: registration of information, storage of information, and retrieval of information. In each of these areas, evidence is accumulating to indicate that the elderly are less capable in comparison to younger adults (Craik, 1977; Hartley, Harker, & Walsh, 1980).

Logical Abilities

In addition to research on learning and memory, numerous studies have been conducted on problem-solving and logical reasoning in the elderly. One group of studies in particular is worth noting—those that have attempted to extend Piagetian theory and research to the thought processes of the aged. Papalia (1972), for example, presented subjects, six to sixty-five years and over, with a battery of conservation tasks (number, mass, weight, and volume). In the older adults, Papalia found a lower level of performance primarily for the more advanced concepts—particularly conservation of volume, for which only 6 percent of the sixty-five and older age group produced correct responses. Similarly, in the area of classification ability, Denny and Cornelius (1975) reported that middle-aged adults significantly outperformed two groups of elderly adults: those who lived in a community and those who were institutionalized. A comparison of the two older groups indicated that institutionalized living was more strongly linked to low-level logical reasoning than was community-based living. The elderly also have been found to be more egocentric than younger adults, and more variable or inconsistent in their moral reasoning (Bielby & Papalia, 1975).

The strongest and most consistent decrements in performance for the elderly, however, has been found in the area of formal operational abilities—the most advanced form of reasoning within Piaget's system (Overton & Clayton, 1976). This has given rise to an interesting hypothesis that the most recent abilities to emerge in development—for example, formal operations—are the first to disappear during aging.

Interpreting Age-Related Cognitive Decline

The pattern of cognitive and intellectual decline during the aging years, which has been documented repeatedly by research studies, has been variously interpreted. Schaie (1974) speaks of the "myth of intellectual decline." When tested in cross-sectional studies, he says, marked differences in the skills of successive generations are found. On nonspeeded tests, at least, the elderly function nearly as well as they did when young. Still, they do not function as well as their well-educated grandchildren. Schaie suggests that in intellectual abilities, old people, if they are reasonably healthy, do not decline—they become obsolete. (There is no way of telling whether this will be true of successive generations.) Similar points have been made with respect to Piagetian task performance. For example, Papalia and Bielby note that one must be cautious about interpreting the apparent decline in formal operational abilities, since many adults never attain this level. Lower performance among the elderly may reflect an initially less competent sample (Papalia & Bielby, 1974). It may also reflect changing expectations. Speaking more generally, Riegel (1973a) has said, "Generation and social change outpace the individual, and while the old person might produce the impression that he has deteriorated in his performance, it might be that he has remained stable but society has changed its conditions and standards."

Other researchers believe that health-related factors, and neurological intactness, are associated with performance decrements in the elderly. In what has now become a classic study, Birren et al. (1963) examined physiological, intellectual, and personality functioning in young and elderly men, the latter of which were grouped into two separate categories: those who were in optimal health in every regard, and those who were without obvious clinical symptoms of disease but were found to have mild or subclinical disease through intensive examinations. In the majority of areas measured, the subclinical older group were functioning not only below younger subjects, but also below optimally healthy older subjects. In the area of intelligence, the subclinical group obtained poorer scores than the healthy older group on twenty-one of twenty-three tests. Of interest, however, was that for verbal intelligence, both older groups outperformed the younger group, whereas in areas measuring psychomotor speed, the reverse was found. This pattern supports the hypothesis that verbal conceptual ability does not decline with age and, in fact, may continue to increase, whereas skills dependent upon speed of central nervous system transmission do show age-related decline.

Elderly artists may be slower to put paintbrush to canvas but conceptual and creative ability are still sharp.

The study by Birren and his associates is important because it points to the adverse impact of disease, even a mild degree of disease, on the adaptive functioning of older people. When the elderly are free of disease, which admittedly is not that common when subclinical problems are included in one's definition of disease, there is relatively little difference between the old and the young with the major exception of a slowing down of central nervous system activity.

One other interpretation of the relatively low test scores achieved by the elderly rests on the distinction between *competence* and *performance* (Flavell & Wohlwill, 1969). Technically, competence is defined as "what the individual knows or could do in a timeless ideal environment," whereas performance represents what the individual actually does in the task at hand. Utilizing this distinction, some psychologists suggest that the decreased performance of the elderly does not necessarily indicate decreased competence. For example, older people may perform poorly because they are not motivated. They may be put off by the toylike materials used in Piagetian tasks. They may be unable to relate to a younger researcher, or even to hear the instructions. In some areas their competence may be high, but their skills may be rusty. Older subjects may be in a position similar to that of the person who remembers having mastered Latin or the violin: they are still capable of functioning at a high level, but probably cannot do so at the present moment. The more years that go by, the greater is the possibility that skills will fall into disuse. The decline in cognitive functions in the elderly may thus represent an increasingly wider gap between competence and performance, rather than regression (Bearison, 1974). If this is so, then the performance of older people might be improved relatively easily. For example, more appropriate rewards might be introduced to counter poor motivation; retraining might be expected to result in higher functioning for skills that have fallen into disuse.

PERSONALITY DEVELOPMENT

There have been many negative stereotypes attached to aging adults. Some of the most common are that they are "set in their ways," "inflexible," "narrow-minded," "self-centered," and "out of date." These terms portray the elderly as somehow rigid, unchangeable, and nonadaptive. They also imply—as all stereotypes do—a uniformity among older people. On both counts nothing could be further from the truth.

Old age brings new challenges and new tasks to be faced and mastered. Most older individuals are just as successful or unsuccessful in confronting and handling the developmental tasks of late adulthood as younger individuals are in dealing with the tasks of their own respective life periods. Furthermore, the styles of adjusting are, if anything, more variable during the later years than earlier in life. This is not to deny, however, the seriousness of the problems confronting the aged. Declining health, loss of functions, widowhood, financial problems, loss of social status, social isolation, susceptibility to crime, and impending death are but some of the real problems that older people face today. Yet face them they do. In fact, the success that most older people have in meeting the challenges of old age speaks to a resiliency not usually associated with this life period in the minds of most individuals. Late adulthood is a time of continued psychological growth—even in the face of physiological decline.

Developmental Tasks in Late Adulthood

During old age, according to Erikson, the individual experiences the crisis of *ego integrity versus despair* (Erikson, 1963). Integrity is experienced as emotional integration; as a transcendence of the limitations of the self, through full acceptance of the one and only life one is granted (Erikson, 1976). Despair expresses itself as a feeling that time is now too short—that there is no further chance of finding an alternate path to an acceptable life. As in earlier stages, there is inner struggle. Even the person who enters old age with a high degree of integrity experiences despair at the momentary thought of death—and disgust at the futility and pettiness of human life. As earlier, it is the favorable ratio that is important. The person who achieves a favorable ratio of integrity over despair in the last years attains wisdom: "the detached and yet active concern with life itself, in the face of death itself." It is this outcome which "maintains the integrity in spite of the decline of bodily and mental functions" (Erikson, 1976).

According to Peck (1968), continued psychological growth in the aging years centers on the outcome of three major developmental tasks. In late adulthood most people must come to grips with *occupational retirement*. They must be able to find personal satisfaction and self-worth beyond the work activities that have been important for self-definition in earlier periods. Peck summarizes this issue in the question which he believes each person must ask himself during late adulthood: "Am I a worthwhile person only insofar as I can do a full-time job; or can I be worthwhile in other, different ways—as a performer of several other roles, and also because of the kind of person I am?" (Peck, 1968). To the extent that older people can redefine themselves meaningfully in areas other than work, they are more likely to face the future with greater interest, vitality, and a sense of integrity.

A second theme of old age, within Peck's theory of personality development, concerns the inevitable *physical decline* that accompanies old age. People who define happiness and well-being primarily along physical dimensions are often seriously disturbed by the bodily changes they experience during aging—even more so than by the changes in middle age. They become preoccupied with these changes; so much so that they may experience a profound sense of despair and disgust—with themselves, and with life itself. Older people, according to Peck, must shift their values away from the physical domain, if they haven't already, and into the domain of interpersonal relations and mental activities. It is through these areas of human functioning, Peck

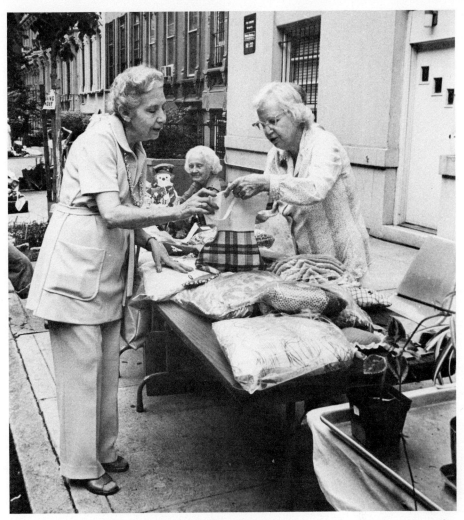

Maintaining a sense of self-worth is important in later years. Involvement in community activities such as a street bazaar or flea market can keep the elderly person feeling healthy and useful.

says, that the elderly are most likely to experience feelings of life satisfaction and fulfillment.

The final theme emphasized by Peck is directly linked to *human mortality.* Each person in old age must face the realization of impending death; must try to accept not only the inevitability of fate, but also find meaning in it. This may well be the most significant and challenging task confronting the aging adult. Like Erikson, Peck believes that the answer is to be found in the feelings of generativity developed by the person over the years. He explains it this way: "To live so generously and unselfishly that the prospect of personal

Erikson's Crises in Psychosocial Development

BASIC TRUST VERSUS BASIC MISTRUST (FIRST YEAR OF LIFE)

AUTONOMY VERSUS SHAME AND DOUBT (SECOND YEAR OF LIFE)

INITIATIVE VERSUS GUILT (THE PRESCHOOL YEARS)

INDUSTRY VERSUS INFERIORITY (MIDDLE CHILDHOOD)

IDENTITY VERSUS ROLE CONFUSION (ADOLESCENCE)

INTIMACY VERSUS ISOLATION (EARLY ADULTHOOD)

GENERATIVITY VERSUS STAGNATION (MIDDLE ADULTHOOD)

EGO INTEGRITY VERSUS DESPAIR (OLD AGE)

Ego integrity is a state of mind characterized by the conviction that there is order and meaning to life, and that the life one has lived is both fully acceptable and necessary. For the older, well-integrated person, the outcome is Wisdom. The person who does not achieve integrity experiences despair and disgust, bitterness and fear, in the terminal stage of life.

death—the night of the ego, it might be called—looks and feels less important than the secure knowledge that one has built for a broader, longer future than any one ego ever could encompass. Through children, through contributions to the culture, through friendships—these are ways in which human beings can achieve enduring significance for their actions which goes beyond the limit of their own skins and their own lives" (Peck, 1968).

It is obvious that there are many common threads in the characterization of old age as portrayed by Erikson and Peck. Each views the central developmental tasks of this period in terms of the challenges of declining health, reduced generativity, acknowledgment and acceptance of one's mortality, and above all, the integration of feelings about the self and life in general. Not as obvious, however, is the assumption made by both researchers, as well as by others (Havighurst, 1974; Neugarten, 1971), that success in meeting these challenges depends, to a great extent, on the success experienced with earlier developmental tasks. The crisis of old age is a culmination of the many psychosocial crises through which the individual has passed. We have already noted that both Erikson and Peck place a great deal of importance on generativity (a central psychosocial task of middle-age) in giving meaning to the final years of life. But the integrity of old age is also an outcome of the love that has emerged in intimacy, and the fidelity to self and to others that has issued from the identity crises. All the earlier conflicts can be seen to reach into, and to be renewed by, the level of this last developmental challenge as they have been on each level in between. It is the primal trust of infancy, writes Erikson, which provides the foundation for some faith necessary both for terminal peace, and for the renewal of life from generation to generation (Erikson, 1976).

Social Image and Self-Concept

Many writers, historians, and psychologists have remarked on the distaste, fear, and negative connotation that is attached to the image of old age in modern societies. And it is certainly true that old age does conjure up some unattractive images. Several classic attitudinal studies have shown that young people perceive the old as lonely, resistant to change, and failing in physical and mental powers (Tuckman & Lorge, 1953). The attitudes of high school and college youth toward the elderly and their social role are mostly negative (Lane, 1964; Kastenbaum & Durkee, 1964). Old age is often perceived as without significant positive values. The older the adult, the more unpleasant he or she appears to the younger subject (Hickey & Kalish, 1968). Researchers note that the young people who make these judgments tend to omit any consideration of their own old age (Kastenbaum & Durkee, 1964). If they do look to the far future, they hope to die before their time (Kastenbaum, 1971).

As for the old themselves, probably one of the most difficult things about aging is learning to define oneself as old. The elderly cannot help but agree with some of the cultural stereotypes of old age. After all, they themselves have held these stereotypes most of their lives. A man who is biased against women, or a white person who dislikes blacks, is never himself in the position of being turned into the object of his prejudice. But the young person *does* eventually become an old person. Activist groups that represent the elderly say that they must combat stereotypes held by the elderly about themselves as well as stereotypes held by younger generations. Psychologists often find that projective tests (in which the subject is asked to tell a story about a picture, for example) elicit unhappy images of old age from older subjects. When shown an older man, for example, older subjects tell stories that allude to the character's weakness or passivity in the family (Neugarten & Gutmann, 1958). Still, the fact that some studies have found a decrease in self-concept and self-esteem in old age must be interpreted with caution. Kaplan and Pokorny (1970), argue that it is not aging per se that influences self-concept, but rather events that the elderly experience during this life phase—for example, a lower income level than one expected and living alone rather than as a couple.

Regardless of long-held prejudices, older people must at some point face up to thinking of themselves as "old" and adjust their self-concepts accordingly. Many factors enter into the definition. One is the awareness of social norms. According to the classic Neugarten study, an "old" man is between sixty-five and seventy-five years of age; an "old" woman between sixty and seventy-five (Neugarten, Moore & Lowe, 1965). According to U.S. Government statistics, people between sixty-five and seventy-four are "aged" and anyone older is "overaged." These definitions are reflected and perpetuated by social policy. Under most circumstances, people become eligible for Social Security at sixty-five. In some cities, they may receive a special senior citizen pass to the movies or on intercity transportation upon reaching their sixtieth or sixty-fifth birthday. All these "rites of passage" may be expected to enter into a person's awareness of advancing age. Joining an activist group for senior citizens may be the final step in accepting and exploiting the social definition.

Another important factor in age awareness becomes apparent in social interaction. Being offered a seat on the bus by a younger person is a typical example of an interaction that underscores one's age. Expressions of consideration—being offered an arm coming down the stairs, or a seat up front "so you can hear"—or disrespect—being told to "watch it, Grandpa"—are socially significant.

Age awareness is also influenced by the age composition of society, that is, by one's relative age. In 1978 there were over 24 million people aged sixty-five or older—or 11 percent of the population (U.S. Department of Commerce, 1979)—a statistic that suggests that we should, perhaps, assign seventy-five as "the marker" (Neugarten, 1971). People in the late sixties or early seventies today need not define themselves as "really old," because they know quite a few eighty- and ninety-year-olds. The degree to which the likely survival of one's peers enters into the self-concept can be seen in a comparison of black and white Americans. Blacks tend to think of themselves as being older than do whites of the same age, in part because proportionately fewer blacks live into their seventies and eighties (Busse, Jeffers, & Christ, 1970).

Although social definitions contribute to age awareness, there is a tradition that states "you are a young as you feel." This implies that subjective or psychological criteria are what are important. Believing that they can still learn (and perhaps returning to school) or finding that they can still perform sexually are indications of youthful well-being. Accordingly, many older people deny the impact of old age, by saying, for example, that they are "eighty years young." People with this attitude may be relatively unaffected by retirement or gray hair. They feel old only if confined by illness, or confronted by a difficult adjustment, such as the death of a spouse.

Personality and Adjustment

With respect to personality, age is a poor index of differences between people (Neugarten, 1971). Work and family roles, financial resources, and physical health appear to be more important to adult adjustment than the exact number of birthdays which the individual has survived. Certainly age brings life developments that work against expression of ingrained personality traits. The aggressively independent person may need to learn graceful reliance on others, for instance. But for the most part, old age brings no abrupt changes. The best indicator of personality in later life is, not surprisingly, personality in middle adulthood.

Without trying to identify any personality-type characteristic of later life, psychologists have studied age-related tendencies in selected areas of personality. They have investigated older persons' perceptions of, and interac-

Older Students

Many college students are no longer surprised to find that the people sitting beside them in history or calculus class are older than they are—by about fifty years. Over 5 percent of the senior citizens in the United States are voluntarily returning to school, often after full and successful careers, to learn for the pleasure of it rather than the promise of economic reward.

There are several reasons for the surge in the number of elderly students: the growing proportion of older persons in the population, the increasing political power of the elderly, and a greater awareness on the part of the government of their special needs and desires. That awareness has been reflected in government spending and encouragement of programs for the elderly.

At least a fifth of American colleges and universities have made provisions for adult education. One example is the University of Kentucky's Donovan Scholars Program—a program that extends the rights and privileges of university students, tuition-free, to retirees from all over the country. The only requirements are a dedication to learning and the scholar's own confidence in his physical and mental health. Secondary schools and noncollege organizations have begun similar programs.

Special arrangements are made to fit these special students. A new set of teaching techniques has evolved that recognizes the independence of the student, gives her credit for life experience, encourages her personal goals, and utilizes practical, off-campus teaching. Since transportation can present a problem to the elderly, many programs arrange for them to live in campus dormitories, thus allowing for fuller participation in the university community.

The coming of the elderly to student life is not without problems—the two main ones being a possible lack of self-confidence, and the preconceptions of teachers and other students. Some professors, uncertain of how to behave, either ignore their new pupils or treat them with an exaggerated deference. But as these problems are worked out, the rewards for both student and school become clear. In the past few years there has been much protest over the separation of the elderly from the general population. They have been segregated into nursing homes, retirement villages, and senior citizen housing projects. Young people have been deprived of their experience and their memories, and everyone has lost from the flow of ideas which could exist between the generations. Campuses unsegregated by age show one way of alleviating this situation. As for the elderly themselves, having contributed to society in terms of money and service, they can now afford to relax and indulge in one of life's pleasures—school.

---

tions with, their particular environments—environments that have become increasingly risky, dangerous, and complex. Such environments are seen as making demands and the self as having to conform to them. The older person has to "go along with things," even though those things may move too fast or be too noisy.

Some laboratory experiments have indicated that older subjects show a preference for uncomplicated situations (Alpaugh & Birren, 1977) and a tendency to avoid risks when given a choice (Botwinick, 1966). They tend to choose relatively easy tasks as a means of protecting themselves against failure (Okun & DiVesta, 1976). In the practical world, too, older people are known to avoid stressful and complicated situations. For example, they may not apply for food stamps and other services if the bureaucracy does not simplify forms and procedures. And yet the elderly are not always more cautious or less risk-taking than the young. In one experimental situation where the size of the reward was contingent on the size of the risk taken, no difference in cautiousness was observed between the young and old (Okun & Elias, 1977). Similarly, in research that eliminated the "no-risk" option—that is, where subjects had to take some risk, no matter how small—both young and elderly subjects displayed the same level of risk-taking (Okun & DiVesta, 1976). It appears, therefore, that the primary difference between younger and older adults is not in risk taking per se, but in the tendency to avoid risks when possible. In situations where risk-taking is unavoidable, however, few if any age differences are evident.

A related finding is that the elderly gradually reduce or simplify their interactions with others. They exhibit less role activity (Neugarten, 1973; 1977); they engage less often in family and community activities. The drop-off in social interaction, however, is not a sharp one, but rather a gradual decline in each successive age group from the mid-fifties on (Havighurst, Neugarten, & Tobin, 1968). This is not, of course, a function of personality alone. Older people may have fewer opportunities to interact with others (just as they have greater reason to avoid the risks of their environment).

A number of researchers have suggested that older people choose, perhaps wisely, to risk less personal investment in their relationships. "There seems to be reduction in drive level, a decrease in ego involvement" (Kuhlen, 1964). Less "ego energy" is available to deal with conflict situations, especially as they involve emotions (Havighurst, Neugarten, & Tobin, 1968). Perhaps for this reason, older people seem less worried than younger people. If something doesn't go right, the tendency is to "let it go," take it in stride. In particular, "it is the privilege of the old to feel less guilt about the undone, and what a joy that is!" writes author May Sarton (1978).

Preoccupation with the inner life seems to become more intense, leading some writers to describe increased *interiority* as a developmental change of this period (Neugarten, 1973). Older people tend to move toward more eccentric and self-preoccupied positions. "I am more interested in myself than in anyone else," Miss Sarton continues. At sixty-five, she says, she feels she has the right to self-interest, self-exploration, and reflection. Some researchers have proposed a *disengagement theory* to account for this change, as well as the reduction in social and psychological investments described earlier. The disengagement theory predicts a decrease in role activity and gradual physical and psychological detachment from others. The process seems to be a reciprocal one between the elderly person and society; as individuals gradually disengage themselves from society, there is less and less of a place for them in the society. If the two processes occur at about the same time, then a good adjustment to aging is likely. However, if a person is cut off from society by early retirement or a loss of social contacts, there are likely to be problems in adjustment (Cumming & Henry, 1961). In commenting on adaptation to life-cycle events and role disengagement, Neugarten (1977) writes,

> ... it is not the occurrence of the life event itself which precipitates an adaptational crisis, for most such events are anticipated and rehearsed and the transition accomplished without shattering the sense of continuity of the life cycle. Instead it is when such events occur "off time" rather than "on time," for example, when grandparenthood, retirement, major illness, or widowhood occur earlier in life than expected, that crisis is experienced.

Gradual disengagement of the person from society is said to lead to a sense of psychological well-being and satisfaction (Cumming & Henry, 1961). That is, disengagement is desired for its own sake. Other researchers have proposed an *activity theory* which suggests the opposite: that maintaining the earlier level of activity results in successful aging. Recent findings suggest that much depends on the individual's style of aging. "Certain personality types, as they age, slough off various role responsibilities with relative comfort and remain highly content with life," writes Neugarten (1973). Other types are depressed by any reduction in social opportunities. Still others who have long had low levels of interaction accompanied by high satisfaction show relatively little change as they grow older. Personality type and long-standing life-styles seem to predict the way in which the individuals adapt to society as they age.

SUMMARY

▶ Findings concerning the physical, emotional, and intellectual decline in old age tend to be contradictory. This is partly because individual differences are so great and partly because the researchers have little personal experience of old age. Changes in physical appearance include wrinkles and age spots, loss of teeth, and postural stoop.

▶ The major systems of the body—cardiovascular, pulmonary, and digestive—continue to decline in efficiency. There is an acceleration in sensory decline, particularly in hearing.

▶ Old people are more susceptible to disease and less likely to recover quickly. In old age, people are more likely to suffer from such mental disorders as depression, chronic anxiety, and hypochondriasis. In extreme old age hardening of the arteries may cause senile dementia. A slowing down of the central nervous system accounts for the slowness of movement and of the mental processes of old people when encountering new situations.

▶ The aging process cannot be satisfactorily explained by a single theory. Some think that aging is a result of an accumulation of errors that occur in the transformation at the cellular level. Some attribute aging to the wear and tear on the body over the years. Aging is also explained by the deprivation theory as due to an inadequate delivery of essential nutrients to the cells, which then deteriorate and die. Aging has been explained in such terms as: a breakdown in the immune system, an accumulation of stresses over the years, and an accumulation of metabolic wastes. For many of these theories it is unclear whether the explanatory factor is a cause of aging or one of the symptoms of aging.

▶ Certain aspects of intelligence seem to decline with age, particularly psychomotor skills, memory, and inductive reasoning. Social knowledge, verbal-conceptual ability, and arithmetic reasoning, however, are not affected by age. Furthermore, declines, if there are any, are not experienced equally by all people. The better educated tend to experience little if any decline in intelligence.

▶ Many factors affect the ability of older people to perform well on intelligence tests, including the pacing of the problems, an overarousal of the autonomic nervous system, and a lack of motivation. Some researchers do not believe that there is a decline in intelligence in older people if they are healthy and active.

▶ According to Erikson the crisis of old age is that of ego-integrity versus despair. Most old people continue to grow psychologically as they face the challenges of old age. Old people must adjust to retirement, physical aging, and the inevitability of their own death. Compounding these problems is the negative image of age held by most members of society including the aged themselves.

▶ There are two opposing theories concerning the best means of adapting to old age. The disengagement theory suggests that old people can adjust to aging best by reducing their involvement with other people and situations and becoming more interested in themselves. Other researchers, however, do not agree. They feel that activity and involvement keep a person healthy and youthful. The way they have lived their lives seems to predict the adaptation to aging of individual old people.

FURTHER READINGS

Baltes, P.B., and Schaie, K.W. (Eds.) *Life-span developmental psychology: Personality and socialization.* New York: Academic Press, 1978.
This book of readings focuses on research about the changes in personality which occur as one ages.

Birren, J.E. *The psychology of aging.* Englewood Cliffs, N.J.: Prentice-Hall, 1964.
This text includes fine chapters on the biological influences of aging on perception, psychomotor skills, and speed and timing.

Butler, Robert N. *Why survive? Being old in America.* **New York: Harper & Row, 1975.**

A grimly realistic book on the tragic conditions of the aged in America. Butler forces us to face the fact that in this country the aged daily confront prejudice, poverty, and discrimination.

Montagu, Ashley. *Immortality, religion, and morals.* **New York: Hawthorn, 1971.**

A witty and literate collection of essays dealing with man's search for immortality, through children, creative works, or the survival of the soul. Montagu supports his text with evidence from the fields of anthropology, sociology, religion, and philosophy.

Olsen, Tillie. "Tell Me a Riddle," in *Tell me a riddle.* **New York: Dell, 1971.**

A deeply moving story about a woman dying of cancer, who converses with and advises each member of her family.

Rosenfeld, Albert. *Prolongevity.* **New York: Knopf, 1976.**

Is it possible to prolong life indefinitely? Rosenfeld maintains that, in the near future, science will have discovered ways to postpone, slow down, or even halt the aging process by means of gene transplants or revising the brain. This controversial and thought-provoking book is well researched and well documented.

Chapter 19

٭٭٭٭٭٭٭

Family Life,
Retirement, and the
Final Years

Barring premature death, each of us will go through the process of aging—the terminal stage of life—yet each of us will experience this process differently. For some, the later years of life are filled with joy, excitement, and a sense of continued involvement—with family, friends, and society as a whole. For other people, however, old age brings with it unhappiness, loneliness, boredom, and regrets. In between these two extremes are the majority of older people—those whose lives continue to be characterized by "ups and downs"; by success and happiness in some areas, and frustration, and possible failure, in others. As one seventy-two-year-old retired carpenter commented:

> In looking back over my life, it is hard to judge whether I've been successful or not . . . My marriage has been a good one; my children are all grown and have children of their own . . . We are a close family . . . I'm proud of them all . . . Other things I'm not so happy about. I never made a lot of money; never had the time or the means to give my family what I wanted to. I feel bad about that . . . But in comparison to others, it hasn't been so bad. When I balance it all up, the pluses and minuses, I guess I feel pretty good about my life. At least I know I tried.

Successful adjustment in old age is dependent on many factors. In Chapter 18 we examined how physical, mental, and personality changes affect the older person. In the present chapter, we focus on adjustment in later adulthood within the broader contexts of family and occupational life. Lifespan psychologists such as Erikson (1963; 1976), Havighurst (1974), and Peck (1968), among others, have noted that some of the most important developmental tasks confronting the elderly are the contexts of family and work—the death of a spouse, retirement, and reduced income, for example.

We shall also take up what is clearly the single most important developmental task of late adulthood—confrontation with death. Human beings are unique within the animal kingdom in their ability to reflect on their own lives, and on their own death. In many ways, however, this capacity is a "double-edged sword." On the one hand, it certainly enriches our life, providing an important dimension of meaning to our existence. And yet for many people, the process of self-reflection, including confrontation with death, results in intense anxiety, dread, and profound regret. Yet death is inevitable and must be confronted. Some kind of accommodation or attempt at adjustment must be made in the waning years of life. This adjustment involves a process of contemplation and evaluation of life's meaning; of integrating the many experiences and facts of life, including the final and most incomprehensible one of all—human mortality. Such an adjustment involves acceptance of the one and only life (and death) one has—with dignity and without too much regret. However, not everyone can accept the life they lived or the death they face. For some older people the challenges of the terminal period cannot be met. Often alone, isolated from those who care, without adequate financial means to make life bearable, let alone comfortable, the dying older person sometimes welcomes death as an escape from an intolerable life. In such cases, the final search for meaning is displaced by the more immediate need for peace.

FAMILY LIFE

Marriage in Late Adulthood

Stereotypes of the aging couple are often rather bleak. Streib (1977) suggests that most people tend to view the older husband and wife as unhappy, isolated, lonely, and rejected by loved ones—especially children and relatives. While this is certainly true for some people, it is the exception rather than the rule. Most research suggests that the quality of marital life in old age is generally quite good. Couples who enter this period together feel especially fortunate. In fact, in one important study, the majority of older couples described this time as the happiest period in their marriage (Stinnett, Carter, & Montgomery, 1972). Among the values important to each were "companionship" and "being able to express true feelings to each other." The factor seen as accounting for marital success was most often "being in love."

Research suggests that the quality of marital life in old age is generally quite good. The majority of older couples describe this time as the happiest period in their marriage.

In part, of course, the adjustment of the older couple represents learning and experience. After forty years or more together, each partner has learned to ignore small irritations and accept what cannot be changed. An age-related decrease in ego energy, one's mental and emotional resources, may also contribute to a more easygoing relationship in late marriage. So too does the tendency to "block out" conflict and other stressful situations. Chiriboga and Cutler (1980) note that while the elderly frequently are confronted with stressful life events, they generally are quite successful in coping with them—usually by "distancing" themselves, psychologically, from the events. In so doing, the elderly experience less disruption in their lives, including their marriage.

According to Adams (1975) the two factors that give the older marriage its unique character are the gradual shift in focus away from the children, and the retirement of the husband (and more recently the wife) from occupational life. Both events provide the couple with increased freedom from outside responsibilities and obligations; in fact, they generally are not expected to do much more than support and sustain each other. Death has usually relieved them of responsibilities toward parents; and their children usually ask only that they remain self-sufficient, which of course, they mean to do. Consequently, husbands and wives often find that they have more time for each other during this period than at any other time in their marriage— a factor that seems to facilitate marital happiness.

Some couples do, certainly, experience problems in late marriage. Retirement—having the man about the house—is sometimes a trial for the wife, at least at first. New routines and household responsibilities must be established now that both partners are at home. In addition, the success with which the husband adapts to retirement also appears to be important (Adams, 1975). One may also speculate that with the increasing number of women in the work force, and the improved opportunities for career development, the relationship between success late in the marriage and adjustment to retirement may soon apply (if it does not already) to wives as well.

Illness also tends to strain the marital relationship, reducing sexual interaction, and perhaps introducing new dependency relationships. Poverty is another source of marital discontent, especially when encountered for the first time in the later years. Retirement brings with it a substantial reduction in financial income. Consequently, the older couple must make drastic adjustments in their standard of living—adjustments that may strain the marriage if adequate decision-making processes for managing scarce resources have not been developed over the years. Generally, most couples who have been relatively well adjusted improve their relationship with old age. On many indices of marital satisfaction, the aging couple come to resemble the young childless couple. Rollins and Feldman (1970), two observers of the marriage relationship, conclude that "perhaps the outstanding characteristic of this group is the general feeling of peacefulness, lack of stress, and satisfaction with marriage, in which they approach the level of the newly married."

One factor that may help to explain the success of some late marriages is an interesting sex-role reversal that characterizes some older couples. It has frequently been noted that parenthood and occupational life sharpens sex-role distinctions in many couples. As couples enter into later life, however, the demands of parenthood and work lessen, often leading to a marked reduction of sex-role differences. Some men begin to recognize and express their more affiliative, nurturant, and emotional needs, while women become more assertive (Gutmann, 1977; Neugarten, 1968). These changes are likely to reduce tension between the couple, allowing for greater ease of communication and increased sharing of feelings—both of which are likely to facilitate marital success.

Finally, it should also be noted that marriage is not only quite satisfying during this age period, but it is also psychologically and biologically beneficial. Research indicates that older individuals who are married are less likely to experience loneliness and depression than are the unmarried elderly (Tibbitts, 1977). They also show less evidence of mental illness (Gove, 1973) and they are likely to live longer (Civia, 1967). It would appear, therefore, that conditions surrounding marriage, particularly the ready availability of a companion, buffer the older individual from many of the stresses and strains of later life.

Psychosexual Adjustment

Until fairly recently, the sexual lives of the elderly were more often the subject of jokes than serious study. Today there is increased sensitivity to the sexual needs and pleasures of older people. A sociologist, writing for a popular retirement-oriented magazine, noted that in one community of 10,000 older people, problems involving sex were brought to therapists about twice as often as anything else (Peterson, 1971, cited in Puner, 1974). The informed public is no longer shocked to read of marriages between nursing-home residents, or of living-together arrangements among older unmarried couples. Masters and Johnson and virtually every modern authority agree that healthy older people are able, and usually interested in participating in sexual activity, and that they can do so with warmth and dignity. To date there have been few large-scale studies of sexual behavior of the elderly, but there are enough data for us to conclude that there is no age cut-off point for sex (Butler & Lewis, 1976).

There are many factors that influence the expression of sexuality in old age; biological and physiological changes are some of the most important ones. For some older people, the superficial changes in overt appearance—wrinkling and sagging of skin, baldness, and so on—contribute to a negative self-image that reduces the desire to seek sexual encounters. Biological changes also contribute directly to sexual functioning. Hormone reduction—testosterone for men and estrogen for women—which began in middle adulthood continues to alter the structure and functioning of reproductive organs in old age. For women, the walls of the vagina become thinner, shorter, and less expansive. Vaginal lubrication also decreases, thereby leading to occasional pain during intercourse. Orgasm is generally shorter and less intense as well (Weg, 1978). For men, more direct stimulation is necessary to achieve erection; and the time it takes for full erection to occur is longer, sometimes as long as thirty to forty minutes (Runciman, 1975). Older men also experience longer times between erections, and less intense orgasms. Yet they are better able to control ejaculation; that is, they are able to maintain erections longer before orgasm. In many cases, this increases the man's ability to satisfy his partner, and to enhance his own pleasurable sensations (Masters & Johnson, 1966). Finally, it is important to note that despite these biological changes, older men and women are still capable of an active sexual life and the experience is still extremely satisfying (Butler & Lewis, 1976). Perhaps it is only the goal that changes. Rather than focusing on performance, the older person appears to be more concerned with pleasure (Kaplan, 1977).

Sexuality in old age is also complicated by medical problems. Diabetes, hypothyroidism, arthritis, alcoholism, drug dependence, and obesity, to name a few health-related factors, frequently contribute to a decreased sexual desire, and at times, even to impotence. Certain surgical procedures are also linked to sexual problems in the elderly. Radical surgery for cancer of the colon or the rectum frequently leads to impotence in older men—sometimes because of surgical damage to the nerves that cause an erection, but more often because of the negative impact of surgery on sexual self-image. Similarly, older women sometimes lose interest in sexual activity following a hysterectomy, not because of some medical complication, but because of the myths surrounding the surgery (Jacobson, 1974).

Besides biological and medical factors, a number of sociopsychological factors contribute to sexual expression in older adults. It appears that most sexual activity is conducted within marriage or marital-like relationships. The older man fears exposure and failure with an unfamiliar woman. The sexual attitudes of the older woman may prevent her from being assertive or from engaging in casual relationships.

A Duke University study found that among older women the presence and intensity of the sexual experience tends to depend upon the availability of the spouse (Pfeiffer, Verwoerdt, & Davis, 1972). The most frequent reason for cessation of sexual relations was death of the husband; the second most frequent reason, illness of the husband. Since most women over sixty-five years are not still married, it is understandable that sexual activity in this group declines dramatically. And yet older women (and men) are still sexual creatures, still desirous of sexual expression. Sviland (1975) reports that 70 percent of aged healthy married couples are "sexually active." Therefore, it is not age that determines sexual expression, but the availability of a willing sexual partner.

One's sexual history and attitude about sexuality also contribute to sexual expression in old age. People who engaged frequently in sexual activity during their earlier years, who found it pleasurable and are comfortable with sexual matters, are much more likely to continue sexual activity in late adulthood (Dresen, 1975).

Aside from the lack of a willing partner, older women also are subject to a "double standard" when it comes to sexual expression. The sexuality of the older woman has traditionally been less acceptable and less visible than that of the older man. This may reflect the association of sexual attractiveness with youth. This association holds more strongly for women than for men—who are sometimes said to become more attractive in later life. It appears, too, that in the past older women have been embarrassed to speak of their sexual needs. One physician (herself an older woman) reported that she found her older women patients had difficulty, even in a climate of relaxed sexuality, admitting that they had sexual desires (Knopf, 1975).

Fortunately, many older women had no difficulty answering questionnaires published in a national magazine. Here is what a sixty-eight-year-old woman told *The Redbook Report on Female Sexuality* (which elicited an unprecedented 100,000 replies):

> We live way out in the country, paradice [sic] lane I call it. There is such a nice place, running water all around, we made our own swimming pond. We love going naked all the time, we even work the garden, swim, saw wood naked ... We don't care what other people think. It's so much fun to put hay in the barn and lay on it and f---. We love saying words like that—they sound so important to us (Tavris and Sadd, 1975).

Perhaps more typical is this statement, made to sociologist John Cuber:

> We don't talk about it to anyone, but you're a professional and not so young either. We're over sixty and have as much fun as we did before we married forty years ago. Maybe one of the things that makes it all so precious, besides the great memories, is that growing awareness that we won't be around forever, that the future gets shorter all the time (Cuber, quoted in Tavris & Sadd, 1975).

Although the idea that they are not interested in sex has been discredited, older people continue to be adversely affected by this myth. For example, friends and relatives react with consternation if an older widow or widower conducts an obviously sexual affair. As a result, many older couples court in an atmosphere of secrecy and near shame (McKain, 1972). When interviewed about their marriages, they pointedly avoid mentioning sex, referring instead to "companionship."

The sexual expression of older people is varied. Those who do not have opportunities for sexual intercourse—or who, from marital boredom, do not avail themselves of opportunities—do not become, in the last years of life, sexless. The expression of sexuality is not dependent upon the sexual act. If it were, we would be sexless creatures until the age at which the norms of our particular societies granted us a sexual partner—until mid- or late adolescence in our own society. Since Freud, most people agree that sexuality exists in some form from the beginning of life. This is so despite the fact that young children are incapable of intercourse. In old age, too, a person is "sexual" whether or not there is opportunity (or healthy capacity) for intercourse. When sexuality is not limited to genital expression, it tends to involve other aspects of the personality, particularly the imagination. It is the older person (and the frustrated adolescent) who has a reputation for fantasy, and for being interested in pornography and erotic art. And it is, significantly, the older person who imagines "the young in one another's arms," more beautifully than the young could have experienced it. (The image is from William Butler Yeats's "Sailing to Byzantium," which opens with the well-known line, "This is no country for old men," and proceeds to describe that country in sensual terms.) In many cases it is the artist as an old man who, believing that he has passed the time for passion, at last feels its meaning (Edel, 1977).

Relations with Children

According to popular images, there is no room in the nuclear family for the older generation, relegating them to a lonely old age. In actuality, the old are neither isolated nor abandoned. The majority prefer to live independently, while actively participating in family life (Yankelovich, Skelly, & White, 1977). About one-third of all people over sixty-five live with children. These tend to move into the "empty nest" of their middle-aged children, creating a two-generation household (Troll, 1971). Other older people live within easy distance of their children—in the same apartment building, city block, or suburb. In one important investigation, it was discovered that approximately 84 percent of Americans over sixty-five lived less than an hour away from one of their children (Shanas et al., 1968). It appears that in the urban working class, nuclear families of several generations are established within a neighborhood. In the more mobile middle class, older couples sometimes find it necessary to move, in order to be near children and grandchildren.

Older people rely primarily upon their children in times of illness, and they receive an almost instantaneous response (Sussman, 1960; 1965). How-

Babysitting is just one type of aid that grandparents can provide for their children.

ever, they usually are not emotionally or financially dependent upon their children. The relationship is one in which they give as well as receive. Among the types of aid that older parents give their children are money, services such as baby-sitting or legal advice, and houshold services such as needlework and woodwork. One group of researchers concluded that "altogether, the proportion of old people who give help to their children tends to exceed the proportion who receive help from their children" (Riley, Riley, & Johnson, 1968). The amount of mutual aid does not seem to depend on how close the generations live, or how often they visit. Some sex-linked patterns do emerge: sons tend to receive money from their elderly parents, whereas daughters receive services (Sussman, 1960; 1965).

Relationships with Grandchildren

In old age, one's grandchildren are no longer toddlers or schoolchildren. They are adolescents, or older. A number of studies suggest that grandparenting in old age is not always as rewarding as it was earlier. As the grandchild becomes older, and perhaps less attentive, the grandparent experiences a kind of "reality shock" that leads to disenchantment (Troll, 1971). One study of older grandparents found that subjects did not feel particularly close to grandchildren, but were "glad to see them come and glad to see them go" (Cumming & Henry, 1961, quoted in Troll, 1971). In some families, of course, there is stronger involvement; for example, a grandmother announces that she "gets a kick out of" the free-wheeling life-style of her college-aged granddaughter; the two identify, sometimes to the dismay of the middle-aged mother between them.

Grandparents and adult grandchildren often acknowledge reciprocal attempts to influence one another. Moreover, they admit that their attempts are often successful—but only in certain areas (Troll, 1980). Interestingly, both groups realize that there are some areas in which influence should be avoided. Hagestad (1978) uses the term *demilitarized zone* in reference to these sensitive areas—sexuality and religion, for example. She suggests that family members, including those from different generations, go to great lengths to avoid interpersonal conflict. By not attempting to influence one another within these sensitive areas—which obviously will vary from one family to another—grandparents and adult grandchildren avoid disrupting the stability of familial relationships.

Relationships with Siblings

Between 75 and 80 percent of people in late adulthood have living brothers and sisters (Shanas et al., 1968). Even very old people are likely to have a surviving sibling. Cicirelli (1979) found that in his sample of midwestern older adults, those over eighty years of age still had, on the average, one living sibling. Furthermore, contact with brothers and sisters is relatively frequent among the aged, although it obviously depends on the distance between residences.

Relationships with siblings play a very important role in the life of the aging adult, particularly for those individuals who have lost a spouse, are divorced, or who never married (Shanas, 1979). Siblings often provide the support and help that normally would come from a spouse. They act as "confidants"; share family occasions, holidays, and recreational activities; aid in decision-making, homemaking, and home repairs; boost morale; lend money in times of financial need; and provide nursing care and emotional support in times of illness. It is understandable, therefore, that the majority of older people feel "close" or "extremely close" to at least one of their siblings (Cicirelli, 1979; 1980).

Research suggests that the influence of siblings on older adults differs depending upon the sex of the sibling and the sex of the individual (Cicirelli, 1977, 1979). Generally, female siblings exert a greater influence on both aged men and women. They are more effective in preserving family relationships and providing emotional support. Furthermore, the presence of sisters tends to reduce the threat of aging for the older man; that is, older men seem happier and less affected by economic and social insecurities when they have living sisters. For aged women, the presence of sisters results in greater concern about social skills, social relationships outside of the family, and community activity. In other words, sisters stimulate each other and tend to facilitate a more stimulating and challenging environment for the older woman.

Singlehood

Older people who have never married are in the special situation of having neither their own children nor grandchildren toward whom to extend themselves. Their adjustment to old age has been of interest not only to psychologists but to every happy single who has heard the threatening question "But

Grandparents sometimes identify with the free-wheeling lifestyles of their college-age grandchildren.

what will you have when you are old and sick?'' At least one study suggests that elderly single people, as lifelong isolates, do not find old age especially lonely (Gubrium, 1975). Indeed, they bristle at the very question of loneliness (''I'm never lonely now, I wasn't lonely when I was forty-five. I think it's rather foolish to answer that . . .'') Single older people appear to feel less lonely than

A close relationship between older siblings is maintained by the provision of support and help that would normally come from a spouse.

those who are unhappily married or widowed. Whether that is because they are lifelong isolates, or simply because they have learned to make use of other emotional resources, probably depends upon the individual. The single older person does tend to maintain closer relationships with siblings than do those who marry and have families (Shanas et al., 1968). Sister-sister ties are usually strongest.

Widowhood

Widowhood represents the greatest emotional and social loss suffered by individuals in the normal course of the life span. (Other major losses, such as the death of a parent in childhood, or the death of a child, represent what we, in a more fortunate time, have come to see as unnatural events.) Between the ages of sixty-five and seventy-four, 41.1 percent of women are widowed; over seventy-five years of age, the figure rises to 69.7 percent. In contrast, the corresponding percentages for men are 9.3 and 24.3, respectively (U.S. Bureau of the Census, 1978). The sex difference in widowhood represents a higher mortality rate for men than women, and the fact that older men are much more likely to remarry following the death of their spouse than are older women. In fact, Treas and Van Hilst (1976) report that among whites there are six times more men than women over sixty-five years who remarry following the death of the spouse.

Widowhood is, first, an experience to be lived through and, secondly, a social status to be lived with. The death of the spouse is an emotional emergency; only later is the bereaved person in a position to adjust, so far as is possible, to a new status and life-style.

In the first stages of grief, the widow may suffer from such physical symptoms associated with grief as loss of appetite and sleep. If the widow has an age-related health problem, such as hypertension, it not infrequently leads to more serious developments such as coronary heart disease. Panic, guilt, depression, and contemplation of one's own death are common psychological reactions. Marital bereavement is first on a list of stressful life events associated with physical and psychological illness. The widowed often die sooner; that is, there is an increased mortality risk for the surviving spouse (Berardo, 1968).

Still, many widows outlive their husbands for what amounts to one or more generations. In the second stage of adjustment, the widow must establish a new relationship with society. According to Lopata, who has studied this stage of the family cycle in depth, the widow has several options (Lopata, 1973). For one, she can return to the medium or high levels of activity she enjoyed before being widowed. This may be difficult if her activities had depended on the presence of a spouse, as is often the case for middle-class, educated women. Or, she can choose to enter a new role and develop new friends (including widows like herself). Or, she can retreat into isolation. Lopata suggests that the first two solutions, or some combination, are ideal from the widow's standpoint.

A more immediate and practical problem for the widow is where she will live (most often expressed in the question "What will you do now?") The widow can live alone, adopt some form of congregate living, live with one of her married children, or remarry (Lopata, 1971). About one-half of Lopata's sample of 301 Chicago women lived alone, primarily because they wanted to be free and independent. Those who lived with relatives or took in roomers were more often than not the head of the household. Only 10 percent lived with married children. Despite the stereotype, this last is not the preferred solution. One widow explained, "I couldn't be as independent as I am living with my children. I've become very independent since I'm a widow and wouldn't give that up for anything. If you lived with one of your kids you'd be subject to their wills and whims. No sir, that's not for me." Widowers, who always relied on their wives for domestic service and social contacts, may find it more difficult to adopt this attitude.

While many widows enjoy living alone, they nevertheless mention loneliness as their most serious problem. The pleasure of having someone near—someone to whom she comes first in life—is greatly missed; chances for intimacy are significantly reduced. In fact, the literature on the psychological adjustment of widows generally suggests that loss of spouse results in depression and low morale (Atchley, 1975; Shanas et al., 1968). A recent study by Morgan (1976), however, challenges this view. Morgan found that it was not widowhood per se that caused low morale, but rather some of the changes in life-style and social standing that accompanied the situation. Specifically, reduced income, a decrease in social standing, loss of health, and a loss of self-image (for those who closely identified with their spouse) were more important in determining the adjustment of the widowed person than was the state of widowhood itself. Other research suggests that having an intimate friend or confidant buffers the person against the enormous social loss resulting from the death of a spouse, and it also serves to reduce depression and raise general morale (Lowenthal & Haven, 1968).

Institutionalization

Some older people who are unable to live in family or home environments, are placed (or place themselves) in institutions variously referred to as nursing homes, geriatric hospitals, hospitals for the chronically ill, and old-age homes.

❖❖

Senior Power

Senior power takes its name from the activist special-interest groups that emerged in the late 1960s and 70s: blacks organized black power groups to combat racism; women joined hands to fight sexism, and gay power groups protested homophobia. The elderly have massed together in such groups as the National Council of Senior Citizens (3.5 million members), which lobbies aggressively in Washington for their rights. The Gray Panthers are a smaller activist organization. Their leader, Margaret Kuhn, who is in her mid-seventies, says that old people should be proud of such marks of age as gray hair and wrinkles (Harris, 1974).

Senior Power is most often directed at economic reform. Eleven million elderly Americans live on yearly incomes that are lower than the government's standards for the cost of living of an older person. Consequently, seniors are demanding tax breaks and increased Social Security, welfare, and medical benefits. The abolition of retirement at age sixty-five is also being advocated.

Old people should be able to work and earn for as long as they wish or can. Discrimination against the elderly in hiring and at promotion time must cease, say those who speak for the movement.

Seniors also want to be treated with more respect and dignity. Tired of being considered wards of society, they demand patient rights for those in nursing homes, tenant rights for those in housing projects, and a greater say in federal projects designed to help the elderly. They want government benefits to be paid directly to individuals, not to middlemen. Older people wishing to live alone or with their children could then do so, rather than being forced into federally funded housing projects.

Seniors, it should be noted, vote in record numbers, whether they are activists or not. As time goes on, politicians will have to pay greater attention to the political demands of senior citizens because of the changing age composition of the population. Not only will a larger percentage of the population fall into the category of aged—and aged people who vote—but they will be a better-educated group. Better-educated voters tend to understand their own interests and tend to vote their own interests. The future aged will be a more homogeneous group, socialized by the mass media and not divided by the language barriers that jeopardize the many immigrant aged today. Since younger people at present show no particular loyalty to either of the two major political parties, when they become senior citizens they are more likely to be catered to by politicians running for office. Age segregation in retirement communities, too, can have an impact, especially at the local level where old people can rally to defeat proposals that do not benefit them. Thus, as the population ages, older people can expect to wield a greater political influence (Peterson, Powell, & Robertson, 1976).

The institutionalized older person receives a great deal of media attention, with the result that many people believe that institutionalization is quite widespread. As we have seen, the majority of older people live independently, an hour or less away from one of their children. Only about 5 percent live in nursing homes (Townsend, 1971). If we include other forms of institutions, however, such as psychiatric or extended-care medical facilities, perhaps as

Economic reform is just one target of senior citizens' activist organizations.

many as 20 percent of the elderly are at some point institutionalized (Kastenbaum & Candy, 1973).

The reasons for entering nursing homes and other long-term care facilities are varied. Some older people enter voluntarily. A debilitating condition may make it impossible for some people to maintain themselves at home. They may be unwilling to become dependent on children, seeking, instead, the impersonal comfort of institutionalized care. Some older people assert their independence by deciding to enter an institution before they become unable to care for themselves (and even to select the institution). Married couples occasionally close up their own home and admit themselves to the facility together—if they can afford it.

In many other cases, institutionalization seems not to be a decision, but an involuntary action on everyone's part. The middle-aged son or daughter say they have no choice. For example, they may be unable, financially or physically, to care for the chronically ill parent within their homes. Even if resources exist, they may feel unable to accommodate the parent without destroying their own family relationships (including, perhaps, the relationship with the ailing parent). No matter the justification, the son or daughter often feels guilty. *Don't Give Up on an Aging Parent* admonishes the title of a popular book (Galton, 1975). To "give up" is to institutionalize or "put away."

The assumption underlying these feelings is that all institutions for the elderly are unpleasant and dehumanizing places. They are often described as places where one goes to die (a seeming judgment as well as a fact), and yet the institutions are so varied that it is difficult to make generalizations. They range from small convalescent homes run by religious orders to large proprietary nursing homes run by operators with "tender loving greed" (Mendelson, 1974). Some facilities resemble country clubs, others resemble prisons. Some serve the well-to-do patient (for $2,000–$3,000 a month), whereas others are the equivalent of the old-fashioned poorhouse. Indirectly, through Medicare, the government pays for (or toward) the hospitalization of most older people—without exercising too much control over services provided.

Because most older people do not reside in nursing homes or other institutions, it has frequently been asked whether those individuals who do become institutionalized differ phsyically, socially, or psychologically from those who do not. In one of the most comprehensive studies on this question, Tobin and Lieberman (1976) found that, surprisingly, there was little difference between the two groups. Nursing-home residents were neither more dependent in personality nor more lacking in a confidant than were same-age residents of the community. Furthermore, both groups seemed to be characterized by the same kind of physical, social, and economic losses. The researchers found that institutionalization was most likely to occur when the person's physical condition showed evidence of increased deterioration, and there was a lack of adequate care facilities (or the inability or unwillingness to provide it) within the family or the community.

Life in the nursing home or extended-care hospital presents a number of adjustment problems to the older person. In our society people are simply not socialized for communal living (as they are, for example, in societies that raise their children in graded children's homes or collectives). In the exploratory stages of youth, the college dorm or an army barracks provides some experience in communal life. However, young people in these settings seldom feel constrained to spend large blocks of time within. By contrast, older people are confined in the insitution—perhaps for the rest of their lives. After living in a family environment for some sixty years, they are confronted with roommates and floormates who are virtual strangers. Lack of privacy is often difficult to get used to. Furthermore, the staff, in many cases, consists of members of ethnic or minority groups with whom the older person has no experience, and whom he or she may therefore distrust.

Perhaps most important is the new identity that attaches to nursing-home residents. They are now patients. A woman is no longer a homemaker (a deprivation that affects some women very strongly). Only when a child visits does the old role of "mother" come into play, and then it's not the same; the institutionalized mother is no longer in a position to serve dinner or give advice. The only topics she is asked to talk about are her health and the institution. And if she complains too much or is too negative, there is always the possibility that the son or daughter will visit less often.

Some older people adapt well to institutionalization and communal life. If admission is voluntary; if the older person has had a part in planning it; if, in fact, it offers solutions to loneliness or other life problems, adjustment may be relatively smooth (Schulz & Brenner, 1977). "Occasionally," writes Simone de Beauvoir, "being put in an institution gives a person back his taste for life; he feels less cut off, he makes friends, and out of a kind of competition he neglects himself less than before" (de Beauvoir, 1972). Others have noted that the enterprising resident may learn to "work the system," and enjoy a special status with the staff. Some residents find opportunities to develop new friends, to court, and even to marry.

Generally, however, the effects are negative. Psychologists who administer cognitive tests to the elderly usually find lower performance among the institutionalized—not only because of physical disabilities that are common in this sample, but because of social losses incurred as a result of institutionalization. Rapid decline in health is often observed upon admisssion; mortality increases among first-year residents. As we have seen, the aged person is especially vulnerable in periods of stress. Lieberman (1961) suggests that it is entering the institution (rather than living in one) that dramatically upsets the equilibrium. Nurses have long known that even a change of rooms or roommate precipitates decline. Schulz and Brenner (1977) suggest that one way of reducing the stress of relocation is through preparatory programs—helping the older person adjust to the idea of institutionalization (or a change from one institution to another) before the relocation actually occurs. Such programs, Schulz and Brenner note, actually reduce postrelocation mortality rates.

In order to minimize some of the discontinuity experienced by the new resident, sympathetic directors of institutions for the elderly have tried to duplicate certain features of the home within the institution. For example, some people live with their spouses within the institution and are encouraged to look upon the staff as a kind of family. Some nursing homes have limited self-government. Recent fieldwork by Rodin and Langer (1977) describes staff interventions that produced beneficial effects by encouraging residents to make choices and accept responsibilities. The researchers observed an experimental group that had been induced to take responsibility for themselves, and a comparison group that had been assured that the staff was there to take responsibility for them. For example, the residents in the experimental group had been given plants to care for themselves, while those in the comparison group were given plants that were watered by the staff. Both groups were compared with a control group. The residents who were encouraged to take responsibility showed higher health and activity patterns, and mood and sociability, which did not decline as greatly as in other residents. In lectures, they were more likely to ask hard and meaningful questions about family problems and the approach of death. Most surprisingly, the experimental group also had lower mortality rates. This suggests that increased choice and responsibility for daily living can slow down or reverse some negative effects of institutionalization.

RETIREMENT

Retirement age is often described as an "artifact" of the Social Security system. As many psychologists, physicians, and social planners have noted, chronological age is a poor indication of one's ability or desire to work. Adopting sixty-five or seventy as a normal retirement age is a device to allow employers to dispense with older workers, and younger workers to enter and advance in the job hierarchies. Most supervisors, when questioned, say that they would prefer a variable retirement age, to account for individual differences in ability and health.

Reasons for retiring vary from individual to individual. Those who choose to retire do so because of adequate financial resources, good pension plans, desire to spend more time with family, or dislike for the job. Involuntary retirement, however, usually results from the mandatory retirement policy of the company or from poor health. In a recent study, Louis Harris and Associates (1975) found that 58 percent of men and 66 percent of women retire voluntarily. People from lower socioeconomic groups, however, are less likely to retire by choice than are people from middle- and high-income groups, primarily because the former are less financially secure.

Not all workers retire, or retire completely. Self-employed people—artists, professional scholars, independent craftsmen, and contractors—are not affected by mandatory retirement. But of those who do retire, an important life adjustment is required. Due to the centrality of work in our culture, retirement represents a loss of an important social role and with daily contact with others at the work place. Retirement affects people in much the same way as other major losses. Like widowhood, retirement is statistically associated with increased mortality in the first year. Retirement can also be seen within the context of the disengagement theory. When someone retires, he or she may withdraw from other social activities—from community events or social outings with associates. Even if they lose only their work-related contacts, social interactions are reduced.

A second career after retirement is often an outlet for one's skills and interests in old age.

Still, except for those who are involuntarily retired, retirement does not seem to be associated with low morale in most cases. Nor does it lead to psychological impairment or mental illness (Lowenthal & Haven, 1968). Retirement, like the empty nest and other age-related periods of change and uncertainty, may seem most unpleasant to those who have not experienced it, or are not about to. One study suggests that middle-aged men view retirement more negatively than do men who are about to retire (Lowenthal, Thurnher, & Chiriboga, 1975). Similarly, it has been shown that the most devastating period of marriage for husbands is the period when they are anticipating retirement (Rollins & Feldman, 1970). The effect of the wife's retirement in a dual-career family has received little attention, perhaps because the dual-career pattern was not so common in the generations that have reached retirement in recent years. One study, however, seems to indicate that women who retire from jobs and careers have as many problems adjusting to retirement as do men (Fox, 1977). Yet regardless of these problems, it is interesting that the retirement period is generally associated with high marital satisfaction for both partners (Rollins & Feldman, 1970).

A number of factors influence people's attitudes toward retirement. First is the amount of choice they can exercise in the matter. This varies with the occupation. People who are self-employed, such as a novelist, carpenter, or physician, have the option of working well beyond normal retirement age. A schoolteacher can choose to retire after twenty or twenty-five years—with different benefit schedules. Members of trade unions may be able to take advantage of a "flexible retirement" clause that allows them to work past normal retirement; or provides an early retirement option that allows full benefits after only thirty years. Other workers have no choice but to accept the gold watch at the specified moment. Interacting with this, of course, is job satisfaction. Unskilled workers (who show less job satisfaction) are likely to opt for early retirement within a corporation that provides this option. More satisfied workers choose retirement at sixty-five or, if possible, later. Who, then, is discontented? As common sense and popular literature would have it, the person for whom adjustment is most difficult is the one who enjoys his work but finds his career, after forty years of competence, "brought to end by unpleasant compulsions." This person is thwarted in his lifelong desire "to go out with his job boots on" (Olmstead, 1975).

Adjustment is also difficult for those who do not have adequate savings or retirement income (Atchley, 1975). It is often said that the majority of older Americans have inadequate income. Although such judgments are necessarily subjective, it does appear that many retired people find, in an inflationary period, that their "nest eggs" and fixed retirement incomes amount to much less than they had foreseen. Postretirement poverty is experienced differently by different retirees. For the person who has always been poor, it is just "one more economic insult." For the majority of retirees it represents a relative deprivation and a discontinuity with the working years (Maddox, 1968). Especially for the latter group, reduced resources represent a difficult adjustment, perhaps a scrapping of retirement plans for travel and other recreations. For retired people generally, a high level of morale may be possible only if their economic status compares favorably with that of working adults (Bromley, 1974).

Perhaps most important to retired people is the question of what they are going to do with their time. Their options seem to include leisure, hobbies or recreation, part-time employment, voluntary service, socializing, or doing nothing (which might mean anything from watching television to contemplating the meaning of life). Though doing nothing might be a reasonable choice after a lifetime of labor—and there are societies that have recognized the older person's privilege to sit and think—this is not thought to be an admirable choice in our culture. Leisure, too, has a bad name in some quarters. For example, gerontologist Alex Comfort advises that leisure is "a con.... What the retired need ... isn't leisure, it's occupation.... Get occupation first. Leisure in the right sense will follow if you have time for it" (Comfort, 1976). This is clearly a cultural attitude rather than a fact, but it appears to have some validity for people in our work-oriented culture. A study of employed people over sixty-five showed that they enjoy their leisure more—with greater intensity and over more activities—than those who have retired and are idle (cited in Puner, 1974).

A study by Harris and Associates (1975) suggests that the most frequent activity engaged in by older people is socializing with friends—47 percent of the aged reported that they spend "a lot of time" in this activity. Other popular activities included gardening and raising plants (39 percent), watching television (36 percent), reading (36 percent), and sitting and thinking (31 percent).

The older person, as well as the middle-aged, is increasingly encouraged to think in terms of a second career. Recognizing that this need not be a career in the traditional sense, Comfort (1976) refers to a "second trajectory" or path. This might involve a new work role, artistic pursuit, voluntary service, neighborhood activism—all the things the individual might have wanted to accomplish earlier, had there been time. Selecting the second trajectory means foreseeing, when young or middle-aged, an outlet for one's skills and interests in old age. Some older people find outlets in part-time work in their own or related fields. For example, a retired teacher may do occasional substitute work or get elected to the school board. A retired dentist may participate in a health education program in the inner city. Some older people develop new roles in voluntary services. There is ample opportunity. Among the many governmental agencies known to value the work of older people are Veterans' Administration Volunteers Service, Foster Grandparents, Small Business Administration, Vista, and Peace Corps (Arthur, 1969). Opportunity for general community service differs, of course, with the community. Some cities have agencies that place older people in other city agencies, matching skills and interests to requirements. Even small towns and rural areas have community self-help programs that depend upon the volunteer efforts of retired residents. Educational opportunities, too, are expanding for the older student, in part as a result of the Adult Education Act of 1972. In exploring these options, today's older person breaks new territory. Never before has a generation seen so many years and so many possibilities at the end of their working life.

THE TERMINAL STAGE

As a continuous series of stages, life includes not only growth and expansion, but aging and death as well. It is only recently, however, that investigators have begun to study the *terminal stage* of life. One researcher, for example, defines the terminal stage as a persistent awareness of the prospect of death from natural causes in later life. The terminal stage might begin when a man develops a chronic illness, such as cancer. Or it might begin when he becomes aware that he has not too much longer to live, and when his behavior is shaped by this realization (Bromley, 1974). A woman who has reached the age of ninety-five, or who finds herself severely weakened and bedridden, might come to this awareness.

For the most part, our socialization processes brush over the final years of life; they emphasize personal growth and achievement, especially during the early and middle years. As a result, many people who reach the stage of advanced age are ill-prepared for living within its limits—living with the certainty that death is not far off. For these people, old age is the period during which they first awaken to intimations of mortality (Kastenbaum, 1969). However, many others develop from their early years a broader perspective on life—one that enables them to be conscious of passing time and the prospect of death. As old people, they are usually able to make a satisfactory adjustment to their later years. Some people step up their participation in life, striving to wring satisfaction from every moment remaining to them.

What exactly does it mean to be old and to face death? What happens to individuals—psychologically, intellectually, and socially—as they enter the terminal stage of life? How does the setting in which they live out their final days affect their state of mind and behavior? These questions have been the subject of recent research. The answers may shed some light not only on the terminal stage, but on all of human life.

Psychological Changes

In the terminal stage of life, the older person may undergo psychological changes; these can be observed and measured as early as four or five years before death. Lieberman (1965), for example, studied twenty-five male and female nursing-home residents who ranged in age from seventy to eighty-nine. Tests were administered to each subject to evaluate various aspects of their ego functioning and emotional states. One test involved copying figures such as patterns of small circles and dots; another called for the subjects to copy a human figure freehand; and a third involved describing line drawings of the human figure in terms of the feelings which the action states of the drawings evoked.

Results over a number of trials showed that those patients who were near death had increasing difficulty in organizing and integrating the stimuli in their environment. Moreover, their energy levels appeared to decrease. Lieberman concludes from these results that systematic psychological changes occur in older people prior to death. He believes that aged people approaching

Double Jeopardy: To Be Old and a Minority Group Member

Although almost everyone in the United States belongs to one or another ethnic group with a unique cultural heritage, members of minority groups based on racial differences share economic and psychological disadvantages because of discrimination. Minority group members are considered to be a population in jeopardy because discrimination and prejudice have affected their ability to make a decent place for themselves in society. Since the aged are also a population in jeopardy, aged minority members are said to be in double jeopardy. An old woman who belonged to a minority group would be in triple jeopardy.

To lump all minority members regardless of race or national origin into one group who are thought to share the common experience of age, however, would be a distortion. In each group different cultural attitudes mitigate the experience of the aged. Unfortunately, compared to the white majority, there is much less known about the old in minority groups. They are less visible, more reluctant to talk to researchers, and have had few advocates in the social sciences outside of their own group members. Nonetheless, in our society an aged member of a minority group accumulates a different experience over the life span than does an aged white person. And although all minority groups share the common experience of a lower standard of living than the rest of society, there are marked differences among the groups.

Aged Black Americans. There are over 25 million black Americans, constituting 11 percent of the population. Less than 7 percent of blacks are 65 years and older, compared to more than 10 percent of whites. The life expectancy for black men in 1976 was 66.5 years as compared to 69.7 for white men; black women had a life expectancy in 1976 of 72.6 compared to 77.3 for white women. As white life expectancies creep up to what seems to be the limits of human life, black life expectancy rates are catching up, reflecting a gain in the standard of living affecting both blacks and whites.

The health of the black aged is poorer than that of whites. They have higher rates of hypertension, dental problems, and diabetes than whites. But they do have better vision and better hearing. Aged blacks have less money to pay for medical services and are in double jeopardy in regard to the medical professions, first because of age and second because of race (Dancy, 1977).

A much higher percentage of aged blacks live in poverty: 36 percent of older blacks compared to 12 percent of aged whites. From ages 45 to 75 there is a 55 percent decline in income compared to a 36 percent decline for whites. Black women are especially disadvantaged economically.

The principal strength of the black aged is the strong kinship bonds that exist into old age. Aged blacks have a important role to play in child care. Most older black families have children in them—either grandchildren or the children of other relatives. Elderly blacks are more likely to continue working than their white counterparts, enabling them to maintain their status as full-fledged contributing members of society. Aged blacks also have a lower suicide rate than whites, possibly reflecting a less drastic change in life-style in old age than that of many whites.

Aged Mexican-Americans. Mexican-Americans are the second largest minority group in the United States after blacks. Only about 4 percent are 65 and over, reflecting the large proportion of children and adolescents in this group and a very low life expectancy. Mexican-Americans generally show the effects of age earlier because of inadequate diet, overcrowded housing, and poor medical care. Like blacks, a little over one-third of aged Mexican-Americans live in poverty. Most have had little schooling and only 8 percent of the aged both read and write English.

Research is contradictory concerning the support aged Mexican-Americans receive from their families. One researcher found that the traditional extended family in which old people are regarded with love and respect is still intact (Carp, 1970). Relationships between grandparents and grandchildren were seen as very close (Carp, 1968). The marriages of aged Mexican-Americans tend to remain intact (if both members are alive) to a greater extent than those of whites and these old people are less likely to be living alone. Men and women have about the same life expectancies, as opposed to the other groups, and have more adult children to look after them. On the other hand, other researchers have found this pattern to be changing. Aged Mexican-Americans did not expect their children to take care of them and did not find old age a desirable state (Crouch, 1972).

Native Americans. To a greater extent than any other group in the United States, Native Americans live a life out of the mainstream because so many live on reservations. Native Americans are the poorest of all the minority groups. Their life expectancy is only about 45 to 50 years (National Tribal Chairman's Association, 1976); they suffer from inadequate medical care, lack of sanitary facilities, poor nutrition, and overcrowded and inadequate housing. Aged Native Americans are more likely than whites to have tuberculosis, gastritis, cirrhosis of the liver, influenza, pneumonia, and diabetes.

Most aged Native Americans live on reservations and are unable to avail themselves of any of the services, such as Meals on Wheels, available to other older people. Furthermore, there are no jobs for the aged on reservations. However, older Indians appear not to experience psychological stress as they grow older. They seem to accept a more passive relationship with the world (Goldstine & Gutmann, 1972).

Some generalization can be made about the aged in minority groups. They are poorer, do not live as long, are not as healthy. Although they seem more isolated from American society than the aged majority members, they appear to enjoy a higher status in their own communities and especially in their own families (Crandall, 1980).

death probably experience a kind of psychological upheaval not because of the fear of death, but because of a disorganization of the mental processes as death approaches. People who withdraw from life in the later years may be building a kind of protective shell around themselves as they "attempt to hold themselves together—to reduce the experience of chaos" (Lieberman, 1965).

Impending death may influence intellectual performance. For example, Riegel and Riegel (1972) conducted a ten-year study of old people in Germany. The subjects were 190 males and 190 females who ranged in age from fifty-five to seventy-five years. The investigators administered a battery of tests to the subjects, including an intelligence test, a word-association test, tests to assess verbal achievement, and a number of attitude and interest tests.

Many people in the terminal stage of life are left with an overwhelming sense of loneliness and their own impending death as spouses and peers die.

Findings showed that subjects whose performance on intelligence tests was below average were closer to death than their more successful peers—indicating a *terminal drop* in intellectual functioning. The Riegels analyzed the subjects' scores by going backward in age, starting with the time of death. They concluded that the decline in performance on intelligence tests was due to a sudden drop in ability that occurred within five years before death. These findings appear to dovetail with Lieberman's conclusion that old people near death experience a systematic disintegration. However, these findings remain somewhat controversial.

As people near death they also seem to engage in a process called *life review*. They organize their memories and reinterpret the actions and decisions that have shaped the course of their life. Ideally, the life review is a positive experience resulting in further integration of the personality in the face of death. For some, the life review leads to less ego involvement with one's own situation and to more concern with the world in general. For others, it produces nostalgia and perhaps a touch of regret. In still others, it engenders anxiety, guilt, and depression: instead of reflecting on a full life, the person feels cheated and enraged. In a small number of cases, the person taking stock of his life may be thrown into a state of panic that may result in suicide (Butler, 1971).

As the literature on life review suggests, the response of older people to the terminal stage is influenced by the sense of the life they have lived. Few valid generalizations can be made. To be sure, the terminal stage is marked by a number of identifiable themes—a general decline in physical, psychological, and intellectual functions and a growing sense of isolation and loneliness. But as Kastenbaum has observed, these phenomena are not handled in the same way by all older people: "... different people selected different ways of living in the valley of the shadow" (Kastenbaum, 1977).

Social Losses

For many older people the terminal stage is characterized by loneliness. Spouses and age peers die, one by one, leaving the survivor bereft and depressed. Often an older person does not have time to get over the passing of one loved one before another dies. This is particularly true for women, who tend to outlive men. When death takes one's spouse, the survivor is left to manage as well as possible and often to think about his or her own impending death. As Kastenbaum (1977) notes, "Somewhat apart from the prospect of one's own death, then, the falling away of significant others is a powerful influence upon the thoughts, feelings, and actions of old people." Understandably, the death of a spouse or close age peer makes the old person feel even lonelier.

The family often tend to ignore older people when they begin talking about impending death—a topic that quite naturally is uppermost in their minds. "Shh. Don't talk about it," the family may say, ignoring the fact that the dying person has a deep need to discuss the situation with someone. Indeed, at times, hospital attendants are the only audience the old person can find.

Terminal Hospitalization

It used to be that aged people died in their own home, surrounded by family and loved ones. This situation not only relieved their loneliness, but also made them aware that they were the living center of concern. Today, however, fewer older people die at home. Lesnoff-Caravaglia (1978–1979) found that currently only 15 percent of the aged die at home. In contrast, 54 percent die in hospitals, 30 percent in extended care facilities, and 19 percent in nursing homes. Moreover, as we have already noted, relocation of the elderly from their homes to nursing homes or hospitals is a very stressful event, associated with increased mortality. Wershaw (1976) found that 3 percent of those admitted to nursing homes died within twenty-four hours; 44 percent died within thirty days of admission.

More and more health-care professionals are becoming aware that large hospitals and extended care facilities are often dehumanizing places in which to spend one's last moments. The professional staff is usually busy taking care of administrative matters and the medical aspects of keeping patients alive. In such surroundings, the dying patient typically feels burdensome and isolated.

One solution to this problem has been to hire paraprofessional health workers who periodically visit and care for chronically ill older people in their homes. The organization known as Cancer Care, for instance, tries to manage the illness within the context of family. But even this arrangement is not without its difficulties. For one thing, the old person must depend on a total stranger for his or her most intimate needs. For another, the patient and the health worker are often from different socioeconomic backgrounds, a situation which engenders misunderstandings and conflicts. One of the newest and most promising solutions to caring for the terminal patient in a more human environment is the *hospice*, a homelike hospital that specializes in care of the dying.

Attitudes About Death

It is often assumed that the elderly, as a group, live in special fear of death. This would make sense since the probability of death is greater for these people than for any other age group. Crandall (1980) lists seven reasons why people fear death and dying: They are:

1. The fear of what happens after death.
2. The fear of a painful death.
3. The fear that dying will drain the family's finances.
4. The fear of what will happen to one's family after death.
5. The fear of the indignities associated with dying.
6. The fear that no one will really care or will remember you after death.
7. The fear that dying will strip away one's defenses and facades, leaving one's "real self" exposed.

Crandall notes that it is natural for people to fear death—it is the "great unknown." But do the elderly actually fear death more than younger people? Research evidence suggests that they do not. In fact, a classic study by Munnichs (1966) found that the most common orientations in individuals seventy and older were acceptance or acquiescence. A more recent study suggests that elderly subjects were less preoccupied with death fears than middle-aged subjects (Bengston et al., 1977). Similarly, Hinton (1967) reported that young terminal patients were more anxious about their illness than were older patients. Munnichs suggests that excessive fear or denial of death in older people represents a general failure to come to terms with their own limitations, which, in turn, may be an indication of psychological immaturity. Fear of death is also associated with lack of ego integrity (Erikson, 1963). On the other hand, a relative lack of fear of death is associated with people's having experienced "purpose in life" (Durlak, 1973), and having achieved integrity.

Although older people in general anticipate death, they do not necessarily live "in the shadow." Perhaps, like the jet passenger moving westward, they live with a movable sunset. Probably they look at death as a younger person looks at aging, as something that inevitably happens, but which cannot be expected to happen at any particular time. In old age, if ever, death is perceived as a natural process. Perhaps for this reason, some older people

❖❖❖

Hospices

Contact with the dying has long inspired the living with fear and revulsion. Primitive tribesmen often abandoned the aged and sick in the wilderness to die alone. Death was regarded as a threat to human society, and contact with the dying was considered polluting and mystically dangerous. Today, terminally ill patients are often isolated in sterile hospital wards and left to face the final end alone, without the loving companionship of friends and family. Even adequate protection against pain is sometimes denied. Modern hospitals, geared to aggressive life-prolonging therapies, are simply not good places to die. But there is a quiet revolution going on toward more humane treatment of the dying—the hospice movement.

Originally hospices were resting places for travelers, the young, and the needy, maintained by religious orders during the Middle Ages. Today, hospices are homes for the care of the dying, specifically those who are incurably ill with diseases such as cancer.

The modern hospice concept is the work of Britain's Dr. Cicely Saunders. The idea was born out of her friendship with a Polish refugee who was dying of cancer in the noisy confusion of a busy London hospital. In 1967, Saunders founded St. Christopher's Hospice in southeast London for those afflicted with terminal cancer. St. Christopher's provides a pain-free, emotionally secure environment for the dying. The atmosphere is warm and friendly, with plenty of sunlight and fresh flowers. Patients may bring in cherished possessions—one woman brought her antique collection! Visiting hours extend from 8 A.M. to 8 P.M., and family and friends help with patients' care—holding hands, giving sponge baths, bringing special foods from home. Sophisticated use of analgesics keeps patients relatively pain-free. Saunders pioneered the use of the "Brompton mix," containing such ingredients as heroin, cocaine, and gin, for the alleviation of terminal cancer pain. Patients may go home to die if feasible.

Hospice, Inc., in New Haven, Connecticut, is at present the only operating hospice in the United States. At Hospice, Inc., great stress is laid on the creation of a harmonious atmosphere for the dying through the use of architectural design. Patients are housed in communal wards rather than isolated cells, and exposure to natural light through extensive use of skylights and picture windows keeps patients aware of the rhythms of nature.

Some doctors say that there is only a limited need for facilities designed to care for the dying, since many hospital patients could die at home—providing they have one—given adequate education, emotional support, and technical aid.

Whatever the future of the hospice, it should lead to a more humane attitude toward the dying—as in the case of the woman who died tranquilly in a Montreal hospice while her two teen-age daughters softly played guitars and sang to her (Holden, 1976).

---

express the belief that death may be merely the ending of one phase of existence and the beginning of another. For example, Eleanor Roosevelt, reflecting on her life (1949), wrote, "I believe that all you go through has some value, therefore there must be some *reason*. And there must be some going on" [after death].

Old age is also a time when people experience many forms of symbolic death. The loss of a spouse after forty or more years of marriage, and the loss of old friends, often leads the older person to say that part of his life has ended. Retirement is also experienced by some (but by no means all) as a kind of death. So is the social rejection which is routinely visited on the older person. "I might as well be dead" states the elderly individual, when he is so treated by relatives or caretakers. Some people in late adulthood show extreme withdrawal or deathlike apathy under conditions of institutionalization or bereavement. Others find, in a time of rapid social change, that they have seemingly passed into another world; the neighborhood has changed drastically, and no one is left who speaks their language or understands their values. In a sense, the world has died.

There are also numerous physical and psychological conditions that older people experience as partial deaths. Among these are sensory loss (blindness or deafness); weakness and immobility; and mental disorganizaton ("senility") that results in confusion of past, present, and future. In the terminal stage the aged patient may be heavily sedated by pain-killing medicines, and may thus be imagined to have entered a state of diminished life. Not uncommonly, many spend their last hours in the deathlike stage we call a coma.

The Dying Process

In some belief systems and personal ideologies, death is not a process, but a moment of extinction. In others it is likened to a journey, with the scenery specified; or a long, restful wait before a final judgment. Some cultures have seen death as the end of all experience, and others as the beginning of salvation.

We do not know today, any more than we knew yesterday, what death is, or what developmental significance it has for the individual. However, we do have the advantages of recent research in the medical, biological, and psychological sciences. These sciences, in studying life, have necessarily granted insights into the dying that is part of life.

One seemingly new viewpoint is that death is not a distinct moment in which the person changes from alive to dead. Rather, we have come to see death as a process, in part because of recent technological advances. Three separate types of death are differentiated (Schulz, 1978). *Clinical death* refers to the cessation of spontaneous respiration and heartbeat. In some cases artificial respiration will revive the patient. *Brain death* occurs when the individual is deprived of oxygen for four to six minutes or more. The cortex, that portion of the brain controlling voluntary actions, thought, and memory, dies first, followed by the midbrain, and finally the most primitive portion of the brain, the brainstem. Finally, *cellular death* involves the physical death of organ systems—the irreversible loss of organ functioning. This form of death—which occurs at different rates for different organs—is the last to occur.

The distinction between these forms of death is hardly trivial. Today people lapse into comas, showing no evidence of life in higher order brain areas, and yet their vital organs continue to live—they may even be able to breathe on their own. Are these people alive? The answer appears debatable.

At present, physicans use brain death as evidence for a final determination of death. Veatch (1976) notes that the various criteria include: unreceptivity and unresponsivity, no movements or breathing, no reflexes, and a flat electroencephalogram (EEG) reading that remains flat for twenty-four hours. As objective as these criteria may appear, the case of Karen Ann Quinlan illustrates how difficult and controversial they are to apply. This young woman, whose tragic story was widely described in the press and on television, was thought to be in an irreversible coma (and hence, medically dead) until the respirators controlling her breathing were turned off. The fact that she continued breathing on her own indicated to her doctors and the lawyers and judges involved in the case that technically she was still alive (and so she remains today).

Cases such as Karen Ann Quinlan, however, have prompted some medical researchers and practitioners to argue that the standard criteria of brain death are outmoded. Schulz (1978) notes that this argument assumes that cerebral death (death of the higher order brain centers) is sufficient to render a decision that the patient is medically dead. Under this condition, the person would be forever unconscious or in a coma, even though he may be able to breathe by himself (as Karen Ann Quinlan is capable of doing).

Clearly, the issues involved here are complex; and it is evident that no solution or answer has been uniformly accepted. Still, one outcome of the controversy has been to put aside the old views of death as an abrupt event. Instead, there is a growing belief in the gradual nature of death—in viewing death as a process that can be studied in developmental terms.

Stages of Dying

Of recent developmental work on dying, one theory has gained recognition, probably on account of its usefulness to those who work with dying patients and their families. This is the *stages theory of dying* formulated by Elisabeth Kübler-Ross. This theory does not propose to cover the dying process as it might develop over the life span; and it does not give much attention to physical aspects of dying. Essentially, it is a description of the way in which people who know they are going to die adjust to that knowledge (Kübler-Ross, 1969). Kübler-Ross's theory is also applicable to situations analogous to death. For example, the person who faces bereavement may progress through the stages of adjustment Kübler-Ross describes. So might the person who is told that she will lose her sight or hearing, her husband, or her political liberty.

In the first stage, *denial*, the person reacts to his serious illness (or loss) by saying, "No, it cannot be me." He may assert that the doctors are incompetent, the diagnosis mistaken. In extreme cases he may refuse treatment and persist in going about business as usual. Most patients who use denial extensively throughout their illness are people who have become accustomed to coping with difficult life situations in this way. (Indeed, the denial habit may contribute to the seriousness of his condition—as, for example, when a person refuses to seek medical attention at the onset of the illness.) Ordinarily the person relies on denial at the beginning of the illness, and perhaps at other moments when facing reality becomes temporarily impossible. For most patients, denial soon becomes difficult and other reactions begin to intrude.

The cry of the dying person at the next stage, *anger,* is "Why me?" The person facing the great loss feels anger, at fate, at God, at powers that be, at everyone who comes uncomprehendingly into his sphere. There is resentment of the healthy, particularly those who must care for him. The person is angry at others for perceiving him as dying or as good as dead. At this stage he is likely to alienate others, for no one can give an answer to the anger he feels at his shortened life span and lost chances.

In the next stage the person changes his attitude and attempts to *bargain* with his fate. For example, he may ask God for a certain amount of time in return for good behavior, stoicism, cooperation in treatment. He may promise a change of ways, even a dedication of his life to the church. He may announce himself ready to settle for a less threatening form of the same illness and begin to bargain with the doctor over his diagnosis. For example, if he submits gracefully to some procedures, might he be rewarded by not progressing to the next stage?

When the terminally ill patient can no longer deny his illness, when he is forced to undergo more surgery or hospitalization, when he begins to have more symptoms or becomes weaker and thinner, he cannot smile it off anymore. His numbness or stoicism, his anger and rage will soon be replaced with a sense of great loss. At this stage the person enters a deep *depression.* He is depressed because of the losses he is incurring, for example, loss of body tissue, loss of job, loss of life savings. And he is depressed about the loss which is to come. The patient is in the process of losing everything and everybody he loves. It is important that he be allowed to express his sorrow.

Finally, the dying person *accepts* death. The struggle is over and the person experiences "a final rest before the long journey." At this point, the person is tired and weak. He sleeps often. In some cases the approach of death feels appropriate or peaceful. The person may limit the number of people he will see, and withdraw his interest from matters of the world. Silence and constancy are appreciated. The person seems to detach himself so as to make death easier.

Not all terminal patients progress through the stages Kübler-Ross describes. For example, a person may die in the denial stage because he is psychologically unable to proceed beyond it or because the course of his illness does not grant him the necessary time to do so. Kübler-Ross notes that patients do not limit their responses at any one stage; a depressed patient may have recurring bursts of anger. She notes, too, that all patients in all stages persist in feeling *hope.* Even the most accepting, the most realistic patients left the possibility open for some cure.

As important as Kübler-Ross's work is, it is not without its critics. Schulz (1978) notes that many researchers have found it difficult to use her system. The stages are highly subjective and therefore difficult to identify in patients. Shneidman (1980) also reports that while he has observed evidence of isolation, envy, bargaining, depression, and acceptance in dying persons, he sees no reason to think of these behaviors and affect states as "stages." Moreover, he does not believe that everyone goes through these stages in the same order. Instead, Shneidman sees the dying person as expressing a constantly alternating display of affect and thought. Feelings of anguish, depression, hope, envy, bewilderment, anger, acceptance, denial, pain, and even yearning are all evident in the dying person—but their appearance, according to Shneidman, would seem to be less predictable than Kübler-Ross's theory suggests. Nevertheless, Shneidman and Kübler-Ross agree that the most important goal in working with dying people is to help them face "that inevitable path" with hope, love, dignity, and as little pain as possible.

❖❖❖

Sunset Walk in Thaw-Time in Vermont

When my son is an old man, and I have not,
For some fifty years, seen his face, and, if seeing it,
Would not even be able to guess what name it wore, what
Blessing should I ask for him?

That some time, in thaw-season, at dusk, standing
At woodside and staring
Red-westward, with the sound of moving water
In his ears, he
Should thus, in that future moment, bless,
Forward into that future's future,
An old man who, as he is mine, had once
Been his small son.

For what blessing may a man hope for but
An immortality in
The loving vigilance of death?

—Robert Penn Warren
(1905–   )

SUMMARY

▶ Many of the adjustments to aging lie within the contexts of family and work, such as the death of a spouse, retirement, and accommodating to a reduced income. Most research seems to indicate that the quality of married life in old age is good. The two factors that characterize the older marriage are the focus away from the children and retirement from work, leaving the couple with more time with each other.

▶ Poverty and illness place a strain on married life. However, people benefit in old age from being married. They live longer, and experience less mental illness and loneliness where there is a spouse to buffer them from the stresses of old age.

▶ Sexual activity is still important to old people. They enjoy sex but usually conduct their sex lives within marriage or marital-like relationships. A sex life, however, is not restricted to genital activity; sexuality can involve the imagination as well.

▶ Most older people are neither abandoned nor isolated. They live independently of their children and, often, nearby. Old people rely on their children in times of illness but give as well as receive. Relationships with grandchildren seem not as close as the grandchildren become adolescents and older. Often a "demilitarized zone" is observed in such relationships to preserve family harmony. Relationships with siblings, especially sisters, enhance old age.

▶ Widowhood represents the single greatest loss suffered by aging individuals. Of women over seventy-five years of age, 70 percent are widowed. Most prefer to maintain their independence despite the problem of loneliness. Some other problems are decreased income and a decrease in social status. A good friend helps.

▶ Only about 5 percent of older people live in nursing homes. About 20 percent will be institutionalized at one time or another in psychiatric or extended-care medical facilities. Usually the institutionalization of an elderly person is a last resort. Generally people enter an institution when their physical condition is increasingly deteriorating and there is no other care available.

▶ Most people have difficulty in adjusting to living in an institution. For some it offers a solution to loneliness, but most find the lack of privacy difficult. It is a stressful change and adjustment is best when an older person is prepared for it.

▶ Retirement cuts off income, social contacts, and social status. People who choose to retire and have planned for it financially have less difficulty in making the adjustment than those who are forced to retire and suffer a loss of income. Retirement is usually associated with high marital satisfaction. A second career or a new pursuit offers an outlet and possible income after retirement.

▶ The terminal stage of life is that time when an individual has a persistent awareness of the prospect of death. In our society people are ill prepared for death. During the terminal stage they have less energy and therefore they have a difficult time arranging the stimuli in their environment. People are likely to score poorly on intelligence tests within five years of their death. This sudden drop in performance is called terminal drop. During the terminal stage a person may engage in a life review, organizing and reinterpreting a lifetime of memories.

▶ Old people suffer many social losses as their contemporaries die, one after another. Only 15 percent of people today die in their homes. The rest die in hospitals, extended-care facilities, or nursing homes—3 percent within twenty-four hours of arrival at the institution.

▶ Although people fear death, the elderly do not seem to fear it more than the young. Old people experience symbolic deaths, such as the death of a spouse, the dying or changing of the neighborhood where they always lived, and blindness or deafness.

▶ We are realizing to a greater extent than ever before that there is no distinct moment of death. Clinical death refers to the moment the heart and breathing stop. Brain death occurs after the individual has been deprived of oxygen for four to six minutes. Cellular death occurs when the physical organs die—the last failure to take place.

▶ Kübler-Ross has identified five stages in the dying process: denial ("No, it cannot be me."), anger ("Why me?"), the bargaining period, a deep depression, and finally, acceptance. She notes that at all stages a dying person, even one who has accepted death, may have hope. Other researchers have not found the stages as clear-cut as has Kübler-Ross.

FURTHER READINGS

Aries, Philippe. *Western attitudes toward death: From the middle ages to the present.* Baltimore: Johns Hopkins, 1974.

In four essays, Aries traces the ways in which human beings face death, from the attitudes of the knights of chivalry in the *Chansons de Geste* to the present day. He finds that death has gradually changed from a public affair with friends and family, faced with resignation, to an emphasis on the importance of one's existence. Death is now "shameful and forbidden," and one dies in a hospital, relatively alone.

Atchley, R. C. *The social forces in later life* (3rd ed.). Belmont, Calif.: Wadsworth, 1980.

This introductory work examines social factors that influence the elderly, and presents social stereotypes and the effects they have on older adults.

Atchley, R. C. *The sociology of retirement.* Cambridge, Mass.: Schenkam, 1976.

This brief book covers the six stages of retirement which one normally experiences.

Becker, Ernest. *The denial of death.* New York: Free Press, 1973.

Ernest Becker won the Pulitzer Prize for General Nonfiction with this book, which examines the concept of death through a synthesis of philosophy and psychoanalytic thought.

Blyth, Ronald. *The view in winter: Reflections on old age.* New York: Penguin Books, 1980.

A collection of interviews with the older residents of a small, rural town in England. The people describe their views on life and how it feels to be old in this time and place. Blyth presents this material beautifully.

Butler, Robert N., and Lewis, Myrna I. *Sex after sixty.* New York: Harper & Row, 1976.

In this wise and compelling book, Butler and Lewis discuss the value of sex, romance, and love among the elderly. Impotence, emotional problems with sex, patterns of love-making, and remarriage are treated openly and honestly.

Kleemeier, Robert W. (Ed.). *Aging and leisure: A research perspective into the meaningful use of time.* New York: Oxford, 1961.

Time is the focus of this collection of essays. A cross-section of different cultures and age groups is represented. The chapters on retirement, family relations, the life cycle, rest homes, and social gerontology are of special interest.

Stoddard, Sandol. *The hospice movement: A better way of caring for the dying.* Briarcliff Manor, N.Y.: Stein and Day, 1978.

Hospices are places which have been set up to help terminally ill patients face death as much as possible without pain or fear. The techniques used involve medication and an environment of support. Stoddard provides a favorable overview of the hospice movement through case studies and the author's personal experience in St. Christopher's Hospice in London.

Observational Activities

Part Eight   Late Adulthood

Media Stereotyping of the Aged

The image of old age in our society is anything but positive. Among other things, older people are said to be lonely, fearful, sexless, rigid, self-centered, and "out-of-date." Research, however, suggests that most of these stereotypes do not accurately represent the majority of older adults. Why then do the stereotypes persist? Some people believe that the media play a major role in fostering the continuation of such stereotyping.

Observe a random selection of television shows during prime time over a two-week period. Focus on the roles and behaviors of older adults in these shows, as well as other people's behavior toward the elderly.

1. To what extent are the elderly portrayed as figures of authority?
2. Are most older adults on televison active and vigorous or are they portrayed as passive and unenergetic?
3. What role does sexuality play in the lives of older television characters?
4. Are the stereotypes attributed to the aged different for men and women? Different for individuals according to racial group or social class?
5. What are the attitudes of most younger adults toward the elderly in the majority of television shows? Do they perceive the elderly as competent and adaptable or as "senile" and unchangeable?

From your observations draw some conclusions concerning the role of television in perpetuating negative stereotypes about the elderly. Are any subgroups of older adults more likely to be stereotyped than others?

Life Review

As people enter the later years of life they usually engage in a process called life review. This involves organizing one's memories and reflecting on the significant actions and developmental milestones that have shaped one's life. It is through the life review that people attempt to gain a final understanding of themselves and the world around them.

Choose an older adult for an in-depth life review interview. Ask the person the following questions.

1. Who were the most important persons that contributed to your development, both as a child and as an adult? In what ways were they important to you?
2. What events or developmental milestones were particularly significant in your life? Why?
3. How has aging affected you—physically, psychologically, socially?
4. How do you feel about your life? Has it been satisfactory? In what areas have you been most satisfied? Least satisfied?
5. How often do you think about your eventual death? What thoughts go through your mind when you think about death?

From your interview, summarize this person's perception about his or her life. Are the significant events and developmental milestones that shaped the person's life the same as those described in the text? How would you evaluate the person's attitude toward life?

Glossary

Accommodation   In Piaget's theory of cognitive development, a person's modification of an action or idea to improve the way it meets the environment.

Accommodation of the lens   The adjustment of lens curvature to focus light rays sharply on the retina of the eye.

Activity theory   The belief of some researchers that maintaining an earlier level of activity results in successful aging; the opposite of disengagement theory.

Adulthood   Physical maturity and adult social identity.

Afterbirth   The placenta and attached membranes and cord which are expelled from the uterus during the final stage of labor.

Alleles   Paired gene factors affecting such characteristics as eye color and blood type.

Amniocentesis   Analysis of fetal cells from a sample of amniotic fluid to detect genetic defects.

Amniotic sac   The thin membrane that holds the embryo and the amniotic fluid bathing it.

Androgynous   Having an equal distribution of feminine and masculine characteristics.

Anorexia nervosa   A psychological disorder chiefly affecting adolescent girls; characterized by voluntary restriction of food intake, resulting in chronic undernutrition and occasionally death.

Anoxia   Deprivation of oxygen in gestation or during the birth process; may cause brain damage.

Assimilation   In Piaget's theory of cognitive development, a person's adaptation of things in the environment to his or her needs; sucking on a thumb instead of a nipple, for example.

Attention span   The length of time a person can focus on a given object or task.

Autism   Psychosis characterized by withdrawal ranging from avoidance of contact to extreme isolation.

Behaviorism   A school of thought that maintains that what we call development is simply what we learn, and which limits its studies to objective, observable behavior.

Biological or physical development   The growth and biological aging of the individual; changes in size and shape and in physical and sensory capacities.

Brain death   Occurs when the individual is deprived of oxygen for four to six minutes or more.

Breech presentation   In birth, the baby's coming out bottom first rather than head first, as most do.

Cellular death   The physical death of organ systems.

Centration   The tendency of a child in Piaget's preoperational period to center attention on a single feature of an object or situation.

Cephalocaudal growth trend   Growth that proceeds in a head-to-toe direction; upper parts of the body develop before lower parts do.

Cesarean birth   Delivery of the baby through a surgical incision in the mother's abdomen and uterus.

Childhood psychosis   Condition characterized by symptoms such as impaired or nonexistent relationships with others, lack of sense of self-identity, inability to talk, inability to understand others, and intolerance of change in the environment.

Classical conditioning   Process developed by Pavlov whereby a learner (in Pavlov's experiments, a dog) can be made to respond (salivate) when exposed to a conditioned stimulus (bell) that it has learned to associate with an unconditioned stimulus (food); see also operant conditioning.

Climacteric   Changes in the reproductive and sexual organs which usually accompany middle age.

Clinical death   Cessation of spontaneous respiration and heartbeat.

Cognition   Knowing, including imagery, perception, thought, reasoning, reflection, problem-solving, and all verbal behavior.

Cognitive or intellectual development   The changes in a variety of operations such as representational thought, reversibility of thought, problem-solving, memory, and abstract thought.

Cognitive style   The individual's manner and form of cognitive performance.

Cohort   A group of individuals born and raised during the same time period.

Colic   The distension of an infant's abdomen with gas, apparently resulting in severe pain.

Compulsion   Irresistible, irrational impulse to act in certain repetitious, stereotyped ways.

Congenital   Existing at birth.

Conservation   The knowledge that certain properties of objects remain invariant despite transformations to which they might be subjected.

Convergence   The ability to focus both eyes to produce a single image; begins during the first hours of life but is not perfected until the end of the second month.

Correlational studies   Research limited to measurement and correlation because the independent variable is not under the researcher's control.

Critical period   In the development of an organ, the phase of rapid growth both in cell number and size; if growth is interfered with during this period, development will be permanently affected.

Cross-sectional studies   Comparisons of same-age individuals and groups designed to note age-related similarities.

Crowning   The appearance of the baby's head with each contraction early in the second stage of labor.

Crystallized abilities   Abilities that depend on the individual's acquisition of information and skills important to his or her culture.

Decentration   The decline of egocentrism (centering on oneself).

Deferred imitation   The ability to imitate a situation that occurred at a previous time.

Dependency   Reliance on others for information, support, and emotional comfort.

Dependent variable   The presumed effect in the relationship under study; varies with changes in the independent variable, which is presumed to be the cause.

Descriptive research   The collection of data about a particular characteristic of the subjects under study.

Development   The processes that are biologically programmed or inherent in the person, and the ways in which the person is irreversibly changed or transformed by interaction with the environment.

Developmental psychology   The study of the physical, cognitive, and psychosocial changes that occur over the lifespan.

Dilation   The first stage of labor, during which the cervix expands enough to let the baby through.

Disengagement theory   An explanation of the changes in elderly people which lead to reflection, self-exploration, and a reduction in social and psychological investments; gradual disengagement of the person from society is said to lead to a sense of well-being and satisfaction.

DNA   Deoxyribonucleic acid; the basic chemical of heredity.

Egocentrism   The self-centered quality of thought and behavior characterizing the preoperational child.

Ego identity   One's feelings about oneself.

Embryo stage   The second stage of gestation, lasting forty-six days, during which differentiated tissues and body systems begin to develop and the embryo begins to take on a human appearance.

Empirical testing   Testing by observation or experimentation.

Endogamy   The practice of choosing a mate's from one's own group.

Experimentation   A research method in which the researcher has direct control over at least one of the independent variables.

Expulsion   The second stage of labor, in which the baby is delivered.

Family cycle   The changes in growth and development that mark the life of the family; the cycle begins with marriage and ends with the death of the surviving spouse.

Fetal stage   The third stage of gestation, lasting about thirty weeks, during which all body systems develop and the fetus grows dramatically in size.

Fluid abilities   The skills that enable a person to perceive complex relations, to conceptualize, and to abstract.

Fontanelles   Soft areas of connective tissue in the neonate's skull.

Gametes   The two germ cells which combine in fertilization.

Gene   Hereditary material that governs one trait.

Gene dominance   When the alleles a child receives consist of one dominant allele and one recessive, then the dominant allele will suppress the recessive one.

Gene recessiveness   When both parents have alleles of mixed genotype (dominant and recessive), then their offspring may have recessive traits.

Gerontology   The study of aging and the old.

Grammar   The system of rules that govern how the parts of a language are put together to create meaningful sentences.

Habituation   The process of becoming familiar with a stimulus and having a decreasing reaction to it; considered one of the best signs of learning in the neonate.

Heterozygous   The condition in which the alleles of a gene pair for a particular trait are different.

Homozygous   The condition in which the alleles of a gene pair for a particular trait are the same.

Hospice   A homelike hospital which specializes in care of the dying.

Hysteria   A type of neurosis characterized by involuntary loss of motor or sensory function; for example, facial tics, or loss of speech or hearing without physical cause.

Imprinting   The fixing of a behavior pattern early in life.

Independent variable   The presumed cause in the relationship under study; manipulation or variation of the independent variable will affect the dependent variable.

Instrumental conditioning   See operant conditioning.

Interiority   Preoccupation with the inner life, rather than with outside things and people.

Language acquisition   Learning words and relating them to experienced objects, actions, or qualities; at the same time, learning not only the grammar of a particular language but the "rule-ness" of grammar itself.

Learning   The process by which a person acquires or modifies a pattern of behavior.

Life review   The process of organizing memories and reinterpreting actions and decisions that have shaped a person's life.

Longitudinal studies   Studies that note changes in individuals over an extended period of time.

Meiosis   Reduction division; the process by which germ cells are produced with twenty-three single chromosomes.

Menarche   First occurrence of menstruation.

Menopause   The cessation of ovulation and menstruation signaling the loss of fertility in women, usually occurring between ages forty-five and fifty-five.

Mentors   Teachers or advisers to whom young adults form "psychological apprentice-ships."

Metacognition   Conscious knowledge people have about the factors involved in learn-ing and problem-solving.

Middlescence   The troubled-midlife passage and the new social role that comes with this period.

Mitosis   The process of cell division in body cells; the resulting cells have twenty-three pairs of chromosomes.

Monozygotic twins   Identical twins; they develop from a single zygote which has be-come separated into two masses.

Moratorium   A period of delay granted or forced onto someone who is not ready to meet an obligation; in Erikson's terms, a delay of adult commitments.

Morpheme   A combination of phonemes; the smallest part of a word that has mean-ing.

Mutuality   A characteristic of adult intimacy in which one cares for the other person as much as one cares for onself.

Negative reinforcement   An unpleasant stimulus is removed in order to encourage a particular response.

Norms   The standards and expectations of one's society.

Obsession   Preoccupation with an idea, feeling, or emotion, often accompanied by anxiety; commonly begins as a phobia.

Operant conditioning   Learning model in which behavior is instrumental in affecting the outcome because the response comes before the reward; also known as instrumental conditioning.

Operational definition   Meaning assigned to research variables by describing activi-ties that the researcher performs to measure the variables.

Ovum stage   First stage of gestation, lasting ten to fourteen days, when the zygote splits into cells as it moves through the fallopian tube to the uterus; there the cell cluster, or blastocyst, implants itself in the uterine wall.

Period of concrete operations   In Piaget's theory, the cognitive stage characterized by development of decentration, conservation, and reversible thinking.

Period of formal operations   In Piaget's theory, cognitive stage characterized by the ability to operate with abstractions, propositions contrary to fact, and symbols of symbols.

Phobia   Severe or excessive fear of and persistent desire to avoid a particular object or situation.

Phonemes   Smallest units of sound that have meaning in the language.

Placenta   Disk-shaped mass of tissue implanted in the inner wall of the uterus and serving as a two-way filter between the bloodstreams of mother and embryo.

Placental   Third stage of labor, when the afterbirth is expelled from the uterus.

Postconventional   In Kohlberg's theory, morality focused on the social contract and on basic human rights that do not have to be earned.

Preoperational period   A period of cognitive development that begins about two years of age and characterizes a child's mental development until he or she is about seven years old.

Prepared childbirth   Childbirth prepared for with breathing routines, study, and exercise.

Presbycusis   A progressive loss of hearing, especially for tones of high frequency, caused by degenerative changes in the auditory system.

Primary memory   Recall of information that is still being attended to "in one's mind."

Primary reinforcer   A reinforcer that meets a basic unlearned need and is intrinsically satisfying, such as food.

Proximodistal growth trend   Growth that proceeds in a center-to-periphery direction; central portions of the body develop before the extremities do.

Psychosocial development   The changes in the personality and emotional structures of individuals, as well as in their usual ways of interacting.

Punishment   An unpleasant or painful stimulus used to discourage a particular behavior.

Pupillary reflex   The automatic narrowing of the pupil of the eye in bright light and its widening in dim light.

Reflex   An involuntary motor response to a specific stimulus.

Reinforcement   A stimulus that follows behavior to motivate learning; a pleasant stimulus, called positive reinforcement, encourages repetition of the behavior; an unpleasant stimulus, called negative reinforcement, discourages repetition of the behavior.

Reliability   Relative certainty that measurement of the same phenomenon by the same researcher at different times, or by different researchers, will produce the same results.

Regression   Behavior that is more suitable to a younger age and may be used to deal with the tensions of frustration.

Sampling   Using a portion of the population as representative of the entire population.

Schema(ta)   Organized pattern(s) of perception and/or behavior.

Schizophrenia   General term for psychosis characterized by regression, bizarre behavior, apathy, destructive rages, and other symptoms of detachment from reality.

Secondary memory   Information that has been encoded but is no longer the focus of active or focused attention.

Secondary reinforcer   Term for a reinforcer that rewards not because of its intrinsic value but because of the things that can be acquired with it; money and power are examples.

Secondary sex characteristics   Physical features other than genitals that distinguish men from women.

Self-concept   The beliefs, hypotheses, and assumptions the individual has about himself, organized into a self-image which reflects his vision of what he is really like; the self-concept acts as a filter for incoming stimuli, an organizer of objects and events, and a guide to conduct.

Sensorimotor intelligence   In Piaget's theory, cognitive processes that regularize sensations and control motor activity.

Separation anxiety   The fear of being left alone and out of reach of the persons who are the child's anchor of safety and familiarity.

Significance, statistical   The probability that the characteristics of an observed sample represent the characteristics of the population from which the sample was drawn and are not due to chance sampling variation.

Social cognition   Knowledge about social relationships and reaction.

Social learning   The process of learning sex roles by observation, reinforced by social approval and the need for cognitive consistency; also known as observational learning.

Social learning theory   School of psychological thought drawing on the behaviorism principles of learning and reinforcement but recognizing that people can learn from the examples of others.

Socialization   The learning process that guides the growth of our social personalities and makes us reasonably acceptable and effective members of our society.

Sociometry   A methodological technique for plotting mutual attractions and rejections in a group.

Stage theory of dying   Kübler-Ross's descriptive theory of the way in which people who know they are going to die adjust to that knowledge; the stages are denial, anger, bargaining, depression, and acceptance.

Status   Relative standing in a group; the dimension of peer acceptance or rejection.

Sutures   Junctures of the several bones in the skull of a neonate.

Syntax   See grammar.

Teratogens   Environmental agents that produce abnormalities in the developing fetus.

Teratology   The study of congenital abnormalities caused by prenatal environmental influences.

Terminal drop   Decline in intellectual performance which frequently occurs within five years before death.

Terminal stage   The time when a person becomes aware of having not much longer to live.

Thanatology   The study of death.

Transition   The phase of labor between the first and second stages.

Type A behavior   Pattern of behavior characterized by a chronic sense of time urgency and an excessive competitive drive; thought to be a factor in heart disease.

Ultrasound   A technique for scanning the uterus with extremely high-level sound waves to get a picture of the outline of the fetus.

Umbilical cord   The cord through which the embryo's blood circulates to and from the placenta, enabling it to take nourishment and oxygen and release waste products.

Validity   In statistical research, correspondence between what a measuring device is supposed to measure and what it actually measures.

Variables   Objects of scientific study.

Visual coordination   Ability of the eye muscles to turn the eyes in the direction of an object, achieved a few weeks after birth.

Youth   An optional period of development in which an individual is legally an adult but has not yet undertaken adult work and roles.

Zygote   The fertilized egg.

Credits (continued from p. 4)

Part One Opener: p. 30, Charles Gatewood

Chapter 1: p. 33 Beryl Goldberg; p. 42 Mimi Cotter; p. 43 Gloria Karlson; p. 45 Charles Gatewood; p. 47 Dorien Grunbaum; p. 52 Dr. John C. Hobbins and Dr. Fred Winsberg, from their book Ultrasound in Obstetrics and Gynecology, © 1977 by the Williams & Wilkins Co.; p. 56 Beryl Goldberg; p. 61 Beryl Goldberg; p. 63 Rodelinde Albrecht; p. 64 E. Trina Lipton

Chapter 2: p. 67 Kathryne Abbe; p. 69 Abigail Heyman/Magnum; p. 73 Mariette Allen/Maternity Center Association; p. 76 Jean Gaumy/Magnum; p. 78 Beryl Goldberg; p. 82 Karen Mantlo; p. 89 Suzanne Karp Krebs

Chapter 3: p. 93 Mimi Cotter; p. 102 Beryl Goldberg; p. 104 Charles Gatewood; p. 106 Mimi Cotter; p. 112 Kathryne Abbe; p. 115 (upper left) Kathryne Abbe; p. 115 (top right) Kathryne Abbe; p. 115 (middle right) Kathryne Abbe; p. 115 (bottom) Richard Daniels; p. 117 Mimi Cotter; p. 120 Charles Gatewood; p. 123 Beryl Goldberg; p. 128 (left) Charles Gatewood; p. 128 (right) Karen Mantlo; p. 129 (upper left) Charles Gatewood; p. 129 (upper right) Gloria Karlson; p. 129 (lower left) Charles Gatewood; p. 129 (lower right) Mimi Cotter; p. 131 Beryl Goldberg

Part Two Opener: p. 140, Mimi Cotter

Chapter 4: p. 143 Mimi Cotter; p. 145 reprinted from Radiographic Atlas of Skeletal Development of the Hand and Wrist, 2nd ed., by William Walter Greulich and S. Idell Pyle, with the permission of the publishers, Stanford University Press. © 1950 and 1959 by the Board of Trustees of the Leland Stanford Junior University; p. 146 Mimi Cotter; p. 148 Mimi Cotter; p. 151 Mimi Cotter; p. 154 Beryl Goldberg; p. 158 Mimi Cotter; p. 162 Blair Seitz/Editorial Photocolor Archives; p. 164 Joel Last/Editorial Photocolor Archives; p. 166 Suzanne Karp Krebs; p. 168 Mimi Cotter; p. 170 Suzanne Karp Krebs; p. 172 Beryl Goldberg; p. 175 Rita Nannini

Chapter 5: p. 181 Laima Druskis/Editorial Photocolor Archives; p. 183 Karen Mantlo; p. 187 Bruce Anspach/Editorial Photocolor Archives; p. 188 Beryl Goldberg; p. 192 Mimi Cotter; p. 193 Mimi Cotter; p. 197 Jean Shapiro; p. 199 Mimi Cotter; p. 201 Laima Druskis/Editorial Photocolor Archives; p. 209 James Foote/Photo Researchers

Part Three Opener: p. 218 Gloria Karlson

Chapter 6: p. 221 Gloria Karlson; p. 228 (upper left) Rhoda Galyn; p. 228 (upper right) Mimi Cotter; p. 228 (lower left) Charles Gatewood; p. 228 (lower right) Beryl Goldberg; p. 230 Charles Gatewood; p. 233 Beryl Goldberg; p. 236 Mimi Cotter

Chapter 7: p. 240 Jan Lukas/Editorial Photocolor Archives; p. 243 Charles Gatewood; p. 248 Mimi Cotter; p. 251 Susan Szasz/Photo Researchers; p. 259 Doug Magee/Editorial Photocolor Archives; p. 261 (top) Bruce Anspach/Editorial Photocolor Archives; p. 261 (lower left) Mimi Cotter; p. 261 (lower right) Daniel Brody/Editorial Photocolor Archives; p. 265 Charles Gatewood; p. 267 Blair Seitz/Editorial Photocolor Archives

Chapter 8: p. 270 Charles Gatewood; p. 272 Gloria Karlson; p. 274 Raimondo Borea/Editorial Photocolor Archives; p. 277 Rhoda Galyn; p. 280 Joseph Szabo; p. 287 Geoffrey Gove; p. 291 Laima Druskis/Editorial Photocolor Archives; p. 294 Beryl Goldberg

Part Four Opener: p. 300, Rhoda Galyn

Chapter 9: p. 303 Charles Gatewood; p. 305 Bruce Anspach/Editorial Photocolor Archives; p. 309 Rita Nannini; p. 311 Gloria Karlson; p. 314 Jean Shapiro; p. 317 Charles Gatewood; p. 319 Marion Bernstein/Editorial Photocolor Archives; p. 325 Suzanne Karp Krebs

Chapter 10: p. 328 Beryl Goldberg; p. 331 Beryl Goldberg; p. 333 Bruce Anspach/Editorial Photocolor Archives; p. 338 Karen Mantlo; p. 341 Karen Mantlo; p. 348 Charles Gatewood; p. 350 Charles Gatewood

Chapter 11: p. 356 Gloria Karlson; p. 358 Jean Shapiro; p. 360 J. Friedman/Editorial Photocolor Archives; p. 363 Marion Bernstein/Editorial Photocolor Archives; p. 365 Beryl Goldberg; p. 368 Susan Szasz; p. 372 Suzanne Karp Krebs; p. 375 Rita Nannini; p. 380 Beryl Goldberg; p. 381 Karen Mantlo; p. 384 Rita Nannini

Part V Opener: p. 390, Joseph Szabo

Chapter 12: p. 393 Mimi Cotter; p. 395 Beryl Goldberg; p. 400 Charles Gatewood; p. 401 Beryl Goldberg; p. 403 Joseph Szabo; p. 407 Joseph Szabo; p. 409 Ann Chwatsky/Editorial Photocolor Archives; p. 413 James Carroll/Editorial Photocolor Archives.

Chapter 13: p. 418 Joseph Szabo; p. 421 Joseph Szabo; p. 424 Beryl Goldberg; p. 426 Rhoda Galyn; p. 427 Joseph Szabo; p. 430 Beryl Goldberg; p. 432 Joseph Szabo; p. 439 Joseph Szabo; p. 440 Rhoda Galyn; p. 442 Daniel Brody/Editorial Photocolor Archives

Part VI Opener: p. 446 Rhoda Galyn

Chapter 14: p. 449 Gloria Karlson; p. 450 Beryl Goldberg; p. 452 Charles Gatewood; p. 453 Rita Nannini; p. 460 Charles Gatewood; p. 463 Charles Gatewood; p. 467 Charles Gatewood; p. 470 Gloria Karlson

Chapter 15: p. 475 Ann Chwatsky/Editorial Photocolor Archives; p. 476 Rita Nannini; p. 477 Charles Gatewood; p. 479 Gloria Karlson; p. 484 Rhoda Galyn; p. 491 Charles Gatewood; p. 493 Gloria Karlson; p. 502 Beryl Goldberg

Part VII Opener: p. 506 Gloria Karlson

Chapter 16: p. 509 Rhoda Galyn; p. 511 Gloria Karlson; p. 514 Bob Adelman/Magnum Photos; p. 515 Gloria Karlson; p. 517 Gloria Karlson; p. 524 Mark Antman; p. 526 Laimute Druskis/Editorial Photocolor Archives; p. 529 Gloria Karlson

Chapter 17: p. 535 Gloria Karlson; p. 537 Charles Gatewood; p. 541 Charles Gatewood; p. 542 Alan Carey; p. 545 Alan Carey; p. 553 Charles Gatewood

Part VIII Opener: p. 560 Herb Taylor/Editorial Photocolor Archives

Chapter 18: p. 563 Rhoda Galyn; p. 565 Charles Gatewood; p. 568 Beryl Goldberg; p. 571 Rhoda Galyn; p. 572 Blair Seitz/Editorial Photocolor Archives; p. 573 Susan McKinney/Editorial Photocolor Archives; p. 578 Judy Rosemarin/Editorial Photocolor Archives; p. 581 Beryl Goldberg

Chapter 19: p. 590 Gloria Karlson; p. 592 Gloria Karlson; p. 597 Beryl Goldberg; p. 599 Alan Carey; p. 600 Rita Nannini; p. 603 Eleanor Pred/Editorial Photocolor Archives; p. 606 Susan McKinney/Editorial Photocolor Archives; p. 612 Woodfin Camp

References

Abramovitch, R., and Grusec, J. E. Peer imitation in a natural setting. *Child Development*, 1978, 49, 60–65.

Adams, B. N. *The family: A sociological interpretation.* Chicago: Rand McNally, 1975.

Adams, G. M., and DeVries, H. A. Physiological effects of an exercise training regimen upon women aged 52–79. *Journal of Gerontology*, 1973, 28, 50–55.

Adelson, J. The political imagination of the young adolescent. In I. Kagan and R. Coles (Eds.), *Twelve to sixteen: Early adolescence.* New York: Norton, 1972.

Adelson, J., and O'Neil, R. P. Growth of political ideas in adolescence: the sense of community. *Journal of Personality and Social Psychology*, 1966, 4, 295–306.

Ahrens, R. Beitrage zur Entwicklung des Physiognomie und Mimikerkennens. *Zeitzschrift fur Experimentelle und Angewandte Psychologie*, 1954, 2, 412–494; 599–633.

Ainsworth, M. D. S. Developmental changes in some attachment behaviors in the first year of life. Symposium presented at the biennial meeting of the Society for Research in Child Development, Minneapolis, April 1971.

Ainsworth, M. D. S., and Bell, S. M. Attachment, exploration, and separation: Illustrated by the behavior of one-year-olds in a strange situation. *Child Development*, 1970, 41, 49–67.

Ainsworth, M. D. S.; Bell, S. M.; and Stayton, D. J. Individual difference in the development of some attachment behaviors. *Merrill-Palmer Quarterly*, 1972, 1S, 123–143.

Ainsworth, M. D. S.; Blehar, M. C.; Waters, E.; and Wall, S. *Patterns of attachment.* Hillside, N.J.: Erlbaum, 1978.

Albin, R. S. Depression appears to afflict thousands of children in U.S. *The New York Times*, March 31, 1981.

Alexander, C. N. Consensus and mutual attraction in natural cliques: A study of adolescent drinkers. *American Journal of Sociology*, 1964, 69, 395–403.

Allport, G. W. *The person in psychology.* Boston: Beacon, 1968.

Allport, G. W. *Pattern and growth in personality.* New York: Holt, Rinehart and Winston, 1961.

Alpaugh, P. K., and Birren, J. E. Variables affecting creative contributions across the adult life span. *Human Development*, 1977, 20, 240–248.

Alpert, J. L., and Richardson, M. S. Parenting. In L. W. Poon (Ed.), *Aging in the 1980s: Psychological issues.* Washington, D.C.: American Psychological Association, 1980.

Ambrus, C. M.; Weintraub, D. M.; Niswander, K. R.; Fischer, L.; Fleischman, J.; Bross, I.D.; and Ambrus, J. L. Evaluation of survivors of respiratory distress syndrome at 4 years of age. *American Journal of Diseases of Children*, 1970, 120, 296–302.

American Psychological Association. *Ethical principles in the conduct of research with human participants.* Washington, D.C.: American Psychological Association, 1973.

Ambron, S. R., and Irwin, D. M. Role-taking and moral judgment in 5- and 7-year olds. *Developmental Psychology*, 1974, 11, 102.

Ames, L. B., and Ilg, F. L. *Your two-year-old.* New York: Delacorte, 1976.

Angelino, H.; Dollins, J.; and Mech, E. V. Trends in the "fears and worries" of school children as related to socioeconomic status and age. *Journal of Genetic Psychology*, 1956, 89, 263–276.

Arenberg, D., and Robertson-Tschabo, E. A. Learning and aging. In J. E. Birren and K. W. Schaie (Eds.), *Handbook of the psychology of aging.* New York: Van Nostrand Reinhold, 1977.

Arlin, P. A. Cognitive development in adulthood: a fifth stage? *Developmental Psychology*, 1975, 11, 602–606.

Arlin, P. A. Piagetian operations in problem finding. *Developmental Psychology*, 1977, 13, 297–298.

Arms, Suzanne. *Immaculate deception: A new look at women and childbirth in America.* Boston: Houghton Mifflin, 1975.

Aronfreed, J. *Conduct and conscience.* New York: Academic Press, 1968.

Arthur, J. K. *Retire to action: A guide to voluntary service.* Nashville, Tenn.: Abingdon, 1969.

Asher, S. R. Children's ability to appraise their own and another person's communication performance. *Developmental Psychology*, 1976, 12, 24–32.

Asher, S. R., and Oden, S. L. Children's failure to communicate: An assessment of comparison and egocentrism explanations. *Developmental Psychology*, 1976, 12, 132–139.

Atchley, R. C. Dimensions of widowhood in later life. *The Gerontologist*, 1975, 15, 176–178.

Athanasiou, R.; Shaver, P.; and Tavris, C. Sex: *Psychology Today* reports back to readers on what they told when they filled out the sex questionnaire. *Psychology Today*, July 1970, 4(2), 39–52.

Bach, G. Young children's play fantasies. *Psychological Monographs*, 1945, 59(2).

Bachtold, L. M., and Rayel de Jackson, O. A culturally based preschool. *Children Today*, 1978, 7, 12–26.

Badger, E., and Burns, D. Impact of a parent education program on the personal development of teen-age mothers. *Journal of Pediatric Psychology*, 1980, 5, 415–422.

Bahr, S. Effects of power and division of labor in the family. In L. Hoffman, and G. Nye (Eds.), *Working mothers.* San Francisco: Jossey-Bass, 1973.

Bailyn, L. Career and family orientation of husbands and wives in relation to marital happiness. In J. M. Bardwick (Ed.), *Readings on the psychology of women.* New York: Harper & Row, 1972.

Ball, S., and Bogatz, G. A. *The first year of Sesame Street: An evaluation.* Princeton, N.J.: Educational Testing Service, 1970.

Bandura, A. The stormy decade: Fact or fiction. *Psychology in the School*, 1964, 1, 224–231.

Bandura, A. The role of modeling processes in personality development. In W. W. Hartup and N. L. Smothergill (Eds.), *The young child: Reviews of research.* Washington, D.C.: National Association for the Education of Young Children, 1967.

Bandura, A. *Aggression: A social learning analysis.* Englewood Cliffs, N.J.: Prentice-Hall, 1973.

Bandura, A., et al. Transmission of aggression through imitation of aggressive models. *Journal of Abnormal Social Psychology*, 1961, 63, 575–582.

Bandura, A., and Walters, R. H. *Social learning and personality development.* New York: Holt, Rinehart and Winston, 1963a.

Bandura, A., and Walters, R. H. Aggression. In H. W. Stevens (Ed.), *Yearbook of the National Society for the Study of Education.* Chicago: University of Chicago Press, 1963b.

Banks, W. C. White preference in blacks: A paradigm in search of a phenomenon. *Psychological Bulletin*, 1976, 83, 1179–1186.

Barnes, A.; Colton, T.; Gunderson, J.; Noller, K.; Tilley, B.; Strama, T.; Townsend, D.; Hatab, P.; and O'Brien, P. Fertility and outcome of pregnancy in women exposed in utero to diethylstilbestrol. *New England Journal of Medicine*, 1980, 302, 609–613.

Barnes, H. V. Physical growth and development during puberty. *Medical Clinics of North America*, 1975, 59(6), 1305–1317.

Barrett, C. J. Effectiveness of widow's groups in facilitating change. *Journal of Consulting and Clinical Psychology*, 1978, 46, 20–31.

Barrett, N. S. Women in the job market: occupations, earnings, and career opportunities. In R. E. Smith (Ed.), *The subtle revolution: women at work*. Washington, D.C.: The Urban Institute, 1979.

Barron, E. *Creativity and psychological health: Origins of personal vitality and creative freedom*. New York: D. Van Nostrand, 1963.

Barry, H.; Bacon, M. K.; and Child, I. L. A cross-cultural survey of some sex differences in socialization. Reprinted in J. M. Bardwick (Ed.) *Readings on the psychology of women*. New York: Harper & Row, 1972.

Barry, W. A. Marriage research and conflict: An integrative review. *Psychological Bulletin*, 1970, 73(1), 41–54.

Bart, P. Mother Portnoy's complaints. *Trans-action*, 1970, 8, 69–74.

Bartz, K. W., and Levine, E. S. Childrearing by black parents: A description and comparison to anglo and chicano parents, *Journal of Marriage and the Family*, 1978, 40, 709–719.

Basseches, M. Dialectical schemata: a framework for the empirical study of the development of dialectical thinking. *Human Development*, 1980, 23, 400–421.

Basow, S. A., and Howe, K. G. Role-model influence: Effects of sex and sex-role attitudes in college students. *Psychology of Women Quarterly*, 1980, 4, 558–572.

Bauer, D. H. An exploratory study of developmental changes in children's fears. *Journal of Child Psychology and Psychiatry*, 1976, 17, 69–74.

Baumrind, D. Current patterns of parental authority. *Developmental Psychology Monographs*, 1971, 4, 99–103.

Baumrind, D. Parental disciplinary patterns and social competence in children. *Youth and Society*, 1978, 9(3), 239–276.

Bayley, N., and Bayer, L. M. The assessment of somatic androgyny. *American Journal of Physical Anthropology*, 1946, 4, 433.

Bayley, N., and Oden, M. H. The maintenance of intellectual ability in gifted adults. *Journal of Gerontology*, 1955, 10, 91–107.

Bearison, D. J. The construct of regression: A Piagetian approach. *Merrill-Palmer Quarterly*, 1974, 20, 21–30.

Bell, R. Q. A reinterpretation of the direction of effects in studies of socialization. *Psychology Review*, 1968, 75, 81–95.

Bell, R. R., and Coughey, K. Premarital sexual experience among college females, 1958, 1968, and 1978. *Family Relations*, 1980, 29, 353–357.

Belsky, J.; Goode, M. K.; and Most, R. K. Maternal stimulation and infant exploratory competence: cross-sectional, correlational, and experimental analyses. *Child Development*, 1980, 51, 1163–1178.

Belsky, J., and Steinberg, L. D. The effects of day care: A critical review. *Child Development*, 1978, 49, 929–949.

Belsky, J., and Steinberg, L. D. What does research teach us about day care: A follow-up report. *Children Today*, July–August 1979, 21–26.

Belsky, J.; Steinberg, L. D.; and Walker, A. The ecology of day care. In M. Lamb (Ed.), *Childrearing in Nontraditional Families*, Hillsdale, N.J.: Erlbaum, 1981.

Bem, S. L. Androgyny vs. the tight lives of fluffy women and chesty men. *Psychology Today*, 1975, 9, 58–62.

Bem, S. L. On the utility of alternative procedures for assessing psychological androgyny. *Journal of Consulting and Clinical Psychology*, 1976, 42(2), 155–162.

Bender, A. E. Nutrition of the elderly. *Royal Society Health Journal*, 1971, 91, 115–121.

Benedek, T. Parenthood as a developmental phase. *American Psychoanalytic Association Journal*, 1959, 7, 389–417.

Bengston, V. L.; Cuellar, J. B.; and Ragan, P. K. Stratum contrasts and similarities in attitudes toward death. *Journal of Gerontology*, 1977, 32, 76–88.

Bengston, V. L., and Troll, L. Youth and their parents: Feedback and intergenerational influence in socialization. In Richard M. Lerner and Graham B. Spencer, *Child influence on marital and family interaction: A life span perspective*. New York: Academic Press, 1978.

Berardo, F. M. Widowhood status in the United States: Perspective on a neglected aspect of the family life cycle. *Family Coordinator*, 1968, 17, 191–202.

Berenda, R. W. *The influence of the group on the judgments of children*. New York: King's Crown, 1950.

Berko, J. The child's learning of English morphology. *Word*, 1958, 14.

Bernard, J. *The Future of Marriage*. New York: World Publishing, 1972.

Berndt, T. J. Developmental changes in conformity to peers and parents. *Developmental Psychology*, 1979, 15, 610–616.

Bettelheim, B. Bringing up children. *Ladies Home Journal*, 1973, 90, 28.

Bielby, D. D., and Papalia, D. E. Moral development and perceptual role-taking egocentrism: Their development and interrelationship across the life span. *International Journal of Aging and Human Development*, 1975, 6(4), 293–308.

Bigelow, B. J. Children's friendship expectations: A cognitive-developmental study. *Child Development*, 1977, 48, 246–253.

Bigelow, B. J., and La Gaipa, J. J. Children's written descriptions of friendship: A multidimensional analysis. *Developmental Psychology*, 1975, 11, 857–858.

Biller, A. B. Father absence and the personality development of the male child. *Developmental Psychology*, 1970, 2, 181–201.

Birnbaum, J. L. A. Life patterns, personality style, and self-esteem in gifted family-oriented and career-committed women. (Doctoral dissertation, University of Michigan) *Dissertation Abstracts International*, 1971, 32, 1834B.

Birren, J. E. Transitions in gerontology—from lab to life: Psychophysiology and speed of response. *American Psychologist*, 1974, 29, 808–815.

Birren, J. E.; Butler, R. N.; Greenhouse, S. W.; Sokoloff, L.; and Yarrow, M. R. (Eds.), *Human aging: a biological and behavioral study*. Publication No. (HSM) 71-9051. Washington, D.C.: U.S. Government Printing Office, 1963.

Birren, J. E.; Woods, A. M.; and Williams, M. V. Behavioral slowing with age: causes, organization, and consequences. In L. W. Poon (Ed.), *Aging in the 1980s: psychological issues*. Washington, D.C.: American Psychological Association, 1980.

Bixenstine, V. E.; Decorte, M. S.; and Bixenstine, B. Conformity to peer-sponsored misconduct at four grade levels. *Developmental Psychology*, 1978, 14, 226–236.

Blum, J. E., and Jarvik, L. F. Intellectual performance of octogenarians as a function of education and initial ability. *Human Development*, 1975, 18, 364–375.

Bond, G., and Tinker, M. *Reading difficulties*. New York: Appleton, 1973.

Bonney, M. E. A sociometric study of some factors of mutual friendships on the elementary, secondary, and college levels. *Sociometry*, 1946, 9, 21–47.

Bonney, M. E., and Powell, J. Differences in social behaviour between sociometrically high and sociometrically low children. *Journal of Educational Research*, 1953, 46, 481–495.

Booth, A. Wife's employment and husband's stress: A replication and refutation. *Journal of Marriage and the Family*, 1977, 39, 645–650.

Borke, H. Interpersonal perception of young children. *Developmental Psychology*, 1971, 5, 263–269.

Bossard, J., and Boll, E. *The sociology of child development*. New York: Harper & Row, 1960.

Botwinick, J. Intellectual abilities. In J. E. Birren and K. W. Schaie (Eds.), *Handbook of the psychology of aging*. New York: Van Nostrand Reinhold, 1977.

Bower, D., and Christopherson, V. University student cohabitation: A regional comparison of selected attitudes and behavior. *Journal of Marriage and the Family*, 1977, *39(3)*, 447–453.

Bowes, W. A.; Brackbill, Y.; Conway, E.; and Steinschneider, A. The effects of obstetrical medication on fetus and infant. *Monographs on Social Research in Child Development*, 1970, *35*, 4.

Bowlby, J. *Attachment and loss: Separation*, vol. 2. New York: Basic Books, 1973.

Bowlby, J. Childhood mourning and psychiatric illness. In P. Lomas (Ed.), *The predicament of the family*. London: Hogarth Press, 1967.

Bradley, R. H.; Caldwell, B. M.; and Elardo, R. Home environment and congitive development in the first 2 years: a cross-lagged panel analysis. *Developmental Psychology*, 1979, *15*, 246–250.

Bradley, S. J. The relationship of early maternal separation to borderline personality in children and adolescents: A pilot study. *American Journal of Psychiatry*, 1979, *136(4A)*, 424–426.

Braine, M. D. S. The ontogeny of English phrase structure: The first phase. *Language*, 1963, *39*, 1–13.

Brandfonbrenner, M.; Landowne, M.; and Shock, W. W. Changes in cardiac output with age. *Circulation*, 1955, *12*, 557–566.

Brazelton, T. B. A child-oriented approach to toilet training. *Pediatrics*, 1962, *29*, 121–128.

Brazelton, T. B. *Neonatal behavioral assessment scale*. London: Heinemann, 1973.

Brecher, E. M., and the Editors of *Consumer Reports*. Marijuana: The health questions, *Consumer Reports*, March 1975, 143–149.

Breckenridge, M. E., and Murphy, M. N. *Growth and development of the young child*. Philadelphia: Saunders, 1969.

Bretheron, I., and Ainsworth, M. D. S. The response of one-year-olds to a stranger in a strange situation. In M. Lewis and L. A. Rosenblum (Eds.), *The origins of fear*. New York: Wiley, 1974.

Brewer, G. S. (Ed.), *The pregnancy after 30 workbook*. Emmaus, Pa.: Rodale Press, 1978.

Brody, J. E. Cancer agency head advises diet changes. *The New York Times*, October 4, 1979.

Brody, J. E. U.S. acts to reshape diets of Americans. *The New York Times*, February 5, 1980.

Brody, J. E. Personal Health, *The New York Times*, December 10, 1980.

Brodzinsky, D. M.; Messer, S. B.; and Tew, J. D. Sex differences in children's expression and control of fantasy and overt aggression. *Child Development*, 1979, *50*, 372–379.

Brodzinsky, D. M.; Pappas, C.; Singer, L. M.; and Braff, A. M. Children's conception of adoption: a preliminary investigation. *Journal of Pediatric Psychology*, 1981a, *6*, 177–189.

Brodzinsky, D. M.; Singer, L. M.; and Braff, A. M. Children's understanding of adoption: a comparison of adopted and non-adopted children. Paper presented at the Society for Research in Child Development, Boston, 1981b.

Broman, S. H. Prenatal anoxia and cognitive development in early childhood. In T. M. Field, A. M. Sostek, S. Goldberg, and H. H. Shuman (Eds.), *Infants born at risk: behavior and development*. New York: Spectrum Publications, 1979.

Bromley, D. Some experimental tests of the effect of age in creative intellectual output. *Journal of Gerontology*, 1956, *11*, 74–82.

Bromley, D. B. *The psychology of human aging*. (2d ed.) Middlesex, England: Penguin, 1974.

Bronfenbrenner, U. Some familial antecedents of responsibility and leadership in adolescents. In L. Petrullo and R. L. Brown (Eds.), *Leadership and interpersonal behavior*. New York: Holt, Rinehart and Winston, 1961.

Bronfenbrenner, U. *Two worlds of childhood: U.S. and U.S.S.R.* New York: Basic Books, 1970.

Bronfenbrenner, U. *Influences on human development*. Hinsdale, Ill.: Dryden Press, 1972.

Bronfenbrenner, U. Contexts of child rearing: Problems and prospects. *American Psychologist*, 1979, *34*, 844–850.

Brooks, J., and Lewis, M. Infants' responses to strangers: Midget, adult, and child. *Child Development*, 1976, *47*, 323–332.

Broverman, I. K.; Broverman, D. M.; Clarkson, F. E.; Rosenkrantz, P. S.; and Vogel, S. R. Sex role stereotypes and clinical judgments of mental health. *Journal of Consulting and Clinical Psychology*, 1970, *34*, 1–7.

Brown, F. Depression and childhood bereavement. *Journal of Mental Science*, 1961.

Brown, F.; Chase, J.; and Winson, J. Studies in infant feeding choice of primiparae: II. Comparison of Rorschach determinants of acceptors and rejectors of breast feeding. *Journal of Projective Technology*, 1961, *25*, 412.

Brown, J. V., and Bakeman, R. Antecedents of emotional involvement in mothers of premature and full-term infants. Paper presented at meeting of Society for Research in Child Development, New Orleans, March 1977.

Brown, P., and Elliot, R. Control of aggression in a nursery school class. *Journal of Experimental Child Psychology*, 1965, *2*, 102–107.

Brown, R. The dialogue in early childhood. Unpublished paper, Harvard University, 1966; quoted in D. I. Slobin, Imitation and grammatical development in children. In N. Endler, L. Boulter, and H. Osser (Eds.), *Contemporary issues in developmental psychology*. New York: Holt, Rinehart and Winston, 1968.

Brown, R. The first sentences of child and chimpanzee. In *Psycholinguistics: Selected papers*. Glencoe, Ill.: The Free Press, 1970.

Brown, R., and Fraser, C. The acquisition of syntax. In C. N. Cofer, and B. S. Musgrave (Eds.), *Verbal behavior and learning: Problems and processes*. New York: McGraw-Hill, 1963.

Bruch, H. Transformation of oral impulses in eating disorders. *Psychiatry Quarterly*, 1961, *35*, 458.

Bruch, H. *Eating disorders*. New York: Basic Books, 1973.

Bruch, H. Anorexia nervosa and its treatment. *Journal of Pediatric Psychology*, 1977, *2(3)*, 110–112.

Bryant, P. E., and Trabasso, T. Transitive inferences and memory in young children. *Nature*, 1971, *232*, 456–458.

Burke, R. I., and Weir, T. Personality differences between members of one-career and two-career families. *Journal of Marriage and the Family*, 1976a, *38*, 453–459.

Burke, R. I., and Weir, T. Relationship of wives' employment status to husband, wife, and pair satisfaction and performance. *Journal of Marriage and the Family*, 1976b, *38*, 279–287.

Burlin, F. The relationship of parental education and maternal work and occupational status to occupational aspiration in adolescent females. *Journal of Vocational Education*, 1976, *9*, 99–104.

Burns, S. M., and Brainerd, C. J. Effects of constructive and dramatic play on perspective taking in very young children. *Developmental Psychology*, 1979, *15(5)*, 512–521.

Buros, O. K. (Ed.). *The seventh mental measurements yearbook*, vol. 1, Edison, N.J.: Gryphon Press, 1972.

Burr, W. R. Satisfaction with various aspects of marriage over the life cycle: A random middle-class sample. *Journal of Marriage and the Family*, 1970, *32*, 29–37.

Busse, E. W.; Jeffers, I. C.; and Christ, W. D. Factors in age awareness. In E. Palmore (Ed.), *Normal aging: Reports from the Duke longitudinal study,* 1955–1969. Durham, N.C.: Duke University Press, 1970.

Butler, R. N. Old age: The life review. *Psychology Today,* December 1971, *5,* 49.

Butler, R. N., and Lewis, M. I. *Love and sex after sixty: A guide for men and women for their later years.* New York: Harper & Row, 1976.

Butler, R. N., and Lewis, M. I. *Aging and mental health* (2nd ed.) St. Louis: Mosby, 1977.

Bybee, R. W. Violence toward youth: A perspective. *Journal of Social Issues,* 1975, *35(2),* 1–14.

Caldeyro-Barcia, R. The influence of maternal position on time of spontaneous rupture of the membranes, progress of labor, and fetal head compression. *Birth and the Family Journal,* Spring 1979, *6(1),* 7–15.

Calhoun, A. C. *A social history of the American family.* New York: Barnes & Noble, 1960.

Campbell, J. D., and Yarrow, M. R. Perceptual and behavioral correlates of social effectiveness. *Sociometry,* 1961, *24,* 1–20.

Carp, F. M. *Factors in Utilization of Services by the Mexican-American elderly.* Palo Alto: American Institute for Research, 1968.

Carp, F. M. Communicating with elderly Mexican-Americans. *The Gerontologist,* 1970, *9(1),* 20–24.

Carter, H., and Glick, P. C. *Marriage and divorce: a social and economic study.* Cambridge, Mass.: Harvard University Press, 1970.

Caster, W. O. *The nutritional problems of the aged.* Athens, Ga.: University of Georgia Press, 1971.

Castleman, M. Why teenagers get pregnant. *The Nation,* November 26, 1977, 549–552.

Cattell, R. B. Theory of fluid and crystallized intelligence: A critical experiment. *Journal of Educational Psychology,* 1963, *36,* 1–22.

Cavior, N., and Dokecki, P. R. Physical attractiveness, perceived attitude similarity, and academic achievement as contributors to interpersonal attraction among adolescents. *Developmental Psychology,* 1973, 44–54.

Cavior, N., and Lombardi, D. A. Developmental aspects of physical attractiveness in children. *Developmental Psychology,* 1973, *8,* 67–71.

Chaillé, C. The child's conceptions of play, pretending, and toys: Sequences and structural parallel. *Human Development,* 1978, *21,* 201–210.

Chagnon, N. A. *Yanomamö: The fierce people.* New York: Holt, Rinehart and Winston, 1968.

Cheyne, J. A., and Walters, R. H. Intensity of punishment, timing of punishment and cognitive structure as determinants of response inhibition. *Journal of Experimental Child Psychology,* 1969, *7,* 231–244.

Chiriboga, D. A., and Cutler, L. Stress and adaptation: life span perspectives. In L. W. Poon (Ed.), *Aging in the 1980s: Psychological issues.* Washington, D.C.: American Psychological Association, 1980.

Chomsky, N. *Syntactic structures.* The Hague, Netherlands: Mouton, 1957.

Chomsky, N. *Aspects of the theory of syntax.* Cambridge, Mass.: M. I. T. Press, 1965.

Chomsky, N. *Language and Mind.* New York: Harcourt Brace Jovanovich, 1968.

Cicirelli, V. G. Relationship of siblings to the elderly person's feelings and concerns. *Journal of Gerontology,* 1977, *131,* 309–317.

Cicirelli, V. G. *Social services for elderly in relation to the kin network.* Report to the NRTA-AARP Andrus Foundation, Washington, D.C., 1979.

Cicirelli, V. G. Sibling relationships in adulthood: a lifespan perspective. In L. W. Poon (Ed.), *Aging in the 1980s: Psychological issues.* Washington, D.C.: American Psychological Association, 1980.

Civia, A. Longevity and environmental factors. *The Gerontologist,* 1967, *7,* 196–205.

Clark, K. B., and Clark, M. P. Racial identity and preferences in Negro children. In T. Newcomb and E. L. Hartley (Eds.), *Readings in social psychology.* New York: Holt, 1947.

Clark, L. D.; Hughes, R.; and Nakashima, E. N. Behavioral effects of marijuana: Experimental studies. *Archives of General Psychiatry,* 1970, *23,* 193–198.

Clarke, A. An examination of the operation of residential propinquity as a factor in mate selection. *American Sociological Review,* 1952, *17,* 17–22.

Clarke-Stewart, K. A. Recasting the love stranger. In J. Glick and K. A. Clarke-Stewart (Eds.), *The development of social understanding.* New York: Gardner Press, 1978.

Clausen, J. Perspectives on childhood socialization. In J. A. Clausen (Ed.), *Socialization and society.* Boston: Little, Brown, 1968.

Clayton, R., and Voss, H. Shacking up: Cohabitation in the 1970s. *Journal of Marriage and the Family,* 1977, *39(2),* 273–283.

Clemens, P. W., and Rust, J. O. Factors in adolescent rebellious feelings. *Adolescence,* 1979, *14(53),* 159–173.

Clore, G. L., and Byrne, D. The process of personality interaction. In R. B. Cottell and R. M. Dreger (Eds.), *Handbook of Modern Personality Theory.* New York: Wiley, 1977.

Coates, B.; Anderson, E. P.; and Hartup, W. W. Interrelations in the attachment behavior of human infants. *Developmental Psychology,* 1972, *6(2),* 218–230.

Coates, B., and Pusser, H. E. Positive reinforcement and punishment in "Sesame Street" and "Mister Rogers' Neighborhood." *Journal of Broadcasting,* 1975, *19,* 143–151.

Coates, B.; Pusser, H. E.; and Goodman, I. The influence of "Sesame Street" and "Mister Rogers' Neighborhood" on children's social behavior in the preschool. *Child Development,* 1976, *47,* 138–144.

Cochran, M. M., and Brassard, J. A. Child development and personal social networks. *Child Development,* 1979, *40,* 601–616.

Coles, R. *Erik H. Erikson: The growth of his work.* Boston: Little, Brown, 1970.

Collard, R. R. Social and play responses of firstborn and later born infants in an unfamiliar situation. *Child Development,* 1968, *39,* 325–334.

Comfort, A. *A good age.* New York: Crown, 1976.

Commons, M. L., and Richards, F. A. The structural analytic stage of development: a Piagetian postformal operational stage. Paper presented at the meeting of the Western Psychological Association, San Francisco, April 1978.

Condon, W. S., and Sander, L. W. Neonate movement is synchronized with adult speech. *Science,* 1974a, *183,* 99–101.

Condon, W. S., and Sander, L. W. Synchrony demonstrated between movements of the neonate and adult speech. *Child Development,* 1974b, *45,* 456–462.

Condry, J., and Condry, S. Sex differences: A study of the eye of the beholder. *Child Development,* 1976, *47,* 812–819.

Conger, J. J. Parent-child relationships, social change, and adolescent vulnerability. *Journal of Pediatric Psychology,* 1977, *2(3),* 93–97.

Conger, J. J. Adolescence: A time for becoming. In Michael E. Lamb (Ed.), *Social and personality development.* New York: Holt, Rinehart and Winston, 1978.

Coopersmith, S. *The antecedents of self-esteem.* San Francisco: Freeman, 1967.

Copans, S. A. Human prenatal effects: methodological problems and some suggested solutions. *Merrill-Palmer Quarterly,* 1974, *20,* 43–52.

Corso, J. F. Auditory perception and communication. In J. E.

Birren and K. W. Schaie (Eds.), *Handbook of the psychology of aging.* New York: Van Nostrand Reinhold, 1977.

Costa, P. T.; McCrae, R. R.; and Arenberg, D. Enduring dispositions in adult males. *Journal of Personality and Social Psychology,* 1980, *38,* 793–800.

Costanzo, P. R. Conformity development as a function of self-blame. *Journal of Personality and Social Psychology,* 1970, *14,* 366–374.

Costanzo, Philip, and Shaw, Marvin E. Conformity as a function of age level. *Child Development,* 1966, *37,* 967–975.

Cottrell, L. S., Jr. The adjustment of the individual to his age and sex roles. *American Sociological Review,* 1942, 617–620.

Cox, R. D. *Youth into maturity.* New York: Mental Health Materials Center, 1970.

Craik, F. I. M. Age differences in human memory. In J. E. Birren and K. W. Schaie (Eds.), *Handbook of the psychology of aging.* New York: Van Nostrand Reinhold, 1977.

Cramer, P., and Bryson, J. The development of sex-related fantasy patterns. *Developmental Psychology,* 1973, *8,* 131–134.

Crandall, R. C. *Gerontology: a behavioral science approach.* Reading, Mass.: Addison-Wesley, 1980.

Crandall, V. J.; Orleans, S.; Preston, A.; and Rabson, A. The development of social compliance in young children. *Child Development,* 1958, *29,* 429–443.

Cross, J. F., and Cross, J. Age, sex, race, and the perception of facial beauty. *Developmental Psychology,* 1971, *5,* 431–439.

Crouch, B. M. Age and institutional support: Perceptions of older Mexican-Americans. *Journal of Gerontology,* 1972, *27,* 524–529.

Cuber, J. F., and Harroff, P. B. *The significant Americans.* New York: Appleton-Century-Crofts, 1965.

Cumming, E., and Henry, W. E. *Growing old.* New York: Basic Books, 1961.

De Beauvoir, S. *The coming of age.* (Trans. by P. O'Brian) New York: Putnam, 1972.

Dale, P. S. *Language development: Structure and function* (2nd ed.). New York: Holt, Rinehart and Winston, 1976.

Damon, W. *The social world of the child.* San Francisco: Jossey-Bass, 1977.

Dancy, J. *The black elderly: A guide for practitioners.* Ann Arbor: The Institute for Gerontology, The University of Michigan-Wayne State University, 1977.

Dasen, P. R. Cross-cultural Piagetian research: A summary. *Journal of Cross-Cultural Psychology,* 1972, *3,* 23–39.

Davidson, S. School phobia as a manifestation of family disturbance. *Journal of Child Psychology and Psychiatry,* 1961, *1,* 270–278.

Davies, J. M.; Latto, I. P.; Jones, J. G.; Veale, A.; and Wardrop, C. A. Effects of stopping smoking for 48 hours on oxygen availability from the blood: A study of pregnant women. *British Medical Journal,* 1979, *2,* 355–356.

Davis, C. M. Self-selection of food by children. *The American Journal of Nursing,* 1935, *35,* 403–410.

Davitz, J. R. Social perception and sociometric choice in children. *Journal of Abnormal Social Psychology,* 1955, *50,* 173–176.

DeFrain, J. S. Parenting by the book. *Human Behavior,* 1978, *7,* 49–50.

DeFries, J. C., and Plomin, R. Behavior genetics. *Annual Review of Psychology,* 1978, *29,* 473–515.

DeLisi, R., and Staudt, J. Individual differences in college students' performances on formal operations tasks. *Journal of Applied Developmental Psychology,* 1980, *1,* 201–208.

Denckla, Martha B. *Minimal brain dysfunction.* Chicago: The National Society for the Study of Education, 1978.

Dennis, W. Creative productivity between the ages of 20 and 80 years. *Journal of Gerontology,* 1966, *21,* 1–18.

Denny, N. W., and Cornelius, S. W. Class inclusion and multiple classification in middle and old age. *Developmental Psychology,* 1975, *11,* 521–522.

Derdeyn, A. P. Adoption and ownership of children. *Child Psychiatry and Human Development,* 1979, *9(4),* 215–226.

Deur, J. L., and Parke, R. D. The effects of inconsistent punishment on aggression in children. *Developmental Psychology,* 1970, *24,* 403–411.

DeVries, H. A. Physiological effects of an exercise training regimen upon men aged 52–88. *Journal of Gerontology,* 1970, *25,* 325–336.

DeVries, H. A. Physiology of exercise and aging. In D. S. Woodruff and J. E. Birren (Eds.), *Aging: Scientific perspectives and social issues.* New York: D. Van Nostrand, 1975. Pp. 257–275.

DeVries, H. A., and Adams, G. M. Electromyographic comparison of single doses of exercise and meprobamate as to effects on muscular relaxation. *American Journal of Physical Medicine,* 1972, *51,* 130–141.

DHEW, *Thinking about Drinking.* U.S. Dept. Health, Education, and Welfare, 1978, 1979, (ADM) 79–27.

Dickstein, E., and Posner, J. M. Self-esteem and relationship with parents. *The Journal of Genetic Psychology,* 1978, *133,* 273–276.

Dine, M.; Gartside, P.; Glueck, C.; Rheines, L.; Greene, G.; and Khoury, P. Where do the heaviest children come from? A prospective study of white children from birth to 5 years of age. *Pediatrics,* 1979, *63,* 1–6.

Dinnerstein, D. *The mermaid and the minotaur: Sexual arrangements and human malaise.* New York, Harper & Row, 1976.

Dionne, E. J., Jr. Stories that test scores don't tell. *The New York Times,* May 1, 1977, p. ED 17.

Division of Youth and Family Services. Considerations on Child Abuse. DYFS 2–31, Revised January 1976.

DiVitto, B., and Goldberg, S. The effect of newborn medical status on early parent-infant interaction. In T. Field, A. Sostek, S. Goldberg, and H. H. Shuman (Eds.), *Infants born at risk.* New York: Spectrum, 1979.

Donaldson, M., and Balfour, G. Less is more: A study of language comprehension in children. *British Journal of Psychology,* 1968, *59,* 461–472.

Douvan, E. Differing view of marriage, 1957–1976. *Center for Continuing Education for Women Newsletter* (University of Michigan), 1978, *12,* 1–2.

Douvan, E., and Adelson, J. *The adolescent experience.* New York: Wiley, 1966.

Dresen, S. E. The sexually active middle adult. *American Journal of Nursing,* 1975, *75,* 1001–1005.

Dullea, G. Vast changes in society traced to the rise of working women. *The New York Times,* November 29, 1977, p. 1.

Durkin, D. *Children who read early.* New York: Teachers College, 1966.

Durlak, J. A. Relationship between attitudes toward life and death among elderly women. *Developmental Psychology,* 1973, *8(1),* 146.

Durrett, M. E.; O'Bryant, S.; and Pennebaker, J. W. Childrearing reports of white, black, and Mexican-American families. *Developmental Psychology,* 1975, *11,* 871.

Duvall, E. *Marriage and family development.* (5th ed.) Philadelphia: Lippincott, 1977.

Dyk, R., and Witkin, H. Family experiences related to the development of differentiation in children. *Child Development,* 1965, *36,* 21–55.

Eckerman, C. O., and Whatley, J. L. Toys and social interaction between infant peers. *Child Development,* 1977, *48,* 1645–1656.

Edel, L. Portrait of the artist as an old man. *American Scholar,* Winter 1977–1978, pp. 52–68.

Eisdorfer, C. Arousal and performance: Experiments in verbal learning and a tentative theory. In G. A. Talland (Ed.), *Human aging and behavior.* New York: Academic Press, 1968.

Eisdorfer, C.; Nowlin, J.; and Wilkie, F. Improvement of learning in the aged by modification of autonomous nervous system activity. *Science*, 1970, *170*, 1327–1329.

Eisdorfer, C., and Wilkie, F. Stress, disease, aging, and behavior. In J. E. Birren and K. W. Schaie (Eds.), *Handbook of the psychology of aging.* New York: Van Nostrand Reinhold, 1977.

Elkind, D. Egocentrism in adolescence. *Child Development*, 1967a, *38*, 1025–1035.

Elkind, D. Middle-class delinquency. *Mental Health*, 1967b, *5*, 80–84.

Elkind, D. Quantity conceptions in junior and senior high school students. *Child Development*, 1961, *32*, 551–560.

Elkind, D. Quantity conceptions in college students. *Journal of Social Psychology*, 1962, *57*, 459–465.

Elkind, D. *A sympathetic understanding of the child six to sixteen.* Boston: Allyn and Bacon, 1971.

Elkind, D.; Koegler, R. R.; and Go, E. Studies in perceptual development: II. Part-whole perception. *Child Development*, 1964, *35*, 81–90.

Elkins, D. Some factors related to the choice status of ninety eighth-grade children in a school society. *Genetic Psychology Monograph*, 1958, *58*, 207–272.

Emmerich, H. J. The influence of parents and peers on choices made by adolescents. *Journal of Youth and Adolescence*, 1978, *7(2)*, 175–180.

Emmerich, W. Parental identification in young children. *Genetic Psychological Monographs*, 1959, *60*, 257–308.

Engel, W. v. R. The development from sound to phoneme in child language. In C. A. Ferguson and D. I. Slobin (Eds.), *Studies of child language development.* New York: Holt, Rinehart and Winston, 1973.

Engen, T. Taste and smell. In J. E. Birren and K. W. Schaie (Eds.), *Handbook of the psychology of aging.* New York: Van Nostrand Reinhold, 1977.

Erikson, E. H. *Identity and the life cycle: Selected papers by Erik H. Erikson.* New York: International Universities Press, 1959.

Erikson, E. H. *Childhood and society.* (2d ed.) New York: W. W. Norton, 1963.

Erikson, E. H. Insight and responsibility: *Lectures on the ethical implications of psychoanalytic insight.* New York: W. W. Norton, 1964.

Erikson, E. H. Generativity and ego integrity. In B. L. Neugarten (Ed.), *Middle age and aging.* Chicago: University of Chicago Press, 1968.

Erikson, E. H. *Identity: Youth and crisis.* New York: W. W. Norton, 1968.

Erikson, E. H. Reflections on Dr. Borg's life cycle. *Daedalus*, Spring 1976, *105(2)*, 1–28.

Eriksson, M.; Larsson, G.; and Zetterstrom, R. Abuse of alcohol, drugs, and tobacco during pregnancy: Consequences for the child. *Paediatrician*, 1979, *8(4)*, 228–242.

Ervin, S. M. Imitation and structural change in children's language. In E. H. Lenneberg, (Ed.), *New directions in the study of language.* Cambridge, Mass.: M. I. T. Press, 1964.

Ervin-Tripp, S. M. Imitation and structural change in children's language. In C. A. Ferguson and D. I. Slobin (Eds.), *Studies of child language development.* New York: Holt, Rinehart and Winston, 1973.

Escalona, S. K., and Corman, H. H. The impact of mother's presence upon behavior in the first year. *Human Development*, 1971, *14*, 2–15.

Eysenck, H. J. *Crime and personality.* Boston: Houghton Mifflin, 1964.

Faber, A., and Mazlish, E. *Liberated parents/liberated children.* New York: Grosset & Dunlap, 1974.

Fagot, B. I. The influence of sex of child on parental reactions to toddler children. *Child Development*, 1978, *49*, 459–465.

Fakouri, M. E. "Cognitive development in adulthood: a fifth stage?" a critique. *Developmental Psychology*, 1976, *12*, 472.

Fantz, R. L. The origins of form perception. *Scientific American*, 1961, *204*, 66–72.

FBI Law Enforcement Bulletin, May 1978, pp. 4–5.

Feingold, B. F. Hyperkinesis and learning disabilities linked to artificial food flavors and colors. *American Journal of Nursing*, 1975, *75*, 797–803.

Fernald, G. *Remedial techniques in basic school subjects.* New York: McGraw-Hill, 1943.

Field, T. M. Effects of early separation, interactive deficits, and experimental manipulations on infant-mother face-to-face interaction. *Child Development*, 1977, *48*, 763–771.

Field, T. M. Interaction patterns of primary versus secondary caretaker fathers. *Developmental Psychology*, 1978, *14*, 183–185.

Field, T. M.; Dempsey, J. R.; and Shuman, H. H. Developmental assessment of infants surviving the respiratory distress syndrome. In T. Field, A. Sostek, S. Goldberg, and H. H. Shuman (Eds.), *Infants Born at Risk.* New York: Spectrum, 1979.

Fink, R. S. Role of imaginative play in cognitive development. *Psychological Reports*, 1976, *39*, 895–906.

Firestone, G., and Brody, N. Longitudinal investigation of teacher-student interactions and their relation to academic performance. *Journal of Educational Psychology*, 1975, *67*, 544–550.

Fitzgerald, H. E., and Brackbill, Y. Classical conditioning in infancy: Development and constraints. *Psychological Bulletin*, 1976, *53*, 353–376.

Fitzhardinge, P. M.; Pape, K.; Arstikaitis, M.; Boyle, M.; Ashby, S.; Rowley, A.; Netley, C.; and Swyer, P. R. Mechanical ventilation of infants of less than 1501 gm birthweight: Health, growth, and neurologic sequelae. *Journal of Pediatrics*, 1976, *88*, 531–541.

Flaherty, J. F., and Dusek, J. B. An investigation of the relationship between psychological androgyny and components of self-concept. *Journal of Personality and Social Psychology*, 1980, *38*, 984–992.

Flavell, J. H. *The developmental psychology of Jean Piaget.* New York: D. Van Nostrand, 1963.

Flavell, J. H. *Cognitive development.* Englewood Cliffs, N.J.: Prentice-Hall, 1977.

Flavell, J. H. Metacognition and cognitive monitoring. *American Psychologist*, 1979, *34*, 906–911.

Flavell, J. H., and Wohlwill, J. F. Formal and functional aspects of cognitive development. In D. Elkind and J. H. Flavell (Eds.), *Studies in cognitive development: Essays in honor of Jean Piaget.* New York: Oxford University Press, 1969.

Fleming, J. B. *Stopping wife abuse.* Garden City, New York: Anchor Press/Doubleday, 1979.

Fontana, V. J. *Somewhere a child is crying.* New York: Macmillan, 1973.

Forbes, D. Recent research on children's social cognition: A brief review. In W. Damon (Ed.), *New directions for child development.* San Francisco: Jossey-Bass, 1978.

Fox, G. L., The family's influence on adolescent sexual behavior. *Children Today*, May–June 1979, pp. 21–25.

Fox, J. H. Effects of retirement and former work life on women's adaptation to old age. *Journal of Gerontology*, 1977, *32*, 196–202.

Fozard, J. L.; Wolf, E.; Bell, B.; McFarland, R.; and Podolsky, S. Visual perception and communication. In J. E. Birren and K. W. Schaie (Eds.), *Handbook of the Psychology of Aging.* New York: Van Nostrand Reinhold, 1977.

Fraiberg, S. H. *The magic years: Understanding and handling the problems of early childhood.* New York: Scribner's, 1959.

Fraiberg, S. H. *Every child's birthright: In defense of mothering.* New York: Basic Books, 1977.

Frederick, C. J. Current trends in suicidal behavior in the United States. *American Journal of Psychotherapy*, 1978, *32(2)*, 172–200.

Freud, S. *A general introduction to psychoanalysis.* London: Boni and Linerright, 1924.

Fried, B. *The middle-age crisis.* New York: Harper & Row, 1967.

Friedenberg, E. Z. *Vanishing adolescence.* Boston: Beacon, 1959.

Friedman, M., and Rosenman, R. H. *Type A behavior and your heart.* New York: Knopf, 1974.

Fuchs, V. R. *Who shall live? Health, economics, and social choice.* New York: Basic Books, 1974.

Gallagher, J. J. *Teaching the gifted child.* 2nd ed. Boston: Allyn and Bacon, 1975.

Galst, J. P., and White, M. A. The unhealthy persuader: The reinforcing value of television and children's purchase-influencing attempts at the supermarket. *Child Development*, 1976, *47*, 1089–1096.

Galton, L. *Don't give up on an aging parent.* New York: Crown, 1975.

Gardner, L. I. Deprivation dwarfism. *Scientific American*, 1972, *227(1)*.

Garvey, C. *Play.* Cambridge, Mass.: Harvard University Press, 1977.

Gay, G. Multicultural preparation and teacher effectiveness in desegregated schools. *Theory Into Practice*, 1978, *11*, 149–156.

Gelfand, D. F. et al. The effects of adult models and described alternatives on children's choice of behavior management techniques. *Child Development*, 1974, *45*, 585–593.

Gelfand, D. M. The influence of self-esteem on rate of verbal conditioning and social matching behaviour. *Journal of Abnormal Social Psychology*, 1962, *65*, 259–265.

Gelles, R. J., and Straus, M. A. Violence in the American family. *Journal of Social Issues*, 1979, *35(2)*, 14–38.

Gelman, R., and Gallistel, C. R. *The child's understanding of number.* Cambridge, Mass.: Harvard University Press, 1978.

Gesell, A., and Amatruda, C. S. *Developmental diagnosis: Normal and abnormal child development.* New York: Hoeber, 1941.

Gesell, A., and Ilg, F. L. *Child development.* New York: Harper & Row, 1949.

Gewirtz, J. L., and Boyd, E. F. Experiments on mother-infant interaction underlying mutual attached acquisition: The infant conditions the mother. In T. Alloway, P. Pliner, and L. Krames (Eds.), *Attachment behavior*, New York, Plenum Press, 1977.

Gibson, E. J. Development of perception: Discrimination of depth compared with discrimination of graphic symbols. In J. C. Wright and J. Kagan (Eds.), Basic cognitive process in children. *Monograph of Social Research in Child Development*, 1963, *28(2)*, 5–32.

Gibson, E. J., and Walk, R. D. The "visual cliff." *Scientific American*, 1960, *202*, 64–71.

Gilder, G. *Naked Nomads.* New York: Quadrangle, 1974.

Gilligan, C., and Kohlberg, L. From adolescence to adulthood: The rediscovery of reality in a postconventional world. In Appel and Preseissen, *Topics in Cognitive Development.* New York: Plenum Press, 1977.

Ginott, C. *Between parent and child.* New York: Macmillan 1965.

Ginsburg, H., and Opper, S. *Piaget's theory of intellectual development: An introduction* (2nd ed.). Englewood Cliffs, N.J.: Prentice-Hall, 1979.

Ginzberg, E. et al. *Occupational choice.* New York: Columbia University Press, 1951.

Glaser, K. The treatment of depressed and suicidal adolescents. *American Journal of Psychotherapy*, 1978, *32(2)*, 252–269.

Glazer, N. The rediscovery of the family. *Commentary*, 1978, *65(3)*, 49–56.

Glick, P. C. A demographer looks at American families. *Journal of Marriage and the Family*, 1975, *37*, 15–26.

Glick, P. C., and Norton, A. J. Frequency, duration, and probability of divorce. *Journal of Marriage and the Family*, 1971, *33*, 307–317.

Glick, P. C., and Norton, A. J. Marrying, divorcing, and living together in the U.S. today. *Population Bulletin.* Washington, D.C.: Population Reference Bulletin, 1977.

Goethals, G. W., and Klos, D. S. *Experiencing youth: First-person accounts.* Boston: Little, Brown, 1976.

Gold, D., and Andres, D. Developmental comparisons between 10-year-old children with employed and nonemployed mothers. *Child Development*, 1978, *49*, 75–84.

Goldberg, S. Social competence in infancy: A model of parent-infant interaction. *Merrill-Palmer Quarterly*, 1977, *23*, 163–177.

Goldberg, S., and Lewis, M. Play behavior in the year-old infant: Early sex differences. *Child Development*, 1969, *40*, 21–31.

Golden, M.; Rosenbluth, L.; Grossi, M.; Policare, H.; Freeman, H.; and Brownlee, E. *The New York City infant day care study.* New York: Medical and Health Research Association of New York City, 1978.

Goldfarb, W. Effects of psychological deprivation in infancy and subsequent stimulation. *American Journal of Psychiatry*, 1945a, *102*, 18–33.

Goldfarb, W. Psychological privation in infancy and subsequent adjustment. *American Journal of Orthopsychiatry*, 1945b, *15*, 247–255.

Goldfarb, W. Childhood psychosis. In Paul H. Mussen (Ed.), *Carmichael's manual of child psychosis.* New York: Wiley, 1970.

Goldstein, E. Effect of same-sex and cross-sex role models on the subsequent academic productivity of scholars. *American Psychologist*, 1979, *34*, 407–410.

Goldstine, T. and Gutmann, D. A TAT study of Navajo aging. *Psychiatry*, 1972, *35*, 373–384.

Golomb, C., and Cornelius, C. B. Symbolic play and its cognitive significance. *Developmental Psychology*, 1977, *13(3)*, 246–252.

Goodenough, F. L. *Anger in young children.* Minneapolis: University of Minnesota Press, 1931.

Goodman, K. S., and Goodman, Y. M. Learning to read is natural. In Resnick and Weaver (Eds.), *Theory and practice of early reading.* Hillsdale, N.J.: Erlbaum, 1980.

Goodman, M. Toward a biology of menopause. *Signs: Journal of Women in Culture and Society*, 1980, *5*, 739–753.

Goodnow, J. J. A test of milieu differences with some of Piaget's tasks. *Psychological Monographs*, 1962, *76(36)*, Whole no. 555.

Gordon, C.; Gaitz, C. M.; and Scott, J. Leisure and lives: personal expressivity across the life span. In R. H. Binstock and E. Shavas (Eds.), *Handbook of aging and the social sciences.* New York: Van Nostrand Reinhold, 1977.

Gordon, S, and Scales, P. The myth of the normal sexual outlet. *Journal of Pediatric Psychology*, 1977, *2(3)*, 101–103.

Gordon, T., and Foss, B. M. The role of stimulation in the delay of onset of crying in the newborn infant. *Quarterly Journal of Experimental Psychology*, 1966, *18*, 79–81.

Goslin, P. A. Accuracy of self-perception and social acceptance. *Sociometry*, 1962, *65*, 283–296.

Gould, R. L. The phases of adult life: A study in developmental psychology. *American Journal of Psychiatry*, 1972, *129(5)*, 33–43.

Gove, W. R. Sex, marital status, and mortality. *American Journal of Sociology*, 1973, *79*, 45–67.

Graham, F. K.; Mantarazzo, R. G.; and Caldwell, B. M. Behavioral differences between normal and traumatized newborns. *Psychological Monographs*, 1956, *70*, Nos. 427 and 428.

Graves, A. J. Attainment of conservation of mass, weight, and volume in minimally educated adults. *Developmental Psychology*, 1972, 7, 223.

Graziano, A. M.; DeGiovanni, I. S.; and Garcia, K. A. Behavioral treatment of children's fears: A review. *Psychological Bulletin*, 1979, 86, 804–830.

Green, C. P., and Polleigen, K. *Teen-age pregnancy: A major problem for minors*. Washington, D.C.: Zero Population Growth, August 1977.

Greenberg, J. H. (Ed.). *Universals of language*. Cambridge, Mass.: M. I. T. Press, 1963.

Gregor, A. J., and McPherson, D. A. Racial attitudes among white and Negro children in a Deep South metropolitan area. *Journal of Social Psychology*, 1966, 68, 95–106.

Gross, B., and Gross, R. Model programs in six cities to teach mothers and children the fundamentals of family life. *Parents'*, July 1978, 53, 72–75.

Gubrium, J. F. Being single in old age. *International Journal on Aging and Human Development*, 1975, 6, 29–41.

Guilford, J. P. The structure of intellect. *Psychological Bulletin*, 1956, 53, 267–293.

Guilford, J. P. *The nature of human intelligence*. New York: McGraw-Hill, 1967.

Guilford, J. P., and Hoepfner, R. *Analysis of intelligence*. New York: McGraw-Hill, 1971.

Guinn, R. Value clarification in the bicultural classroom. *Journal of Teacher Education*, 1977, 28, 46–47.

Gump, P.; Schoggen, P.; and Redl, F. The camp milieu and its immediate effects. *Journal of Social Issues*, 1957, 13, 40–46.

Gurin, G.; Veroff, J.; and Feld, S. *Americans view their mental health*. New York: Basic Books, 1960.

Guthrie, K., and Hudson, L. M. Training conservation through symbolic play: A second look. *Child Development*, 1979, 50, 1269–1271.

Guttman, D. The cross-cultural perspective: Notes toward a comprehensive psychology of aging. In J. E. Birren and K. W. Schaie (Eds.), *Handbook of the Psychology of Aging*. New York: Van Nostrand Reinhold, 1977.

Haaf, R. A., and Bell, R. Q. A facial dimension in visual discrimination by human infants. *Child Development*, 1967, 38, 893–899.

Haan, N., and Day, D. A longitudinal study of change and sameness in personality development: Adolescence to later adulthood. *International Journal of Aging and Human Development*. 1974, 5, 11–39.

Hagestad, G. Pattern of communication and influence between grandparents and grandchildren in a changing society. Paper presented at the World Congress of Sociology, Sweden, 1978.

Halverson, C. F., and Waldrop, M. F. Relations between preschool activity and aspects of intellectual and social behavior at age 7½. *Developmental Psychology*, 1976, 12, 107–112.

Harding, C. G., and Golinkoff, R. M. The origins of intentional vocalizations in prelinguistic infants. *Child Development*, 1979, 50, 33–40.

Hare, A. P. Small group discussions with participatory and supervisory leadership. *Journal of Abnormal Psychology*, 1953, 48, 273–275.

Harkins, E. B. Effects of empty-nest transition on self-report of psychological and physical well-being. *Journal of Marriage and the Family*, 1978, 40, 549–558.

Harlow, H. F. The heterosexual affectional system in monkeys. *American Psychologist*, 1962, 17, 1–9.

Harlow, H. F., and Harlow, M. K. Learning to love. *American Scientist*, 1966, 54(3), 244–272.

Harris, C. S. *Fact book on aging: A profile of America's older population*. Washington, D.C.: The National Council on the Aging, Inc., 1978.

Harris, D. D., and Tseng, S. Children's attitudes toward peers and parents revealed by sentence completions. *Child Development*, 1957, 28, 401–411.

Harris, F. Fighting agism: Old people power. New Republic, 1974, March 23, pp 10–11.

Harris, L. and Associates, Inc. *The myth and reality of aging in America*. Washington, D.C.: The National Council on the Aging, Inc., 1975.

Harris, S., and Braun, J. Self-esteem and racial preference in black children. *Proceedings of the 79th Annual Convention of the American Psychological Association*, 1971, 6, 259.

Harrod, H. R.; L'Heureux, R.; Wangensteen, D. O.; and Hunt, C. D. Long-term follow-up of severe respiratory distress syndrome treated with IPPV. *Journal of Pediatrics*, 1974, 84, 277–286.

Hartley, J. T.; Harker, J. O.; and Walsh, D. A. Contemporary issues and new directions in adult development of learning and memory. In L. W. Poon (Ed.), *Aging in the 1980s: Psychological issues*. Washington, D.C.: American Psychological Association, 1980.

Harvey, O. J., and Rutherford, J. Status in the informal group: Influence and influenceability at differing age levels. *Child Development*, 1957, 28, 377–385.

Havens, E. M. Women, work, and wedlock: A note on female marital patterns in the United States. *American Journal of Sociology*, 1973, 78, 975–981.

Havighurst, R. J. *Developmental tasks and education* (3rd ed.). New York: David McKay, 1974.

Havighurst, R. J. Youth in exploration and man emergent. In H. Borrow (Ed.), *Man in a world of work*. Boston: Houghton Mifflin, 1964.

Havighurst, R. J.; Neugarten, B. L.; and Tobin, S. S. Disengagement and patterns of aging. In B. L. Neugarten (Ed.), *Middle age and aging*. Chicago: University of Chicago Press, 1968. Pp. 161–172.

Haynes, H.; White, B. L.; and Held, R. Visual accommodation in human infants. *Science*, 1965, 148, 528–530.

Hazen, N. L.; Lockman, J. J.; and Pick, H. L., Jr. The development of children's representations of large-scale environments. *Child Development*, 1978, 49, 623–636.

Hechinger, F. M. Limits sought on discipline of students. *The New York Times*, February 5, 1979, p. C1.

Heller, Celia. S., *Mexican-American youth: Forgotten youth at the crossroads*. New York: Random House, 1967.

Helson, R. Personality characteristics and developmental history of creative college women. *Genetic Psychological Monograph* 1967, 76, 205–256.

Hendry, L. B., and Gillies, P. Body type, body esteem, school, and leisure: A study of overweight, average and underweight adolescents. *Journal of Youth and Adolescence*, 1978, 7(2), 181–195.

Hersov, L. A. Refusal to go to school. *Journal of Child Psychology and Psychiatry*, 1960, 1, 137–146.

Hess, E.; Roth, R. B.; and Kaminsky, A. F. Is there a male climacteric? *Geriatrics*, 1955, 10, 170–173.

Hess, R. D. Political socialization in the schools. *Harvard Educational Review*, 1968, 38, 528–536.

Hetherington, E. M. A developmental study of the effects of sex of the dominant parent on sex-role preference, identification, and imitation in children. *Journal of Personality and Social Psychology*, 1965, 2, 188–194.

Hetherington, E. M. Effects of paternal absence on sex-types behaviors in Negro and white preadolescent males. *Journal of Personality and Social Psychology*, 1966, 4, 87–91.

Hetherington, E. M. Effects of father absence on personality development in adolescent daughters. *Developmental Psychology*, 1972, 7, 313–326.

Hetherington, E. M. Divorce: A child's perspective. *American Psychologist*, 1979, *34(10)*, 851–858.

Hetherington, E. M., and Deur, J. The effects of father absence on child development. *Young Children*, 1971, *26*, 233–248.

Hetherington, E. M., and Parke, R. D. *Child psychology*. New York: McGraw-Hill, 1975.

Hetherington, E. M.; Stouwie, R. J.; and Ridberg, E. H. Patterns of family interaction and child-rearing attitudes related to three dimensions of juvenile delinquency. *Journal of Abnormal Psychology*, 1971, *78*, 160–176.

Hickey, T., and Kalish, R. A. Young people's perceptions of adults. *Journal of Gerontology*, 1968, *23*, 215–219.

Hilger, Inez. The Chippewa child's life and its cultural background. Washington, D.C.: U.S. Government Printing Office, 1951.

Hilger, Inez. *Arapaho child life and its cultural background*. Washington, D.C.: U.S. Government Printing Office, 1972.

Hinton, J. *Dying*. Baltimore, Penguin Books, 1967.

Hock, E. Working and nonworking mothers with infants: Perceptions of their careers, the infants' needs, and satisfaction with mothering. *Developmental Psychology*, 1978, *14*, 37–43.

Hock, E.; Christman, K.; and Hock, M. Factors associated with decisions about return to work in mothers of infants. *Developmental Psychology*, 1980, *16*, 535–536.

Hoffman, L. W. Effects of maternal employment on the child—A review of the research. *Developmental Psychology*, 1974, *10*, 204–228.

Hoffman, L. W. Maternal employment: 1979. *American Psychologist*, 1979a, *34(10)*, 859–865.

Hoffman, L. W. The value of children in the United States. Paper presented at the East-West Population Center, Honolulu, 1979b.

Hoffman, L. W., and Mavis, J. D. Influences of children on marital interaction and parental satisfactions and dissatisfactions. In R. M. Lerner and G. B. Spanier (Eds.), *Child influences on marriage and family interaction: A lifespan perspective*. New York: Academic Press, 1978.

Hogan, D. The variable order of events in the life course. *American Sociological Review*, 1978, *43*, 573–586.

Holden, C. Hospices: For the dying, relief from pain and fear. *Science*, 1976, *193*, 389–391.

Holland, J. L. *Making vocational choices: A theory of careers*. Englewood Cliffs, N.J.: Prentice-Hall, 1973.

Hollingworth, L. S. What we know about the early selection and training of leaders. *Teachers College Record*, 1939, *40(7)*, 583.

Holmes, F. B. An experimental study of the fears of young children. *Child Development Monographs*, No. 20, Pt. 3. New York: Teachers College, 1935.

Holmes, L. B. Genetic counseling for the older pregnant woman: New data and questions. *New England Journal of Medicine*, 1978, *298*, 1419–1421.

Holt, J. *How children learn*. New York: Dell, 1970.

Hooper, F. H., and Sheehan, N. W. Logical concept attainment during the aging years: Issues in the neo-Piagetian research literature. In W. F. Overton and J. M. Gallagher (Eds.), *Knowledge and development* (Vol. 1). New York: Plenum Press, 1977.

Horn, J. L. Organization of data on lifespan development of human abilities. In L. R. Goulet and P. B. Baltes (Eds.), *Lifespan developmental psychology: Research and theory*. New York: Academic Press, 1970.

Horn, J. L. Intelligence: Why it grows, why it declines. In J. M. Hunt (Ed.), *Human intelligence*. New Brunswick, N.J.: Transaction Books, 1972.

Horn, J. L., and Cattell, R. B. Refinement and test of the theory of fluid and crystallized intelligence. *Journal of Educational Psychology*, 1966, *57*, 253–270.

Horn, J. L., and Donaldson, G. Cognitive development in adulthood. In O. B. Brim and J. Kagan (Eds.), *Constancy and change in human development*. Cambridge, Mass.: Harvard University Press, 1980.

Horner, M. F. Fail: Bright women. *Psychology Today*, November 1969, 36–38.

Horney, K. *The neurotic personality of our time*. New York: W. W. Norton, 1937.

Horowitz, J. Artistry grows with age, says Arrau at 75. *The New York Times*, February 5, 1978, sec. 2, p. 1.

Houts, P. L. IQ tests once again disturb educators. *The New York Times*, May 1, 1977, p. ED 21.

Hugin, F.; Norris, A.; and Shock, N. W. Skin reflex and voluntary reaction time in young and old males. *Journal of Gerontology*, 1960, *14*, 338–391.

Hulicka, I. M. Age differences in retention as a function of interference. *Journal of Gerontology*, 1967, *22*, 274–280.

Human Behavior: Adolescent alcoholics. 1978, *7(57)*, 474.

Hunt, B., and Hunt, M. *Prime time: A guide to the pleasures and opportunities of the new middle age*. New York: Stein and Day, 1975.

Hunt, M. *Sexual behavior in the 1970s*. Chicago: Playboy Press, 1974.

Hunt, M., and Hunt, B. *The divorce experience*. New York: McGraw-Hill, 1977.

Hunter, R. S.; Kilstrom, N.; Kraybill, E. N.; and Loda, F. Antecedents of child abuse and neglect in premature infants: A prospective study in a newborn intensive care unit. *Pediatrics*, 1978, *61(4)*, 629–635.

Hyde, J. S., and Rosenberg, B. G. *Half the human experience: The psychology of women*. (2nd ed.). Lexington, Mass.: D. C. Heath, 1980.

Inhelder, B., and Piaget, J. *The growth of logical thinking from childhood to adolescence*. New York: Basic Books, 1958.

Inhelder, B., and Piaget, J. *The early growth of logic in the child*. New York: Harper & Row, 1964.

Inhelder, B.; Sinclair, H.; and Bovet, M. *Learning and the development of cognition*. Cambridge, Mass.: Harvard University Press, 1974.

Interprofessional Task Force on Health and Children. Joint position statement on the development of family-centered maternity/newborn care in hospitals. Chicago: American College of Obstetrics and Gynecology, June 1978.

Irwin, D., and Moore, S. The young child's understanding of social justice. *Developmental Psychology*, 1971, *5*, 406–410.

Iscoe, I.; Willing, M.; and Harvey, J. Modification of children's judgments by a simulated group technique: A normative study. *Child Development*, 1963, *34*, 963–978.

Jacobson, L. Illness and human sexuality. *Nursing Outlook*, 1974, *22*, 50–53.

Jacques, E. Death and the midlife crisis. *International Journal of Psychoanalysis*, 1964, *46*, 502–514.

Jacques, J. M., and Chason, K. J. Cohabitation: Its impact on marital success. *Family Coordinator*, 1979, *28*, 35–45.

Jelliffe, D. B. Culture, social changes and infant feeding: Current trends in tropical regions. *American Journal of Clinical Nutrition*, 1962, *10*, 19–45.

Jenkins, C. D.; Rosenman, R. H.; and Zyzanski, S. J. Prediction of clinical coronary heart disease by a test for the coronary-prone behavior pattern. *New England Journal of Medicine*, 1974, *290*, 1271–1275.

Jensen, A. R. How much can we boost IQ and scholastic achievement? *Harvard Educational Review*, 1969, *39*, 1–123.

Joffe, C. Taking young children seriously. In N. K. Denzin (Ed.), *Children and their caretakers*. New Brunswick, N.J.: Transaction Books, 1973.

Jones, H. E., and Conrad, H. S. The growth and decline of intelligence: A study of a homogeneous group between the ages of ten and sixty. *Genetic Psychology Monographs*, 1933, *13*, 223–294.

Johnson, J. D.; Malachawski, N. C.; Grobstein, R.; Dailig, W. J. R.; and Sunshine, P. Prognosis of children surviving with the aid of mechanical ventilation in the newborn period. *Journal of Pediatrics*, 1974, *84*, 272–276.

Johnstone, J. W. C. Juvenile delinquency and the family: A contextual interpretation. *Youth & Society*, 1978, *9(3)*, 299–313.

Kagan, J. Do infants think? *Scientific American*, 1972, *226(3)*, 74–82.

Kagan, J. Family experience and the child's development. *American Psychologist*, 1979, *34(10)*, 886–891.

Kagan, J.; Kearsley, R.; and Zelazo, P. The effects of infant day care on psychological development. Paper presented at the meeting of the American Association for the Advancement of Science, Boston, 1976.

Kagan, J., and Kogan, N. Individual variation in cognitive process. In P. H. Gussen (Ed.), *Carmichael's Manual of Child Psychology*, vol. I. New York: Wiley, 1970.

Kagan, J., and Moss, H. A. *Birth to maturity*. New York: Wiley, 1962.

Kalish, R. A., and Knudtson, F. W. Attachment versus disengagement: A lifespan conceptualization. *Human Development*, 1976, *19*, 171–181.

Kallman, F. J. *The genetics of schizophrenia: A study of heredity and reproduction in the families of 1,087 schizophrenics*. New York: Augustin, 1938.

Kallman, F. J., and Sander, G. Twin studies on senescence. *American Journal of Psychiatry*, 1949, *106*, 29–36.

Kane, B. Children's concepts of death. *The Journal of Genetic Psychology*, 1979, *134*, 141–153.

Kaplan, H. S. Sex at menopause. In L. Rose (Ed.), *The menopause book*. New York: Hawthorn, 1977, 112–129.

Kaplan, H. S., and Pokorny, A. P. Aging and self-attitude: A conditional relationship. *International Journal of Aging and Human Development*, 1970, *1*, 241–250.

Kaplan, R. Personal correspondence, 1980.

Kappelman, M. M. *Sex and the American teen-ager: The problems of adolescent sexuality—and how to cope with them—in today's changing world*. New York: Readers Digest Press, 1977.

Kastenbaum, R. The foreshortened life perspective. *Geriatrics*, 1969, *24*, 126–133.

Kastenbaum, R. Getting there. *Psychology Today*, December 1971, *5*, 53.

Kastenbaum, R. Death and development throughout the life span. In H. Feifel (Ed.), *New meanings of death*. New York: McGraw-Hill, 1977, 18–45.

Kastenbaum, R., and Candy, S. E. The 4% fallacy: a methodological and empirical critique of extended care facility population statistics. *Aging and Human Development*, 1973, *4*, 15–21.

Kastenbaum, R., and Durkee, N. Young people view old age. In R. Kastenbaum (Ed.), *New thoughts on old age*. New York: Springer Publishing, 1964. Pp. 237–249.

Katchadourian, H. A. *The biology of adolescence*. San Francisco: Freeman, 1977.

Katz, L. Sibling rivalry. *Parents*, January 1979, p. 78.

Kaye, H. The conditioned Babkin reflex in human newborns. *Psychonomic Science*, 1965, *2*, 287–288.

Keislar, E. R.; Hsieh, E.; and Bhasin, C. An intercultural study: Discrimination and informal experience. *Reading Teacher*, November 1972.

Kemler, D. G. Patterns of hypothesis testing in children's discriminative learning: A study of the development of problem-solving strategies. *Developmental Psychology*, 1978, *14*, 653–673.

Keniston, K. Youth: A "new" stage of life. *The American Scholar*, Autumn 1970, pp. 631–654.

Keniston, K. *Youth and dissent: The rise of a new opposition*. New York: Harcourt Brace Jovanovich, 1971.

Keniston, K. The future of the American family. *Parents*, 1978, *53*, 46–47.

Kenkel, W. F. *The family in perspective*. New York: Appleton-Century-Crofts, 1966.

Kessen, W.; Haith, M. M.; and Salapatek, P. H. Human infancy: A bibliography and guide. In P. H. Mussen (Ed.), *Carmichael's manual of child psychology* (3rd ed.), New York: Wiley, 1970.

Kessler, J. W. Neurosis in childhood. In B. Wolman (Ed.), *Manual of child psychopathology*. New York: McGraw-Hill, 1972.

Keyserling, M. D. *Windows on day care*. New York: National Council of Jewish Women, 1972.

Kimmel, D. C. *Adulthood and aging*. New York: Wiley, 1974 (2nd ed.).

Kinsey, A. C.; Pomeroy, W. B.; and Martin, C. C. *Sexual behavior in the human male*. Philadelphia: Saunders, 1948.

Kinsey, A. C.; Pomeroy, W. B., and Martin, C. C. *Sexual behavior in the human female*. Philadelphia: Saunders, 1953.

Klaus, M. H., and Kennell, J. H. *Maternal-infant bonding*. St. Louis: C. V. Mosby, 1976.

Klaus, M. H., and Kennell, J. H. Parent-to-infant attachment. In J. H. Stevens, Jr., and M. Mathews (Eds.), *Mother/child, father/child relationships*. Washington, D.C.: National Association for the Education of Young Children, 1978, p. 20.

Klein, C. *The single parent experience*. New York: Avon, 1973.

Klein, M., and Stern, L. Low birth weight and the battered child syndrome. *American Journal of Diseases of Children*, 1971, *122*, 15–18.

Klocke, R. A. Influence of aging on the lung. In C. E. Finch and L. Hayflick (Eds.), *Handbook of the biology of aging*. New York: Van Nostrand Reinhold, 1977.

Klonoff, H.; Low, M.; and Marcus, A. Neuropsychological effects of marijuana. *Canadian Medical Association Journal*, 1973, *108*, 150–156.

Knopf, O. *Successful aging: The facts and fallacies of growing old*. New York: Viking, 1975.

Kobasa, S. C. Stressful life events, personality, and health: An inquiry into hardiness. *Journal of Personality and Social Psychology*, 1979, *37*, 1–11.

Kohl, H. *36 children*, New York: New American Library, 1967.

Kohlberg, L. The development of children's orientations towards a moral order: I. Sequence in the development of moral thought. *Vita Humana*, 1963, 6, 11–33.

Kohlberg, L. Development of moral character and moral ideology. In M. L. Hoffman and L. Hoffman (Eds.), *Review of child development research*. New York: Russell Sage Foundation, 1964, *1*, 383.

Kohlberg, L. A cognitive-developmental analysis of children's sex-role concepts and attitudes. In E. F. Maccoby (Ed.), *The development of sex differences*. Stanford: Stanford University Press, 1966.

Kohlberg, L. Continuities in child and adult moral development revisited. In P. B. Baltes and K. W. Schaie (Eds.), *Lifespan developmental psychology: Personality and socialization*. New York: Academic Press, 1973. Pp. 179–204.

Kohlberg, L., and Kramer, R. Continuities and discontinuities in childhood and adult moral development. *Human Development*, 1969, *12*, 93–120.

Kohn, R. R. Heart and cardiovascular system. In C. E. Finch and L. Hayflick (Eds.), *Handbook of the biology of aging*. New York: Van Nostrand Reinhold, 1977.

Kolata, G. B. Behavioral teratology: Birth defects of the mind. *Science*, 1978, *202*, 732–734.

Kübler-Ross, E. *On death and dying*. New York: Macmillan, 1969.

Kuhlen, R. G. Developmental changes in motivation during the adult years. In J. E. Birren (Ed.), *Relations of development and aging.* Springfield, Ill.: Charles C Thomas, 1964. Pp. 209–246.

Kuhn, D.; Nash, S. C.; Brucken, L. Sex role concepts of two- and three-year-olds. *Child Development,* 1978, *49,* 445–451.

Kurtines, W., and Greif, E. B. The development of moral thought: Review and evaluation of Kohlberg's approach. *Psychological Bulletin,* 1974, *81(8),* 453–470.

Kushnir, T. A review of the evidence for birth order differences in anxiety and affiliation in stressful situations. *Social Behavior and Personality,* 1978, *6(2),* 179–186.

Ladd, G. W., and Oden, S. The relationship between peer acceptance and children's ideas about helpfulness. *Child Development,* 1979, *50,* 402–408.

Lamb, M. The role of the father: An overview. In M. Lamb (Ed.), *The role of the father in child development.* New York: Wiley, 1976.

Lamb, M. Father-infant and mother-infant interaction in the first year of life. *Child Development,* 1977, *48,* 167–181.

Lamb, M. Paternal influences and the father's role. *American Psychologist,* 1979, *34(10),* 938–943.

Lane, B. Attitudes of youth toward the aged. *Journal of Marriage and the Family,* 1964, 26, 229–231.

Lansky, L. M. The family structure also affects the model: Sex-role attitudes in parents of preschool children. *Merrill-Palmer Quarterly,* 1967, *13,* 139–150.

Lapouse, R., and Monk, M. A. An epidemiologic study of behavior characteristics in children. In H. Quay (Ed.), *Children's behavior disorders.* Princeton: D. Van Nostrand, 1968.

Laska, S. B., and Micklin, M. The knowledge dimension of occupational socialization: Role models and their social influences. *Youth & Society,* 1979, *10(4),* 360–378.

LaVoie, J. C. Punishment and adolescent self-control. *Developmental Psychology,* 1973, *8,* 16–24.

Leahy, R. L., and Eiter, M. Moral judgment and the development of real and ideal androgynous self-image during adolescence and young adulthood. *Developmental Psychology,* 1980, *16,* 362–370.

Lehman, H. C. *Age and achievement.* Princeton, N.J.: Princeton University Press, 1953.

Leifer, A. D.; Leiderman, P. H.; Barnett, C. R.; and Williams, J. A. Effects of mother-infant separation on maternal behavior. *Child Development,* 1972, *43,* 1203–1218.

Lenneberg, E. H. A biological perspective of language. In Eric H. Lenneberg (Ed.), *New directions in the study of language.* Cambridge, Mass.: M. I. T. Press, 1964a.

Lenneberg, E. H. (Ed.). *New directions in the study of language.* Cambridge, Mass.: M. I. T. Press, 1964b.

Leonard, Carol H. et al. Preliminary observations on the behavior of children present at the birth of a sibling. *Pediatrics,* 1979, *64(6),* 949–951.

Lerner, R. M., and Korn, S. J. Development of body build stereotypes in males. *Child Development,* 1972, *45,* 908–920.

Le Shan, E. *The wonderful crisis of middle age.* New York: David McKay, 1973.

Leon, G. R.; Gillum, B.; Gillum, R.; and Gouze, M. Personality stability and change over a 30-year-period—middle age to old age. *Journal of Consulting and Clinical Psychology,* 1979, *47,* 517–524.

Leskow, S., and Smock, C. D. Developmental changes in problem-solving strategies: Permutations. *Developmental Psychology,* 1970, *2,* 412–422.

Leventhal, A. S., and Lipsitt, L. P. Adaptation, pitch discrimination, and sound localization in the neonate. *Child Development,* 1964, *35,* 759–767.

Levin, I. The development of time concepts in young children: Reasoning about duration. *Child Development,* 1977, *48,* 435–448.

Levin, I.; Israel, E.; and Darom, E. The development of time concepts in young children: The relation between duration and succession. *Child Development,* 1978, *49,* 755–764.

Levinson, D. *The seasons of a man's life.* New York: Knopf, 1978.

Levinson, D.; Darrow, C.; Klein, E.; Levinson, M.; and McKee, B. Periods in the adult development of men: Ages 18 to 45. *The Counseling Psychologist,* 1976, *6,* 1.

Levinson, D.; Darrow, C.; Klein, E.; Levinson, M.; and McKee, B. Periods in the adult development of men: Ages 18 to 45. In A. G. Sargent (Ed.), *Beyond the sex roles.* New York: West Publishing, 1977.

Lewis, R. A. A longitudinal test of a development framework for premarital dyadic formation. *Journal of Marriage and the Family,* 1973, *35,* 16–25.

Lewis, R. A.; Frenau, P. J.; and Roberts, C. L. Fathers and the postparental transition. *Family Coordinator,* 1979, *28,* 514–520.

Lewis, R. A., and Spanier, G. B. Theorizing about the quality and stability of marriage. In W. R. Bun, R. Hill, F. I. Nye, and I. L. Reiss (Eds.), *Contemporary theories about the family.* Vol. I. New York: The Free Press, 1979.

Liben, L. S. Memory from a cognitive-developmental perspective: A theoretical and empirical review. In W. F. Overton and J. M. Gallagher (Eds.), *Knowledge and development.* New York: Plenum Press, 1977.

Lieberman, M. A. The relationship of mortality rates to entrance to a home for aged. *Geriatrics,* 1961, *16,* 515–519.

Lieberman, M. A. Psychological correlates of impending death: Some preliminary observations. *Journals of Gerontology,* 1965, *20(2),* 181–190.

Lindeman, B. *The twins who found each other.* New York: Morrow, 1969.

Linden, E. Apes, men, and language. New York: Dutton, 1975.

Ling, D. Acoustic stimulus duration in relation to behavioral responses of newborn infants. *Journal of Speech and Hearing Research,* 1972, *15,* 567–571.

Lipsitt, L. P.; Sturner, W. Q.; and Burke, P. Perinatal indicators and subsequent crib death. *Infant Behavior and Development,* 1979, *2,* 325–328.

Lipsitz, J. S. Adolescent development: Myths and realities. *Children Today,* October 1979, pp. 2–7.

Little, A. H. Eyelid conditioning in the human infant as a function of ISI. Paper presented at the meeting of the Society for Research in Child Development, Minneapolis, April 1971.

Livson, N. Developmental dimensions of personality: A lifespan formulation. In P. B. Baltes and K. W. Schaie (Eds.), *Lifespan developmental psychology: Personality and socialization.* New York: Academic Press, 1973.

Looft, W. R. Egocentrism and social interaction across the life span. *Psychological Bulletin,* 1972, *78(2),* 73–92.

Lopata, H. Z. Widows as a minority group. *Gerontologist,* 1971, *11(1),* Part 2.

Lopata, H. Z. Living through widowhood. *Psychology Today,* July 1973, *7,* 87–98.

Losnoff-Caravaglia, G. The five-percent fallacy. *International Journal of Aging and Human Development,* 1978–1979, *9,* 187–192.

Love, K. For first time in U.S. divorces pass one million. *The New York Times,* February 18, 1976, p. 49.

Lowenthal, M. F., and Haven, C. Interaction and adaptation: Intimacy as a critical variable. *American Sociological Review,* 1968, *33,* 20–30.

Lowenthal, M. F. et al. *Four stages of life: A comparative study of men and women facing transitions.* San Francisco: Jossey-Bass, 1975.

Luce, G. G., and Segal, J. *Sleep.* New York: Coward-McCann, 1966.

Lynn, D. B. *The father: His role in child development.* Monterey, Calif.: Brooks/Cole Publishing Co., 1974.

Maccoby, E. E., and Jacklin, C. N. *The psychology of sex differences.* Stanford, Calif.: Stanford University Press, 1974.

McConnell, T. Suggestibility in children as a function of chronological age. *Journal of Abnormal Social Psychology,* 1963, *67,* 286–289.

McCord, W.; McCord, J.; and Howard, A. Familial correlates of aggression in non-delinquent male children. *Journal of Abnormal and Social Psychology,* 1961, *62,* 79–93.

McGhee, P. E. *Humor: Its origin and development.* San Francisco: W. H. Freeman, 1979.

McGurk, H., Turnura, C., and Creighton, S. J. Auditory-visual coordination in neonates. *Child Development,* 1977, *48,* 138–143.

McKain, W. C. A new look at older marriages. *Family Coordinator,* 1972, *21,* 61–69.

Macrae, J. W., and Herbert-Jackson, E. Are behavioral effects of infant day care programs specific? *Developmental Psychology,* 1975, *12,* 269–270.

Maddox, G. L. Retirement as a social event in the United States. In B. L. Neugarten (Ed.), *Middle age and aging.* Chicago: University of Chicago Press, 1968.

Made, M. F., and Wrench, D. F. Significant findings in child abuse research. *Victimology,* 1977, *2,* 196–224.

Magenis, R. E.; Overton, K. M.; Chamberlin, J.; Brady, T.; and Lovrein, E. Paternal origin of the extra chromosome in Down's syndrome. *Human Genetics,* 1977, *37,* 7–16.

Makinodan, T. Immunity and aging. In C. E. Finch and L. Hayflick (Eds.), *Handbook of the biology of aging.* New York: Van Nostrand Reinhold, 1977.

Malina, R. M. Secular changes in size and maturity: Causes and effects. In Alex F. Roche et al. (Eds.), Secular trends in human growth, maturation, and development, *Monographs of the Society for Research in Child Development,* 1979, *44* (3–4), Serial no. 179, 59–102.

Mannarino, A. Friendship patterns and self-concept development in preadolescent males. *Journal of Genetic Psychology,* 1978, *133,* 105–110.

Manosevitz, M.; Prentice, N. M.; and Wilson, F. Individual and family correlates of imaginary companions in preschool children. *Developmental Psychology,* 1973, *8,* 72–79.

Marcia, J. E. Development and validation of ego-identity status. *Journal of Personality and Social Psychology,* 1966, *3,* 551–558.

Marcia, J. E. Identity six years later: A follow-up study. *Journal of Youth and Adolescence,* 1976, *5,* 145–160.

Marland, S. P. *Education of the gifted and talented.* A report submitted to the citizens of the United States by the Commissioner of Education. Washington, D.C.: U.S. Office of Education, 1972.

Marsh, G. R., and Thompson, L. W. Psychophysiology of aging. In J. E. Birren and K. W. Schaie (Eds.), *Handbook of the psychology of aging.* New York: Van Nostrand Reinhold, 1977.

Marshall, W. A. The body. In R. R. Sears and S. Feldman (Eds.), *The seven ages of man.* Los Altos, Calif.: William Kaufmann, 1964.

Masters, J. C., and Mokros, J. R. Self-reinforcement processes in children. In H. W. Reese (Ed.), *Advances in child development and behavior.* Vol. 19. New York: Academic Press, 1974.

Masters, W. H., and Johnson, V. E. *Human sexual response.* Boston: Little, Brown, 1966.

Masters, W. H., and Johnson, V. E. *Human sexual inadequacy.* Boston: Little, Brown, 1970.

Masters, W. H., and Johnson, V. E. *The pleasure bond: A new look at sexuality and commitment.* Boston: Little, Brown, 1975.

Matas, L.; Arend, R. A.; and Sroufe, L. A. Continuity of adaptation in the second year: The relationship between quality of attachment and later competence. *Child Development,* 1978, *49,* 547–556.

Matheny, A. P., Jr. Bayley's infant behavior record: Behavioral components and twin analyses. *Child Development,* 1980, *51,* 1157–1167.

Mathes, E. The effects of physical attractiveness and anxiety on heterosexual adjustment over a series of five encounters. *Journal of Marriage and the Family,* 1975, *37,* 769–773.

Mathews, K. A., and Brunson, B. I. Allocation of attention and the Type A coronary-prone behavior pattern. *Journal of Personality and Social Psychology,* 1979, *37,* 2081–2090.

Matteson, D. R. *Adolescence today: Sex roles and the search for identity.* Homewood, Ill.: Dorsey Press, 1975.

Mead, G. H. *Mind, self, and society.* Chicago: University of Chicago Press, 1934.

Mead, M. *Coming of age in Samoa.* New York: Morrow, 1928.

Mead, M. *Male and female: A study of the sexes in a changing world.* New York: Morrow, 1949.

Mead, M. *Culture and commitment: A study of the generation gap.* Garden City, N.Y.: Doubleday, 1970.

Mears, C. Play and development of cosmic confidence. *Developmental Psychology,* 1978, *14(4),* 371–378.

Mech, E. V. Adoption: A policy perspective. In B. Caldwell and H. Riccuiti (Eds.), *Review of child development research,* vol. 3. Chicago: University of Chicago Press, 1973.

Medawar, P. W. Unnatural science. *New York Review of Books,* February 3, 1977, pp. 13–18.

Mednick, S. A.; Schulsinger, H.; and Schulsinger, F. Schizophrenia in children of schizophrenic mothers. In A. Davies (Ed.), *Child personality and psychopathology,* vol. 2. New York: Wiley, 1975.

Meislin, R. J. Poll finds more liberal beliefs on marriage and sex roles, especially among the young. *The New York Times,* November 27, 1977, sec. 1, p. 75.

Mendelson, M. A. *Tender loving greed: How the incredibly lucrative nursing home "industry" is exploiting old people and defrauding us all.* New York: Knopf, 1974.

Mendelson, M. J., and Haith, M. M. The relation between audition and vision in the human newborn. *Monographs of the Society for Research in Child Development,* 1976, *41(4),* serial no. 167.

Meredith, H. V. Body size of contemporary groups of preschool children studied in different parts of the world. *Child Development,* 1968, *39,* 335–369.

Messer, S. B. Reflection-impulsivity. A review. *Psychological Bulletin,* 1976, *83,* 1026–1052.

Midgley, M. Beast and man. Ithaca, N.Y.: Cornell University Press, 1978.

Millar, S. *The psychology of play.* New York: Jason Aronson, 1974.

Miller, G. A. Language and psychology. In Eric H. Lenneberg (Ed.), *New directions in the study of language.* Cambridge, Mass.: M. I. T. Press, 1964

Miller, N., and Dollard, J. *Social learning theory and imitation.* New Haven, Conn.: Yale University Press, 1941.

Mills, E. W. Career development in middle life. In W. E. Bartlett (Ed.), *Evolving religious careers.* Washington, D.C.: CARA, 1970.

Milman, D. H. School phobia: Clinical experience. *New York State Journal of Medicine,* 1966, *66,* 1887–1891.

Money, J. Influence of hormones on sexual behavior. *Annual Review of Medicine,* 1965, *16,* 67–82.

Money, J., and Ehrhardt, A. A. *Man and woman, boy and girl.* Baltimore: Johns Hopkins Press, 1972.

Money, J., and Tucker, P. *Sexual signatures: On being a man or a woman.* Boston: Little, Brown, 1975.

Montrose, Myryame. New options in childbirth, Part I: Family centered maternity care. *American Baby,* May 1978, 52–54, 58ff.

Moore, K., and Waite, L. Early childbearing and educational attainment. *Family Planning Perspectives,* 1977, *9,* 220–225.

Morgan, L. A. A reexamination of widowhood and morale. *Journal of Gerontology*, 1976, *31*, 687–695.

Morison, P., and Gardner, H. Dragons and dinosaurs: The child's capacity to differentiate fantasy from reality. *Child Development*, 1978, *49*, 642–648.

Morland, J. K. Racial recognition by nursery-school children in Lynchburg, Virginia. *Social Forces*, 1958, *37*, 132–137.

Morrison, Ian. The elderly primigravida. *American Journal of Obstetrics and Gynecology*, 1975, *15*, 465–470.

Moskowitz, B. A. The acquisition of language. *Scientific American*, 1978, *239*, 92–108.

Mowrer, O. H. Learning theory and the symbolic process. New York: Wiley, 1960.

Mueller, E., and Lucas, T. A developmental analysis of peer interaction in a playgroup setting. In M. Lewis and L. A. Rosenblum (Eds.), *Friendship and peer relations*. New York: Wiley, 1975.

Munnichs, J. M. A. *Old age and finitude*. Basel, Switzerland: Karger, 1966.

Munsinger, H. The adopted child's IQ: A critical review. *Psychological Bulletin*, 1975, *82*, 623–659.

Murphy, J. M., and Gilligan, C. Moral development in late adolescence and adulthood: A critique and reconstruction of Kohlberg's theory. *Human Development*, 1980, *23*, 77–104.

Murphy, L. B. Infants' play and cognitive development. In Maria W. Piers (Ed.), *Play and development: A symposium*. New York: Norton, 1972.

Mussen, P. H. (Ed.). *Handbook of research methods in child development*, New York: Wiley, 1960.

Mussen, P. H. *The psychological development of the child*. Englewood Cliffs, N.J.: Prentice-Hall, 1973.

Muuss, R. E. Adolescent development and the secular trend. *Adolescence*, 1970, *5*, 267–286.

Myers, M. L. et al. A nutritional study of school children in a depressed urban district. II. Physical and biochemical findings. *Journal American Dietetic Association*, 1968, *53*, 226–234.

National Institutes of Health. Antenatal diagnosis: Report of a consensus development conference sponsored by the National Institute of Child Health and Human Development. Bethesda, Md.: NIH Publication No. 79–1973, April 1979.

National Tribal Chairmen's Association. National Indian Conference on Aging. Phoenix, Ariz., 1976.

Neilon, P. Shirley's babies after fifteen years: A personality study. *Journal of Genetic Psychology*, 1948, *73*, 175–186.

Neimark, E. Intellectual development during adolescence. In F. Horowitz (Ed.), *Review of child development research*, vol. 4, Chicago: University of Chicago Press, 1975.

Neimark, E. D. Confounding with cognitive-style factors: An artifact explanation for the apparent nonuniversal incidence of formal operations. In I. E. Sigel, D. M. Brodzinsky, and R. Gollinkoff (Eds.), *Piagetian theory and research: New directions and applications*. Hillsdale, N.J.: Erlbaum, 1981.

Neimark, E.; Slotnik, N.; and Ulrich, T. Development of memorization strategies. *Developmental Psychology*, 1971, *5*, 427–432.

Nelson, H.; Enkin, M.; Saigal, S.; Bennett, K.; Milner, R.; and Sackett, D. A randomized clinical trial of the Leboyer approach to childbirth. *New England Journal of Medicine*, 1980, *302*, 655–660.

Neugarten, B. L. *Personality in middle and late life*. New York: Atherton Press, 1964.

Neugarten, B. L. The awareness of middle age. In R. Owen (Ed.), *Middle age*. London: British Broadcasting Corporation, 1967.

Neugarten, B. L. Adult personality: Toward a psychology of the life cycle. In B. L. Neugarten (Ed.), *Middle age and aging*. Chicago: University of Chicago Press, 1968.

Neugarten, B. L. Personality change in late life: A developmental perspective. In C. Eisdorfer and M. P. Lawton (Eds.), *Psychology of adult development and aging*. Washington, D.C.: American Psychological Association, 1973.

Neugarten, B. L. Personality and aging. In J. E. Birren and K. W. Schaie (Eds.), *Handbook of the psychology of aging*. New York: Van Nostrand Reinhold, 1977.

Neugarten, B. L., and Gutmann, D. Age-sex roles and personality in middle age: A thematic apperception study. *Psychological Monographs*, 1958, 72(17, Whole No. 470).

Neugarten, B. L.; Moore, J. W.; and Lowe, J. C. Age norms, age constraints, and adult socialization. *American Journal of Sociology*, 1965, *70*, 710–717.

Neugarten, B. L., and Weinstein, K. K. The changing American grandparent. *Journal of Marriage and the Family*, 1964, *26(2)*, 199–203.

Neugarten, B. L.; Wood, V.; Kraines, R.; and Loomis, B. Women's attitudes toward the menopause. *Vita Humana*, 1963, *6*, 140–151.

Newcomb, P. R. Cohabitation in America: An assessment of consequences. *Journal of Marriage and the Family*, 1979, *41*, 597–603.

Newmann, H. H.; Freeman, F. N.; and Holzinger, K. J. *Twins: A study of heredity and environment*. Chicago: University of Chicago Press, 1937.

Newsweek. Teen-age suicide. August 28, 1978, 74–77.

Newton, N. Battle between breast and bottle. *Psychology Today*, 1972, *6*, 68–70, 88–89.

Newton, N.; Peeler, D.; and Rawlins, C. Effect of lactation on maternal behavior in mice with comparative data on humans. *Lying-in: Journal of Reproductive Medicine*, 1968, *1*, 257.

Niemi, R. G., and Sobieszek, B. I. Political socialization. *Annual Review of Sociology*, 1977, *3*, 209-233.

Nisbet, J. D. Intelligence and age: Retesting with twenty-four years' interval. *British Journal of Educational Psychology*, 1957, *27*, 190–198.

Novak, M. The family out of favor. *Harper's*. April 1976, pp. 37–46.

NYCA. Facts on alcoholism. National Council on Alcoholism, N.Y., 1978.

O'Brien, P.; Noller, K.; Robboy, S.; Barnes, A.; Kaufman, R.; Tilley, B.; and Townsend, D. Vaginal epithelial changes in young women enrolled in the National Cooperative Diethylstilbestrol Adenosis (DESAD) Project. *Obstetrics and Gynecology*, 1979, *53*, 300–304.

Okun, M. A., and DiVesta, F. J. Cautiousness in adulthood as a function of age and instructions. *Journal of Gerontology*, 1976, *31(3)*, 371–376.

Okun, M. A., and Elias, C. S. Cautiousness in adulthood as a function of age and payoff structure. *Journal of Gerontology*, 1977, *32*, 311–316.

Olmstead, A. H. From the journal of a newly retired man. *The New York Times*. August 13, 1975, p. 33.

Olweus, D. Stability of aggressive reaction patterns in males: A review. *Psychological Bulletin*, 1979, *86*, 852–875.

Orlofsky, J. L.; Marcia, J. E.; and Lesser, I. M. Ego identity status and the intimacy versus isolation crisis of young adulthood. *Journal of Personality and Social Psychology*, 1973, *27*, 211–219.

Orton, S. *Reading, writing, and speech problems in children*. New York: W. W. Norton, 1937.

Overton, W. F., and Reese, H. W. Models of development: Methodological implications. In J. R. Nesselroade and H. W. Reese (Eds.), *Lifespan developmental psychology: Methodological issues*. New York: Academic Press, 1973.

Pagelow, M. D. Research on woman battering. In J. B. Fleming, *Stopping wife abuse*. Garden City, N.Y.: Anchor Press/Doubleday, 1979.

Papalia, D. E. The status of several conservation abilities across the life span. *Human Development*, 1972, *15*, 229–243.

Papalia, D. E., and Bielby, D. Cognitive functioning in middle-

and old-age adults: A review of research based on Piaget's theory. *Human Development*, 1974, *17*, 424–443.

Parents. The facts of adolescent life. February 1979, *54*, 69.

Parke, R. D. Punishment in children: Effects, side effects, and alternative strategies. In Hom and Robinson (Eds.), *Psychological processes in early education*. New York: Academic Press, 1977, pp. 71–97.

Parke, R. D. Introduction to emerging themes for social-emotional development. *American Psychologist*, 1979a, *34*, 930–931.

Parke, R. D. Perspectives on father-infant interaction. In J. D. Osofsky, *Handbook of infant development*, New York: Wiley, 1979b.

Parke, R. D. et al. Child and adult perceptions of the impact of reactions to discipline on adult behavior. Unpublished research, Fels Research Institute, 1974.

Parke, R. D., and Murray, S. Reinstatement: A technique for increasing stability of inhibition in children. Unpublished manuscript, University of Wisconsin, 1971.

Parke, R. D., and O'Leary, S. E. Father-mother-infant interaction in the newborn period: Some findings, some observations and some unresolved issues. In K. Riegel and J. Meachem (Eds.), *The developing individual in a changing world. Vol. 2: Social and environmental issues*. The Hague, Netherlands: Mouton, 1976.

Parke, R. D., and Sawin, D. B. The impact of children's reactions to discipline on adult disciplinary choices. Unpublished manuscript, Fels Research Institute, 1975.

Parke, R. D., and Sawin, D. B. Fathering: It's a major role. *Psychology Today*, November 1977, 109–112.

Parke, R. D., and Walters, R. H. Some factors determining the efficacy of punishment for reducing response inhibition. *Monographs of Society for Research in Child Development*, 1967, *32*, (serial no. 109).

Parmelee, A. H.; Schultz, H. R.; and Disbrow, M. A. Sleep patterns of the newborn. *Journal of Pediatrics*, 1961, *58*, 241–250.

Parness, E. Effects of experiences with loss and death among preschool children. *Children Today*, November–December 1975, pp. 2–7.

Patterson, M., and Engelberg, L. Women in male-dominated professions. In Stromberg and Harkess (Eds.), *Women working: Theories and facts in perspective*. Palo Alto, Calif.: Mayfield, 1978.

Peck, R. Psychological developments in the second half of life. In B. L. Neugarten (Ed.), *Middle age and aging*. Chicago: University of Chicago Press, 1968.

Pederson, D. R, and Ter Vrugt, D. The influence of amplitude and frequency of vestibular stimulation of the activity of two-month-old infants. *Child Development*, 1973, *44*, 122–128.

Perry, D. G., and Parke, R. D. Punishment and alternative response training as determinants of response inhibition in children. *Genetic Psychology Monographs*, 1975, *91*, 257–279.

Perry, J. C. Neonate-adult head movement: No and yes revisited. *Developmental Psychology*, 1980, *16*, 245–250.

Peterson, D. S.; Powell, C.; and Robertson, L. Aging in America: Toward the year 2000. *The Gerontologist*, 1976, *16(3)*, 264–269.

Peterson, J. A. Marriage and sex and the older man and woman. *Modern Maturity*, December 1970–January 1971.

Pfeiffer, E. Psychopathology and social pathology. In J. E. Birren and K. W. Schaie (Eds.), *Handbook of the psychology of aging*. New York: Van Nostrand Reinhold, 1977.

Pfeiffer, E.; Verwoerdt, A.; and Davis, G C. Sexual behavior in middle life. *American Journal of Psychiatry*, 1972, *128(10)*, 82–87.

Piaget, J. *Language and thought of the child*. London: Routledge, Kegan Paul, 1926.

Piaget, J. *The psychology of intelligence*. New York: Harcourt, 1950.

Piaget, J. *The origins of intelligence in children*. New York: International Universities Press, 1952.

Piaget, J. *The construction of reality in the child*. (trans. M. Cook). New York: Basic Books, 1954.

Piaget, J. The definition of stages of development. In J. Tanner and B. Inhelder (Eds.), *Discussions on child development*, vol. 4, New York: International University Press, 1960.

Piaget, J. *Play, dreams and imitation in childhood*. New York: Norton, 1962.

Piaget, J. *The moral judgment of the child*. New York: The Free Press, 1965.

Piaget, J. *Judgment and reasoning in the child*. Totowa, N.J.: Littlefield, Adams, 1968.

Piaget, J. *Genetic epistomology*. New York: W. W. Norton, 1970a.

Piaget, J. The definition of stages of development. In J. Tanner and B. Inhelder (Eds.), *Discussions on child development*, vol. 4. New York: International University Press, 1970b.

Piaget, J. *Mental imagery in the child*. New York: Basic Books, 1971.

Piaget, J. Intellectual evolution from adolescence to adulthood. *Human Development*, 1972, *15*, 1–12.

Piaget, J., and Inhelder, B. *Psychology of the child*. New York: Basic Books, 1969.

Piaget, J., and Inhelder, B. *Memory and intelligence*. New York: Basic Books, 1973.

Pick, A. D.; Hales, J. J.; Christy, M. D.; Frankel, G. W.; and Glick, J. H. The effect of a human facial context on the discrimination and recognition of curved lines. *Psychonomic Science*, 1972, *27(4)*, 239–242.

Pick, H. L., Jr. Mapping children—Mapping space. Paper presented at the meeting of the American Psychological Association, Honolulu, September, 1972.

Pineo, P. C. Disenchantment in the later years of marriage. *Marriage and Family Living*, 1961, *23*, 3–11.

Planned Parenthood. *11 million teen-agers: What can be done about the epidemic of adolescent pregnancies in the United States*. New York: PPFA, 1976.

Plomin, R., and DeFries, J. C. Multivariate behavioral genetic analysis of twin data on scholastic abilities. *Behavioral Genetics*, 1979, *9*, 505–517.

Pohlman, E. Childlessness, intentional and unintentional: Psychological and social aspects. *Journal of Nervous and Mental Disease*, 1970, *151*, 2–12.

Population Institute. *The youth values project: An inquiry conducted by teen-agers themselves, into the attitudes, values and experiences of teen-agers in New York City regarding sex, contraception and their life goals*. Washington, D.C.: 1978.

Poussaint, A. F., and Comer, J. F. What white parents should know about children and prejudice. *Redbook*, May 1972.

Powell, G. F.; Brasel, J. A.; and Blizzard, R. M. Emotional deprivation and growth retardation simulating idiopathic hypopituitarism. *New England Journal of Medicine*, 1967, *276*, 1271–1278.

Powell, R. R. Psychological effects of exercise therapy upon institutionalized geriatric mental patients. *Journal of Gerontology*, 1974, *29*, 157–161.

Presser, H. Social factors affecting the timing of the first child. In W. Miller and F. Newman (Eds.), *The first child and family formation*. Chapel Hill: Carolina Population Center, 1978.

Provence, S., and Lipton, R. C. *Infants in institutions: A comparison of their development with family-reared infants during the first year of life*. New York: International Universities Press, 1962.

Puner, M. *To the good long life: What we know about growing old*. New York: Universe Books, 1974.

Quindlen, A. Relationships: Independence vs. intimacy. *The New York Times*, November 28, 1977, p. 36.

Quinn, B., and Goldberg, S. Feeding and fussing: Parent-infant interaction as a function of neonatal medical status. Paper presented at meeting of Society for Research on Child Development, New Orleans, March 1977.

Quinn, R.; Staines, G.; and McCullough, M. *Job satisfaction: Is there a trend?* U.S. Department of Labor, Manpower Research Monograph No. 30. Washington, D.C.: Government Printing Office, 1974.

Rahe, H.; Mahan, J.; and Arthur, R. J. Prediction of near future health; change from subjects preceding life change. *Journal of Psychosomatic Research*, 1970, *14*, 401–406.

Ramey, C., and Smith, B. Assessing the intellectual consequences of early intervention with high-risk infants. In P. Mittler (Ed.), *Research to practice in mental retardation*, vol. 1: *Care and intervention*. Baltimore: University Park Press, 1977.

Ramey, C., and Smith, B. Assessing the intellectual consequences of early intervention with high-risk infants. *American Journal of Mental Deficiency*, 1976, *81*, 318–324.

Ramsey, C. E. *Problems of youth: A social problems perspective.* Encino, Calif.: Dickenson, 1967.

Rattner, S. In business terms, testing is a success. *The New York Times*, May 1, 1977, p. ED 16.

Rebelsky, F., and Hanks, C. Fathers' verbal interaction with infants in the first three months of life. *Child Development*, 1971, *42*, 63–66.

Redd, W. H.; Morris, E. K.; and Martin, J. A. Effects of positive and negative adult-child interactions on children's social preferences. *Journal of Experimental Child Psychology*, 1975, *19*, 153–164.

Reedy, M., and Birren, J. E. *How do lovers grow older together? Types of love and age.* Paper presented at the Gerontological Society Meetings, 1978.

Rees, L. Psychosomatic aspects of premenstrual tension syndrome. *Journal of Mental Science*, 1953, *99*, 62–73.

Reese, H. W., and Overton, W. F. Models of development and theories of development. In L. R. Goulet and P. B. Baltes (Eds.), *Lifespan developmental psychology: Theory and research*. New York: Academic Press, 1970.

Reinisch, J. M. Prenatal exposure to synthetic progestins increases potential for aggression in humans. *Science*, 1981, *211*, 1171–1173.

Reisman, J. M., and Schorr, S. I. Friendship claims and expectations among children and adults. *Child Development*, 1978, *49*, 913–916.

Rhead, W. J. Smoking and SIDS. *Pediatrics*, 1977, *59(5)*, 791–792.

Rheingold, H.; Gewirtz, J.; and Ross, H. Social conditioning of vocalizations in the infant. *Journal of Comparative Physiological Psychology*, 1959, *52*, 68–73.

Ricciuti, H. Fear and development of social attachments in the first year of life. In M. Lewis and L. A. Rosenblum (Eds.), *The origins of human behavior: Fear*. New York: Wiley, 1974.

Richard, J. The parent place. *Human Behavior*, September 1978, 36–37.

Riegel, K. F. Developmental psychology and society: Some historical and ethical considerations. In J. R. Nesselrode and H. W. Reese (Eds.), *Lifespan developmental psychology: Methodological issues*. New York: Academic Press, 1973a.

Riegel, K. F. Dialectic operations: The final period of cognitive development. *Human Development*, 1973b, *16*, 346–370.

Riegel, K. F. Adult life crises: A dialectical interpretation of development. In N. Datan and L. H. Ginsberg (Eds.), *Lifespan developmental psychology: Normative life crises*. New York: Academic Press, 1975.

Riegel, K. F., and Riegel, R. M. Development, drop and death. *Developmental Psychology*, 1972, *6*, 306–319.

Riley, M. W.; Riley, J. W., Jr.; and Johnson, M. F. *Aging and society.* Vol. 1. *An inventory of research findings.* New York: Russell Sage, 1968.

Ringness, T. A. Identification patterns, motivation, and school achievement of bright junior high school boys. *Journal of Educational Psychology*, 1967, *58*, 93–102.

Rist, R. Student social class and teacher expectations. The self-fulfilling prophecy in ghetto education. *Harvard Educational Review*, 1970, *40*, 411–458.

Robertson, J. F. Grandparenthood: A study of role conceptions. *Journal of Marriage and the Family*, 1977, *39*, 165–174.

Roche, A. F. (Ed.) *Secular trends in human growth, maturation, and development*, Monographs of the Society for Research in Child Development, vol. 44, no. 3–4. Chicago: University of Chicago Press for the Society for Research in Child Development, 1979.

Roche, A. F. Secular trends in stature, weight, and maturation. In A. F. Roche (Ed.), Secular trends in human growth, maturation, and development. *Monographs of the Society for Research in Child Development*, 1979, *44* (Serial No. 179), 3–27.

Roche, A. F. The adipocyte-number hypotheses. *Child Development*, 1981, *52*, 31–63.

Roche, A. F., and Davila, G. H. Late adolescent growth in stature. *Pediatrics*, 1972, *50*, 874–880.

Rodin, J., and Langer, E. J. Long-term effects of a control-relevant intervention with the institutionalized aged. *Journal of Personality and Social Psychology*, 1977, *22*, 897–902.

Rollins, B. C., and Feldman, H. Marital satisfaction over the family life-cycle. *Journal of Marriage and the Family*, 1970, *32*, 20–37.

Rollins, H., and Genser, L. Role of cognitive style in a cognitive task: A case savoring the impulsive approach to problem solving. *Journal of Educational Psychology*, 1977, *69*, 281–287.

Roman, M., and Haddad, W. The case for joint custody. *Psychology Today*, September 1978, pp. 96–104.

Roopnarine, J. L., and Lamb, M. E. The effects of day care on attachment and exploratory behavior in a strange situation. *Merrill-Palmer Quarterly*, 1978, *24(2)*, 85–95.

Roosevelt, E. *This I remember.* New York: Harper & Row, 1949.

Rosen, B. C., and Aneshensel, C. S. Sex differences in the educational-occupational expectation process. *Journal of Social Forces*, 1978, *57(1)*, 164–186.

Rosen, C. E. The effects of sociodramatic play on problem-solving behavior among culturally disadvantaged preschool children. *Child Development*, 1974, *45*, 920–927.

Rosenberg, M. *Society and the adolescent self-image.* Princeton, N.J.: Princeton University Press, 1965.

Rosenthal, R., and Jacobson, L. *Pygmalion in the classroom: Teacher expectation and pupils' intellectual development.* New York: Holt, Rinehart and Winston, 1968.

Ross, D. M., and Ross, S. A. Leniency toward cheating in preschool children. *Journal of Educational Psychology*, 1968, *60*, 483–487.

Ross, D. M., and Ross, S. A. *Hyperactivity: Research, theory, and action.* New York: Wiley, 1976.

Ross, M. B., and Salvia, J. Attractiveness as a biasing factor in teacher judgments. *American Journal of Mental Deficiency*, 1975, *80(1)*, 96–98.

Rossi, A. S. Transitions to parenthood. *Journal of Marriage and the Family*, 1968, *30*, 26–39.

Rossi, E. Development of classification behavior. *Child Development*, 1966, *37*, 137–142.

Rossman, I. Anatomic and body composition changes with aging. In C. E. Finch and L. Hayflick (Eds.), *Handbook of the biology of aging*. New York: Van Nostrand Reinhold, 1977.

Routh, D. K.; Mushak, P.; and Boone, L. A. A new syndrome of elevated blood lead and microcephaly. *Journal of Pediatric Psychology*, 1979, *4(1)*, 67–76.

Rowe, M. Wait time and rewards as instructional variables: Their influence on language, logic, and fate control. *Journal of Research in Science*, 1974. *11*, 291–308.

Rubenstein, J., and Howe, C. Caregiving in infant behavior in day care and homes. *Developmental Psychology*, 1979, *15(1)*, 1–23.

Ruble, D. Premenstrual symptoms: A reinterpretation. *Science*, 1977, *197*, 291–292.

Runciman, A. Problems older clients present in counseling about sexuality. In I. M. Burnside (Ed.), *Sexuality and aging*. Los Angeles: University of Southern California Press, 1975.

Ruopp, R. et al. *Children at the center: Final report of the national day care study* (Executive summary). Cambridge, Mass.: Abt Associates, 1979.

Russac, R. J. The relation between two strategies of cardinal number: Correspondence and counting. *Child Development*, 1978, *49*, 728–735.

Russell, C. S. Transition to parenthood: Problems and gratifications. *Journal of Marriage and the Family*, 1974, *36*, 294–301.

Rutherford, E., and Mussen, P. Generosity in nursery school boys. *Child Development*, 1968, *39*, 755–765.

Rutter, M. Maternal deprivation, 1972–1978: New findings, new concepts, new approaches. *Child Development*, 1979, *50*, 283–305.

Salapatek, P., and Kessen, W. Prolonged investigation of a plane geometric triangle by the human newborn. *Journal of Experimental Child Psychology*, 1973, *15*, 22–29.

Salkind, N. J. *Theories of human development*. New York: D. Van Nostrand, 1981.

Salkind, N. J., and Nelson, C. F. A note on the development of reflection-impulsivity. *Developmental Psychology*, 1980, *16*, 237–238.

Sallade, J. B. A comparison of psychological adjustment of obese vs. non-obese children. *Journal of Psychosomatic Research*, 1973, *17*, 89–96.

Saltin, B. et al. Response to exercise after bed rest and after training. *American Heart Association Monograph #23*. New York: The American Heart Association, 1969.

Sameroff, A. J. Learning and adaptation in infancy: A comparison of models. In Reese (Ed.), *Advances in child development and behavior*, 1972, 7, 169–214.

Sarton, M. More light. *The New York Times*, January 30, 1978, p. A21.

Scanlon, J. W.; Brown, W. V., Jr.; Weiss, J. B.; and Alper, M. H. Neurobehavioral responses of newborn infants after maternal epidural anesthesia. *Anesthesiology*, 1974, *40(2)*, 121–128.

Scanzoni, J. *Sex roles, life-styles, and childbearing*. New York: The Free Press, 1975.

Scarf, M. The anatomy of fear. *The New York Times Magazine*, June 16, 1974, 10.

Scarr, S., and Weinberg, R. A. IQ test performance of black children adopted by white families. *American Psychologist*, 1976, *31*, 726–739.

Scarr-Salapatek, S. Genetics and the development of intelligence. In F. D. Horowitz (Ed.), *Review of child development research*. Vol. 4. Chicago: University of Chicago Press, 1975.

Schachter, S. *The psychology of affiliation*. Stanford, Calif.: Stanford University Press, 1959.

Schaefer, A. E., and Johnson, O. C. Are we well fed? The searches for an answer. *Nutrition Today*, 1969, *41(1)*, 2–11.

Schaeffer, W. W., and Bayley, N. Maternal behavior, child behavior, and their intercorrelations from infancy through adolescence. *Monographs of the Society for Research in Child Development*, 1963, *28*, serial No. 87, 1–127.

Schaffer, H. R. (Ed.). *The origins of human social relations*. New York: Academic Press, 1971.

Schaffer, H. R., and Emerson, P. E. The development of social attachments in infancy. *Monographs of the Society for Research in Child Development*, 1964, *29(3)*, serial no. 94.

Schaie, K. W. Transitions in gerontology—from lab to life: Intellectual functioning. *American Psychologist*, November 1974, *29*, 802–807.

Schaie, K. W. Age changes in intelligence. In D. S. Woodruff and J. E. Birren (Eds.), *Aging: Scientific perspectives and social issues*. New York: D. Van Nostrand, 1975. Pp. 111–124.

Schaie, K. W., and Parham, I. A. Stability of adult personality traits: Fact or fable? *Journal of Personality and Social Psychology*, 1976, *34*, 146–158.

Schmitt, M. H. Superiority of breast-feeding: Fact or fancy? *American Journal of Nursing*, July 1970, 1488–1493.

Schneidman, E. S. Death work and stages of dying. In E. S. Schneidman (Ed.). *Death: Current perspectives* (2nd ed.). Palo Alto, Calif.: Mayfield Publishing, 1980.

Schoen, R., and Nelson, V. E. Marriage, divorce and mortality: A life table analysis. *Demography*, 1974, *11(2)*, 267–290.

Schonfield, D. Transitions in gerontology—from lab to life: Utilizing information. *American Psychologist*, 1974, *29*, 796–801.

Schorr, A., and Moen, P. The single parent and public policy, *Social Policy*, 1979, *9(5)*, 15–21.

Schram, R. W. Marital satisfaction over the family life-cycle: A critique and proposal. *Journal of Marriage and the Family*, 1979, *41*, 7–40.

Schramm, W.; Lyle, J.; and Parker, E. G. *Television in the lives of our children*. Stanford, Calif.: Stanford University Press, 1961.

Schulz, D. A. *The changing family: Its function and future*. Englewood Cliffs, N.J.: Prentice-Hall, 1972.

Schulz, R. *The psychology of death, dying, and bereavement*. Reading, Mass.: Addison-Wesley, 1978.

Schulz, R., and Brenner, A. Relocation of the aged: A review and theoretical analysis. *Journal of Gerontology*, 1977, *32*, 323–333.

Scott, E. M. et al. A psychological investigation of primigravidae. *Journal of Obstetrical Gynecology*, British Empire, 1956, *63*, 338–343.

Scott, R., and Smith, J. Ethnic and demographic variables and achievement scores of preschool children. *Psychology in Schools*, 1972, *9*, 174–182.

Scottish Council for Research in Education. *Social implications of the 1947 Scottish Mental Survey*. London: University Press, 1953.

Sears, R. R.; Maccoby, E. E.; and Levin, H. *Patterns of child rearing*. Evanston, Ill.: Row, Peterson, 1957.

Seavy, C; Katz, P.; and Zalk, S. Baby X: The effect of gender labels on adult responses to infants. *Sex Roles*, 1975, *1*, 103–109.

Sells, S. F., and Roff, M. Peer acceptance and rejection and personality development. Final report, Project No. OE-0417, U.S. Department of Health, Education and Welfare, 1967.

Selman, R. L., and Selman, A. P. Children's ideas about friendship: A new theory. *Psychology Today*, October 1979, pp. 71, 114.

Shanas, E. Social myth as hypothesis: The case of the family relations of old people. *The Gerontologist*, 1979, *19*, 3–9.

Shanas, E.; Townsend, P.; Wedderburn, D.; Friis, H.; Milhoj, P.; and Stehouwer, I., *Older people in three industrial societies*. New York: Atherton, 1968.

Shantz, C. The development of social cognition. In E. M. Hetherington (Ed.), *Review of child development research*, vol. 5. Chicago: University of Chicago Press, 1975.

Shaywitz, B. A.; Finkelstein, J.; Hellman, L.; and Weitzman, E. D. Growth hormone in newborn infants during sleep-wake periods. *Pediatrics*, 1971, *48(1)*, 103–109.

Sheehy, G. *Passages: Predictable crises of adult life*. New York: E. P. Dutton, 1976.

Sheldon, W. H. *The varieties of human physique*. New York: Harper & Row, 1940.

Sherif, M.; Harvey, O. J.; White, B. J.; Hood, W. R.; and Sherif, C. W. *Intergroup conflict and cooperation: The Robber's Cave experiment*. Norman: University of Oklahoma Press, 1961.

Sherif, M., and Sherif, C. W. *Groups in harmony and tension*. New York: Harper & Row, 1953.

Shields, J. *Monozygotic twins: Brought up apart and brought up together*. London: Oxford University Press, 1962.

Shock, N. W. Biological theories of aging. In J. E. Birren and K. W. Schaie (Eds.), *Handbook of the psychology of aging*. New York: Van Nostrand Reinhold, 1977.

Sidel, R. *Women and child care in China: A firsthand report*. New York: Hill & Wang, 1972.

Sidorowicz, L., and Lunney, G. S. Baby X revisited. *Sex Roles*, 1980, *6*, 67–73.

Sigel, I. E., and Brodzinsky, D. M. Individual differences: A perspective for understanding intellectual development. In H. L. Hom and P. A. Robinson (Eds.), *Psychological processes in early education*. New York: Academic Press, 1977.

Sigel, R. S. Students' comprehension of democracy and its application to conflict situations. *International Journal of Political Education*, 1979, *2*, 47–65.

Sigel, R. S., and Hoskin, M. B. *The political involvement of adolescents*. New Brunswick, N.J.: Rutgers University Press, 1981.

Silverman, P. R. Widowhood and preventive intervention. *The Family Coordinator*, 1972, *21*, 95–102.

Skeels, H. M. Adult status of children with contrasting early life experience. *Monographs of the Society for Research in Child Development*, 1966, *31*, 1–65.

Skinner, B. F. *The behavior of organisms: An experimental analysis*. New York: Appleton, 1938.

Skinner, B. F. *Verbal behavior*. New York: Appleton, 1957.

Skinner, B. F. *Technology of teaching*. New York: Appleton-Century-Crofts, 1968.

Slobin, D. I. Imitation and grammatical development in children. In N. Endler, L. Boulter, and H. Osser (Eds.), *Contemporary issues in developmental psychology*. New York: Holt, Rinehart and Winston, 1968.

Slobin, D. I. Cognitive prerequisites for the development of grammar. In C. A. Ferguson and D. I. Slobin (Eds.), *Studies of child language development*. New York: Holt, Rinehart and Winston, 1973.

Smethurst, W. *Teaching young children to read at home*. New York: McGraw-Hill, 1975.

Smith, C., and Lloyd, B. Maternal behavior and perceived sex of infant: Revisited. *Child Development*, 1978, *49*.

Smith, D. C.; Prentice, R.; Thompson, D. J.; and Herrmann, W. L. Association of exogenous estrogen and endometrial carcinoma. *New England Journal of Medicine*, 1975. *293(23)*, 1164–1167.

Smith, G. H. Sociometric study of best-liked and least-liked children. *Elementary School Journal*, 1950, *51*, 77–85.

Smith, S. M. *The battered child syndrome*. London: Butterworth, 1973.

Smith, R. E. *Women in the labor force in 1990*. Washington, D.C.: The Urban Institute, 1979.

Smith, S. N. Recent cross-ethnic research on the adolescent. *Journal of Negro Education*, 1979, *48(2)*, 302–323.

Sontag, S. The double standard of aging. In L. R. Allman and D. T. Joffe (Eds.), *Readings in adult psychology: Contemporary perspectives*. New York: Harper & Row, 1977.

Sontag, L. W. Differences in modifiability of fetal behavior and psychology. *Psychosomatic Medicine*, 1944, *6*, 151–154.

Sorensen, R. C. *Adolescent sexuality in contemporary America*. New York: World, 1973.

Sorosky, A. D., Baran, A., and Pannor, R. *The adoption triangle*. Garden City, N.Y.: Anchor Press, 1979.

Sostek, A. M. Infant scales in the pediatric setting: The Brazelton Neonatal Behavioral Assessment Scale, and the Carey Infant Temperament Questionnaire. *Journal of Pediatric Psychology*, 1978, *3(3)*, 113–121.

Spelke, E. S. *Perceiving bimodally specified events*. Paper presented at the International Conference on Infant Studies, Providence, R.I., March 1978.

Spence, J. T.; Helmreich, R.; and Stapp, J. Ratings of self and peers on sex role attributes and their relation to self-esteem and conceptions of masculinity and femininity. *Journal of Personality and Social Psychology*, 1975, *32*, 23–39.

Spencer-Booth, Y., and Hinde, R. A. The effects of separating rhesus monkey infants from their mothers for six days. *Journal of Child Psychology and Psychiatry*, 1966, *7*, 179–197.

Spinetta, J., and Rigler, D. The child-abusing parent: A psychological review. *Psychological Bulletin*, 1972, *77(4)*, 296–304.

Spitz, R. A. Hospitalization: An inquiry into the genesis of psychiatric conditions of early childhood. In A. Freud et al. (Eds.), *The psychoanalytic study of the child*. New York: International Universities Press, 1945.

Spock, B. *Baby and child care*. New York: Hawthorn, 1976.

Spreitzer, E., and Riley, L. E. Factors associated with singlehood. *Journal of Marriage and the Family*, 1974, *36*, 533–542.

Sroufe, L. A. Drug treatment of children with behavior problems. In F. D. Horowitz (Ed.), *Review of child development research*. Vol. 4. Chicago, University of Chicago Press, 1975.

Sroufe, L. A. The coherence of individual development: Family care, attachment, and subsequent developmental issues. *American Psychologist*, 1979, *34(10)*, 834–841.

Sroufe, L. A., and Waters, E. Attachment as an organizational construct. *Child Development*, 1977, *48*, 1184–1199.

Sroufe, L. A., and Wunsch, J. P. The development of laughter in the first year of life. *Child Development*, 1972, *43*, 1326–1344.

Staples, R. Toward a sociology of the black family: A theoretical and methodological assessment, *Journal of Marriage and the Family*, 1971, *33*, 119–137.

Stark, R., and McEvoy, J. Middle class violence. *Psychology Today*, 1970, *4*, 52–65.

Stein, A. H., and Friedrich, L. K. Television content and young children's behavior. In J. P. Murray, E. A. Rubinstein, and G. A. Comstock (Eds.), *Televison and social behavior*, Vol. 2, Washington, D.C.: U.S. Government Printing Office, 1972.

Stein, A. H., and Friedrich, L. K. Impact of television on children and youth. In E. M. Hetherington (Ed.), *Review of child development research*, vol 5. Chicago: University of Chicago Press, 1976.

Stevens-Long, J. *Adult life: Developmental processes*. Palo Alto, Calif.: Mayfield Publishing, 1979.

Stinnett, N.; Carter, L. M.; and Montgomery, J. E. Older persons' perceptions of their marriages. *Journal of Marriage and the Family*, 1972, *34*, 665–670.

Stinnett, N., and Walters, J. *Relationships in marriage and family*. New York: Macmillan, 1977.

Straus, M. A. Family patterns and child abuse in a nationally representative sample. *Child Abuse and Neglect*.

Streib, G. F. Social stratification and aging. In R. H. Binstock and E. Shanas (Eds.), *Handbook of aging and the social sciences*. New York: Van Nostrand Reinhold, 1977.

Strong, L. D. Alternative marital and family forms: Their relative attractiveness to college students and correlates of willingness to participate in nontraditional forms. *Journal of Marriage and the Family*, 1978, *40*, 493–503.

Stults, H. Obesity in adolescents: Prognosis, etiology, and management. *Journal of Pediatric Psychology*, 1977, *2(3)*, 122–126.

Sullivan, H. S. *The interpersonal theory of psychiatry*. New York: W. W. Norton, 1953.

Super, D. E. *The psychology of careers*. New York: Harper & Row, 1957.

Super, D. E. *Career development: Self-concept theory*. New York: College Entrance Examination Board, 1963.

Sussman, M. B. Intergenerational family relationships and social role changes in middle age. *Journal of Gerontology*, 1960, *15(1)*, 71–75.

Sussman, M. B. Relationships of adult children with their parents in the United States. In E. Shanas and G. Streib (Eds.),

Social structure and the family: Generational relations. Englewood Cliffs, N.J.: Prentice-Hall, 1965.

Sutherland, D. Childbirth is not for mothers only. *Ms.* May 1974, *2(11)*, 47–51.

Sutton-Smith, B., and Rosenberg, B. G. *The sibling.* New York: Holt, Rinehart and Winston, 1970.

Svejda, M. J.; Campos, J. J., and Emde, R. N. Mother-infant "bonding": Failure to generalize. *Child Development,* 1980, *51,* 775–779.

Sviland, M. A. Helping elderly couples become sexually liberated: Psycho-social issues. *Counseling Psychologist,* 1975, *5,* 67–72.

Sweetland, J. *Mid-career perspectives: The middle-aged and older population.* Scarsdale: Work in American Institute, Inc., 1978.

Szasz, T. *Sex by prescription.* Garden City, N.Y.: Doubleday/Anchor Press, 1980.

Tagiuri, R.; Kogan, N.; and Long, L. M. K. Differentiation of sociometric and status relations in a group. *Psychology Report,* 1958, *4,* 523–526.

Tangri, S. S. Determinants of occupational role innovation among college women. In M. T. S. Mednick, S. S. Tangri, and L. W. Hoffman (Eds.), *Women and achievement: social and motivational analysis.* Washington, D.C.: Hemisphere Publishing Co., 1975.

Tanner, J. M. *Growth at adolescence.* Oxford, England: Blackwell Scientific Publications, 1962.

Tanner, J. M. *The physique of the Olympic athlete.* London: G. Allen and Unwin, 1964.

Tanner, J. M. Galtonian eugenics and the study of growth. *Eugenics Review,* 1966, *58,* 122–135.

Tavris, C., and Sadd, S. *The Redbook report on female sexuality: 100,000 married women disclose the good news about sex.* New York: Delacorte, 1975.

Teller, M. N. Age changes and immune resistance to cancer. *Advances of Gerontological Research,* 1972, *4,* 25–43.

Terkel, S. *Working.* New York: Random House/Pantheon, 1972.

Tessman, L. H. *Children of parting parents.* New York: Aronson, 1978.

Tharp, R. G. Psychological patterning in marriage. *Psychological Bulletin,* 1963, *60,* 97–117.

Theorell, T., and Rahe, R. H. Psychosocial factors and myocardial infarction I: An inpatient study in Sweden. *Journal of Psychosomatic Research,* 1974, *15,* 25–31.

Thomas, A., and Chess, S. *Temperament and development.* New York: Brunner/Mazel, 1977.

Thomas, A.; Chess, S.; and Birch, H. The origin of personality. *Scientific American,* 1968, *233,* 102.

Thompson, A. M. Maternal stature and reproductive efficiency. *Eugenics Review,* 1959, *51,* 157–162.

Thompson, R. J. Effects of maternal alcohol consumption on offspring: Review, critical assessment and further directions. *Journal of Pediatric Psychology,* 1979, *4(3).*

Thurnher, M.; Spence, D.; and Lowenthal, M. F. Value conflict and behavioral conflict in intergenerational relations. *Journal of Marriage and the Family,* 1974, *36,* 308–319.

Tibbitts, C. Older Americans in the family context. *Aging,* 1977, 270–271, 6–11.

Time. Parental line: Same old birds and bees. December 25, 1978, p. 60.

Timiras, P. S. *Developmental physiology and aging.* New York: Macmillan, 1972.

Tinklenberg, J. R., and Darley, C. F. Psychological and cognitive effects of cannabis. In P. H. Cornell and N. Dorn (Eds.), *Cannabis and man.* New York: Churchill Livingstone, 1975.

Tobin, S. S., and Lieberman, M. A. *Last home for the aged.* San Francisco: Jossey-Bass, 1976.

Toner, I. J.; Moore, L. P.; and Ashley, P. K. The effect of serving as a model of self-control on subsequent resistance to deviation in children. *Journal of Experimental Child Psychology.* 1978, *26,* 85–91.

Toner, I. J.; Parke, R. D.; and Yussen, S. R. The effect of observation of model behavior on the establishment and stability of resistance to deviations in children. *The Journal of Genetic Psychology,* 1978, *132,* 283–290.

Toolan, J. M. Depression in children and adolescents. *American Journal of Orthopsychiatry,* 1962, 22, 404–415.

Toolan, J. M. Therapy of depressed and suicidal children. *American Journal of Psychotherapy,* 1978, *32(2),* 243–251.

Torgersen, A. M., and Kringlen, E. Genetic aspects of temperamental differences in twins. *Journal of the American Academy of Child Psychiatry,* 1978, *17,* 433–444.

Townsend, C. *Old age, the last segregation: The report on nursing homes.* Ralph Nader's Study Group Reports. New York: Grossman, 1971.

Trabasso, T. The role of memory as a system in making transitive inferences. In R. V. Kail and J. W. Hagen (Eds.), *Perspectives on the development of memory and cognition.* Hillsdale, N.J.: Erlbaum, 1977.

Treas, J., and Van Hilst, A. Marriage and remarriage rates among older Americans. *The Gerontologist,* 1976, *16,* 132–136.

Treffert, D. A. Marijuana use in schizophrenia: A clear hazard. *American Journal of Psychology,* 1978, *135,* 10.

Trevarthen, C. Conversations with a 2-month-old. *New Scientist,* May 2, 1974, 230–235.

Tritremmel, H., and Ferrara, D. *Child abuse and neglect in New Jersey,* revised. Department of Human Services, State of New Jersey, April 1977.

Troll, L. E. The family of later life: A decade review. *Journal of Marriage and the Family,* 1971, *33,* 263–290.

Troll, L. E. *Early and middle adulthood.* Monterey, Calif.: Brooks/Cole, 1975.

Troll, L. E. Grandparenting. In L. W. Poon (Ed.), *Aging in the 1980s: Psychological issues.* Washington, D.C.: American Psychological Association, 1980.

Troll, L. E.; Miller, S. J.; and Atchley, R.C. *Families in later life.* Belmont, Calif.: Wadsworth, 1979.

Troll, L. E., and Smith, J. Attachment through the life span: Some questions about dyadic bonds among adults. *Human Development,* 1976, *19,* 156–170.

Tryon, C. M. Evaluation of adolescent personality by adolescents. *Monograph of Social Research and Child Development,* 1939, *4(4).*

Tuckman, J., and Lorge, I. Attitudes toward old people. *Journal of Social Psychology,* 1953, *37,* 249–260.

Tuddenham, R. D. The constancy of personality ratings over two decades. *Genetic Psychology Monographs,* 1959, *60,* 3–29.

Turiel, E. The development of concepts of social structure: Social convention. In J. Glick and Clarke-Stewart, K. Alison (Eds.), *The development of social understanding.* New York: Halsted Press, 1978.

Turiel, E. Domains and categories in social cognitive development. In W. Overton (Ed.), *The relationship between social and cognitive development.* Hillsdale, N.J.: Erlbaum, in press.

Unger, R. K. *Female and male: Psychological perspectives.* New York: Harper & Row, 1979.

U.S. Bureau of the Census. Fertility of American women: June 1976. *Current Population Reports,* Series P-20, No. 308. Washington, D.C.: GPO, 1977.

U.S. Bureau of the Census. *Statistical Abstracts of the United States, 1978* (99th Annual Edition). Washington, D.C.: GPO, 1978.

U.S. Bureau of Labor Statistics, *March Population Survey.* Washington, D.C.: U.S. Department of Labor, 1978.

U.S. Department of Commerce, Bureau of the Census. The sex differential in earnings, by age. 1975. *Current Population Reports*, Series P-60, No. 105. Washington, D.C.: GPO, 1977.

U.S. Department of Commerce, Bureau of the Census. Estimates of the population of the United States by age, sex, and race. *Current Population Reports*, Series P-25, No. 805. Washington, D.C.: GPO, 1979.

U.S. Department of Health, Education, and Welfare. *Monthly vital statistics report; final mortality statistics, 1976*. Washington, D.C.: GPO, 1978.

U.S. Department of Labor, Bureau of Labor Statistics. *Going back to school at 35 and over*. Special Labor Force Report, No. 204, prepared by A. M. Young. Washington, D.C.: GPO, 1977.

U.S. News & World Report. Why a surge of suicide among the young. July 10, 1978, p. 49.

U.S. Public Health Service. The health consequences of smoking for women: A Report of the Surgeon General. Washington, D.C.: U.S. Dept. of Health and Human Services, 1980 (prepublication copy).

Vaillant, G. E. *Adaptation to life*. Boston: Little, Brown, 1977.

Vaughan, W. T., Jr. Children in crisis. *Mental Hygiene*, 1961, *45*, 354–359.

Veatch, R. M. Brain death. In E. S. Shneidman (Ed.), *Death: Current perspectives*. Palo Alto, Calif.: Mayfield Publishing, 1976.

Veevers, J. E. Voluntary childlessness: A neglected area of family study. *Family Coordinator*, 1973, *22*, 199–205.

Veroff, J., and Feld, S. *Marriage and work in America: A study of motives and roles*. New York: Van Nostrand Reinhold, 1970.

Veroff, J.; Feld, S.; and Gurin, G. Dimensions of subjective adjustment. *Journal of Abnormal and Social Psychology*, 1962, *64(3)*, 192–205.

Vincent, C. E. Socialization data in research on young marrieds. *Acta Sociologica*, August 1964, *8*.

Vore, D. A. Prenatal nutrition and postnatal intellectual development. *Merrill-Palmer Quarterly*, 1973, *19*, 253–260.

Vygotsky, L. *Thought and language*. Cambridge, Mass.: M. I. T. Press, 1962.

Wagner, C. A. Adolescent sexuality. In J. F. Adams (Ed.), *Understanding adolescence: Current developments in adolescent psychology* (4th ed.). Boston: Allyn Bacon, 1980.

Walk, R. D. The development of depth perception in animals and human infants. *Monographs of the Society for Research in Child Development*, 1966, *31*, 82–108.

Walker, K. Time spent by husbands in household work. *Family Economics Review*, *14*, 1970, 8–11.

Walster, E.; Aronson, V.; Abrahams, D.; and Rottmann, L. Importance of physical attractiveness in dating behavior. *Journal of Personality and Social Psychology*, 1966, *4*, 508–516.

Waterman, A. S.; Geary, P. S.; and Waterman, C. K. A longitudinal study of changes in ego identity status from the freshman to the senior year at college. *Developmental Psychology*, 1974, *10*, 387–392.

Waters, E. The reliability and stability of individual differences in infant-mother attachment. *Child Development*, 1978, *49*, 483–494.

Waters, E.; Vaughn, B. E.; and Egeland, B. R. Individual differences in infant-mother attachment relationships at age one: Antecedents in neonatal behavior in an urban, economically disadvantaged sample. *Child Development*, 1980, *51*, 208–216.

Watson, J. B. *Behaviorism*. New York: W. W. Norton, 1930.

Waugh, W. C., and Norman, D. A. Primary memory. *Psychological Review*, 1965, *72*, 89–104.

Weg, R. B. Changing physiology of aging: Normal and pathological. In D. S. Woodruff and J. E. Birren (Eds.), *Aging: Scientific perspectives and social issues*. New York: D. Van Nostrand, 1975.

Weg, R. B. The physiology of sexuality in aging. In R. L. Solnick (Ed.), *Sexuality and aging*. Los Angeles: University of Southern California Press, 1978.

Weideger, P. *Menstruation and menopause: The physiology and psychology, the myth and the reality*. New York: Knopf, 1976.

Weidner, G., and Mathews, K. A. Reported physical symptoms elicited by unpredictable events and the Type A coronary-prone behavior pattern. *Journal of Personality and Social Psychology*, 1978, *36*, 1213–1220.

Weiner, A. S. Cognitive and social-emotional development in adolescence. *Journal of Pediatric Psychology*, 1977, *2(3)*, 87–92.

Weisler, A., and McCall, R. B. Exploration and play. *American Psychologist*, 1976, *31*, 492–508.

Welford, A. T. *Aging and human skill*. London: Oxford University Press, 1958.

Welford, A. T. Psychomotor performance. In J. E. Birren (Ed.), *Handbook of aging and the individual*. Chicago: University of Chicago Press, 1959.

Wellman, H. M. Knowledge of the interaction of memory variables: A developmental study of metamemory. *Developmental Psychology*, 1978, *14*, 24–29.

Wershaw, H. J. The four percent fallacy: Some further evidence and policy implications. *The Gerontologist*, 1976, *16*, 52–55.

Wessel, J. A., and Van Huss, W. D. The influence of physical activity and age on exercise adaptation of men 20–69 years. *Journal of Sports Medicine*, 1969, *9*, 173–180.

Wetstone, H., and Friedlander, B. The effect of word order on young children's responses to simple questions and commands. *Child Development*, 1973, *44*, 734–740.

Whitbourne, S. K., and Weinstock, C. S. *Adult development: The differentiation of experience*. New York: Holt, Rinehart and Winston, 1979.

White, B. L. *The first three years of life*. Englewood Cliffs, N.J.: Prentice-Hall, 1975.

White, B. L., and Watts, J. *Experience and environment*. Englewood Cliffs, N.J.: Prentice-Hall, 1973.

White, L. K. Sex differentials in the effect of remarriage on global happiness. *Journal of Marriage and the Family*, 1979, *41*, 869–876.

White, R. W. *Lives in progress*. (3rd ed.) New York: Holt, Rinehart and Winston, 1975.

Whiting, J. M., and Child, I. L. *Child training and personality: A cross-cultural study*. New Haven, Conn.: Yale University Press, 1953.

Whorf, B. L. *Language, thought and reality*. New York: Wiley, 1956.

Wibberley, D. G.; Khera, A. K.; Edwards, J. H.; and Rushton, D. K. Lead levels in human placenta from normal and malformed births. *Journal of Medical Genetics*, 1977, *14*, 339–345.

Wilkes, P. Robert L. Coles: Doctor of crisis. *New York Times Magazine*, March 26, 1978, p. 14.

Williams, D. *The search for leadership*. Unpublished manuscript, prepared for The Conference Board, New York, 1977.

Wilson, A. B. Social stratification and academic achievement. In A. H. Passow (Ed.), *Education in depressed areas*. New York: Teachers College, Columbia University, 1963.

Winch, R. F. Complementary needs and related notions about voluntary mate selection. In R. F. Winch and G. B. Spanier (Eds.), *Selected studies in marriage and the family*. New York: Holt, Rinehart and Winston, 1974.

Winder, C. L., and Rau, L. Parental attitudes associated with social deviance in preadolescent boys. *Journal of Abnormal Social Psychology*, 1962, *64*, 418–424.

Wiseman, R. Crisis theory and the process of divorce. *Social Casework*, 1975, *56*, 205–212.

Witkin, H. A., and Goodenough, D. R. Field dependence and interpersonal behavior. *Psychological Bulletin*, 1977, *84*, 661–689.

Witkin, H.; Moore, C.; Goodenough, D.; and Cox, P. Field-dependent and field-independent cognitive styles and their educational implications. *Review of Educational Research*, 1977, *47*, 1–64.

Witkin, H. A.; Mednick, S. A.; Schulsinger, F.; Bakkestrom, E.; Christiansen, K. O.; Goodenough, D. R.; Hirschhorn, K.; Lundsteen, C.; Owen, D. R.; Philip, J.; Rubin, D. B.; and Stocking, M. Criminality in XYY and XXY men. *Science*, 1976, *193*, 547–555.

Witryol, S. L., and Calkins, J. E. Marginal social values of rural school children. *Journal of Genetic Psychology*, 1958, *64*, 418–424.

Wolman, B. B. *Children's fears*. New York: Grosset & Dunlap, 1978.

Woodruff, D. S., and Birren, J. E. Age changes and cohort differences in personality. *Developmental Psychology*, 1972, *6*, 252–259.

Wright, H. F. Recording and analyzing child behavior. New York: Harper & Row, 1967.

Yankelovich, Skelly, & White, Inc. *Raising children in a changing society*. Minneapolis, Minn.: General Mills, 1977.

Yarrow, L. Everything you want to know about teen-agers (but are afraid to ask). *Parents'*, 1979, *54*, 68.

Yarrow, L. J. Separation from parents during early childhood. In M. L. Hoffman and L. W. Hoffman (Eds.), *Review of child development research*. New York: Russell Sage Foundation, 1964.

Yllo, K. Nonmarital cohabitation: Beyond the college campus. *Alternative Lifestyles*, 1978, *1*, 37–54.

Yogman, M.; Dixon, S.; Tronick, E.; and Brazelton, T. B. *Development of infant social interaction with fathers*. Paper presented at the meeting of the Eastern Psychological Association, Chicago, September 1977.

Young, R. D., and Avdze, A. The effects of obedience/disobedience and obese/nonobese body type on social acceptance by peers. *The Journal of Genetic Psychology*, 1979, *134*, 43–49.

Young, W. C.; Goy, R. W.; and Phoenix, C. H. Hormones and sexual behavior. *Science*, 1964, *143*, 212–218.

Zacharias, L. et al. Sexual maturation in contemporary American girls. *Journal of Obstetrics and Gynecology*, 1970, *108*, 833.

Zahn-Waxler, C.; Radke-Yarrow, M.; and King, R. A. Child rearing and children's prosocial initiations toward victims of distress. *Child Development*, 1979, *50*, 319–330.

Zegans, S., and Zegans, L. S. Fear of strangers in children and the orienting reaction. *Behavioral Science*, 1972, *17*, 407–419.

Zintz, Miles V., American Indians. In Thomas D. Horn (Ed.), *Reading for the disadvantaged*. New York: Harcourt Brace Jovanovich, 1970, pp. 41–48.

Name Index

Subject Index